THE NATIONAL GEOGRAPHIC TRAVELER

ITALY

THE NATIONAL
GEOGRAPHIC TRAVELER

ITALY

Tim Jepson

Contents

Page 1: Farmer picking grapes
Pages 2–3: Fall in the Val d'Orcia, southern Tuscany
Left: View of Vernazza, one of the Cinque Terre villages

How to use this guide

See back flap for keys of text and map symbols

The *National Geographic Traveler* brings you the best of Italy in text, pictures, and maps. Divided into three main sections, the guide begins with an overview of history and culture. Following are 11 regional chapters with featured sites selected by the author for their particular interest and treated in depth. Each chapter opens with its own contents list for easy reference.

The regions, and sites within them, are arranged geographically, each one introduced with a map highlighting the featured sites. Walks and drives, plotted on their own maps, suggest routes for discovering an area. Features and sidebars offer intriguing detail on history, culture, or contemporary life. A More Places to Visit page generally rounds off the regional chapters.

The final section, Travelwise, lists essential information for the traveler—pre-trip planning, getting around, communications, money matters, and emergencies—plus a selection of hotels and restaurants arranged by region, shops, and entertainment.

To the best of our knowledge, site information is accurate as of the press date. However, it is always advisable to call ahead when possible.

84

Color coding

Each region is color coded for easy reference. Find the region you want on the map on the front flap, and look for the color flash at the top of the pages of the relevant chapter. Information in **Travelwise** is also color coded to each region.

San Giovanni in Laterano

- 47 F2
- Piazza di San Giovanni in Laterano
- 06 6988 6433 or 6988 6452
- Scala Santa closed a.m. in summer
- Church, Baptistery, & Scala Santa: free Cloister: $
- Metro: San Giovanni

Visitor information

Practical information is given in the side column by each major site (see key to symbols on back flap). The map reference gives the page number of the map and grid reference. Other details are the site's address, telephone number, days closed, entrance charge in a range from $ (under $4) to $$$$$ (over $25), and public transportation. Other sites have visitor information in italics and parentheses in the text.

TRAVELWISE

Color-coded region name

Town or area name

Hotel name, price range, & star rating

Address, telephone, & fax numbers

Brief description of hotel

Hotel facilities & credit card details

Town or area name

Restaurant name & price range

Address & telephone number

Brief description of restaurant

Restaurant facilities & credit card details

Hotel and restaurant prices

An explanation of the price ranges used in entries is given in the Hotels and Restaurants section (see p. 352).

REGIONAL MAPS

Regional name

Adjoining chapter

Important featured town

Map reference

Point of interest

Road number

Drive start point

- A locator map accompanies each regional map and shows the location of that region in the country.
- Adjacent regions are shown, with page references.

WALKING TOURS

Direction of route

Start point

Red numbered bullet links site on map to description in the text

Walk route

Building outline

Featured site (in bold) on walk route

Point of interest not on walk route

- An information box gives the starting and finishing points, time and length of walk, and places not to be missed along the route.

DRIVING TOURS

Drive start point

Red numbered bullets link sites on map to descriptions in the text

Road number

Line of route

Detour

Important place of interest

- An information box provides details including starting and finishing points, places not to be missed along the route, time and length of drive, and tips on the terrain.

THE NATIONAL GEOGRAPHIC TRAVELER

ITALY

About the author

Tim Jepson has been a passionate and lifelong devotee of Italy. Since graduating from Oxford, he has spent long periods of time living and traveling in the country, including a year in a remote Umbrian village—where he learned fluent Italian—and five years as a writer and journalist in Rome. Over the years he has written some 15 books on the country, as well as numerous articles for the *Daily Telegraph, Vogue, Condé Nast Traveller,* and other publications.

Now based in London with the *Daily Telegraph,* Tim continues to visit Italy regularly, and, as a keen hiker and outdoor enthusiast, he takes a particular interest in the country's mountain and wilderness areas. He also revels in Italy's more sedentary pleasures—the food, wine, art, and culture—and hopes one day to indulge them all from a small Venetian apartment of his own.

Tim has also worked on Italian programs for the BBC and commercial television, and his career has included spells in a slaughterhouse, on building sites, and as a musician playing piano and guitar in streets and bars across Europe.

History & culture

Botticelli's Venus

Italy today

ITALY HAS CREATED MANY OF THE WORLD'S MOST SUBLIME WORKS OF ART, literature, and architecture, spawned some of the greatest empires of the ancient and medieval world, and, since World War II, has emerged as one of Europe's wealthiest and most economically vibrant countries. It also designs and produces many of the world's most exquisite clothes, has evolved one of the world's finest cuisines, and possesses a medley of landscapes as beautiful and varied as any in Europe. Few cultures are as beguiling, few countries as rich and endlessly fascinating.

PEOPLE

In 1860, the year of Italian unification, Prime Minister Camillo Cavour made a comment that has haunted politicians ever since. "We have made Italy," he remarked, "now we must make Italians." Some 140 years later—when "Italians" number around 57 million—it is a moot point whether he and his like-minded followers succeeded. For there has never been, and probably never will be, a typical Italian despite the clichéd archetypes with which we're all familiar—possessive *mamma*, Latin Lothario, olive-skinned beauty (think Sophia Loren), Mafia godfather....

Italy's history has been too long and divisive for uniformity. Southern Italy includes Arabs, Greeks, Phoenicians, Normans, Spanish, and others among its ethnic mix. In the northwest, the Valle d'Aosta and Piedmont have strong French ties; German is the first language of many in Alto-Adige to the north; and, in the northeast, the linguistic and ethnic cocktail embraces Slovenian. Dotted across the country there are even pockets of Arbëresh (Albanian), Occitan (Provençal), and Ladin (Old Swiss) culture. Sardinia, with its unique language and people—blends of Italian, Spanish, and other elements—is a law unto itself.

Modern mass media is producing a degree of cultural homogenization, but for the most part Italians retain regional loyalties that reflect their history. A Tuscan is a Tuscan, first and foremost, not an Italian; and then not just a Tuscan, but a Pisan, Florentine, or Sienese. The Italian word for it is *campanilismo*—the idea that your loyalties and worldly concerns extend no farther than the reach of your church belltower, or *campanile*.

Taken to their logical conclusion, these tightly focused loyalties end with that most close-knit of all social groupings—the Latin family. Although demographic and social changes are weakening this most basic unit, even in Italy, the livelihoods of at least 65 percent of working Italians are still bound to a family business. At the same time, Italy's birthrate, averaging less than one child per couple, is among the lowest in Western Europe, giving the lie to the notion of Italy as a country of large families, or of one in thrall to the Roman Catholic church. Some 97 percent of Italians are baptized, but only 10 percent now regularly attend Mass. Divorce, birth control, and abortion have all been freely available since the 1970s.

In emphasizing Italians' diversity, however, we should not underestimate their common traits. Most are pragmatic and spontaneous. Most are realists, many are self-reliant. They are also rather formal and conservative—the notion of *bella figura*, of cutting a "beautiful figure," by dressing well and not making a fool of yourself, is an important one. Many have flair and it is not surprising that Italian fashion and design are big business. Most have a sensual appreciation of the finer things of life—and no wonder in a country where the finer things of life are so prevalent.

POLITICS

Italians are naturally wary and weary of authority—the country was long fragmented and ruled, often badly, by foreigners down the centuries. The experience of the last 50 years has hardly helped. The republican constitution framed in 1948 with good intentions—to prevent a return to fascism—produced a weak and often corrupt form of government.

A gown by Versace highlights the long-standing Italian tradition of flair in fashion, art, and design.

The political upheavals of the early 1990s, which appeared to mark the system's death throes, have so far proved a false dawn.

Closer ties with Europe through the European Union, and the financial and institutional disciplines these demand, are now forcing change on recalcitrant politicians. No one would be surprised, however, if the Italians merely pay lip service to this new conceit—one more authoritarian body far removed from the realities of daily life.

Why blame them when self-reliance has served Italians well, allowing them to transform their country in less than a generation? And make no mistake, Italy has been transformed. Half a century ago, this was an agricultural backwater: Poverty was rife and emigration a fact of life. Today, it is one of the world's most powerful economies—region for region, experts say, only California outperforms northern Italy. The change has been abrupt—statistics show that for the first time,

only as recently as 1972, more people entered Italy than left it—and has been achieved despite, rather than because of, its politicians.

THE LAND

Italy is a small country. From north to south, the distinctive "boot" measures barely 800 miles (1,300 km) and covers 116,000 square miles (300,000 sq km). Of this, 35 percent is mountainous, rising to over 2,300 feet (700 m), 40 percent hilly, and just 21 percent plain.

Food and family are two of the pillars of Italian life. The traditional large family, however, is increasingly a thing of the past.

The main relief features are the high, rugged mountains of the Alps, which range in a broad arc across the north of the country—Monte Rosa, the highest point, reaches 15,203 feet (4,634 m); the lower central mountains of the Apennines, hunched in a narrow spine along the length of the peninsula; and the broad

An elderly monk in Assisi: Religion plays an increasingly small part in the mainstream of Italian life.

plains of the Po, Italy's longest river, which stretches 405 miles (650 km) and drains a densely populated area between the Alps and the Apennines.

Italy's oft-ignored coastline extends for 4,660 miles (7,500 km) and is washed by two major seas—the Tyrrhenian to the west, and the Adriatic to the east. Scattered off their shores are numerous islands, of which Sicily and Sardinia, the first and second largest islands in the Mediterranean, are the most notable.

Italy's basic landscape, however, is riddled with anomalies. Of these, the most famous are the active volcanoes of Vesuvius, Etna, and Stromboli, all linked to the residual movement of the tectonic plates that formed the Apennines. The same movement accounts for the seismic activity in parts of central and southern Italy, which produces earthquakes such as the powerful tremors that shook Naples in 1980 and Umbria in 1997.

Climate divides into three broad bands: alpine in the north, characterized by cold winters and warm summers; temperate across the Po plains, with cold, damp winters and hot, humid summers; and Mediterranean across most of the peninsula and islands, with mild winters and long, hot, dry summers. This said, all manner of variations pertain: Icy blasts from central Asia can produce freezing conditions in the north, while the sirocco (a warm dust-laden wind) and heat of North Africa can bring blast furnace conditions to Sicily and the south. Vegetation mirrors the variety of climate and relief, ranging from the pine forests of the Alpine north to the familiar vines, olive and fruit trees of the Mediterranean south.

FOOD & DRINK

Imagine you are on a desert island, a special sort of desert island. Here you are allowed to enjoy the cuisine of any country in the world. The only catch—you have to eat it for the rest of your life. What is it to be? French? Chinese? Japanese? Mexican? None seem quite right… but Italian? Well, most of us could probably live with Italian food for the rest of our days, and live quite happily.

The food is healthy; the ingredients— meat, fish, fruit, and vegetables—are fresh; the quality is first-rate; there is huge regional and

Turning their backs on the past: Italians have transformed their country from a predominantly agricultural backwater to a modern economic state in less than a generation.

local variety; and the cooking methods are quick and simple. The principal staple—pasta—is endlessly versatile. The fast food—pizza—has no peers; and as for dessert—well, where would we be without ice cream?

Italian cuisine is actually many regional cuisines rolled into one. In Milan, rice rather than pasta dominates; in the far north, where Austrian influences are strong, you'll be offered dumplings and apple strudel; and, in Sicily, where the influence of the sea and North Africa prevail, you might dine on tuna, couscous, and spicy Arabian-style peppers. The variety is endless. The only rough rule of thumb is that the farther south you go, the simpler the cuisine, poverty in the peasant south having long been the culinary mother of invention.

But few rules are hard and fast. Even in the poorest areas, where tomato, olive oil, and pasta reign, you'll find endless regional specialties. Umbria and Piedmont offer one of the world's rarest foodstuffs—the truffle (see pp. 90–91); Parma has two great Italian staples—Parma ham and Parmesan cheese; Campania has mozzarella cheese; and Liguria has created *pesto alla Genovese* (a blend of oil, basil, garlic, cheese,

and pine nuts), one of many sauces to have reached beyond Italian shores.

Certain items are universal—olive oil is invariably excellent, as is the coffee. So, too, is the Italian passion for the social and sensual side of eating. Italians, like the French, live to eat, but without their northern neighbors' fuss and fanfare. It follows that food should be one of the great pleasures of an Italian sojourn—anything from a oven-fresh roll (brioche) with your morning cappuccino to the final mouthful of gelato or zabaglione last thing at night. Try experimenting from region to region and seek out the more obscure restaurants—a far cry from the obvious tourist traps that will leave you thinking you could have done better at home.

Wine

While you might happily live on Italian food forever, no one is pretending that Italian wine rivals the world's best (although, most years, Italy produces more wine than any other country in the world). The country's wine has long had to live with the image of the wicker-covered Chianti flask, for years the mainstay

of old-time Italian restaurants at home and abroad. Fortunately, the enamel-stripping tannins of the rough, watery reds are largely a distant memory. A new breed of producers has sprung up, casting off the old-fashioned techniques and prejudices of centuries in favor of innovative methods and new grape varieties. The result has been the revitalization of some familiar names—Frascati, Soave, Asti Spumante, Chianti, Valpolicella—and the creation of new ones. So-called Super Tuscans—full-bodied, ripe reds such as Tignanello and Sassicaia—epitomize the new wave.

Some older wines have always been highly prized. Barolo and Barbaresco, from the region of Piedmont, are two of Europe's foremost reds; Prosecco is a light, sparkling white of sublime quality from the Veneto; and, in Tuscany, Brunello and Vino Nobile are reds of the highest distinction.

As with food, regional variety is enormous. Indeed, one of the great pleasures of traveling

in Italy is the chance to taste the many local wines. In Sicily, for example, there is Marsala, a dark and powerful dessert wine, as well as the lighter Malvasia wines of Etna and Lipari; in Umbria, try Sagrantino, a voluptuous red made from a grape found nowhere else in Europe; and, in Campania, one of the favorite tipples is *Lacryma Christi* (Tears of Christ), a white wine teased from vines grown on rich volcanic soils.

This said, Italian table wine will rarely match its French or New World cousins—

Festivals play a significant role in Italian life. Here, Siena's *alfieri*, or flag-throwers, demonstrate their skills in front of the city's cathedral.

where it does, it will be expensive—but it is nearly always a perfect accompaniment to the food. And, if the wine doesn't please, ask for one of Italy's famed aperitifs or liqueurs—grappa, *limoncello*, Cinzano, Campari, and Sambuca are just some worth sampling. ∎

History of Italy

MANY OF THE FIRST "ITALIANS" SAILED TO ITALY FROM ELSEWHERE IN THE Mediterranean, settling in the southern part of the country around 5000 B.C. Others were of Indo-European extraction and occupied northern and central Italy around 3000 B.C. More clearly defined tribes emerged around 1800 B.C., notably the Nuraghic people of Sardinia, the Liguri, who settled in present-day Liguria, and the Siculi, who prospered across southern Italy and modern-day Lazio. Later came the Picini and Messapiens, migratory peoples from the Balkans who settled on Italy's Adriatic coast. These were followed by the so-called Italic peoples—the Umbrians, Samnites, Latins, Volscians, Venitii, and others—who colonized areas in the north and center of the peninsula. The Phoenicians of North Africa founded colonies in Sicily and Sardinia about 800 B.C., while French-born Celts arrived about 600 B.C.

THE GREEKS

Settlement patterns achieved greater coherence in the south with the arrival of the Greeks around 735 B.C. Greece had long traded with parts of Italy, and it was inevitable that Greek migrants would make their presence permanent. Independent Greek cities such as Acragas and Catana (known today as Agrigento and Catania) grew up across southern Italy and Sicily, creating a region known as Magna Graecia (Greater Greece). In the process they enriched the artistic, cultural, and agricultural prowess of Italy's indigenous populations.

Many of the new colonies eventually eclipsed the cities of Greece itself, leading to friction between Magna Graecia and the mother country. In 415 B.C., a naval attack by Athens on Syracuse, the most powerful of Sicily's Greek cities, was repulsed in one of the greatest sea battles of the ancient world. Further challenges to Magna Graecia came from the Etruscans to the north (see below) and from Carthage in nearby North Africa.

Carthage

Carthage began life as a Phoenician colony on the North African coast. By Magna Graecia's heyday, it had become a power in its own right and soon established colonies alongside those of the Greeks in Sicily and elsewhere. Conflict followed. Only in the third century B.C. did the two enemies set aside their differences, and only then in the face of a new superpower that threatened both rivals—Rome. Syracuse fell to the new power in 211 B.C. Carthage put up more of a fight—and survived a little longer.

THE ETRUSCANS

While the Greeks and Carthaginians fought over southern Italy, another major civilization, the Etruscans, imposed a degree of hegemony on the fractured domains to the north. Who these people were and where they came from are two of archaeology's great mysteries. First recorded around 800–900 B.C., they were probably a mixture of indigenous and foreign peoples who assimilated other tribes—notably the Umbrians—and eventually developed a common language and shared social, artistic, and cultural outlook.

Society was structured around a loosely affiliated 12-city federation and ruled by priestly kings. Evidence of their art and culture is scant, however, as many of their cities were built from wood and quickly succumbed to the passage of time. Virtually the only archaeological evidence of their existence comes from their tombs. Their technical and cultural sophistication kept them unchallenged in central Italy for some 400 years, only to fall eventual prey to the Romans, who by 350 B.C. had defeated or absorbed most of their cities.

THE ROMAN EMPIRE

Legend claims Rome was founded in 753 B.C., but evidence suggests the date was nearer 1200 or 1400 B.C., the age of the earliest shards of pottery found on the city's

A couple visiting the Vatican Museums in Rome sit dwarfed beneath a massive sculpted head.

Capitoline Hill. By the ninth century B.C., the low hills on the banks of the Tiber were probably covered with scattered villages. The site then assumed a position of strategic importance between the territories of the Etruscans to the north and the Latins—another central Italian race—to the south. Over the next three centuries, the region prospered through

Julius Caesar, ancient Rome's most famous leader, enjoyed absolute power for just four years before being assassinated.

trade and came under the control of the Etruscan kings.

In 509 B.C., Rome's citizens overthrew their Etruscan overlords, installing a system they called a *res publica*, or republic, a state where the "people were kings." The city then continued to prosper, its only weakness a growing gulf between the "common people," who became known as plebians, and the burgeoning political and military elite—the patricians. This and other failings were addressed in 494 B.C., when a Tribune, or magistracy, was created to protect plebian interests.

A more robust political base, of which the Tribune was a part, allowed Rome to embark on a program of conquest. Etruscan, Samnite, and Greek-dominated areas of southern Italy soon fell, leading to confrontation with Carthage, a stand-off that resulted in three protracted campaigns known as the Punic Wars. The first of these (264–241 B.C.) saw

Rome capture the main Mediterranean islands of Sicily, Sardinia, and Corsica. The second (218–202 B.C.) pitched Rome against Hannibal, a Carthaginian general who inflicted stunning defeats on Rome before his campaigns collapsed in 202 B.C. Carthage finally succumbed during the Third Punic War (149–146 B.C.), an encounter that left Rome dominant across much of the the Mediterranean.

While Rome prospered abroad, at home it was increasingly ravaged by civil strife. Repression and placatory measures alike failed to resolve renewed disputes between patricians and plebians, disputes that found their most violent expression in the so-called Social Wars of 92 to 89 B.C. Unrest resulted in a military clampdown under the leadership of Sulla, a general whose brutal regime marked the emergence of the army as a political force. His period in power is best remembered for the Slaves' Revolt (73–71 B.C.), an ultimately doomed rebellion led by a former gladiator called Spartacus.

Another general, Pompey, came to the fore after Sulla's death. He ruled in conjunction with Crassus, an ultimately peripheral patrician figure. When military matters plucked Pompey from Rome, a third leader, Julius Caesar, appeared. Caesar had joined the army in 81 B.C. to pay off debts, but by 63 B.C. had achieved the office of *Pontifex Maximus*, Rome's ceremonial high priest. In 59 B.C., he joined Crassus and Pompey in a power-sharing triangle known as the First Triumvirate.

Originally distinguished by his powers of oratory and financial acumen, Caesar quickly proved his ability in the military sphere, embarking on a ten-year campaign that saw him win notable victories in present-day Britain, Germany, and France. These triumphs rankled with Pompey, who attempted to turn Rome against his partner, thus presenting Caesar with the pretext for retaliation. Returning to Italy in 49 B.C., Caesar marched his armies across the Rubicon, a river close to modern-day Bologna, thus flaunting a decree that forbade armies from breaching the river without senatorial permission. Pompey fled, forewarned of Caesar's advance, causing political resistance in Rome to crumble.

In 48 B.C., Caesar was appointed Rome's ruler for life. He then embarked on a policy of reform and renewal, encouraging a sustained construction program and rejuvenating legal and other institutions. However, the new dictator's powers provoked jealousy and on March 15, 44 B.C. (the Ides of March) a clique of conspirators, which included his adopted son Brutus, murdered Caesar as he walked to the Senate.

Bedlam followed Caesar's assassination. The so-called Second Triumvirate took initial charge, a coalition of prominent Romans— Mark Antony, Lepidus, and Octavius (Caesar's great-nephew and designated heir). This was followed by 12 years of turbulence during which Mark Antony and Octavius vied for control. Antony's liaison with the Egyptian queen, Cleopatra, ultimately undermined his ambitions, his final defeat coming with Octavius' victory at the Battle of Actium in 31 B.C. Octavius then changed his name to Augustus, and in 27 B.C. adopted the title of emperor, ushering in the Augustan Age, the heyday of Imperial Rome.

Augustus' rule was inspired. Expansion was reined in, military successes were consolidated, and massive building projects were instigated across the empire. Augustus' boast would be that he "found Rome brick and left it marble." Cultural life blossomed, particularly in literature, where writers such as Ovid, Virgil, and Horace produced some of the masterpieces of the classical canon.

Augustus' successors—members of the Julio-Claudian dynasty—proved less adept. Emperors Tiberius (A.D. 14–37), Claudius (A.D. 41–54), and Nero (A.D. 54–68) were mostly venal and decadent, successful only in squandering their considerable inheritance. Only the great riches of the empire masked the period's economic and bureaucratic shortcomings. Nero's tenure proved particularly traumatic, and saw the start of widespread persecution of Christians.

The Flavian dynasty (A.D. 69–96)— emperors Vespasian, Titus, and Domitian— was generally more accomplished, as was the Antonine (A.D. 96–192) and its incumbents Nerva, Trajan, Hadrian, Antoninus, and Marcus Aurelius. The empire reached its greatest territorial extent under Trajan in A.D. 117, while in Hadrian, Rome found the most cultured and astute of its leaders.

DECLINE & FALL

The death of Marcus Aurelius (A.D. 161–180) proved a watershed, and saw the first genuine threats to the Roman Empire from external foes. Rome's deficiencies, long masked by imperial bluster, now came home to roost. Inflation raged and the economy faltered. Imperial assets were mortgaged to pay debts.

A gold *solidus* coin bearing the head of Constantine the Great, Rome's first Christian emperor

Cultural life withered and emperors began to come and go with increasing regularity. Agriculture and trade at home collapsed as the spoils of empire dried up. Social, military, and other institutions became weak and moribund.

Attempts were made to arrest the process, notably the division of the empire in A.D. 286 into eastern and western dominions, each with emperors in Rome and Constantinople. Such measures brought temporary respite, as did the appearance of an unusually robust emperor. Rome prospered under Constantine (A.D. 306– 337), the first emperor to extend freedom of worship to Christians. Such respites proved temporary. In A.D. 395, the western empire's capital was moved from Rome to the more easily defended Ravenna in the northeast. Fifteen years later, Rome was sacked by Alaric the Goth, the leader of a tribe of Baltic origin and one of the first so-called Barbarians. The end was approaching. In A.D. 475, another Goth,

Odoacer, displaced Romulus Augustulus, the western empire's last emperor. In A.D. 493, Odoacer was followed by Theodoric, who ruled most of Italy from the empire's last capital, Ravenna.

FRANKS & BYZANTINES

Across the Mediterranean, however, the old eastern empire, or Byzantium, escaped the fate of its western neighbor. Between 536 and 552, its emperor, Justinian, reconquered large areas of Italy, imposing a Byzantine hold that would linger across much of the country for centuries. Complete hegemony was prevented by the arrival of the Lombards (567–774), a mostly pagan Germanic people who established powerful duchies across non-Byzantine areas of northern and central Italy.

The peninsula's territorial jigsaw was further complicated by the involvement of the Franks, a Christian race from Gaul (modern-day France). The Franks' position in Gaul was weakened by the existence of two rival royal dynasties, the Carolingian and Merovingian, a conflict addressed by Pepin the Short, the Carolingian leader, who appealed to the papacy, an institution with increasing temporal authority, to arbitrate in the affair. Pope Stephen III sanctioned Pepin's rule in 754, but demanded in return that the Franks drive the Lombards from Italy.

This they did, partly under Pepin, and partly under Pepin's more famous son, Charlemagne, who was crowned Holy Roman Emperor by Pope Leo III on Christmas Day, A.D. 800, in an act of immense symbolic importance. Charlemagne then awarded the papacy the central Italian territories captured from the Lombards, thus creating the germ of the Papal States, territories which for the first time provided the papacy with the financial resources to wield genuine political power.

The transfer of territory also forged enduring links between the papacy and empire. These ties remained largely friendly while Charlemagne and his more powerful successors controlled the empire (while the Frankish empire eventually disintegrated, the Holy Roman Empire remained a coherent entity). As time passed, however, and the fortunes of the popes and emperors wavered, so relations between the two became strained.

When issues of legitimacy arose, both parties harked back to Charlemagne's fateful coronation: Popes claimed the right to sanction emperors, emperors the right to appoint popes. The consequences of the standoff, as well the names of the respective camps and their supporters—Guelphs (the papal party) and Ghibellines (the imperial party)—would resonate through Italian history for centuries.

ARABS & NORMANS

Events in southern Italy followed a different course. In its day, the Roman Empire had been forced to fight off a challenge from North Africa, defeating the Carthaginians during the Punic Wars. During the ninth century, the African challenge was resurrected, this time in the shape of the Arabs, or Saracens, who invaded Sicily from North Africa in 827. They remained on the island for almost two centuries, introducing countless cultural, architectural, gastronomic, and other innovations, many of which (such as ice cream!) enrich our lives to this day.

Both Arabs and Byzantines, the latter still dominant elsewhere in southern Italy, eventually fell prey to the Normans, a race of Scandinavian descent who had settled in Normandy in northern France. Far-ranging in their search for plunder, they arrived in southern Italy as mercenaries, but by 1030 had established a self-contained kingdom in Puglia as a springboard for conquest. From here, they invaded Sicily in 1061, establishing a royal dynasty—kings Roger I and II were the most notable incumbents—that had kinship with England's 11th-century nemesis, William the Conqueror.

Events during this period colored southern Italy's development for centuries. When Roger II was crowned king of Sicily, for example, he united a kingdom—the Kingdom of Naples and Sicily—that survived in one form or another until 1860. In the short term, however, Norman hegemony was soon undermined. The main culprits here, as in the north, were the papacy and the Holy Roman Empire.

The Norman decline was sparked by the marriage in 1186 between Henry VI, the Holy Roman Emperor, and Constance of Hautville, a Norman princess. When the Norman royal line died out in 1194, Henry's fortuitous union

A 19th-century painting from the French school shows Charlemagne crowned Holy Roman Emperor in A.D. 800.

made him heir to the Norman throne. The papacy had sanctioned Norman rule in the south, much as it had done with Charlemagne, and deeply resented the appearance of the empire. Henry's son, Frederick Hohenstaufen (1197–1250), one of the great figures of the Middle Ages, proved impervious to papal resentment—he simply ignored his excommunication in 1228, for example—and ruled the south adroitly, acquiring the title *Stupor Mundi* (Wonder of the World) in recognition of his artistic, scientific, and military achievements.

Frederick's son, Manfred, proved less adept, and was defeated in 1266 by Charles of Anjou, the son of King Louis VIII of France, to whom the popes had appealed in 1260 to rid them of the Hohenstaufens. Charles then moved his capital to Naples, where he and his Anjou (or Angevin) successors established a dynasty that ruled the south for two centuries. Only Sicily, always something of a law unto itself, slipped from their control, a lapse precipitated by the Sicilian Vespers, an anti-Anjou uprising in 1282 (the revolt was sparked at the hour of vespers on March 30 of that year,

hence its name). During the revolt, Sicily's nobles looked to outside powers for help, this time to Spain's Peter III of Aragon. Not only did the Aragonese seize Sicily, but in 1442, in one of history's ironic twists, the Aragonese ruler, Alfonso V, was later named as heir to the last of Naples' Angevins, thus uniting the south under Spanish control until the 18th century.

CITY STATES

Northern Italy, meanwhile, had seen the emergence of the *comuni*, or city states, during the 11th and 12th centuries. In the first instance, these independent enclaves were nurtured by the weakness of the papacy and the Holy Roman Empire, the two bodies who should have exercised power in the region. Most emperors proved unable to combine their imperial obligations in northern Europe—their main power base—with the task of imposing authority in Italy. The papacy, for its part, was weakened by its bickering with the empire, and eventually fell prey to French domination, being forced to move to Avignon in 1309, where it remained under French "protection" until 1377.

Cities took advantage of the power vacuum to forge increasingly independent identities. The so-called Maritime Republics—Genoa, Pisa, Amalfi, and above all Venice—grew rich through overseas trade. Cities such as Florence and Siena prospered through textiles and banking. Others—Milan, Bologna, and Verona—flourished astride important trade routes. Eventually, some 400 city states stretched across the north of the country. Only in the south, where the Spanish and the old feudal system held sway, was progress stifled, a situation that prevailed until the 20th century.

Initially, most of the cities enjoyed a degree of democratic rule, electing merchants and minor nobles to their ruling bodies. As time went by, however, cities were increasingly riven by internal dissent and disputes with rival cities. Against this background, there often emerged a single powerful figure or wealthy family, the only people able to exert authority in troubled times—the Medici in Florence, Visconti in Milan, Montefeltro in Urbino, Este in Ferrara, Gonzaga in Mantua, Scaligeri in Verona were among the many.

Although often despotic, these wealthy clans provided the stability required for economic prosperity. They were also often enlightened artistic patrons, and the cities they controlled became sophisticated centers of learning. The result was an unparalleled explosion of artistic and cultural endeavor. In the literary field, the period saw the emergence of Dante (1265–1321), Petrarch (1304–1374), and Boccaccio (1313–1375). In painting, it produced innovators such as Giotto (1266–1337), Cimabue (1240–1302), and Duccio (1255–1318). In architecture, it spawned Arnolfo di Cambio (1245–1302), responsible for Florence's great cathedral, and, in sculpture, the figures of Giovanni Pisano, Nicola Pisano, and many others. The age's dynamism was also reflected in spiritual matters, where figures such as St. Francis (1182–1226) revitalized and challenged the prevailing religious orthodoxies. It was also manifest in the area of scholarship, which saw a revival of classical learning and the creation of some of Europe's oldest universities (notably Padua and Bologna).

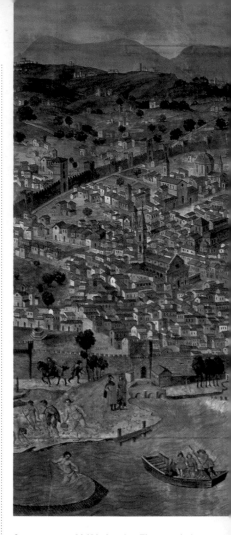

A panorama of 1490 showing Florence in its Renaissance heyday. The city was then one of about 400 independent Italian states.

Lay patronage freed artists from their earlier obligations to religious art, obligations that resulted in conservative modes of expression. Similar freedoms appeared in scholarship, where writers and thinkers were able to turn from theology to the study of classical and humanist texts. From here it was a short step to a revival of the classical ideal in art, and to the vast upsurge in artistic and other cultural activity known as the Renaissance (from the Italian *rinascimento*, or rebirth; see pp. 33–34).

But even as Italy was enjoying what in retrospect would be seen as a golden age,

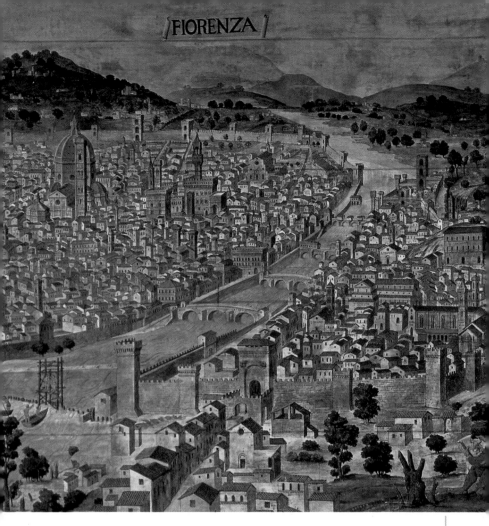

the first powerful hints of its eventual demise were already evident. Spain and Portugal's discovery of the New World and of improved trade routes to the east undermined the Mediterranean and mainland trade on which the considerable prosperity of Venice and other maritime powers was based. The rise of the Ottoman (Turkish) Empire also threatened the power of Venice, and by implication Italy, while the increased prominence of the Italian states on the European stage inevitably brought them into greater contact with the continent's other major powers.

FRANCE & SPAIN

The turning point came with the death in 1492 of Lorenzo de' Medici, whose control of Florence had helped ensure a period of relative peace. Henceforth, foreign powers began to turn on Italy with an ever greater vengeance. The first was Charles VIII in 1494. The French king entered Italy at the "request" of the Duke of Milan, who had become embroiled in an argument with the Kingdom of Naples. Charles justified his interference on the basis that his French Anjou ancestors had once ruled Naples and much of southern Italy (see p. 23). Within three months he had seized, looted, and then abandoned Naples.

In 1526, it was the turn of Charles V (1500–1558), the Holy Roman Emperor and heir to the Austrian and Spanish thrones. Within a short time he had defeated the French, captured Rome, and established puppet regimes in Milan, Tuscany, and Genoa. In 1559, the power of his Spanish successors in Italy was formalized by the Treaty of Cateau-Cambrésis, an agreement that left virtually only Venice and the Papal States free of foreign control.

In the 17th century, Spain's grip on its foreign dominions was weakened by internal and the Veneto were controlled by the Austrians; in central Italy, power was held by the papacy; and in Naples and the south, authority was wielded by the Bourbons. Unification had been an issue for centuries, but only became a serious possibility when Napoleon's integration of the peninsula underlined the potential for a unified state.

Count Camillo Cavour (left) and Guiseppe Garibaldi, founding fathers of Italian unification.

conflict—the Wars of the Spanish Succession (1701–1713)—precipitating a further fragmenting of Italy's political jigsaw. The Treaty of Utrecht (1713) saw Sardinia pass to Austria; Piedmont and Sicily were handed to the French House of Savoy in 1720; and, in 1734, Naples and southern Italy were given to the Bourbons. Later in the century, Napoleon's campaigns (1796–1800) briefly made him master of the Italian peninsula, a short-lived interruption to the Italian status quo, which was restored by the Congress of Vienna in 1815.

UNIFICATION

The move toward Italian unification—known in Italian as the Risorgimento (Resurgence)—was hampered by the variety of forces ranged against it. In the north, much of Lombardy

The first hints of change were contained in the so-called Carbonari, secret societies active against the Austrians and Papal States in the 1820s. These were followed in 1831 by the foundation of a political movement known as *Giovane Italia* (Young Italy), whose aim was the creation of an Italian republic. Its leader was Giuseppe Mazzini (1805–1872), one of unification's three founding fathers.

Unification's second major proponent was Count Camillo Cavour (1810–1861), prime minister of Piedmont, an independent kingdom whose Savoy rulers Cavour hoped to install as kings of a united Italy. Its third was Giuseppe Garibaldi (1807–1882), a charismatic military leader who would help unite the opposing republican and royalist ambitions of Mazzini and Cavour.

The first efforts at change came during the revolutionary turmoil that swept Europe in 1848. Cavour and Garibaldi declared a republic in Rome, while ill-fated uprisings against the Austrians were led in Venice by Daniele Manin (1804–1857) and Carlo Alberto, the Savoy king, in Lombardy. The Austrian army crushed the revolts in the north, while the

by the *Mille* (Thousand), his famous troop of red-shirted volunteers. The Papal States fell soon after, save for Rome, still protected by its French garrison. The kingdom of Italy was proclaimed in Turin on March 14, 1861. Venice and the Veneto region joined in 1866, when Austria was defeated by Bismarck and the Prussians at the Battle of Sadova. Rome,

Mussolini flanked by black-shirted supporters. The dictator ruled Italy for almost 20 years.

French, under Napoleon III, restored the power of their papal allies in Rome.

Things would change, however, over the next ten years. First, Piedmont sided with Britain, France, and Turkey against Russia in the Crimean War, winning increased sympathy from its allies with regard to what had become known as the "Italian Question." Second, Cavour's political skill produced an alliance with the French against Austria, resulting in a combined French-Piedmontese force: In 1859, it defeated the Austrians in northern Italy at the battles of Magenta and Solferino. Lombardy then fell to the Savoys, followed soon afterward by Tuscany and Emilia, both the scene of spontaneous uprisings.

Within four months, Garibaldi had captured the south from the Bourbons, aided

the final link, was occupied in 1870, when the French withdrew following their defeat in the Franco-Prussian War. Rome was declared capital of the new country a year later.

ITALY UNITED

Politicians made concerted efforts to modernize Italy in the decades after unification. Highways and railroads were built, education improved, and industry encouraged. Colonies were acquired—parts of Eritrea (1885) and Libya (1911–12) were conquered in North Africa—and, in 1913, the first elections were held with universal male suffrage (women had to wait until 1946 for the vote).

Italy remained neutral at the outbreak of World War I in 1914, but within nine months (on May 24, 1915) had rallied to the Allied cause, seduced by the possibility of further colonial gains in Africa and the acquisition of the so-called *terre irredente* (Italian-speaking areas of northeast Italy still held by the Austrians). Italy's nascent army initially proved no match for the Austrians, and lost several major battles before a remarkable rear-guard victory at Vittorio Veneto in 1918.

Italy received some of what it had hoped for from the peace treaty of 1919, but still suffered grievously in the economic and social upheavals that followed the war. Political chaos ensued, providing a fertile breeding ground for extremism. A former socialist journalist, Benito Mussolini, adroitly exploited the situation, using his black-shirted followers to foment unrest on the streets and seducing Italy's nervous upper- and middle-classes with the power of his rhetoric.

A threatened general strike in 1922 provided the catalyst for change. Mussolini made his famous "March on Rome" from Milan, leading King Vittore Emanuele III—fearful of civil war—to sanction Mussolini as prime minister, despite the still paltry showing of his Fascist Party in parliament. Mussolini quickly consolidated power, eventually assuming the title of *Duce,* or Leader. By 1925, he had forged a dictatorial fascist state that drifted inexorably toward alliance with Nazi Germany in the buildup to war.

Italy made common cause with the Nazis in 1940, expecting easy gains on the back of sweeping German victories in Poland and France. But the Italian armies were ill-prepared and ill-motivated, and suffered losses in Greece, Ethiopia, and elsewhere that culminated in the Allied invasion of Sicily in July 1943. An armistice followed in September 1943, Mussolini was imprisoned, and—amid chaotic scenes—a new Italian government declared war on Germany. Hitler then freed Mussolini by force, installed him as head of a puppet state in northern Italy, and began a hard-fought war of attrition against the advancing Allies.

Rome was eventually taken on June 4, 1944, but the Allies would not cross the Po in northern Italy until April 24, 1945. Mussolini was captured by partisans attempting to escape to Switzerland, and executed on April 28.

TO THE PRESENT

Italy's remarkable postwar transformation began in June 1946, when a national referendum narrowly voted to replace the country's monarchy with a republic. The Marshall Plan then provided the catalyst for an economic boom, fueled by the availability of cheap labor and the Italians' voracious appetite for material change. The country's emergence into the European mainstream was symbolized by the 1957 Treaty of Rome, a document that laid the foundations of the European Union, of which Italy was one of the six founding members. It was further cemented when Rome hosted the 1960 Olympic Games, the same year as Federico Fellini's famous *La Dolce Vita,* a movie that captured the flavor of Italy during a decade of extraordinary change.

Italy's transformation was not without its problems. By the 1960s, the boom had largely

run its course. Coalition governments became weaker, and the economy faltered, leading to violent social tensions. Unrest exploded in the so-called *autunno caldo* (literally, "hot fall") of 1968, when worker and student demonstrations swept the country.

Worse was to come in the next few years, when Italy was ravaged by political terrorism of all political shades. The low point came in 1978, when the most feared of the terrorist groups, the Brigate Rosse (Red Brigades), kidnapped and murdered the former prime minister, Aldo Moro. No sooner had the terrorist menace been nullified, however, than Italy's moribund political system was wracked by the corruption scandals of the early 1990s. At the time it seemed the experience had precipitated a sea change, demonstrating for the first time Italy's genuine desire for institutional and constitutional change. In the event, the Second Republic,

An American-style billboard for designer Giorgio Armani in central Milan, a city whose art, culture, and economic prosperity epitomizes much of modern Italy

proclaimed in 1994, proved something of a false dawn, although the country's ever closer ties with the European Union have recently produced a degree of change by default.

Italy today continues to appear fractured, much as it has done for centuries. The impoverished south remains a problem; the Mafia flourishes; voices seek independence for northern Italy; many Italians hold authority in contempt; and politicians seem more or less unable to effect genuine reforms. And yet the country prospers, overcoming circumstance and political incoherence in the same inspired and ultimately triumphant manner it has for much of its checkered past. ■

The arts

ITALY'S IMMENSE ARTISTIC AND CULTURAL HERITAGE IS ITS GREATEST legacy. Over almost 3,000 years, the paintings, sculptures, mosaics, operas, and works of literature of the country's countless artists, composers, and writers have helped shape and define Western civilization.

PAINTING & SCULPTURE

Greece & Rome

Greek art was introduced to Sicily and southern Italy in the eighth century B.C. with the arrival of Greek settlers to Magna Graecia (see p. 18). Its most obvious memorials are the temples of Paestum, Agrigento, and elsewhere, and the semicircular theaters of Taormina and Syracuse. Little survives of Hellenistic painting of the time, although its influence can be seen in the tomb and vase paintings of the Etruscans in central Italy, and in the fresco decoration of Roman villas, of which the most exhilarating examples survive at Pompeii and Naples' Museo Archeologico Nazionale.

Etruscan and Roman art also looked to Greece for the mosaic, a medium that found favor on the walls and floors of domestic and religious buildings across Italy. Naples and Pompeii again preserve fine Roman-era mosaics, although the best of all belong to the third-century A.D. hunting lodge at Piazza Armerina in Sicily. Of still greater influence was Hellenistic sculpture, whose impact was felt not only during the Roman period, but also during the Renaissance and the neoclassic revival of the 18th and 19th centuries. Museums across Italy, but especially in Rome, contain numerous masterpieces of Roman sculpture, works whose debt to Greece is belied by exquisite execution. Much the same can be said of Etruscan sculpture, examples of which are rarer—the best are found in Rome's Villa Giulia and the smaller provincial museums of Tuscany, Umbria, and Lazio.

Byzantine empire

Byzantine art was the art of the Byzantine empire, an entity born of the decision to divide the old Roman empire in two: a western empire with its capital in Rome and an eastern empire centered on Constantinople (Istanbul). Given its eastern and Roman roots, Byzantine art developed along distinctive lines, emerging as a hybrid of classical and more ornate oriental styles. Its most dominant medium was the mosaic, a form that proved perfectly suited to the Byzantine penchant for ornamentation, abstraction, and the characteristic use of gold and other richly colored backgrounds.

Byzantium's first major incursion onto Italian soil came with Justinian, the Byzantine emperor who reconquered areas of Italy from the Goths, invaders from central Europe, in the sixth century. He established his capital at Ravenna, a town still graced with Europe's finest Byzantine mosaics, although other magnificent Byzantine-influenced mosaics exist in Aquileia, Milan, Rome, and elsewhere. One of Byzantium's most remarkable aspects was its longevity, the mosaic tradition having remained a component of buildings such as St. Mark's Basilica in Venice and Florence's Baptistery until the 12th century and beyond.

Pre-Renaissance

Byzantine's grip was especially slow to loosen in the sphere of painting, where three stylized images dominated Italian art for more than 500 years: portraits of saints; the iconic Madonna and child; and *Christus Triumphans,* a painted figure of Christ on the cross. But by the 14th century, as the increasing wealth and cultural sophistication of the city states took hold, these images had begun to seem tired and anachronistic. However, the move to new idioms—harbingers of the Renaissance—was gradual.

One of the first artists to grapple with new forms of expression was the Roman Pietro Cavallini (circa 1250–circa 1330), a Byzantine-trained mosaicist who began in mid-career to explore the possibilities of fresco painting. For a while he worked in the Basilica of

A 6th-century Madonna and child mosaic in Sant' Apollinare Nuovo, Ravenna

Botticelli's "The Birth of Venus" is typical of many Renaissance works in its use of classical rather than Christian imagery.

St. Francis (1228) in Assisi, a seminal building in the development of Italian art. Here he met Cimabue (circa 1240–circa 1302), famously described by the Renaissance art critic Giorgio Vasari as the "father of Italian painting." Soon after, he worked with Cimabue's pupil, Giotto di Bondone (circa 1266–1337), the single most influential figure in European pre-Renaissance art. Building on the tentative advance of Cimabue and others, Giotto introduced realism, narrative, emotion, and spatial depth into paintings, breaking Byzantium's stilted stranglehold on both the style and substance of Italian art. Similar advances were made in sculpture, a long neglected art form, in particular by the Tuscan-based artists Nicola Pisano (1220–1284) and Arnolfo di Cambio (circa 1245–1302).

The Renaissance

The great cultural Renaissance, or rebirth, that enveloped Italy and elsewhere during the 15th and 16th centuries was not an overnight phenomenon. Changes had been taking place in art and society for two or three hundred years, precipitated by the increased wealth and sophistication of the city states, the upsurge in scholarship, the revival of interest in classical art and ideas, the allure of humanism—the notion that humankind and not the divine

was at the heart of all things—and by the growth of lay patrons such as the Medici in Florence, whose commissions freed artists from the need to produce the conservative art demanded (and paid for) by the Church.

Innovation duly appeared, particularly in Florence, where all the conditions for artistic renewal came to fruition. Filippo Brunelleschi (1377–1446) flew the flag for architecture, Donatello (1386–1466) pioneered advances in sculpture, and Masaccio (1401–1428) set new

Venice's Palazzo Ducale by Antonio Canal, better known as Canaletto (1697–1768)

standards in painting. Thereafter, the floodgates of genius and achievement opened, not only in Florence, but in cities across Italy. The most notable center was Venice, whose immense wealth and cosmopolitan élan found artistic expression in the works of Vittore Carpaccio, Giovanni Bellini, Titian, Jacopo Tintoretto, and many others.

Mannerism & the High Renaissance

The Renaissance can be said to have lasted the best part of the 15th century, at least as far as parameters can be defined. Its final years, more or less the first quarter of the 16th century, are referred to as the High Renaissance. Three hallowed names dominate this period, Leonardo da Vinci (1452–1519), Michelangelo (1475–1564), and Raphael (1483–1520), men of consummate individual genius whose work transcends category or classification.

Renaissance self-confidence was eventually punctured by Italy's increasingly troubled political situation, whose perilous state found its most dramatic expression in 1527 with the attack on Rome and the papacy by Charles V's imperial army. The uncertainty of the times was reflected in Mannerism, the artistic genre that bridged the Renaissance and baroque periods. As the name suggests, its approach was more mannered, putting style above substance and artifice above naturalism. Previously unquestioned conventions such as color, proportion, and composition were deliberately subverted. Michelangelo's and Raphael's late work displayed Mannerist hints, many of which were taken up and developed by artists such as Pontormo (1494–1556), Rosso Fiorentino (1494–1540), and Parmigianino (1503–1540).

The baroque

Baroque art was an expression of the new spirit of self-confidence engendered during the late 16th century by the Counter Reformation, a movement promulgated by the Catholic Church to challenge the rise of Protestantism. The Italian writer, Luigi Barzini, produced a view shared by many of much of baroque art, describing it as "anything pointlessly complicated, otiose, capricious and eccentric" (*The Italians*, 1964). The style prospered hugely in

"Soothsayer's Recompense," by internationally renowned surrealist Giorgio de Chirico

Rome, where the papacy became Italy's greatest 17th-century patron, but also found triumphant expression in Naples, Lecce, Turin, and Palermo. Its most obvious memorials are sculptural and architectural, its greatest exponents the exuberant Gianlorenzo Bernini (1598–1680) and his more troubled and introverted rival, Francesco Borromini (1599–1667).

Baroque painting, while less high profile, also had its masters, principally Caravaggio (1573–1610), who produced works of graphic and revolutionary realism, and the Carracci dynasty (Ludovico, Annibale, and Agostino), whose approach tended toward the cooler and more restrained precepts of classical art.

To the present
The approach exemplified by the Carraccis was also pursued in the 18th century, when Europe was swept by a renewed passion for the classical ideal in art. Neoclassicism, as the movement was known, was most marked in sculpture, where the style's sober virtuosity was exemplified by artists such as Antonio Canova (1757–1822). Painting of the period tended more to the florid world of rococo, a

sensual style born in France that found a natural home in the decadent world of 18th-century Venice and painters such as Giovanni Battista Tiepolo (1696–1770).

The middle of the 19th century was enlivened by the Macchiaoli, a Tuscan-based group of painters whose new approach to style and color mirrored that of the French Impressionists. Paris seduced Italy's most celebrated late 19th-century painter, Amedeo Modigliani (1884–1920), who spent much of his life in the city. It was also the birthplace of futurism, a movement founded in 1909 by a group of Italians in Paris, which aimed to embody the drama and dynamism of the mechanical age.

During the 20th century, Italy's artistic influence was peripheral—surrealist Giorgio de Chirico (1888–1978) was the country's last painter of true international renown. Today, its long artistic tradition finds more oblique, but no less glorious expression in other areas—those of design and high fashion—where Michelangelo, Leonardo, and other past greats would doubtless be working were they alive today.

ARCHITECTURE

Among Italy's first architectural creations were the prehistoric *nuraghi* of Sardinia, circular stone dwellings of which extremely little is known. Then came the great temples and theaters of Magna Graecia, the area of southern Italy colonized by the Greeks from about 800 B.C. The classical elements of these and

Marble detailing used to decorate buildings

other buildings influenced Etruscan and Roman architecture, although little survives of the Etruscans save their central Italian necropoli, or burial grounds (most Etruscan buildings were made from wood and so perished over the years). All but a handful of Roman architectural forms were derivative— the triumphal arch and basilica were notable exceptions—although the innovative use of the arch and new materials such as concrete (in the Pantheon, for example) allowed the Romans to build on a grander scale than the Greeks.

Byzantine architecture borrowed both from Rome (and therefore Greece) and the Orient. Many of its buildings were based on the basilica or the Greek cross, the latter a design in which a dome was raised above a square or rectangular base. The Orient's heavily decorated traditions are seen to best effect in the basilicas of St. Mark's in Venice and San Vitale in Ravenna, and to a lesser extent in the cathedral of Monreale in Sicily,

where Byzantine forms were mixed with exotic and northern European elements introduced by Arab and Norman invaders.

This intermingling of traditions influenced Italian architecture for centuries, particularly the Romanesque styles that developed around the tenth century. The style's simple, round-arched forms varied greatly by region, from the buildings of Sicily and Puglia, often tinged with ornate Arab-influenced decorative details, to the black and white marble-striped and sculpture-embellished appearance of Lombard- and Pisan-Romanesque buildings in the north. Used extensively across the country, the Romanesque style's popularity was fostered by the spate of church building that followed the emergence of city states after the Dark Ages.

From about the 13th century, the Romanesque was enlivened and eventually replaced by Gothic architecture, a style that at its most basic is identified by a pointed arch, vaulting, and rose windows, and by its propensity for airy interiors and an emphasis on verticality. The form was largely introduced from France, finding its earliest expression in simple but influential buildings such as the Basilica of St. Francis in Assisi. Like the Romanesque, it proliferated and mutated quickly, its spread facilitated by the profusion of civic and church building in the wealthy and now well-established city states. Romanesque-Gothic hybrids predominated, largely because of the length of time it took to complete buildings, a fusion most notable in the great cathedrals and public palaces of Siena, Pisa,

Buildings of the size and decorative complexity of Siena cathedral (above) often took hundreds of years to complete.

Florence, and Orvieto. Only rarely did the Gothic predominate, most gloriously in Milan's cathedral and the Doge's Palace in Venice.

Renaissance architecture saw the reemergence of classical forms and ideals. Even as the Gothic reached its apogee, architects such as the Florentine Filippo Brunelleschi (1337–1446) were adapting ancient forms to new buildings. Brunelleschi's work was developed by Michelozzo, Leon Battista Alberti, and Bramante—who conceived the basic plan for St. Peter's Basilica in Rome—although the most important architect of the period was Andrea Palladio (1508–1580), whose reworking of classical idioms in Venice, Vicenza, and elsewhere continues to influence architecture to the present day.

Renaissance purity of line and form eventually gave way to the baroque, an exuberant style whose complex, theatrical, and highly decorated elements expressed the self-confident optimism of the Counter Reformation. Religious

given renewed impetus to a distinguished 3,000-year-old tradition.

MUSIC

Italy's immense contribution to the world of classical music bore early fruit in the 11th century when a Tuscan monk, Guido Monaco (995–1050), devised the musical scale and

Composer Giuseppe Verdi (1813–1901)

Composer Gioacchino Rossini (1792–1868)

and architectural ebullience found their greatest expression in Rome, where papal patronage fueled a 17th-century building boom led by the style's greatest exponents, Gianlorenzo Bernini (1598–1680) and Francesco Borromini (1599–1667).

Baroque's energy and invention eventually gave way to the bland creations of 18th-century neoclassicism, a further reworking of classical forms that lacked the earlier subtlety of Palladio and his contemporaries. Art nouveau also made a brief 19th-century appearance, most notably in the covered glass arcades of Milan and Naples. In the modern age, Italian architecture has mirrored the burgeoning fortunes of Italian design, cele-brated architects such as Renzo Piano, responsible for Paris's CentrePompidou, have

forms of notation still used today. The country also produced one of the world's first documented composers, Francesco Landini (circa 1325–1397). Religious and choral music predominated during much of the Middle Ages, culminating in the work of Giovanni Palestrina (1524–1594). Secular music of the period often took the form of madrigals, a genre in which poems were set to music, or of wedding entertainments, both of which helped lay the foundations of Italy's greatest musical legacy—opera (see facing page).

Opera's earliest manifestations, however, were largely overshadowed by the development of instrumental music. A triumvirate of composers perfected and advanced the cause of such music: Girolamo Frescobaldi (1583–1643) wrote largely for the organ,

Arcangelo Corelli (1653–1713) for the violin, and Domenico Scarlatti (1685–1757) for the harpsichord. Venice, then one of the great centers of Italian music, thanks in part to the choir and orchestra of St. Mark's, gave birth to Antonio Vivaldi (1678–1741), somewhat passed over in his own day—he died impoverished in Vienna—but now celebrated for

musical declamation. In 1597, two of the academy's members, Jacopo Peri and Ottavio Rinucci, produced *Dafne*, what many consider to be the first opera, as well as *Euridice*, the first opera to have survived in its complete form (the work was originally performed at Florence's Palazzo Pitti to celebrate the marriage of Maria de' Medici to Henry IV).

Opera singer Luciano Pavarotti singing *Un Ballo in Maschera* with Lillian Watson

works such as *The Four Seasons*. The composer wrote some 454 concertos, helping to establish the concerto's classic three-movement structure (fast-slow-fast). Tomaso Albinoni (1671–1750), a similar composer and close contemporary of Vivaldi, has also achieved modern fame—his stately *Canon* is perhaps his best known work.

Opera

Opera's precise origins are disputed. Many trace the genre to the *intermedii* of Florentine and other wedding ceremonies, entertainments that included a series of tableaus involving singing, dancing, and static performance. Members of a Florentine academy known as the Camerata, inspired by these entertainments, then began to combine elements of Greek drama with

The first well-known composer to grapple with the new form was Claudio Monteverdi (1567–1643), master of music at St. Mark's, whose *Orfeo* (1607) first established opera in the musical mainstream. Various refinements to the form then took place during the 17th century, notably the division between *opera seria*, which dealt with weightier themes—usually drawn from mythology—and *opera buffa*, or comic opera, which frequently drew on the stock characters and situations of Commedia dell'Arte. Every major Italian city soon had its own opera house, and in Naples Alessandro Scarlatti (1660–1725) established the opera's classic opening overture and the division between the individually sung arias and the joint recitative essential for the development of plot.

Henceforth, virtually all the great names of opera were Italian. The notable exception was, of course, Mozart (although it was an Italian, Lorenzo da Ponte, who wrote the librettos for the maestro's greatest operas, *Don Giovanni, Così fan tutte,* and *Le Nozze di Figaro).* Giochino Rossini (1792–1868) was one of the earliest masters of comic or light opera *(William Tell, The Barber of Seville).* Contemporaries who worked in a similar vein included Vincenzo Bellini (1801–1831), whose melodic genius found expression in works such as *Norma,* and Gaetano Donizetti (1797–1848), who combined melodrama *(Lucia di Lammermoor)* with more lightweight fare *(L'Elisir d'Amore).*

Opera's golden age dawned at the end of the 19th century with the arrival of the genre's giants—Giuseppe Verdi (1813–1901) and Giacomo Puccini (1858–1924). Verdi's lush, romantic works, with those of Mozart, form the bedrock of the operatic canon *(Aida, Rigoletto, Nabucco,* and *La Traviata).* Puccini, no less performed, explored more modern themes, embracing the trend toward *verismo,* or realism, in operas such as *Tosca, Madame Butterfly,* and *La Bohème.*

Modern Italian music stands in opera's long shadow, and it is an opera star, Luciano Pavarotti, rather than a composer, who ranks as Italy's best known contemporary musician. Italy's musical heritage, however, is celebrated in numerous prestigious festivals across the country, most notably Verona's Festival della Lirica, Florence's Maggio Musicale, and Spoleto's Festival dei Due Mondi.

CINEMA

Italian cinema accounts for much of what we know, or think we know, of modern Italy. Neorealist movie makers after World War II, Federico Fellini's *La Dolce Vita,* and stars such as Sophia Loren and Marcello Mastroianni, have all contributed to our idea of how Italians look and behave.

The industry's roots are old. The first Italian movie studio was built in Turin in 1905. The first full-length movie, *Cabiria,* appeared in 1914. Within a few years the business had moved to Rome, lured by the capital's kinder weather and impressive range of locations.

Fascism, when it came, proved a boon, but only in terms of quantity—numerous movies were made in the thirties. Quality was another matter. Most movies of the time were light-weight baubles, escapist fare that pandered to the streak of sentimentality in the Italian character. Others were little more than propaganda: When Mussolini opened Rome's famous Cinecittà studios in 1938 it was with the boast that movies would be "our greatest weapon."

Postwar Italian moviemaking came of age. A new generation of directors pioneered a genre known as neorealism, a gritty style grounded in hard-hitting social *vérité.* Roberto Rossellini's *Roma, Città Aperta* (1945) was its first masterpiece, an almost documentary-style movie of deliberately jerky camera work, real locations, and a narrative that rarely pulled its punches.

Rossellini's lead was followed by Luchino Visconti, Michelangelo Antonioni, and Vittorio de Sica, and later by Pier Paolo Pasolini and Federico Fellini, each of whom, in his own way, explored the changing face of postwar Italy. Neorealism quickly colored Hollywood's approach to films noirs and the French New Wave, as well as drawing foreign mainstream moviemakers to the Italian studios *(Cleopatra* and *Ben Hur* were just two of the blockbuster movies partly made at Cinecittà).

The glory days were soon over. Neorealism's iconoclasm—although influential—proved short-lived, while rising costs pushed Italian studios into soft porn and spaghetti westerns to make ends meet. The old names—Fellini and Visconti—worked on, and still sprung the odd surprise, but by the late seventies the pioneering fervor of 20 years earlier had vanished.

These days, Italian moviemakers only occasionally hit the mainstream. Franco Zeffirelli *(Romeo and Juliet, Hamlet)* and Bernardo Bertolucci *(Last Tango in Paris, The Last Emperor)* are the only current directors of international stature, although films such as Giuseppe Tornatore's *Cinema Paradiso* (1988) and Roberto Benigni's *Life is Beautiful* (1998) have charmed audiences worldwide.

Anita Ekberg trails through Rome's Trevi Fountain in a scene from Federico Fellini's classic 1960 movie, *La Dolce Vita.*

LITERATURE

Early Italian literature is the literature of the classical canon, notably the Roman poets Virgil and Ovid, authors of *The Aeneid* and *Metamorphoses,* respectively, and writers such as Pliny *(Historia Naturalis),* Julius Caesar *(The Gallic Wars)* and Suetonius *(The Twelve Caesars),* who chronicled the history of Rome and its empire. In drama, Seneca explored the tragic idiom, while Plautus was the master of comedy. Juvenal stands out among the satirists—he coined the phrase *panem et circenses* (bread and circuses) to mock the decadence of a Roman populace that bartered its freedom for food and entertainment.

Latin's linguistic primacy continued until the 13th century, when Franciscan poets such as Jacopone da Todi and St. Francis of Assisi, borrowing from the troubador traditions of Provence, began to write in the everyday Italian of the period. This trend was continued by three of Italy's greatest literary figures: Dante Alighieri (1265–1321), Petrarch (1304–1374), and Giovanni Boccaccio (1313–1375). Dante's *Divine Comedy* (circa 1321) is one of the finest epic poems of any age or language, an all encompassing work inspired by the poet's doomed love for Beatrice. Love also inspired Petrarch, whose passion for Laura produced the lyrical sonnets of the *Canzoniere,* or Songs. Boccaccio is remembered for the narrative finesse of *Il Decamerone* (1348–1353), a series of 100 tales told by ten people over ten days as the Black Death raged in Florence.

Petrarch and Boccaccio were not entirely wedded to the vernacular, but joined attempts to revive Latin and Greek as literary languages, forming part of the humanistic and classical vanguard that paved the way for the Renaissance. Classical ideals found expression in the works of humanists such as Leonardo Bruni and Poliziano, and in the verse of Michelangelo, who, as well as being a painter, sculptor, and architect, also wrote accomplished sonnets and other poetry.

Other hugely influential works of the period included Baldassare Castiglione's *The Courtier* (1528), a handbook of courtly manners read across Europe, and Ariosto's *Orlando Furioso,* an epic poem based on the exploits of the knight Orlando and his paramour Angelica. Less influential in its own day, but infamous today, is Machiavelli's *The Prince,* a masterly political analysis that combined political science with an unerring study of human nature.

Italian literature after the Renaissance continued to produce outstanding individual exponents of the various literary movements that swept Europe in the 18th and 19th centuries. Alessandro Manzoni's *I Promessi Sposi* reflected the development of the novel as a form—his epic tale of young love written in idiomatic Italian (a revolution in literary terms) remains required reading for Italian school children to this day. In drama, the dominant figure was Carlo Goldoni (1707–1793), whose bright incisive comedies bear similarities to the plays of the 17th-century French dramatist, Molière. In poetry, the lyrical poems of Giacomo Leopardi (1798–1837) represented Italian Romanticism at its best, while the similar, if darker works of Giosuè Carducci (1835–1907) presaged the more troubled undercurrents of the modern age.

These undercurrents found expression in the novels of Italo Svevo (1861–1928), whose existential and psychoanalytical concerns mirrored those of contemporaries such as Czech-born Franz Kafka and France's Marcel Proust. Similar concerns were addressed in the plays of Luigi Pirandello (1867–1936), whose work explores human alienation and the contradictions of personality. The 20th century also marked the emergence of women writers, in particular Grazia Deledda (1875–1936), winner of the Nobel Prize in literature in 1926.

Fascist repression produced its own masterpieces, notably Primo Levi's powerful accounts of his experiences in the Nazi death camps, and Carlo Levi's *Christ Stopped at Eboli* (1945), an account of the poverty encountered by a writer exiled to southern Italy. Both were starkly realistic, as were the works of Alberto Moravia (1907–1990), a writer whose portrayal of the rapidly changing Italy of the postwar era found an audience beyond his home country. The same can be said of Umberto Eco *(The Name of the Rose),* and of Italy's greatest modern writer, Italo Calvino (1923–1989), whose subtle and often magical novels and short stories have been widely translated. ■

Rome is a city of popes, emperors, romance, sunny days, and fountain-filled piazzas; a city filled with museums, galleries, churches, and glorious monuments to almost a thousand years of empire.

Rome

Swiss guard

Rome

ROME (ROMA) IS WITHOUT EQUAL. NO OTHER CITY CAN MATCH ITS artistic, historical, or architectural riches, and no city presents quite such an intimidating sight-seeing prospect—merely visiting the absolute highlights will take you several days. It also has more than its share of modern problems—namely noise, traffic, and pollution—and on first acquaintance, especially during the sweltering summers, can seem too busy and bustling for comfort. Although this may sound off-putting, it only serves as a warning—it is easy to forget that Rome has a problematic present as well as a glorious past.

Your best approach to the city is an oblique one. Avoid the big-name sights at the outset, and ease yourself gently into the city with a coffee or a stroll around its more intimate squares—Piazza Navona and the market-filled Campo de' Fiori are two of the best. Remember that enjoying a city is not only about seeing the monuments, so leave time for aimless exploration of these districts and others like Trastevere and the Ghetto, two of the most rewarding old quarters.

Once you are ready for the sights, a clear map and basic sense of direction will stand you in good stead, as orientation around the

Enjoying a balmy summer's night on the Spanish Steps and Piazza di Spagna, one of Rome's most celebrated squares

and two of the city's most interesting churches, San Clemente and San Giovanni in Laterano. All of these sights could be comfortably seen in a day, although the last major church in this district, Santa Maria Maggiore, lies in a slightly isolated position in the unlovely area around Termini, Rome's main train station.

West of Piazza Venezia runs Corso Vittorio Emanuele II, the second of Rome's principal thoroughfares, cutting through what is often called the city's medieval and Renaissance heart. In truth, as elsewhere in Rome, the district it divides—the city's most appealing— is a medley of monuments from every era. Its key sights are the Palazzo Doria Pamphili, one of the city's top art galleries, and two major squares: Piazza Navona and Campo de' Fiori.

All manner of other churches, palaces, and nameless little nooks and corners lie scattered around the area, and you could spend a couple of days exploring this quarter alone (see pp. 66–67). If time is short, stick to the Pantheon, Rome's best-preserved ancient monument, and the churches of San Luigi dei Francesi (paintings by Caravaggio) and Santa Maria sopra Minerva (a fine Michelangelo sculpture).

An almost equally appealing area lies astride the third of Piazza Venezia's thoroughfares, the Via del Corso running to the north, whose side streets conceal such well-known attractions as the Trevi Fountain and Spanish Steps, not to mention the Palazzo Barberini (a major gallery), and a grid of streets around Via Condotti that make up the city's main shopping district. At its northern end, the Corso opens out into Piazza del Popolo, beyond which stretches the Villa Borghese, Rome's main park and the setting for two leading museums: the Galleria Borghese (paintings and sculpture) and Villa Giulia (ancient art and artifacts).

Across the Tevere (Tiber), Rome's principal river, stands St. Peter's Basilica, which requires most of a morning to see, including about an hour in the nearby Castel Sant'Angelo (see p. 82). In the same area, the tiny independent state of the Vatican City, are the Vatican Museums, home to the Sistine Chapel and the world's single greatest museum complex. ∎

old city is not difficult. Head first for Piazza Venezia, a vast traffic-filled square that lies more or less at the city's heart. Overlooking it is the Monumento a Vittore Emanuele II, a colossal shrine to Italian unification, flanked on its right by the Capitoline Hill, the core of the ancient city. Three principal roads lead from the square, each providing a useful focus for sight-seeing expeditions.

First of these is the Via dei Fori Imperiali, which runs south past the Roman Forum and Colosseum, two of the city's big set pieces. It also provides easy access to the Imperial Fora, San Pietro in Vincoli (known for its huge Michelangelo statue of Moses),

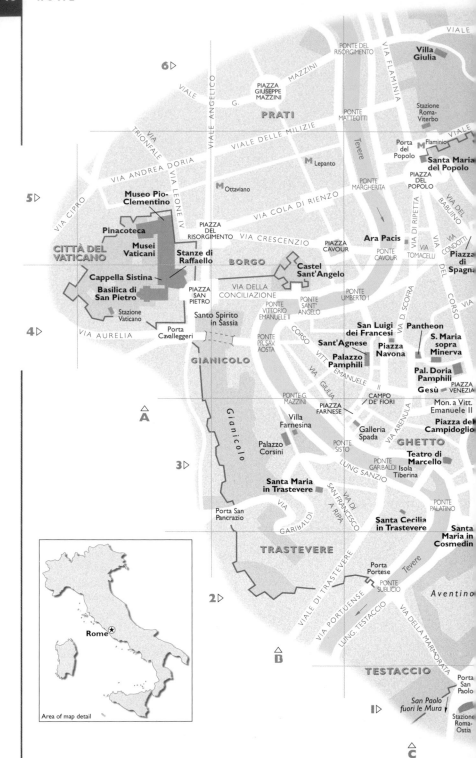

VIALE

6▷

PONTE DEL
RISORGIMENTO

**Villa
Giulia**

PRATI

VIALE ANGELICO

VIALE DELLE MILIZIE

PIAZZA
GIUSEPPE
MAZZINI

MAZZINI

VIA FLAMINIA

PONTE
MATTEOTTI

Stazione
Roma-
Viterbo

VIALE

G.

VIA TRIONFALE

VIA ANDREA DORIA

VIA LEONE IV

Tevere

M Lepanto

Porta
del
Popolo

M Flaminio

**Santa Maria
del Popolo**

5▷

**Museo Pio-
Clementino**

M Ottaviano

VIA COLA DI RIENZO

PONTE
MARGHERITA

PIAZZA
DEL
POPOLO

VIA DEL BABUINO

VIA CIPRO

Pinacoteca

PIAZZA
DEL
RISORGIMENTO

VIA CRESCENZIO

PIAZZA
CAVOUR

Ara Pacis

VIA DI RIPETTA

VIA
TOMACELLI

VIA
CONDOTTI

**CITTÀ DEL
VATICANO**

**Musei
Vaticani**

**Stanze di
Raffaello**

BORGO

**Castel
Sant'Angelo**

PONTE
CAVOUR

**Piazza
di
Spagna**

Cappella Sistina

VIA DELLA
CONCILIAZIONE

PONTE
UMBERTO I

VIA D. SCROFA

VIA DEL CORSO

**Basilica di
San Pietro**

PIAZZA
SAN
PIETRO

PONTE
VITTORIO
EMANUELE II

PONTE
SANT'
ANGELO

**San Luigi
dei Francesi**

Pantheon

Stazione
Vaticano

Santo Spirito
in Sassia

CORSO

Sant'Agnese

**Piazza
Navona**

**S. Maria
sopra
Minerva**

4▷

Porta
Cavalleggeri

VIA AURELIA

PONTE PR. SAV.
AOSTA

VIA GIULIA

**Palazzo
Pamphili**

**Pal. Doria
Pamphili**

GIANICOLO

VITT.

EMANUELE

Il

Gesù

PIAZZA
VENEZIA

VIA ARENULA

CAMPO
DE' FIORI

Mon. a Vitt.
Emanuele II

△
A

PONTE G.
MAZZINI

PIAZZA
FARNESE

**Piazza del
Campidoglio**

Gianicolo

Villa
Farnesina

Galleria
Spada

GHETTO

3▷

Palazzo
Corsini

PONTE
SISTO

**Teatro di
Marcello**

PONTE
GARIBALDI

Isola
Tiberina

PONTE
PALATINO

**Santa Maria
in Trastevere**

LUNG. SANZIO

VIA DI RIPA

VIA SAN FRANCESCO A RIPA

**Santa Cecilia
in Trastevere**

**Santa
Maria in
Cosmedin**

Porta San
Pancrazio

VIA
GARIBALDI

TRASTEVERE

Porta
Portese

Tevere

Aventino

2▷

VIALE DI TRASTEVERE

PONTE
SUBLICIO

△
B

Rome ★

Area of map detail

VIA PORTUENSE

LUNG. TESTACCIO

VIA DELLA MARMORATA

TESTACCIO

Porta
San
Paolo

I▷

San Paolo
fuori le Mura

Stazione
Roma-
Ostia

△
C

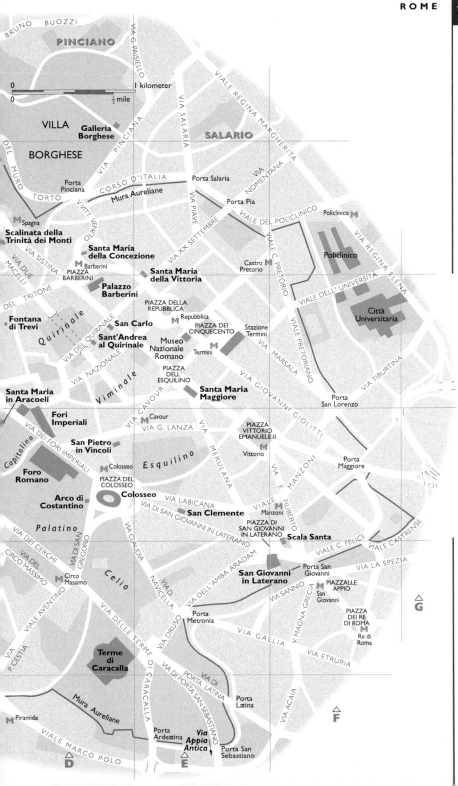

PINCIANO

VILLA
BORGHESE

Galleria
Borghese

SALARIO

0 | 1 kilometer
0 | ½ mile

Porta
Pinciana

CORSO D'ITALIA

Mura Aureliane

Porta Salaria

Porta Pia

VIA G. PAISIELLO

VIA PINCIANA

VIA SALARIA

VIALE REGINA MARGHERITA

VIA NOMENTANA

DEL MURO TORTO

V. VIT. VENETO

Policlinico

VIALE DEL POLICLINICO

Spagna

Scalinata della
Trinità dei Monti

Santa Maria
della Concezione

Barberini

PIAZZA
BARBERINI

Palazzo
Barberini

Fontana
di Trevi

San Carlo

Sant'Andrea
al Quirinale

Santa Maria
in Aracoeli

Fori
Imperiali

San Pietro
in Vincoli

Foro
Romano

Arco di
Costantino

Quirinale

Viminale

Museo
Nazionale
Romano

PIAZZA
DELL'
ESQUILINO

Cavour

Cavour

VIA G. LANZA

Colosseo

PIAZZA DEL
COLOSSEO

Colosseo

Palatino

VIA XX SETTEMBRE

VIA PIAVE

Santa Maria
della Vittoria

PIAZZA DELLA
REPUBBLICA

Repubblica

PIAZZA DELLA
REPUBBLICA

PIAZZA DEI
CINQUECENTO

Castro
Pretorio

VIA C. PRETORIO

Stazione
Termini

Termini

Santa Maria
Maggiore

PIAZZA
VITTORIO
EMANUELE II

Vittorio

San Clemente

Policlinico

Città
Universitaria

VIALE DELL' UNIVERSITA

VIA REGINA ELENA

VIA PRETORIANO

VIA MARSALA

VIA GIOVANNI GIOLITTI

Porta
San Lorenzo

VIA TIBURTINA

Porta
Maggiore

VIA E. FILIBERTO

Manzoni

PIAZZA DI
SAN GIOVANNI
IN LATERANO

Scala Santa

VIALE C. FELICE

VIALE CASTRENSE

VIA LA SPEZIA

Porta San
Giovanni

San Giovanni
in Laterano

PIAZZALLE
APPIO

San
Giovanni

PIAZZA
DEI RE
DI ROMA

Re di
Roma

Esquilino

VIA MERULANA

VIA DI SAN GIOVANNI IN LATERANO

VIA LABICANA

VIA CLAUDIA

Celio

Circo
Massimo

Terme
di
Caracalla

Mura Aureliane

Piramide

VIALE MARCO POLO

VIA DEI CERCHI

VIA DEL CIRCO MASSIMO

VIALE AVENTINO

P. CESTIA

VIA DELLE TERME DI CARACALLA

VIA DRUSO

VIA NAVICELLA

Porta
Metronia

VIA DELL' AMBA ARADAM

VIA DI PORTA SAN SEBASTIANO

VIA DI PORTA LATINA

Porta
Latina

VIA GALLIA

V. MAGNA GRECIA

VIA SANNIO

VIA ETRURIA

VIA ACAIA

Porta
Ardeatina

Porta
Latina

Via
Appia
Antica

Porta San
Sebastiano

Castro
Pretorio

VIALE C. PRETORIO

Stazione
Termini

D

E

F

G

An equestrian statue of Emperor Marcus Aurelius serves as the centerpiece of Piazza del Campidoglio.

Campidoglio

PIAZZA VENEZIA IS DOMINATED BY THE MONUMENTO A Vittorio Emanuele II, a shrine to Italian unification known locally as the "typewriter" or "wedding cake" after the shape and dazzling white-ness of its marble bulwarks. Its construction resulted in the destruction of countless medieval buildings and altered forever the contours of the Campidoglio or Capitolino (Capitoline Hill), the heart of ancient Rome and the most important of the city's original Seven Hills.

Campidoglio

🗺 46 C3

Musei Capitolini

✉ Piazza del Campidoglio

☎ 06 671 0207

🕐 Closed Sun. p.m. & Mon.

💲 $. Free last Sun. of the month

🚌 Bus: 56, 60, 64, 81, 87, & all other buses to Piazza Venezia

Inhabited since the Bronze Age, the Capitoline's southern summit once contained the city's most venerated temple, a shrine to Jupiter, while its northern promontory housed the Arx, Rome's earliest defensive citadel. Today, its main focus is the **Piazza del Campidoglio,** completed to an original design by Michelangelo in the 17th century. Palaces on either side contain

the linked **Musei Capitolini** (Capitoline Museums), home to a picture gallery and some of the city's most remarkable pieces of Roman and Greek statuary. The most impressive of all is the second-century equestrian statue of Emperor Marcus Aurelius, installed in the portico of the Palazzo del Museo Capitolino on the right (the statue in the square is

his successors after the original Roman forum became too crowded for further building. Many of their monuments now lie entombed beneath the Via dei Fori Imperiali, a road scythed through the area by Mussolini in 1932. Estimates suggest only one-fifth of the original area remains above ground.

Julius Caesar was the first to build on any scale outside the original forum, but time has been unkind to his creation, the **Foro di Cesare** (54–46 B.C.). His imperial successor, Augustus, was equally undermined by posterity—the ruins of the Tempio di Mars Ultor, flanked by columns on three sides, is more or less all that survives of his **Foro di Augusto** (2 B.C.– A.D. 14). Two large columns and a delightful frieze are the highlights of the **Foro di Nerva,** built by an emperor who reigned for just two years (A.D. 96–98). However, most people overlook this, and the **Foro di Vespasiano** (A.D. 71–75), in favor of the Emperor Trajan's **Foro Traiano** (A.D. 107–113), the most extravagant of the five fora.

Trajan's forum is dominated by Trajan's Column, the Imperial Fora's centerpiece. The top of the 97-foot (30 m) pillar was once the same height as the surrounding land, emphasizing the scale of the quarrying required to excavate the forum. The superbly preserved monument—widely considered the masterpiece of all Roman carving—was raised in A.D. 113 to commemorate victories over the Dacians, a warrior tribe who occupied much of present-day Romania. An intricate spiraling frieze 656 feet (200 m) in length winds around the column's 18 marble drums. Woven into its majestic marble narrative are scenes from Trajan's victorious campaigns—including some 2,500 figures. ∎

a copy). Walk to the rear left of the piazza for some memorable views over the Roman forum.

A flight of 112 steps leads to the church of **Santa Maria in Aracoeli,** an approach built in 1348 as a votive offering to cele-brate the passing of the Black Death. A less demanding approach is possible from the rear of Piazza del Campidoglio. Inside, the building has a musty, magical charm, particularly at dusk, when delicate chandeliers illuminate the gold-tinged ceiling and shadowy ancient columns. Artistic highlights include Pinturicchio's frescoes on the "Life of San Bernardino" (1486), in the first chapel in the south aisle.

The **Fori Imperiali** (Imperial Fora) is the name given to the five fora created by Julius Caesar and

The hundreds of figures on Trajan's Column have provided scholars with vital information regarding war and warfare in ancient Rome.

Foro Romano

FOR ALMOST A THOUSAND YEARS, THE FORO ROMANO (Roman Forum) was the heart of ancient Rome and the nerve center of an empire that extended across most of the known world. Today, all that remains is a jumble of romantic ruins, although its wistful beauty and myriad historical echoes still make it Europe's most important archaeological site. Altered and rebuilt over many centuries, its monuments—one superimposed on another—are often confusing. Don't expect to be overwhelmed by ancient grandeur—come instead to enjoy the hints of past splendors and the gentle charm of a once great site.

The forum began life as a marshy valley between the Palatine and Capitoline hills. During the Iron Age, it served as the cemetery on the fringes of a village, a location giving rise perhaps to the name (the Latin *forum* means "outside"). Later, it became a garbage dump for nearby settlements, and later still a communal market place. Its first distinct monuments probably appeared in the seventh century B.C. during the reigns of the first Etruscan kings.

As the empire flourished, so the forum began to accumulate all the structures of civic, religious, and political life. Patrician houses, shops, temples, and markets jostled for space and merchants, politicians, and emperors competed to fill the area with ever more magnificent monuments.

By the second century A.D., the building frenzy had run its course, largely because all available room had been taken up. The site remained a vital symbolic focus, however, despite the shift of political power to the Palatine, trade to the Mercato Traiano (Trajan's

The Roman Forum's scattered ruins include the Arco di Settimio Severo (right), a triumphal arch raised in A.D. 203.

Vestal Virgins

Vestal Virgins were required to tend Rome's sacred flame, a perpetually burning symbol of Rome's eternal character kept in the Tempio di Vesta. All were aged between six and ten at induction and were chosen only from the grandest patrician families. They served 30 years before being awarded a state pension and allowed to marry. Ten years were spent in learning, ten in performing, and ten in teaching their ritual tasks.

Incumbents who lost their virginity—a vestal's blood could not be spilt—were buried alive and the offending male flogged to death.

Those allowing the flame to die were whipped by the Pontifex Maximus, Rome's high priest, and forced to rekindle the fire using sacred pieces of wood. In return for their services, the virgins enjoyed high social esteem and had special rights, among them the power of mercy over condemned criminals, the right of way on all streets, permission to drive in carriages within the city limits (a right usually granted only to empresses), and the safekeeping of wills, including those of the emperor. Any injury inflicted on a virgin was punishable by death. ■

Market), and new building to the Imperial Fora.

After Rome's fall, time began to take its toll. Fire had ravaged the site in the third century, followed by earthquakes and the assaults of barbarian invaders in the fifth century. During the Middle Ages, stone was pillaged for churches and palaces and precious marbles reduced to dust in the lime kilns of builders. Eventually, the forum was so reduced that it became known as *campo vaccino*, or cow pasture. Coherent excavations only began toward the end of the 18th century and continue to this day.

THE SITE

Be sure to grasp an overview of the forum before exploring the site, the best of which can be obtained from Via del Campidoglio and the steps behind the Palazzo Senatorio on Piazza del Campidoglio. You need a good site plan and a great deal of imagination to make full sense of the ruins. What follows is a guide only to the better-preserved and more evocative monuments.

From the main entrance on Via dei Fori Imperiali, bear right on the Via Sacra, the ancient forum's most important street, and follow a roughly counter-clockwise route. This will leave you at the Arco di Tito exit, where you have the choice of walking up to the Palatine (see box, p. 52) or proceeding directly to the Colosseum (see pp. 54–57).

The first temple on your right, the **Tempio di Antonino e Faustina** (A.D. 141), is one of the forum's best preserved, largely because it was converted in the

Foro Romano

🅰 47 D3

✉ Entrances at Largo Romolo e Remo (at the junction of Via dei Fori Imperiali and Via Cavour) & Via di San Gregorio

☎ 06 699 0110

🕐 Closed Sun. p.m. & Mon.

💲 Forum: free. Palatine: $$

🚌 Bus: 85, 87, 175, & all other buses to Piazza Venezia. Metro: Colosseo

In a valley at the foot of the Palatine lie the remains of the Circo Massimo, where thousands of imperial chariot races once took place.

11th century to the church of San Lorenzo in Miranda. The original temple was raised by the Emperor Antoninus Pius in honor of his wife, Faustina (Roman gossip at the time suggests the emperor was the only man in the city unaware of his wife's numerous infidelities). Beyond on the right lies the **Basilica Aemilia** (179 B.C.), once a business and banking complex and reputedly among the forum's most beautiful buildings (it was all but destroyed during Alaric the Goth's attack on Rome in A.D. 410).

At the end of the Via Sacra stand two unmistakable monuments: the austere, brick built **Curia** and the

Arco di Settimio Severo. The space in front of them was known as the **Comitium,** probably the forum's first important meeting place and the hub of its early social, judicial, and civic life. Processions, funerals, and sacrifices took place here, local politicians met and voted in its halls, and judgments were handed down by the *praetor* in its law courts. The Curia was home to the Roman senate and its 300 senators (it became a church in the seventh century). The Arco (A.D. 203), or arch, was raised to celebrate the military triumphs of the Emperor Septimius, its four principal reliefs decorated with battle

Palatino

The Palatino (Palatine) was one of Rome's original Seven Hills. It was also the site of the city's earliest settlement—predating the forum—and the spot on which the legendary she-wolf is said to have suckled the twins Romulus and Remus.

One of Rome's earliest residential districts, it later became a favored location for the city's grandest imperial palaces (the word "palace" derives from the Latin *palatino*). Its ruins are now more confusing than those of the forum, but its views, lovely gardens, shady orange groves, and peaceful corners make this a wonderful area in which to take a break from sight-seeing. ■

scenes, the goddess of victory, and panels lauding Septimius' sons, Geta and Caracalla.

Below the arch stretches a ruined brick wall, all that remains of the **Imperial Rostra,** orators' platforms that took their name from the bronze ships' *rostra,* or prows, used to ram other boats in battle. Such prows were taken as spoils of war and once adorned the platforms. It was here that Mark Antony reputedly delivered his "Friends, Romans, and countrymen…" speech after the murder of Julius Caesar. Behind the arch to the left stand the eight red-gray columns of the **Tempio di Saturno** (479 B.C.), the oldest and most venerated of the forum's early temples. It was dedicated to Saturn, god of agriculture, Rome's early power having been deemed to stem from its agricultural prowess. The temple also housed the State's treasury of gold and silver.

With your back to the temple, the area in front of you to the right is the **Basilica Giulia** (54 B.C.), once a central courthouse. Beyond it are the three lonely columns of the **Tempio di Castore e Polluce.** Farther beyond lie two of the forum's most evocative sights, the **Tempio di Vesta** and **Atrium Vestae,** respectively the Temple of Vesta, goddess of the hearth, and the House of the Vestal Virgins (see box, p. 50). The former held Rome's eternal "sacred flame," a symbol of the city's well-being. Citizens ritually extinguished their fires on the first day of the Roman New Year (March 1) before relighting them with tapers taken from the flame. The extinguishing of the flame, tended by the Vestal Virgins, was considered the worst of all possible portents, foretelling the fall of Rome. Ashes from the fire were scattered on the Tiber on June 15 each year as part of a pagan ritual of continuity and regeneration.

On the left beyond the Atrium rises the **Basilica di Massenzio** (A.D. 306), whose vast trio of vaults make up one of the forum's most physically impressive sights. The **Arco di Tito** near the exit is an arch built in A.D. 81 to commemorate the capture of Jerusalem by the Emperor Titus. Its reliefs show Titus's triumphal return to Rome and the removal of treasures from the holy city. ■

Colosseo

THE COLOSSEO (COLOSSEUM) IS THE ROMAN WORLD'S largest surviving structure, its majestic impact undimmed either by the passage of time or the blight of today's encircling traffic. Once its walls echoed to the sounds of gladiatorial combat and the roar of the Roman mob, and later to the chink of hammers as its stones were pillaged to build Rome's medieval churches and palaces. Today, its walls are still standing, albeit half-ravaged, defying the famous prophecy that "while the Colosseum stands, Rome shall stand; when the Colosseum falls, Rome shall fall; when Rome falls, the world shall fall."

Colosseo

🏛 47 D3

✉ Piazza del Colosseo

☎ 06 700 4261

🕐 1st floor closed Sun. p.m. & Mon. p.m.

💲 Ground floor: free. 1st floor: $$

🚌 Bus: 85, 87, & 175. Tram: 30 to Piazza del Colosseo. Metro: Colosseo

Opposite:
The three tiers
of the Colosseum
feature the three
main classical
orders of pillars
and capitals:
Doric, Ionic,
and Corinthian.

RISE & FALL

The Colosseum was the brainchild of the Emperor Vespasian in A.D. 70, who wanted a monument to celebrate his military triumphs in the Middle East. Unfinished at his death in A.D. 79, the building was continued by Vespasian's son, Titus, its inauguration taking place in A.D. 80. Finishing touches were added by Titus's successor, Domitian (A.D. 81–96), who like his predecessors was a member of the Flavian dynasty, hence the name by which the arena was originally known— the Amphitheatrum Flavianum. Its present name may derive simply from its size, or, more probably, from the presence (it is now lost) of the nearby Colossus of Nero, once the world's largest bronze statue.

The Colosseum's vast scale presented huge engineering problems, not least those offered by the marshy site—chosen for its proximity to the Forum and Palatine Hill—previously used as a ceremonial lake for the Domus Aurea, or Golden House, of the Emperor Nero. Immense drainage channels, many still extant, honeycombed the foundations, while huge quantities of light volcanic tufa and brick-clad cement were used to form the walls. More than a million cubic feet (100,000 cubic meters) of travertine marble gilded its surfaces, a decorative veneer held in place by 300 tons of iron brackets (these brackets were wrenched out in A.D. 664, hence the puzzling holes that pockmark the building's exterior).

The completed amphitheater was a model of simplicity and function, providing a template not only for other Roman amphitheaters, but also for numerous stadiums of the modern age. Some 50,000 spectators could enter and leave by one of the 80 numbered *vomitoria*, or exits, while 240 wooden masts on the upper story supported a broad *velarium*, or sailcloth awning, swung into place to protect crowds from the sun by sailors of the imperial fleet. Sand covered the amphitheater's floor, its purpose to prevent combatants slipping and to soak up the blood of gladitorial combat (the Latin *arena* [sand] would be used from this time on to describe places of spectacle). All manner of understage tunnels, pulleys, and lifts enabled animals and contestants to be brought to the arena, while conduits and aqueducts were used to flood the arena to allow the staging of *naumachiae*, or mock sea battles.

The building fell into decline early. A fire in A.D. 240 destroyed much of the stage area and upper seating, both of which were constructed largely of wood. Further conflagrations and earthquakes compounded the damage over the

Bloodthirsty combats between gladiators were some of the most popular events staged in the Colosseum.

next two centuries. After Rome's fall, a small church was built nearby and the stage area used as a cemetery. Some parts of the monument then became a fortress, others homes, or shops. Stone was ruthlessly plundered from the site, finding its way in to the Palazzo Farnese, Palazzo Venezia, Palazzo Barberini, and any number of smaller palaces, churches, and latter-day bridges. Two-thirds of the monument vanished over the years—more would have gone had it not been for Pope Benedict XIV, who consecrated the site in 1749 in honor of the Christians supposedly martyred here. Subsequent popes and administrators then began a process of restoration, excavation, and consolidation that continues to the present day.

THE GAMES

One of the Colosseum's most enduring myths—that it ran red with the blood of Christian martyrs—is just that: a myth. Evidence suggests few, if any, Christians died here, Rome's great religious persecutions having taken place during Emperor Nero's reign some 30 years before the building's completion. Many others, however, certainly did die here.

Gladiators had originally fought in ritual combat to prepare for battle, a practice inherited by the Romans from the Samnites and Etruscans. By Vespasian's time, the practice had been debased, the games, or *munera* (dutiful gifts),

Vomitoria (exits)

Upper story

Corinthian columns

Ionic columns

Doric columns

Internal corridor

having become part of the decline of a population, which, in Juvenal's famous phrase, had sold its soul for free food and entertainment, or *panem et circenses* (bread and circuses). Individuals initially sponsored the events, but by Domitian's time, the games were so important that they were the gift of emperors alone.

Daily performances usually followed a timetable. First came the *venationes,* or animal hunts: Trajan's victories in Dacia in A.D. 107, for example, were followed by 123 days of games involving some 10,000 gladiators and the deaths of 10,000 animals. Then came public killings, often preceded by bouts of torture and completed with the use of gruesomely complicated instruments of death. The playing out of macabre episodes from Greek and Roman mythology were added refinements. The main highlight, the gladitorial games themselves, came last.

Ever more ingenious variations were used to spice up the games. Men, women, animals—even midgets—fought one another. Criminals and slaves often grappled to the death, with spectators gambling on a contest's outcome. Slaves could be won in an imperial lottery, while spectators held a combatant's fate—literally—in their hands: A waved handkerchief signified salvation, the more famous—and more usual—down-turned thumb meant death. Even those who survived often had their throats cut, while the dead were teased with red-hot pokers to ensure they had actually died. Gladiatorial contests survived until A.D. 438, while the last animal extravaganza was recorded in A.D. 523. ■

A detail from the Arco di Costantino, a fourth-century triumphal arch raised in the shadow of the Colosseum.

Understage tunnels

Holes left after the removal of iron brackets

ARCO DI COSTANTINO

Immediately alongside the Colosseum, stands the Arco di Costantino, a triumphal arch built in A.D. 315 to celebrate the Emperor Constantine's victory three years earlier over his rival, Maxentius. One of Imperial Rome's last great monuments, it used many decorative reliefs pilfered from earlier classical buildings. ■

Michelangelo's "Moses," flanked by "Leah" and "Rachel," symbols of the active and contemplative life.

San Pietro in Vincoli

SAN PIETRO IN VINCOLI WOULD BE JUST ANOTHER CHURCH, barely worth the five-minute stroll from the Colosseum, were it not for one astounding statue and a relic of tantalizing repute. According to tradition, the church was founded in A.D. 442, supposedly on the spot where four centuries earlier St. Peter had been condemned to death during the persecutions of the Emperor Nero.

San Pietro in Vincoli

 47 D3

✉ Piazza San Pietro in Vincoli 4a

☎ 06 488 2865

🚌 Bus: 62 & 64 Tram: 30 to Colosseo. Metro: Colosseo

San Pietro's original purpose was to house the *vincoli*, or chains, allegedly used to bind St. Peter in Jerusalem, relics given to Pope Leo I by the Empress Eudoxia, wife of the Roman Emperor Valentinian III. Some time later, a second set of chains, reputedly used to shackle the saint in Rome, were brought here from Constantinople. On being united, the chains fused miraculously and you can see them preserved in this state in a casket below the high altar.

A more persuasive sight awaits you at the top of the right nave, a monumental **"Moses"** by Michelangelo, one of 42 proposed figures for the sepulchre of Pope Julius II. This "tragedy of a tomb," as Michelangelo called it, occupied the

sculptor for years, but only this statue and a handful of fragments were ever completed. Julius kept Michelangelo busy in the Sistine Chapel instead, and, once Julius died, few subsequent popes felt inclined to lavish funds on the glorification of a predecessor. Yet in the powerful and spiritually charged figure of Moses, Michelangelo produced one of his greatest masterpieces, capturing the prophet at the moment he receives the tablets of the Ten Commandments. The figure's horns represent beams of light, features frequently attributed to the prophet in medieval art, while the beard contains a faint but distinctive signature—a self-portrait of the sculptor. ■

San Clemente

SAN CLEMENTE IS A GEM OF A CHURCH, A PLACE WHERE three phases of Rome's long religious history lie layered one above another. The first is encapsulated by a peerless medieval church (1108–1130), beneath which lies a second older church, founded in A.D. 392, perhaps earlier. Below this again extend the ruins of a temple dedicated to one of Rome's most important pre-Christian cults.

The highlights of the medieval church are many. Most eye-catching are the nave's *schola cantorum,* or **choir screen,** pulpits, and parts of the *baldacchino,* or altar canopy. A 12th-century **mosaic** behind the altar depicts "The Triumph of the Cross," below which stands a 14th-century marble tabernacle by Arnolfo di Cambio and frescoes of saints. Important paintings on the "Life of St. Catherine" (1428), the work of Florentine artist Masolino da Panicale, swathe a chapel next to the church's side entrance.

Steps lead down to the older church, built in honor of San Clemente, Rome's fourth bishop and pope. It was destroyed by the Normans in 1084, but preserves faded frescoes from the fifth or sixth century. The church was only discovered in 1857.

More steps go down to the oldest area of the complex (first century A.D.), a series of chambers and tunnels that include the remains of a **Mithraic temple** and the partially excavated remains of a Roman street, warehouse, and patrician palace. The sound of running water comes from an underground stream that runs to the Cloaca Maxima, ancient Rome's principal sewer. ∎

San Clemente
- 47 E3
- Via di San Giovanni in Laterano
- 06 7045 1018
- Bus: 85 to Via di San Giovanni in Laterano, or 87 & 186 to Via Labicana

Much of San Clemente's beautiful medieval interior was salvaged from an earlier church destroyed by the Normans.

San Giovanni in Laterano

**San Giovanni
in Laterano**

🅰 47 F2

✉ Piazza di San
Giovanni in
Laterano

☎ 06 6988 6433 or
06 6988 6452

🕐 Scala Santa closed
a.m. in summer

💲 Church, Baptistery,
& Scala Santa: free.
Cloister: $

🚇 Metro: San Giovanni

SAN GIOVANNI IS ROME'S CATHEDRAL CHURCH, NOT St. Peter's as many visitors assume. It is also the "Mother and head of all the churches of the city and the world," according to the Latin inscription across its towering facade. Built around A.D. 314 by Constantine, the first Christian emperor, the church has witnessed all manner of historical events: Charlemagne was baptized here in 774, popes were crowned at its altar until the 19th century, and, with the signing of the Lateran Treaty in 1929, it saw Mussolini and the papacy formalize relations between Church and State.

The interior, much altered by fire, earthquakes, and rebuilding over the centuries, is largely the work of Borromini, a tortured baroque genius who remodeled much of the church between 1646 and 1650. Certain earlier parts of the building survive, notably the superlative wooden ceiling, the Gothic tabernacle (1367) above the altar—said to contain the skulls of saints Peter and Paul—and a patch of fresco, possibly by Giotto, showing Boniface proclaiming the first Holy Year in 1300 (first pillar, right aisle). However, all these pale beside the **cloister,** a sublime ensemble located off the north aisle.

Linked to the church, but entered separately, is Italy's earliest **Baptistery,** whose octagonal form was the model for similar buildings across the country. Although much restored, it is the only surviving fragment of the original fourth-century church: Its centerpiece is a scintillating fifth-century mosaic. On the northeast flank of the church square lies the **Scala Santa,** reputedly the marble staircase from Pontius Pilate's Jerusalem palace that Christ ascended during his trial. Penitents who mount the stairs on their knees believe they will gain nine years respite from purgatory for every step climbed. ∎

The facade (1735) of San Giovanni in Laterano is known for its statues of Christ and the Apostles, visible for miles around, and for its magnificent bronze doors.

Santa Maria Maggiore

The mosaics in Santa Maria Maggiore, some over 1,400 years old, are among the most impressive in Rome.

SANTA MARIA MAGGIORE IS ONE OF ROME'S FOUR GREAT basilican churches, along with St. Peter's, San Giovanni, and San Paolo fuori le Mura. Founded around A.D. 420, it was built to celebrate a summer snowfall in A.D. 358, during which the snow reputedly marked the outlines of the future church. Today it is Rome's finest early Christian basilica, an important point of pilgrimage, and the largest of the city's churches devoted to the Virgin.

The first feature to catch the eye is the sumptuous ceiling, supported by 40 massive columns removed from ancient Roman buildings. Swathes of decoration cover nearly every surface: The most outstanding is the mosaic (1290–95) in the apse by Jacopo Torriti, widely considered the apogee of Rome's medieval mosaic tradition. Equally important mosaics adorn the nave and triumphal arch, a more extensive sequence than Torriti's, dating from the fifth century. Elsewhere, be sure to look at the **Cappella Sistina** (1585), off the south aisle, almost a church within a church. It was built by Dominico Fontana for Pope Sixtus V. Across the nave lies the **Cappella Paolina** (1611), commissioned by two popes, Paul V and Clement VIII. Its orgy of decorative excess was deliberately designed to outshine Sixtus' chapel opposite.

Within the **high altar** are the relics that draw most of the church's pilgrims: five pieces of iron-bound wood said to be fragments of Christ's Bethlehem crib, a prize revealed to public scrutiny on the 25th of every month (it is only brought out into the basilica itself on Christmas Eve). Almost immediately to the altar's right lies the church's loveliest sepulchral monument, the "Tomb of Cardinal Cosalvo Rodriguez" (died 1299), adorned with beautiful marble inlay by Giovanni Cosmati, one of a family of craftsmen that gave its name to this much-copied form of decoration. ∎

Santa Maria Maggiore

🅰 47 E4

✉ Entrances on Piazza dell'Esquilino & Piazza Santa Maria Maggiore

☎ 06 483 195

🚌 Bus: 4, 9, 16, & all other buses to Piazza dei Cinquecento. Metro: Cavour

Piazza Navona

PIAZZA NAVONA IS ROME'S LOVELIEST SQUARE, A NATURAL
magnet for visitors by day or night, and an ideal place to spend
an hour or so people-watching while ensconced at one of its many
cafés. Broadly elliptical in shape, the piazza's outline matches that of
the Circus Agonalis—from which the square's name derives—a vast
30,000-seat stadium inaugurated by the Emperor Domitian in A.D. 86.

Piazza Navona

🅰 46 C4

🚌 Bus: 81 & 87 to
Corso del Rinasci-
mento

The square underwent its most
significant transformation in 1644,
when Pope Innocent X embarked
on a radical program of baroque
rebuilding. Chief among the resulting monuments were two outstanding fountains by Bernini, the
Fontana del Moro (at the square's
southern end), and the central
Fontana dei Quattro Fiumi,
or Fountain of the Four Rivers.
Statues on the latter symbolize the
four Rivers of Paradise, the Danube,

Nile, Plate, and Ganges, and the
four corners of the known world—
Asia, Africa, Europe, and America.

On the square's western side is
the church of **Sant' Agnese,** its
concave facade (1653–57) the work
of Bernini's great rival, Francesco
Borromini. It stands on the site
of the martyrdom of St. Agnes, a
13-year-old virgin killed for refusing
to marry a pagan. One of Innocent
X's many palaces, the **Palazzo
Pamphili** stands alongside. ∎

Campo de' Fiori

Campo de' Fiori (literally "field of flowers") has a wonderful street market, where every day except Sunday the ramshackle square overflows with fruit, fish, flower, and vegetable stands and stallholders who look as though they have stepped straight out of a Fellini movie.

Campo de' Fiori does not have a church—a rare occurrence in Rome. It has also long been one of the city's more down-at-heel districts: It was here, for example, that the painter Caravaggio murdered an acquaintance after losing a game of tennis. Nothing symbolizes the piazza's secular nature better than the half-hidden statue at its heart, the somber, cowled figure of Giordano Bruno, a humanist philosopher burned for heresy here in 1600.

Piazza Farnese, a bright, open square to the south, provides a counterpoint to the Campo's more

cramped charms. Here all is decorum and refinement, thanks mainly to the **Palazzo Farnese** (1515), now the French Embassy, part of whose facade is the work of Michelangelo. Be sure to explore **Via Giulia,** one of Rome's most elegant streets, to the rear of the palace. ∎

Stallholders in the Campo de' Fiori market, held in one of Rome's most appealing squares

Palazzo Doria Pamphili

Strands of Rome's long past are still woven into the city's present, few of them more marked than the Palazzo Doria Pamphili, a rambling 1,000-room palace that still belongs to the Pamphili, one of Rome's preeminent medieval patrician families. Part of the palace is given over to the family's private art collection, a collection that ranks with those of the Vatican and Galleria Borghese as one of the finest in the city.

The collection was founded by Pope Innocent X, a member of the Pamphili dynasty, and augmented when subsequent family members married into the equally elevated Doria and Borghese clans. Today, the paintings are ranged around

part of the palace's first floor, their beautifully appointed setting almost as splendid as the works of art themselves. Guided tours around other areas of the palace are available most mornings for a small additional fee.

The pictorial highlights are many. Make a special point of seeking out Velázquez's celebrated portrait of "Innocent X" (1650), a picture that captures all too clearly the man's suspicious and feeble-minded nature. Pope Innocent himself is said to have complained that the portrait was "too true, too true." Also look for works by Titian, Tintoretto, Filippo Lippi, Caravaggio, and Raphael's magnificent "Portrait of Two Venetians." ∎

Palazzo Doria Pamphili
🗺 46 C4
✉ Piazza del Collegio Romano 1a-Via del Corso
☎ 06 679 7323
🕐 Apartments closed p.m.
💲 Gallery: $$. Apartments: $$
🚌 Bus: 44, 46, 56, 60, 61, 64, & all other buses to Piazza Venezia

Pantheon

Only from
the Pantheon's
interior can you
appreciate the
scale of the 1,900-
year-old dome.

AFTER THE RAVAGED BUT ROMANTIC BEAUTY OF THE Forum and the shattered majesty of the Colosseum, the pristine grandeur of the Pantheon provides Rome's most powerful illustration of how the ancient city might once have appeared. It is also centrally located and within easy reach of several other sights, most notably Santa Maria sopra Minerva, a rare medieval fossil among Rome's surfeit of baroque churches, and the church of San Luigi dei Francesi (see p. 82), best known for an outstanding trio of paintings by Caravaggio.

Pantheon
- 46 C4
- Piazza della Rotonda
- 06 6830 0230
- Closed Sun. p m
- Bus: 116 to Piazza della Rotonda, or 81 & 87 to Corso del Rinascimento

The Emperor Hadrian completed the Pantheon in A.D. 128—probably to his own design—replacing much of an earlier temple on the site raised in 27 B.C. by Marcus Agrippa, son in law of the Emperor Augustus. Hadrian retained the pediment's imposing inscription, which attributed the building to Agrippa: The Latin text reads

"Marcus Agrippa, son of Lucius, consul for the third time, built this."

The building's miraculous state of preservation stems from its conversion to a Christian church in A.D. 609, a transformation that ensured that the removal of even a single stone would constitute a mortal sin. On November 1 of the same year the church was christened Santa

Maria ad Martyres (the Virgin and all the Martyrs), a date commemorated ever since as All Saints' Day.

Today the building is still a church, and both its interior and exterior look virtually as they did in the second century. Not all the interior marbles are original, although their patterning and arrangement are believed to conform to Hadrian's original scheme. Around the walls lie the **tombs** of Raphael and two Italian kings, Umberto I and Vittore Emanuele I.

The **dome** is one of the masterpieces of Roman engineering. Larger than St. Peter's, it was the largest concrete construction undertaken until the 20th century, and the world's largest freestanding dome until as recently as 1960. The dome's *oculus,* the circular hole that opens to the sky, was a key feature of Hadrian's original plan, its purpose being both practical—it helped illuminate the interior—and spiritual, allowing those in the temple direct contemplation of the heavens. ■

Santa Maria sopra Minerva

Santa Maria sopra Minerva

- 46 C4
- Piazza della Minerva 42
- 06 679 3926
- Closed during services
- Bus: 119 to Piazza della Rotonda

The delightful marble elephant in Piazza della Minerva was designed by Bernini and sculpted by Ercole Ferrata in 1667.

Santa Maria's plain Gothic facade is unique in Rome, a city where most churches were reworked along baroque lines during the 16th and 17th centuries. As singular in its way is Bernini's elephant statue (1667) in front of the church, an idiosyncratic work in which the elephant is supposed to represent piety and wisdom, Christianity's founding virtues; the Egyptian obelisk on the elephant's back dates from the sixth century B.C. The present church (1280) was originally built over *(sopra)* an earlier Roman temple to Minerva—hence its name.

Pride of place among the interior's many paintings goes to a series of frescoes (1488–1492) by the Florentine artist Filippino Lippi. They portray the "Annunciation" and "Episodes from the Life of St. Thomas Aquinas" (first chapel of the south transept). Another Florentine painter, Fra Angelico, is buried near the high altar, as is one of Italy's patron saints, Catherine of Siena (minus her head, which is in Siena). The church's sculptural masterpiece is Michelangelo's "Redeemer" (1519–1521), criticized on its unveiling for appearing too much like a pagan god. ■

A walking tour of medieval Rome

From Piazza Colonna, this walk explores some of Rome's more enchanting back streets, wending through artisans' quarters and the old Ghetto before crossing the Tiber River to finish in the atmospheric district of Trastevere.

Start at **Piazza Colonna ❶**, named after the Colonna di Marco Aurelio, a relief-covered column raised in the second century to celebrate the military triumphs of the Emperor Aurelius. Beyond it stands Bernini's Palazzo di Montecitorio (1650), now the lower house of the Italian parliament. Then walk west on Via Uffici di Vicario past the venerable Caffè Giolitti at No. 40, aiming for **Sant' Agostino,** a Renaissance church off Via della Scrofa known for paintings by Caravaggio and Raphael. More canvases by the former lie in **San Luigi dei Francesi ❷** (see p. 82) to the south, from whence you should walk east on Via Giustiniani to visit the **Pantheon ❸** (see pp. 64–65) and **Santa Maria sopra Minerva ❹** (see p. 65).

From the Piazza della Rotonda next to the Pantheon, walk west to Corso del Rinascimento by way of Piazza Sant'Eustachio. On the way, note the Palazzo della Sapienza, whose courtyard contains the entrance to Sant'Ivo alla Sapienza (1602–1660), an eccentric-looking church—the twisting tower is modeled on a bee's sting—designed by Francesco Borromini. Cross the Corso and enter **Piazza Navona ❺** (see p. 62), leaving the square midway down its western side on Via di Tor Millina. The Bar della Pace at the end of this street is an attractive spot to break for coffee.

Bear right (north) toward Via dei Coronari, a street known for its antique shops. Follow it west until Via del Panico, where you should turn left and twist through the back streets to the **Chiesa Nuova ❻**, a church celebrated for paintings by Rubens and a baroque fresco cycle by Pietro da Cortona. Cross Corso Vittorio Emanuele II in front of the church and continue straight before turning left on Via del Pellegrino and then almost immediately right onto Via dei Cappellari. Lined with dusty furniture workshops, the latter presents a picturesque view of old Rome.

Follow the street to **Campo de' Fiori ❼** (see p. 63) and then turn right into Piazza Farnese. Take Via di Monserrato from this square's southern corner past the **Palazzo Spada** (*Piazza Capo di Ferro, tel 06 686 1158, closed Sun. p.m. & Mon.*), known for its decorated facade, a modest art gallery, and Borromini's trompe l'oeil colonnade (a pillar-lined corridor cleverly made to look longer than it is).

Turn left on Via Arco del Monte and then right on Via Giubbonari. Cross Via Arenula and follow Via dei Falegnami into the pretty web of streets that once made up Rome's Jewish Ghetto. In Piazza Mattei, a short distance farther down the street, is one of the city's most charming fountains, the **Fontana delle Tartarughe** (1581), named after Bernini's quaint bronze *tartarughe* (tortoises).

Turn right out of the piazza heading south and then left on Via del Portico d'Ottavia, a street named after the Roman ruins at its eastern end, once the *portico* (entrance) to a vast library and temple complex. Follow the street as it bends right, passing Rome's main synagogue and the circular bulwarks of the **Teatro di Marcello ❽**, a first-century B.C. amphitheater later covered by medieval

---

- 🅜 Also see area map, p. 46 C4
- ▶ Piazza Colonna
- 🕒 3.25 miles (5.25 km)
- 🕓 5 hours
- ▶ Piazza Santa Maria in Trastevere

NOT TO BE MISSED
- San Luigi dei Francesi
- Pantheon
- Santa Maria sopra Minerva
- Piazza Navona
- Campo de' Fiori
- Trastevere
- Santa Maria in Trastevere

houses. Cross the riverside street, the Lungotevere, and take the Ponte Fabricio ahead to the **Isola Tiberina ⑨**, an island largely given over to a hospital dating from 1538. Stroll the island's walkways and drop into the church of **San Bartolomeo,** built in the 11th century over a pagan temple to Aesculapius, god of the healing arts.

Cross the Ponte Cestio to the district known as **Trastevere** (literally "over the Tiber"). Traditionally a blue-collar enclave, this is a colorful area known for its restaurants

and nightlife, though the trendier bars and clubs are increasingly shifting farther south to a more downbeat area around Testaccio. Beyond the Lungotevere, walk south on Via Anicia from Piazza in Piscinula, to look at the church of **Santa Cecilia in Trastevere** (see p. 82), known for its ninth-century mosaic, and then double back to pick up Via della Lungaretta. Follow this to **Santa Maria in Trastevere ⑩** (see p. 82), another fine mosaic-laden church set in a lovely square at the heart of Trastevere. ■

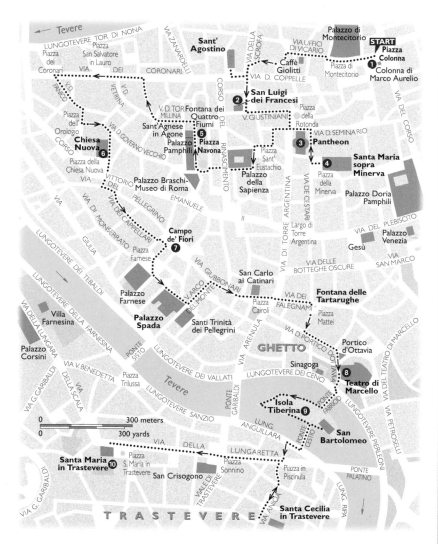

Fontana di Trevi

IT HAS TO BE ONE OF THE MOST MEMORABLE IMAGES
from postwar movies: Anita Ekberg, black-clad and bosom heaving,
trails through the placid waters of the Fontana di Trevi in *La Dolce
Vita*, Fellini's paen to the indolent, easy-living days of Rome in the late
1950s. The director chose his backdrop with care—the Trevi Fountain
is the most beautiful of all the city's many silvery fountains.

Fontana di Trevi

 47 D4

✉ Piazza di Trevi

The first fountain on this site was
built in 1453 for Pope Nicholas V,
taking its waters from the Acqua
Vergine, an aqueduct built by
Augustus in A.D. 19. The present
fountain, modeled on the Arco
di Costantino (see p. 57), was built
between 1732 and 1762 for Clement
XII, although the designer's identity
remains uncertain. Few sights in
Rome are as lovely at first glimpse,
narrow cobbled lanes suddenly
opening up to reveal the *fontana*

ranged across an entire wall of the
Palazzo Poli. The fountain's name
derives from these lanes—the *tre vie*
(three streets) that meet here.

At the fountain's center stands
a statue of "Oceanus" (Neptune),
flanked by horse-riding tritons
that symbolize a stormy sea (left)
and the sea in repose (right). The
niche statues behind "Oceanus"
represent Health and Abundance,
the pediment statues the four
seasons with their gifts. ■

Piazza di Spagna

The Piazza di Spagna and the Spanish Steps are one of Rome's great set pieces. Both the square and its famous flight of steps take their name from the Palazzo Spagna, built in 1622 as the residence of the Spanish Ambassador to the Holy See. Long one of the city's focal points, the piazza is as renowned today as a meeting place as for its surfeit of monuments. During the heyday of the Grand Tour (see pp. 72–73), the square and its surrounding streets provided a magnet for artists and foreign visitors. Hotels, studios, and cafés attracted many famous names, among them Byron, Liszt, Stendhal, and Wagner—you can sample something of the flavor of the times at a survivor of the period, the nearby **Caffè Greco** at Via Condotti 86.

No single character is more associated with the piazza than the English Romantic poet John Keats, who came to Rome in 1821 seeking a cure from tuberculosis, only to die in a house alongside the Spanish Steps. Today the building houses a fascinating museum given over to Keats, Shelley (who also died in Italy), and other 19th-century literary figures.

Other sights on the square include the eccentric little **Fontana della Barcaccia** at the foot of the steps, deliberately designed—possibly by Bernini—to resemble a half-submerged boat, in memory of the floods of 1598. Many visitors will also be seduced by the fine stores and galleries on surrounding streets—the area is Rome's premier shopping district. ■

Piazza di Spagna

🅰 46 C5

Keats-Shelley Memorial House

✉ Piazza di Spagna 26
☎ 06 678 4235
🕐 Closed Sun.
💲 $
🚌 Bus: 119.
Metro: Spagna

Palazzo Barberini

🅰 47 D4
✉ Via delle Quattro Fontane 13
☎ 06 481 4591
🕐 Closed Mon.
💲 $$
🚌 Bus: 58, 71, & 160.
Metro: Barberini

Palazzo Barberini

The Palazzo Barberini has a distinguished pedigree: Its architects were three of the biggest names of their day—Bernini, Carlo Maderno, and Borromini—while its founding family, the Barberini, was one of Rome's greatest medieval dynasties. Today, its magnificent baroque interior houses the Galleria Nazionale d'Arte Antica, part of Italy's national art collection and one of Rome's premier galleries.

The palace is an attraction in itself, all sweeping staircases, grandiose suites, and labyrinthine apartments. Few rooms, even in Rome, can match the almost overblown splendor of its great set piece, the **Gran Salone,** crowned with a dazzling ceiling

fresco by Pietro da Cortona depicting an "Allegory of Divine Providence" (1638–39).

Only paintings of the first rank can compete with such surroundings, paintings such as Raphael's famous "La Fornarinia," possibly a portrait of the artist's mistress, a baker's daughter (*fornaio* means "baker"). The work was completed in the year the painter died, a demise reputedly hastened by his mistress's voracious sexual demands. Other exceptional works from the early Renaissance period include pictures by Fra Angelico, Filippo Lippi, and Perugino, while the late Renaissance is represented by, among others, Titian, Tintoretto, Lorenzo Lotto, Caravaggio, and Andrea del Sarto. ■

"Conversion of St. Paul" (1601), one of two masterpieces by Caravaggio in Santa Maria del Popolo

Santa Maria del Popolo

- 46 C5
- ✉ Piazza del Popolo 12
- ☎ 06 361 0836
- 🚇 Bus: 119. Metro: Flaminio

A marble tomb with relic in Santa Maria del Popolo

Santa Maria del Popolo

SANTA MARIA DEL POPOLO STANDS ON THE EDGE OF Piazza del Popolo, a broad square close to the city's old northern gateway. Church and square both take their name from the *populus,* or hamlet, which stood here during the Middle Ages. The church is laden with interior treasures and makes an essential stopover before exploring the park and galleries of the nearby Villa Borghese.

Santa Maria was founded in 1099 over the tomb of the Emperor Nero, its purpose to reclaim for Christianity ground sullied by contact with the pagan demagogue. Much of the present building is by Bramante and Bernini and dates from the 16th and 17th centuries.

The interior's most prized sight is the **Cappella Chigi** (1513), commissioned from Raphael by the Sienese banker Agostino Chigi, who instructed the artist that his chapel should "convert earthly things into heavenly." All the decoration here is by Raphael, except for a handful of Bernini medallions on the Chigi tombs and Sebastiano del Piombo's altarpiece painting of the "Birth of the Virgin." Other treasures include two paintings by Caravaggio (north transept), a set of **frescoes** (1485–89) by Pinturicchio behind the high altar, and a pair of tombs (1505–1507) in the choir by Andrea da Sansovino. ■

Villa Borghese

THE OPEN SPACES AND SHADY WALKS OF ROME'S MOST central park act like a soothing balm after the maelstrom of much of the city center. They're also home to two of the city's most important galleries: the Galleria Borghese, crammed with priceless paintings and sculptures, and the Villa Giulia, widely considered the world's greatest museum of Etruscan art and artifacts.

The splendor of a 17th-century patrician summerhouse forms the backdrop for the Galleria Borghese's sublime works of art.

The park, the first of its kind in Rome, was originally laid out between 1613 and 1616 for the Borghese family, providing them with a shady country retreat during the fierce heat of the Roman summer. Today, the lakes, fountains, woods, and grassy spaces make it perfect for a stroll or siesta. It offers plenty of chances to escape the crowds, even on Sundays, when the park is at its busiest.

The **Galleria Borghese** at its heart was once the Villa Borghese's *casino* (little house), the name given to the principal building of an Italian country estate. The word's later association with gambling stems from the fact this was often the major pursuit of such houses' inhabitants. Although smaller than many galleries in Rome, the Borghese's collection is widely considered the city's most ravishing.

Many of the works were commissioned by Cardinal Scipione Borghese, a nephew of Pope Paul V, and bought by the state in 1902. Scipione was a great patron of Bernini, one of the baroque's leading lights, whose works dominate the gallery's sculpture sections. The most notorious sculpture, however, is by Antonio Canova: an erotic statue (1805–1808) of Paolina Borghese, sister of Napoleon and husband of Camillo Borghese. Among the many valuable paintings are works by Raphael, Titian, Botticelli, and Caravaggio.

The **Villa Giulia** nearby was built as a pleasure palace for

Pope Julius III, a man who was so compulsive a collector of classical sculpture that on his death in 1555 some 160 boat journeys up and down the Tiber were required to clear his collection from the villa. Today, the villa's artistic emphasis is slightly different, but the sheer quantity of material on display—devoted almost entirely to the Etruscans—is almost equally staggering.

The Etruscans and their art are not to all tastes, but there is much to admire here if you ignore the endless lines of funerary vases. Highlights include the terra-cotta statues of Apollo and Herakles, the contents of the Bernardini Tomb, and the sixth-century B.C. Sarcofago degli Sposi, a statue of a reclining and enigmatically smiling married couple. ∎

Galleria Borghese
- 47 D6
- Piazzale Scipione Borghese 5
- 06 328 101 (information); 06 328 101 (required reservations 9 a.m.– 6 p.m. Mon.–Fri.)
- Closed Mon.
- $$
- Bus: 19 & 30. Metro: Flaminio

Villa Giulia
- Piazzale di Villa Giulia 9, Viale delle Belle Arti
- 06 320 1951 or 06 3326 6571
- Closed Sun. p.m. & Mon.
- $$

The Grand Tour

Italy has long seduced the curious and world weary of colder climes, bewitching with its art and culture, befuddling with its charm, inexpensive wine, and siren call to the senses. However, modern tourism is a far cry from the decorous days of the Grand Tour, a ritualized progression through the cities of Europe without which the education of 18th-century gentlemen—rarely ladies—was deemed incomplete.

For most Grand Tourists, the attraction was the lure of imperial Rome, and the city's great monuments of antiquity—the Colosseum, Pantheon, Palatine hill, and Roman Forum. Close behind came the collections of classical statuary, notably the Capitoline Museums and the Vatican's Bramante Courtyard, whose peerless statues—the "Laocoön" and "Apollo Belvedere"—made it the Tour's Holy of Holies.

Not all visitors came for culture. In 1765, the British diarist James Boswell caught venereal disease and crab lice during an orgy of nocturnal sight-seeing. The Duchess of Devonshire and Lady Elizabeth Foster (two among many) came to conceal the birth of illegitimate children. In 1594, the English dramatist, Thomas Nashe—no sightseer he—boasted, "I was at *Pontius Pilate's* house and pissed against it." Other visitors formed part of the tribe of foreign eccentrics who have found refuge in travel. The aristocratic Thomas Hackman walked to Rome from London studiously "taking no notice of anything," while George Hutchinson, a Presbyterian firebrand, came to Rome in 1750 "by God's command," his mission to "preach mightily against statues, pictures, umbrellas, bag-wigs, and hoop petticoats."

Many had equally pressing, but more poignant reasons for a visit, none more so than the English poet John Keats, who arrived in 1820 desperately seeking deliverance from tuberculosis. It proved a wretched affair, the poet describing his stay in the city—where he was to die after three months—as a "posthumous life" in which he "already seemed to feel the flowers growing over" him.

"At Florence, you think," runs an old Italian proverb, "at Rome, you pray; at Venice you love; at Naples, you look." Only a handful of visitors to the capital, however, spent any time on their knees. Far more hedonistic pleasures filled their days. Breakfast, often after a night of whoring, might be taken in the infamous Caffè degli Inglesi near the Spanish Steps, a "filthy vaulted room" and favored den of gossip and drink. Mornings would be spent seeing the sights, often in the company of the so-called bear leaders, the much put-upon tutors detailed to chaperone the wayward *milordi*, as the English (noble or otherwise) were known. Afternoons meant tea at Babington's in Piazza di Spagna (still serving today) or a nap in the English Club on Via Condotti.

For those not engaged in Boswellian pursuits, evenings were a fashionable time to visit the catacombs or sculpture galleries, where guttering candles added to the erotic charm of the latter and the eerie romanticism of the former. At some point, virtually every visitor of means found time to sit for a portrait, a pastime that by the mid-18th century had become an integral part of the Tour. The main reason was cost: In 1760, Sir Joshua Reynolds' fee for a half-length painting in London was over £150. Rome's leading practitioner, Pompeo Batoni, would produce one for £25.

And not for the milordi the present-day keepsakes of T-shirts, cheap art, and religious kitsch. A Grand Tour souvenir meant the real thing—statues, furniture, prints, and paintings. Such was the obsession with artifacts that many echoed the sentiments of the Earl of Chesterfield, who despaired, as he put it, of those who "run through Italy *knick-knackically*." British writer Horace Walpole admitted in 1740 that "I am far gone in medals, lamps, idols, prints," adding that he "would buy the Coliseum [sic] if I could…." One of the keenest collectors, Charles Townley, whose collection was sold to the British Museum, sacked Rome of its treasures on no fewer than three Grand Tours. ∎

The Colosseum was one of Rome's most popular attractions among Grand Tourists. Visitors included German writer Johan Goethe (above) and Lord Byron (below).

Basilica di San Pietro

THE BASILICA DI SAN PIETRO (ST. PETER'S BASILICA) CAN hardly fail to impress: It is the largest church in Christendom (capable of accommodating an estimated 60,000 people), represents the heart of Roman Catholicism, serves as a seminal point of pilgrimage, and is crowned by a stupendous Michelangelo-designed dome that offers sweeping views across much of the Eternal City. The church owes its site and spiritual legitimacy to Peter the Apostle, the first pope, who is believed to have been buried here after his crucifixion close by in the Imperial Gardens in either A.D. 64 or 67.

Basilica di San Pietro

🚇 46 A4
✉ Piazza San Pietro
☎ 06 6988 3712
🕐 Church & dome closed during religious services
💲 Church: free. Dome: $
📷 64

Note: A dress code applies—no shorts, short skirts, or bare shoulders.

Bernini's bronze altar canopy at the heart of St. Peter's stands above the supposed tomb of St. Peter the Apostle.

A shrine was probably built on the site around A.D. 155, perhaps earlier, but the first church for which records survive was begun around A.D. 326 by Pope Sylvester I during the reign of Constantine the Great, the first Christian emperor. This church was to survive until 1452, when its perilous state prompted Pope Nicholas V to consider the creation of a new basilica. Almost 200 years elapsed before this church was completed, during which time the leading architects of their day produced a succession of different plans, false starts, and half-baked or half-finished schemes.

The first significant proposal came from Bramante in 1506, a design built around a church arranged in the form of a Greek cross. The next was delivered by Antonio da Sangallo in 1539, a plan that required the alteration of work in progress to accommodate a church based on a Latin cross. Raphael, Baldassare Peruzzi, and Giuliano da Sangallo then had their say. In 1546 it was the turn of Michelangelo, then 72, appointed to make sense of the increasingly muddled project. He promptly obliterated Sangallo's work and embarked on the construction of the dome—both the drum and cupola's distinctive twin columns are his.

By 1605, Carlo Maderno had reinstated the Latin cross, as well as widening the facade to more or less its present width. Bernini then created the magnificent square outside—Piazza San Pietro—and made a few modest alterations to the interior. The new church was finally consecrated in 1626, exactly 1,300 years after the original basilica.

THE BASILICA

Bramante spared little of the original St. Peter's, for which he earned the damning nickname Bramante Ruinante—Bramante the Destroyer. Among the handful of works to escape his modernizing zeal were the church's **central doors** and a mosaic fragment above them on their inner arch. The latter is the work of Giotto and portrays the Apostles' ship, the *Navicella,* and the figure of Christ walking on water. (Incidentally, the Porta Santa —the farthest right of St. Peter's five doors—is opened only once every 25 years during Holy Years.) The equestrian statues flanking the doors depict Charlemagne (on the left) and Constantine (by Bernini) on the right.

Once inside the church, the first breathtaking impressions are of its staggering size, although after wandering endlessly amid the cascades of marble, somber tombs, and mountains of baroque decor, you realize that the interior is surprisingly bereft of major works of art. One notable exception

Clerics and onlookers hold palms and olive branches after the pope's traditional Palm Sunday address in Piazza San Pietro.

is Michelangelo's **"Pietà"** (1499), located in the first chapel off the south aisle.

Moving down the church, note the measurements set into the nave, markers indicating the size of other churches in relation to St. Peter's. The crossing is dominated by the unmistakable bulk of the *baldacchino* (1678), or **altar canopy,** a work created by Bernini using bronze melted down from the Pantheon's ancient doors. Behind it, at the rear of the church lies the **Cathedra Petri** (1656), also by Bernini, an ornate throne crafted to enclose a wood and ivory chair reputedly used by St. Peter to address his first sermon to the Romans (scholars believe it actually dates from the fourth century).

On either side of the Cathedra are two of the more outstanding of the church's plethora of tombs and statues: On the left stands Guglielmo della Porta's Tomb of Pope Paul III, while on the right lies Bernini's **Tomb of Urban VIII** (1647), a model for countless funerary monuments that followed. Also hunt out Antonio del Pollaiuolo's Tomb of

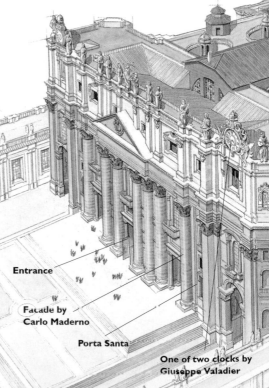

Entrance

Façade by Carlo Maderno

Porta Santa

One of two clocks by Giuseppe Valadier

Innocent VIII (1498), a lovely Renaissance work located between the second and third bays of the left aisle. Don't miss the bronze **statue of St. Peter,** attributed to Arnolfo di Cambio and located by the front right of the crossing's four pillars. It is an unmistakable work, thanks to its worn right foot, caressed by millions since Pius IX granted a 50-day indulgence to anyone kissing it following confession.

Finally, on no account fail to explore the so-called Vatican Grottoes, tomb-filled underground chambers below the church, nor—more importantly—to climb the dome for some unforgettable views of Piazza San Pietro and the city beyond. The dome's entrance lies off the south aisle; access is by stairs or elevator. ■

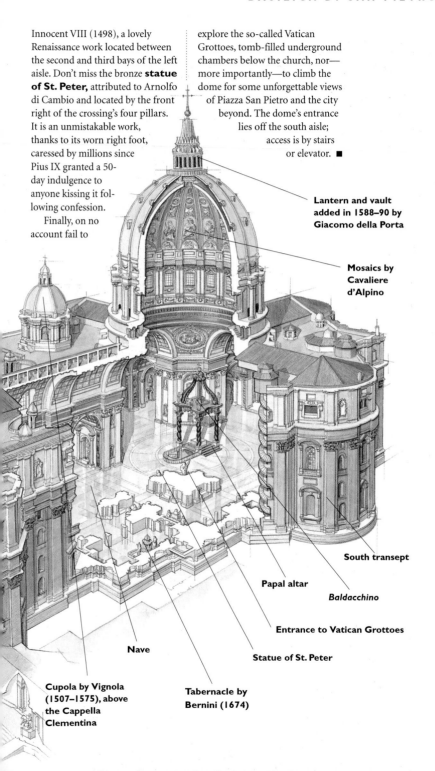

Lantern and vault added in 1588–90 by Giacomo della Porta

Mosaics by Cavaliere d'Alpino

South transept

Papal altar

Baldacchino

Entrance to Vatican Grottoes

Nave

Statue of St. Peter

Cupola by Vignola (1507–1575), above the Cappella Clementina

Tabernacle by Bernini (1674)

Musei Vaticani

IT IS HARD TO THINK OF ANY GREATER MUSEUMS THAN those of the Vatican. Other galleries may match the broad span and myriad origins of its artifacts, but none can also offer works of art that include entire rooms painted by Raphael and the ceiling frescoes of the Sistine Chapel. Exhibits are scattered around many separate museums and several hundred rooms, and to see them all involves a walk of some 5 miles (8 km).

Musei Vaticani

- 46 A5
- Main entrance on Viale Vaticano
- 06 6988 3333
- Closed Sat. p.m. & Sun. (except last Sun. of month) mid-March–Oct., & p.m. Mon.–Sat. & all Sun. (except last Sun. of month) Nov.–mid-March
- $$ (free last Sun. of month)
- Bus: 19, 51, 81, & 492 to Piazza del Risorgimento

The ceiling of the Sistine Chapel, where Michelangelo's frescoes tell the story of Genesis and the history of humanity before the coming of Christ.

See the obvious highlights—the Museo Pio-Clementino, Sistine Chapel, Raphael Rooms, and Pinacoteca (picture gallery)—and then make for museums that reflect your own interests. This might mean choosing between the ancient Egyptian exhibits of the Museo Gregoriano Egizio and the Etruscan offerings of the Museo Gregoriano Etrusco. Or it might involve deciding between rooms devoted to modern or pagan art, admiring tapestries and precious manuscripts, wandering corridors lined with ancient maps, or enjoying rooms crammed with medieval furniture and classical sculpture. Whatever your choice, allow plenty of time and try to arrive early—the high-season crowds can be overwhelming.

The Vatican Museums contain enough classical sculpture to last a lifetime. If you want to see the best, make straight for the **Museo Pio-Clementino,** laid out in the 18th century by popes Pius VI and Clement XIV. The museum's finest pieces are arranged in the Cortile Ottagono, or **Octagonal Courtyard.** Here you'll find the famous "Laocoön," carved on the island of Rhodes in 50 B.C. but only rediscovered close to the Colosseum in 1506. The sculpture exerted much influence on the art of the High Renaissance, as did another of the courtyard's works, the celebrated **"Apollo Belvedere,"** a Roman work of A.D. 130 copied from a Greek original (330 B.C.).

The museum's many other highlights include the first-century **"Apoxyomenos"** (literally the "Scraper"), which shows an athlete scraping the sweat and dust from his body after a wrestling match; the first-century **"Belvedere Torso,"** a work that greatly impressed Michelangelo; a figure of Hermes shown throwing a cloak over her shoulders; the statue of **"Apollo Sauroktonos,"** which portrays the god about to kill a lizard; Canova's neoclassic **"Perseus"** (1800); and the Candelabri Barberini, a pair of second-century lamps from Hadrian's Villa at Tivoli.

STANZE DI RAFFAELLO

In 1503, Pope Julius II commissioned the young Raphael, then just 26, to decorate a suite of four modestly sized rooms in the Vatican. The result was the Stanze di Raffaello, or Raphael Rooms, one of the supreme masterpieces of Western European art. The first area to be painted was the **Stanza della Segnatura** (1508–1511), Julius's library and the room where papal bulls, or documents, received his signature *(segnatura)*. The four principal paintings here explore the themes of Theology, Poetry, Philosophy, and Justice, each of them a complex interweaving of classical, religious, and contemporary characters and allusions. Raphael then moved to the **Stanza d'Eliodoro** (1512–14), a private antechamber, where the main

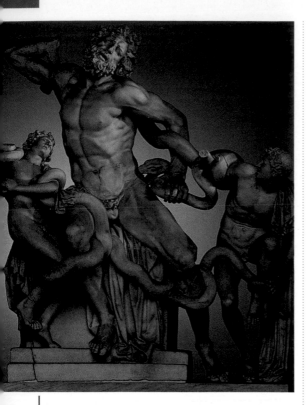

The Laocöon sculpture dates from 50 B.C. One of the Vatican's most celebrated works, it shows a Trojan priest and his sons grappling with sea serpents.

marked. It is thought the change owed much to the influence of Michelangelo, then working close by in the Sistine Chapel. Further development of Raphael's style was cut short by his premature death in 1520, and only one painting in the final room, the **Sala di Costantino** (1517–1524), is based on his drawings.

CAPPELLA SISTINA

Western art's most famous masterpiece started life as a humble chapel built for Pope Sixtus IV in 1475. Its earliest decoration began in 1481, when the lower walls were painted by a group of leading artists who included Botticelli, Perugino, Pinturicchio, and Luca Signorelli. The now famous ceiling remained relatively unadorned until 1508, the year Pope Julius II approached Michelangelo to begin one of the world's most celebrated paintings.

The work took four years to complete, four years in which Michelangelo endured the most trying of conditions—extremes of heat and cold and weeks of cramped misery spent painting on his back. Over 300 figures populate the scenes, which divide into nine basic sections. Each is read chronologically in the order you walk through the chapel. First come the five seminal events from the Book of Genesis: the "Separation of Light and Darkness," the "Creation of the Heavenly Bodies," the "Separation of Land and Sea," the "Creation of Adam," and the "Creation of Eve." These are followed by the "Fall and Expulsion from Paradise," the "Sacrifice of Noah," the "Flood," and the "Drunkenness of Noah."

Rome was a different city and Michelangelo a different man when he came to paint the Sistine Chapel's other masterpiece, the vast fresco of the **"Last Judgment"** (1534–1541), which covers the

quartet of paintings explore the theme of Divine Providence intervening to defend Faith.

A new pope, Leo X, ascended the papal throne during work on the room, which is why one of the walls depicts a scene of "Leo I Repulsing Attila the Hun." Leo's insistence on the inclusion of his illustrious namesake, Leo I, was intended to secure glory for himself by proxy. This less than subtle form of self-promotion was carried over into the third room, the **Stanza dell' Incendio del Borgo** (1514–17). Most of the paintings here involve previous Leonine popes, although their content is less eye-catching than their manner, which reveals Raphael painting in a grander style than in earlier rooms, his color more virulent, his emphasis on the human figure more

chapel's rear wall. Over 20 years had elapsed since his work on the ceiling, during which time Rome had been traumatized by the 1527 sack of the city by Charles V. For his part, Michelangelo had become embittered by, among other things, his work on the tomb of Julius II, his former employer. As a result, the painter's vision of the Day of Judgment is dark and uncompromising, its content a departure from earlier interpretations of the theme in which forgiveness and redemption had laced vengeance and Divine ire. The doomed are shown sinking to their fate on the painting's right, faces and bodies contorted with terror, while the saved—merely relieved rather than overjoyed at their salvation—rise powerfully on the painting's left.

OTHER ATTRACTIONS

The minor Vatican Museum with the most general appeal is the **Pinacoteca,** or art gallery, whose 20 or more rooms contain the cream of the Vatican's collection of medieval and Renaissance paintings.

The most celebrated pictures here are Raphael's last work, the **"Transfiguration"** (1517), hung above the artist as he lay in state; the same artist's "Madonna of Foligno" (1512); Giotto's "Stefaneschi Triptych"; a "Deposition" by Caravaggio; and Melozzo da Forlì's portrait of Sixtus IV and his librarian, Platina. The gallery also contains Rome's only painting by Leonardo da Vinci, an unfinished monochrome of St. Jerome, as well as works by virtually every other Italian and European artist of note.

Other areas worth seeing if you have time include the **Galleria delle Carte Geografiche,** whose walls are decorated with a 40-panel sequence of pictorial maps (1580). The **Cappella di Niccolò V,** close to the Raphael Rooms, contains frescoes by Fra Angelico on the "Life of St. Stephen and St. Lawrence" (1447–1451), while the nearby **Appartamento Borgia** features equally celebrated frescoes by the Umbrian artist Pinturicchio. The **Museo Gregoriano-Etrusco** boasts the world's finest collection of Etruscan art after the Villa Giulia, while the **Museo Gregoriano Egizio** is a treasure chest of Egyptian artifacts. ∎

"God Creating the Earth" by Raphael, in the Stanze di Raffaello

More places to visit in Rome

MUSEUMS & MONUMENTS

Few ancient Roman reliefs are as well-preserved as those adorning the **Ara Pacis** *(Map 46 C5, Via di Ripetta, tel 06 6880 6848, closed Sun. p.m. & Mon.)*, a masterpiece of the Augustan era, and few as imposing as the **Teatro di Marcello** *(Map 46 C3, Via del Teatro di Marcello, closed to the public)*, in its day one of Rome's largest theaters. Roman remains on the old city's fringes include the **Terme di Caracalla** *(Map 47 D2, Via Antonina, closed Mon. p.m. & Sun. p.m.)*, a colossal bath complex, and **Via Appia Antica** *(Off map 47 E1)*, a superbly preserved and tomb-lined portion of Roman road. Close to the latter lie several sets of early Christian catacombs—of those open to the public the best are **San Sebastiano** *(Via Appia Antica, tel 06 788 7035, closed Thurs. & Nov.)*, **San Callisto** *(Via Appia Antica 110, tel 06 513 6725, closed Wed. & Nov.)*, and **San Domitilla** *(Via delle Sette Chiese 282, tel 06 511 0342, closed Tues.)*.

Many minor Roman museums would be the pride and joy of most other cities. Among these the most notable is the **Castel Sant'Angelo** *(Map 46 B4, Lungotevere Castello 50, tel 06 687 5036 or 06 681 9111, closed Mon.)* near St. Peter's, a fortress-cum-mausoleum built in A.D. 135 and now a museum of medieval and other artifacts. Outstanding classical art resides in the **Museo Nazionale Romano,** while medieval, Renaissance and later masterpieces fill the gilded salons of the **Galleria Spada, Villa Farnesina,** and **Palazzo Corsini.**

SAN LUIGI DEI FRANCESI

San Luigi is dedicated to St. Louis (Luigi in Italian), better known as Louis IX of France. Since its completion in 1589, it has been the French national church in Rome. The blank Renaissance facade barely hints at its interior treasures —three masterpieces by Caravaggio tucked away in the Cappella Contarelli, the fifth chapel of the north aisle.

These intense and dramatic paintings (1597–1602) may not suit all tastes—their groundbreaking realism certainly found little favor with the church authorities who commissioned them—but their energy and Caravaggio's virtuoso handling of chiaroscuro (light and shade) are beyond reproach. Each picture portrays a scene from the life of Matthew the Apostle: The "Calling" shows Matthew summoned by God as he collects taxes; the "Martyrdom" portrays his death; while "St. Matthew and the Angel" depicts a winged man who resembles an angel, the saint's symbol.

🅜 46 C4 ✉ Via Santa Giovanna d'Arco ☎ 06 6880 3629 🕒 Closed Thurs. p.m. & Sun. p.m. 🚌 Bus: 81 or 87 to Corso del Rinascimento

OTHER CHURCHES

In Trastevere try to visit **Santa Maria in Trastevere** *(Map 46 B3, Piazza di Santa Maria in Trastevere)*, renowned for the 12th-century mosaics that adorn both its facade and dusky interior. Nearby **Santa Cecilia in Trastevere** *(Map 46 C3, Piazza Santa Cecilia)* contains more mosaics (ninth century) and an altar canopy (1293) by Arnolfo di Cambio. Across the river, the portico of **Santa Maria in Cosmedin** *(Map 46 C3, Piazza Bocca della Verità)* houses the famous Bocca della Verità, the so-called Mouth of Truth, whose stone jaws are supposed to clamp shut on the hands of dissemblers.

Santa Maria's medieval interior provides a contrast to the prevailing baroque tone of most of the city's churches. Foremost among these are the **Gesù** *(Map 46 C4, Piazza del Gesù)*, mother church of the Jesuits, and two more modest but no less architecturally distinguished churches— **San Carlo** *(Map 47 D4, Via del Quirinale 23)* and **Sant'Andrea al Quirinale** *(Map 47 D4, Via del Quirinale 29)*, designed by Borromini and Bernini respectively, the baroque's leading lights. One of Bernini's most famous sculptures, the erotically charged "Ecstasy of St. Theresa," graces the church of **Santa Maria della Vittoria** *(Map 47 E4–E5, Via XX Settembre 17)*. Equally memorable, but more macabre, is the decoration of **Santa Maria della Concezione** *(Map 47 D5, Via Vittorio Veneto 27)*, much of which consists of skulls and lovingly arranged human bones. ∎

Northwest Italy boasts two major cities—Turin and Genoa—but its greatest lures are sublime food and wine, its many outdoor activities, and the beauty of its magnificent mountain and coastal landscapes.

Northwest Italy

The insignia of Ferrari

Northwest Italy

NORTHWEST ITALY INTRODUCES THREE REGIONS—PIEMONTE (PIEDMONT), Liguria, and the Valle d'Aosta—and three very different types of landscape—the peaks, forests, and deep-cut valleys of the Alps; the flatlands and meandering rivers of the Po plain; and the cliffs, coves, and beaches of the Mediterranean coast.

Piedmont takes its name from *piede dei monti*—the foot of the mountains—after the vast alpine wall that guards its mist-shrouded plains, tidy provincial towns, and pastoral, vine-covered hills. At its heart lies Turin, an underrated city whose bleak industrial reputation is belied by its beautiful baroque heritage and the refined air of its cobbled streets, shady arcades, and elegant sidewalk cafés. In the past, it was the cradle of Italy's unification movement, home to the Savoy, ancient dukes of Piedmont and first kings of a united Italy.

Agriculture thrives in the region while the dulcet chalk hills of Monferrato, south of Turin, yield truffles, wonderful cheeses, Asti Spumante, and two of the country's premier red wines—Barolo and Barbaresco. Vermouth and *grissini* (bread sticks), mainstays of bars and Italian restaurants across the world, also have their origins here.

Wedged hard up against the Alps is the Valle d'Aosta, containing some of Italy's grandest scenery, including its greatest national park—the Parco Nazionale del Gran Paradiso—and three of Europe's highest mountains: Mont Blanc, Monte Rosa, and Monte Cervino (the Matterhorn).

The Gran Paradiso park is an obvious target, but almost all the smaller alpine valleys—notably the Val d'Ayas or Val di Gressoney—offer scenic rewards. Aosta is the main town, its lovely churches and Roman remains best seen as part of a one- or two-day tour of the Valle d'Aosta. Along the valley floor looms a succession of gaunt castles, monuments to a time when mountain passes such as the Great St. Bernard made the region a strategic corridor between Italy, France, and Switzerland. Today, tunnels like the St. Bernard maintain the area's role as a vital European routeway.

Liguria is Italy's maritime region par excellence. Genoa, its briny capital, is the country's largest port and birthplace of Christopher Columbus (1451–1506), while the nooks and crannies of its fractured coastline contain some of Europe's most beguiling scenery. A narrow sliver of territory, the region runs from the French border as far as Tuscany, forming a long coastal strip—the so-called Italian Riviera—sheltered by the Ligurian Alps.

West of Genoa, the palm-fringed coast is known as the Riviera di Ponete; to the east is the Riviera di Levante. Both rivieras are strung with resorts and towns, many of them spoiled, like so much of the Italian coast, by unregulated development. Only a few blessed spots remain. The best are the Cinque Terre, five little cliff-hung villages, and Portofino, a romantic jewel set on a beautiful coastal promontory. ■

Area of map detail

Turin

"TURIN IS NOT A CITY...TO MAKE A FUSS ABOUT," complained Henry James in *Italy Revisited* (1877), a still common belief among those unacquainted with this largely unsung and unvisited city. Dour and un-Italian, at least by reputation, its center at first glance is a grid of mostly 19th-century streets, its outskirts a tangle of industrial suburbs. On closer inspection, it emerges as a city of considerable elegance, full of parks, palaces, rattling trams, venerable cafés, old-fashioned arcades, and some of Italy's finest baroque architecture outside Rome. It is also home to the much disputed Turin Shroud and—more prosaically—to the giant Fiat corporation, bulwark of the city's industrial might.

Turin

84 C3

Visitor information

Piazza Castello 161

011 535 901

Turin (Torino) began life as the capital of the Taurini, a tribe of Celtic origin. Later it became a modest Roman military outpost. Its rise to real prominence came when the princes of Savoy, an ancient Italo-French dynasty, made the city the seat of their royal court in 1574. Savoy patronage and two outstanding baroque architects, Guarino Guarini (1624–1683) and Filippo Juvarra (1676–1736), then turned the city into a social and architectural showcase. In the 19th century, the family became prime movers in the unification movement and the

first kings of a united Italy. In the 20th century, large companies such as Fiat, founded in 1899, attracted vast pools of migrant labor, particularly from southern Italy, leading to the growth of major new suburbs during the 1950s and '60s.

Central Turin is a close-knit area that is easy and pleasant to explore on foot. On its western side lies the fashionable Piazza San Carlo, the most architecturally distinguished of the city's squares. On one of the piazza's flanks stands the Palazzo dell'Accademia delle Scienze, a 17th-century palace by Guarini

that houses the city's principal museums—the Museo Egizio and Galleria Sabauda. Opposite stand the churches of San Carlo and Santa Cristina, the latter's striking facade designed by Juvarra. Turin's attractive main street, Via Roma, all cobbled squares and tempting stores, leads east to the Piazza Castello, the city's other main square. On and around it lie Palazzo Madama and Palazzo Carignano, the cathedral (home to the famed Turin Shroud), and the Palazzo Reale, the Savoy's former residence.

Turin is not where you would expect to find one of the world's greatest museums of ancient Egyptian artifacts. Only London and Cairo, however, have comparable collections to that of the **Museo Egizio.** The city owes its windfall to the Savoys, who in 1824 brought the artifacts accumulated by Bernardo Drovetti, a Piedmont-born French consul general posted to Egypt during the Napoleonic Wars. To these were added finds from excavations made by Italian archaeologists in 1911, as well as outstanding treasures such as the rock temple of Thutmose II (1450

B.C.) from Ellessya, gifted by the United Arab Republic to the museum in 1967 for its help during the excavations that preceded the building of the Aswan Dam.

The museum's lower floor is given over largely to monumental sculpture, its highlights a black diorite statue of Ramses II (1299–33 B.C.) and the huge Colossus of Sethi II. Upstairs, the exhibits run the gamut of Egyptian civilization, embracing everything from objects linked to weaving, farming, fishing, and hunting to fully reconstructed tombs such as the sepulchres of Khaiè and Meriè (14th century B.C.) and a collection of papyri that includes what is reputedly the world's oldest topographical map.

The **Galleria Sabauda** has paintings accumulated by the Savoy from the 15th century onward, a collection donated to the state following unification in 1860. Among the many Dutch and Flemish works, look for Rembrandt's "Old Man Asleep," possibly a portrait of the artist's father; Hans Memling's "Passion of Christ"; a "Madonna and Child" by Antony Van Dyck and Holbein the Younger; and Van

Piazza San Carlo, Turin's airy main square, is dominated by long arcades lined with elegant shops and cafés.

Museo Egizio

⊠ Via Accademia delle Scienze 6

☎ 011 561 7776

🕐 Closed Mon.

💲 $$

Galleria Sabauda

⊠ Via Accademia delle Scienze 6

☎ 011 547 440

🕐 Closed p.m. daily except Thurs. (closed a.m.) & all Mon.

💲 $$

Just outside
Turin, the Basilica
di Superga (see
sidebar p. 89) was
built in fulfillment
of a vow made to
the Virgin Mary
while French
troops were
besieging Turin
in 1706.

Dyck's "Children of Charles I of England." Italian painters include Mantegna, whose wistful "Madonna" is one the loveliest works in the gallery; members of the Venetian school such as Giovanni Bellini, Tiepolo ("The Triumph of Aurelius"), Veronese ("The Meal at the House of Simon"), and Tintoretto; and an impressive roster of Tuscan artists—Fra Angelico ("Madonna"), Filippino Lippi ("Three Archangels"), Sodoma ("Madonna and Saints"), and Antonio and Piero Pollaiuolo ("St. Tobias and the Archangel Raphael"). Also keep an eye open for Orazio Gentileschi's "Annunciation" and Bernardo Bellotto's views of 18th-century Turin.

Close to the Galleria Sabauda lies the **Palazzo Carignano** (*Via Accademia delle Scienze 5, tel 011 562 1147, closed Sun. p.m. & Mon.*), built between 1679 and 1684 for the Carignano, a branch of the Savoy family, and distinguished by Guarini's unusual curved brick facade. Italy's first king, Vittore Emanuele II, was born here in 1820, and between 1861 and 1864 the palace served as the seat of

Italy's first parliament. Today, it houses the 27-room **Museo Nazionale del Risorgimento,** a museum devoted to the 19th-century unification of Italy.

At the center of a huge square, north of the palace, stands the **Palazzo Madama** (*Piazza Castello, tel 011 442 5901, closed for restoration—reopens 2001*). It owes its present appearance to Filippo Juvarra (see p. 86), but has its origins in the Roman fortifications and medieval fortress that once stood on the site. The palace is named for its 17th-century occupant, "Madama" Marie-Christine of France, mother of Carlo Emanuele of Savoy. Inside it houses the **Museo Civico d'Arte Antica,** a museum whose wide-ranging collection includes paintings and objets d'art spanning some three millennia. Its undoubted highlights are the famous "Portrait of a Man" (1476) by the Sicilian painter Antonello da Messina and the Duc de Berry's sumptuously illustrated *Book of Hours* (1450).

Turin's cathedral, the **Duomo di San Giovanni** (*Piazza San*

Giovanni), was begun by Tuscan architects in 1491. Today, it is the city's only major Renaissance monument, although even here the city's presiding baroque geniuses could not hold their hand—Juvarra designed the crown (1720) of the restrained brick campanile (1468–1470), while inside Guarini was responsible for the **Cappella della Santa Sindone** (1668–1694). This magnificent chapel was badly damaged by fire in 1997, but its most precious relic, the *Sindone*, or Holy Shroud, escaped the conflagration unscathed.

To believers, this controversial relic, better known as the **Turin Shroud,** is the winding sheet used to wrap Christ after his crucifixion. To doubters, it is a 13th-century fake. Carbon dating in 1988 seemed to vindicate the skeptics, but many have since questioned the validity of the dating techniques. The shroud is supposed to have been taken from Jerusalem to Cyprus, and from there to France, where it came into the possession of the Savoys in 1453. First displayed in the cathedral in 1694, it is now shown to visitors only intermittently. Fake or otherwise, no one has been able to give a plausible explanation for the cloth's image, a shadowy outline of a crucified man, complete with wounds and the marks consistent with a crown of thorns.

The **Palazzo Reale,** or Royal Palace, immediately east of the Duomo, was the Savoy's principal seat from 1646 to 1865. Today, it is visited for its gardens and lavish state apartments *(Piazzetta Reale, tel 011 436 1455, guided tours daily except Mon.)*, and for the **Armeria Reale,** or Royal Armory *(Piazza Castello 191, tel 011 543 889, closed Mon.–Tues., & Thurs. p.m.)*. Housed in one of the palace's wings, this is one of the world's largest and most important

collections of arms and military memorabilia. The collection was amassed by the Savoy and comprises weapons from Greek and Roman times, majestic medieval and Renaissance items, and military hardware from as far afield as China and Japan.

Walk east from the Armeria Reale and Piazza Castello on Via Giuseppe Verdi and you come to the **Mole Antonelliana** *(Via Montebello 20, tel 011 817 0496, closed—reopens 2000)*, Turin's most prominent monument. For a while during the 19th century, this was one of the world's highest buildings, standing at 548 feet (167 m). Begun as a synagogue by architect Alessandro Antonelli in 1862, it was eventually completed by the Turin city council in 1897. These days the Mole—which simply means the massive structure—serves as an exhibition center and home to the **Museo Nazionale del Cinema,** a museum that traces the Italian movie industry from its earliest days in Turin. Be sure to ride the elevator to the viewing platform midway up for airy views across the city to the Alps and Po Valley. ∎

Try one of the rich pastries at Caffè Platti on Corso Vittorio Emanuele II.

SUPERGA

Superga *(Strada di Superga 73, tel 011 898 0083, closed Fri.)*, a stupendous baroque basilica, is the masterpiece of the architect, Juvarra. Built between 1717 and 1731, on top of a 2,198-foot (670 m) hill, 6 miles (9.6 km) east of the city, it was raised in thanksgiving for the city's deliverance from the French army in 1706. The exterior terraces offer superlative views of the city and its surroundings, while the interior contains the royal tombs of the Savoy. ∎

Truffles

Piedmont is one of Italy's great truffle capitals, home to the fabled white truffle—*tuber magnatum*—one of the world's rarest foodstuffs. Truffles have been known, if not understood, since ancient times. The first written record dates from the fifth century B.C. They were enjoyed by the Babylonians, the Greeks, and the Romans, who consumed them as much for their reputed aphrodisiacal qualities as their gastronomic allure.

Classical writers were mystified by truffles. Plutarch believed they were mud cooked by lightning; Juvenal that they were the product of thunder and rain. Pliny, bewildered by their origins, considered them nature's greatest miracle. During the Middle Ages, they were considered a manifestation of the devil. And no wonder, for here was a "plant" apparently without root, branch, or stem; without leaf, fruit, or flower; lacking, in fact, all visible means of growth.

Truffles are actually a form of fungus that has sunk underground, probably as part of an evolutionary defense against the elements. Unlike a normal mushroom, therefore, their spores are spread not by the wind, but by various truffle-eating animals such as rodents, deer, slugs, and wild boar. Their underground home precludes photosynthesis, meaning they rely for nutrients on a symbiotic relationship with the roots of certain trees, most commonly oak, hazel, beech, and lime.

Truffles usually attain their final dimensions anything from the size of a pea to the size of a soccer ball—over a few days during the spring. Protected from the weather, they are then able to mature slowly, often over the course of several months. Only when ripe—from about November onward—do they give off the distinctive perfume, and only then for about ten days, thus ensuring they are snaffled up only when laden with viable spores. Thereafter, they become poisonous and rot. But to ensure they're rooted out, they need to advertise their presence.

This is where the truffle's famous perfume comes in, not to mention dogs and pigs, foremost among the ragbag of sleuths used to nose out the prized tuber (goats, foxes, and ferrets are also used, even bear cubs, in Russia). Pigs love truffles, at least female ones, for among the countless volatile compounds exuded by the truffle is one that closely resembles the musky sexual pheromones of the wild boar. In fact, a truffle gives off almost twice the amount of this scent as the male boar, the idea being to attract the sow and so disperse its spores. Sows are huge and unmanageable, however, and they're also prone to attacks of sexual frenzy when close to the truffle, the main reasons they've been replaced by dogs.

But why the fuss and mystique surrounding truffles? They are nothing to look at and the perfume, best described as "essence of undergrowth," has been compared to leaf mold, overripe cheese, garlic, herbs, methane, and sweaty armpits. For cooks, the appeal is the truffles' unique and subtle flavor. Elizabeth David, in her classic cookbook, *Italian Food* (1954), called them the "most delicious of all foods anywhere." Brillat-Saverin, the distinguished 19th-century French gastronome, went further, stating that "without truffles there can be no truly gastronomic meal."

The truffle's mystery, its seemingly spontaneous appearance and ethereal existence, is also significant. (Lord Byron, the early 19th-century English poet, kept one on his desk to "aid creativity.") Equally important is the rarity and thrill of the hunt—it is the only gourmet food, indeed one of the only foods of any description, that cannot be grown to order. It is also gloriously unpredictable, something that has made cultivation something of an agricultural Holy Grail. One tree will yield truffles while its apparently identical neighbor will not—and no one knows why. Money also plays a part. Weight for weight, truffles are among the world's costliest foodstuffs: Only saffron costs more.

Only a relatively modest amount, however, needs to be spent to enjoy the truffle's exalted qualities. Nowhere, with the exception of central France, can you relish their sublime flavor better than in the restaurants of Piedmont, Umbria, and—to a lesser extent—Tuscany and the Marche. ∎

Above: Dogs rather than pigs are used to hunt truffles in Italy. A good truffle dog can be worth several thousand dollars.

Right: A nose for quality: The distinctive perfume of the truffle is its most prized characteristic.

Below: Truffles are extremely delicate and must be processed carefully within a few hours of discovery.

Parco Nazionale del Gran Paradiso

ITALY'S FIRST NATIONAL PARK BEGAN LIFE AS A ROYAL hunting reserve maintained exclusively for Vittore Emanuele II of Savoy and his family in 1856. In 1920, Vittore Emanuele III presented the reserve to the state, and three years later the area was declared a national park. Today, the Parco Nazionale del Gran Paradiso extends across 270 square miles (70,000 ha), spanning the regions of Piedmont and the Valle d'Aosta, and protecting the majestic mountain scenery on and around the 13,323-foot (4,061 m) Gran Paradiso massif, the only wholly Italian peak over 13,123 feet (4,000 m).

Landscapes in the park's alpine region are a patchwork of high mountain wilderness, alpine meadows, and dulcet valley bottoms. Permanent snow and glaciers shroud in its inner fastness, a bleak redoubt of rock and ice from which crashing streams plunge into flower-strewn pastures and forests of larch, fir, and pine. Waterfalls, deep-cut valleys, and pastoral corners also abound, all within easy reach, thanks to the park's good roads and well-maintained trails.

The region can be reached from Piedmont in the south, but for many visitors the most convenient and interesting approach is from the **Valle d'Aosta** and the north (see drive, pp. 94–95). The best tactic is to take one of the trio of roads that follow the major valleys on the park's northern flanks—the Val di

Rhêmes, Val Savarenche, and Val di Cogne. Any of these roads offers prodigious views, wonderful landscapes, and the opportunity to pick up trails for hikes of varying lengths and difficulty.

In an ideal world, you would explore all three roads, but if time is short the best route is the SS507 along the Val di Cogne, an approach that brings you to the park's major resort at Cogne, a busy little place some 30 minutes' drive from Aosta. En route you can stop off to admire the castle at **Aymavilles** and follow the short signposted road diversion to **Pondel**, a tiny hamlet famed for its superb third-century B.C. Roman bridge and aqueduct.

Cogne (*Visitor information, Piazza Chanoux 36, tel 0165 74 040*) is a good place to stay and pick up trail details (trails are indicated by the Italian Alpine Club's official trail numbers and markings), although for the best scenery you need to follow two smaller roads that push a couple of miles deeper into the park. One finishes at **Lillaz**, a relatively peaceful little village where many of the houses still preserve their traditional slate roofs (you can also walk here along the river from Cogne). The nicest short hike from the village is along

Gran Paradiso National Park protects some of Italy's finest alpine scenery and (left) one of Europe's endangered species, the ibex.

Parco Nazionale del Gran Paradiso
🗺 84 B4
Visitor information
✉ Via Umberto I, Noasca
☎ 0124 901 070

the valley to the east, where the Cascata di Balma is one of the area's many dramatic waterfalls.

Alternatively, follow the minor road south to **Valnontey,** a busier village, and the trailhead for one of the park's most deservedly popular hikes, the walk to the **Vittorio Sella** mountain refuge (trail 106/36) and back via the Lago di Lauson (trail 39) and Sella Herbetet refuge (trail 33). Allow a full day for the walk and try to avoid weekends, when the route is busy. Valnontey is also known for the **Giardino Alpino Paradisia** *(Closed Oct.–mid-June),* founded in 1955, where you can admire some of the park's many wild alpine plants and flowers growing in controlled conditions.

Scenery aside, one of the Gran Paradiso's major attractions is its wildlife, and the ease with which much of it can be seen. Chief among its animals, and chosen as the park's symbol, is the *stambecco* (ibex), a member of the deer family. Virtually extinct elsewhere in Europe, the animal thrives in the region—the park has some 5,000—where it has been protected since 1821. If anything, there are too many, the lack of predators allowing herds to proliferate beyond naturally sustainable limits. Plans to introduce wolves and even lynx have so far proved unsuccessful. Numbers of deerlike chamois are also considerable, as are those of marmots, a small furry mammal whose piercing warning whistle is a common sound on the park's trails. The Valnontey walk has almost guaranteed sightings of ibex and chamois. ■

A drive along the Valle d'Aosta

This stunning drive takes you through high alpine scenery from Pont-St.-Martin to Courmayeur and the foot of Mont Blanc via the historic town of Aosta.

Pont-St.-Martin ❶ is known for its vineyards and the small first-century B.C. Roman bridge at its heart. Consider a diversion here on the SS505 along the **Val di Gressoney,** a perfect alpine valley of meadows, traditional houses, and soaring mountains whose inhabitants, the Walser, descendants of 12th-century Swiss migrants, still speak an ancient German dialect.

A few minutes beyond Pont-St.-Martin on the SS26 lies the brooding **Fortezza di Bard** (Closed to the public), first of the 70 or more fortresses for which the Valley d'Aosta is renowned. Dismantled on Napoleon's orders, it was largely rebuilt in the 19th century. A little farther along the same road is the superb **Castello di Issogne ❷,** built in 1498 by Georges de Challant, a member of the family that controlled much of the Valle d'Aosta for centuries. Across the river lies the **Castello di Verrès** (Closed Wed.), also built by the Challant, but more gaunt in

appearance as its purpose was more defensive than residential.

A side road at Verrès, the SS506, leads north along the **Val d'Ayas ❸,** the prettiest of all the side valleys on the drive: Cable cars from the village of **Champoluc** at its head run to one of the Alps' grandest viewpoints, with vistas of Monte Rosa and Monte Cervino, the two highest mountains in Europe after Mont Blanc.

Hotel-filled **St.-Vincent** is known for its casino, and for the road up the Valtournenche to **Breuil-Cervinia,** a winter resort. This is one of the drive's less enticing diversions, so press on to the **Castello di Fénis ❹,** an outstanding castle renowned for its 15th-century frescoes and exquisite furniture.

> 🅰 Also see area map,
>   p. 84 C4–C5
> ▶ Pont-St.-Martin
> ⟷ 90 miles (145 km)
> 🕐 I day
> ▶ Courmayeur-La Palud
>
> **NOT TO BE MISSED**
> - Val d'Ayas
> - Castello di Fénis
> - Aosta
> - Parco Nazionale del Gran Paradiso
> - Mont Blanc cable car

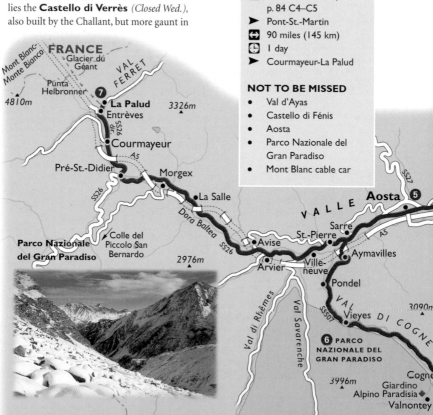

Don't despair at the industrial suburbs of **Aosta** ➎ (*Visitor information, Piazza Chanoux 8, tel 0165 236 627*), for at its heart the region's capital is a pleasant historic town of Roman ruins, medieval churches, and tranquil old squares. Captured from the local Salassi tribe by the Romans, the town was christened Augusta Praetoria in honor of the Emperor Augustus—Aosta is a corruption of Augustus. Over the centuries, its strategic position brought it considerable wealth, its current prosperity bolstered by tourism, trade, and the Mont Blanc and St. Bernard tunnels.

Aosta's nickname, the "Rome of the Alps," overstates things just a touch, but the tally of Roman remains is still impressive. In the old center, see the Roman forum, theater, and amphitheater; farther afield visit the Porta Pretoria, Arch of Augustus, and old Roman bridge. Roman and other early artifacts are the mainstay of the **Museo Archeologico Regionale** (*Piazza Giovanni XXIII, tel 0165 236 627*), a modest museum situated alongside the forum.

Close by stands the town's 12th-century **Cattedrale,** or Cathedral, filled with fine tombs, choir stalls, and mosaic pavements. It also has a little treasure-house of a museum, the **Museo del Tesoro** (*Via Monsignor de Sales, tel 0165 363 589, closed a.m. in winter*). The town's other main church is the lovely 11th-century **Collegiata di Sant'Orso** (*Via Sant'Orso, tel 0165 262 026*), a beguiling medieval complex comprising a priory, a jewel of a Romanesque cloister, an ancient crypt, frescoes, a Gothic choir, and a baroque rood screen.

A side road beyond Aosta at Sarre leads to Cogne on the SS507 and the **Parco Nazionale del Gran Paradiso** ➏ (see pp. 92–93). After this essential detour, return to the main SS26, which climbs ever closer to the vast peaks at the head of the valley. Sarre has yet another castle, as do the picturesque villages of St.-Pierre and Avise. At Pré-St.-Didier, the SS26 toward the Colle del Piccolo San Bernardo offers more scenic diversions. Above all, allow time for the celebrated **cable car** ride (10–12 departures daily) up and over Mont Blanc (or Monte Bianco). The well-signposted ride starts at **La Palud** ➐, a hamlet close to the resort town of Courmayeur. Most people ride as far as Punta Helbronner, but another two stages (*April–Sept. only*) will take you over the Géant glacier and across the mountain into France. Return to La Palud by cable car. ■

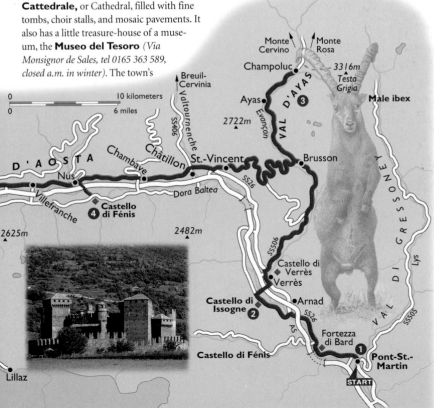

Genoa

"MISTRESS OF THE SEA," SAID PETRARCH, THE 14TH-CENTURY poet, of Genoa (Genova), capturing the maritime prowess—past and present—of a city whose fame has been built on the seafaring exploits of its mariners and the trading potential of Italy's premier port. Visitors to *La Superba* (The Proud), as the city is known, are few, partly because of the lack of obvious sights, partly because of the unedifying suburbs and whiff of squalor characteristic of all large ports. By burrowing beneath the city's rumpled appearance, however, and confining yourself to the historic core, you will uncover Genoa's eclectic wealth of churches, palaces, and galleries.

With its strategic position and fine natural harbor, Genoa's historical rise was almost inevitable. During its 14th-century heyday, the territories of this city state extended as far as Syria, North Africa, and the Crimea. Defeat by Venice in 1380 curtailed maritime expansion, but within two centuries, diversification into banking and other areas of trade had restored its primacy. Great dynastic families, most notably the Doria, then enriched the city with palaces, parks, and works of art, a second golden age undermined by the eventual loss of colonies to Venice and the Ottomans and the increasing share of trade taken by other Mediterranean ports. If you get lost, take a street that leads downward and you will find yourself near the port. From here you can easily catch a bus to any part of Genoa.

Forget any notion of making a logical tour of Genoa's historic center, whose jumble of streets and alleys (*caruggi* in local parlance), with their twists, turns, and ever-changing levels, makes a non-sense of pre-planned itineraries. Instead, get hold of a good map and abandon yourself to random exploration. Revel in the rough-edged charm of the area's teetering houses, crumbling wayside shrines, and washing-hung streets—but avoid some of the dingier corners

after dark, sometimes the haunt of the city's lowlife.

Begin a tour in **Piazza Matteotti,** one of the larger squares, dominated by the gargantuan **Palazzo Ducale** (*Tel 010 557 4000*). Built over several centuries as the erstwhile home of Genoa's ruling medieval doges, it is now given over to exhibitions and other cultural events. From here, walk a few steps west to San Lorenzo. Thereafter, trust your map (available from the visitor center).

SAN LORENZO

Cattedrale di San Lorenzo (*Piazza San Lorenzo, tel 010 247 1831, closed Sun.*) is Genoa's cathedral. Begun in the ninth century and completed in 1118, it received countless embellishments over the centuries. Thus the portal of San Giovanni on its north side is 12th-century Romanesque, while the main facade's doorways and rose window echo later French Gothic models. A similar medley of styles is found in the interior, whose broadly baroque appearance is tempered by the great **Cappella di San Giovanni,** a glorious Renaissance chapel (1451–1465) dedicated to St. John the Baptist, Genoa's patron saint.

Religious relics of all descriptions abound, not least in the cappella, which contains a 13th-century

Genoa
🗺 84 D2
Visitor information
✉ Palazzina Santa Maria, Via al Porto Antico
☎ 010 248 711

"In the wonderful, crooked, twisting, climbing, soaring, burrowing Genoese alleys the traveller is really up to his neck in the old Italian sketchability....Genoa is the crookedest and most incoherent of cities; tossed about on the sides and crests of a dozen hills, it is seamed with gullies and ravines that bristle with innumerable palaces..."
—Henry James, *Italy Revisited* (1877) ■

Opposite: The Gothic portal of San Lorenzo Cathedral was created by French craftsmen in the 13th century.

The Palazzo di San Giorgio on Piazza Caricamento once housed the Banca di San Giorgio upon which much of Genoa's medieval prosperity was based.

"The dock front of Genoa is marvellous. Such heat and colours and dirt and noise and loud wicked alleys with all the washing of the world hanging from the high windows."
—Dylan Thomas, Letter to his parents (1947) ∎

French sarcophagus once said to have concealed the remains of St. John the Baptist. In the church's **treasury,** entered from the sacristy, is the "Sacro Catino," a blue platter reputedly used to serve up the saint's head to Salome. Also here is a green glass bowl said to have been used during the Last Supper.

Just north of San Lorenzo stands **Piazza San Matteo,** one of Genoa's most quaint squares—its small church and old houses were rebuilt and restored by the Doria family in 1278. To the south lie the best of old Genoa's many churches. Charming **San Donato** has a lovely octagonal bell tower, doorway, and a painting of the "Adoration of the Magi" by Joos van Cleve, while Gothic **Sant' Agostino** nearby is worth a look for its museum of frescoes, sculptures, and archaeological fragments (Piazza Sarzano 35, tel 010 251 1263, closed Sun. p.m. & Mon.).

Romanesque **Santa Maria Castello** (Off Piazza Embriaci) owes its name to an earlier Roman castrum (castle) on the site—a few ruins from that period still survive. The church also has several worthwhile frescoes and sculptures, but its most compelling treasures lie in the adjoining Dominican convent. Here the lower loggia of the second cloister features captivating 15th-century frescoes, while the upper loggia has a

monochrome fresco of St. Dominic and a tabernacle of the Trinity, both late 15th-century Genoese works. There are also broad views over the port and city center.

VIA GARIBALDI
Emperor Charles V described the 16th century as the "century of the Genoese," and strolling along Via Garibaldi, often called the most beautiful street in Italy, you can see why. Laid out between 1551 and 1558, the Strada Nuova, or New Road, as it was then called, was created for newly rich merchants anxious to escape the cramped confines of the medieval quarter. Today, many of its palaces have been converted into offices or dazzling stores, although the facades, fountains, frescoes, and half-hidden interior gardens remain as grand as ever.

Palace follows palace in a splendid parade: the Palazzo Cambiaso at No. 1, Palazzo Carrega-Cataldi (No. 2), Palazzo Parodi (No. 3), Palazzo Doria (No. 6), and Palazzo Podestà (No. 7). The **Palazzo Doria-Tursi** (No. 9) is now the town hall and home to a municipal art museum that includes three letters by Christopher Columbus and a violin that belonged to the famous Genoa-born violinist Nicolò Paganini (1784–1840).

Another essential stop is the **Palazzo Bianco** at No. 11, home

Christopher Columbus

Remarkably little is known of Christopher Columbus (1451–1506). The navigator's handwritten will of 1498 states he was born in Genoa, while old city registers record the name of his father, a weaver. Some scholars claim he was born in Piacenza in Emilia-Romagna, others have him as Swiss, Corsican, French, or English. Some

say he was a Spanish Jew forced into Italian exile by persecution, while a handful claim he was a Levantine corsair, Giorgio Bissipat. Genoa does not care: Cristoforo Colombo, as he is known in Italian, appears at every turn, from numerous statues and paintings to the streets, piazzas, fountains, bars, and city airport that bear his name. ∎

to one of the city's principal art collections *(Via Garibaldi 11, tel 010 557 3499, closed Mon. & p.m. Tues., Thurs., Fri., & Sun.)*. Some of the paintings are by worthy but otherwise little known Genoese artists, but there are also pieces by high-profile Italian masters—Caravaggio, Veronese, and Filippino Lippi among them—as well as exceptional Dutch and Flemish works by Memling ("Christ Blessing"), Joos van Cleve ("Madonna and Child"), and Jan Provost ("St. Peter," an "Annunciation," and "St. Elizabeth").

Virtually opposite the Palazzo Bianco lies the **Palazzo Rosso** *(Via Garibaldi 18, tel 010 557 4700, closed Mon. & p.m. Tues., Thurs., Fri., & Sun.)*, where you can admire similarly outstanding paintings. These include portraits by Antony Van Dyck, who worked in the city between 1621 and 1627, and paintings by Dürer, Veronese, Palma il Vecchio, and lesser Genoese artists.

The third of Genoa's triumvirate of galleries, the **Palazzo Spinola** *(Piazza Pellicceria 1, tel 010 270 5300, closed Mon. a.m.)* lies to the southwest of the Palazzo Rosso. As so often in Italian galleries, the rooms in which exhibits are hung—here beautifully appointed salons from the 17th and 18th centuries—are almost as beguiling as the works of art themselves. Genoese artists naturally figure large—Lazzaro Tavarone's ceiling frescoes (1615) are particularly fine—but there are also paintings of wider renown, notably Joos van Cleve's sublime "Adoration of the Magi," Antonello da Messina's "Ecce Homo," Rubens' equestrian portrait of Gio Carlo Doria, and Van Dyck's winsome "Portrait of Lady and Child."

Celebrations in 1992 to commemorate the 500th anniversary of Columbus's voyage to the New World saw much of Genoa spruced up and adorned with new

or renovated buildings. Many of the improvements took place in the port, where Renzo Piano, one of Europe's leading architects, transformed previously derelict swathes of waterfront. One of the most popular new sights is the **Acquario** *(Ponte Spinola, Strada Aldo Moro, tel 010 248 8011, closed Mon. Oct.–March)*, a state-of-the-art aquarium—Europe's largest—based around 50 vast basins and containing some 20,000 marine creatures. Here you can see dolphins, seals, sharks, and penguins, along with countless smaller fish and miscellaneous marine life. Underwater environments such as the Red Sea and a Caribbean coral reef have also been re-created, and numerous exhibits and movies give you the chance for some interactive participation. ∎

The palaces on Via Garibaldi contain sumptuously decorated rooms, such as the Salone Dorato, or Golden Room, of the Palazzo Carrega-Cataldi.

The harbor at Portofino, one of Italy's prettiest villages and a favorite of the rich and famous

Portofino

PORTOFINO IS THE JEWEL OF AN ALREADY GLORIOUSLY embellished coastline. Romantic and beautiful, this former fishing village is now one of Italy's most exclusive and expensive little resorts. When you tire of the yachts, the exclusive stores, the summer crowds, the tangle of cobbled streets, the chic cafés, and the candlelit restaurants, then you can stroll amid pine-scented woodlands or follow one of the easy trails that crisscross the promontory above the village.

Portofino
🅰 85 E2
Visitor information
✉ Via Roma 35
☎ 0185 269 024

Explore the village and then walk to the church of **San Giorgio** *(Salita San Giorgio),* home to what are reputed to be the relics of San Giorgio (St. George), brought from the Holy Land in the 12th century by homeward-bound crusaders. Then go past the old castle and follow the path to the lighthouse, a walk of about 2.5 miles (4 km). This is the most popular of many local walks, and you can see why, for the views, particularly at dusk, are ones you will take to the grave. Almost equally magical vistas are possible from the corniche road linking the village with the resort town of Santa Margherita Ligure.

Much of the promontory above Portofino is protected by the **Parco Naturale di Monte di Portofino,** where trees such as aleppo and maritime pines flourish on the hilly slopes along with a fragrant undergrowth of herbs, juniper, heathers, cistus, and over 700 species of wildflowers. All manner of tranquil paths fan out across the area from Portofino, and from **Camogli,** a fishing village on the promontory's western edge. The best of the longer walks from Portofino is to **San Fruttuoso,** an 11th-century monastery idyllically set amid olives and pines at the head of a narrow bay. This 9-mile (14.5 km) walk takes some four hours round-trip, but you could make either outward or return legs (or both) by boat, an unbeatable way to enjoy the area's coastal scenery first hand. ∎

Cinque Terre

MOST SECRETS ARE EVENTUALLY DISCOVERED, AND THIS, sadly, is true of the Cinque Terre (Five Lands), a quintet of tiny seafront villages that until recently were all but inaccessible by road and all but unknown to visitors. So far the villages' charms remain unspoiled, as does the allure of their surrounding countryside, which is a jumble of plunging cliffs, vineyards, olive groves, and steeply terraced slopes.

You can take a car to most of the villages, but parking is all but impossible and the roads are a nightmare of twists, turns, and hellish grades. Instead, take the train, which stops at all the villages, and either base yourself in one place or shuttle from village to village on foot, by rail, or—best of all— by boat. Accommodations are often in short supply, but try **Levanto,** a pleasant town to the north with plenty of hotels.

The attractions of all five villages are similar: intimate pebbly beaches, tiny coves, crisp white wines, romantic fish restaurants, or quaint huddles of pastel-colored houses. None should disappoint, and you'll soon find your own favorite. When you do want to move on, the trains and boats can whisk you to a neighboring village in minutes.

For many, **Manarola** is the favorite village, closely followed by **Vernazza.** The biggest, most popular, and, perhaps, least alluring village is **Monterosso,** but it has the largest beach and best choice of accommodations. **Riomaggiore,** too, has plenty of places to stay and is prettier. **Corniglia,** high above the sea, is the smallest village, a farming rather than fishing community, but privy to a long shingle beach. Be sure to try a little hiking—local visitor centers have details. The well-signed Via dell'Amore (Path of Love) between Manarola and Riomaggiore is the most famous hike and covers just 1 mile (1.6 km). ■

Perched on cliffs above the sea, Manarola, like all of the Cinque Terre villages, was largely cut off from the outside world for centuries.

Levanto
🗺 85 E2
Visitor information
✉ Piazza Cavour
☎ 0187 808 125

Monterosso
🗺 85 E2
Visitor information
✉ Via Fegina
☎ 0187 817 506

More places to visit in Northwest Italy

ASTI

The Piedmontese town of Asti sits at the heart of some of northern Italy's finest wine country, one reason it is best known for its eponymous sparkling white wine, Asti Spumante. The town's most dramatic festival, an annual horse race combined with much medieval pageantry, is timed to coincide with its wine fair and the first hints of the wine harvest, or *vendemmia,* at the end of September.

Many of the town's older monuments lie on or close to the main street, Corso Vittorio Alfieri, named after local poet and dramatist, Vittorio Alfieri (1749–1803). Worth seeing are the crop of medieval towers at the street's western end, the 14th-century Gothic **Duomo,** and the 15th-century church of **San Pietro in Consavia,** celebrated for its 17th-century frescoes, cloister, and circular Romanesque Baptistery. The last was built between the 10th and 12th centuries and once belonged to a group of medieval knights known as the Order of St. John of Jerusalem. Just west of the central Piazza Alfieri lies the church of **Collegiata di San Secondo,** founded in the 13th century and distinguished by a series of 15th-century frescoes and a fine Renaissance altarpiece by Gandolfino d'Asti.

🏛 84 C3 **Visitor information** ✉ Piazza Alfieri 34 ☎ 0141 530 357 or 0141 538 200

LERICI

The Ligurian coast is studded with beach resorts and seaside towns, many of them bland and forgettable. Lerici is a notable exception, and a favorite among Italian and foreign visitors who enjoy its quiet and unpretentious air. Past visitors have included numerous literary figures, among them writer D. H. Lawrence and poet W. B. Yeats, and it was from a village nearby (San Terenzo), that the English Romantic poet Shelley set sail in 1822 on the fateful voyage that would end with his death by drowning off the Tuscan coast to the south. A former fishing village, Lerici sits on a lovely bay under a glowering 13th century Pisan fortress, from which there are superb views. Prettily painted houses and villas line the waterfront, where you can watch boats come and go, eat and drink in the many bars and restaurants, or relax on the modest beaches.

🏛 85 F1 **Visitor information** ✉ Via Gerini 40 ☎ 0187 967 346

PORTOVENERE

Portovenere may not be as exclusive as Portofino, farther north on the Riviera di Levante, but it is almost as seductive, with its harbor, brightly colored houses, and knot of little streets and alleys. Sights include the church of **San Pietro,** founded in the sixth century. From its location at the end of the waterfront, known as the Palazzata, you can enjoy views of the offshore island of Palmaria. In the upper village, visit the 12th-century church of San Lorenzo (St. Laurence). Note the relief above the door that shows the saint's martyrdom—he was killed by being roasted on a griddle. Then clamber to the ramparts around the village's 16th-century fortress for a breathtaking panorama that takes in the pretty resort town of Lerici and the great wall of cliffs girding the Cinque Terre to the west.

🏛 85 E1 **Visitor information** ✉ Piazza Bastreri ☎ 0187 790 961

SACRA DI SAN MICHELE

Movie location scouts looking for the quintessential medieval monastery need go no farther than Sacra di San Michele. Founded around the year 1000, the abbey lay astride one of the main pilgrim routes to Rome. Eventually, it became one of Europe's most powerful religious foundations, controlling more than 140 sister houses across Italy, France, and Spain.

From the outside it might as well be a fortress, so dark and forbidding are its walls, so lofty and lonely its position—perched at a height of 3,156 feet (962 m). Some 154 rock-hewn steps, the Scalone dei Morti (Stairs of the Dead), lead to the main Porta del Zodiaco, a Romanesque portal adorned with fine early carvings. Inside, the monastery church features a variety of medieval paintings, less memorable, if truth be told, than the magnificent view from the church's esplanade.

🏛 84 B4 ✉ Strada Sacra di San Michele, Monte Pirchiriano, near Avigliana ☎ 011 939 130 🕐 Closed Mon. 🚆 Train from Turin to Avigliana, then infrequent bus ∎

The idyllic lakes and mountains of Lombardy provide a contrast to the mercantile bustle of Milan, Italy's business capital, and to the beauty and variety of the region's many smaller historical towns and villages.

Lombardy & the Lakes

Making instruments in Cremona

Lombardy & the Lakes

LOMBARDY RISES FROM THE ALPINE HEIGHTS RANGED ALONG ITS BORDER with Switzerland, meanders through the lower and more lyrical landscapes of the Italian Lakes, and then expires gently on the great city-studded plains of the Po River. Named after the Lombards, sixth-century invaders from northern Europe, the region has a long and distinguished history, the artistic fruits of which fill its many cities and small towns.

The Lombard plain offers little by way of scenic reward, save for the shadowy outline of the Alps on the distant horizon. Cities are its raison d'être, commerce its driving force. The biggest city, Milan, is Italy's mercantile heart, the place where the money is made and the deals are done. Lombardy is also an agricultural region, however, its vast fields and floodplains perfectly suited to farming on an almost industrial scale: Fruit, cereals, and market gardening are all big business and *risotto* (rice), not pasta, is the region's gastronomic mainstay.

Lombardy's prosperity is not a modern phenomenon, for powerful city states held sway in the region throughout much of the medieval period. And where there were powerful city states in Italy, backed by powerful noble families with powers of patronage, there were usually jewel-like medieval city centers, majestic palaces, and sublime works of art. Thus in Milan, where the presiding dynastic families were the Sforzas and Visconti, the city's modern appearance is belied by an extraordinary range of art-filled palaces and galleries. In Mantua, one of Italy's most unexpected treasures, the Gonzaga family oversaw the creation of a flourishing court and two stupendous palaces. Smaller centers are no less alluring, not least Bergamo, a lofty hilltop citadel, and sleepy Cremona, birthplace of the violin maker Antonio Stradivari.

THE LAKES

Carved by alpine glaciers, the lakes strung across northern Italy have been celebrated by poets and painters for centuries. Their mild-weathered margins are scattered with quaint villages, venerable resorts, soaring mountains, and a wonderful array of villas and luxuriant gardens. Few areas are as romantic or as scenically blessed, at least at their best, for in places the region's beauty and tranquility have been compromised by the march of progress. Fast,

modern roads bring crowds to the resorts in summer and on weekends; pollution has often taken its toll on the lakes' once pristine waters; and modern building occasionally sullies the shorelines and their once peerless vistas.

This is just a gentle word of warning, for the good far outweighs the bad. Como,

Maggiore, and Garda are the most celebrated; Orta and Iseo are smaller and less known, while Lugano is shared with Switzerland. Maggiore is the most visited, Como the most beautiful. Spring, when the gardens are in bloom, is sublime. Twisting lakeside roads offer excellent touring routes, and you can just as easily get around by train. Traveling by boat is a sight-seeing must—all the lakes are criss-crossed by numerous car and passenger ferries.

There are endless opportunities for out-door activities, all easily arranged on the spot. Local visitor centers can provide details of golf courses, watersport centers, and the many well-mapped and well-worn hiking trails in the area.

If the lake scenery seems too gentle, then head north to the rugged beauty of the Alps, in particular the Parco Nazionale dello Stelvio, one of the country's premier national parks. ■

Milan

ITALY'S SECOND CITY (POPULATION 1.3 MILLION) IS A BRISK businesslike metropolis a world away from the medieval sublimities of Rome, Florence, or Venice. Modern and northern European in manner and appearance, it seems at first glance to have sacrificed art and beauty to the material demands of style, fashion, and high finance. Amid the smart stores and sleek office blocks, however, there are less worldly distractions, among them Europe's most extravagant Gothic cathedral, the world's most famous opera house, northern Italy's finest art gallery, and Leonardo da Vinci's celebrated masterpiece, the "Last Supper."

Milan

◭ 104 B3

Visitor information

✉ Via Marconi 1, off Piazza del Duomo

☎ 02 809 662 or 02 7202 2999

Opposite: The facade of Milan's cathedral is a dazzling marriage of Gothic and baroque styles.

Central Milan is not a difficult area to explore. Begin your tour in **Piazza del Duomo,** easily reached on foot, by cab, or by subway (*La Metropolitana* or *Metro* in Italian). From here you can see the Duomo (Cathedral) before walking north to take in the nearby Teatro alla Scala opera house. Still on foot, you can then visit a trio of galleries to the north, among them the Brera, Milan's principal art gallery. Nearby is the so-called Quadrilatero, or rectangle, the name given to an area of fashion houses and luxury stores bounded by four streets: Via Monte Napoleone, Via della Spiga, Via Borgospesso, and Via Sant'Andrea. Moving west, and still within walking distance, lies the Castello Sforzesco, a bristling medieval fortress. The only major sight that you need transportation to visit is Leonardo's "Last Supper."

HISTORY

Location has long been Milan's strong suit—the city's power grew from its position astride vital trad-ing routes. Home to the bulk of the Roman army in the third century B.C., Mediolanum, as the city was known, functioned as the empire's effective capital from A.D. 286 to 403—it was here, for example, in A.D. 313, that the Emperor Constantine issued his edict recognizing Christianity.

In the Middle Ages, the city became one of Italy's most powerful city states, ruled by the Visconti and Sforza families, under whom it acquired the title of the "New Athens," due to the cultural sophistication of its dynastic courts. Capitulation to the French in 1499 prefaced several centuries of foreign interference, including periods of Spanish, Austrian, and Napoleonic domination. More recently, Milan bore the brunt of the corruption scandals of the early 1990s, almost inevitably given that the country's major political and economic deals are brokered here.

PIAZZA DEL DUOMO

The **Duomo,** Milan's cathedral, is not to all tastes. To fans of Gothic architecture, it is a masterpiece of decorative elaboration: "A poem in marble," remarked Mark Twain in *Innocents Abroad* (1869). The exterior alone is adorned with 2,245 statues, 135 spires, 96 gargoyles, and around half a mile (1 km) of tracery. To more demanding palates it is all too much: "an awful failure," according to Oscar Wilde (1854–1900). "Outside the design is monstrous and inartistic, the over-elaborated details stuck high up where no one can see them; everything is vile in it..."

Founded in 1386, the building was instigated by Gian Galeazzo

flayed alive (the statue depicts the saint carrying his folded skin). The same transept contains a lavish "Monument to Gian Giacomo Medici" (1560–63) and the entrance to the roof, a spot you must visit to enjoy the exterior's decoration—some wonderful gables, pinnacles, and gargoyles—and views to the distant Alps that on a clear day extend to the Matterhorn.

Just south of the cathedral stands the **Palazzo Reale,** a royal palace built for the Austrian Grand Dukes in the 18th century. Today one wing contains the modest cathedral museum, the **Museo del Duomo** (*Piazza del Duomo 14, tel 02 860 358, closed Mon.*), whose highlights

Left: The cathedral's exterior contains over 135 spires, a wealth of statues, gargoyles, and other decoration.

Visconti, Milan's ruler of the time, hopeful that the commission would persuade Heaven to reward him with a male heir. Heaven obliged, although the Visconti progeny, the barbarous Giovanni Maria, was assassinated shortly after assuming power in the early 1400s. Work continued for almost five centuries, the finishing touches being added on Napoleon's orders in 1809.

After the exterior's pyrotechnics the bland interior disappoints. Size is the abiding impression—it comes as no surprise to discover that, at 515 feet long by 301 feet wide (157 m by 92 m), this is Europe's third largest church after St. Peter's in the Vatican City and Spain's Seville Cathedral. The stained glass, however, dating back in places to the 15th century, is some of Europe's most extensive, while embedded in the nave near the entrance is the world's largest sundial (1786).

Other key works of art include a seven-branched, bronze candleabrum (14th century) of French or German origin in the north transept, and in the south transept, a macabre statue (1562) of St. Bartholomew, martyred by being

Nearly all of the cathedral's spires and pinnacles were added in the 19th century.

Central portal by Pelegrino Tabaldi

are a variety of casts taken from the cathedral's statues, a lovely wooden model (1519) of the Duomo, and Tintoretto's "The Infant Christ Among the Doctors of the Church." The palace's second floor houses the **Museo Civico d'Arte Contemporanea** (*Piazza del Duomo 12, tel 02 6208 3219, closed—reopens 2000*), a starkly exhibited display of modern art with works by Matisse, Picasso, Braque, and Umberto Boccioni (1882–1916), the leading light of Milan's futurist painters.

To the north of the cathedral lies the **Galleria Vittorio**

Emanuele II, a beautiful glass-enclosed arcade (1865): A belle epoque masterpiece, it is best admired from one of the cafés nestled between its chic offices and luxury stores. Known to the Milanese as the city's *salotto*, or salon, it is a great place to escape sight-seeing duties and watch the locals preen and parade.

Its unfortunate designer, one Giuseppe Mengoni, tumbled through the roof and was killed just days before its inauguration in 1877. Watch to see if anyone pays special attention to the zodiac mosaic

Duomo

✉ Piazza del Duomo 14

☎ 02 8646 3456

🕐 Cathedral, Crypt, & Treasury closed Sun. a.m. & during services

💲 Cathedral: free. Crypt & Treasury: $

🚇 Metro: Duomo

Octagonal drum by Giovanni Antonio Amadeo (1490–1500)

Stained-glass window

Two 16th-century organs

One of 52 piers supporting the cathedral's weight

Pulpits (1585–1602)

Neo-Gothic buttress

enchanting collection bequeathed to the city by wealthy aristocrat Giacomo Poldi-Pezzoli in 1879. Giacomo's eclectic taste ensured a wonderfully diverse collection of art and artifacts—everything from weapons, clocks, cutlery, and fabrics to bronzes, jewelry, paintings, porcelain, and furniture. The carpet and fabric collections, in particular, are outstanding.

Foremost among the paintings are a "Madonna and Child" and "Portrait of a Man" by Mantegna; "St. Nicholas of Tolentino" by Piero della Francesca; a "Madonna" and a "Pietà" by Botticelli; a picture of "Artemesia," possibly by Luca Signorelli; the "Dead Christ" by

The **Galleria Vittorio Emanuele II** is an elegant 19th-century arcade of shops and restaurants.

Museo Teatrale alla Scala

- ⊠ Piazza della Scala
- ☎ 02 887 9478
- 🕒 Closed Sun. Nov.–April
- 💲 $
- Ⓜ Metro: Duomo

Museo Poldi-Pezzoli

- ⊠ Via Alessandro Manzoni 12
- ☎ 02 794 889
- 🕒 Closed Mon., & Sun. p.m. in summer
- 💲 $$
- Ⓜ Metro: Duomo, Manzoni

on the pavement beneath the main cupola—standing on Taurus's testicles is supposed to bring good luck. Walk through the Galleria and you come to Piazza della Scala. On your left stands the world's most distinguished opera house, **Teatro alla Scala.** Inaugurated in 1778, the building took its name from an earlier church on the site, although much of the present plain-faced building dates from 1946, when it was reopened after extensive war damage. To see the 2,800-seat auditorium and its vast stage—Europe's largest—you need to visit the **Museo Teatrale alla Scala,** entered via a door to the left of the opera house entrance. This museum contains all manner of operatic memorabilia, including past sets, costumes, portraits, and Verdi's top hat. More importantly, it allows you into one of the theater's boxes for a peek at the sumptuous interior and its famous gargantuan chandelier.

North of Piazza della Scala stretches Via Alessandro Manzoni, one of the city's busier and more fashionable streets. A short way up on the right stands the **Museo Poldi-Pezzoli,** home to an

Giovanni Bellini; and the gallery's most famous work, Antonio or Piero Pollaiuolo's "Portrait of a Young Woman." Many of these works generally hang in the Salone Dorato, or Golden Salon, the grandest of a series of rooms whose magnificent decoration is as alluring as the works of art themselves.

MUSEO BAGATTI VALSECCHI

After the Poldi-Pezzoli collection, you have a choice between another palace or more paintings. Turn left on Via Borgonuovo and you come to the Pinacoteca di Brera (see p. 112), turn right on Via Monte Napoleone, one of Milan's

premier shopping streets, and you reach the **Palazzo Bagatti Valsecchi.** Begun in 1876, the palace is a Renaissance pastiche inside and out, the interior having been decorated after 1887 by its owners, Fausto and Giuseppe Bagatti Valsecchi, with original works of art or persuasive 19th-century copies. The house remained in the Valsecchi family until 1974 and opened as a museum in 1994. Like the Poldi-Pezzoli, the palace interior is as interesting for its decor as its art and artifacts, its decorative style reflecting the taste for Renaissance ornamentation that prevailed in much of late 19th-century Italy.

Most of Milan's designer stores are found on the fashionable shopping streets north of the Duomo.

Museo Bagatti Valsecchi

Via del Gesù 5, off Via Monte Napoleone

02 7600 6132

Closed Mon. & a.m. Tues.–Sun.

$$

Metro: Montenapoleone

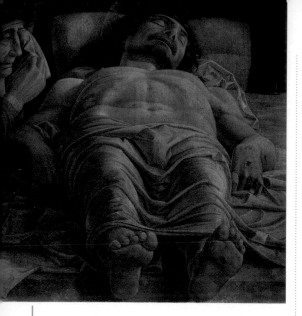

Pinacoteca
di Brera

✉ Via Brera 28

☎ 02 722 631

🕐 Closed Mon.

💲 $$. Free some Sat.
& Sun.

Ⓜ Metro: Manzoni,
Lanza, & Monte

Castello Sforzesco

✉ Piazza Castello

☎ 02 6208 3940

🕐 Closed Mon.

💲 $$

Ⓜ Metro: Cadorna,
Lanzu, & Cairoli

PINACOTECA DI BRERA

The Brera art gallery contains
northern Italy's finest collection
of paintings after Venice's Gallerie
dell'Accademia. Although founded
in the 18th century, it owes much
to the efforts of Napoleon, who
gathered works from churches
and palaces across Italy to create a
collection worthy of a city he had
earmarked as capital of his
proposed "Cisalpine Republic."

In **Rooms 2–15,** painters
of the Venetian school figure large,
most notably Giovanni Bellini, with
a poignant "Pietà," and Mantegna,
whose "Dead Christ" is among
the gallery's most famous works.
Tintoretto's "Miracle of St. Mark,"
Veronese's "Supper at the House
Simon," and "St. Mark Preaching
in Alexandria," by Gentile and
Giovanni Bellini, also clamor for
attention. This said, there are almost
equally compelling works by all the
great Venetian names, among them
Carpaccio, Tintoretto, Lorenzo
Lotto, and Cima di Conegliano.

Painters with Lombard connections are also prominent in
Rooms 15–19, three of the most
appealing works being Bernardino

Luini's "Madonna del Roseto,"
Vicenzo Foppa's "Madonna and
Saints," and Giovanni Boltraffio's
"Gerolamo Casio." Caravaggio is
represented by the superb "Supper
at Erasmus," although, as is often
the case, the central Italians are the
ones to have the last word. Their
most celebrated works here are
Raphael's "Marriage of the Virgin"
and Piero della Francesca's last documented work, the "Montefeltro
Altarpiece," which portrays the
Madonna surrounded by saints
and members of Urbino's ruling
Montefeltro family.

CASTELLO SFORZESCO

West of the Brera rises Milan's most
imperious monument, the gaunt
Castello Sforzesco, a huge redbrick fortress of high towers and
bristling defensive walls. Begun by
the Visconti in the 14th century, it
was virtually destroyed in 1447 by
mobs demonstrating against the
family's monopoly of power, only
to be rebuilt soon after by another
dynastic clan, the Sforzas. It was
never quite the same after Milan's
defeat by the French in 1499, serving as little more than a glorified
barracks until its conversion, in
1904, for use as a library, archive,
and municipal museum.

Today, it contains four museums. The art gallery and fine arts
museum are essential ports of call,
but the two others are minor affairs
devoted to musical instruments and
archaeological exhibits. Highlights
of the former, the Pinacoteca and
Museo d'Arte Atica, are a polyptych
by Mantegna, the "Pala Trivulzio"
(1497), Bambaia's 1525 tomb and
tomb reliefs of Gaston de Foix,
and the unfinished "Rondanini
Pictà," the last known work of
Michelangelo. To the castle's north
stretches the **Parco Sempione**
(1893), Milan's largest, and most
central, public park.

PALAZZO DELL'AMBROSIANA

Milan's parade of art-filled palaces and galleries continues with the **Palazzo dell'Ambrosiana** (1609), home to a famous library founded in the 17th century by Cardinal Federico Borromeo (1564–1631), archbishop of Milan, and to a first-floor gallery crammed with Lombard, Venetian, and Florentine masterpieces. Among the library's 750,000 volumes and 35,000 manuscripts are drawings by Leonardo da Vinci, a fifth-century copy of the *Illiad,* and early editions of Dante (1353), Virgil (1470), and Boccaccio (1471).

Among the works of art, the prize exhibits are a cartoon by Raphael of his painting "The School of Athens" (now in the Vatican), a "Portrait of a Musician" (1485) by Leonardo da Vinci, and a fine "Portrait of a Young Woman" by one of Leonardo da Vinci's pupils, Ambrogio de Predis. Other paintings worthy of note are Caravaggio's "Basket of Fruit" (1596), one of the first still lifes in Italian art, and works by Botticelli, Ghirlandaio, Pinturicchio, Titian, and Tintoretto.

SANT'AMBROGIO

About half a mile (1 km) west of the Palazzo dell'Ambrosiana, Sant'Ambrogio is the most important of Milan's many churches. Founded in 379 by Milan's patron saint (the remains of German-born St. Ambrose, who died in 390, still reside in the crypt), the building's 12th-century Romanesque form served as a model for countless Lombard Romanesque basilica churches across northern Italy.

Twin bell towers flank the austere facade and its stunning atrium (1088), one from the 9th century on the right, another from the 12th century on the left. The restored main portal features 9th-century bronze panels, probably made at about the same time as the interior's superb ciborium (in the sanctuary) and ravishing gold, silver, and jewel-studded high altar front. Also search out the 11th-century pulpit, among Italy's foremost Romanesque works, and the 4th-century sarcophagus beneath it. At the end of the south aisle, seek out the Sacello di San Vittore, a crepuscular chapel built in the 4th century over the site of

The Parco Sempione is a popular place to escape the heat and hustle of Milan's city center.

Palazzo dell'Ambrosiana

✉ Piazza Pio XI 2

☎ 02 806 921

🕐 Closed Mon.

💲 $$

🚇 Metro: Duomo

Despite the controversy surrounding the restoration of Leonardo da Vinci's "Last Supper," the painting remains one of the most famous artworks in the world.

an earlier Christian cemetery: Its mosaics and gold-domed ceiling date from the 5th century.

MILAN ENVIRONS

An easy day trip 24 miles (38 km) to the south of Milan takes you to **Pavia,** a delightful historical

town beside the Ticino River. Once the capital city of the Lombards, Pavia is rich in buildings from the Romanesque and Renaissance periods, none more so than the nearby Certosa di Pavia (see facing page). Be sure to visit the town's cathedral in Piazza Vittoria, the

"Last Supper"

✉ Piazza Santa Maria delle Grazie 2

☎ 02 498 7588

🕐 Closed Mon.

💲 $$

Ⓜ Metro: Cadorna

Note: Advance reservations are required (Tel 199 199 100), for which there is an additional charge ($).

"Last Supper"

Few paintings are as familiar as Leonardo da Vinci's "Last Supper" (1494–97), and few, it must be said, are quite as disappointing in the flesh. The "saddest painting in the world," wrote Aldous Huxley in Along the Road (1925). Painted on the refectory wall of Bramante's Santa Maria delle Grazie—a Renaissance church worth a look in its own right—the "Last Supper" owes its decay to Leonardo's predilection for oil over the traditional techniques of fresco. Painted on to wet plaster, pigments bind powerfully to a porous wall in a strong chemical reaction. Painted as oil, they simply rest on a surface and become prone to damp and weathering. Oil allows greater choice of color and tone, however,

and, in the short term, produces dazzling frescoes. In the long term, the result is often catastrophic deterioration.

Matters were made worse, in this case, by clumsy restoration and by sheer bad luck: At one point, the resident monks whitewashed part of the painting, at another Napoleonic troops billeted here used the wall for target practice, and in 1943 much of the building was destroyed by a World War II bomb. Today, the painting has been restored again to portray its former grandeur, sublime coloring, and dramatic composition—elements which, had the original survived intact, might have made it the world's single greatest painting. ■

outstanding churches of **San Michele,** on Via Capsoni, and **San Pietro,** on Via Griziotti. The former Visconti castle is home to a rewarding little museum and art gallery *(Castello Visconteo, Piazza Castello, tel 0382 33 853, closed Mon.).*

Certosa, Chartreuse, and Charterhouse are the Italian, French, and English names respectively for a Carthusian monastery, of which the most beautiful in Europe is the **Certosa di Pavia.** Intended as a mausoleum for the Visconti, Milan's ruling medieval dynasty, the building is the supreme expression of Lombard Gothic and Renaissance architecture, the decorative majesty of its exterior rivaled by very few buildings in Italy.

Pavia was a natural choice for a monument intended by the Visconti to rival Milan's cathedral. As early as the fifth century, it had been capital of the Lombards' most important Italian duchy, and later witnessed the coronation of emperors such as Charlemagne (in 774) and Frederick Barbarossa (in 1155).

Work on the Certosa began in 1396 on the orders of Gian Galeazzo

Visconti. No expense was spared. Marble was brought from as far away as Carrara on the Tuscan coast, while craftsmen were removed from their labors on Milan's cathedral to satisfy the Visconti whim. Work proceeded for some 200 years, its defining moments provided mostly by Antonio Amadeo, the architect responsible, among other elements, for much of the superlative facade and its bewildering multicolored collection of statues and intricate marble ornament.

Decoration inside is equally excessive, some of it outstanding, some of it superficial froth. Highlights, located in the south and north transepts respectively, include the fresco-framed "Tomb of Gian Galeazzo Visconti" (1493–97), the only Visconti buried here, and the monument (1497) dedicated to Lodovico Sforza and his child bride, Beatrice d'Este. Also look for the altarpiece of "St. Ambrose" (1492) by Bergognone in the Cappella di Sant'Ambrogio (sixth chapel of the north aisle), the inlaid wooden stalls of the choir (1498), and the dazzling ivory altarpiece of the old sacristy, a 15th-century Florentine work. ■

The stunning facade of the Certosa di Pavia reflects the wealth and power of its patrons, the Visconti and Sforza families.

Pavia
 104 B2
Visitor information
✉ Via Fabio Filzi 2
☎ 0382 22 156

Certosa di Pavia
✉ Viale Monumento, 6 miles (9 km) N of Pavia
☎ 0382 925 613
🕐 Guided tours except Mon.
💲 Donation
🚌 Bus: (board Piazza Piave) from Pavia to Certosa

Lago di Como

LAGO DI COMO, OR LAKE COMO, IS THE MOST VARIED AND
most dramatic of the Italian Lakes. Its banks are fringed with villas,
lush gardens, and bucolic villages, while its hinterland is a patchwork
of wood-swathed hills and rugged mountains. The best approach
to sight-seeing is to pick a base—Como is the largest town, Bellagio
the prettiest village—and then explore by driving the scenic lakeshore
roads or boarding one of the many ferries that link the lake's far-
flung settlements.

COMO

"Bosomed deep in chestnut groves,"
wrote William Wordsworth, the
English poet, of Lake Como's capital
in 1791, although these days a faint
industrial fringe—silk and other
textiles are big business here—
slightly tarnishes the town's lakeside
allure. In the old center, close to the
water, however, you can still happily
wander the park-lined promenades
and relax in pleasant waterfront
cafés. Boats embark here for all
points of the lake, and there is also
a little sight-seeing for rainy days.

Principal sights in Como's
historic town center include the
Duomo (Via Plinio), founded
in the 14th century: It has a fine
facade and several interior treasures, of which several tapestries
(1598) and the Renaissance altarpieces by Tommaso Rodari and
Bernardino Lini are the most memorable. Next door stands the arched
Broletto, the town's 13th-century
town hall, while farther afield lie
San Fedele (Piazza di San Fedele)
and Sant'Abbondio (Via Regina
Feodolinda), two perfect Lombard
Romanesque churches.

TREMEZZO

Just north of Como lies the village
of Cernobbio, famed for the 16th-
century Villa d'Este and its splendid
garden, now part of a magnificent
hotel and thus only open to lucky
patrons. All and sundry, however,
can visit two sets of gardens in

Tremezzo, a village to the north:
the **Parco Comunale,** and the
more elaborate **Villa Carlotta**
(Tel 0344 40 405, closed Nov.–mid-
March)—the one garden on the
lake you should visit if you see no
other. The 18th-century villa also
contains a small sculpture gallery.
Take excursions by boat from nearby Sala or other village ports to the
wooded **Isola Comacina,** Lake
Como's principal island, and to
the romantic gardens at **Villa del
Balbianello** near Lenno (Tel 0344
561 102, villa closed Nov.–March,
gardens closed Mon. & Wed.).

BELLAGIO

Bellagio is a dream of a place,
nestled on a hilly promontory that
overlooks both of Lake Como's
watery arms. Its name comes from
the Latin bi-lacus, meaning between
the lakes. Views are matchless, the
cobbled streets quaint, and the gardens of the **Villa Serbelloni** (Tel
031 950 204, twice-daily guided tours
April–Oct. Tues.–Sun., reserve at
visitor center) and **Villa Melzi
D'Eryl** (Closed Nov.–Feb.) as pretty
and perfumed as any in Italy. The
Serbelloni, owned by the Rockefeller
Foundation, was reputedly built
over a villa belonging to Pliny the
Younger (A.D. 61–112), a noted
Roman man of letters born nearby.

Bellagio's central position makes
it an ideal base, but even if you are
only visiting the village for the day, it
is still worth taking a ferry from here

Como
🗺 104 B3
Visitor information
✉ Piazza Cavour 17
☎ 031 265 244

Bellagio
🗺 104 B4
Visitor information
✉ Piazza della
    Chiesa 14
☎ 031 950 318

Menaggio
🗺 104 B4
Visitor information
✉ Piazza Garibaldi 8
☎ 0344 32 924

to the lake's eastern shore to visit **Varenna.** The best of this village's many leafy retreats are the **Villa Cipressi** *(Closed in winter)* and **Villa Monastero** *(Closed Nov.– April),* the latter built over a former convent dissolved in the 16th century due to its nuns' wayward behavior! The village, like most on the lake, offers some lovely strolls, notably up to the ruined Castello Vezio for breathtaking views of the lake; along the shoreline to the Fiumelatte, reputedly Italy's shortest river; and from Fiumelatte to Baluardo, another lofty viewpoint.

MENAGGIO

Back on the lake's western shore, you come eventually to Menaggio, probably the most fashionable resort and an ideal base for a sporting or hiking interlude. There is also an 18-hole golf course above the village, while **Monte Bregagno,** one of the region's more rewarding mountain peaks at 6,913 feet (2,107 m), lies close by. Consult local visitor centers for details of trails and water- or land-based sporting options in or near the lake's villages. ■

A poet's perspective

" This lake exceeds any thing I ever beheld in beauty…. The union of culture and the untameable profusion and loveliness of nature here is so close, that the line where they are divided can hardly be discovered." —Percy Bysshe Shelley, Letter to Thomas Love Peacock (1818) ■

A mild climate allows luxuriant gardens to thrive on the shores of Lake Como.

Lake Maggiore drive

This drive takes you along the attractive western shore of Lake Maggiore, probably the best known of the Italian Lakes, with the option of a diversion at Stresa to the celebrated Isole Borromee.

The best route to Lake Maggiore from the south is via Autostrada A8/26, but it is not an approach that raises high scenic expectations. First impressions of a lake renowned across centuries for its romantic beauty involve a rather drab, factory-pocked shoreline and the no-nonsense market town of **Arona ❶** (*Visitor information, Piazzale Duca d'Aosta, tel 0322 243 601*), best known for its colossal statue of Cardinal Charles Borromeo (1538–1584). Borromeo's family has long been the lake's leading light—even today it owns all of the lake's islands and its fishing rights, as it has done for some 500 years. Charles became Archbishop of Milan at 22, thanks to the influence of his uncle, Pope Pius IV. (The word "nepotism" derives from the Italian *nipote,* meaning nephew, after the considerable number of papal nephews raised to high office.) After exploring the older upper town and climbing the 120-foot (36 m) statue *(Tel 0322 249 669, closed Mon.–Fri. in winter),* you have a choice of two routes north, both equally appealing. The SS33 follows the lake shore, with worthwhile stops at **Lesa ❷** to see San Sebastiano, the lake's best Romanesque church, and the pleasing resort of **Belgirate,** where the lake's scenery begins to improve. The other leads inland on the SS142 and runs through the pretty hill country of the Vergante region and its string of appealing villages. Both routes meet just south of **Stresa ❸** *(Visitor information, Via Canonica 3, tel 0323 30 150 or 0323 31 308).*

This mild-weather town is the lake's principal resort, known for its lovely mountain-backed setting, sedate waterfront promenades, luxuriant gardens—all palms and orange blossoms—and some heart-melting views of the nearby Isole Borromee. Two local villas, blessed with luxuriant lakeside gardens, merit a visit: the **Villa Ducale** and **Villa Pallavicino.** Take time to stroll the town's placid cobbled streets, then spend time exploring the **Isole Borromee ❹** (see p. 120) and

Monte Mottarone ❺, the mountain rising 4,891 feet (1,491m) above the town. Make the ascent by the zigzagging tollroad, signed off the SS33 west, just south of Stresa at Alpino, or by cable car from Stresa Lido *(Tel 0323 30 295, daily every 20 minutes).* On a clear day, the views from the summit are magnificent, embracing Lake Maggiore, the Lombard plain, a wide swathe of the Alps, and many of the region's other lakes.

Proceed on the main lakeside SS33 as far as sleepy **Baveno.** Squeezed between crags and lakeshore, it has been a desirable resort since 1879, when Great Britain's Queen Victoria graced the village with her presence. German composer Richard Wagner also stayed here. Today there is little specific to see—just the plain-faced 11th-century church of Santi Gervasio e Protasio and an octagonal baptistery with fifth-century origins. Curving northward you come to **Pallanza ❻,** best known for the **Villa Taranto** *(Tel 0323 556 667, open daily April–Oct.),* built in 1831. It was rescued from semi-dereliction in 1931 by its Scottish owner, Neil McEachern, who replanted the gardens with some 20,000 often rare and imported flowers, shrubs, and trees.

The lake and its villages become quieter as you follow the SS34 north of Pallanza. To continue northward eventually means either doubling back or following the road into Switzerland, before reentering Italy for the run down Maggiore's peaceful, although less engaging, eastern shore. Resorts such as **Ghiffa, Cannero Riviera,** and **Cannobio** are charming as far as they go, but there are several alternatives to the Swiss diversion. Heading west from Cannobio, for example, you could follow the Valle Cannobina to Domodossola, a dramatic ride through high alpine scenery. Better still, especially if time is short, leave Maggiore at Pallanza and take the road via Gravellona Toce to explore the easily accessible confines of **Lago d'Orta** (see p. 121). ■

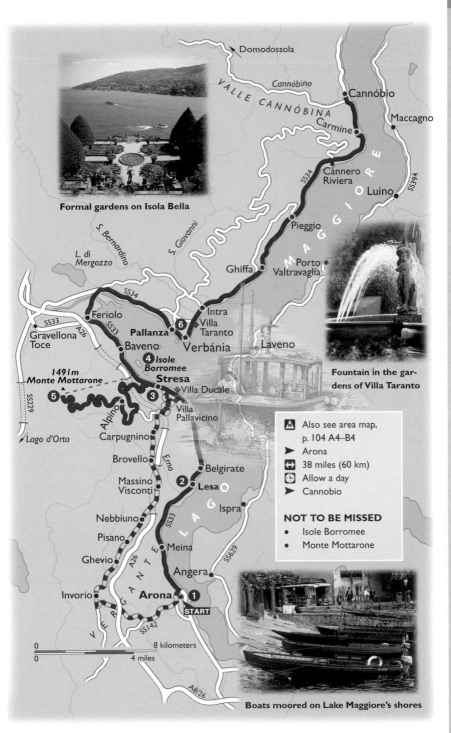

Formal gardens on Isola Bella

Fountain in the gardens of Villa Taranto

Boats moored on Lake Maggiore's shores

Also see area map, p. 104 A4–B4
Arona
38 miles (60 km)
Allow a day
Cannobio

NOT TO BE MISSED
- Isole Borromee
- Monte Mottarone

The ornate gardens and extravagant architectural flourishes of Isola Bella's Palazzo Borromeo make it the most visited of the Borromean Islands.

Isole Borromee

THE ISOLE BORROMEE, OR BORROMEAN ISLANDS, ARE A trio of almost impossibly idyllic islands lapped by the waters of Lake Maggiore. All three—Bella, Pescatori, and Madre—are usually jam-packed in high season, but it is worth putting up with people and high prices to enjoy the villas, gardens, and peerless views of the archipelago's loveliest retreats—the Isola Bella and Isola Madre.

Isole Borromee

- 104 A4
- ☎ 0323 30 556
- ⊕ Palaces & gardens on both islands closed late Oct.–late March
- $ $$ (combined ticket to villa & gardens on each island)
- ⛴ Boats to the islands leave regularly throughout the year from Arona, Stresa, Baveno, & other local towns. Excursion tickets give you the freedom to move between the islands.

The **Isola Bella,** the best known of the islands, was a rocky wasteland until 1670, when Count Carlo III Borromeo decided to transform it into a garden for his wife, Isabella. (A more salacious version of the story suggests the island was intended as a rendezvous for Borromeo and his mistresses.) Huge quantities of soil and plants were brought from the mainland, creating a beautifully theatrical garden arranged over ten terraces, each terrace a luxuriant mixture of laurel, cypresses, camellias, box hedges, and creamy magnolias. Work on the adjoining Palazzo Borromeo went on for generations, with the finishing touches made as late as 1959. The end result is less an architectural triumph than an amusing monument to decorative kitsch.

Sheer weight of numbers spoils the **Isola Pescatori,** writer Ernest Hemingway's favorite island, a place almost too quaint for its own good. It is probably only worth a passing visit en route to the **Isola Madre,** which is larger, less-inundated, and, in many ways, scenically superior to the other islands. The Borromeos also toiled here for generations to produce a magnificent garden, perfect for a languorous couple of hours spent strolling and relaxing. Pheasants, peacocks, and parrots add an exotic touch to the grounds, which are filled with early-blooming camellias, Europe's largest Kashmir cypress, and a wide variety of other rare plants and trees. ■

Lago d'Orta

LAGO D'ORTA, OR LAKE ORTA, IS A VISION FROM A BYGONE age, its almost unsullied beauty a hint of how Como and Maggiore, its near neighbors, might once have appeared before crowds and commercialism took their toll. Both its tranquil capital, Orta San Giulio, and its island hideaway, the Isola San Giulio, are unspoiled gems, ideal for a few days relaxation and gentle sight-seeing.

Orta San Giulio is a perfect base from which to explore the lake, a stretch of water described by French novelist Balzac as a "gray pearl in a green basket." Intimate and peaceful, the village and its leafy peninsula offer lovely views and a tangle of cobbled streets. Village life revolves around Piazza Motta, a lakeside square dominated by the arcaded Palazzotto (1582), Orta's former town hall. Walk up to the **Sacro Monte** above the village, a pretty group of tiny chapels (1590–1770) overlooking the lake. Still lovelier views can be enjoyed from the **Passeggiata del Movero,** a headland path near the village.

Boats from Orta run to the **Isola di San Giulio,** named after the fourth-century saint credited with clearing the island of snakes and dragons. Having first sailed to its shores on his cloak (the local fishermen were too afraid to row him across), he then yoked wolves to a cart and proceeded to construct a church. For this reason, Giulio was annointed patron saint of builders.

Today, the successor to his church is the baroque **Basilica di San Giulio,** whose crypt reputedly contains the saint's relics. It also features some beautiful fourth-century sculptural fragments, probably from the saint's original tomb. The main body of the church boasts an 11th-century black marble pulpit adorned with reliefs of scenes from Giulio's life, also celebrated in accomplished 15th-century frescoes off the church's north aisle. ∎

The island of San Giulio lies at the heart of Lake Orta.

Lago d'Orta
🅐 104 A3
Visitor information
✉ Via Bossi 7, Orta San Giulio
☎ 0322 911 937

BOAT SERVICES
Navigazione Lago d'Orta *(Tel 0322 844 862)* operate frequent services from Orta *(Piazza Motta)* to the Isola San Giulio. They also run two or more services daily between Orta and eight other villages on the lake, as well as a midnight cruise during July and August. ∎

Bergamo

BERGAMO IS A TALE OF TWO CITIES: THE LOWER AND mostly modern Bergamo Basso, built across the Lombard plain at the confluence of the Brembo and Serio Rivers; and Bergamo Alta, an older and mainly medieval quarter perched on one of the foothills of the Orobian Alps. Bergamo Basso boasts the region's finest provincial art gallery, while Bergamo Alto, all towers, spires, and city walls, has an ensemble of medieval buildings described by French writer Stendhal as "the most beautiful place on earth…the prettiest I have ever seen."

The highlight of the Cappella Colleoni is an equestrian statue of the 15th-century mercenary leader, Bartolomeo Colleoni.

Bergamo

Ⓜ 105 C3

Visitor information

✉ Vicolo Aquila Nero 2, Bergamo Basso

☎ 035 242 226

Bergamo Basso, the lower town, has its medieval moments, the best of them found on and around the palace-lined Via Pignolo, the street that climbs toward the upper town. Near it stands a trio of churches known for the altarpieces by Lorenzo Lotto (1480–1556), who was born in Bergamo: **Santo Spirito** *(Corner of Via Torquato Tasso),* **San Bernardino** *(Via San Giovanni),* and **Sant'Alessandro** *(Piazzetta del Delfino).* Lotto also left a wonderful "Madonna and Saints" in **San Bartolomeo,** a church overlooking Piazza Matteotti, Bergamo Basso's broad main square.

The beauty of Lotto's paintings prepares you for the **Accademia Carrara,** an outstanding provincial art gallery full of great names, in particular those of the great 15th-century Venetians. Gentile Bellini is

represented by several ethereal portraits, his brother Giovanni by a forceful "St. Sebastian," and Carpaccio by a stately "Portrait of the Doge Leonardo Loredan." Other Venetian offerings include paintings by Antonio Vivarini, Titian, Tintoretto, Canaletto, Carlo Crivelli, Veronese, Tiepolo, and Guardi. The Florentines are not forgotten— Raphael's "St. Sebastian" and Botticelli's stern-faced "Giuliano de' Medici" would shine in any company—nor are non-Italians such as Holbein, Brueghel, Van Dyck, Velázquez, and Dürer.

The imperious position of **Bergamo Alto,** or Upper Town, attracted Ligurian settlers from as early as 1200 B.C. Later, the site was adopted by the Celts, who named it Bergheim or Berghem (hill town), then by the Romans, who renamed it Bergomum. During the Middle Ages, it became an independent city state before falling first to Milan's Visconti and then to Venice. The *condottiere,* or mercenary leader, Bartolomeo Colleoni (1400–1475), was born here—although he devoted most of his active life to Venice— as was the composer Gaetano Donizetti (1797–1848), who also died in the city. The medieval Bergamask dance originated here, as did the commedia dell'arte, comedy drama known for its stock characters, Harlequin, Pulcinella, Scaramouche, and Columbine.

Bergamo's old town huddles within ancient walls built by the Venetians, at its heart two closely linked squares: **Piazza Vecchia** and **Piazza del Duomo.** The former, with its delightful ensemble of medieval buildings includes the **Palazzo della Ragione,** one of Italy's oldest civic palaces (1199). Be sure to take the elevator ride up the square's 12th-century **Torre Civica** for a bird's-eye view of the city *(Tel 035 224 700, closed Mon.– Fri. Nov.–Feb.).*

Pride of place in the neighboring square goes to the exquisitely decorated **Cappella Colleoni** *(Piazza Duomo, tel 035 226 331, closed Mon. Nov.–Feb.),* commissioned in 1470–76 as a mausoleum by the eponymous condottiere from Giovanni Antonio Amadeo, the architect responsible for much of the equally extravagant Certosa di Pavia (see p. 115). Alongside it stand the Baptistery (1340) and **Basilica di Santa Maria Maggiore** (begun in 1137), the latter an outstanding piece of Lombard Romanesque architecture spoiled only by its later baroque interior. Several outstanding Flemish and Florentine tapestries redeem the baroque meddling, however, as do the lavish *intarsia* (inlaid wood) panels of the chancel and choir.

North of the piazza, clamber up to the ruined **Rocca,** or fortress, for views over the town. Then follow Via Porta Dipinta to the north, pausing to admire the medieval frescoes in the church of **San Michele** and the **Convento di Sant' Agostino.** South of the piazza, take the funicular up to the **Castello** for more sweeping vistas. ■

Medieval squares in Bergamo, such as the **Piazza Vecchia,** have been much admired by modern architects such as Le Corbusier and Frank Lloyd Wright.

Accademia Carrara

✉ Piazza dell' Accademia 82a, Bergamo Basso

☎ 035 399 643

🕐 Closed Tues.

💲 $$. Free on Sun.

The Palazzo Ducale in Mantua contains hundreds of beautifully decorated rooms.

Mantova

INSPIRED BY ITS CANALS, LAKE-RINGED SURROUNDINGS, and almost faultless medieval center, Aldous Huxley described Mantova (Mantua) as the world's most romantic city. Locals know it as *la piccola Venezia*, or little Venice. The beautifully arcaded streets are among northern Italy's most evocative and, in the Palazzo Ducale and extraordinary Palazzo del Tè, the town boasts two of the country's most remarkable palaces.

Mantova
⚑ 105 E2
Visitor information
✉ Piazza delle Erbe-
Piazza Andrea
Mantegna 6
☎ 0376 328 253 or
0376 350 681

Mantua lies among marshy lowlands—hence its lakes and canals—and was probably founded as an island refuge by the Etruscans during the fifth or sixth century B.C. During the Middle Ages, the ruling Gonzaga family turned the town into a byword for courtly life and cultural endeavor, their patronage attracting the likes of Leon Battista Alberti (1404–1472), the great Renaissance architectural theorist,

and painters such as Mantegna, Pisanello, and Giulio Romano.

Like most Italian towns, Mantua has its share of dispiriting suburbs, but once through its industrial fringes the historic center is an unmitigated delight. Here, three squares create a focus—Piazza Sordello, Piazza Broletto, and Piazza delle Erbe—each bristling with medieval buildings and flanked with cobbled lanes and

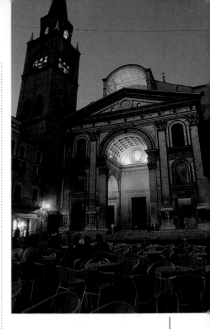

Right: The facade of Sant'Andrea, a church designed in 1470 by the great Renaissance architect and theorist, Leon Battista Alberti

Palazzo Ducale
✉ Piazza Sordello
☎ 0376 320 283
🕐 Closed Sun. p.m. & Mon.
💲 $$

Palazzo del Tè
✉ Viale Tè
☎ 0376 323 266 or 0376 325 886
🕐 Closed Mon. a.m.
💲 $$

ancient arcaded streets. Piazza delle Erbe plays host to **Sant'Andrea,** an imposing 15th-century church designed by Leon Battista Alberti (the painter Mantegna is buried in one of its chapels) and to the 11th-century **Rotonda di San Lorenzo,** a restrained Romanesque church with lovely loggia and a colonnaded ambulatory.

Mantua's great sight, indeed one of northern Italy's greatest sights, is the **Palazzo Ducale,** or Ducal Palace, a vast edifice begun in the 14th century and expanded over several centuries, largely on behalf of the Gonzaga dukes. In its day, it was Europe's largest palace. When the building was sacked by the Austrian Habsburgs in 1630, some 80 carriages were used to remove 2,000 works of art from its 500 rooms. A staff of around 1,000 catered to the dukes' every whim.

Room follows room in a majestic parade, some immeasurably grand, others tiny decorative fresco-filled jewels. Among their more notable works are a series of courtly frescoes by the Veronese artist Pisanello (1395–1450), most of them inspired by episodes from the tales of King Arthur and the Knights of the Round Table. Also outstanding is the Appartamento degli Arazzi, or Room of the Tapestries, hung with Flemish tapestries crafted to designs by Raphael. Best of all is the **Camera degli Sposi,** or Room of the Spouses, so called because marriages were recorded here. Although tiny in extent, the room is almost entirely covered in one of the most breathtaking Renaissance fresco cycles (1465–1474), Mantegna's sublimely lyrical portraits of the Gonzaga family and the splendors of courtly life.

The **Palazzo del Tè,** situated in parkland on the edge of the old town, was conceived as a country retreat for the Gonzaga family. Built later than the Palazzo Ducale— between 1525 and 1535—it is a smaller and very different creature to its more central rival. Both the design and many of the interior frescoes were the work of Giulio Romano (1492–1546), one of the age's most accomplished mannerist artists and architects.

Stylized and deliberately shocking, the palace was conceived primarily as a pleasure dome, the preoccupation with hedonism most obvious in the **Sala di Psiche** (Room of Psyche), whose languo-rous frescoes—all satiated satyrs and frolicking nymphs— must be some of Italy's most erotic and sexually explicit paintings. The scenes, like many in the palace, borrow heavily from classical myth, although contemporary gossip suggested they were intended as an earthy celebration of Federico Gonzaga's passion for his mistress.

Still more extraordinary paintings adorn the neighboring **Sala dei Giganti** (Room of the Giants), where looming and grotesquely distorted figures act out Jupiter's rage against the Titans. ■

More places to visit in Lombardy & the Lakes

BRESCIA

As Lombardy's second largest city, Brescia deserves only a brief mention, for in the flesh it is a dispiriting mixture of industry, modern streets, and drab architecture. Redeeming features include the **Pinacoteca Civica** *(Via Martinengo da Barco, tel 030 375 7776, closed Mon.)*, a gallery with paintings by Raphael, Tintoretto, and local Renaissance artists, and the **Museo Romano** *(Via Musei 57a, tel 030 46 031, closed Mon.)*, a museum of Roman art and artifacts.

⚑ 105 D3   **Visitor information** ✉ Corso Zanardelli 38   ☎ 030 45 052

CREMONA

Cremona has its attractions—namely a fine cathedral, lovely central square, and Italy's tallest medieval tower—but is only worth a special visit if your interests include violins and violin maker Antonio Stradivari (1644–1737). Stradivari was part of Cremona's long instrument-making tradition, a tradition that continues to this day: As many as 1,000 violins a year may be crafted in the town's 60 or so workshops. Displays in the unremarkable **Museo Civico** *(Via Ugolani Dati 40, tel 0372 461 885, closed Mon.)* explore the history of violinmaking. To see Cremona's very own Stradivarius you need to consult the visitor center.

⚑ 105 D2   **Visitor information** ✉ Piazza del Comune 5   ☎ 0372 23 233

LAGO D'ISEO

Lago d'Isco, or Lake Isco, is often seen as the poor relation of the Italian Lakes, overshadowed by the splendors of Como, Garda, and Maggiore. In truth, its wild scenery, high mountains, and small villages are worth a look, and can easily be incorporated on an itinerary that takes in the Dolomites to the north.

Its major centers—both on the eastern shore—are **Iseo,** whose pleasant main square is graced with the pretty fresco-filled church of Sant'Andrea, and **Pisogne** to the north, whose church, Santa Maria della Neve, is also extensively frescoed. Be warned, however, that these and other lakeside centers are popular—and busy—with Italians on weekends. The western shore, and the villages of Sarnico, Tavernola, and Riva di Solto, are usually a touch quieter.

The single best sight on the lake is **Monte Isola** *(regular boat connections from several lake towns)*, a verdant lake island crowned by the hilltop church of Madonna della Ceriola, from whence tremendous views of the lake and surrounding mountains abound.

A short excursion by road from Marone on the lake's eastern shore takes you to **Cislano,** 3 miles (5 km) away, where you can admire one of the region's more unusual natural phenomena—the so-called Fairies of the Forest. These consist of thin and strangely eroded rock spires and towers, most of them crowned with a precariously perched boulder.

⚑ 105 D3   **Visitor information** ✉ Lungolago Marconi 23, Iseo ☎ 030 980 209

PARCO NAZIONALE DELLO STELVIO

Lombardy's prime slice of alpine scenery is protected by the Parco Nazionale dello Stelvio, Italy's largest national park, a mountain playground with plenty of skiing opportunities and almost 1,000 miles (1,600 km) of marked hiking trails. The town of **Bormio** is the best base, the **Valle dello Zebrù,** a spectacular valley to its east, a good target for first-time visitors wishing to hike.

⚑ 105 D5   **Visitor information** ✉ Via Roma 13/b   ☎ 0342 903 300

SABBIONETA

Stranded on the Lombard plains southwest of Mantua, Sabbioneta is a planned town begun in 1558 by Vespasiano Gonzaga, a cultured mercenary leader who made his fortune in the service of Philip II of Spain. Hemmed in by a hexagon of walls, the Renaissance experiment is a delight, full of ordered streets, and fine buildings that include the **Palazzo Ducale, Palazzo del Giardino,** and the church of the Incoronata (Vespasiano's burial place). The **Teatro Olimpico** was designed by Vicentino Scamozzi, a leading pupil of Palladio.

⚑ 105 D1   **Visitor information** ✉ Via Vespasiano Gonzaga 31   ☎ 0375 52 039 ■

Venice is a city beyond description and compare. Or as the English poet Elizabeth Barrett Browning put it in 1851: "Nothing is like it, nothing is equal to it, not a second Venice in the world."

Venice

The Lion of St. Mark

Venice

THE WORLD'S MOST BEAUTIFUL CITY RARELY DISAPPOINTS. "I'D RATHER BE in Venice on a rainy day than in any other capital on a fine one," was how the author Herman Melville put it in 1857, capturing the allure of a city whose magic casts its spell year-round—whether you visit in the depths of winter, an icy mist spreading chill over the encircling lagoon, or in the shimmering, enervating heat of summer, when the canals, ancient churches, and endless palaces are dappled with the shifting light of the Mediterranean sun. Although threatened on many fronts—pollution and depopulation are real problems—the city remains as close as the real world gets to a fairy tale.

Venice (Venezia) is a relatively recent city—compared to Rome, London, or Paris—yet few places have remained as unsullied by the passing of time. Its lagoon was probably inhabited during the time of Christ, albeit sparsely, and small groups of refugees may have settled its islands following barbarian raids in the fifth century (myth dates the city's foundation to March 25, 421). The first doge, or ruler, was elected in 726, but presided over a loose confederation of settlements rather than a single city. Later, the Frankish invasions of the eighth century forced some of the lagoon's inhabitants to the so-called Rivus Altus, or high bank, a group of more easily defended islets that in time would become the Rialto, the cornerstone of present-day Venice.

By the tenth century, the nascent city had established trading links with the East and elsewhere. Prosperity increased during the Crusades and in the wake of the city's growing maritime prowess. Firm government provided political and social cohesion at home, and by the 13th century the city was mistress, in an oft-quoted phrase, of "one quarter and one half-quarter" of the old Roman empire. On the mainland the city subdued its main maritime rivals, notably Genoa, and extended its reach across much of northeast Italy, an empire that remained intact until the arrival of Napoleon. Decline was due largely to the rise of the Turks from about the 14th century, who gradually absorbed Venice's maritime empire, and to the long-standing emnity of other Italian and European powers. The republic's final dissolution came in 1797, courtesy of Napoleon, after which the city passed under Austrian control before joining a united Italy in 1866.

WHAT TO SEE

Venice is divided into six *sestieri*, or districts, three on either side of the Grand Canal, the city's watery main thoroughfare. (Rather than base your sight-seeing around the sestieri, however, concentrate instead on small clusters of adjoining sights.) Before embarking on the sights, take a ride along the Grand Canal (see pp. 132–33), by far the best introduction to the city. Above all, don't plunge straight into St. Mark's, where the crowds could put you off the city before you even start. Instead, make for one of the city's smaller squares—Campo Santo Stefano or Campo Santa Margherita are the best—to sample areas of the city not entirely given over to tourism. Only then, acquainted with the more intimate side of Venice, should you surrender to the demands of sight-seeing.

The city's two key churches are Santa Maria Gloriosa dei Frari and Santi Giovanni e Paolo (known as San Zanipolo), its principal art galleries the Accademia and Collezione Peggy Guggenheim. The major *scuole*, ancient art-filled buildings, are the Scuola Grande di San Rocco and the smaller Scuola di San Giorgio degli Schiavoni. Second-ranked galleries include the Museo Civico Correr, Ca' d' Oro, and Ca' Rezzonico, while lesser churches—a relative term in Venice, given that even the smallest Venetian churches have charm and treasures beyond compare—include Santa Maria della Salute and San Zaccaria. Finally, steel yourself for the "big two"—the Doge's Palace and St. Mark's Basilica.

Masks were banned in Venice under Mussolini, but they have been made and sold in shops across the city since the revival of the Carnival in 1979.

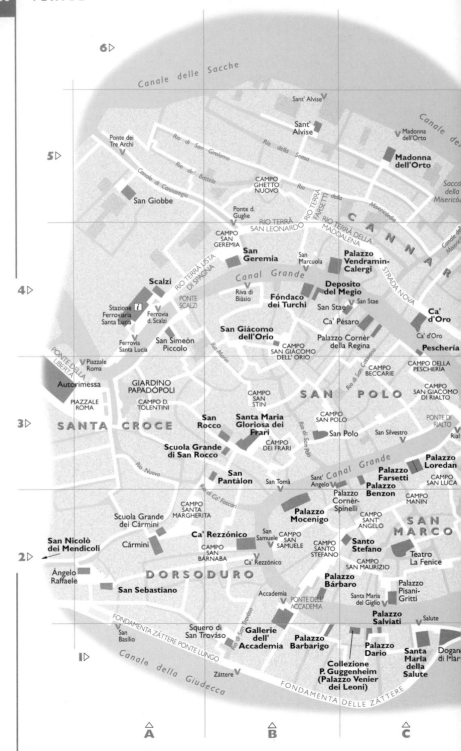

6▷

Canale delle Sacche

Sant' Alvise

Sant'
Alvise

Madonna
dell'Orto

Canale de

Ponte dei
Tre Archi

Rio di San Girolamo

Rio della Sensa

Madonna
dell'Orto

5▷

Canale di Cannaregio

Rio del Battelo

CAMPO
GHETTO
NUOVO

Rio

Sacca
della
Misericó

San Giobbe

Ponte d.
Guglie

RIO TERRÀ
SAN LEONARDO

RIO TERRA
FARSETTI
della

della
Misericórdia

Canale Miseri

CAMPO
SAN
GEREMIA

RIO TERRÀ DELLA
MADDALENA

C A N N A R

San
Geremia

San
Marcuola

Palazzo
Vendramin-
Calergi

STRADA NOVA

4▷

RIO TERRÀ LISTA
DI SPAGNA

Scalzi

Canal Grande

Deposito
del Megio

Stazione
Ferroviaria
Santa Lucia

Ferrovia
d. Scalzi

PONTE
SCALZI

Riva di
Biásio

Fóndaco
dei Turchi

San Stae

San Stae

R

Ca'
d'Oro

Ca' Pésaro

Ferrovia
Santa Lucia

San Simeòn
Piccolo

Rio Marin

San Giácomo
dell'Orio

Ca' d'Oro

Peschería

PONTE DELLA
LIBERTÀ

Piazzale
Roma

CAMPO
SAN GIÀCOMO
DELL' ORIO

Palazzo Cornèr
della Regina

Rio di Sant Cassiano

CAMPO DELLA
PESCHERÍA

Autorimessa

GIARDINO
PAPADÓPOLI

CAMPO
BECCARIE

CAMPO
SAN GIACOMO
DI RIALTO

PIAZZALE
ROMA

CAMPO D.
TOLENTINI

CAMPO
SAN
STIN

S A N   P O L O

3▷

SANTA   CROCE

Rio Nuovo

San
Rocco

Santa Maria
Gloriosa dei
Frari

Rio di San Polo

CAMPO
SAN POLO

San Polo

San Silvestro

PONTE DI
RIALTO

Rial

Scuola Grande
di San Rocco

CAMPO
DEI FRARI

Rio di Ca' Foscari

San
Pantàlon

San Tomà

Sant'
Angelo

Canal Grande

Palazzo
Farsetti

Palazzo
Loredan

CAMPO
SAN LUCA

Palazzo
Benzon

2▷

Scuola Grande
dei Cármini

CAMPO
SANTA
MARGHERITA

Palazzo
Mocenigo

Palazzo
Cornèr-
Spinelli

CAMPO
SANT'
ANGELO

CAMPO
MANIN

S A N
M A R C O

San Nicolò
dei Mendicoli

Cármini

Ca' Rezzónico

CAMPO
SAN
BÁRNABA

San
Samuele

CAMPO
SAN
SAMUELE

CAMPO
SANTO
STEFANO

Santo
Stefano

Teatro
La Fenice

Ángelo
Raffaele

San Sebastiano

Ca' Rezzónico

D O R S O D U R O

CAMPO
SAN MAURÍZIO

Palazzo
Bárbaro

Palazzo
Pisani-
Gritti

FONDAMENTA ZÁTTERE PONTE LUNGO

Accademia

Santa Maria
del Giglio

Santa Maria
del Giglio

Palazzo
Salviati

Salute

San
Basilio

Squero di
San Trováso

Rio di San Trováso

PONTE DELL'
ACCADEMIA

Salute

1▷

Gallerie
dell'
Accademia

Palazzo
Barbarigo

Palazzo
Dario

Santa
María
della
Salute

Dogan
di Mar

Canale della Giudecca

Záttere

Collezione
P. Guggenheim
(Palazzo Venier
dei Leoni)

FONDAMENTA DELLE ZÁTTERE

△   △   △
A   B   C

Venice's greatest attraction is Venice itself and you should allow plenty of time simply to wander its magical labyrinth. Nighttime exploration, when the streets are virtually deserted, is particularly rewarding (and safe). Don't ignore the city's fringes, notably the quiet area to the west around San Nicolò dei Mendicoli and the residential district around the Biennale gardens to the east. Also try to see the Giudecca, an undervisited island south of the city, but don't waste time on another outlying sight, the famous but disappointing Lido. Head instead for the island of San Giorgio Maggiore—the view from its church is one of Venice's most memorable—and on no account miss the island of Torcello, one of Venice's most enchanting spots.

But if Torcello shows the city at close to its best, it's worth remembering that Venice is also a city with problems. It may no longer, strictly speaking, be sinking, but its position still makes it a constant prey to floods, while the combination of sea, salt water, and the corrosive effects of airborne pollution from factories on the mainland greatly affects the city's fabric. Depopulation is also a problem, as is the sense that the numbers of visitors are more than the city can sustain. Venice may be a fairy tale, but it may not necessarily be a fairy tale with a happy ending. ■

Area of map detail

Canal Grande

THERE CAN BE NO MORE BEAUTIFUL URBAN THOROUGH-
fare than the Canal Grande (Grand Canal), the broad watery artery
that winds in a mesmerizing and serpentine loop through the ancient
heart of Venice. Wherever and however you arrive in the city, your
first thought should be to board one of the lumbering *vaporetti*, or
water buses, that ply its palace-lined length, an unforgettable odyssey
of sights and sounds, and an eye-opening first glimpse of the water-
borne eccentricities of Venetian daily life.

TO THE RIALTO

Board a boat at Piazzale Roma or
the railroad station for San Marco.
The first church you see on
your left beyond the bridge is
the **Scalzi**, designed in 1656 by
Baldassare Longhena (1604–1682),
architect of Santa Maria della
Salute (see p. 151) and several of
the canal's most prestigious palaces.
Farther down on the left stands
San Geremia, home to the
prized relics of St. Lucy, a fourth-
century martyr. On the opposite
(south) bank, the arched **Fondaco
dei Turchi,** now Venice's natural
history museum, was the headquarters between 1621 and 1838 of
Turchi (Ottoman) merchants, while
the plain 15th-century **Deposito
del Megio** to its left served as an
emergency grain store for use during famine or siege.

Mauro Coducci's **Palazzo
Vendramin-Calergi,** one of
the canal's most famous palaces,
is now home to the Casinò. One of
its suites was occupied by the composer Richard Wagner between 1882
and 1883 during the last months of
his life. Two other great palaces lie
a short way beyond, the Ca' Pesaro
and stunning **Ca' d'Oro** (see
p. 134), now museums of modern
and medieval art respectively.
Almost opposite the Ca' d'Oro
stands the neo-Gothic **Pescheria,**
or fish market, heralding the arrival
of the **Rialto,** the city's ancient
heart, and the unmistakeable outlines of the 16th-century **Ponte
di Rialto,** or Rialto Bridge.

Beyond the Rialto, the 13th-
century **Palazzo Loredan** and
Palazzo Farsetti on the left
form Venice's town hall, once home
to the neoclassic sculptor Antonio
Canova. Among the former inhabitants of the **Palazzo Benzon,** a
few palaces down on the same side,
was the Contessa Benzon, a leading
19th-century socialite whose overnight guests included such lumi-
naries as Lord Byron. The poet
himself lodged close by, in one
of four palaces owned by the
Mocenigo family on the Volta del
Canal, the canal's great bend. With
Byron during his two-year stay in
the haunted **Palazzo Mocenigo,**
located opposite the San Tomà
landing stage, were a dog, a wolf,
and a monkey. Short-stay guests

**Left: The Ponte di
Rialto (1588) is
the last in a series
of bridges built on
the site dating
back to 1172.**

Visitor information

☒ Giardini ex Reali,
Fondamenta delle
Farine

☎ 041 522 6356 or
041 529 8740

🚤 1, 82, & all boats to
San Marco

☒ Aeroporto Marco Polo
☎ 041 541 5887

☒ Ferroviaria Santa
Lucia (railroad
station)
☎ 041 529 8727

included Margherita Cogni, one of Byron's many lovers, who reacted to his rejection of her by attacking him with a knife and then jumping into the canal. (Byron also took to the water, but for heroic swims to the Lido and back.) On the opposite bank, right on the canal's bend, stands the **Ca' Rezzonico,** now devoted to a museum of Venice in the 18th century (see p. 135).

On the left beyond the Ponte dell'Accademia, last of the canal's three bridges, stands the 15th-century **Palazzo Barbaro,** bought in 1885 by the Curtis family, a Boston dynasty whose guests included Claude Monet, John Singer Sargent, Cole Porter, and Henry James (his novel *The Wings of a Dove* [1902] was set here). The garish, modern mosaics on the palace almost opposite mark

the **Palazzo Barbarigo,** now owned by a glass company. A short way down on the same bank stands the truncated **Palazzo Venier dei Leoni,** where the Collezione Peggy Guggenheim is housed (see p. 150). Immediately beyond is the perilously leaning **Palazzo Dario,** one of the canal's most charming looking palaces but also one of the least desirable to own—Venetians have long considered it cursed. The mosaic-fronted **Palazzo Salviati** two palaces farther down, like the Barbarigo, is owned by a glass company. Just beyond the Santa Maria del Giglio landing stage rises the Palazzo Pisani-Gritti, Venice's premier hotel, almost overshadowed by the church of **Santa Maria della Salute** (see p. 151). Soon afterward comes the first glimpse of the Doge's Palace and Piazza San Marco. ■

The Regata Storica, or Historic Regatta, is one of several pageants held each year on the Grand Canal.

Canal Grande

- Vaporetto 1, 82 (year-round); 3, 4 (summer only)
- Vaporetto tickets: single journey, 24-hour tourist ticket, and 3- and 7-day tourist tickets available

Note: Vaporetto 1 stops at every landing stage on the Grand Canal; the faster 82 service makes fewer stops.

Ca' d'Oro

Ca' d'Oro

🗺 130 C4

✉ Canal Grande or Calle di Ca' d'Oro, off the Strada Nuova

☎ 041 523 8790

💲 $

🚤 1 to the Ca' d'Oro

THE CA' D'ORO, OR HOUSE OF GOLD, TAKES IT NAME FROM the veneer of gilt and other precious materials that once adorned its magnificent facade. Begun in its present guise in 1420, the palace endured a succession of lackadaisical owners and clumsy restorations before being bequeathed to the state and opened to the public in 1927. After many more years of restoration, the facade has been returned to its ornate splendor and the interior now houses the Galleria Franchetti, an outstanding potpourri of medieval paintings and sculpture.

The Ca' d'Oro, once intended to be the most magnificent palace on the Grand Canal

The gallery is not large—just two floors, each with a handful of modestly sized side rooms and a large *portego* (this was an area that divided most Venetian palaces, its purpose to promote cooling breezes in summer). Nor are the works of art numerous, although they are often exquisite, none more so than the first floor's pictorial masterpiece, Mantegna's **"St. Sebastian"** (1506). As a saint invoked against disease, Sebastian was a popular pictorial subject in plague-ridden Venice. He also suited Mantegna's famously gloomy outlook, exemplified by the painting's symbolically guttering candle and its Latin inscription: "Only the Divine is eternal, all else is but smoke."

Other highlights here include the 15th-century "Bust Of Young Couple" by Tullio Lombardo, six 15th-century bronze reliefs by Andrea Briscio, paintings by Carpaccio, Giovanni Bellini, and Antonio Vivarini, and works of art by Florentine masters such as Luca Signorelli and Antonio da Firenze.

A glorious age-worn staircase leads to the second floor and a room full of Flemish **tapestries,** in their day a far more valuable commodity than paintings. Secreted amid the hangings are a "Venus" by Titian and portraits by Tintoretto and Van Dyck, artistic preludes to several faded frescoes by Pordenone, Titian, and Gorgione in the nearby portego. A poignant reminder of the works lost to Venice over the centuries—not least the Ca' d'Oro's embellished facade—the damaged paintings were removed for safekeeping from churches and other buildings around the city. ∎

Ca' Rezzonico

VENICE HAS ENJOYED MANY A COLORFUL PERIOD, BUT FEW have been as striking as the decadent years of its 18th-century dotage, a period when, according to one popular adage, the "Venetians did not taste their pleasures but swallowed them whole." The Ca' Rezzonico, or Museo del Settecento Veneziano, is a museum devoted to the period, its displays and palatial interior fashioned to reflect the artistic and social tastes of the city during the years of its often frivolous decline.

The Ca' Rezzonico was begun circa 1667 by Baldassare Longhena (1598–1682), the leading baroque architect of his day, and completed in fits and starts over the next hundred years. Among its long line of owners was Pen Browning, son of the English poet Robert Browning, who bought the palace with the help of his wealthy American wife— Browning *père* died here in 1889. The building was bought by the state and opened as a museum devoted to 18th-century Venice in 1935.

The first eye-opener on a tour of the palace is the magnificent **ballroom,** spoiled only by the renowned but vulgar furniture of Andrea Brustolon (1662–1732), whose shackled wooden slaves make dispiriting viewing. Soon after comes the **Sala dell'Allegoria Nuziale,** with 18th-century ceiling frescoes by Giambattista Tiepolo (1696–1770), and then rooms adorned with portraits in pastel by Rosalba Carriera, Flemish tapestries, and beautiful lacquerwork furniture.

Part of the second floor is given over to an art gallery, where the highlights are works by Canaletto, Franceso Guardi's vignettes of Venetian high society, and Pietro Longhi's fascinating snapshots of Venetian daily life. Pride of place, however, goes to Giandomenico Tiepolo's satirical frescoes (1793–97) in the last few rooms, a sequence moved here from the artist's country villa. ■

Look up to see the glittering chandeliers and beautifully decorated ceiling of the ballroom in the Ca' Rezzonico.

Ca' Rezzonico
- 🅰 130 B2
- ✉ Fondamenta Rezzonico 3316
- ☎ 041 241 0100
- 💲 $$
- 🚤 1 to Ca' Rezzonico

Piazza San Marco

"THE MOST BEAUTIFUL DRAWING ROOM IN EUROPE," SAID
Napoleon of the Piazza San Marco, or St. Mark's Square, Venice's
famous central square, which provides not only the setting for two of
the city's foremost buildings—St. Mark's Basilica (see pp. 138–143) and
the Doge's Palace (see pp. 144–45)—but also the home to historic cafés,
to the Campanile, and to the Correr Museum, whose displays provide
a fascinating insight into Venice's long history.

Piazza San Marco

 131 D2

1, 82, & all boats
to San Marco

Campanile

Piazza San Marco

041 522 4064

$

Note: Arrive early to
avoid lines. Ascent
is by elevator.

The piazza's most distinctive smaller
monuments are the two **columns**
near the waterfront, brought from
the eastern Mediterranean in 1170.
One is topped with the lion of St.
Mark, the other with St. Theodore,
one of Venice's patron saints,
flanked by a creature of unknown
type or symbolic significance. The
area between the pillars was once
a place of execution, and Venetians
still consider it an unlucky place to
walk. To the west lies Jacopo
Sansovino's **Zecca** (1545), the
city's mint until 1870, one of the few
buildings in the city built entirely
of stone, a precaution against fire.
Alongside stands the **Libreria
Sansoviniana** (1588), or state
library, also by Sansovino, entered
under the portico at No. 13a.

To the left (north) of the
Basilica, look up at the **Torre
dell'Orologio** (1499), a clock

tower whose Latin legend reads "I number only the happy hours." The two distinctive bronze figures are known as *I Mori*, or the Moors, after their dark patina.

The **Campanile,** Venice's tallest building at 323 feet (98.5 m), offers one of Europe's most entrancing viewpoints, but when it was first built around 912, it had three very different purposes: to act as bell tower for the Basilica, to provide a lookout for the harbor below, and to serve as a lighthouse for ships at sea. Over the centuries, it received all manner of minor alterations, none of them, unfortunately, directed at the foundations, which, unknown to anyone, were barely 65 feet (20 m) deep.

Lashed by wind and rain, corroded by salt water, and struck repeatedly by lightning, the tower grew ever weaker. When it finally collapsed on July 14, 1902, the only wonder was that it had not crumbled earlier. No one was killed in the disaster, cracks having provided warning of the imminent catastrophe (the only casualty was the caretaker's cat). Within hours the city council vowed to rebuild the tower "dov' era e com' era" (where it was and how it was). The pledge was realized ten years later in 1912, when a new tower, identical but for the fact it was 600 tons lighter and better supported, was inaugurated on the Feast of St. Mark (April 25), exactly a thousand years after the first campanile.

Flanking the piazza on three sides are the **Procuratie,** the arcaded buildings that once served as offices for the *Procuratie,* the upper tier of Venice's administrative bureaucracy. Within part of these buildings is the **Museo Civico Correr** (Correr Museum), whose exhibits offer a wonderful and often eccentric survey of Venice's long history. Ranged over the three floors,

Right: Legend claims the Venetians blinded the creators of the clock on the Torre dell'Orologio to prevent them from producing similar works for rival cities.

Museo Civico Correr

✉ Procuratie Nuove-Ala Napoleonica, Piazza San Marco

☎ 041 522 5625

💲 $$

the museum consists of a historical section, a picture gallery, and a more specialized section devoted to Italian unification. There is also a salon with early masterpieces by the sculptor Antonio Canova (1757–1822).

Rooms in the first section are arranged by theme, beginning with a section devoted to topographical and other views of the city. Then come areas devoted to costumes, coins, flags, glassware, weapons, and maritime ephemera, although most people's favorite is the special footwear section and the extraordinary *zoccoli,* or platform clogs, once worn by Venetian women. Outstanding paintings in the surprisingly rich picture gallery include Carpaccio's famous "Two Women" (1507), also known as "The Courtesans," and a "Pietà" (1476) by the Sicilian artist Antonello da Messina. ∎

Basilica di San Marco

IT IS HARD TO IMAGINE ANOTHER BUILDING IN WESTERN Europe more beautifully or richly embellished with the architectural and artistic legacy of the centuries than the Basilica di San Marco (St. Mark's Basilica). A magnificent hybrid of a church, it served for almost a thousand years as the tomb of St. Mark, the private chapel of the doges (Venice's rulers), and the spiritual fulcrum and ultimate symbol of the power, authority, and continuity of the Venetian state, the world's longest-standing republic.

**Basilica di
San Marco**

- 131 D2
- Piazza San Marco
- 041 522 5697 or
  041 522 5205
- Basilica, Loggia dei
  Cavalli-Museo, &
  Sanctuary closed
  Sun. a.m.
- Basilica: free.
  Loggia dei Cavalli-
  Museo, Sanctuary, &
  Treasury: $
- 1, 82, & all boats
  to San Marco

St. Mark's first resting place was a modest chapel within the Doge's Palace, a sanctuary replaced first in 832, and again in 978, when rioting destroyed the earlier church and mausoleum. In 1063, Doge Contarini instigated a fourth building, demanding a church that would be "the most beautiful ever seen."

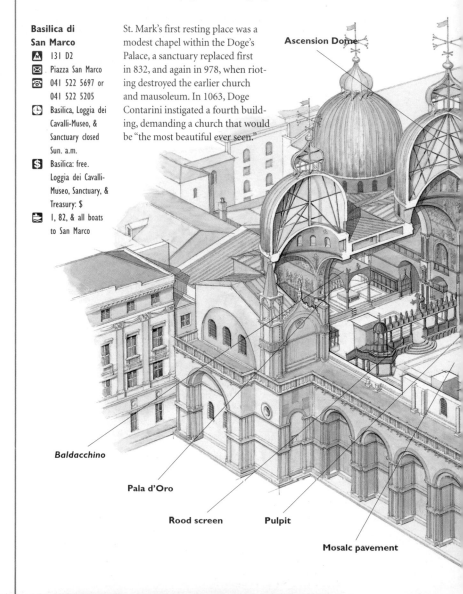

Ascension Dome

Baldacchino

Pala d'Oro

Rood screen

Pulpit

Mosaic pavement

Work on this *nonpareil* culminated in 1094, when the new Basilica was consecrated and designated Venice's "official church of state." This is more or less the building you see today, although in 1094 it had yet to acquire its vast array of artistic and architectural embellishment. Work on the mosaics began around 1100, but the vast bulk of the ornamentation appeared in 1204, much of it

Pentecost Dome

See the mosaics close up on the **Loggia dei Cavalli**, St. Mark's external balcony, which offers sweeping views over the **Piazza San Marco**.

Loggia dei Cavalli

Copies of the Horses of St. Mark

Romanesque carvings

Main entrance

Original facade mosaic: "Translation of the Body of St. Mark to the Basilica"

shamelessly looted by the Venetians from Constantinople during the Fourth Crusade.

EXTERIOR

At first glance, the Basilica appears an intimidating sight-seeing prospect. In truth, the exterior, at least, is relatively straightforward. There are three facades: Start your visit beneath the right (south) facade, the side facing the water, where the outline of what was once the Basilica's main entrance can still be seen.

The two freestanding **columns** against this facade, fifth-century Syrian works, came either from Constantinople or from Acre (in present-day Israel), where the Venetians defeated a Genoese force in 1256. The smaller column stump nearby, the **Pietro del Bando,** almost certainly hails from Acre, and was one of two such columns— the other is in the Rialto markets— once used to proclaim state decrees; it was also used to display the heads of executed criminals. High up on the facade is a small mosaic Madonna flanked by ever-burning oil lamps, originally lit to mark executions, when the condemned would turn to the Madonna with the cry of "Salve Regina." Others claim the mosaic was commissioned by the authorities to atone for a wrongful execution, or in fulfilment of a promise made by an old sailor lost at sea and saved by the Virgin's intercession.

Many of the apparent treasures on the **main facade** are copies, most notably the famous bronze horses (the originals are inside) and the vast majority of the mosaics, only one of which is original: the **"Translation of the Body of St. Mark to the Basilica"** (1260–1270), above the door on the extreme left. This same door, one of five, contains 14th-century

sandstone bas-reliefs portraying the symbols of the Evangelists, together with an attractive architrave of panels and figures dating from either the 5th or 13th century. The facade's greatest works are the 13th-century **Romanesque carvings** above the central (third) portal, whose broad range of themes and figures includes (on the outer arch) the famous statue of a man biting his nails; Venetians claim he represents an 11th-century Greek architect chewing his nails in fury at criticism of his work.

Sights on the oft-ignored **north facade** include the Porta dei Fiori, or Door of Flowers, whose arches enclose a charming nativity scene. Alongside is the tomb of Daniele Manin (1804–1857), leader of a heroic but unsuccessful 19th-century uprising against the Austrians. At the center of the first arch lies an eighth-century Byzantine relief of the Twelve Apostles, while between the arch and its neighbor is a quaint tenth-century relief portraying Alexander the Great's mythical quest to reach heaven on a chariot pulled by two griffons.

INTERIOR

Crowds and services within the Basilica are such that you cannot always wander at will or choose which of the many treasures you wish to see. (Nor can a short account do justice to the sights on show, and in order to make the most of your visit and, in particular, to make sense of the quite bewildering array of mosaics, it pays to buy a specialist guidebook at the Basilica's shop.) Aim to arrive early in the morning or late in the afternoon to avoid the worst of the crowds. And note that while admission is free to the main interior space, you need separate tickets to view most of the Basilica's real treasures.

**Opposite:
Mosaics—some
more than 900
years old—cover
almost every
surface of the
Basilica's interior.**

The Basilica's famous bronze horses were probably scratched deliberately to catch the sun.

Opposite: The Pala d'Oro, or Screen of Gold, comprises many illustrated enameled plaques. This one depicts the boat carrying St. Mark's body from Alexandria to Venice.

Mosaics

Almost every available surface of the Basilica—some 43,000 square feet (4,000 sq m) in all— is blanketed with golden-hued mosaics, an artistic medium, like the church's Greek cross plan, that was adopted from the Byzantine tradition. The earliest examples date from around 1100, but new additions were still being made 700 years later. Down the centuries, the leading artists of their day, notably Titian, Tintoretto, and Veronese, often contributed the designs for new panels. Mosaics in the Basilica's dusky interior largely portray episodes from the New Testament, while those in the **narthex,** or vestibule, the first area you come to just inside the Basilica's main door, depict scenes from the Old Testament.

Loggia dei Cavalli

Stairs from the narthex lead to the Loggia dei Cavalli, or the Loggia of the Horses, an external balcony that offers a lofty view across Piazza San Marco. It is also home to the Basilica's famous **bronze horses,** brought from Constantinople in 1204, or rather copies of these horses, as the originals are now kept far from the corrosive assault of airborne pollution in the adjoining Museo or Galleria Marciano. Part of a *quadriga*, or four-horsed chariot team, the gilded creatures are the only such artifact to have survived from classical antiquity, although whether they are of Greek (fourth century B.C.) or Roman (third century A.D.) provenance is uncertain. All four found their way to Paris in 1797, courtesy of Napoleon, but were returned to Italy 18 years later—unlike many Italian works of art looted by the French emperor.

Sanctuary

The Basilica's most compelling sight after the horses and the solemn beauty of the dimly lit interior is the area behind the high altar—the

St. Mark

Venice has long enjoyed a special relationship with St. Mark, Apostle and Evangelist. Not that St. Mark enjoyed any relationship with Venice, a city still several centuries from existence during the saint's lifetime. The nearest he supposedly came to the city's site was on his return to Rome from Aquileia, a Roman colony on the Adriatic, when an angel appeared to the saint as he passed through the lagoon with the words, "Pax tibi Marce, evangelist meus. Hic requiescet corpus tuum" (Peace be with you Mark, my Evangelist. Here shall your body rest.).

The story is probably a myth of Venetian invention, used to justify the theft of the saint's body and to lend valuable spiritual sanction to the foundation of a city that, in truth, had been disappointingly banal in its origins. The theft, a seminal moment in Venetian history, occurred in 828, although details of the event are encrusted in myth. The authorized version suggests the custodians of the saint's body, then in Alexandria in Egypt, became concerned at the Alexandrian king's plundering of the saint's tomb. Fearing further assault, they agreed to help the Venetians steal the body, hiding the relics beneath mounds of pork to distract the Muslim guards. After a tumultuous sea voyage, the remains were presented to the doge and Mark was duly declared Venice's patron saint. ∎

Sanctuary—and its monumental altarpiece, the **Pala d'Oro** (Screen of Gold). This altarpiece lies to the rear of the altar, reputed final resting place of St. Mark, although many claim the saint's relics were destroyed in a fire of 976. The Pala is Europe's greatest piece of medieval gold and silverware, its dazzling frontage adorned with 15 rubies, 100 amethysts, 300 sapphires, 300 emeralds, 400 garnets, 1,300 pearls, and some 200 miscellaneous stones. Begun in 976, it was reworked in 1105 and again in 1209, when it was embellished with some of the flood tide of jewels looted from Constantinople during the Fourth Crusade.

Note the **pulpit** on exiting the Sanctuary, traditionally the spot where a new doge was presented to the people, and the vast iconostasis, or **rood screen,** which is topped with 14th-century statues of the Virgin, St. Mark, and the Apostles.

Treasury

Booty from the Fourth Crusade makes up much of the collection in the Basilica's **Tesoro,** or Treasury, located off the transept midway down the church's right (south) side. Made up largely of religious and other early Byzantine silverware, the collection is the finest of its kind in Europe, and, but for the antics of Napoleon, would have been finer still—some 55 gold and silver ingots were all that remained once he had melted down the cream of the collection. Note the large throne by the turnstile, the so-called **Throne of St. Mark,** carved in Alexandria and presented to one of the lagoon's earliest religious rulers in 690. Note, too, the Treasury's redoubtable **walls,** probably part of the original ninth-century Doge's Palace. ∎

The ornate central window of the Palazzo Ducale's waterfront facade is topped by "Justice," dating from 1579.

Palazzo Ducale

THE PALAZZO DUCALE, OR DOGE'S PALACE, WAS HOME FOR almost a thousand years not only to Venice's ruling doges, secret police, and principal law courts, but also to its municipal prisons, torture chambers, and many of the city's myriad administrative institutions. One of the world's finest Gothic buildings, the exterior is a beautiful mingling of columns, quatrefoils, and intricately patterned marbles. The interior is a labyrinth of gilt- and painting-smothered rooms, as well as a series of dark and intimidating dungeons that once confined the 18th-century adventurer Casanova, among others.

Palazzo Ducale
- 🏠 131 D2
- ✉ Piazzetta-Piazza San Marco
- ☎ 041 522 4951
- 💲 Palace: $$. Guided tours: $$$
- 🚤 1, 82, & other boats to San Marco
- Note: Guided tours: 2–3 daily, a.m. only. Reserve places two days in advance by calling the above number or stopping by the office at the foot of the Scala d'Oro.

The first palace, a fortresslike structure, was built in 814, but succumbed to fires in 976 and 1106. The present building began to take shape in 1314, when work started on a great hall for the Maggior Consiglio, the Republic's parliamentary lower house. Three years after this was completed, in 1422, remaining parts of the older palazzo were razed to make way for the palace's present main facade. Thereafter, the interior was constantly modified as the machinery of government grew, the palace attaining more or less its present shape in 1550. Major fires in 1574 and 1577 brought the building close

to collapse, and for a while there were plans to demolish the palace and rebuild it along High Renaissance lines. As it turned out, a more modest restoration scheme saved the Gothic palace for posterity.

EXTERIOR
Start your visit by walking to the bridge, the Ponte della Paglia, at the far end of the palace's waterfront facade. From the little bridge, you can admire the inexplicably famous Ponte dei Sospiri (1600), or **Bridge of Sighs,** reputedly named after the sighs of condemned men being led from the palace to the city's prisons. Then

look up to the left to admire "The Drunkenness of Noah," one of three statues adorning each corner of the palace—the other two represent "Adam and Eve" and "The Judgment of Solomon." Walking back along the waterfront facade, note the statue of "Justice" (1579) above the central window. The capitals of the many pillars below are carved with allegories of the vices and virtues.

Around the corner, on the palace's other principal facade, look up to the loggia and its two anomalous red columns, reputedly stained by the blood of the tortured criminals who were hung here before execution. Left of the palace's flamboyant main entrance, the **Porta della Carta** (1443), stand the famous **Tetrachs,** a group of maroon-colored porphyry knights, probably fourth-century statues representing the Emperor Diocletian and three co-rulers of the Roman empire.

Right: Mystery surrounds the sculpted Tetrarchs at the entrance to the Palazzo Ducale. One legend claims they were Moors who raided the Treasury and subsequently plotted to murder each other in a squabble over the spoils.

INTERIOR

Beyond the Porta della Carta is the Scala dei Giganti, or Giants' Staircase (1501), named after Jacopo Sansovino's statues of "Mars" and "Neptune" (1567), emblems of Venice's command of land and sea respectively. Purchase an entrance ticket before climbing Sansovino's **Scala d'Oro,** or Golden Staircase (1550), to the start of a set itinerary through the palace's long succession of magnificently decorated rooms. The first of these, the **Sala dell'Anticollegio,** acted as an anteroom for visiting dignitaries, who, while awaiting an audience, could admire paintings by Tintoretto and Veronese. The same painters decorated the **Sala del Collegio,** home to the Collegio, Venice's ruling council, and the Signoria, the Collegio's more powerful inner sanctum.

Highlights among the stream of rooms that follow include the gilt-laden **Sala del Senato** and the **Sala del Consiglio dei Dieci,** the latter a meeting place for the Council of Ten, magistrates and overseers of Venice's feared secret police. The **Sala della Bussola** next door contains a *Bocca di Lione* (Lion's Mouth), a form of mailbox into which citizens could drop accusations against fellow Venetians. The Sala's rear door led to a small inner courtroom, and from thence to the torture chamber and prisons.

A four-room armory follows until the itinerary, somewhat circuitous by this stage, arrives at the palace's star turn, the immense **Sala del Maggior Consiglio,** dominated by the world's largest oil painting, Tintoretto's gargantuan "Paradiso" (1592). The old prisons follow, reached via the Bridge of Sighs, strikingly dark and somber after the preceding splendor.

In addition to the public rooms, you can see more of the palace, including the old dungeons, by joining the Itinerari Segreti, the palazzo's excellent guided tours. ■

Gallerie dell'Accademia

IT WAS NO SURPRISE THAT A CITY AS SINGULAR AS VENICE should produce its own artists and its own artistic style. "All Venice was both model and painter," observed novelist Henry James, "and life was so pictorial that art could not help becoming so." German writer Johann Goethe concurred, observing that "since our eyes are educated from childhood on by the subjects we see around us, a Venetian painter is bound to see the world as a brighter and more joyful place than most people" *(Italian Journey, 1786)*.

Gallerie dell'Accademia

🅰 130 B1
✉ Ponte dell' Accademia, Campo della Carità
☎ 041 522 2247
🕐 Closed Sun. p.m.
🚤 1, 82 to Accademia
💲 $$

Venetian art was transcendent across several centuries, and not only those spanning the Renaissance and High Renaissance, Italy's obvious artistic zenith. It was also outstanding across earlier and later centuries, from the gold-backed Byzantine mosaics of Torcello and St. Mark's Basilica, to the camera-sharp 18th-century cityscapes of Canaletto.

One of Venice's glories is the preponderance of art still nestled, sometimes half-hidden, often proudly displayed, in the churches

"Vitruvian Man" by Leonardo da Vinci

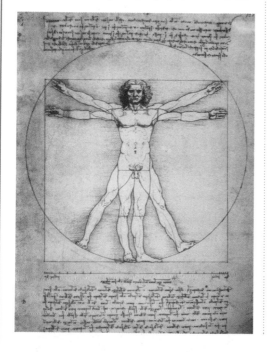

and palaces for which it was first produced. Some of the greatest of its paintings, however, are gathered in a single gallery, the Gallerie dell'Accademia, founded in 1750 as an academy of the arts. Much of its collection was acquired in 1807, the year the academy moved to its present home. Most was collected from churches, convents, and monasteries suppressed and cleared by Napoleonic decree. Little in the gallery disappoints, but it still pays to be discriminating. Many of the more famous paintings are in Rooms 1–5, in Rooms 10 and 11, and amid the two *storie*, or narrative fresco cycles, that provide the Accademia's dazzling grand finale.

BYZANTINE BEGINNINGS

The Accademia's opening room augurs well, its glorious gold-tinged ceilings providing a beautiful foil for the array of largely Byzantine-influenced paintings below. The star turn is the glorious "Coronation of the Virgin" (1365) by Paolo Veneziano (active 1335–1360), one of the city's first great painters, and an artist who played a prominent role in transforming Venice's previous artistic preoccupation with the mosaic into a preference for painting. Moving to **Room 2,** you skip a century to find yourself among early Renaissance masterpieces: Giovanni Bellini (1435 1516), perhaps the most sublime of all Venetian painters, is represented by

a "Madonna and Saints" (1485), while another big name, Vittore Carpaccio (circa 1460–1526), makes an early appearance with the seductive "Presentation of Jesus in the Temple" and the graphic "Ten Thousand Martyrs of Mount Ararat." The latter alludes to the legend of 10,000 defeated Roman soldiers martyred by Armenian rebels.

GREAT NAMES

Rooms 4 and **5,** two of the Accademia's tiniest, contain some its greatest paintings. Among them is one of the most remarkable and mysterious of all Renaissance works, Giorgione's "The Tempest" (1500), a work so enigmatic that no one has been able to explain its allegorical meaning (if one exists) with any success. Nearby is Giorgione's "Col Tempo" (With Time), a more easily understood allegory of old age and passing time. The Tuscan, Piero della Francesca (1416–1492), an almost equally enigmatic painter, is represented by a curious "St. Jerome," arranged alongside an almost indecent number of paintings by Giovanni Bellini—a painter heavily influenced by Piero—the most beguiling of which is the "Madonna and Child with Saints."

HIGH RENAISSANCE

Rooms 6–9 mark something of a hiatus in proceedings, a lull interrupted in spectacular fashion by Paolo Veronese's colossal "Supper in the House of Levi" (1573) in **Room 10.** Originally intended as a depiction of the Last Supper, Veronese (1528–1588) was forced to change the painting's title—but not its content—when the Inquisition objected to its inappropriate portrayal of what it termed "buffoons, drunkards, Germans, dwarfs, and similar indecencies." Two less controversial, but infinitely more bizarre, paintings hang close by, both by Jacopo Tintoretto (1519–1594), one of the giants of the Venetian High Renaissance, the "Miracle of the Slave" (1548) and the "Translation of the Body of St. Mark" (1560). On the opposite wall hangs a "Pietà" (1576), a masterpiece by Titian (1485–1576), Tintoretto's foil and rival. Painted when the artist was over 90, the red-cloaked figure to the right of Christ is probably a self-portrait.

MIRACLES OF THE TRUE CROSS

The gallery's main corridor and **Rooms 12–19** provide a handful of worthwhile distractions, most notably several works by Canaletto, pastels by Rosalba Carriera (1675–1757), one of Venice's best-known women artists, and several fascinating little 18th-century vignettes of Venetian daily life by Pietro Longhi (1702–1785). Make sure you reserve energy for "Miracles of the True Cross" (1494–1510) in **Room 20,** an eight-painting sequence created by a variety of artists for the city's Scuola Grande di San Giovanni Evangelista. Each work ostensibly portrays a miracle associated with a fragment of the cross from the Crucifixion, presented to the *scuola*,

Left: Carpaccio's "Dream of St. Ursula"—note the angel and creeping dawn light on the right of the painting.

although much of the painting's charm derives from the cycle's wonderful accumulation of incidental narrative detail. Gentile Bellini's "Procession of the Holy Relic," for example, offers a marvelous portrait of Piazza San Marco as it appeared in 1496.

CARPACCIO'S ST. URSULA

Another painting cycle, with similar narrative appeal, fills **Room 21,** but this time the nine-work sequence is by a single artist, Carpaccio, and the theme is the life and grisly death of St. Ursula. Daughter of a Breton king, Ursula promises to marry an English prince on condition he accompany her and a train of 11,000 virgins on a pilgrimage to Rome. Carpaccio portrays a variety of scenes, often compressing several events into a single frame. Some of the best are the "Arrival of the English Ambassadors," the "Conditions of Marriage," the "Return of the Ambassadors," and Ursula's "Departure for Rome" (the last panel depicts no fewer than four distinct events). "London" is portrayed on the right, dark and barbaric (note the symbolic sunken ship). The Breton capital, by contrast—founded on Humanist principles—is shown bright and marble decked. Each painting is crammed with the sort of incidental detail for which Carpaccio is famous (his little dog a favored motif). Few scenes are as action-packed as the penultimate panel, which combines the martyrdom of the saint and her followers in Cologne—massacred by the Huns then besieging the city— and her subsequent funeral. ∎

Gentile Bellini's "Procession of the Holy Relic" (1496) shows the doge and his entourage entering the Piazza San Marco from the Palazzo Ducale (right).

The late Peggy Guggenheim, pictured in the Palazzo Nonfinito with some of her much-loved dogs

Collezione Peggy Guggenheim

PEGGY GUGGENHEIM ADORED VENICE AND VENICE adored her in turn, making the American-born heiress an honorary citizen of the city she adopted as her own in 1949. Born in 1898, she moved to Europe in 1921, where she became a leading light in artistic circles—she enjoyed a brief marriage to painter Max Ernst—and a collector of the finest avant-garde art of her day. Much of her collection is now on show in the Palazzo Venier dei Leoni.

Collezione Peggy Guggenheim

- 130 C1
- Palazzo Venier dei Leoni, S. Gregorio, Dorsoduro
- 041 520 6288
- Closed Tues.
- $$
- 1, 82 to the Accademia or Salute

The palace gardens, on the banks of the Grand Canal, are a delight, thanks to their scattered works of sculpture including pieces by Paolozzi, Giacometti, and Henry Moore. The 18th-century palace, while superbly adapted to the demands of the collection, is less alluring, partly because it was never completed—hence its nickname, the "Nonfinito," the Unfinished.

Guggenheim had a matchless eye for the exquisite, and virtually every exhibit is scintillating, even for those whose taste does not normally extend to the modern or avant-garde. Her enthusiasms were also wide-ranging, and most broad

movements within modern 20th-century art are represented. Thus Picasso and Braque fly the flag for cubism, Francis Bacon for English modernism, and Mondrian, Malevich, and Pevsner for constructivism. Among the surrealists, one of Guggenheim's chief passions, the works of Dalí, Max Ernst, and Magritte stand out, as do those of Americans such as Jackson Pollock, Willem de Kooning, and Mark Rothko. Italian Marino Marini, however, produced the gallery's most provocative work, "Angel of the Citadel," an equestrian statue complete with nude rider and erect phallus, overlooking the Grand Canal. ■

Santa Maria della Salute

REMOVE THE TOWERING RENAISSANCE CHURCH OF SANTA Maria della Salute from Venice and you would lose one of the city's most distinctive landmarks. Perched at the mouth of the Grand Canal, the great white-domed edifice has occupied a pivotal point on the Venetian skyline for more than 350 years.

Santa Maria was built in 1631 to fulfill a pledge made a year earlier by the Venetian Senate. The vow promised the building of a church in honor of the Virgin should she deliver Venice from a plague that had claimed more than 45,000 lives, around a third of the city's population. When the pestilence lifted— a result of cold weather rather than divine intervention, according to the cynics—a competition was launched to choose the church's architect, a man who had to fulfill the Senate's demand that the building should "make a good impression without costing too much." The winner was Baldassare Longhena, who would go on to design the facades of the Scalzi and Scuola Grande dei Carmini, and palaces on the Grand Canal such as the Ca' Pesaro and Ca' Rezzonico. His winning entry was christened the Salute, meaning both health and salvation in Italian.

Santa Maria's main portal is opened only during the Festa della Salute, a festival held on November 21 to commemorate the passing of the 1630 epidemic. Entry via the small side door scarcely diminishes the impact of the interior—the beautiful marble pavement at your feet and the soaring dome above. The high altar features the "Virgin Casting Out the Plague" (1670), a sculpture designed by Longhena and executed by Juste le Court. The figure on the Virgin's left symbolizes Venice, the figure to the right the banished plague.

Other major works of art include Titian's "Descent of the Holy Spirit"

(1550), the third of three paintings on the church's left side, and a dozen or so paintings in the sacristy, of which the most notable are Tintoretto's "Feast at Cana" (1561), Titian's trio of ceiling paintings, and the same artist's majestic "St. Mark and Saints Damian, Cosmas, Roch, and Sebastian" (1510). ■

Santa Maria della Salute

- 130 C1
- Campo della Salute–Fondamenta della Salute
- 041 522 5558
- Church: free. Sacristy: $
- 1 to the Salute

The huge scrolls, or volutes, surrounding the dome of Santa Maria della Salute are known as *orrechioni*, or big ears.

Santa Maria Gloriosa dei Frari

Titian's immense altarpiece of the "Assumption" is artfully framed by the entrance to the Frari's choir.

SANTA MARIA GLORIOSA DEI FRARI IS VENICE'S MOST important religious building after St. Mark's. Begun around 1250, the colossal Gothic church was built for the Franciscans, from whom it takes its colloquial name, the Frari, a corruption of *frati*, meaning friars. It boasts a surfeit of sculpture and paintings completely at odds with the Franciscans' belief in the ideals of poverty and humility, and claims three of Italy's greatest Renaissance paintings.

Santa Maria Gloriosa dei Frari

- 130 B3
- San Polo, Campo dei Frari
- 041 275 0462
- $
- 1, 82 to San Tomà

The first of these paintings, Titian's gargantuan **"Assumption"** (1518), proclaims its glory in no uncertain terms, dominating the church from its position above the high altar. Everything in the Frari contrives to focus your attention on the work, most notably the 124-stall wooden choir (1468)—itself a masterpiece—whose arched entrance frames the painting from the church's rear.

The Frari's second great painting could hardly be more different. Quiet and restrained where Titian is loud and assertive, Giovanni Bellini's sublime **triptych** in the sacristy is the essence of meditative calm. The painting portrays the Madonna and Child between Saints Peter, Nicholas, Mark, and Benedict (1488), its saints the namesakes of those who commissioned it—Pietro Pesaro and his sons Niccolò, Marco, and Benedetto.

While this picture offers only restrained beauty, the third major painting, Titian's **"Madonna di Ca' Pesaro"** (1526), provides more by way of incidental distraction. Commissioned by Iacopo Pesaro, who lies buried in a tomb to the painting's right, the work contains several portraits of the Pesaro family. The most obvious is Iacopo's nephew and heir, Lunardo, the small boy who stares out at the onlooker in one of the painting's most familiar compositional flourishes. Iacopo himself is the figure on the left in front of the knight (possibly a self-portrait of Titian), while Iacopo's brother, Francesco, is the figure between Lunardo and San Francesco (St. Francis). Pesaro was a bishop and admiral, and, in 1502, led a campaign against the Turks on the prompting of the Borgia pope, Alexander VI. This accounts for the Borgia and Pesaro coats of arms on the red banner and the turbaned Turk and slave on the left being led toward St. Peter, symbolizing their conversion and the Christian impulse behind Iacopo's campaign.

TOMBS

There is no mistaking the Frari's most distinctive tomb: a huge white marble pyramid created in honor of Antonio Canova (1827). All that

remains of the noted neoclassic sculptor within it, however, is his heart, the rest of his remains having been removed to his birthplace in the Veneto. Canova himself had originally designed the tomb as a new mausoleum for Titian (died 1576), who lies across the nave in a second-rate tomb designed by Canova's pupils. To the right of Canova's pyramid stands the extraordinary "Monument to Doge Giovanni Pesaro" (died 1659), a kitschy but oddly beguiling tomb.

Three tombs of greater intrinsic merit occupy the end wall of the south transept: These are monuments to Paolo Savelli (1407), Benedetto Pesaro (died 1503), and Beato Pacifico (1437). Savelli was a Roman *condottiere*, or mercenary, who died of the plague while leading Venice's army against Padua

(his tomb includes the city's first equestrian monument). Pesaro, by contrast, was a Venetian admiral who died in Corfu, hence the reliefs of ships and naval fortresses adorning his tomb. The tomb of Pacifico, a religious figure, is a rare Florentine work, its canopy and terra-cotta figures some of the prettiest objects in the church.

Two tombs in the second chapel to the right of the high altar are almost equally pleasing, particularly the disarmingly modest effigy of Duccio degli Uberti (died 1336) on the left, with its protective and quaintly hovering statue of the Madonna and Child. The chapel to the left features another Florentine work, a statue of "St. John the Baptist" (1438) by Donatello, the Tuscan sculptor's only work in Venice. ■

The majestic arched frame of Giovanni Bellini's "Madonna and Child with Saints" was created specially to complement the domed space above the figure of the Virgin.

Scuola Grande di San Rocco

THE VENETIAN *SCUOLA* WAS A COMBINATION OF GUILD, charity, and religious confraternity. Some were designed to unite merchants, craftspeople, or those with similar professions, others to link groups of expatriates, religious orders, and individuals with charitable and humanitarian aims. Most were lay organizations with firm religious ties, their main purpose mutual assistance and charitable works. By the fall of the Republic in 1797, there were more than 300 in Venice, of which the six largest and most prosperous had acquired the title of Scuola Grande.

Of these half dozen, the most important was the Scuola Grande di San Rocco, founded in 1478 in honor of San Rocco (St. Roch), a French-born saint widely invoked against infectious diseases. These credentials made him a prime candidate for veneration in plague-battered Venice (he is the city's co-patron with St. Mark), and the obvious inspiration for an institution devoted to healing the sick, hence the considerable sum paid by the scuola to bring his relics from Germany to Venice in 1485.

As well as patron saints such as Roch, each scuola often had its own church and specially commissioned meeting place, the latter usually a two-story building divided into an albergo (a committee room) and sala del capitolo (used for services and ceremonies). The arrival of Roch's relics brought the scuola a flood of donations, allowing it to commission a magnificent new home from architect Bartolomeo Bon, in 1516. On completion, the interior remained relatively unadorned until 1564, when Tintoretto won a commission to decorate the sala dell'albergo, beginning an association with San Rocco that would last 25 years and produce 54 extraordinary paintings.

To follow the chronological course of Tintoretto's artistic progress through the scuola you should initially ignore the paintings on the ground and first floors and make for the small annex on the first floor known as the **sala dell'albergo.** Decorated between 1564 and 1567, it features the ceiling painting of "St. Roch in Glory" that first won Tintoretto his commission. In a celebrated ruse, Tintoretto trumped other painters competing for the commission by creating a finished painting—his rivals produced only sketches—and then had it secretly placed in situ on the ceiling before the judges' arrival. Like everything else in the room, however, the winning picture is overshadowed by the painter's vast "Crucifixion" (1565), widely considered one of the finest paintings in Italy. John Ruskin, the eminent Victorian critic, thought it "beyond all analysis and above all praise," while Henry James wrote "it is one of the greatest things in art," adding that "surely no picture in the world contains more of human life…there is everything in it."

Most other paintings would disappoint after such a tour de force. Not in San Rocco, where the rest of the upper floor, the **Sala Grande,** features the main body of Tintoretto's work (1575–1581). The artist began his labors on the ceiling, where a multitude of paintings depict episodes from the Old Testament. Although often

**Scuola Grande
di San Rocco**
🅜 130 B3
✉ Campo San Rocco
☎ 041 523 4864
💲 $$
🚢 1, 82 to San Tomà

obscure in their inspiration, all were carefully selected to draw some parallel with the scuola's humanitarian aims—thus the obvious relevance of such scenes as "The Feeding of the Five Thousand" or "Christ's Healing of the Paralytic." The ten wall paintings deal with episodes from the New Testament, their volatile composition, unworldly coloring, and generally iconoclastic approach making them some of the city's most striking works of art. Don't, however, miss the wonderful collection of 17th-century **wooden carvings** around the walls. The two most famous are the "Painter," a caricature of Tintoretto, complete with brushes (near the altar), and "Curiosity," a macabre, spy-like figure in cocked hat and one sinister eye peering over his cloak (left and below Tintoretto's "Resurrection.")

Tintoretto was in his sixties when he moved to the scuola's **lower hall,** where eight huge canvases (1583–87) pick up from the New Testament scenes upstairs. The painter's invention here is equally breathtaking. Rarely can the subject of the Annunciation, for example, have been painted with such vigor, or with quite such disregard for the conventions usually demanded of the subject. The Virgin's home is a shattered chaos of splintered wood and tumbledown brick, her expression one of startled disbelief as the angel Gabriel descends from the darkened heavens with a cohort of dive-bombing cherubs.

If you have not had your fill already, you can see more of Tintoretto's paintings in the church of **San Rocco** immediately outside the scuola. ∎

Tintoretto completed some 54 paintings—all free of charge—over the course of 25 years. This one illustrates the "Glory of St. Roch."

A walking tour of San Marco & Dorsoduro

This walk runs west from Piazza San Marco through the heart of Venice, crossing the Accademia bridge to explore the Dorsoduro district before reaching the Scuola Grande dei Carmini, headquarters of the Carmelite confraternity.

Leaving **Piazza San Marco** ❶ (see pp. 136–37) walk past the **Palazzo Ducale** (see pp. 144–45) to the waterfront and bear right. Go past the Giardini ex Reali, and Harry's Bar, and turn right up Calle del Ridotto to the church of **San Moisè,** noted for its exuberant baroque facade created by Alessandro Tremignon in 1668. From here, cross the bridge over the Rio di San Moisè to reach Calle Larga XXII Marzo and take a short detour north on Calle delle Veste to Teatro La Fenice, Venice's opera house, undergoing restoration after a devastating fire. Follow the shop-lined Calle Larga XII Marzo west to Campo Santa Maria Zobenigo, where you should drop into Santa Maria del Giglio, a

church crammed with a bizarre assortment of saintly relics. Continue west through Campo San Maurizio to Campo Santo Stefano.

Leave this square after visiting the church of **Santo Stefano** ❷, with its fine ceiling and calm interior, followed by a rejuvenating drink or ice cream at Paolin, a café in the Campo's northwest corner. Campo San Vidal leads from the square's southern flank to the **Ponte dell'Accademia,** a bridge over the Grand Canal. Here you can absorb one of Venice's most mesmerizing views.

Follow the street named Rio Terrà A. Foscarini to the left of the **Gallerie dell' Accademia** ❸ (see pp. 146–49), and then bear left on Calle Nuova Sant'Agnese. Continue

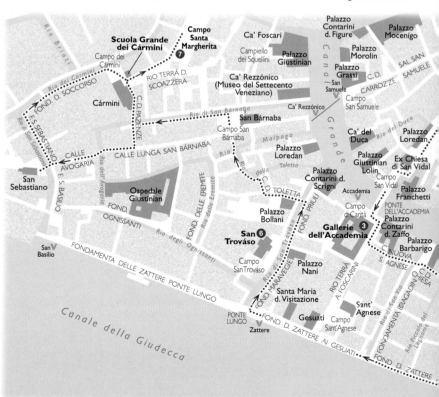

due east, passing the **Collezione Peggy Guggenheim** ④ (see p. 150), to emerge in front of **Santa Maria della Salute** ⑤ (see p. 151). From here, follow the waterfront promenade all the way around the Punta della Dogana and the Zattere, a route that offers views across to the island of the Giudecca and the Palladian church of San Giorgio Maggiore. Pass the church of the Gesuati and turn north on Fondamenta Maravegie along the Rio di San Trovaso canal. Note the picturesque *squero* (one of the few remaining gondola boatyards in the city) across the canal in front of the church of **San Trovaso** ⑥.

Cross the second bridge and follow Calle delle Toletta and its continuation to emerge in Campo San Barnaba. Follow the line of the canal left from the top of the square. Cross the bridge before the canal bends left and take Calle del Pazienze north to the church of the Carmine, which has two excellent paintings by Lorenzo Lotto and Cima da Conegliano. Directly opposite stands the **Scuola Grande dei Carmini** (*Campo Santa Margherita, tel*

041 528 9420, closed Sun.), noted for Tiepolo's 18th-century ceiling frescoes.

An optional loop west on Calle San Pazienza, Calle Lunga San Barnaba, and Calle Avogaria takes you to the church of **San Sebastiano,** with paintings by Veronese. Continue north on Fondamenta San Sebastiano and east on Fondamenta del Soccorso, past the Carmine, to reach **Campo Santa Margherita** ⑦, one of Venice's prettiest piazzas. ∎

🗺 Also see map, p. 131 D2

➤ San Marco: vaporetti 1, 3, 4, 82

🔄 3.5 miles (5.5 km)

🕐 3–5 hours

➤ Campo Santa Margherita

NOT TO BE MISSED

- Santo Stefano
- Ponte dell'Accademia
- Collezione Peggy Guggenheim
- Santa Maria della Salute
- Scuola Grande dei Carmini

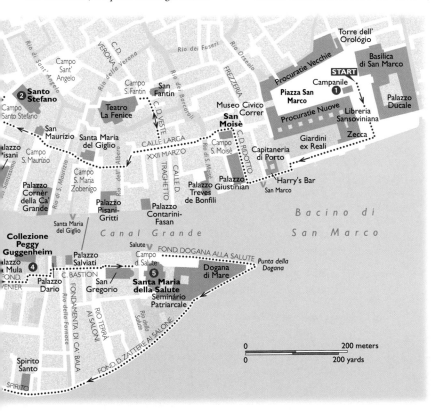

"St. George
Slaying the
Dragon" (1502),
by Carpaccio

Scuola di San Giorgio degli Schiavoni

**Scuola di San
Giorgio degli
Schiavoni**

- 131 E3
- Calle dei Furlani
- 041 522 8828
- Closed Mon.
- $
- 1, 52, 82 to San Zaccaria

Few works of art in Venice are as charming as the painting cycle of this tiny *scuola,* founded in 1451 to serve the city's large *Schiavioni* (Slav) population. The work of Carpaccio, the cycle deals mainly with events from the lives of Dalmatia's three patron saints: George, Tryphon, and Jerome. The nine-painting cycle (1502) starts on the left wall with "St. George Slaying the Dragon." Panels to the right portray "The Triumph of St. George," "St. George Baptizing the Gentiles," and the "Miracle of St. Tryphon," which captures the boy-saint exorcizing a demon. The central saintly theme, abandoned in the following paintings, "The Agony in the Garden" and "The Calling of St. Matthew," is picked up again in the last three pictures, each of which recalls an episode from the life of St. Jerome. ■

San Zaccaria

San Zaccaria

- 131 E2
- Campo San Zaccaria
- 041 522 1257
- 1, 10, 20, 52, 82 to San Zaccaria

The church of San Zaccaria is dedicated to Zacharias, the father of St. John the Baptist, whose relics it reputedly houses. It embraces a wide range of architectural styles and boasts a variety of outstanding frescoes and paintings.

Gothic and Renaissance elements compete in the markedly different styles of the upper and lower sections of the facade. Inside, the second altar on the left contains Giovanni Bellini's "Madonna and Saints" (1505), considered among the city's greatest altarpieces. Across the nave, the second altar on the north wall contains the relics of St. Zacharias, while alongside lies the entrance to a small museum, part of an earlier 12th-century Romanesque church on the site. The vaults in the second of its two rooms, the Cappella di San Tarasio, feature important early Renaissance **frescoes** (1442) by the Florentine artist Andrea de Castagno, while around the walls are three resplendent altarpieces (1443) by the Venetian painters Antonio Vivarini and Giovanni d'Alemagna. ■

Santa Maria dei Miracoli

Santa Maria dei Miracoli
🗺 131 D3
✉ Campo dei Miracoli
☎ 041 275 0462
🕐 Closed Sun. a.m.
💲 $
🚤 1, 82 to the Rialto

The "Archangel Gabriel" is one of several carvings by Pietro Lombardo and his sons in Santa Maria dei Miracoli.

If San Giorgio has one of Venice's most pleasing little interiors, then nearby Santa Maria dei Miracoli, a half-hidden jewel of a church swathed in precious colored marbles, has one of its most immediately beguiling exteriors.

Pietro Lombardo (1438–1515), one of the leading architects of his day, began Santa Maria in 1480, its purpose to house a miraculous image of the Virgin painted in 1409. Lombardo ignored structural complexity in favor of a church that relied for its exterior effect almost entirely on color. Inside, he was responsible, along with his sons Tullio and Antonio, for the fine carving on the pillars of the nuns' choir (near the entrance) and the pillars and balustrade of the raised choir by the altar. On the altar is the miracle-working image of the Virgin that gave the church its name (*miracoli* means "miracles"). ∎

Madonna dell'Orto

Madonna dell'Orto
🗺 130 C5
✉ Campo Madonna dell'Orto
☎ 041 719 933 or 041 275 0462
🕐 Closed Sun. a.m.
💲 $
🚤 52 to Madonna dell'Orto

Madonna dell'Orto was the parish church of Tintoretto. Best known for its large number of paintings by the artist, it is also worth a visit for the tranquility of its setting, in Venice's less-visited northern district, and for the redbrick beauty of its Gothic facade.

The first church here was founded in 1350 and dedicated to St. Christopher, whose statue still stands above the main portal. It was rededicated to the Madonna in 1377 following the discovery of a statue of the Virgin with miraculous powers in a nearby *orto* (vegetable garden). For years the church's pride and joy was a Bellini altarpiece, but after its theft in 1993 (it was never recov-

ered) the interior's artistic interest shifted to Cima da Conegliano's painting of "St. John the Baptist" (1493) on the first altar of the south wall. Almost every other work of note belongs to Tintoretto, who is buried, along with his children, in the chapel to the right of the choir. The choir itself contains two of the painter's masterpieces, the towering "Last Judgment" and "The Making of the Golden Calf." The artist completed all the paintings in the church free of charge, asking only for the cost of his materials.

Just south of the church, be sure to find the three statues of Moors embedded in the wall of Campo dei Mori. ∎

Santi Giovanni e Paolo

Santi Giovanni e Paolo

🗺 131 D3

✉ Campo Santi Giovanni e Paolo

☎ 041 523 7510

🕐 Closed Sun. a.m.

🚤 1, 82 to the Rialto

The tomb of Doge Nicolò Marcello by Pietro Lombardo, one of the finest of San Zanipolo's funerary monuments

SANTI GIOVANNI E PAOLO, OR SAN ZANIPOLO, IS VENICE'S second most important church after Santa Maria Gloriosa dei Frari. Where the Frari was the work of the Franciscans, San Zanipolo was the mother church of the city's Dominicans, who began the present building in 1333. Its fame rests on a profusion of superlative funerary monuments—no fewer than 25 doges are buried here.

San Zanipolo's lovely main portal ushers you in to the church's solemn interior, its unadorned **nave,** characteristic of Dominican churches, designed primarily to preach to as large a congregation as possible. On the way in, you pass the tomb of one doge, Giacomo Tiepolo (died 1249), buried in the most ornate of the four tombs on the exterior facade. Three more tombs lie across the facade's interior wall, all devoted to members of the Mocenigo family, and all sculpted by Pietro, Tullio, and Antonio Lombardo, three of the most accomplished sculptors of their day. The finest belongs to Doge Pietro Mocenigo, remarkable for the fact that while glorifying Pietro, the haughty figure framed by a triumphal arch, it contains barely a hint of the religious iconography often found in church tombs.

The second altar on the south wall features the church's greatest painting, Giovanni Bellini's "St. Vincent Ferrer with Sts. Christopher and Sebastian" (1465). To its right is an urn associated with one of Venice's most stomach-churning episodes. Inside lies the skin of Marcantonio Bragadino, a Venetian general captured by the Turks in 1571 and tortured before being flayed alive. Across the nave, on the north wall, the highlights are three more tombs by the Lombardos. Pietro Lombardo's "Monumento al Doge Nicolò Marcello" (died 1474) is the finest: a mature Renaissance work that contrasts with the same sculptor's canopied Gothic tomb—three altars to the right—of Doge Pasquale Malipiero (died 1462), carved some 15 years earlier.

The **south transept** features three eye-catching paintings: Alvise Vivarini's "Christ Carrying the Cross," "The Coronation of the Virgin," attributed to Cima

Bartolomeo Colleoni

To San Zanipolo's left stands the **Scuola Grande di San Marco,** with its sublime facade (1495), now a hospital but once the wealthiest of all Venice's many *scuole.* To the right stands Europe's finest equestrian monument, Andrea Verrocchio's 15th-century statue of Bartolomeo Colleoni, a mercenary soldier who served Venice for much of his life. Colleoni had hoped to be commemorated in Piazza San Marco. Indeed, he left the bulk of his vast fortune to the city on condition that he be honored accordingly. Venice never encouraged the cult of the individual, however, and certainly not in its main square. But it wanted Colleoni's money, and so cheated the mercenary by raising a statue in Campo San Marco. ■

The equestrian monument to Bartolomeo Colleoni, by Florentine artist Andrea Verrocchio, stands outside the church of Santi Giovanni e Paolo, and not on Piazza San Marco, as was Colleoni's wish.

da Conegliano, and Lorenzo Lotto's marvelous "St. Antoninus Peruzzi Giving Alms to the Poor" (1542). Moving to the high altar, note the tomb of Doge Michele Morosini (died 1382) on the right-hand wall, a beautiful Byzantine-Gothic hybrid and one of the church's loveliest monuments. High up on the opposite wall is an almost equally lovely Gothic tomb, the five-figured "Monumento al Doge Marco Corner" (died 1368), while to its right lies the "Monumento al Doge Andrea Vendramin" (died 1478), a vast white marble edifice by Antonio and Tullio Lombardo.

The **north transept** walls belong to the Venier, once among Venice's leading patrician families. The most eminent of the family members interred here is Doge Sebastiano Venier (died 1578), victorious commander of the fleet that confronted the Turks at the Battle of Lepanto (1571). A door leads to the **Cappella del Rosario,** built to celebrate the battle, fought on the feast day of the Madonna del Rosario. Its best artworks are ceiling panels by Veronese. ■

Gondolas

Dark, silent, and oddly sinister, the gondola, for all its romantic allure, is an equivocal vessel. "Moths of which coffins might have been the chrysalis," mused Percy Bysshe Shelley in 1818; "black as nothing else on earth except a coffin," wrote the German author Thomas Mann. Nothing summons Venice so swiftly to mind as the gondola's sleek shape and its easy gliding motion along mirror-smooth canals. Yet few objects so emblematic of a city are so mysterious in their origins, so rigid in their present-day appearance, or so convoluted in their evolution over the centuries.

Gondolas today are remarkably uniform. All weigh around 1,500 pounds (700 kg), comprise 280 components, and employ eight different types of wood—lime, larch, oak, fir, cherry, walnut, elm, and mahogony. All have an oar—made from beech—and a *forcola*, or carved oarlock, each of which is custom-made to suit individual gondoliers and allows the oar to be manhandled in eight distinct maneuvers. All are 35.5 feet (exactly 10.87 m) long and four and a half feet wide (exactly 1.42 m), and all have one side ten inches (24 cm) longer than the other. This last feature, oddly enough, was one of the last in the boat's evolutionary process. Added by a boatyard during the 19th century to compensate for the weight of the gondolier, the imbalance lends the gondola its distinctive lean and lopsided appearance.

Other refinements are much older. Some scholars claim the vessel dates back to 697. Most agree on a first documentary reference in 1094, when the word appears in part of a decree aimed at regulating boats using the lagoon. The name is a matter of debate—some claim Maltese or Turkish origins, others that it derives from the Greek for "cup" or "mussel." The most macabre theory links the name to classical mythology and the ferry used by Charon to carry the dead to the underworld.

Decoration on gondolas has been kept to a minimum since a law of 1562 was introduced to curb excessive ornamentation.

Left: A newly married couple ride in the world's most romantic vessel through the world's most romantic city.

In reality, the gondola's evolution was gradual. The lagoon's shallows and mud flats required a shallow-drafted vessel from earliest times. In the 13th century, the requisite boat had 12 oars; by the 15th the "gondola" had shrunk in size but acquired a *felze,* or cabin. By 1562, it had accumulated such a wealth of decoration that a special law banning ostentation of almost any kind was introduced. Henceforth, gondolas became a uniform black, while their exteriors were restricted to just three decorative flourishes—a curly tail, a pair of seahorses, and the familiar multi-pronged *ferro,* or prow.

The origin and symbolism of the prow are even more contentious than the gondola's origins. Some ferri have five prongs, some six— emblematic perhaps of Venice's six districts. The single prong facing aft is described alternatively as a symbol for the Doge's Palace, the Giudecca, Cyprus (part of Venice's former empire), or Piazza San Marco. Meanwhile, the broad-edged "blade" above may represent the sea, a lily, a doge's hat, a Venetian halberd,

or the Rialto bridge. Depending on your source, the ferro was inspired by Roman galleys, the funerary barges of ancient Egypt, or a judicial axe.

Gondola rides

Venice's cheapest gondola rides involve the *traghetti* (ferries) that ply across the Grand Canal at regular intervals. (A Venetian stands up, but a *foresta,* or outsider, usually finds it safer to sit.) Tariffs are set for the "genuine" gondola excursions. You pay more between 8 p.m. and 8 a.m., and additional rates apply for every 25 minutes over the standard 50-minute ride. Musical entertainment also costs more. In practice, gondoliers are open to negotiation—you may want to follow a particular route, for example— but always confirm the price and duration of any trip *before* setting out. Remember prices are per boat (not per person), up to a five-passenger limit. To avoid rip-offs, consult visitor centers for current rates and location of official stands. ■

The island of
Burano, in the
Venetian lagoon,
is celebrated for
its painted houses
and exquisite lace.

The Lagoon

THE LAGOON HAS BEEN VENICE'S SALVATION, AND ITS
curse. Once its watery embrace provided a defensive barrier against
the outside world and later helped foster a maritime tradition that
secured a far-flung empire. But its high tides also flood the city and
its waters are a dumping ground for industrial waste from mainland
factories. Few visitors will be aware of such problems, however, as
they take a boat trip to one or more of its many outlying islands.

The Lagoon

See map inset
p. 131
Note: For information on
getting to the
islands, see p. 166.

Murano is the closest, most
famous, and least pretty of the
islands. Although inhabited since
Roman times, it only prospered after
1291 when Venice's glass furnaces
were moved here as precaution
against fire. Today, it is worth a visit
for its glass shops, glass museum, a
pair of churches, and the chance to
look at **San Michele,** Venice's main
island cemetery, along the way.

Fondamenta dei Vetrai has
many of the largest glass shops and
foundries. The church at its northern end, **San Pietro Martire,**
is also home to some grandiose
wooden carvings, several Murano
chandeliers, and one of the city's
foremost altarpieces—Giovanni
Bellini's "Madonna and Child with
Doge Barbarigo and Saints Mark
and Augustine" (1488). Close by is

Museo Vetrario

✉ Palazzo Giustinian, Fondamenta Giustinian 8

☎ 041 739 586

🕐 Closed Wed.

💲 $$

Scuola di Merletti

✉ Piazza Baldassare Galuppi

☎ 041 730 034

🕐 Closed Tues.

💲 $

the **Museo Vetrario,** or Glass Museum, whose intriguing displays document the history and techniques of glassmaking with the help of some lovely glassware. To the museum's right stands the seventh-century church of **Santi Maria e Donato,** notable for its unusual arcaded apse, a 6th-century pulpit, and a breathtaking 12th-century mosaic pavement.

Whereas Murano's lure is glass, **Burano** is known for its lace, made on the island since at least the 15th century. Today much of the material on sale is imported, although a handful of older women still make the fine *punta in aria* (points in air) for which the island is famous. Some teach in the **Scuola di Merletti,** a museum-cum-school where you can watch work in progress or admire ravishing older pieces of lace.

Burano is considerably prettier than Murano, thanks to its brightly colored houses, reputedly painted to help husbands identify their homes from boats far out at sea. The island also preserves the air of a genuine fishing community, with boats moored on its grassy banks and nets strung to dry across cobbled streets. This makes the island somewhere to explore for its own sake, the old fish market and peaceful shoreline being the best targets. It is also perfect for a morning's excursion when combined with **Torcello,** just five minutes away by boat.

Move heaven and earth to visit Torcello, one of the loveliest places in Venice. Now virtually deserted, the island was probably the first part of the lagoon settled in the fifth century—which makes it Venice's birthplace. Malaria and the silting of its canals sealed its fate in the 12th century. Today, the island has only a single huddle of buildings, easily reached by a pastoral canal-side walk from the landing stage. On your right stands **Santa Fosca,** an 11th-century Byzantine church, and to the left the **Museo dell' Estuario** *(Tel 041 730 761, closed Mon.),* a small museum devoted to the history of the lagoon. Straight ahead stands **Santa Maria Assunta** *(Tel 041 730 084),* arguably the most glorious church in Venice. Founded in 639, everything in its interior is matchless, from the elegant 11th-century wooden ceiling and marble pavement to the rood screen, choir, and apse mosaic of the Virgin. The main body of the building dates from 1008, the facade and portico from about 864, and the crypt and high altar from the original 7th-century church. Don't miss the 11th-century mosaics in the chapel to the right of the altar or the ghoulish 12th-century mosaic of the Last Judgment on the rear wall. ∎

More places to visit in Venice

CHURCHES

Venice's most charming small church is **San Giovanni in Bragora** *(Map 131 E2, Campo Bandiera e Moro, tel 041 520 5906)*. Once the parish church of composer Antonio Vivaldi (look for his baptismal font on the left as you enter), it features magnificent Renaissance paintings by Antonio and Bartolomeo Vivarini, as well as a glorious altarpiece, Cima da Conegliano's "Baptism of Christ" (1494).

Another fascinating small church, ninth-century **San Giacomo dell'Orio** *(Map 130 B4, Campo San Giacomo dell'Orio, tel 041 275 0462)* contains paintings by Veronese and a stunning altarpiece (1546) by Lorenzo Lotto.

You can see more superlative paintings in **San Sebastiano** *(Map 130 A2, Campo San Sebastiano, tel 041 275 0462)*. Here, the interior is filled with works by Veronese, who lived locally and was buried in the church. **San Pantàlon** *(Map 130 B3, Campo San Pantàlon, tel 041 523 5893)* nearby is dominated by the work of the lesser-known Antonio Fumiani, whose gargantuan ceiling painting is reputedly the world's largest area of painted canvas. Don't miss Antonio Vivarini's more intimate "Coronation of the Virgin" (1444) in the chapel to the left of the high altar.

Close to the Rialto, **San Giovanni Crisostomo** *(Map 131 D3, Campo San Giovanni Crisostomo, tel 041 522 7155)* has an altarpiece by Giovanni Bellini, while, east of the Rialto, **Santa Maria Formosa** *(Map 131 D3, Campo Santa Maria Formosa, tel 041 277 0233)* offers a painting by Palma il Vecchio of St. Barbara (1522–24), patron saint of gunners, hence the cannon balls in and around the painting. Santa Maria is located in a lovely piazza. So, too, is **Santo Stefano** *(Map 130 C2, Campo Santo Stefano, tel 041 275 0462)*, its pretty and peaceful interior as captivating as any individual works of art.

Movie buffs may recognize the outlying **San Nicolò dei Mendicoli** *(Off map 130 A2, Campo San Nicolò, tel 041 275 0387)*—it was the church Donald Sutherland helped restore in Nic Roeg's *Don't Look Now* (1973). There are few treasures here, but the interior is sumptuously decorated. Finally, don't miss another peripheral church—Palladio's **San Giorgio Maggiore** *(Map 131 D1, Isola di San Giorgio Maggiore, tel 041 522 7827)*, reached by vaporetto 82 from Zaccaria. The view from its campanile is the best in Venice.

Chorus Pass

The Chorus Association *(Tel 041 275 0462)* is a nonprofit organization that aims to protect the heritage of Venice's churches. The Chorus Pass ($$$), valid for three months, allows you to visit some 13 churches participating in the scheme. A minipass ($$) gives access to six churches, or you can buy single tickets ($). Both passes include entrance fees, a color guide, and a map of Venice. The churches are open seven days a week *(Closed Sun. a.m.)*. ∎

Getting to the islands

Purchase standard boat tickets for a trip to Murano unless you are visiting Burano and Torcello at the same time, in which case a joint one-way boat pass, the *Biglietto Isole*, is available for visiting Murano, Burano, Mazzorbo (near Burano), and Torcello. You need a separate one-way ticket for the return leg from the last island you visit.

Murano
- 🚤 52 from Zaccaria or the Fondamente Nuove to Colonna
- ⊕ Journey time is 7 minutes
- 💲 $

Burano
- 🚤 12 from the Fondamente Nuove (every 60–90 minutes)
- ⊕ Journey time is 40 minutes
- 💲 $$. Purchase the special *Biglietto Isole*

Torcello
- 🚤 12 from Fondamente Nuove (every 60–90 minutes)
- ⊕ Journey time is 45 minutes
- 💲 $$. Purchase the special *Biglietto Isole*

For information on what to see and do on the islands, see pp. 164–65. ∎

The great cities of Northeast Italy—Verona, Padua, and Vicenza—provide the perfect historic foil to Venice, while in Lake Garda and the Dolomites the region boasts the country's largest lake and Europe's most spectacular mountain range.

Northeast Italy

Climbing in the Dolomites

Northeast Italy

NORTHEAST ITALY IS DOMINATED BY VENICE, A CITY WHOSE SIREN CALL TO visitors often diverts attention from one of the country's most scenically and ethnically diverse corners. Comprising three regions, the Veneto, Trentino-Alto Adige, and Friuli-Venezia Giulia, this is an area of lakes, city-scattered plains, and spectacular alpine peaks.

If you can only spare a short time in the northeast, make for the Veneto, a prosperous region that corresponds roughly to the limits of Venetia, the mainland territory once ruled by the Venetian Republic. In earlier times, the region lay astride important Roman lines of communication, a strategic position that led to the growth of colonies that evolved into the latter-day cities of Padua, Vicenza, and Verona. These ancient foundations are still the region's main attractions: Padua boasts one of Italy's most celebrated fresco cycles, Vicenza is an urbane little city known for the architecture of Palladio, while Verona—by far the region's most alluring urban focus—is a treasure-house of art and architecture from a variety of historical eras. Verona is also a mere whisker away from Lake Garda, Italy's largest lake and the region's premier scenic attraction.

North of Lake Garda, the Veneto's densely populated plains and rippling hills give way to the Alps, and in particular to the Dolomites, easily the most sensational mountains in Italy. If you are tempted by only one major Italian landscape, make it this one. Bolzano (Bozen) is the main center, but virtually every town and village in the region makes a suitable base.

The Veneto shares several of the Dolomites' 30 or more massifs with Trentino-Alto Adige, a curious hybrid of a region cobbled together from two historically and ethnically disparate areas. Trentino in the south, named after the regional capital, Trento, is distinctly Italian. The mainly German-speaking Alto Adige in the north extends across a region ceded to Italy from the former Austro-Hungarian empire after World War I (it is sometimes referred to as the Südtirol, or South Tyrol). German remains the predominant language and there is a distinctly Teutonic flavor to everything from food to architecture, not to mention an undeniably brisk and efficient air to all matters practical and bureaucratic.

All this makes the region a fascinating one

for visitors. Architecture is enlivened by Austrian onion-domed churches, and the wooden balconies of the traditional Tyrolean houses are invariably garlanded in summer with geraniums and other flowers. In the kitchen, Italian staples are complemented, or replaced, by *knödel* (dumplings) and other specialties such as *blau forelle* (mountain trout), *speck* (cured ham), goulash, and the ubiquitous apple strudel.

Similar ethnic complexities shape the northeast's third region, Friuli-Venezia Giulia, an area whose position on the fringes of the Balkans and central Europe has made it a melting pot of Italian, Slavic, and Austro-German cultures. Its position, out on a limb, has discouraged visitors, who may only have heard of Trieste, an intriguing city, but too far from the rest of the country to merit a diversion if your stay is short. ■

Map labels:

3498m
Pico dei Trei Signori
Valle Aurina
Canova
3510m
Gran Pilastro
Campo Túres (Sand in Taufers)
Brunico (Bruneck)
A22
Val Pustéria
Bressanone (Brixen)
San Cándido (Innichen)
SS49
Dobbiaco (Toblach)
Sesto (Sexten)
SS214
Val Badia
AUSTRIA
Val di Funes
Chiusa (Klausen)
Ortisei (St. Ulrich)
SS51
3094m
Dolomiti di Sesto
2780m
Mte. Cogliáns
Siusi (Seis)
Val Gardena
Canazei
Tires (Tiers)
3342m
Marmolada
SS48
Cortina d'Ampezzo
Auronzo di Cadore
Santo Stéfano di Cadore
Paluzza
Pontebba
Tarvisio
Álleghe
3220m
Mte. Civetta
Pieve di Cadore
Ampezzo
Tolmezzo
Chiusaforte
Moena
Forno di Zoldo
SS52
Predazzo
San Martino di Castrozza
Longarone
Ágordo
SS203
2563m
Mte. Schiara
FRIULI-VENÉZIA GIULIA
Venzone
A23
Gemona del Friuli
2847m
Cima d'Asta
PARCO NAZIONALE DELLE DOLOMITI-BELLUNESI
Belluno
Sédico
Ponte nelle Alpi
Maniago
Spilimbergo
San Daniele del Friuli
Tarcento
Tricésimo
Cividale del Friuli
Fonzaso
SS50
Trichiana
Mel
Feltre
Aviano
Údine
SLOVENIA
Grigno
Arsiè
Vittório Véneto
Pordenone
SS13
Gorizia
1775m
M. Grappa
Valdobbiádene
Conegliano
Codróipo
Palmanova
Gradisca d'Ísonzo
Ásolo
Cornuda
Maser
Spresiano
Azzano Décimo
San Vito al Tagliamento
Castions di Strada
Monfalcone
Maróstica
Bassano del Grappa
Montebelluna
A27
A28
A4
Cervignano del Friuli
Duino
A4
Treviso
Ponte di Piave
Oderzo
Latisana
Portogruaro
Aquiléia
TRIESTE
Cittadella
Castelfranco Veneto
Roncade
San Donà di Piave
Santo Stino di Livenza
Lignano Sabbiadoro
Grado
Múggia
Dueville
Scorzè
Preganziol
A4
SS14
Eraclea
Cáorle
Golfo di Trieste
A31
VENETO
Vicenza
SS47
Campodarsego
Iésolo
Lido di Iésolo
Longare
Cadóneghe
Mira
VENÉZIA (VENICE)
Rubano
Dolo
Golfo di Venézia
Abano Terme
PÁDOVA (PADUA)
Albignasego
Noventa Vicentina
Monsélice
Piove di Sacco
SS309
Laguna Véneta
SS10
Este
Conselve
Chioggia
A13
Cavázere
Lendinara
Rosolina
Rovigo
SS443
Ádria
Contarina
Polesella
Táglio di Po
EMILIA-ROMAGNA
p. 183
Pórto Tolle
Delta

Inset map:
Rome
Area of map detail

C   D   E   F

Piazza Brà, home to Verona's Roman amphitheater, is the best place to begin a tour of the city.

Verona

REFINED, RELAXED, AND ROMANTIC, VERONA IS THE northeast's second most alluring historic city after Venice. It is also one of the country's most prosperous cities, thanks to its position astride trade routes to the north, south, east, and west. In the past, it was a thriving Roman colony for the same reasons, and later became a prominent city state under the rule of the Scaligeri, its medieval overlords. Subjection to Milan's Visconti and the Venetian Republic followed, with Venice holding control until the arrival of Napoleon. From then on, it remained under the Austrian yoke until Italian unification.

Verona

◪ 168 B2

Visitor information

✉ Palazzo Barbieri, Piazza Brà-Via Leoncino 61

☎ 045 806 8680

Arena

✉ Piazza Brà

☎ 045 800 3204

🕓 Closed p.m. July–Aug., & Mon. year-round

💲 $

Exploring the old city is straightforward and enjoyable. Museums and monuments abound, most of them within easy walking distance of one another. Begin a tour in the vast **Piazza Brà** (from the German *breit*, meaning "spacious") and its cavernous **Arena,** the third largest amphitheater in the Roman world after Capua's, near Naples, and Rome's Colosseum. Completed in A.D. 30, the structure is in remarkably good shape: Only its original third tier has vanished, toppled by an earthquake in 1183. The 44

ranks of stone seats accommodate more than 20,000 people—roughly Verona's Roman-era population—and are now used for Verona's renowned summer opera festival. Be sure to clamber to the interior's upper reaches for some far-reaching views over the city.

On leaving the Arena, walk northeast on the pedestrians-only Via Mazzini, one of the city's premier shopping streets. This brings you to **Piazza delle Erbe,** site of the Roman forum and heart of the medieval city. Gathered around a

bustling market, the cramped square is lined with tempting cafés and many varied period buildings, most notably the **Casa dei Mercanti** (corner of Via Pellicai). Built in 1301 as an exchange and merchants' storehouse, it is all brick and bristling battlements.

The heart of the square contains several smaller monuments: the **Capitello,** a four-columned tribune from which medieval decrees were proclaimed; the Berlina, to which 16th-century convicts were tied and pelted with moldering fruit; the Colonna di San Marco (1523), topped by the Venetian lion of St. Mark; and a delightful fountain (1523) graced with a Roman statue known as the "Verona Madonna." Midway along the

square's east side, hunt for the medieval **Arco della Costa** (Arch of the Rib), named after the whale's rib hung beneath it. Local legend claims the arch will tumble if a married virgin walks beneath it.

Walking through the Arco della Costa ushers you into **Piazza dei Signori,** once Verona's principal public square, its array of buildings lovelier even than those of Piazza delle Erbe. To your right, as you enter the piazza, rises the striped **Palazzo del Comune** (begun in 1193). Once the town hall, it is also known as the Palazzo della Ragione, or Palace of Reason, after its later use as a law court. Turn sharply right and climb the palace's unmistakable **Torre dei Lamberti** for some lofty city views. Straight

ahead stands the brick-fronted Palazzo degli Scaligeri, or Prefettura, built as a palace for the Scaligeri, Verona's dynastic overlords, and later appropriated by the city's Venetian governors. To your left lies the Loggia del Consiglio (1493): An attractive Renaissance arcade with frescoed upper level, it served as a council chamber during Venetian rule.

The statue (1865) at the piazza's heart represents a stern-faced Dante, who, in 1301, was welcomed to the city by the Scaligeri, a family who for all their ruthless rise to power proved relatively just and cultured in office. (In fact, Dante dedicated the final part of *The Divine Comedy* to one of their number.)

Leave Piazza dei Signori under its eastern arch and you come to the Romanesque church of **Santa Maria Antica,** former parish church of the Scaligeri, whose remarkable tombs, the so-called Arche Scaligeri, lie ranged behind the adjacent iron grille. Notice the grille's repeated ladder motif, a pun on the Scaligeri's name *(scala* means "ladder"). Above the church's side door stands the tomb of the family's godfather, Cangrande I, literally Big Dog, who died in 1329. His smirking figure stares down from the reproduction equestrian monument (the original is in the Castelvecchio). Other family worthies behind the palisade include the dynasty's founder, Mastino I, or Little Mastiff, who resides in a plain tomb against the church wall. He died in 1277, assassinated in Piazza dei Signori.

Visitors to Verona invariably get caught up in the *Romeo and Juliet* myth—Shakespeare's romantic tragedy is set in the city. Sooner or later you will have to visit the so-called **Casa di Giulietta,** or Juliet's House. Located close to the Scaligeri tombs, the building

certainly looks the part, complete with balcony and much-groped statue of the eponymous heroine. However, the whole thing is a fraud. Although the Bard's fictional Capulets and Montagues were based on actual families, the Cappello and Montecchi, there is no evidence of any real Juliet, still less of any star-crossed lovers and blood-soaked vendettas. The house itself is a 13th-century inn, notable these days mostly for the crowds cramming its courtyard and the extraordinary variety of lovers' graffiti plastered across its entrance.

Walk northeast from Piazza dei Signori and you reach the riverside **Sant'Anastasia,** Verona's largest church, built for the Dominicans between 1290 and 1481. Beyond the main portal—the best part of an otherwise drab Gothic facade— note the two holy water stoups, each supported by bizarre crouching figures known locally as *i gobbi* (the hunchbacks). Then pray that you find the **sacristy** open, for it conceals the church's main sight, Pisanello's damaged fresco, "St. George Freeing the Princess of Trebizond" (1436). Elsewhere, the chapel to the right of the high altar, the **Cappella dei Pellegrini,** is adorned with terra-cotta bas-reliefs by the 15th-century Tuscan sculptor, Michele da Firenze. The first chapel in the south transept has a much prized fresco, "The Presentation of the Cavalli Family to the Virgin" (1380) by the local artist Altichero.

DUOMO

Verona's cathedral lies north of Sant'Anastasia in Piazza del Duomo. Begun about 1120, its facade is striped with local *rosso di Verona,* the pinky-hued stone that lends many of Verona's churches and palaces their warm, rose-colored appearance. The **west portal**

Torre dei Lamberti

✉ Cortile Mercato Vecchio, Piazza dei Signori

☎ 045 803 2726

🕐 Closed Mon.

💲 $

Casa di Giulietta

✉ Via Cappello 27

☎ 045 803 4303

🕐 Closed Mon.

💲 Courtyard: free. Interior: $

(1139) is the work of Nicolò, one of two master craftsmen also responsible for the facade of San Zeno Maggiore (see p. 174), the city's other sculptural master-piece. Try to identify the statues of Roland and Oliver among the carvings, two of Charlemagne's generals and favorite characters in medieval art and literature—Roland's name appears on his stone sword. The south portal, with old Roman pillars, is almost equally impressive—here the reliefs deal largely with the story of Jonah and the whale.

Chief attractions inside are a painting of the **"Assumption"** (1540) by Titian (first chapel of the north aisle), Michele Sanmicheli's pink and gray marble choir screen (1534), Francesco Torbido's choir frescoes (1534), and the anonymous sculptural work of the Cappella Mazzanti (end of the south aisle). The cathedral complex also includes the entrance to **San Giovanni in Fonte,** part of an eighth-century baptistery built over a fourth-century church, remains of which are nearby. Parts of another church, the 12th-century **Sant'Elena,** can also be seen, while a passageway to the cathedral's left leads to a Romanesque cloister, built over the remains of a fifth-century basilica.

Sant'Anastasia
- ✉ Piazza Sant'Anastasia
- ☎ 045 592 813
- 🕐 Closed Sun. p.m.
- 💲 Cappella Giusti: $

Duomo
- ✉ Piazza del Duomo
- 🕐 Closed Sun. p.m.
- 💲 $

Verona's Roman amphitheater is the setting for Italy's most important opera festival.

Bronze reliefs adorn the main portals of San Zeno Maggiore, Verona's most important church.

Castelvecchio

✉ Corso Castelvecchio 2

☎ 045 594 734

🕐 Closed Mon.

💲 $

CHURCHES

Several of Verona's churches charge an admission fee ($). A *Biglietto Unico*, or combined ticket ($$), however, offers admission to all participating churches (where tickets are on sale), which includes San Zeno Maggiore, the Duomo, and Sant'Anastasia. ∎

CASTELVECCHIO

Verona's main art collection resides in the Castelvecchio, a wonderfully evocative riverside palace-cum-fortress begun by Cangrande II in 1354. Alongside stands the most beautiful of Verona's many bridges, the **Ponte Scaligero,** painstakingly rebuilt after its destruction by the retreating Nazis in 1945. The 27-room **gallery,** opened in 1925, is one of northern Italy's most important, its collection running the gamut from Roman remains to Renaissance paintings.

Highlights among the works of art on display include Pisanello's "Madonna della Quaglia," Carlo Crivelli's "Madonna della Passione," the "Holy Family" by Mantegna, Veronese's "Descent from the Cross," and two Madonnas by Giovanni Bellini. Local and other Venetian and northern Italian artists are also well represented, illustrating the broad development and interchange of ideas among the region's various schools of painting. Other exhibits include glassware, weapons, jewelry, and sculpture, the most noteworthy of which is the equestrian statue

removed from the tomb of Cangrande I (see p. 172).

SAN ZENO MAGGIORE

Be sure to follow the river west or wander through the Parco dell'Arsenale, Verona's main park, to see San Zeno Maggiore *(Closed Sun. a.m.),* northern Italy's finest Romanesque church. Built in its present guise at the beginning of the 12th century, the church began life much earlier, probably as a small chapel over the tomb of St. Zeno, Verona's fourth-century patron saint.

Its treasures begin immediately, with the wonderful canopied **porch** (1138) flanked by carvings and polychrome reliefs (1140). These frame the church's mighty main doors, gilded with 48 important 12th-century bronze reliefs, among the first such works attempted since antiquity. Byzantine in inspiration, the reliefs depict biblical scenes and episodes from the life of St. Zeno, and are probably the work of two or more sculptors: Those on the left date from around 1030, those on the right from 1137.

Inside, your eye is drawn to the magnificent ship's keel ceiling (1386), so-called because it resembles the wooden interior of an upturned boat. The nave's design copies that of an old Roman basilica, many of the capitals on the supporting columns having been salvaged from earlier classical buildings. Faded but lovely patches of fresco adorn the otherwise bare walls, a prelude to the interior's masterpiece, Mantegna's high altarpiece of the "Madonna and Child with Saints" (1457–59). Notice how Mantegna has painted the Virgin's halo as a deliberate echo of the church's 12th-century rose window. Be sure to explore the adjoining cloister (1123) and the church's ancient and atmospheric crypt. ∎

Vicenza

POSSESSED OF "ALL THE ADVANTAGES OF A GREAT CITY," wrote Johann Goethe in 1786 of Vicenza, an observation as true as ever of this sophisticated little town. Renowned above all for the buildings of Palladio, one of the most influential of all medieval architects, its streets are some of the most urbane and architecturally distinguished in Italy.

Vicenza's modern suburbs quickly give way to a glorious old center hinged around a single main street—**Corso Palladio**—and a single spectacular square, the **Piazza dei Signori.** The latter is dominated by Palladio's **Basilica,** a gargantuan medieval building that had been close to collapse until the architect enclosed it in a cradle of columns and arcades. The square also contains the **Loggia del Capitaniato** (1571), another Palladian building, and the Venetian lion of St. Mark atop a lonely column: Vicenza enjoyed centuries of glory as a Roman *municipium* and independent city state before falling to Venice in 1404. Wander into the adjoining Piazza delle Erbe, site of a colorful market, and then to the **Casa Pigafetta** (*Contrà Pigafetta*), an ornate house begun in 1441 and once owned by a crew member of Magellan's around-the-world voyage (1519–1522).

Architectural buffs could have a field day (or two) exploring the finer points of Palladio's many Vicentine buildings. Nonspecialists should stick to the fantastic **Teatro Olimpico** (1580), the architect's last work and Europe's oldest surviving indoor theater— Goethe called its interior "indescribably beautiful." Just off the Corso stands the city's most important church, **Santa Corona,** best known for Giovanni Bellini's "Baptism of Christ" (fifth altar on the north wall). Opposite the theater, housed in Palladio's Palazzo Chiericati (1551–57), is the **Museo Civico Pinacoteca,** whose

La Rotonda outside Vicenza is Palladio's single most famous building.

Villa Valmarana ai Nani

✉ Via dei Nani 2–8

☎ 0444 543 976 or 0444 321 803

🕐 Closed Nov.–mid-March & a.m. Mon., Tues., & Fri.

💲 $$

La Rotonda

✉ Via Rotonda 29

☎ 0444 321 793

🕐 Villa: generally closed Thurs.–Tues. Gardens: Mon.

💲 Villa: $. Gardens: $$

superbly presented collection includes a wide range of medieval and Renaissance works by Vicentine, Venetian, and other northern Italian painters.

The Vicenzan countryside is scattered with villas by Palladio and others, although only two are readily seen from the city itself. Before visiting either, however, you should take a cab to Monte Berico, the cypress-dotted hill that cradles Vicenza, and to the **Basilica** *(Closed Sun. a.m.)* at its summit, built to commemorate a double apparition of the Virgin during a 15th-century plague epidemic. Take in the views of the city from the nearby esplanade, then visit the Basilica's old refectory to admire Veronese's "Supper of St. Gregory the Great."

The **Villa Valmarana ai Nani,** ten minutes' walk from the Basilica, has sweet-smelling gardens that look out over vineyards, green-clad hills, and feathery lines of poplars. The real reason for a visit, however, are the principal buildings which preserve much of their original furniture, rippling old stone floors, and some majestic wooden ceilings. The highlights—a series of often salacious 18th-century **frescoes** by Giovanni Tiepolo and his son, Gian Domenico.

Palladio's Villa Capra Valmarana, better known as **La Rotonda,** is also easily reached from the Basilica. Begun around 1551, it was frequently copied by other architects, not least Inigo Jones in England and Thomas Jefferson in America. ∎

Palladio

Palladio was born in Padua in 1508. He moved to Vicenza at the age of 16, working first as a stone mason and then as the protégé of Giangiorgio Trissano, a nobleman who introduced him to a series of wealthy patrons. Until Palladio's death in 1580, he built palaces and villas in Vicenza and elsewhere—principally Venice—that reinvented and redefined the idioms of classical architecture in a way that influenced architects for generations to come. ∎

Padova

CENTURIES OF ARTISTIC AND CULTURAL SPLENDOR IN Padova (Padua) were destroyed by just a few days' bombing during World War II. The miraculous survival of one of Italy's major fresco cycles, however, and the shrine of one of the country's best-loved saints, means that the city still deserves a visit.

Padua's most important sight is the **Cappella degli Scrovegni.** Commissioned in 1303 by local nobleman Enrico Scrovegni, this vastly important chapel owes its fame to Giotto's exquisite sequence of paintings (1303–1305) bathed in the ethereal blue light of the chapel's modestly sized interior. The best painting is the scene on the rear (entrance) wall, the "Last Judgment," in which a small vignette immediately above the door shows Scrovegni presenting his chapel.

Be sure to explore the adjoining museum complex, the **Musei Civici,** a superb modern ensemble filled with coins, paintings, sculpture, and archaeological exhibits.

Padua's other treasure is the 14th-century **Basilica di Sant' Antonio** (*Piazza del Santo*), burial place of St. Antony of Padua, one

of Italy's venerated saints. Pilgrims stream into the church past Italy's finest equestrian monument, Donatello's statue (1453) of the mercenary leader Gattamelata. Highlights of the basilica's interior include Donatello's high altar reliefs and bronze statues, the intriguing collection of relics at the church's rear, and the nine bas-reliefs (1505–1507) around the saint's tomb, the work mostly of Tullio and Antonio Lombardo, and Jacopo Sansovino—each portrays an episode from the saint's life.

Also worth visiting in old Padua are two squares, Piazza della Frutta and Piazza dei Signori, the beautifully frescoed **Baptistery** (1376), and the gargantuan **Palazzo della Ragione** (1218), one of Italy's largest medieval halls (*Closed Mon.*). ■

The Cappella degli Scrovegni, adorned with important and influential 14th-century frescoes by Giotto

Padova
🅰 169 C2
Visitor information
✉ Stazione Ferrovie (railroad station)
☎ 049 875 2077

Cappella degli Scrovegni & Musei Civici
✉ Piazza Eremitani
☎ 049 820 4550 or 049 875 1153
🕐 Museum closed Mon.
💲 Joint ticket for chapel, museums, & other monuments: $$

A drive around the shores of Lake Garda

This drive takes you around Italy's largest and most scenically diverse lake, beginning on its verdant southern coast and hugging the hillier slopes and cliffs of its northern reaches, before returning in the shadow of its mountain-backed eastern flanks.

Start at **Peschiera del Garda,** a village nestled in a snug harbor and dominated by a redoubtable Venetian fortress. Follow the SS11 west toward **Sirmione** ❶ *(Visitor information, Viale Marconi 2, tel 030 916 245),* the lake's most popular resort. Another fortress, **Rocca Scaligera** *(Closed Mon. & p.m. daily Oct.–March),* built by Verona's Scaligeri family, broods over the village's tidy harbor and attractive huddle of houses. Boats embark here for most of the lakeside villages, which are worth taking for views of the lake, villas, and gardens invisible from the road. Local visitor centers have details of swimming, golfing, boating, and hiking options.

Head west on the lakeside road to **Desenzano del Garda,** Garda's largest town, known for its wines and the proximity of Solferino, site of the bloody battle in 1859 that led to the foundation of the Red Cross. Beyond Desanzano, on the SS45 bis, lies **Salò** ❷, remembered as the capital of the short-lived republic created by Mussolini after the Italian armistice of 1943. The western coast's most attractive base, it has a traditional air and a ravishing 15th-century cathedral.

Gardone Riviera *(Visitor information, Via Repubblica 39, tel 0365 20 347)* lies 3 miles (5 km) northeast of Salò on the SS45 bis. Once the lake's most elegant resort, it marks the start of Garda's more spectacular upland scenery. It is also just half a mile (1 km) from the region's most extraordinary sight, the **Villa Il Vittoriale** ❸ *(Tel 0365 20 130, closed Mon.),* a villa transformed into a treasure-house of kitsch by Gabriele d'Annunzio (1863–1938), a noted poet, soldier, socialite, womanizer, and fascist sympathizer. Look for the bizarre decorative flourishes—everything from an embalmed tortoise to a World War I biplane.

Moving north, you pass through several pretty villages—**Gargnano** ❹ is especially charming—and get the chance to make several scenic diversions away from the lake. The best

run to stunning viewpoints at the sanctuary of **Madonna di Monte Castello** ❺ and the **Pieve di Tremosine** near Campione. (Take the signed road off the SS45 bis north of the road tunnel beyond Gargnano.) Inland and lakeside roads meet at **Limone sul Garda,** one of the lake's more developed resorts. Take the SS45 bis from Limone to **Riva del Garda** ❻ *(Visitor information, Giardini di Porta Orientale 8, tel 0464 554 444),* at the lake's northern tip. This is Garda's best-known resort and is popular with windsurfers and other watersports enthusiasts. Its waterfront and medieval quarters, as in most of Garda's villages, preserve much of their Old World charm.

Heading south along the lakeshore on the SS249, you come to **Malcesine** ❼ *(Visitor information, Via Capitanato 6–8, tel 045 740 0044),* the east coast's prettiest resort, known for its well-preserved fortress and the highly recommended cable car ride to **Monte Baldo.** Views from the upper ridges of this 7,277-foot (2,218 m) mountain are sensational, and there are opportunities to follow numerous marked hiking trails. The area is also renowned for its flora, and was once known as the *hortus europae,* or garden of Europe, after the huge variety of floral species that grow here. The lake's waters and the sheltering arc of the Dolomites to the north create mild and varied microclimates, and favor floral variety and anomalous vegetation—olives, figs, citrus, vines, and cypress. The balmy climate also encourages swimming and sunbathing at Malcesine and elsewhere.

Moving south on the SS249 along the olive tree-swathed coast, you pass **Torri del Banaco,** home to another Scaligeri castle, and the headland at **Punta di San Vigilio,** one of the lake's most romantic spots—more than can be said for nearby **Garda,** a popular but unprepossessing resort developed after World War II. ■

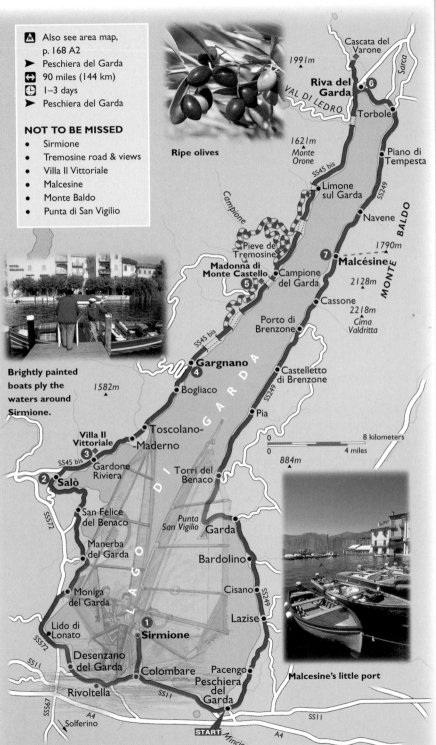

Also see area map,
p. 168 A2

Peschiera del Garda

90 miles (144 km)

1–3 days

Peschiera del Garda

NOT TO BE MISSED

- Sirmione
- Tremosine road & views
- Villa Il Vittoriale
- Malcesine
- Monte Baldo
- Punta di San Vigilio

Ripe olives

Brightly painted boats ply the waters around Sirmione.

Cascata del Varone

1991m

Riva del Garda ⑥

VAL DI LEDRO

Sarca

Torbole

1621m
Monte
Orone

Piano di Tempesta

SS45 bis

Limone
sul Garda

SS249

Navene

MONTE BALDO

1790m

Campione

Pieve de
Tremosine

**Madonna di
Monte Castello** ⑤

Campione
del Garda

⑦ **Malcésine**

2128m

2218m
Cima
Valdritta

Cassone

Porto di
Brenzone

SS45 bis

Gargnano ④

Castelletto
di Brenzone

SS249

Bogliaco

Pia

1582m

**Villa Il
Vittoriale** ③

Toscolano-
-Maderno

LAGO DI GARDA

0   8 kilometers
0   4 miles

884m

SS45 bis

Gardone
Riviera

② **Salò**

SS572

San Felice
del Benaco

Torri del
Benaco

Punta
San Vigilio

Garda

Manerba
del Garda

Bardolino

Moniga
del Garda

Cisano

SS249

Lido di
Lonato

SS572

① **Sirmione**

Lazise

Desenzano
del Garda

Colombare

Pacengo

SS11

Peschiera
del Garda

Rivoltella

SS567

SS11

START Mincio

A4

Solferino

SS11

A4

Malcesine's little port

Dolomiti

OF ALL THE MAJESTIC RANGES CONTAINED IN THE ALPS'
broad sweep, none quite compare with the Dolomiti, or Dolomites,
a tightly packed collection of massifs in Italy's northeast corner whose
peaks and pinnacles make this the most beguiling mountain region in
the country. Wildlife and high alpine flora are superb, while in the
pastoral depths of the valleys you can enjoy flower-strewn meadows
and the rural tranquility of age-old villages.

**Madonna di
Campiglio**
168 A4
Visitor information
Via Pradalago 4
0465 442 000

None of the Dolomites' 30 or more
massifs will disappoint. From a hiking point of view, the best approach
is to pick one or two massifs and
explore them in depth—the
Dolomiti di Brenta are perfect
for the first-time visitor. If you prefer to tour or admire the scenery
from a car, then follow the **Grande
Strada delle Dolomiti,** or Great
Dolomites Road, which runs from
the region's German-speaking capital at Bolzano (Bozen) to Cortina
d'Ampezzo, the most prestigious
of the area's many skiing resorts.

Italians, on the whole, are not
great walkers, but, in terms of culture and tradition, the Dolomites
are not Italy, or at least not the Italy
of popular imagination. Much of

the region still has strong Austro-
German leanings, among which
the Teutonic propensity for healthy
exercise and the great outdoors
loom large. Perhaps it is this more
northern European attitude
to landscape, together with the
Dolomites' supreme natural beauty,
that gives the region its immensely
hiker-friendly infrastructure.

Arrive in any town or village and
a comfortable and reasonably priced
hotel is assured. Ask at any visitor
center and you will be plied with
maps and recommendations for
walks to suit all abilities. Strike into
the mountains and you will find
well-marked and well-worn trails,
not to mention numerous mountain
huts (*rifugi*), where you can stay

overnight in simple dormitories or pause for refreshments before continuing your walk (details from visitor information centers). Towns and villages are often on the upper slopes, so trails quickly reach high altitudes (in summer you can make the ascent by cable car, allowing you to follow high-line paths with minimal effort). All the massifs are mapped (trail numbers are designated by the Club Alpino Italiano), although paths are so well signed that maps are rarely necessary. Every town has outdoor stores selling boots and specialist equipment.

The **Dolomiti di Brenta** are a good place to start hiking, using the resort town of **Madonna di Campiglio** as a base. Numerous circular walks begin close to the town located at 4,921 feet (1,500 m), with cable cars to take you into the mountains. A good option is to take the Grosté cable car to the Graffer refuge at 5,355 feet (2,348 m) and then follow the official trail 316 to the Rifugio Tuckett before dropping back to Madonna on trail 317 or 328/318. Other options include low altitude lake strolls near the village of **Molveno.**

Not everyone, however, wants to hike amid the high peaks or indulge in low-level lakeside and forest strolls. The roads are so good here, and the mountains so scenic, that touring by car still offers you excellent firsthand views of the scenery. The options are many. In the north, you could take the Autostrada A22 from Bolzano (Bozen) to Bressanone (Brixen) and then follow the glorious SS49 road along the Val Pusteria. From here you could head south on the SS244, either at Brunico (Bruneck) down the Val Badia or take the SS51 at Dobbiaco (Toblach) through the Dolomiti di Sesto, one of the range's more noted massifs, to Cortina d'Ampezzo. From Cortina d'Ampezzo you can return to Bolzano (Bozen) on the 68-mile (110 km) Great Dolomite Road (SS48/SS241), built in 1909, which threads through the Catinaccio, Latemar, Marmolada, and other massifs. Alternatively, you can leave the designated route and detour along the Val Gardena (SS242), or follow higher mountain roads via Siusi (Seis) or Tires (Tiers). ■

Jagged limestone rock pinnacles are the hallmark of the Dolomites. Opportunities for hiking and other outdoor activities here are almost endless.

ORIGINS

The Dolomites are set apart from the Alps' main thrust both geographically and geologically. Most of the massifs began life as ancient coral reefs lifted from the seabed, hence the distinctive orange-pink hue of their stone—a rare *dolomia* limestone—and the still more distinctive eroded appearance of their soaring rock towers, pillars, and cliffs. ■

More places to visit in Northeast Italy

AQUILEIA

Now little more than a sleepy village, Aquileia in its day was an important early Christian center and the Roman Empire's fourth-ranking Italian colony after Rome, Milan, and Capua. Finds from its extensive Roman excavations are displayed in a pair of archaeological museums, the **Museo Paleocristiano** *(Closed p.m. daily)* and the **Museo Archeologico** *(Closed Mon. p.m.)*. More impressive than anything in the museums, however, is the **Basilica** on Piazza del Capitolo. Founded in A.D. 313, it preserves large areas of its breathtaking fourth-century mosaic floor. Also worth seeing are the Basilica's **Cripta degli Scavi,** which includes parts of the original church; the Cripta degli Affreschi, filled with 12th-century frescoes; and the tombs of the region's early Patriarchs, or Christian rulers.

Ⓜ 169 E3   **Visitor information** ✉ Piazza Capitolo   ☎ No phone

Twelfth-century frescoes cover the vaults of the Cripta degli Scavi in Aquileia.

ASOLO

Northeast Italy is filled with pleasing little towns—among them Cividale del Friuli, Castelfranco Veneto, and Conegliano—but none are quite as pretty as Asolo, a medieval gem set amid rolling hill country. Like its neighbors, it has little specific to see, but is ideal if you want a taste of small-town life and the guarantee of quiet and relaxation. Excursions can be made to the Palladian villa at Maser, 6 miles (10 km) to the east, and to the interesting towns of Feltre, Castelfranco Veneto, and Bassano del Grappa, the last famous for its grappa, a fiery after-dinner drink.

Ⓜ 169 C3   **Visitor information** ✉ Piazza D'Annunzio 2   ☎ 0423 529 046

TRENTO

Main routes north to the Dolomites pass through Trento, a tidy medieval town near the boundary of the Italian- and German-speaking portions of Trentino-Alto Adige. Its name is closely associated with the Council of Trent (1545–1563), convened to consider ways of combating the rise of Lutheranism. Several of the council's sessions were held in the Duomo (Cathedral), worth visiting for its fine exterior stonework. The nearby **Museo Diocesano** *(Piazza del Duomo, closed Sun.)* contains treasures removed from the cathedral. Also worth seeing is the **Castello del Buon Consiglio** *(Via Bernardo Clesio, tel 0461 233 770, closed Mon.)*, a 13th-century fortress whose museum contains an interesting collection of paintings, sculpture, ceramics, and other objets d'art.

Ⓜ 168 B3   **Visitor information** ✉ Via Alfieri 4   ☎ 0461 983 880

TREVISO

Treviso sees relatively few visitors for it is invariably passed by in favor of Venice. Yet the old walled town has a pleasant mixture of tree-lined canals, old balconied buildings, frescoed facades, and shady arcades. The main square is **Piazza dei Signori,** ringed by medieval and Renaissance towers and palaces, while close by lies Piazza San Vito, home to two churches: **San Vito** and **Santa Lucia,** the latter graced with frescoes by the important north Italian master, Tommaso da Modena (1325–1379). The artist also worked in the town's main sight, **San Nicolò** (across the Sile River), a Romanesque Gothic Dominican church, where he painted several frescoes on the church's interior columns and left portraits of famous Dominicans in the adjoining monastery.

Ⓜ 169 D2   **Visitor information** ✉ Piazza Monte di Pietà 8   ☎ 0422 547 632 ∎

Emilia-Romagna is one of Italy's gastronomic centers, home to Parma ham, Parmesan cheese, and the culinary capital of Bologna. The Marche is less well known, a region graced with lovely countryside and the unsung historic town of Urbino.

Emilia-Romagna & the Marche

A Byzantine mosaic from Ravenna

Emilia-Romagna & the Marche

TOSCANA (TUSCANY) p. 241

RICH IN INDUSTRY AND AGRICULTURE, EMILIA-ROMAGNA IS ONE OF THE COUNTRY'S wealthiest regions. The Marche is a more rural redoubt, its attractions are mostly scenic where Emilia-Romagna's are cultural and culinary.

Emilia-Romagna's position has long made it one of Italy's pivotal regions. Towns developed under the Romans along the line of the Via Aemilia, a Roman road built in 187 B.C. to bind the Adriatic coast with the vital garrison town of Piacenza. Attention during the empire's dying days moved to Ravenna, the capital of Rome's western empire before becoming a major artistic and administrative satellite of Constantinople and the Byzantine empire.

City states emerged in the aftermath of the Dark Ages, states that in time fell prey to great noble families, notably the Benivoglio in Bologna, the Este in Ferrara, and the Farnese in Parma. Court life flourished as patronage on a grand scale attracted writers, poets, and painters—Dante, for example, exiled from Florence, died in Ravenna—yielding a cultural heritage that illuminates the region's historic

cities to this day. Under the heavy hand of Church rule, Emilia and Romagna then developed as separate papal states until 1860.

The Marche knew no such divisions, having existed for centuries as a largely forgotten backwater. The region takes its name from a Germanic word meaning edge or border, underlining a peripheral position that even today sees it isolated from the mainstream of Italian life. A long, narrow, and mostly agricultural region, it is separated from Rome, Tuscany, and the rest of central Italy by the mountain barrier of the Apennines. Historically, its moments of renown have been few, rising above the humdrum only in the 15th century, when the dukes of Montefeltro, financed by their mercenary undertakings, turned Urbino into one of Europe's most dazzling courts. Today it is one of Italy's great unsung towns. Other Marche towns are less exalted—Ascoli Piceno and its perfect medieval center is a notable exception.

Among Italians, the Marche is known primarily for its long string of beach resorts—Pesaro, Fano, San Benedetto del Tronto, and many others. Those with time to spare, however, should ignore the region's beaches in favor of its unspoiled pastoral hill country. To the west, this hill country merges with the high mountains of the Apennines, culminating in the Sibillini massif, beyond which you could visit Umbria by way of the Piano Grande.

Emilia-Romagna has no such scenic glories. Here the distractions are urban, namely the historic towns of Ferrara and Ravenna and the cities of Bologna and Parma, celebrated as much for their gastronomy as their art and architecture. Food and restaurants in the cities are widely held to be some of the country's best, a worthy accolade in a country of Italy's culinary stature. ∎

Bologna's *torre pendenti,* or leaning towers, cast long shadows over the city's medieval heart.

Bologna

BOLOGNA'S FOOD IS REPUTEDLY ITALY'S BEST, HENCE THE nickname *La Grassa,* or The Fat, while its university, one of Europe's oldest, has earned the city another plaudit, *La Dotta,* or The Learned. Better still, its tightly knit old center is a pleasing medieval patchwork of brick arcades, towers, churches, palaces, and fascinating mueums. It is also a city of great cultural energy, enlivened by festivals, theater, music, and summer events. Yet for all this Bologna is surprisingly undervisited, its culinary and cultural allure better known to Italians than foreigners, who tend to pass through without stopping.

Bologna
184 D4
Visitor information
Galleria d'Accursio,
Piazza Maggiore 6
051 239 660

Bologna's central position has long been its strength—roads and railroads still converge on the city from the rest of northern Italy. Of Etruscan or earlier foundation, its early history has a familiar ring—overrun by the Gauls in the fourth century B.C., conquered by the Romans, and then ravaged by the Barbarians. From about 1300 to 1500, it prospered as an independent city state—historians rank it among the top ten European cities of the time—a period of well-being cut short by violent aristocratic feuding. Here, as ever, one clan emerged triumphant, in this case the Bentivoglio. After some 50 years

of autocratic rule, power passed to the papacy, which after 1506 ruled unchallenged until the appearance of Napoleon and Austria.

For so large a city, Bologna's medieval heart is surprisingly small—you could easily see the main sights in a day. Most places of interest—stores and cafés included —lie within easy walking distance of the main Piazza Maggiore and the adjacent **Piazza Nettuno.** Pride of place in the latter goes to Giambologna's central **Fontana del Nettuno** (1566), or Neptune Fountain, a vast bronze affair that spouts water from every orifice— the locals call it *Il Gigante,* or The Giant. Also worth a look is the **Palazzo Comunale,** a huge building from different eras whose modest civic museum, the Collezioni Comunali d'Arte, con-

tains a number of paintings by Bolognese painters spanning several centuries. Finer buildings still line Piazza Maggiore, including the 13th-century **Palazzo del Podestà,** the former governors' palace, and the magnificent church of **San Petronio.** This, Bologna's largest and most important church, is dedicated to St. Petronius, a fifth-century bishop and the city's patron saint. Founded in 1390, the church was originally intended to be twice its present size (this would have made it larger than St. Peter's in the Vatican City), but was constantly starved of funds during the 300 years it took to build. This left the brick-built facade shorn of its planned patterning and marble veneer, one of many aspects to suffer. Money was found to complete the main portal, however, which is

Palazzo Comunale

- ✉ Collezioni Comunali d'Arte, Piazza Maggiore 6
- ☎ 051 203 629
- 🕐 Closed Mon.
- 💲 $$

BALONEY

"First thing at Bologna I tried Bologna sausage, on the principle that at Rome you go first to St. Peter's."
—Herman Melville, *Journal* (1857) ∎

Bologna is one of Italy's gastronomic capitals, and its food stores brim with a tantalizing choice of cheeses, hams, and sausages.

Museo Civico Medievale

✉ Palazzo Ghisilardi-Fava, Via Manzoni-Via dell' Indipendenza

☎ 051 203 930

🕐 Closed Tues. & p.m. Mon.–Fri.

💲 $$

Museo Civico Archeologico

✉ Via dell' Archiginnasio-Piazza Maggiore

☎ 051 233 849

🕐 Closed Mon. & p.m. Tues.–Fri.

💲 $$

adorned with a "Madonna and Child" (1425–1438) and other carvings by the great Sienese sculptor, Jacopo della Quercia.

Inside, your attention is drawn to the nave's soaring Gothic vaulting, part of an architectural scheme that has seen the church described as Italy's greatest brick-built structure. Such was the money lavished here, financial shortfalls notwithstanding, that the extravagance is said to have heavily influenced Martin Luther's revolt against Catholicism. This said, outstanding works of art are surprisingly few and far between. The Cappella Bolognini, the fourth chapel off the north aisle, contains the best—a series of 15th-century frescoes by Giovanni da Modena and an altarpiece (1410) by Jacopo di Paolo.

The baroque Duomo, or Cathedral, to the north of Piazza Nettuno is a disappointing affair. Not so the civic museum, the **Museo Civico Medievale,** that lies opposite, which contains a first-rate collection of medieval and Renaissance paintings, sculpture, and applied arts. Sculptural highlights include Alessandro Algardi's

"St. Michael and the Devil," works by Bernini, a magical "Madonna and Child with Saints" by Jacopo della Quercia, and a "Mercury" and working model for the Neptune fountain by Giambologna. Among the applied arts, watch for several fine 13th-century bronzes and a sumptuous 14th-century cope, a peerless example of *opus anglicanum,* or English medieval embroidery work. The museum also contains notable collections of armor, glassware, ivories, ceramics, and musical instruments.

Bologna's archaeological museum is located east of San Petronio. Like many similar museums in Italy, the collection at the **Museo Civico Archeologico** is poorly displayed and its exhibits likely to appeal mainly to specialists, in this case devotees of Egyptian and Etruscan art. Etruscan influence reached as far north as Bologna, as did that of the Umbrians, a central Italian tribe eventually absorbed by the Etruscans. Tomb remains from both cultures make up many of the displays, the best of which were removed from the necropoli of Felsina, the sixth-century B.C.

Umbro-Etruscan settlement on Bologna's present-day site. Highlights among the Egyptian exhibits are stone reliefs from the 14th-century B.C. tomb of Horemheb. The museum also preserves prehistoric, Roman, and Greek artifacts.

South of the museum lies the **Palazzo dell'Archiginnasio** (1562–63), built by the papal legate in place of what would have been San Petronio's north transept. For centuries the palace formed part of Bologna's prestigious university, and today is worth visiting for the beautiful wood-paneled Teatro Anatomico (1637), the old medical faculty's dissection theater (*Tel 051 236 488, closed Sun. & p.m. daily*). Students once sat in the tiered seats to watch the dissection of human corpses, a form of instruction first introduced in this university school.

City views are hard to resist, and in Bologna the best are to be had from one of its twin *torri pendenti*, or leaning towers, located just to the east of Piazza Nettuno. Begun around 1109, the **Torre Garisenda** and **Torre degli Asinelli** are two of only a handful of survivors of the 180 or more medieval towers that distinguished

The Palazzo Comunale in Bologna's Piazza Nettuno. The central statue portrays Pope Gregory XIII.

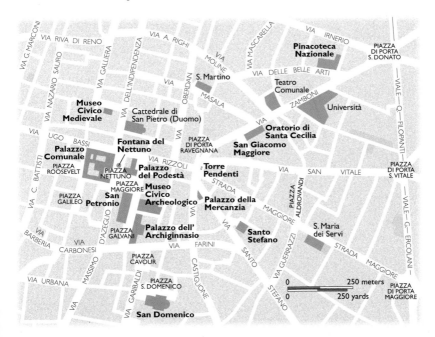

Take time out from sight-seeing to enjoy a cappuccino.

MONUMENT

"Bologna is to the Middle Ages what Pompeii has been to antiquity—a monument to the manner of their domestic existence."
—Lady Morgan, *Italy* (1820) ∎

Pinacoteca Nazionale

✉ Accademia di Belle Arti, Via delle Belle Arti 56

☎ 051 243 222

🕐 Closed Mon. & p.m. daily

💲 $$

Bologna's skyline. Both belonged to leading noble families, were towers of the first rank, even in their own day, and merited a mention in Dante's *Inferno*. The 164-foot (50 m) Garisenda was left unfinished and shortened in the 14th century to prevent its collapse—even today the lean still looks alarming. Its 320-foot (97.5 m) rival lies fourth in the overall Italian league table: Only the towers of Cremona, Siena, and Venice are taller. A lung-busting haul up its 486 steps, acccessible from Via di Porta Ravegnana, is rewarded with a glorious citywide panorama.

Before leaving the area around the towers, take a look at the **Palazzo della Mercanzia** (1382–84) in the adjacent Piazza Mercanzia. A former guild and merchants' meeting place, it is among the city's finest pieces of Gothic architecture. Also be sure to explore the nearby **Strada Maggiore,** the most captivating of Bologna's old streets.

A few minutes' walk from the towers on Via Zamboni lies **San Giacomo Maggiore,** a pleasing Romanesque-Gothic church

founded by the Augustinians in 1267. It has a fine exterior—seek out the lovely portal (1481) on the north side—and a passable assortment of interior paintings and frescoes. The main reason for a visit, however, is the **Cappella Bentivoglio** (1486) at the end of the north aisle, created in 1445 as a mausoleum for the Bentivoglio family, Bologna's erstwhile rulers. Its **altarpiece** (1488) is the work of the painter Francesco Francia, while Lorenzo Costa was responsible for the frescoes of the "Apocalypse," the "Triumph of Death," and portraits of the Bentivoglio family in the company of the Madonna and various saints. In the ambulatory, or walkway, opposite the chapel stands the "Tomb of Anton Galeazzo Bentivoglio" (1435), of the last works of the Sienese sculptor Jacopo della Quercia.

Spare a minute on exiting the church for the **Oratorio di Santa Cecilia,** entered via the church's side portico, which contains more frescoes and paintings (1506) by Francia and Lorenzo Costa.

Paintings by medieval Bolognese artists dominate the **Pinacoteca Nazionale,** the city's premier art gallery, beginning with early painters such as Simone de' Crocefissi and Vitale da Bologna, men heavily influenced by the stylized conventions of Byzantine art. Later works by local Renaissance artists occupy the so-called **long gallery,** although the artists here, notably Francesco Francia, known for his "Felecini Altarpiece," are often outshone by competing works by Giotto (a Maestà), prominent Venetians such as Cima da Conegliano (a touching Madonna), and members of the Ferrara school such as Francesco del Cossa (another Maestà).

The most astounding painting is Raphael's "Ecstasy of St. Cecilia"

(1515), one of the painter's most celebrated works. It shows the patron saint of musicians with instruments at her feet, clutching an organ, which she is said to have invented. Other notable paintings include Parmigianino's "Madonna and Saints" and Guido Reni's "Pietà dei Mendicanti," plus works by masters such as Perugino, Giotto, Titian, El Greco, and Caracci.

Santo Stefano *(Via Santo Stefano, tel 051 223 256)* is not one church but several, part of a pretty monastic complex first mentioned in 887 that originally comprised at least seven separate churches. The lackluster **Crocefisso,** restored in 1924 is followed by the more interesting **San Sepolcro,** home to the shrine of Bologna's patron saint, St. Petronius. Beyond these lie the Cortile di Pilato and a lovely Romanesque cloister, the latter providing access to a small museum *(Tel 051 223 256)* of paintings and religious ephemera. The cortile (courtyard) contains a large eighth-century basin with Lombard inscriptions, reputedly the bowl used by Pontius Pilate to wash his hands and absolve himself of responsibility for Christ's death. At the top of the courtyard lies the 13th-century church of the Trinità, while alongside San Sepolcro stands the disappointing **Santi Vitale e Agricola,** Bologna's oldest church. Dating from the fifth century, it has been much altered since.

Churches belonging to the Dominicans, one of the most severe medieval orders, are generally gaunt and intimidating places. This is partly because the Dominicans were Catholicism's self-appointed moral enforcers—they reveled in the pun on the Latin *domines canes,* or hounds of the Lord. Bologna's church of **San Domenico** *(Piazza San Domenico),* however, is an exception, chiefly because it is the burial place of St. Dominic himself, who died in the city in 1221. The tomb is a showcase of medieval art, featuring funerary carvings (1267) by the Tuscan masters Nicola Pisano and Arnolfo di Cambio, magnificent sculpted reliefs (1468–1473) by Niccolò da Bari, and a kneeling angel and two saints (1494) by the young Michelangelo. Other must-sees include Filippino Lippi's painting of the "Mystic Marriage of St. Catherine" (1501), some beautiful inlaid choir stalls (1451), and—in the sacristy museum *(Closed Sun.)*—a bust (1474) of St. Dominic in polychrome terra-cotta by Niccolò da Bari. ∎

The "Ecstasy of St. Cecilia" by Raphael hangs in the Pinacoteca Nazionale. Cecilia is the patron saint of musicians, hence the instruments.

Parma

NORTHERN ITALY HAS MANY A WELL-HEELED CITY, BUT
none perhaps quite so prosperous or quietly devoted to the finer things
of life as Parma. A byword for fine food—Parma ham and Parmesan
cheese both come from here—this is a refined and genteel city that is
crammed with elegant cafés, superlative restaurants, and tempting luxury stores. If you want to treat yourself to an expensive meal or make
some special purchases—and in between times visit a memorable
museum and marvelous medieval square—then Parma is for you.

The city's historical core is smaller
than many in Italy, but what it lacks
in size it more than makes up for in
appearance. Pride of place goes to
the buildings around **Piazza del
Duomo,** a faultless ensemble dominated by the 11th-century **Duomo**
and its graceful Gothic campanile
(1284–1294). A Romanesque masterpiece, the cathedral is best known
for the frescoes of the "Assumption"
(1522–1530) in its main cupola, the
work of Correggio (1489–1534),
the leading light, with Parmigianino
(1503–1540), of the so-called
Parma school of painting. Its other
major work of art is a relief of the
"Deposition" (1178) in the south
transept, the earliest known work

of the local sculptor Benedetto
Antelami (active 1178–1230).

Antelami was also responsible
for much of the square's other
principal building, the exquisite
octagonal Baptistery (begun in
1196), a distinctive and harmonious
building built largely in Verona's
orange-red marble. The sculptor
designed the structure and created
the sumptuous carving flanking the
three main portals, as well as the
interior's holy water stoup, altar,
and many of the capitals and reliefs
above the doors. The interior's most
stunning feature, however, is its
many frescoes (1260 1270), anonymous Byzantine-influenced works
portraying biblical episodes.

More frescoes, this time by Correggio, can be seen in **San Giovanni Evangelista,** immediately behind the Duomo, and in the **Camera di Correggio,** or Camera di San Paolo *(Via Melloni, tel 0521 282 217, closed p.m. daily).*

There is no mistaking the **Palazzo della Pilotta,** a colossal brick edifice built for the Farnese, a powerful Roman papal family who succeeded the Milan-based Visconti and Sforza dynasties as rulers of Parma between 1545 and 1731. Today, it is given over to three separate sights: the Museo Archeologico Nazionale, the Teatro Farnese, and the Pinacoteca Nazionale.

The **Museo Archeologico Nazionale** occupies much of the first and lower floors, its 15 or so rooms embracing a wide range of prehistoric, Greek, Etruscan, Egyptian, and Roman exhibits. Parma was probably founded by the Etruscans in the sixth-century B.C., and later became a prominent Roman colony on the Via Aemilia.

Of more general appeal is the **Teatro Farnese** (1617–18), an extraordinary wood and stucco stage and auditorium based on Palladio's Teatro Olimpico in Vicenza (see p. 175). The superb **Pinacoteca Nazionale,** or art gallery, in Piazza Pilotta presents its myriad paintings in huge, airy salons, many of them graced with clever modern walkways and other high-tech displays. The works of Emilian painters naturally take center stage, with an obvious bias toward local artists such as Parmigianino and Correggio. The latter's "Madonna della Scodella" (1525–1530) is one of the gallery's star turns, although it is run close by Leonardo da Vinci's "La Scapiliata" and Cima da Conegliano's "Madonna and Child with Saints." Other paintings of note are by Fra Angelico, Van Dyck, Holbein, Canaletto, and Giulio Romano.

Overcome any museum fatigue by walking in the **Parco Ducale** (1560), laid out as a summer retreat for the Farnese, just across the river from the Palazzo della Pilotta. Near its southeast corner lies the **Casa Toscanini,** birthplace of the conductor Arturo Toscanini (1867–1957). The house contains a small museum *(Borgo delle Grazie, tel 0521 816 939, closed Sun. p.m. & Mon.).* ■

Who painted the beautiful 13th-century frescoes in Parma's Baptistery? No one knows.

Parma

🅰 184 C5

Visitor information

✉ Via Melloni 1b

☎ 0521 218 889 or 0521 234 735

Palazzo della Pilotta

✉ Piazzale della Pilotta 15

☎ 0521 233 309 or 0521 233 617

🕐 Museo Archeologico: closed Mon. Pinacoteca & Museum: closed p.m. daily

💲 Museo Archeologico: $$. Teatro Farnese: $. Galleria Nazionale: $$$

Ferrara

FERRARA IS A SLEEPY MEDIEVAL TOWN STRANDED ON THE
Emilian plains a long way from more famous destinations. Its historical heritage owes much to the efforts of a single family, the Este,
whose often despotic behavior did little to temper the growth of a
civilized court during the long years—1208 to 1598—when they controlled the town's destiny. Palaces, castles, and a magnificent set of
walls are their most enduring legacy.

Head first for Piazza della
Repubblica, the square at the
town's heart and the stage for
the **Castello Estense** (begun
in 1385), a grandiose fortress complete with towers, moat, draw-
bridges, and soaring buttressed
ramparts. The Este's principal seat,
its wonderful medieval interior
once played host to numerous writers and artists seduced by the family's largesse. Painters included

members of the so-called Ferrara
school, led by Cosmé Tura,
Francesco del Cossa, Lorenzo
Costa, and Ercole de' Roberti.
Writers included Tasso, Petrarch,
and the author of the medieval epic
Orlando Furioso, Ludovico Ariosto
(1474–1533), whose house can seen
at Via Ariosto 67.

Close to the castle stands the
cathedral, fronted by a superb
facade. Sadly, the effect inside is less

spectacular, the result of dull interior remodeling during the 18th century. The best of the surviving works of art reside in the excellent **Museo della Cattedrale** (*Piazza Trento e Trieste, tel 0532 207 449, closed Sun.*), and include a collection of tapestries, illustrated manuscripts, Romanesque reliefs, painted organ panels by Cosmè Tura featuring a "St. George" and "Annunciation" (1469), and a "Madonna" (1408) by the Sienese sculptor Jacopo della Quercia.

Beyond the Castello Estense, Ferrara's spacious northern margins are different in look and feel to the rest of the town, largely because they form part of the so-called Addizione Erculea, or Herculean Addition, an urban development program commissioned by Duke Ercole I d'Este in 1492. His aim—consummately realized—was to transform the area into a model Renaissance quarter. The district is arranged around Corso Ercole I d'Este, the main street, while its chief focus is the **Palazzo Diamanti** (begun in 1492). Today, it houses the Pinacoteca Nazionale, an art gallery given over largely—but not entirely—to paintings by artists of the Ferrara school.

The fourth of Ferrara's great set piece buildings, the Palazzo Schifanoia, lies in the town's southwest corner. Walking there from the cathedral, you should follow Via Savonarola to see the **Casa Romei** (*Tel 0532 240 341, closed Mon. & p.m. daily*), a fine 15th-century town house with many original fittings and frescoed decoration. Then detour a little to the north to admire the furniture, gardens, and elaborate ceilings of the **Palazzina di Marfisa d'Este** (1559).

The **Palazzo Schifanoia** was begun in 1385 as the Este's summer residence—its name means carefree. Today, it is celebrated chiefly

for the stucco work of the Sala dei Stucchi (1470) and the **Salone dei Mesi** (1460–1471), the latter a room frescoed by Cossa and others with pretty, if faded allegorical and court scenes representing the "Months of the Year."

A little to the south stands the **Palazzo Ludovico il Moro** (*Via XX Settembre 124, tel 0532 66 299, closed Mon.& p.m. daily*), an outstanding but unfinished 15th-century palace now used to house the Museo Archeologico Nazionale di Spina, given over largely to finds from Spina, a former Greco-Etruscan port on the Po delta. The church of the nearby convent of **Sant'Antonio in Polesine** (*Vicolo del Gambone, tel 0532 64 068, closed Sat.–Sun.*) has several chapels smothered in early medieval frescoes. ∎

Palazzo dei Diamanti (Pinacoteca Nazionale)
✉ Corso Ercole d'Este 121
☎ 0532 209 988
🕐 Closed p.m. daily & Mon.
💲 $$

Palazzina di Marfisa d'Este
✉ Corso della Giovecca 170
☎ 0532 207 450
💲 $

Palazzo Schifanoia
✉ Via Scandiana 23
☎ 0532 64 178
💲 $$

Ravenna

RAVENNA ACQUIRED WESTERN EUROPE'S FINEST
Byzantine and early Christian mosaics almost by accident. In A.D.
401, as the power of Rome declined, it was made capital of the
Roman Empire, its port a lifeline to the rest of the world, its marshy
surroundings a bulwark against invading barbarian armies. After
the empire's collapse, the town continued to prosper. The
Ostrogothic king, Theodoric, ruled much of Italy from the city
after A.D. 493, as did the Byzantine emperor Justinian after A.D.
540, both men greatly embellishing its churches and other religious monuments.

Ravenna
🗺 185 E4
Visitor information
✉ Via Salara 8–12
☎ 0544 35 404

DYING EMPIRE

"We ended at
Ravenna and felt the
splendour of Rome
dying among the
barbarians in a way
that I never felt
again until I reached
the ruins of the
Levant."
—Freya Stark,
Traveller's Prelude
(1950) ∎

**Above and
opposite: Ravenna
boasts some of
the world's finest
mosaics. In the
Mausoleo di Galla
Placidia (right),
begun in A.D. 430,
the mosaic to the
rear of the tomb
depicts "The
Good Shepherd."**

BASILICA DI SAN VITALE

Ravenna's star attraction is the
Basilica di San Vitale (*Via
Fiandrini, tel 0544 34 266*), begun
by Theodoric in A.D. 521 and completed in A.D. 547 by Justinian. On
its own, the vast octagonal building
would be judged an architectural
masterpiece. What makes it still
more remarkable are the number
and quality of its sixth-century
mosaics. The most fascinating of
these adorn the side walls of the
apse and portray the courtly ret-
inues of Justinian (on the left) and
his wife Theodora (on the right).

On the basilica's grounds stands
a still more magical monument, the
fifth-century **Mausoleo di Galla
Placidia,** or tomb of Galla Placidia,
sister of Emperor Honorious I who
sanctioned Ravenna's elevation to
capital city in A.D. 401. The tiny
chapel is studded with Italy's most
beautiful mosaics, a glittering decorative spectacle presented in a quite
breathtaking array of colors.

Elsewhere, part of San Vitale's
tenth-century convent building
is given over to the **Museo
Nazionale,** a museum noted
in particular for its collection of
ivories and old coins, but also for
its archaeological exhibits, bronzes,
fabrics, weapons, ceramics, and
Roman, Byzantine, and early
Christian mosaics.

THE TOWN

Mosaics aside, Ravenna is a surprisingly pleasant and prosperous town
in its own right. Its medieval quarter centers on **Piazza del
Popolo,** a square lined with fine
old buildings and plenty of appealing cafés. You come here not for
the duomo, a disappointing 18th-
century remodeling of a fifth-century original, but for the scattering
of interesting buildings around it.

Chief among these is the
Battistero Neoniano (*Via
Battistero, tel 0544 218 559*), converted from a Roman bathhouse
by Bishop Neon in the fifth century.
Inside, the walls are almost entirely
covered in mosaic, stucco, and
other decoration (the lower
mosaics are poorly preserved
Roman originals, the higher ones
better-conserved fifth-century
examples). Compare the building
with the equally important
Battistero degli Ariani (*Via
degli Ariani, tel 0544 34 424*), whose
slightly later mosaics depict almost
identical subjects.

Behind the cathedral, the first
floor of the Arcivescovado, or
Archbishops' Palace, contains the
Museo Arcivescovile, a museum dominated by four outstanding
exhibits: the ivory "Throne of
Maximian," a sixth-century work
carved with biblical scenes; the

silver "Cross of St. Agnellus" (A.D. 556–569); and two entire chapels adorned with fifth- and sixth-century mosaics.

South of Piazza del Duomo is the **Tomba di Dante,** burial place of the great medieval poet who died in the city in 1321 after being exiled from Florence. The tenth-century church of **San Francesco** alongside, largely rebuilt in 1793, preserves several early Christian sarcophagi, a high altar fashioned from the fourth-century tomb of St. Liberius, and the original tenth-century crypt.

Mosaics also dominate the peripheral but outstanding **Sant'Apollinare Nuovo** (*Via Roma, tel 0544 39 081*), begun in A.D. 519 by Theodoric. The golden-hued, sixth-century mosaics run in bands along each side of the upper nave: The right (south) side portrays an array of 26 martyrs approaching Christ, the left a procession of 22 virgin martyrs behind the gift-bearing Magi. Above the bands on both sides are figures of the prophets, fathers of the Church, and episodes from the life of Christ. Don't confuse the church with **Sant'Apollinare in Classe,** a sixth-century building some 3 miles (5 km) south of Ravenna. This building is almost all that remains of the old Roman port of Classis, and though in rather unlovely surroundings, its mosaics are as important as any in the town itself. ■

Tickets

A single ticket is available for admission to San Vitale, the Mausoleo di Galla Placidia, Museo Nazionale, the Battistero Neoniano, Museo Archivescovile, and Sant'Apollinare Nuovo. Tickets are sold at the participating sights (*all open daily*). For further details contact the visitor information center. ■

The Venetians laid out the Piazza del Popolo, Ravenna's medieval heart, in the 15th century.

Urbino

URBINO WAS ONCE ONE OF EUROPE'S GREAT RENAISSANCE courts. Its artistic and cultural life was promoted by the ruling Montefeltro dukes, and reached its zenith during the reign of Duke Federico da Montefeltro between 1444 and 1482. Today, it is one of Italy's best kept secrets, its urbane streets and magnificent ducal palace little known to most foreign visitors. In truth, Urbino is the superior of many more famous towns in neighboring Tuscany and Umbria.

The **Palazzo Ducale,** or Ducal Palace, dominates hilltop Urbino, its towers and honey-colored stone bulwarks soaring above the pretty, rolling countryside that reaches up to the town's medieval walls. Its main architect was Dalmation-born Luciano Laurana (1420–1479), who produced an almost perfect Renaissance palace, with a serene inner courtyard (based on Florentine models), a harmonious interplay of brick and stone, and a faultless purity of line and ornamentation. Against this setting, it is hardly surprising that cultural life flourished: Raphael and the architect Bramante were born in the town, and Baldassare Castiglione drew from his experience at the Montefeltro court for his work, *The Courtier,* a 16th-century handbook of Renaissance manners that was disseminated across Europe.

The Palazzo Ducale in Urbino was begun in 1465 by Federico da Montefeltro, a man who made his fortune as a mercenary soldier.

Urbino

🅰 185 F3

Visitor information

✉ Piazza Duca Federico 35

☎ 0722 2613 or 0722 2788

The meaning of Piero della Francesca's unusual painting of the "Flagellation of Christ" continues to elude scholars. The handsome youth in the foreground may be Federico's assassinated half brother.

Palazzo Ducale-Galleria Nazionale

- ✉ Piazza Duca Federico
- ☎ 0722 2760
- 🕐 Closed Mon. p.m.
- 💲 $$

Casa Natale di Raffaello

- ✉ Via di Raffaello 57
- ☎ 0722 320 105
- 🕐 Closed p.m. daily in summer, also Mon. & Wed. in winter

Merely wandering the palace's stately rooms is a pleasure in itself. As you explore, look for the eagle symbol emblazoned throughout, part of the Montefeltro crest, and for the words Fe Dux, from Federicus Dux—Duke Federico. Make a point, too, of seeking out the studiolo, the duke's private study, whose *intarsia* (inlaid wood) was crafted in places to designs by Botticelli.

The palace's relative lack of original fittings may disappoint, although any sense of anticlimax is quickly tempered by the first-floor **Galleria Nazionale delle Marche,** or National Gallery of the Marches. This contains a wealth of Italian painting, including three of Italy's greatest masterpieces: Raphael's "La Muta" and two mysterious works by Piero della Francesca: the "Madonna di Senigallia" and "Flagellation of Christ." Also noteworthy is Luciano Laurena's painting of the "Ideal City."

Small and contained within its walls, Urbino, like its palace, is a pleasure to explore for its own sake. The first stop is a place of artistic pilgrimage, the **Casa Natale di Raffaello,** birthplace of Raphael

(1483–1520), who lived in the town until he was 14 before moving to Umbria and Rome. Inside, the house preserves much of its period charm.

On Via Barocci, make a point of seeing two small oratories *(both closed Sun. p.m.)*: the **Oratorio di San Giuseppe,** known for its 16th-century stucco presepio, or Christmas crib, and the **Oratorio di San Giovanni Battista,** whose interior is adorned with 14th-century frescoes portraying the "Crucifixion" and the "Life of St. John the Baptist." Elsewhere, spare a moment for the **Duomo,** spoiled by neoclassic alterations, but home to a celebrated 16th-century painting of the "Last Supper" by Federico Barocci. The nearby **Museo Diocesano,** or Diocesan Museum *(Piazza Pascoli 2, tel 0722 2850, closed winter & Sun. rest of year)*, is also worth a look for its collection of ceramics, glassware, and ecclesiastical ephemera. Finally, be sure to walk part of the Strada Panoramica, a scenic street leading from Piazza Roma, and to climb to the park above the town. Both offer rewarding views of Urbino and the surrounding countryside. ■

Ascoli Piceno

The 13th-century Palazzo dei Capitani del Popolo dominates the Piazza del Popolo in Ascoli Piceno.

FEW SQUARES, EVEN IN ITALY, ARE QUITE AS ALLURING AS Ascoli Piceno's Piazza del Popolo, the centerpiece of the most beautiful town in the Marche after Urbino. Nestled in the pastoral upper reaches of the Tronto valley, the town lies far from the commercial taint of the region's coastal resorts, its walled old quarter still laid out in the gridiron pattern of the old Roman colony, Asculum Picenum.

Restrained Renaissance buildings in the **Piazza del Popolo** stand cheek by jowl with more forceful Gothic palaces. Among them is the Palazzo dei Capitani del Popolo, whose facade is adorned with a Renaissance portal and statue (1549) of Pope Paul III by the local painter Cola dell'Amatrice (1480–1559). Almost equally prominent is the church of San Francesco, begun in 1262, its austere appearance softened by the adjacent Loggia dei Mercanti, or Merchants' Loggia, a Tuscan-influenced edifice dating from 1513.

Elsewhere in town, make first for Piazza Arrigo, just east of Piazza del Popolo. The duomo and baptistery are here, along with the Palazzo Comunale, once the town hall and currently home to the **Pinacoteca Civica,** or civic art gallery. The 12th-century duomo has another facade by Cola dell'Amatrice, while inside the main focal point is a stunning polyptych (1473) by Carlo Crivelli, an artist of Venetian origins who based himself in the town in 1470. There are more paintings by the same artist in the Pinacoteca, along with works by Titian, Van Dyck, Guido Reni, and others.

Wander down **Corso Mazzini,** to take in the church of Sant' Agostino, noted for a fresco of "Christ Carrying the Cross" by Cola dell'Amatrice. Then head north on Via dei Torri to visit the adjacent churches of 13th-century San Pietro Martire and the Romanesque Santi Vincenzo e Anastasia. ■

Ascoli Piceno
🅰 185 G1
Visitor information
✉ Piazza del Popolo 1
☎ 0736 253 045

Pinacoteca Civica
✉ Palazzo Comunale, Piazza Arringo
☎ 0736 298 213
🕐 Closed Sun. p.m. & from 3 p.m. daily
💲 $

More places to visit in Emila-Romagna & the Marche

FIDENZA

Fidenza's modern suburbs crowd in on a compact medieval center, visited principally for its 13th-century cathedral, an accomplished piece of composite Lombard-Romanesque and Gothic architecture in Piazza del Duomo.
🅰 184 B5 **Visitor information** ✉ Via Melloni 1b, Parma ☎ 0521 218 889

MODENA

Modena has several cultural distractions—its cathedral is one of northern Italy's greatest, and the **Palazzo dei Musei** contains a complex of museums bursting with paintings, sculptures, and precious manuscripts. To most Italians, however, the city's attractions are mechanical, for the firms of Ferrari and Maserati both build their famous sports cars nearby. The **Galleria Ferrari** in Maranello (*Via Dino Ferrari 43, tel 0536 943 204, closed Mon.*), 12 miles (20 km) to the south, has a museum dedicated to Ferrari memorabilia and vintage cars.
🅰 184 D4 **Visitor information** ✉ Piazza Grande 17 ☎ 059 206 660

DELTA DEL PO

Italy is not a bird-watching destination—too many of the birds have been shot by the country's overenthusiastic hunters. But one area where you may still see birds in considerable numbers, particularly in the spring and fall migration periods, is the Po Delta, north of Ravenna. Much of the area is a park, **Parco Regionale del Delta del Po,** with key smaller reserves found near Comacchio, the region's main center, and the ancient woodlands of the Bosco della Mesola. Watch for avocets, herons, egrets, terns, and other waterfowl. The delta's ethereal landscapes can be enjoyed by driving along the SS309 road, or by taking boat trips from villages such as Taglio di Po.
🅰 185 E5 **Visitor information** ✉ Environmental Education Center, Mesola ☎ 0533 993 644 🕒 Closed Sun. p.m. & Mon., & mid-Sept.–mid-June

PIACENZA

A settlement of Roman origin, Piacenza's pivotal position on the Po plain made it an important garrison town. The old center's rigid street plan still corresponds to the grid of the old Roman colony.

The principal attraction is the **Museo Civico** (*Piazza Cittadella, tel 0523 328 270, closed Mon. & Tues.–Fri. p.m.*), housed in the colossal Palazzo Farnese, begun in 1558. Its star turns are a painting of the "Madonna and Child with St. John the Baptist" by Sandro Botticelli and the curious and rare "Fegato di Pienza," or "Liver of Piacenza," an Etruscan bronze depicting sliced sheep's liver and marked with the names of Etruscan deities. Animal parts were used by priests as aids to divination.

Other sights include the **Piazza dei Cavalli,** the main square, named after the two bronze statues of horses (*cavalli*) and riders on either side of the square. Sculpted by Francesco Mochi, they depict Alessandro Farnese, a noble and mercenary solider, and his son, Ranuccio.

From the square walk to the Lombard-Romanesque **cathedral** (1122–1233) at the end of Via XX Settembre, the main street. The cathedral's plain but lovely interior warrants a few minutes' attention, as does the church of **Sant'Antonino** (*reached from the cathedral on Via Chiapponi*), celebrated for the 12th-century bas-reliefs on its main door.
🅰 184 B5 **Visitor information** ✉ Piazzetta dei Mercanti 7 ☎ 0523 329 324

SAN LEO

Many people have heard of **San Marino,** a tiny independent republic in the Marche. From a distance, its impressive hilltop location holds out great promise but, close up, the streets are crammed with visitors and ghastly souvenir stores. Only the views are worth the journey. Fewer people have heard of nearby **San Leo,** a smaller and far more alluring hill town with an equally commanding position. Machiavelli, the medieval political philosopher, called its fortress Italy's finest military redoubt, while Dante drew inspiration from the castle for parts of his *Purgatorio* The castle survives, looking down from its craggy ramparts on to a quaint cobbled square flanked by a ninth-century parish church and Romanesque cathedral.
🅰 185 F3 **Visitor information** ✉ Piazza Dante 14 ☎ 0541 916 306 ∎

Florence overflows with art and architecture, a city-size shrine to the Renaissance whose streets and galleries are filled with the paintings and sculptures of Europe's greatest artistic flowering.

Florence

Bronze by Lorenzo Ghiberti

Florence

FLORENCE (FIRENZE), EUROPE'S PREMIER ARTISTIC CAPITAL, IS CRAMMED with paintings, frescoes, and sculptures from the richest cultural flowering the world has known. Renaissance treasures fill a host of museums, churches, and galleries, while the roll call of famous names from the city's past—Dante, Machiavelli, Michelangelo, and Galileo among them—are some of the most resonant of the medieval age. The large number of galleries make this a predominantly indoor city but the lively markets, pretty piazzas, and Italy's most visited garden provide ample outdoor respite from the surfeit of art.

Florence was founded in 59 B.C., superseding an earlier Etruscan settlement (present-day Fiesole) in the hills above the modern city. The colony owed much of its prosperity to the Arno River, navigable to this point and crossed by the Via Cassia, one of the Romans' strategic road links to the north. The city emerged from the Dark Ages as an independent city state and quickly prospered as a result of its banking and textile industries. During the 13th century, it enjoyed a sophisticated form of republican government, but in the 14th century fell prey to a powerful banking family—the Medici.

The Medici fortune was established by Giovanni de' Medici (1360–1429) and consolidated by Cosimo de' Medici, also known as Cosimo the Elder (1389–1464). Its fruits were enjoyed by Cosimo's heir, Lorenzo de' Medici, better known as Lorenzo the Magnificent (1449–1492). The enlightened patronage of the Medici and others, together with an upsurge in classical and humanist scholarship, provided the spur for the Renaissance, a long-flowering artistic reawakening that found a fertile breeding ground in Florence, then Europe's most dynamic, cosmopolitan, and sophisticated city.

Medici power faltered in the 1490s with Lorenzo's death, leaving the way clear for Girolamo Savonarola (1452–1498), a charismatic monk eventually removed by the papacy in 1498. By 1512, the Medici were back, albeit with reduced power, only to be ousted again in 1527 by Emperor Charles V. Just two years later, the family had returned again, this time in the shape of Cosimo I, who took control of Tuscany and assumed the title of grand duke. The last Medici died in 1737, after a succession of increasingly inept rulers, the city passing by treaty to Francesco of Lorraine, the future

Emperor Francis I of Austria. The city remained under the Austrian yoke—bar 15 years of Napoleonic rule—until Italian unification in 1860. Since then, its most publicized event was the catastrophic flood of 1966 that killed several people and destroyed or damaged thousands of works of art. Today, the city is as wealthy as ever, grown fat from tourism and its still-thriving textile industry.

Start your artistic odyssey with the two main squares: Piazza della Signoria and Piazza del Duomo, the latter home to the cathedral, Baptistery, and Campanile, making sure you climb the cathedral dome or Campanile for some fabulous views of Florence and its surroundings. From the squares, you can tackle three of the city's main galleries: the Uffizi (paintings), the Bargello (sculpture), and Museo dell'Opera del Duomo (sculpture).

Next come two major churches, Santa Croce and Santa Maria Novella, and then the sights with one-off attractions: the Galleria dell'Accademia (Michelangelo's "David"); the Palazzo Medici-Riccardi (a fresco cycle by Benozzo Gozzoli); the Museo di San Marco (paintings by Fra Angelico); and the Cappelle Medicee (sculptures by Michelangleo).

At some point, cross the river, preferably via the celebrated Ponte Vecchio, and explore the district known as the Oltrarno. Here, you can discover the Palazzo Pitti, whose art gallery is second only to the Uffizi, and the Cappella Brancacci, filled with the city's most important fresco cycle. You will also find the Giardino di Boboli, the city's loveliest garden, as well as numerous artisans' workshops, antique stores, and quieter, more traditional streets and squares. Finally, don't miss the only sight beyond easy walking distance of the center—the superlative church of San Miniato al Monte. ■

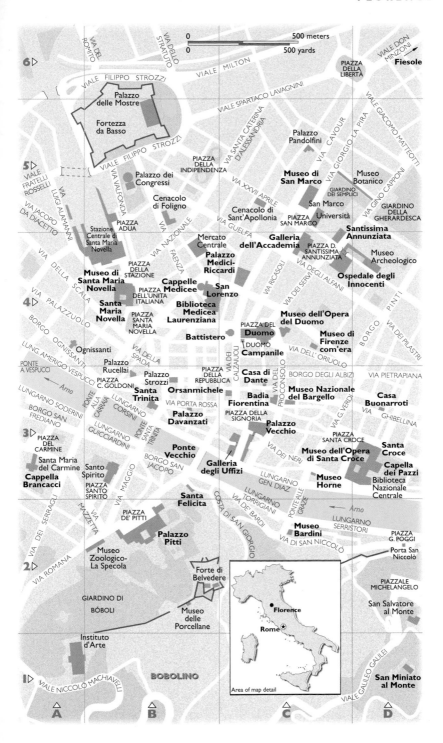

500 meters
500 yards

6

VIA DEL ROMITO
VIA DELLO STRATUTO
VIALE MILTON
VIALE FILIPPO STROZZI
VIALE SPARTACO LAVAGNINI
VIALE DON MINZONI
Fiesole
PIAZZA DELLA LIBERTA

Palazzo delle Mostre
Fortezza da Basso
VIALE FILIPPO STROZZI
VIA SANTA CATERINA D'ALESSANDRIA
Palazzo Pandolfini
VIA CAVOUR
VIA GIORGIO LA PIRA
VIALE GIACOMO MATTEOTTI

5

VIALE FRATELLI ROSSELLI
VIA LUIGI ALAMANNI
VIA VALFONDA
PIAZZA DELLA INDIPENDENZA
Palazzo dei Congressi
Cenacolo di Foligno
VIA XXVII APRILE
Museo di San Marco
GIARDINO DEI SEMPLICI
Museo Botanico
GIARDINO DELLA GHERARDESCA
VIA GINO CAPPONI

VIA JACOPO DA DIACETO
PIAZZA ADUA
VIA NAZIONALE
Cenacolo di Sant'Apollonia
VIA GUELFA
San Marco
PIAZZA SAN MARCO
Università
Stazione Centrale di Santa Maria Novella
VIA FAENZA
Mercato Centrale
Galleria dell'Accademia
Santissima Annunziata
PIAZZA D. SANTISSIMA ANNUNZIATA
Museo Archeologico

Palazzo Medici-Riccardi
VIA RICASOLI
VIA DEGLI ALFANI
VIA DEI SERVI
Ospedale degli Innocenti

VIA DELLA SCALA
Museo di Santa Maria Novella
PIAZZA DELLA STAZIONE
Cappelle Medicee
PIAZZA DELL'UNITA ITALIANA
San Lorenzo

4

VIA PALAZZUOLO
BORGO OGNISSANTI
Santa Maria Novella
PIAZZA SANTA MARIA NOVELLA
Biblioteca Medicea Laurenziana
Battistero
PIAZZA DEL **Duomo**
DUOMO
Campanile
Museo dell'Opera del Duomo
VIA DELL'ORIUOLO
Museo di Firenze com'era
BORGO PINTI
VIA DEI PILASTRI

LUNG. AMERIGO VESPUCCI
Ognissanti
Palazzo Rucellai
VIA DELLA SPADA
PIAZZA DELLA REPUBBLICA
VIA DEI CALZAIUOLI
Casa di Dante
VIA DEL PROCONSOLO
BORGO DEGLI ALBIZI
VIA PIETRAPIANA

PONTE A. VESPUCCI
LUNGARNO VESPUCCI
PIAZZA C. GOLDONI
Palazzo Strozzi
Santa Trinita
Palazzo
Orsanmichele
VIA PORTA ROSSA
Badia Fiorentina
PIAZZA DELLA SIGNORIA
Museo Nazionale del Bargello
VIA G. VERDI
Casa Buonarroti
VIA GHIBELLINA

Arno
LUNGARNO SODERINI
BORGO SAN FREDIANO
PIAZZA ALLA CARRAIA
LUNGARNO CORSINI
PONTE SANTA TRINITA
Palazzo Davanzati
Palazzo Vecchio
PIAZZA SANTA CROCE
Santa Croce

3

PIAZZA DEL CARMINE
LUNGARNO GUICCIARDINI
Ponte Vecchio
BORGO SAN JACOPO
Galleria degli Uffizi
VIA DEI NERI
LUNGARNO GEN. DIAZ
Museo dell'Opera di Santa Croce
Museo Horne
Capella dei Pazzi
Biblioteca Nazionale Centrale

Santa Maria del Carmine
Santo Spirito
PIAZZA SANTO SPIRITO
VIA MAGGIO
Santa Felicita
LUNGARNO TORRIGIANI
PONTE ALLE GRAZIE
Arno
LUNGARNO SERRISTORI

Cappella Brancacci
VIA DEI SERRAGLI
VIA MAZZETTA
PIAZZA DE' PITTI
COSTA DI SAN GIORGIO
VIA DE' BARDI
Museo Bardini
VIA DI SAN NICCOLÒ
PIAZZA G. POGGI
Porta San Niccolò

2

VIA ROMANA
Palazzo Pitti
Museo Zoologico-La Specola
Forte di Belvedere
Florence
Rome
PIAZZALE MICHELANGELO

GIARDINO DI BÓBOLI
Museo delle Porcellane
San Salvatore al Monte

Instituto d'Arte

1

VIALE NICCOLÒ MACHIAVELLI
BOBOLINO
Area of map detail
VIALE GALILEO GALILEI
San Miniato al Monte

A **B** **C** **D**

Florence
243 C4
Visitor information
Via Cavour 1r
055 290 832 or
055 290 833

Borgo Santa Croce
29r
055 234 0444

Piazza della
Stazione
055 212 245

Note: In Florence, business
addresses are suf-
fixed with "r," which
stands for *rosso*
(red). These numbers
are displayed in red
on the street.

Piazza del Duomo

PIAZZA DEL DUOMO IS FLORENCE'S RELIGIOUS HEART. Here stands the Duomo (cathedral) and its imperious dome, one of the city's great symbols, flanked by its freestanding campanile, or bell tower. In the cathedral's shadow stands the Baptistery, Florence's oldest building, a place of spiritual and artistic importance for well over a thousand years. Some of the many works of art produced for these buildings over the years have been removed for safekeeping to the square's fourth major component, the Museo dell'Opera del Duomo, a museum tucked away behind the cathedral.

The **Duomo,** Europe's fourth largest cathedral, was begun in 1296 by the architect Arnolfo di Cambio (1245–1302). Its vast scope was designed to reflect Florence's burgeoning importance as a city and to outshine the recent cathedrals of rivals Siena and Pisa. Consecrated in 1436, it was crowned with the largest dome since antiquity, a masterpiece of medieval engineering designed by Filippo Brunelleschi (1377–1466). The multicolored facade, a Gothic pastiche, dates from as recently as 1887, Arnolfo di Cambio's quarter-finished frontage having been pulled down in 1587.

The contrast between the cathedral's ornate exterior and apparently plain interior could hardly be greater. Size for its own sake seems to be the latter's overriding preoccupation. Closer investigation, however, reveals a surprising number of artistic treasures, as well as two worthwhile side attractions: one the cathedral's crypt, where you can see the remains of **Santa Reparata,** an earlier church on the site; the other the cathedral's **dome,** which offers an insight into Brunelleschi's engineering genius and a glorious panorama of Florence and its surrounding countryside.

Before you explore either of these, however, see the interior's other highlights. Start with three paintings on the left (north) wall: "Dante Explaining the Divine Comedy" (1465) is by Domenico di Michelino, the other two are equestrian portraits of the mercenary soldiers Sir John Hawkwood (1436) and Niccolò da Tolentino (1456) by Paolo Uccello and Andrea del Castagno respectively. Colorful but trite frescoes (1572–79) by Giorgio Vasari of the "Last Judgment" adorn the interior of the dome, distracting from the genuine treasures of the twin sacristies below. On the left, as you face the high altar, is the **Sacrestia Nuova,** or New Sacristy, decorated with exquisite 15th-century inlaid wood paneling and protected by bronze doors (1446–1467) designed by Michelozzo and Luca della Robbia. Above the doors is a bluish white terra-cotta lunette (1442), also by Luca della Robbia. An almost identical lunette (1446–1451) by the

The Florentine skyline, dominated by the cathedral dome (right), Campanile (center), and Palazzo Vecchio (far left)

Duomo

- 205 C4
- Piazza del Duomo
- 055 230 2855
- Closed Sun. a.m. & p.m. 1st Sat. of month

Battistero

- 205 C4
- Piazza San Giovanni-Piazza del Duomo
- 055 230 2885
- Closed Sun. p.m.
- $$

BATTISTERO

The Battistero, or Baptistery, is the city's oldest building. Constructed on the site of a first-century Roman building, it probably dates from around the sixth or seventh century, although the earliest documentary reference comes in 897, when it was mentioned as the city's first cathedral. Much of its classically inspired decoration dates from 1059 to 1128, a period of remodeling that saw the addition of the exterior's geometric medley of pillars, cornices, and colored marble friezes. By far the Baptistery's most eminent features are its **doors.** Those on the south face were the first to be made (1328–1336),

Visitors gather around the Baptistery's east doors, christened by Michelangelo the "Gates of Paradise."

same artist graces the **Sacrestia Vecchia,** or Old Sacristy, on the other side of the church. Between the two sacristies, in the central apse, is a magnificent bronze reliquary (1432–1442) by Lorenzo Ghiberti that holds the remains of St. Zenobius, Florence's first bishop.

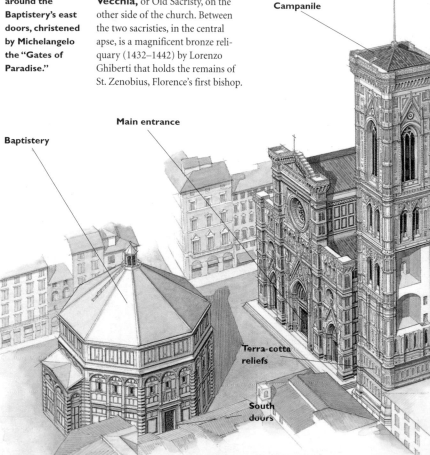

Campanile

Main entrance

Baptistery

Terra-cotta reliefs

South doors

designed by Andrea Pisano, a Pisan sculptor. They are decorated with 28 panels depicting scenes from the life of Florence's patron saint, St. John the Baptist, to whom the building is dedicated. The north doors (1403–1424) were commissioned from Lorenzo Ghiberti after a competition in 1401, a date often seen as marking the beginning of the Italian Renaissance. While following Pisano's earlier 28-panel scheme,

Ghiberti's panels display far greater artistic ambition than their predecessors—their subjects are episodes from the life of Christ, the Evangelists, and Doctors of the Church.

Still greater refinement appear in the most famous of the three portals, Ghiberti's east doors (1425–1452), the so-called **Gates of Paradise,** whose ten panels depict Old Testament scenes with a previous-

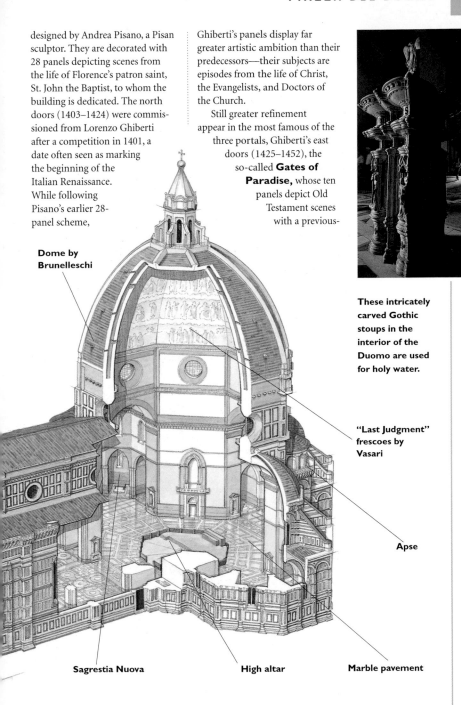

These intricately carved Gothic stoups in the interior of the Duomo are used for holy water.

Dome by Brunelleschi

"Last Judgment" frescoes by Vasari

Apse

Sagrestia Nuova

High altar

Marble pavement

Many panels of the Baptistery's mosaic ceiling were the work of Venetian craftsmen.

Campanile

🅼 205 C4

✉ Piazza del Duomo

☎ 055 230 2885

💲 $$

ly unseen measure of narrative and technical sophistication. The present panels are copies—the originals are in the Museo dell' Opera del Duomo (see facing page). The first impression of the Baptistery's interior is of a bland shell. A glance upward, however, reveals a majestic mosaic-covered **ceiling,** a largely 13th-century work begun by Venetian craftsmen (the Florentines had no grounding in the art of mosaic). Its immensely complex narrative embraces episodes from the lives of Christ, Joseph, the Virgin, and John the Baptist. To the right of the *scarsella,* or apse, lies Donatello and Michelozzos' **tomb of John XXIII,** an adviser and friend of the Medici who died in the city in 1419. Also worthy of note are the interior's band of granite columns,

probably removed from the old Roman Capitol, and the intricately tessellated marble pavement, where the outline of the original octagonal font can still be seen.

CAMPANILE

The Campanile is the cathedral's bell tower. It was begun in 1334 under the guidance of the painter Giotto, then the city's *capo maestro,* or master of works. He completed only the first of the tower's five stories before his death in 1337. Work then proceeded in two phases, the first (1337–1342) under Andrea Pisano, designer of the Baptistery's north doors, the second (1348–1359) under Francesco Talenti. Giotto probably left blueprints for the tower's decoration, although most of the first-story reliefs—the tower's decorative highlights—were

The "Pietà" by Michelangelo in the Museo dell' Opera. The sculptor smashed Christ's arm and leg—later restored—in a fit of rage.

Museo dell'Opera del Duomo

🅰 205 C4

✉ Piazza del Duomo 9

☎ 055 230 2885

🕐 Closed—reopens 2000

💲 $$

executed by Pisano, Luca della Robbia, and assistants. The present reliefs are copies (the age-darkened originals reside in the Museo dell'Opera). A strenuous climb to the top of the 269-foot (82 m) tower—there is no elevator—is rewarded by sensational views of the city.

MUSEO DELL' OPERA DEL DUOMO

The Opera del Duomo was a body created in 1296 to care for the fabric of the cathedral. Since 1891, its former headquarters has been used to safeguard works of art removed over the centuries from the Duomo, Baptistery, and Campanile. Its sculpture collection is second only to that of the nearby Bargello, but the museum's early rooms also contain a range of exhibits devoted to Brunelleschi, most notably a series of tools and other equipment used during the construction of the cathedral dome.

The ground floor's first principal room features a host of statues, most of them rescued from Arnolfo di Cambio's demolished cathedral facade. The most eye-catching are a figure of "St. John" by Donatello and two works by di Cambio: the "Madonna of the Glass Eyes," famous for its otherworldly gaze, and an almost comical statue of "Boniface VIII," a vicious medieval pope identified here by his distinctive hat. The second room contains illustrated manuscripts and several models entered for a 1588 competition to design a new cathedral facade.

Moving upstairs you pass Michelangelo's **"Pietà"** (circa 1550), a late work probably intended for the sculptor's own tomb (the New Testament figure of Nicodemus may be a self-portrait). Michelangelo became disillusioned by the piece, and in his frustration

smashed its left arm and leg. The damage was later repaired by a pupil, but signs of the damage and the obvious discrepancy in styles are still evident.

The upper floor's first room contains two stunning and contrasting *cantorie*, or **choir lofts,** one by Donatello (1433–39), the other by Luca della Robbia (1431–38). Both were removed from the entrances to the cathedral's sacristies. Also here are Donatello's celebrated wooden statue of "Mary Magdalene" (1455) and the bald-headed Old Testament prophet "Abacuc," or Habbakuk (1423–25), one of 16 figures removed here from the Campanile. The room to the left features more refugees from the bell tower, this time the first-story allegorical reliefs by Andrea Pisano, Luca della Robbia, and their pupils. The third major room to the right features Ghiberti's original **panels** from the Baptistery's east doors, as well as a range of sublime paintings and a stupendous 14th-century gold and silver altarpiece. ■

Orsanmichele

Orsanmichele

🏛 205 C3

✉ Via dei
Calzaiuoli 42

☎ 055 284 944

🕐 Closed 1st & last
Mon. of the month

**The painting
at the heart of
Orcagna's taber-
nacle in Orsan-
michele is said
to have miracu-
lous powers.**

WALK SOUTH FROM PIAZZA DEL DUOMO ALONG VIA DEI
Calzaiuoli, Florence's pedestrians-only main street, and about
midway down on the right you pass the church of Orsanmichele,
known chiefly for the extraordinary range of sculptures that adorns
its otherwise plain exterior. The church takes its name from
San Michele ad Hortum, the name of a seventh-century oratory that
once occupied the *hortum* or *orto* (garden) of a Benedictine
monastery on the site.

This oratory was replaced around
1280 by a grain market, although
the site retained its religious associations thanks to an image of the
Virgin accredited with miraculous
powers painted on one of its pillars.

Over the next century, the building
was rebuilt on several occasions,
and by 1380 its lower half had once
again become a church—more or
less the building you see today—
while its upper levels were used
as a granary during times of siege
and famine.

As early as 1339, the city's guilds
had been entrusted with the building's decoration, each of the exterior
niches to be filled with a statue of
a particular guild's patron saint.
Some of the great names of early
Renaissance sculpture eventually
worked on the site, among them
Donatello, Ghiberti, Verrocchio,
and Luca della Robbia, crafting the
niche statues and their ornate surrounds (some of the present works
are copies).

Inside, the church provides a
peaceful retreat from the crowds
on Via dei Calzaiuoli. Patches of
frescoes appear around the walls
as your eyes become accustomed
to the gloom—most portray the
guilds' patron saints. To the rear
stands a magnificent **tabernacle**
(1348–1359) by Andrea Orcagna,
built partly to house a painting of
the "Madonna and Child" (1347)
by Bernardo Daddi, a work said
to have inherited the miraculous
powers of the Virgin on the pillar,
which had been destroyed in a fire.
The greatest work of its kind in
Italy, the tabernacle was financed by
a flood of votive offerings prompted by the Black Death of 1348. ∎

Piazza della Signoria

WHERE PIAZZA DEL DUOMO SERVES AS FLORENCE'S religious heart, the city's second great square, Piazza della Signoria, has long been its civic focus. It is home to the Palazzo Vecchio, the seat of city government for seven centuries, and plays hosts to several notable pieces of public sculpture. It is also a meeting place for visitors and Florentines alike: Rivoire, one of the city's most distinguished cafés is here, while close by lies the entrance to the most celebrated of all Florence's museums, the Uffizi.

The battlements and clocktower of the Palazzo Vecchio, the centerpiece of Piazza della Signoria

Dominating the Piazza della Signoria is the fortresslike bulk of the **Palazzo Vecchio.** Work started on the building in 1299, probably to a plan by the cathedral's architect, Arnolfo di Cambio. Initially it housed the Priori, or Signoria, the city's ruling council, but in 1540 it became home to Grand Duke Cosimo I. Cosimo

remained just nine years before moving to the Palazzo Pitti, the point at which his old *(vecchio)* palace acquired its present name.

Today the palace once again houses the city's council, although much of its interior is also open to the public. You enter the complex via an inner **courtyard** (1555–1574), beautifully decorated by

Piazza della Signoria
🗺 205 C3

Palazzo Vecchio
✉ Piazza della Signoria
☎ 055 276 8465
🕐 Closed Sun. p.m. & all Thurs.
💲 $$

A fellow sculptor described Bandinelli's statue "Hercules and Cacus" in Piazza della Signoria as resembling a "sackful of melons."

Opposite: Evening shoppers linger in the shadow of the Palazzo Vecchio and its imposing bell tower.

Giorgio Vasari, and then climb to the **Salone dei Cinquecento**, the palace's vast centerpiece, designed to accommodate the members of the Consiglio Maggiore, the republic's ruling assembly. Its ceiling painting, the "Apotheosis of Cosimo I," and bombastic wall paintings—illustrations of Florentine military triumphs—are the work of Vasari.

Of greater interest are Michelangelo's statue, "Victory" (1525), almost opposite the room's entrance, and the small **Studiolo di Francesco I** (1569–1573), a study adorned with the decorative efforts of more than 30 artists. Turn left on the stairs from the Salone and a suite of rooms, the Quartiere degli Elementi, leads to the Terrazzo dei Saturno, which offers some intriguing city views. Turn right and you enter the Quartiere di Eleonora, the apartments of Cosimo I's wife. The highlight here is the tiny **Cappella di Eleonora** (1540–45), sumptuously decorated by the mannerist artist Bronzino.

Among the following rooms, the **Sala dell'Udienza** has good views over the Piazza della Signoria and a glorious ceiling (1472–76) by Giuliano da Maiano, who was also responsible, with his brother, for the carved doorway to the neighboring **Sala dei Gigli.** Named

after its decorative lilies *(gigli),* this room features another fine Maiano ceiling, a fresco sequence by Domenico Ghirlandaio (1481–85), and Donatello's sublime statue of "Judith and Holofernes" (1455–1460). The adjacent **Cancelleria** was once Niccolò Machiavelli's office, while the **Sala delle Carte** next door, now filled with lovely 16th-century maps, once housed Cosimo I's costumes of state.

The triple-arched **Loggia della Signoria** on the piazza's eastern side was begun in 1376, possibly to a design by Orcagna, to protect city officials from the weather during Florence's numerous public ceremonies. In time it was also used to meet visiting foreign dignitaries, and as a shelter for the Swiss *lanzi* (lancers) of Cosimo I's personal guard—hence its alternative name, the Loggia dei Lanzi. Today, it acts as a small outdoor museum for two major and several minor pieces of sculpture. The most famous work is Benvenuto Cellini's prodigious "Perseus" (1545–1553), one of Europe's greatest bronze statues. To its right stands Giambologna's "Rape of the Sabine Women" (1583), carved from a single piece of flawed marble. Despite its title, it was originally intended simply as a study of old age, male strength, and female beauty. ∎

Statues

From left to right as you face the Palazzo Vecchio, the statues across the Piazza della Signoria's eastern flank are as follows: "Cosimo I" (1587–1594), an equestrian monument to the Medici duke by Giambologna; "Neptune" (1565–1575) by Ammannati, a work much ridiculed by Michelangelo, among others; Donatello's "Il Marzocco" (1418–1420), a copy of a statue of Florence's heraldic symbol (the original is in the Museo Nazionale del Bargello); Donatello's "Judith and Holofernes," another copy of an original statue now in the Palazzo Vecchio; "David," a copy of Michelangelo's original, now in the Galleria dell'Accademia; and "Hercules and Cacus" (1534), carved by Bandinelli to act as a companion piece for the "David." ∎

Galleria degli Uffizi

GREAT IS AN OVERWORKED ADJECTIVE IN ITALY, WHERE SO many of the country's monuments and works of art command the highest praise. In the case of the Galleria degli Uffizi, or Uffizi, it barely does justice to a gallery that holds the world's finest collection of Renaissance paintings. All the famous names of Italian art are here, not only the Renaissance masters, but also painters from the country's early medieval, baroque, and Mannerist heyday. So, too, are artists from farther afield, notably from Holland, Spain, and Germany.

Visitors to the Uffizi admire Botticelli's "The Birth of Venus," one of the gallery's most popular paintings.

Galleria degli Uffizi

- 205 C3
- Loggiato degli Uffizi 6, off Piazza della Signoria
- 055 234 7941 or 055 23 885
- Closed Mon.
- $$

Florence has the Medici family to thank for the Uffizi. The building that houses the collection was designed in 1560 as a suite of offices *(uffizi)* for Cosimo I, the family's first grand duke, while the collection itself, accumulated by the family over the centuries, was bequeathed to the city (on condition that it never leave Florence) by Anna Maria Luisa, sister of the last grand duke, Gian Gastone Medici. Sculpture from the collection went to the Bargello; Etruscan and other antique art to the Museo Archeologico; and paintings to the Uffizi and Palazzo Pitti.

The gallery spreads across some 45 rooms, and any brief survey can only touch on its absolute highlights. Dedicated visitors may want to make two visits: one to take in the first 15 rooms, home

to the works of the Florentine Renaissance, some of the gallery's best-known paintings, and another to enjoy the works of the other Italian and foreign schools displayed in the remaining 30 rooms. You should be prepared to wait in line at almost any time of the day and in any season, although note that tickets guaranteeing entry at a specific time can be arranged (see p. 218).

An assortment of sculptures and ground-floor frescoes by Andrea del Castagno provide the Uffizi's prelude, and it is only with three great depictions of the **Maestà**, or Madonna Enthroned, in **Room 3** that the gallery gets into its stride. Italy's three finest 13th-century artists were responsible for the paintings—Giotto, Cimabue, and Duccio—each of whom pioneered a distinct move away from the stylized and iconic conventions of Byzantine art that had dominated Italian and other art for centuries. Thus Cimabue's depiction of the saints around the Virgin's throne improves on those of Duccio: Cimabue's saints stand in fixed positions, while those of Duccio, a painter more wedded to Byzantine tradition, seem to float haphazardly. Giotto makes the largest leap of all, adding light and shadow to denote the folds of the Madonna's cloak, one of several realistic and revolutionary departures from the stilted artificiality of the Byzantine approach.

Paintings from Italy's Gothic masters fill **Rooms 3–6,** beginning with works from the city of Siena, where painters continued to borrow heavily from the fading conventions of Byzantine art. Finest of all are Simone Martini's "Annunciation" (1333) and the works by Pietro and Ambrogio Lorenzetti, two brothers who probably died during the plague epidemic that swept Italy in 1348. Then come exponents of the so-called International Gothic, a highly detailed and courtly style exemplified by Gentile da Fabriano's exquisite "Adoration of the Magi" (1423) and Lorenzo Monaco's "Coronation of the Virgin" (1413).

The first flowering of the Renaissance is seen in **Room 7,** which presents works by early iconoclasts such as Masaccio, Masolino, and Fra Angelico. The same room also features a painting by one of the rarest of Italian painters, Domenico Veneziano, an artist with only 12 confidently attributed paintings to his name. Nearby hang two well-known paintings by one of Veneziano's pupils, Piero della Francesca—portraits (1460) of Federico da Montefeltro, Duke of Urbino, and his wife, Battista Sforza. Federico was always portrayed in left profile, as here, after a jousting accident disfigured the right side of his face.

Duke Federico da Montefeltro by Piero della Francesca. The artist admired the duke, but was unsparingly realistic in his portrait.

Botticelli
You can almost guarantee that **Rooms 10–14** will be the Uffizi's most crowded, for this is the suite given over to the gallery's most famous paintings: Botticelli's "Primavera" (1478) and "Birth of Venus" (1485). The latter, the famous girl in a half shell, was the first pagan nude of the Renaissance, and, like the "Primavera" (Spring), drew heavily on classical myth and contemporary humanist scholarship. Venus was impregnated following the castration of Uranus and then rose from the sea, suggesting beauty (Venus) was the result of a union of the physical and spiritual (Uranus). In the myth—and painting—the nymphs Chloris and Zephyr blow the risen Venus to the shore, where she is cloaked by the figure of Hora. The theme of the "Primavera" is more uncertain. Some critics suggest it is an allegory of spring or all four seasons, others that it represents the Triumph of Venus, the attendant Graces representing her beauty, Flora her fecundity.

Leonardo to Michelangelo
Room 15 contains two of only a handful of paintings in Florence

Titian's "Venus of Urbino." The artist's clever use of color, red in particular, gives added compositional strength to the painting.

attributed to Leonardo da Vinci: an "Annunciation" (1475) and the "Adoration of the Magi" (1481), works that rather overshadow paintings by Luca Signorelli and Perugino elsewhere in the room.

The octagonal Tribune, now **Room 18,** was specially built by

the Medici to house their most precious works of art, among which the "Medici Venus," a first-century B.C. Roman statue, figured large. Widely celebrated as Europe's most erotic statue—Lord Byron stood before it "dazzled and drunk with beauty"—the figure was the only Florentine statue removed

Advance tickets

Lines for the Uffizi are horrendously long nearly all year-round, and at any time of day. To reserve tickets, call 055 234 7941 or 055 294 883 between 8 a.m. and 6:30 p.m. Monday to Saturday. (Most staff speak English, but telephone lines are frequently busy for long periods.) If spaces are available, you will receive a

reservation number for the day of your visit. Tickets are held at the meeting point for advance reservations to the left of the main gallery entrance. Pick them up at the allotted time and then enter the gallery directly. A small reservation fee ($) is charged over and above the cost of normal admittance. ■

to France by Napoleon after his invasion of Italy.

The next six rooms are devoted to Florentine, Venetian, German, and Flemish canvases. It is only in **Room 25,** well over half way around the gallery, that you come to the Uffizi's only painting by Michelangelo: the "Doni Tondo" or "Holy Family" (1504).

Raphael & the Mannerists

Little of the content of Michelangelo's "Doni Tondo" is understood, but its deliberately obscure meaning, contorted composition, and often virulent coloring profoundly influenced a style of painting known as Mannerism, a genre whose leading lights are represented in the next four rooms. Look in particular for Pontormo's "Supper at Erasmus" (1525) in **Room 27** and Parmigianino's "Madonna and Child with Angels" (1534–1540), the latter famous for the Virgin's peculiarly etiolated neck **(Room 29).**

Another late Renaissance painter who significantly influenced the Mannerists was Raphael, the cream of whose Uffizi paintings are found in **Room 26.** The most notable are the "Madonna of the Goldfinch" (1506) and unflinching portraits (1506) of the Medici pope, Leo X, and cardinals Giulio de' Medici and Luigi de' Rossi. Raphael also influenced Titian, whose infamous "Venus of Urbino" (1538), one of the most explicit nudes in Western art, led Mark Twain to describe it as "the foulest, the vilest, the obscenest picture the world possesses."

Right: Michelangelo painted the "Holy Family with St. John" or "Doni Tondo" to celebrate the marriage of Angelo Doni and Maddalena Strozzi in 1504.

Rembrant & Caravaggio

Rooms 30–35 deal largely in paintings by artists from areas of northern Italy, notably Venice and Emilia-Romagna, but you may as well hurry past these and reserve energy for the high quality works in the gallery's final rooms. **Room 41** is dominated by Van Dyck and Rubens, and in particular the paintings commissioned from Rubens following the marriage of King Henry IV of France to Marie de' Medici. Caravaggio bears the standard for Italy in **Room 43,** his pomposity in marked contrast to two introspective self-portraits by Rembrandt in the following room.

Many more paintings by artists you have already seen—and many you have not—hang in the **Corridoio Vasariano,** a gallery built by Cosimo I to link the Uffizi with the Palazzo Pitti across the river. It is only intermittently open, however, so inquire at the city's visitor centers or the Uffizi ticket office about the opening times. ∎

Museo Nazionale del Bargello

THE BARGELLO'S COLLECTION OF GOTHIC AND Renaissance sculpture is one of the most important in Italy. Only one other gallery in Florence—the Uffizi—is more notable. The museum takes its name from the palace in which it is housed, the Bargello, a palace built in 1255 and used as the seat of the Podestà, the city's main magistrate. Later it became a law court, prison, torture chamber, and place of execution, taking its present name in 1574 after the Medici abolished the position of Podestà and made the building over to the *bargello*, the chief of police.

"Lamentation" by Giovanni della Robbia. The della Robbia family produced several artists famous for this type of glazed and colored terra-cotta.

Museo Nazionale del Bargello

🅰 205 C3
✉ Via del Proconsolo 4
☎ 055 238 8606
🕑 Closed Mon. & p.m. Tues.–Sun., but open a.m. 1st, 3rd, 5th Mon., & 2nd & 4th Sun. of the month
💲 $$

Opposite: Donatello's "David" (1430–1440) In the Bargello. The figure is shown standing over the head of Goliath.

The Bargello's sculptural highlights occupy two large salons, one on the ground floor and one on the first floor, although it is worth noting that the gallery also devotes many rooms to a scintillating collection of carpets, tapestries, silverware, enamels, ivories, glassware, and other precious objets d'art.

The first room on the ground floor to the right after the ticket hall contains the best of the gallery's late Renaissance sculpture. Most people make directly for three works by Michelangelo: a lurching and very obviously drunk **"Bacchus"** (1497), carved when the sculptor was just 22; a delicate tondo of the **"Madonna and Child"** (1503–05); and a proud-faced bust of **"Brutus"** (1539–1540), the only work of its kind completed by the artist.

Scattered around the room are works by Michelangelo's contemporaries. Among other pieces, a swashbuckling character, Benvenuto Cellini, was responsible for a **"Bust of Cosimo I"** and several preparatory bronzes for his great statue of "Perseus" in the Loggia della Signoria (see p. 213). Giambologna is represented by his famous winged **"Mercury,"** an image that has become the standard representation of the god. In any other company, the works of Bandinelli, Ammannati, and other sculptors on display would shine. Here, they somehow appear second-rate.

Cross the Bargello's courtyard, formerly the scene of executions, to take in the less arresting Gothic works in the ground floor's remaining two rooms (the crests around the courtyard walls, incidentally, belong to the palace's various Podestà over the centuries). Then climb the courtyard's external stairs to the first floor, where you come across a wonderfully eccentric menagerie of bronze animals by Giambologna. Turn right and you reach the gallery's second major salon, the **Salone del Consiglio Generale.**

Sculptures here represent the pinnacle of Renaissance achievement. Michelangelo's preeminent role downstairs is assumed by Donatello, whose most famous sculpture, the androgynous **"David"** (1430–1440), was described by American writer Mary McCarthy in The Stones of Florence (1959) as a "transvestite's and fetishist's dream of alluring ambiguity." Other more restrained masterpieces by the same artist include "St. George" (1416), made for the Armaiuoli, or armorers' guild; "St. George and the Dragon" (1430–1440), sculpted for Orsanmichele; a marble "David" (1408); a stone "Marzocco" (1420), Florence's heraldic symbol; and the **"Atys-Amorino"** (1440), a frivolous putto of unknown mythical origin.

Two other works of immense historical and artistic importance worth seeking out are a pair of **reliefs** depicting the **"Sacrifice of Isaac"** by Lorenzo Ghiberti and Filippo Brunelleschi. These were the joint winning entries of a 1401 competition to choose a sculptor for the Baptistery doors (see pp. 208–209). Also noteworthy are the distinctive 15th-century polychrome terra-cottas of Luca della Robbia, as well as works from most of the great names of Renaissance sculpture—Michelozzo, Vecchietta, Agostino di Duccio, Desiderio da Settignano, and many more.

Most of the rest of the first floor and the entire second floor of the Bargello are given over to a ravishing collection of the **decorative arts** spanning many centuries. Highlights on the second floor include the collections of Islamic art, ivories, and the beautifully decorated Cappella di Santa Maria di Maddalena. The first contains frescoes (1340) by the school of Giotto discovered in 1840 when the chapel was being converted from a prison cell. The fine painting of "Il Paradiso" on the end wall features a depiction of Dante (in maroon in the right-hand group of the saved, fifth from the right). Many Renaissance critics believed the figure was Giotto himself. The chapel's lovely pulpit, lectern, and stalls (all 1483–88) were originally carved for the church of San Miniato al Monte (see p. 239).

On the third floor, look for the enameled terra-cottas of the della Robbia family (Andrea, Luca, and Giovanni); bronzes and other sculptures by Antonio del Pollaiuolo and the Sienese artist Vecchietta; the Sala delle Armi, a display of arms and armor; and the Salone del Camino, home to Italy's finest collection of miniature bronzes. ■

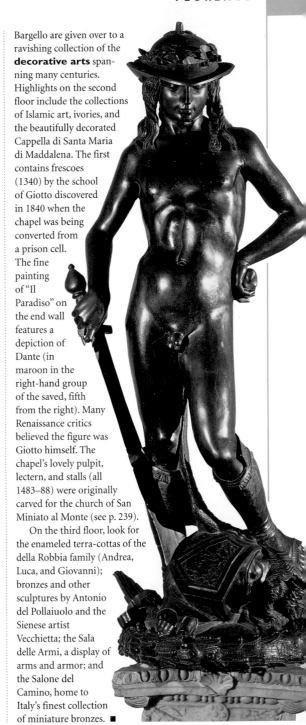

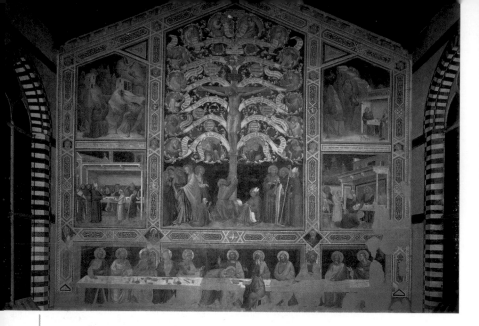

Santa Croce

FLORENCE'S MOST COMPELLING CHURCH IS NOT ONLY AN
artistic shrine—with frescoes by Giotto and others—but also the
burial place of 270 of the city's most eminent inhabitants, among
them Galileo, Michelangelo, and Machiavelli. In the cloisters next
door stands the Cappella dei Pazzi, the church's former chapter
house, widely regarded as one of the most perfect early Renaissance
creations. Finally, the broad square outside, Piazza Santa Croce, lies at
the heart of one of the city's most interesting older quarters.

Santa Croce
- 205 D3
- Piazza Santa Croce
- 055 244 619
- Closed Sun. am.

Santa Croce was commissioned
by the Franciscans and probably
designed by Arnolfo di Cambio.
Begun around 1294, its purpose was
partly to rival Santa Maria Novella,
mother church of the city's
Dominicans, then being built on
the other side of the city. Vast sums
were spent on the church, much
of the money coming from wealthy
Florentine families. Rich Florentines
saw it as an act of humility to be
involved with, and better still buried
among, the humble Franciscans,
while wealthy bankers saw sponsor-
ship of religious buildings as a way
of assuaging the guilt of usury, then
still considered a sin by the Church.

The patronage lavished on Santa
Croce accounts for the ostentation

of its many chapels, most of which
were named after the families that
sponsored them. It also explains the
splendor of its numerous **tombs,**
which begin as soon as you enter
the splendid interior with Giorgio
Vasari's 1570 **monument to
Michelangelo** (opposite the first
pillar on the south wall). Alongside
stands a cenotaph to Dante—the
poet is buried in Ravenna, where
he died in exile in 1321. Beyond this
comes a fine pulpit (1472–76) by
Benedetto da Maiano (third
pillar), and then the **tomb of
Machiavelli** (1787). Beyond these,
and past a gilded stone relief of
the "Annunciation" (1435) by
Donatello, are the tombs of the
opera composer Gioacchino Rossini

(1792–1868) and the 15th-century humanist scholar Leonardo Bruni.

The last (1446–47) was the work of Bernardo Rossellino, and became one of the most influential of all early Renaissance funerary monuments, mainly because it was the first time a human figure was the focus of a secular tomb. Among the works it influenced was the church's other great secular tomb, Desiderio da Settignano's monument (1453) to Carlo Marsuppini, another humanist scholar: It lies across the nave almost opposite the Bruni tomb. Moving back down the church on the north side, look for the **tomb of Galileo** (1737), situated near the entrance opposite the monument to Michelangelo.

Patches of faded fresco adorn many of Santa Croce's walls, sharpening the appetite for the church's pictorial highlights: the Cappella Bardi and Cappella Peruzzi, two chapels to the right of the high altar frescoed by Giotto between about 1315 and 1330. The murals in the latter portray scenes from the lives of St. John the Baptist and St. John the Evangelist, while those in the former depict episodes from the "Life of St. Francis."

Fresco cycles by artists influenced or taught by Giotto fill several nearby chapels. To the left of the **Cappella Bardi,** the chancel area around the high altar is frescoed with the "Legend of the True Cross" (1380) by Agnolo Gaddi (1333–1396). The same artist was responsible for the **Cappella Castellani** (first chapel on the right in the south transept), whose left wall has episodes from the life of St. Antony Abbot and its right scenes from the lives of St. John the Baptist and St. Nicholas (1385). To the chapel's left, the **Cappella Baroncelli** contains a cycle by Agnolo's father, Taddeo,

devoted mostly to scenes from the life of the Virgin (1332–38).

More works by Taddeo and others adorn the nearby sacristy and its adjacent little Cappella Rinuccini. Other paintings, including a celebrated 13th-century "Crucifix" by Cimabue, can be seen in the **Museo dell'Opera di Santa Croce,** a museum entered to the right of the church. The museum ticket also grants entry to the **Cappella dei Pazzi** (1429–1470), an architectural masterpiece designed by Brunelleschi and decorated by Luca della Robbia, Giuliano Maiano, and Desiderio da Settignano. ■

Museo dell'Opera di Santa Croce–Cappella dei Pazzi

✉ Piazza Santa Croce 16

☎ 055 244 619

🕐 Closed Wed.

💲 $

Vasari's 1570 tomb of Michelangelo. The sculptor's body was moved here from Rome ten years after his death.

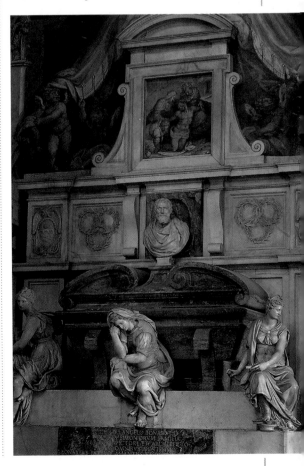

San Lorenzo

San Lorenzo

205 B4

Piazza San Lorenzo

055 216 634

SAN LORENZO IS FLORENCE'S OLDEST CHURCH—IT WAS founded in 393—and served for many years as the city's cathedral. It was also the Medici's parish church, and several vast grants from the family in the 15th century helped transform the old 11th-century Romanesque church on the site into the present-day structure, a restrained Renaissance masterpiece designed by Filippo Brunelleschi.

Bronzino's "Martyrdom of St. Lawrence" shows the saint being roasted to death on a griddle.

The church's first artistic highlight is Rosso Fiorentino's painting of the "Marriage of the Virgin" (1523) in the second chapel on the south wall. In the middle of the nave stand two pulpits (1460), their superb bronze reliefs among the last works of Donatello, who is buried in the church. To their right lies a tabernacle, the "Pala del Sacramento" (1458–1461) by Desiderio da Settignano, while beneath the dome an inscription marks the tomb of Cosimo de' Medici, Donatello's chief patron and the church's main benefactor.

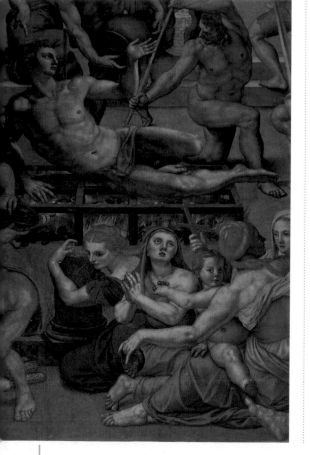

Additional Medici tombs lie to the left of the altar, in the **Sacrestia Vecchia,** or Old Sacristy (1421–26), commissioned as a private chapel by Cosimo's father, Giovanni Bicci de' Medici. Giovanni and his wife are buried beneath the marble slab at the center of the chapel, while their grandsons, Giovanni and Piero de' Medici, lie in a tomb (1472) by Andrea del Verrocchio to the left of the entrance door. Donatello was responsible for the eight colored tondi (round reliefs), the frieze of cherubs, and the two large reliefs and bronze doors of the end wall.

Exit the church at the top of the north aisle, pausing to admire Filippino Lippi's altarpiece of the "Annunciation" (1440). Before the cloister, a door on your right leads to the **Biblioteca Medicea Laurenziana** (Tel 055 210 760, closed Sun. & p.m. Mon.–Sat.), a library created by Pope Clement VII, nephew of Lorenzo the Magnificent, to house the 15,000 manuscripts accumulated by Lorenzo and Cosimo de' Medici. The vestibule, or Ricetto (1559–1571), with its jet black steps, was designed by Michelangelo, as was the reading room at the top of the stairs. ∎

Cappelle Medicee

THE CAPPELLE MEDICEE, OR MEDICI CHAPELS, FORM THE
Medici mausoleum, a three-part complex annexed to San Lorenzo. Its
first section contains countless minor members of the family, while
the second part, the gaudy Cappella dei Principi, is the burial place
of six Medici Grand Dukes. The third part, the Segrestia Nuova, is the
main draw, for it features three major sculptures by Michelangelo.

Beyond the ticket hall, amid the
gloom of the **crypt,** lie the bodies
of 49 of the Medici's lesser lights,
most them placed here in 1791
by Grand Duke Ferdinand III.
According to one contemporary
account, the duke threw the corpses
"together pell-mell…caring scarcely to distinguish one from the
other." The bodies were exhumed in
1857 and arranged in their present,
more dignified manner.

Steps lead from here to the
Cappella dei Principi, or
Chapel of the Princes, the most
expensive project ever undertaken
by the Medici. Begun in 1604, it
was still being paid for when the
family line died out in 1743. The
gargantuan interior features the
tombs of the six Medici grand
dukes—Cosimo I first adopted
the ducal title in 1570. All are
grotesque affairs as are the gaudy
marbles swathing the walls. The
main points of interest are the
stone coats of arms of the 16 major
Tuscan towns under Medici control.

More beautiful examples of
Medici patronage are found in the
Sacrestia Nuova, designed by
Michelangelo as a riposte to
Brunelleschi's Sacrestia Vecchia in
San Lorenzo. The sculptor was also
responsible for the sacristy's **three
tombs** (1520–1534): The one on
the right belongs to Lorenzo, the
arrogant grandson of Lorenzo the
Magnificent, depicted here as a man
of thought; the tomb's two atten-
dant figures represent Dawn and
Dusk. Opposite stands the tomb of

Giuliano, Lorenzo the Magnificent's
feckless youngest son, portrayed as
a man of action with the attendant
figures of Day and Night. The third
sculpture, an unfinished "Madonna
and Child," was intended to grace
the tombs of Lorenzo the Magnificent and his brother, Giuliano. ■

Cappelle Medicee
- 205 B4
- Piazza Madonna
  degli Aldobrandini
- 055 238 8602
- Closed 2nd & 4th
  Sun. & 1st, 3rd, and
  5th Mon. of the
  month.
- $$

**The tomb of
Giuliano de'
Medici by
Michelangelo**

Benozzo Gozzoli's "Journey of the Magi" contains portraits of Lorenzo the Magnificent and other leading Medici.

Palazzo Medici-Riccardi

Cappella dei Magi

- 205 C4
- Palazzo Medici-Riccardi, Via Cavour 1
- 055 276 0340
- Closed Sun. p.m. & Wed.
- $$

TICKETS

The palace's ticket office is located off the garden through the palace courtyard. The stairs to the chapel are off the courtyard immediately on the right after you enter. Lines can be long, as a maximum of 15 people are allowed in the chapel at a time. ■

THE PALAZZO MEDICI-RICCARDI WAS BUILT FOR COSIMO de' Medici between 1444 and 1462, possibly to a plan by Brunelleschi. It remained the Medici's family home and business headquarters until 1540, when Cosimo I moved to the Palazzo Vecchio. Although deliberately understated, the palace and its use of rustication—a facing of rough-cut pieces of stone—would influence other Florentine palaces for generations to come.

Today's visitors come for the **Cappella dei Magi,** a tiny chapel decorated with a three-panel fresco cycle (1460) by Benozzo Gozzoli, a pupil of Fra Angelico. The cycle is one of the most charming objects in Florence—and heavily visited as a result.

Ostensibly, its subject is the "Journey of the Magi." Its actual subject is probably the annual procession of the Compagnia dei Magi, the most prestigious of Florence's medieval confraternities. Several Medici were members of the order, among them Piero de' Medici, who may have commissioned the frescoes. Given the Medici's involvement, it comes as little surprise to find that many of

the family feature as protagonists in the paintings.

Putting names to faces, however, has proved difficult. The obvious figure leading the procession on a white horse is believed to be Piero; the red-hatted figure astride a mule may be Cosimo de' Medici; while the gold-cloaked king riding the gray horse, detached from the rest of the cavalcade, is probably Lorenzo the Magnificent. Lorenzo's brother, Giuliano may be the figure preceded by the bowman. Gozzoli has also included himself in the crowd: He stands on the left a couple of rows from the rear with the words OPUS BENOTTI—the Work of Benozzo—picked out in gold on his red cap. ■

Galleria dell'Accademia

ONLY THE UFFIZI IS MORE VISITED THAN THE GALLERIA dell'Accademia, whose crowds are lured by the most famous Renaissance image of them all—Michelangelo's "David." The statue's home was created by Grand Duke Pietro Leopoldo I in 1784 to house a collection of Florentine paintings and sculpture, the purpose of which was to act as a study aid for students of the city's arts academy.

Galleria dell' Accademia

🅰 205 C4

✉ Via Ricasoli 60

☎ 055 238 8609.
Ticket reservations
055 294 883

🕐 Closed Sun. p.m.
in winter & Mon.
year-round

💲 $$

Michelangelo's "David," was intended to be outdoors.

Michelangelo's **"David"** was commissioned in 1501 by the Opera del Duomo, the body responsible for the upkeep of the cathedral. Its theme—David slaying Goliath—was chosen for its parallels with Florence's recent history, evoking the city's belated liberation from Medici rule and its ability to withstand more powerful foes.

Michelangelo's achievement becomes more remarkable when you realize that not only was the statue carved from a single piece of marble, but also that the marble in question—a thin and fault-riddled block—was considered too damaged to work with. Several artists, Leonardo da Vinci among them, had failed to make anything of the stone, which had been quarried from the Tuscan hills some 40 years previously. Michelangelo confounded the doubters, completing the work in three years, whereupon it was installed in the Piazza della Signoria.

The statue remained in the square until 1873, where its long exposure to the elements resulted in the loss of the gilding that once adorned its hair and chest. Also gone is the skirt of copper leaves designed to placate Florence's more prudish citizens. What remain are the figure's strange proportions—notably the disproportionately long arms and overly large head and hands—created to emphasize the statue's monumentality in its original outdoor setting.

Away from the "David," the gallery contains a variety of pleasing paintings and other works by Michelangelo, notably a statue of **"St. Matthew"** (1504–1508) and four **"Slaves"** (or prisoners). All five (uncompleted) sculptures were originally intended for the tomb of Pope Julius II. ■

Museo di San Marco

THE MUSEO DI SAN MARCO ONCE FORMED PART OF THE Dominican convent of San Marco, a building heavily patronized by Cosimo de' Medici, who backed the creation of a majestic library within its walls and paid for the enlargement of its conventual buildings between 1437 and 1452. Today, the convent is a museum given over to the works of Fra Angelico, an erstwhile monk and prior of the convent, but remembered as one of the most sublime of all Renaissance painters.

Museo di San Marco

🅰 205 C5

✉ Piazza San Marco 1

☎ 055 238 8608

🕐 Closed p.m. daily & 3rd & 5th Sun. & 2nd & 4th Mon. of the month

💲 $$

On entering the former monastic complex you find yourself in the **Chiostro di Sant'Antonino,** a cloister designed in the 1440s by Michelozzo, one of the Medici's preferred architects. It takes its name from Antonino Pierozzi (1389–1459), archbishop of Florence, the convent's first prior and Fra Angelico's religious mentor. You should look first at the faded frescoes in the cloister's four corners, all painted by Fra Angelico, before moving to the far greater works by the artist in the **Ospizio dei Pellegrini** (off the cloister on the right), a room previously used to offer hospitality to visiting pilgrims. Paintings here have been garnered from churches and other buildings around Florence, and include two of the artist's greatest works: the "Madonna dei Linaiuoli"

(1433), commissioned by the linen-weavers' guild (the Linaiuoli), and the "San Marco Altarpiece" (1440), commissioned by the Medici for the church of San Marco, which you can visit next door to the convent. Note the presence in the altarpiece of the saints Cosmas and Damian, chosen by the Medici as their patron saints because of their status as *medici,* or doctors.

A door off the top right-hand corner of the cloister opens into the **Sala del Lavabo,** where the monks washed before eating *(lavare* means "to wash"). The entrance walls contain more frescoes by Fra Angelico, while the large refectory off to the right is dominated by a painting of the "Last Supper," the work of 16th-century artist Giovanni Sogliani.

The *Cenacolo,* or Last Supper, was a common subject, for obvious reasons, of paintings in monastic refectories (rooms where the monks gathered to eat). Several versions are found in buildings around Florence, and there is another, superior, version dating from 1480 by Domenico Ghirlandaio in San Marco's **Refettorio Piccolo** (Small Refectory). This is reached via a passage off the cloister by the old convent bell. The adjacent **Chapter House,** by the bell, retains an impressive fresco of the "Crucifixion" (1441) by Fra Angelico. Beyond the refectory a passage leads to the **Foresteria,**

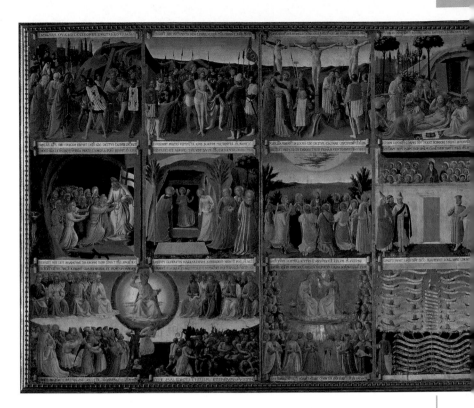

the convent's former guest rooms—today it is full of archaeological fragments and offers goods views of the Cloister of San Domenico, which is closed to the public.

Florence has many artistic surprises, but none as wonderful as the sudden vision of Fra Angelico's **"Annunciation,"** a sublime painting at the top of the stairs leading to San Marco's upper floor. Note the work's inscription, which reminded monks to say a Hail Mary as they passed the image.

Next to catch the eye is the magnificent wooden ceiling, followed by two corridors containing 44 **dormitory cells.** Most of the latter are painted with simple, pious frescoes by Fra Angelico and his assistants, each designed as an aid to devotion for the monks. Fra Angelico's hand is most present in

the frescoes of cells 1 to 11 in the corridor straight ahead of you; numbers 1, 3, 6, and 9 are worthy of special attention—these portray a "Noli mi Tangere" (literally Don't Touch Me), "Annunciation," "Transfiguration," and "Coronation of the Virgin" respectively.

Turn right at the end of this corridor, and you come to a trio of rooms once occupied by Girolamo Savonorola, the monk who held Florence in thrall after the Medici's temporary fall from power in 1494. Turn right by the "Annunciation" along the nearer corridor and you pass the entrance (on the right) to the Michelozzo-designed and Medici-donated **library** (1441–44). Beyond this, the last two cells on the right, both larger than their neighbors, were reserved for the use of Cosimo de' Medici. ■

Scenes from the "Passion of Christ" and the "Last Judgment" by Fra Angelico. The paintings were originally drawers from a chest used to store silver.

A walk from Santissima Annunziata to Santa Trìnita

This is a good walk to follow after visiting the Galleria dell'Accademia or Museo di San Marco, as both are close to its starting point in Piazza Santissima Annunziata.

Admire Giambologna's statue of "Grand Duke Ferdinand I" (1608) at the center of **Piazza della Santissima Annunziata,** a stately square laid out in 1420 by Brunelleschi, before visiting the church of **Santissima Annunziata** ❶ on its northern flank. The church's vestibule, known as the Chiostrino dei Voti, features an accomplished fresco cycle on the "Life of the Virgin" and "Life of St. Filippo Benizzi" by Andrea del Sarto, Pontormo, and Rosso Fiorentino. The interior's chief attraction is Michelozzo's ornate tabernacle (1448–1461), commissioned by the Medici to enshrine a miraculous 13th-century image of the Virgin.

On the square's eastern margin stands the **Ospedale degli Innocenti** *(Tel 055 249 1708, closed Wed.).* Created as an orphanage in 1445, it is known for Brunelleschi's delightful facade (1419–1426) and two interior courtyards, and for a modest museum of Renaissance paintings and sculptures.

Walk south on Via dei Servi, turning left at Via Bufalini, then right onto Via F. Portinari. At the end of the street, stop by the **Museo di Firenze com'era** ❷ *(Via dell'Oriuolo 24, tel 055 261 654, closed Sun. p.m. & Thurs.),* an intimate museum whose beguiling collection of topographical prints and paintings presents the city com'era, or as it was. Flemish artist Justus Utens' 12 lunette pictures (1599) of the Medici villas are especially charming.

Walk west to **Piazza del Duomo** (see pp. 206–11) and then south on Via dello Studio. The poet Dante Alighieri was born somewhere in the tangle of streets here in 1265, although not in the so-called **Casa di Dante** *(Via Santa Margherita 1, tel 055 219 416, closed Tues.),* a mock medieval pastiche given over to a modest museum devoted to the poet. Two nearby churches have associations with Dante: Santa Margherita de' Cerchi was the parish church of the Portinari, the family name of Dante's beloved Beatrice, while San Martino del Vescovo, opposite the Casa di

Dante, was the Alighieri family church.

Walk east on Via Dante Alighieri and you pass the **Badia Fiorentina** ❸, a tenth-century abbey church where Dante is said to have first glimpsed Beatrice. Its highlights are Filippino Lippi's painting of the "Apparition of the Virgin to St. Bernard" (1485) and the Choistro degli Aranci, a cloister with an anonymous fresco cycle on the "Life of St. Benedict" (1436–39).

Turn right, then left onto Via Ghibellina, stopping at the **Museo Nazionale del Bargello** ❹ (see pp. 220–21), before continuing to **Santa Croce** ❺ (see pp. 222–23). If time allows, make a detour to Vivoli, makers of Florence's best ice cream *(Via Isola delle Stinche 7r).* Devotees of Michelangelo may wish to deviate north to the **Casa Buonarroti** *(Via Ghibellina 70, tel 055 241 752, closed Tues.),* a slick museum with a handful of minor works and much miscellaneous ephemera connected with the sculptor.

South of Santa Croce stands the **Museo Horne** *(Via de' Benci 6, tel 055 244 661, closed Sun. & p.m. daily),* a small but high quality art collection amassed by the English art historian Herbert Percy Horne (1864–1916). Now cross the Ponte alle Grazie to visit the similar **Museo Bardini** ❻ *(Piazza de' Mozzi 1,*

🅜 Also see map, p. 205 C4
► Piazza della Santissima Annunziata
⬌ 2 miles (3 km)
🕐 Allow at least half a day
► Piazza Santa Trìnita

NOT TO BE MISSED
- Chiostrino dei Voti
- Museo di Firenze com'era
- Museo Bardini
- Santa Felicita
- Palazzo Davanzati
- Santa Trìnita

tel 055 234 2427, closed p.m. daily & Wed.), a wonderfully eclectic collection put together by Sergio Bardini (1836–1922), the greatest international art dealer of his day.

From the museum, walk west on Via de' Bardi to the Ponte Vecchio (see p. 234), where a left turn brings you to the church of **Santa Felicita ❼**, worth a quick visit for the Cappella Capponi, known for Pontormo's strange painting of the "Deposition" (1525–28). Return to the Ponte Vecchio and cross the river. Head north and on reaching the Mercato

Nuovo, bear west on Via Porta Rossa. Midway down the street on the left is one of the city's most charming museums, the **Palazzo Davanzati ❽** *(Via Porta Rossa 13, tel 055 23 885 for latest details, closed for restoration),* whose interior preserves the decor and appearance of a medieval Florentine house. The piazza at the end of the street contains the interesting church of **Santa Trìnita ❾**, renowned for Domenico Ghirlandaio's fresco cycle (1483–86) and altarpiece in the Cappella Sassetti to the right of the high altar. ∎

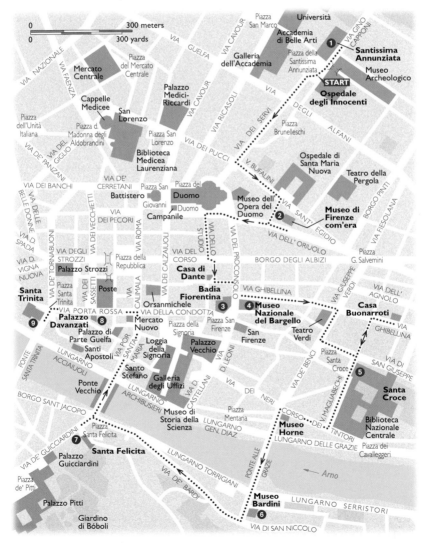

Santa Maria Novella

SANTA MARIA NOVELLA RANKS JUST BEHIND SANTA CROCE
as Florence's most important church. The mother church of the city's
Dominican order, it was begun in 1246, replacing an earlier 11th-
century church on the site. Both the facade and interior are outstanding, the latter home to a trio of captivating fresco cycles and one
of the most influential paintings of the early Renaissance.

**Santa Maria
Novella**

🅜 205 B4

✉ Piazza Santa Maria
Novella

☎ 055 210 113

Santa Maria's interior was
completed in 1360, although its
Romanesque facade remained half-
finished until 1456, when Giovanni
Rucellai, a textile merchant, commissioned Leon Battisti Alberti
to complete the frontage in a more
modern, classical-influenced style.
A Latinized version of Rucellai's
name—Iohanes Oricellarius—is
stamped across the facade, together
with his family emblem, the billow-
ing sail of Fortune. Inside, the
church's overriding impressions are
of size and sobriety. Note how the
columns of the aisles become pro-
gressively closer, a trick designed to
confuse your sense of perspective.

Another triumph of perspective
lies halfway down the nave on the
left, Masaccio's fresco of the
"Trinity" (1427) was one of the
first Renaissance works in which
the new ideas of mathematical

proportion were successfully employed. Florentines lined up for days in 1427 to share in the miracle of a picture that apparently created a three-dimensional space in a solid wall. Note the skeleton with its chilling epigram: "I was that which you are, you will be that which I am."

Santa Maria's first fresco cycle lies in the **Cappella di Filippo Strozzi,** the chapel immediately to the right of the chancel, the area around the high altar. Sponsored by the banker Filippo Strozzi, the paintings (1489–1502) are the work of Filippino Lippi and deal with episodes from the life of Strozzi's namesake, St. Filippo the Apostle (Filippo is Philip). At the rear of the chapel stands the banker's tomb (1491–95), an accomplished work by Benedetto da Maiano.

The church's second, and most important cycle, a work by Domenico Ghirlandaio, is ranged around the **chancel.** It, too, was commissioned by a banker— Giovanni Tornabuoni. Here the themes are the "Life of John the Baptist" (right wall) and the "Life of the Virgin" (1485–1490), although the cycle is crammed with numerous portraits—including members of the Tornabuoni family—and a wealth of insights into the daily life of 15th-century Florence.

The third cycle lies in the **Cappella Strozzi,** the raised chapel in the north transept. Its paintings (1350–57) were paid for by Tommaso Strozzi, a banking ancestor of Filippo Strozzi. They are the work of Nardo di Cione (died 1366), brother of the more celebrated Orcagna (Andrea di Cione), who was responsible for the chapel's main altarpiece. The principal frescoes depict "Paradiso" (left wall) and a pictorial version of Dante's "Inferno" (right wall).

Almost immediately inside Santa Maria's museum (entered to

Right: The kneeling figures in Masaccio's "Trinity" represent the Florentine judge and his wife who paid for the painting.

Museo di Santa Maria Novella

✉ Piazza Santa Maria Novella

☎ 055 244 619

🕐 Closed Sun. p.m. & Fri.

💲 $

the left of the church) lies the **Chiostro Verde** (1332–1350), or Green Cloister, named after the *terra verde* pigment of its frescoes. The frescoes (1425–1430) are the work of Paolo Uccello and depict "Stories from Genesis." The most famous panel is "The Flood" on the right (east) wall, with its twin depictions of the ark before and after the deluge.

Leading off the cloister is the **Cappellone degli Spagnuoli** or Spanish Chapel, most of whose interior is adorned with magnificent frescoes (1367–69) by the little-known painter Andrea da Firenze (active 1343–1377): Those on the left wall portray "The Triumph of Divine Wisdom," those on the right wall "The Mission, Work, and Triumph of the Dominican Order." ∎

The Ponte
Vecchio was the
only Florentine
bridge spared by
the Nazis in 1944
as they fled the
United States'
Fifth Army.

Ponte Vecchio

THE PONTE VECCHIO, WITH ITS LOAD OF OVERHANGING
shops and buildings, is one of Florence's most familiar images. Over
the centuries, it has survived countless floods and the havoc of war
and civil strife. In World War II, only the intervention of Hitler himself is said to have saved it, Field Marshal Kesseling having been
ordered to spare the bridge during the Nazi retreat from the city.

Ponte Vecchio
205 B3

There has probably been a bridge
on the site, the Arno's narrowest
point, since Etruscan times. Under
the Romans, it carried the Via
Cassia, an important highway that
linked Rome to the principal cities
to the north. For centuries
thereafter, the crossing remained
the city's only trans-Arno link,
although its wooden superstructure
was replaced often in the wake
of floods. The present bridge was
built in 1345, whereupon it took its
current name, Ponte Vecchio (old
bridge), coined by the Florentines
to distinguish it from the Ponte alla
Carraia (1218), then known as the
Ponte Nuovo (new bridge).

Shops first appeared on the earlier bridge during the 13th century.
Most were fishmongers and
butchers attracted by the river, a
convenient dump for their waste.
Next came the tanners, who used
the river to soak their hides before
tanning them in horses' urine. In
time, a space was opened at the
center of the bridge—still there
today—to allow the tipping of
rubbish straight into the water.

By 1593, Grand Duke
Ferdinando I banished what he
called the practitioners of these "vile
arts." In their place—at double the
rent—he installed some 50 jewelers
and goldsmiths, many of whose
descendants still trade from the
bridge's pretty wooden-shuttered
shops. A bust (1900) of one of
Florence's most famous goldsmiths,
Benvenuto Cellini, stands at the
middle of the bridge. ■

Cappella Brancacci

IN A CITY OF MAGNIFICENT PAINTINGS, FEW COMMAND AS much attention as the frescoes of the Cappella Brancacci. The work of Masaccio, Masolino da Panicale, and Filippino Lippi, the paintings are considered some of the most important in Western art, executed on the cusp of the Renaissance in a manner whose innovation and invention would influence painters for generations to come.

Cappella Brancacci
- 205 A3
- Santa Maria del Carmine, Piazza del Carmine. Entrance to the right of the church
- 055 238 2195. Reservations 055 294 883
- Closed Sun. a.m. & Tues. Groups of 30 admitted to the chapel for a maximum of 15 minutes
- $

The paintings were commissioned by Filippo Brancacci, a silk merchant and diplomat, and begun in 1424 by Masolino (1383–1447) and his young assistant, Masaccio (1401–1428), or "Mad Tom." In 1426, Masolino was called to Budapest, where he was official painter to the Hungarian court. In his absence, Masaccio's genius blossomed, so much so that when Masolino returned in 1427 he became the junior partner.

The pair's frescoes surpassed anything seen in Italy, dazzling in their realism, dramatic narrative, and mastery of perspective: In the words of Giorgio Vasari, the 16th-century artist and art historian, the "most celebrated sculptors and painters...became excellent and illustrious in studying their art."

Masaccio, however, would die aged just 28, while, in 1428, Masolino was called to Rome, never to return. When Brancacci was exiled in 1436, all work on the chapel ceased. The frescoes were only completed some 50 years later, by Filippino Lippi, whose copying skills proved so consummate that his part in the chapel was only recognized as recently as 1838. Masaccio was responsible for the cycle's most famous image, the stark, emotionally charged panel portraying "The Expulsion of Adam and Eve from Paradise" (left of the entrance arch as you look at the frescoes). Compare this with Masolino's more anodyne rendering of "Adam and Eve" on the

opposite wall. Other panels in the cycle deal with episodes from the life of St. Peter, of which the three most striking, all by Masaccio, are "Christ and the Tribute Money," "St. Peter Healing the Sick," and the combined "Raising of Theophilus's Son" and "St. Peter Enthroned." ■

Right: "The Expulsion of Adam and Eve from Paradise" by Masaccio, one of an influential series of frescoes in the Brancacci Chapel

Floods

Florence is famously prone to flooding. The notorious deluge of 1966, in which several lives and myriad works of art were lost, was only the most recent of a succession of inundations to have plagued the city. The main culprits are the Arno—a river once described by Dante as "a cursed and luckless ditch"—and the surging meltwaters of the Apennine mountains. Also at fault is the position of Florence itself—ringed by hills, close to the river's floodplain, and situated just downstream of the Sieve, the Arno's major tributary.

Florence was so blighted by floods that early chroniclers concluded the city must have been founded by Noah. Accounts over the years abound with tales of watery disaster. "A great part of the city became a lake," lamented one source in 1269, when torrents swept away the Carraia and Trinìta bridges. In 1333 a four-day storm unleashed floods so violent that the city's bells were tolled to drive away the demons blamed for the inundation. And in 1557, Cosimo I introduced primitive city defenses when a flash flood crashed over the Trinìta bridge. On this last occasion, everyone standing on the bridge was killed, all except for two children, who were left stranded on a pillar for two days before being rescued.

Today most visitors see the Arno at its kindest, in summer, when the lazy-flowing waters appear benign. Mark Twain, writing of the river in *Innocents Abroad* in 1869, could not see what all the fuss was about: "This great historical creek," he wrote, "with four feet in the channel…would be a very plausible river if they would pump some water into it." Compare this with the account of another American writer, K. K. Taylor, who described a very different scene in her 1966 *Diary of Florence in Flood:* "A tumultuous mass of water stretches from bank to bank," she wrote, "a snarling brown torrent of terrific velocity, spiraling in whirlpools and countercurrents…this tremendous water carries mats of debris: straw, twigs, leafy branches, rags, a litter that the river sucks down and spews up again in a swelling turbulence."

This apocalyptic scene followed 40 days of almost continuous rain. Around 19 inches (53 cm) fell on November 2 and 3 alone, the days preceding the flood. The final straw came on the night of November 4, when sluice gates above Florence were opened to prevent the imminent collapse of a dam. Apparently, the only people warned of the river's further rise were the jewelers of the Ponte Vecchio, summoned by a night watchman to save their stock as the famous old bridge began to shudder.

At dawn, some 500,000 tons of water crashed through the city, moving with such ferocity that commuters in the train station underpass were drowned where they stood. In all, 35 Florentines perished, and many hundreds were made homeless. Women and children were winched from the roof tops. More than 16,000 cars were destroyed, and gas, water, and electricity were disrupted for days.

Longer term damage was inflicted on buildings and works of art, many of which were submerged beneath water that in places reached 20 feet (6 m) above street level. Damage was

Above: The Ponte Vecchio came close to collapse as the waters rose.

Right: Such was the power of the torrent that five bronze panels were torn from the Baptistery doors and dumped a mile away.

exacerbated by vast quantities of heating oil, recently delivered for the winter and flushed out of basements by the surge of water. Slurry slopped around 8,000 paintings in the Uffizi's cellars and damaged 1.5 million books and manuscripts in the Biblioteca Nazionale.

Donations and volunteers flowed into the stricken city—the so-called Angels of Florence—to help with the cleanup. Huge progress was subsequently made in restoration techniques, albeit at vast human and artistic cost. Even today, only two-thirds of the ravaged paintings are on show, while two huge laboratories, one for sculpture, one for painting, still operate full time to repair the damage of a single night. ■

Palazzo Pitti

FEW PALACES ARE AS COLOSSAL AS THE PALAZZO PITTI, begun by the Pitti family, a banking dynasty, in 1460. So financially draining was the project that the family was forced to sell its creation in 1549, when the palace was bought and further enlarged by Cosimo I. Today, it contains a cluster of museums, of which the most important is the Galleria Palatina, home to much of the Medici art collecion.

Orientation around the gallery's many rooms can be confusing. The collection's real highlights lie in the six ornate state rooms, where the paintings are arranged three or four deep. This is confusing for the modern visitor, but was the preferred arrangement of Cosimo and

the Medici. Any systematic exploration is almost impossible, so wander more at less at will until a painting catches your eye.

Your attention will be drawn quickly for the masterpieces are many. The gallery has no fewer than 11 works by Raphael, the finest being the "Madonna della Seggiola"

(1515), or Madonna of the Chair, and the "Donna Velata" (1516), or Veiled Woman (the subject was reputedly the painter's mistress, a Roman baker's daughter). Several penetrating portraits figure among the 14 paintings by Titian: The most celebrated is the "Portrait of an Englishman" (1540) in the second room.

Another work worth tracking down is Cristofani Allori's erotic and curiously bloodless "Judith and Holofernes" (1610–12), one of the pictures most admired by the palace's 17th-century visitors. It hangs in Room 8, one of seven smaller rooms parallel to the state rooms. The many other painters represented include Caravaggio, Filippo Lippi, Andrea del Sarto, Rubens, and Tintoretto.

The ticket for the Palatina also admits you to the **Appartamenti Reali,** the palace's lavishly decorated state apartments. You need a separate ticket for the **Museo degli Argenti,** whose collection embraces silverware and other decorative arts. ∎

Boboli Garden

Behind the Palazzo Pitti lies Florence's principal park, the Giardino di Boboli, or Boboli Garden, begun by Cosimo I in 1549. Open to the public since 1766, the park's trees, formal gardens, walkways, and fountains provide a green and peaceful retreat. ∎

Palazzo Pitti
🅰 205 B2
✉ Piazza de'Pitti

Galleria Palatina
☎ 055 238 8614
🕐 Closed Mon. year-round & Sun p.m. in winter
💲 $$

Museo degli Argenti
☎ 055 238 88710
🕐 Closed p.m. daily, all Mon., & Sun. p.m. except 1st, 3rd, & 5th Sun., & 2nd & 4th Mon. of the month
💲 $

Left: Raphael painted the "Portrait of Agnolo Doni" to celebrate his marriage to the Florentine noblewoman, Maddalena Strozzi.

Giardino di Boboli
☎ 055 238 8616
🕐 Closed Mon.
💲 $

San Miniato al Monte

SAN MINIATO IS THE MOST BEAUTIFUL CHURCH IN Florence, perhaps even in Tuscany, its glorious colored marble facade visible from across the city atop its hill on the Oltrarno's leafy fringes. Begun in 1013, it sits over the site of an earlier chapel to San Miniato, a saint martyred and buried on the spot in A.D. 250.

The columns on the 13th-century apse and high altar of San Miniato al Monte probably come from an earlier Roman building.

The church was often mistaken for an antique Roman building during the Middle Ages, as was the Baptistery, whose patterned exterior it deliberately copies. The facade's lower section is probably 11th century, its upper reaches 12th century. The mosaic depicting "Christ between the Virgin and St. Minias" dates from 1260. Notice the eagle (1401) with its bale of cloth, a symbol of the Arte di Calimala, the cloth merchants' guild, the body entrusted with the church's upkeep after 1288.

The interior is beyond compare. The beautiful pavement dates from 1207, while many of the pillars and capitals were salvaged from earlier Roman and Byzantine buildings. The center of the nave is dominated by Michelozzo's **Cappella del Crocefisso** (1448), created to house a miraculous Crucifix (now removed) and graced with painted panels (1394–96) by Agnolo Gaddi. Steps to its side lead to the **crypt.**

Other steps lead up to the church's raised choir, dominated by a superlative Romanesque **pulpit, screen** (1207), and glittering apse mosaic (1297). Off to the right stands the sacristy, whose walls are covered in a memorable fresco cycle by Spinello Aretino on the "Life of St. Benedict" (1387). Back in the lower church, off the north aisle, is the **Cappella del Cardinale del Portogallo** (1473), one of Italy's great Renaissance ensembles and a unified composite of sculpture and paintings by Antonio Rossellino, Alesso Baldovinetti, and Luca della Robbia. ■

San Miniato al Monte

🅰 205 D1

✉ Via del Monte alle Croci–Viale Galileo Galilei

☎ 055 234 2731

🚶 It is a pleasant but uphill walk from the Ponte Vecchio to San Miniato via the Costa di San Giorgio, Forte di Belvedere, and Via di Belvedere. Alternatively, take bus 13 to Piazzale Michelangelo.

Fiesole

THE SMALL TOWN OF FIESOLE IS THE MOST POPULAR short excursion from Florence. Cradled in the cypress-scattered hills above the city, roots date back to Etruscan times (around 600 B.C.), predating Florence by several centuries. It fell to its more famous neighbor in 1125, since when it has been a favored rural retreat for Florentines and visitors alike.

Fiesole

🅰 243 D6

Visitor information

✉ Piazza Mino da Fiesole 37

☎ 055 598 720

🚌 Bus: 7 from outside Florence's Santa Maria Novella train station runs regularly to Fiesole's Piazza Mino da Fiesole.

Fiesole's **Duomo,** or cathedral, founded in 1028, has a plain 19th-century facade masking an interior enlivened by Bicci di Lorenzo's dazzling high altarpiece (1450); the **Cappella Salutati** (right of the choir) contains an altar frontal and tomb (1466) by Mino da Fiesole.

A steep lane, Via San Francesco, leads from the edge to the churches of **Sant'Alessandro** and **San Francesco.** Both are worth a look, although the main reason for the climb is to enjoy the fine views of Florence below. Back in the square, another street leads to the pretty **archaeological zone** *(Via Portigiani 1, tel 055 59 477, closed 1st Tues. of every month),* home to the remains of a Roman theater, bath complex, temples, Etruscan walls, and an archaeological

museum. Nearby stands the **Museo Bandini** *(Via Dupre, tel 055 59 477, closed 1st Tues. of every month),* devoted mainly to ivories, ceramics, and Florentine paintings.

If you can take a 1.5-mile (2.5 km) round-trip walk, follow Via Vecchia Fiesolana from the southern side of Piazza Mino. Dropping steeply, the lane passes the **Villa Medici** *(Gardens closed p.m. & Sun.),* built for Cosimo de' Medici, before arriving at the church and convent of **San Domenico.** Once the home of painter and monk Fra Angelico, it contains his "Madonna with Saints and Angels" (1430). Via della Badia then leads to the **Badia Fiesolana,** the town's cathedral until 1028. The lovely Romanesque facade survives, enclosed by a later 15th-century frontage. ■

Tuscany is a pastoral paradise of vineyards, poppy-strewn fields, olive groves, and sun-dappled hills. Age-old towns and villages, all overflowing with churches, galleries, and half-hidden medieval corners, scatter its beautiful countryside.

Tuscany

A cypress-shaded Tuscan chapel

Tuscany

TUSCANY IS ITALY AT ITS BEST. IN Florence, it has the country's greatest Renaissance city, in Siena, one of its most perfect medieval towns, and, in San Gimignano, its single most celebrated village. It also has lesser historical centers—among them Lucca, Pisa, and Pienza—of which any country would be proud, and landscapes whose pastoral glories fully embody the popular image of rural Italy. And as if art, architecture, and countryside were not enough, the region also offers beaches, lots of outdoor activities, and some of Italy's best food and wine.

No trip here is complete without a visit to Siena, one of Italy's most gracious and perfect medieval towns. Less well-known Lucca is almost equally appealing, and shares Siena's combination of churches, galleries, and stunning historical core. Nearby Pisa can hardly be missed—its Leaning Tower is probably the country's most familiar sight.

If Siena is the town you should visit before any other, then San Gimignano is the village you should see if no other. Conveniently located just north of Siena, this quintessential medieval village is best known for its crop of ancient towers.

Foremost among the villages south of Siena, the region's heartland, is tiny Pienza, planned as a model Renaissance city in the 15th century but now little more than a sleepy backwater. Nearby Montalcino is another charming village renowned for two prized red wines, Brunello and Rosso di Montalcino. Slightly farther afield lies Montepulciano, an archetypal Tuscan hill town also known for its wine, Vino Nobile di Montepulciano. North of Siena, the main scenic attraction is Chianti, a region of wooded hills and vineyards that is synonymous with Italy's most famous—although not its best—red wine.

If time is short, keep to the landscapes of Chianti and southern Tuscany, both of which conform to the region's famous rural archetypes: cypress-topped hills, fields of wheat and summer poppies, rustic stone farmhouses, refined Renaissance villas, vineyards, and age-old olive groves. Those with more time on their hands, however, can explore the more rugged reaches of the Garfagnana, a region north of Lucca that embraces the high mountain scenery of the Orecchiella and Alpi Apuane.

Tuscany also has a long coastline, with plenty of places to swim, sail, and sunbathe. Viareggio and Forte dei Marmi are two of the most popular resorts in the north, Castiglione della Pescaia, Talamone, and the exclusive Porto Ercole and Porto Santo Stefano the best to the south, and an archipelago of offshore islands that includes Elba. ■

0 ___ 50 kilometers
0 ___ 30 miles

EMILIA-ROMAGNA
p. 183

MARCHE
p. 183

UMBRIA
p. 269

LAZIO

SS12
San Marcello
Pistoiese
Bagni di Lucca
Vérnio
Firenzuolo
Marradi
Mugello
A1
SS65
SS64
Collodi
árlia
Pescia
Pistoia
SS325
San Piero
a Sieve
Borgo San Lorenzo
Montecatini
Terme
Prato
Dicomano
Mte. Falterona
1654m
PARCO NAZ. DELLE
FORESTE CASENTINESI-
MONTE FALTERONA-
CAMPIGNA
A11
Monsummano
Terme
Sesto
Fiorentino
Fiesole
Stia
Camaldoli
Badia
Prataglia
Lastra a
Signa
Pontassieve
SS70
SS71
Chiusi della
Verna
Vinci
FIRENZE
(FLORENCE)
Scandicci
Reggello
Poppi
Bibbiena
Pieve Santo
Stefano
Fucécchio
Empoli
Figline
Valdarno
1591m
Caprese
Michelangelo
Pontedera
San Miniato
San Casciano
in Val di Pesa
Greve
in Chianti
Pratomagno
Subbiano
Sansepolcro
Ponsaco
Castelfiorentino
San Giovanni
Valdarno
Grópina
Anghiari
Péccioli
Certaldo
SS429
Radda
in Chianti
Montevarchi
Arezzo
Monterchi
Poggibonsi
Gaiole
in Chianti
Búcine
A1
San Gimignano
Castellina
in Chianti
Chianti
SS73
SS439
Volterra
Colle di
Val d'Elsa
Monteriggioni
Castello
di Brolio
Monte
San Savino
Castiglion
Fiorentino
SS71
Cécina
SS541
Siena
Rapolano
Terme
Brólio
Montécchio
SS68
Pomarance
Colline Metallifere
Le Crete
Foiano
della Chiana
Cortona
Castagneto
Carducci
Monticiano
Asciano
Sinalunga
SS326
Torrita di
Siena
TOSCANA
Abbazia di Monte
Oliveto Maggiore
Montepulciano
Campíglia
Maríttima
Massa
Maríttima
Buonconvento
San Quírico
d'Orcia
Pienza
Chianciano
Terme
A1
(TUSCANY)
Montalcino
Bagno
Vignoni
SS1
SS439
Roccastrada
SS73
Abbazia di
Sant'Antimo
Castiglione
d'Orcia
Chiusi
Follónica
SS223
Cinigiano
Cetona
SS2
Punta Ala
SS327
Arcidosso
1738m
Mte. Amiata
Grosseto
Roccalbegna
Castiglione
della Pescáia
Scansano
Sorano
M. dell'Uccellina
Maremma
Marina di Alberese
Magliano
in Toscana
Albegna
Sovana
Parco naturale
della Maremma
Pitigliano
Manciano
Talamone
Capálbio
Porto Santo Stéfano
Orbetello
Ansedonia
Monte
Argentario
Porto
Ercole
Isola del
Giglio
Isola di
Giannutri

Area of map detail
Rome

C   D   E

Siena

SIENA IS ITALY'S MOST PERFECT MEDIEVAL TOWN. AT ITS heart lies the Campo, Italy's most glorious square and the stage for the city's renowned annual horse race—the Palio—as well as the art-filled chambers of the majestic Palazzo Pubblico. Nearby are the Duomo, one of Italy's finest Gothic buildings, and the treasures of the cathedral museum, while all around a magical labyrinth of palace-lined streets and peaceful corners provide a happy hunting ground for hours of aimless exploration.

Your first stop in Siena should be the **Campo**—literally the "field"—a scallop-shaped piazza that has long served as the city's civic and social heart. Located at the convergence of three hilly ridges—known today as the *terzi,* or thirds—its pivotal position made it an obvious site for development. The area was also a point of intersection for the city's fiercely independent *contrade,* or parishes, and therefore the only neutral patch of ground in a combative city. The piazza probably marked the site of the Roman forum and later served as the city's principal marketplace. It acquired its present appearance around 1293, when the city's then ruling body, the Council of Nine, began acquiring land with a view to creating a new public piazza.

A broad arc of palaces grew up around the square, chief among them the **Palazzo Pubblico** (1297–1342), now the city's town hall. Enter the palazzo, bear right up the stairs, and you come to the **Museo Civico,** a rambling collection of state and other apartments adorned with frescoes and paintings. Its two most significant rooms lie side by side: the **Sala del Mappamundo** and Sala della Pace. The end walls of the former are decorated with a beautiful Maestà (1315) by Simone Martini and an "Equestrian Portrait" (1328) of Sienese general Guidoriccio da Foligno, a painting long attributed to Martini (the two painted saintly

figures below the portrait, dating from 1529, are by Sodama). In the **Sala della Pace** is the city's most renowned fresco cycle, Ambrogio Lorenzetti's faded "Allegories of Good and Bad Government" (1337–39). The **Sala dei Pilastri** off the Sala della Pace contains a grand 13th-century Maestà by Guido da Siena and a violent 15th-century "Massacre of the Innocents" by Matteo di Giovanni.

Your eyes are drawn to the **Sala del Concistoro,** whose vaults are covered in frescoes of mythical and allegorical scenes by the Sienese mannerist painter, Domenico Beccafumi (1485–1551). Also noteworthy is the **Cappella del Consiglio,** graced with some beautiful inlaid choir stalls (1415–1428), an intricate screen in wrought iron (1435–1445) by Jacopo della Quercia, an altarpiece (1530) by Sodoma, and frescoes on the "Life of the Virgin" (1407–1408) by Taddeo di Bartolo.

Turn left in the Palazzo's courtyard and climb the 503 steps of the 330-foot (102 m) **Torre del Mangia** (1338–1348), designed by a leading Sienese painter, Lippo Memmi. The bell tower was reputedly named after its first watchman and bell ringer, Giovanni di Balduccio, a notable profligate, or *mangiaguadagni,* literally "eater of profits." (A statue dedicated to him is in the courtyard.) The views are magnificent, particularly those

Siena
 243 D3
Visitor information
✉ Piazza del Campo 56
☎ 0577 280 551

Museo Civico & Torre del Mangia
✉ Palazzo Pubblico, Piazza del Campo
☎ 0577 292 263
🕐 Closed Sun. p.m.
💲 Museum: $$. Tower: $$

over the Campo below, where you can clearly make out the square's nine segments, designed to symbolize the nine members of the Council of Nine and the cloak of the Madonna cast protectively over the city. The tower's great bell was originally used to mark the end of the working day, and the opening and closing of the city gates in the morning and evening.

In front of the tower is the distinctive **Cappella di Piazza,** a stone loggia begun in 1348 to mark the passing of the Black Death. The fountain at the top of the piazza, the Fonte Gaia, is a 19th-century copy of a 15th-century original.

Dominating the Piazza del Duomo is Siena's **Duomo**—a sensational building to which only the cathedrals of Milan and Orvieto come close. Its awe-inspiring **facade** (1284–1296), a Gothic and Romanesque mix of carvings, pillars, and intricate decorative detail,

was largely the work of the Pisan architect and sculptor, Giovanna Pisano (1245–1320). In the interior, your attention is drawn first to the ceiling, whose stone heads represent busts of countless popes, and then to the **marble pavement,** which consists of 56 narrative panels (1349–1547) designed by a succession of Siena's leading artists.

Midway down the north aisle is the interior's first sculptural masterpiece, the **Piccolomini Altarpiece** (1503), whose lower four niche statues are the work of the young Michelangelo. Alongside lies the entrance to the **Libreria Piccolomini** *(Tel 0577 47 321),* a 16th-century library with a fresco cycle (1502–1509) by the Umbrian artist Pinturicchio. The vibrant paintings portray episodes from the life of local-born Aeneas Piccolomini (Pope Pius II).

The chancel features a notable set of inlaid wooden choir stalls,

Siena's magnificent cathedral rises on a site originally occupied by a Roman temple to Minerva.

Battistero di San Giovanni

✉ Piazza San Giovanni (entrance down steps behind cathedral)

☎ 0577 283 048

💲 $

TICKETS

A *Biglietto Cumulativo*, or combined ticket, is available for admission to the Libreria Piccolomini, the Museo dell'Opera del Duomo, Baptistery, and Oratorio di San Bernardino. Buy one at any of the participating sights. ■

while close by stands the building's foremost masterpiece: Nicola Pisano's celebrated **pulpit** and its sculpted reliefs of episodes from the "Life of Christ" (1266–68). Just ahead of it, the wall on the left contains Tino da Camanio's "Tomb of Cardinal Petroni" (1318), a model for many subsequent funerary monuments. In front of this lies the "Tomb of Bishop Pecci" (1426), a bronze pavement memorial by Donatello. The **Cappella di San Giovanni Battista,** in the corner of the north transept, sports a statue of John the Baptist (1457) and more frescoes (1504) by Pinturicchio.

Don't skip the **Battistero di San Giovanni,** the cathedral's subterranean Baptistery, for it shelters the baptismal font (1417–1430), one of the city's best works of sculpture. Its decorative panels were executed by the most exalted

Sienese and Florentine sculptors of their day—Lorenzo Ghiberti (the "Baptism of Christ" and "John in Prison"), Donatello ("Herod's Feast"), and Jacopo della Quercia ("The Angel Announcing the Baptist's Birth"). Jacopo also crafted the font's statue of the Baptist and its marble tabernacle, while Donatello produced two of the font's corner angels. As an added bonus, the Baptistery's walls are swathed in 14th-century frescoes, the work mostly of Vecchietta (1410–1480), an influential Sienese painter and sculptor.

The innocuous looking building opposite the cathedral's facade is the **Ospedale di Santa Maria della Scala.** For almost 800 years it served as Siena's main hospital. Today, it is being converted to the city's premier art and exhibition space. Little that will be introduced

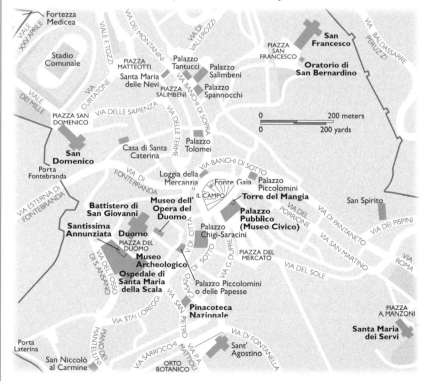

here, however, is likely to overshadow the works of art already in situ. The first of these, in the small vestibule beyond the ticket office, is a fresco of "St. Anne and St. Joachim" (1512) by Beccafumi. Off to the left lie two vast halls—former hospital wards—the second of which contains an extraordinary **fresco cycle** (1440) by Vecchietta and his fellow Sienese artist Domenico di Bartolo (1400–1445). Like other works in the hospital, its cost was met by the many charitable bequests made to the institution over the centuries. Its theme is the hospital's history and its secular content, unusual at the time, offers countless insights into Sienna's 15th-century daily life.

The smaller **Sagrestia Vecchia** nearby has another fresco cycle, Vecchietta's "Articles of the Creed," and an altarpiece of the "Madonna della Misericordia" (1444) by Domenico di Bartolo.

Vecchietta was also responsible for the statue of the "Risen Christ" (1476) on the main altar of the adjoining church, **Santissima Annunziata.** Other highlights include the eerie Oratorio di Santa Caterina della Notte, a lavishly decorated underground oratory, and the hospital's huge, and often bizarre, collection of religious relics.

Tucked away in Piazza del Duomo's southern corner is the **Museo Archeologico** (*Piazza del Duomo, tel 0577 280 551, closed p.m.*), a small but spritely collection of mainly Etruscan artifacts. A spruce, frescoed entrance hall sets the tone for the well-presented displays, with finds from Pienza, Casole d'Elsa, and Siena itself, small centers some distance from the mainstream of Etruscan life in central Italy. The jewelry and goldware in Rooms 8 and 9, removed from a tomb near Monteriggioni, are particularly appealing.

Siena's Piazza del Campo seen from the Torre del Mangia. Its shape symbolized the cloak of the Madonna sheltering the city under its protective embrace.

Ospedale di Santa Maria della Scala
✉ Piazza del Duomo
☎ 0577 224 811
$ $$

The devil—part of a fresco in the Palazzo Pubblico in Piazza del Campo

Museo dell'Opera del Duomo

- ✉ Piazza del Duomo 8
- ☎ 0577 283 048
- 🕐 Closed p.m. Nov.–March
- 💲 $$

Pinacoteca Nazionale

- ✉ Via San Pietro 29
- ☎ 0577 281 161
- 🕐 Closed Mon. p.m. & Sun. p.m.
- 💲 $$

Before you leave the Piazza del Duomo, be sure to visit the **Museo dell'Opera del Duomo,** with its many outstanding paintings and sculptures, most of them removed over the years from the cathedral and Baptistery. The lower-floor Galleria delle Statue kicks off with sculptures, most notably a graceful tondo, or round relief, by Donatello, a bas-relief by Jacopo della Quercia, and several age-worn Gothic statues by Giovanni Pisano. Upstairs, the darkened Sala di Duccio contains the greatest of all Sienese paintings, Duccio's monumental **"Maestà,"** painted for the cathedral's high altar in 1313. Beyond it lies a room with drawings of the cathedral's decorative pavement and the Sala di Tesoro, the highlight of which is an unusual "Christ on the Cross" (1280) by Giovanni Pisano. Another painting-filled room beyond is dominated by the "Madonna dagli Occhi Grossi" (1220–1230) or "Madonna of the Large Eyes," a haunting Byzantine icon that served as the cathedral's pre-Duccio altarpiece. Walk from this room to the museum's external terrace for quite sensational views.

PINACOTECA NAZIONALE

Siena's superb main art gallery is housed in the imposing 15th-century **Palazzo Buonsignori.** Its many rooms offer an in-depth look at the city's Gothic school of painting, a genre heavily influenced in its early days by the stylized composition, intense coloring, and gold backgrounds of Byzantine art. All the major—and many minor—Sienese names are represented, including several of the great masters encountered in the Palazzo Pubblico and Museo dell'Opera. Rooms and paintings proceed in chronological order, revealing the ever greater influence of Florentine art on the more backward-looking Sienese. Later rooms deal with offshoots such as Sienese mannerism, a genre exemplified by the 16th-century works of painters such as Sodoma.

Siena has three principal churches. **Santa Maria dei Servi** lies some way from the center of Siena, but the walk is worth the effort, both for the church itself and the magnificent views from its tree-lined piazza. The oldest of its paintings (first altar of the south aisle) is the "Madonna di Bordone" (1261) by Coppo da Marcovaldo, a Florentine artist captured in battle by the Sienese and forced to paint this picture as part of his ransom. At the end of the same aisle is Matteo di Giovanni's harrowing "Massacre of the Innocents" (1491). A similarly violent depiction of the same event by Pietro Lorenzetti graces the right wall of the second chapel to the right of the high altar. Lorenzetti also painted in the second chapel, left of the altar, along with one of his followers, Taddeo di Bartolo, whose "Adoration of the Shepherds" (1404) also hangs here. Taddeo's pupil, Giovanni di Paolo, painted the "Madonna della Misericordia" (1431) in the north transept.

Fire and heavy-handed restoration have battered **San Francesco** over the years, leaving the church's gloomy interior almost bereft of character and works of art. Its best remaining artifacts are the 14th-century tombs of the Tolomei at the end of the south aisle, burial places of several members of one of the city's leading medieval families. Also worth searching out are frescoes by Sassetta (right of the main door) and Pietro and Ambrogio Lorenzetti (first and third chapels left of the high altar). More remarkable still is the **Oratorio di San Bernardino** *(Piazza San Francesco, tel 0577 280 55)* to the south of the church, whose lovely wood-paneled salon upstairs contains frescoes on the "Life of the Virgin" (1496–1518) by Sodoma, Beccafumi, and Giralmo del Pacchia.

The Gothic outline of the third church, **San Domenico,** dominates northern Siena. Begun in 1226, the austere, brick-built church is closely associated with St. Catherine of Siena, patron saint of both Siena and (with St. Francis) of Italy. It was here that she performed miracles, became a Dominican nun, and received the stigmata. Her links with the church are commemorated

in the **Cappella delle Volte,** which contains her portrait, and in the **Cappella di Santa Caterina** (midway down the south aisle), whose tabernacle (1466) contains part of her skull. The latter chapel also boasts two frescoes (1526) by Sodoma of episodes from her life. Chapels flanking the high altar feature several Sienese paintings, while the high altar itself is adorned with a tabernacle and angels (1465) by Benedetto da Maiano. ■

The "Three Graces" and 16th-century frescoes by Pinturicchio in the Libreria Piccolomini in Siena cathedral

Siena's history

Myth claims Siena was founded by Senius and Acius, sons of Remus, hence the statues around the city of the she-wolf who suckled Rome's mythical founders, Romulus and Remus. In fact, Siena began life as an Etruscan settlement, evolving into a Roman colony, Saena Julia, at the beginning of the first century. Flourishing banking and textile concerns in the Middle Ages then made it one of Europe's most important medieval cities. Its stature inevitably drew it into conflict with Florence, with first one, then the other city achieving dominance. The scales tipped decisively in Florence's favor in 1348, when the Black Death wiped out 70,000 of Siena's 100,000-strong population. The city struggled on until 1554, when the Sienese Republic finally surrendered. Thereafter, Florence deliberately suppressed the city, its decline into a rural backwater one reason for its remarkably unsullied appearance today. ■

The Palio

Siena's Palio is Italy's most spectacular festival. Held twice yearly, it involves a breathtaking bareback horse race around the Campo, together with many preparatory days of drama, processions, drumming, flag waving, and colorful pageantry. The spectacle and celebration are living and vivid expressions of rivalries and traditions that stretch back over 700 years.

A *palio* of some description has taken place in Siena virtually every year since the 13th century. In the early days, it was run around the city streets—only since 1656 has it followed its famous three-lap circuit of the Campo. The prize has always been the same: the embroidered banner, or *pallium*, from which the race takes its name. So, too, is the dedication to the Virgin, the reason why races are run on, or close to, feast days devoted to the Madonna. The July 2 race takes place on the Feast of the Visitation, the August 16 contest on the day after the Feast of the Assumption. Very occasionally, a race is staged to mark another event, the most notable examples being the palios held to commemorate the end of World War II (1945), the sixth centennial of St. Catherine's birth (1947), and the first lunar landing (1969).

Race contestants represent Siena's *contrade*, the districts into which the city has been divided since the 13th century. Today, there are 17 such districts, fewer than in centuries past when there were anything up to 42. Each contrada has its own church, social club, heraldic device, museum, flag, and symbolic animal (from which a contrada usually derives its name). Allegiance to your district is absolute: Church baptisms of new contrada babies, for example, are followed by baptisms in the infants' contrada fountain. Each district also holds its own annual procession and supports a band of *tamborini* (drummers) and *alfiere* (flag throwers), many of whom can be seen practicing on the streets during the year.

Only ten contrade can take part in the Palio. These are drawn by lot, riders from the unlucky seven losers being allowed to accompany the *carroccio*, or chariot, that bears the pallium in the prerace procession. Each contrada has its own particular rival, and as much thought goes into ensuring a rival's defeat as securing one's own victory. Alliances are forged, and bribes offered (and accepted). Horses may be doped, and it has been known for men and animals to be kidnapped. Riders and animals are therefore watched day and night, communication with the outside world being possible only through riders' bodyguards.

The day of the race involves endless ceremonials, all of which make wonderful viewing whether or not you are able to squeeze into the Campo for the race itself. Horses gather for the 90-second dash at around 7 p.m. All but one of the riders are then corralled together. The race begins when the lone rider charges his rivals. From this point, almost

The Palio horse race lasts just 90 seconds, but the pageantry beforehand and celebration afterward, can go on for many weeks.

anything goes. The only rule is that jockeys cannot interfere with another rider's reins. The race is hectic, fast, violent, and dangerous, both for riders and horses. Sand and mattresses are laid out to help prevent serious injury.

Victory is sweet. Thousands of people sit down to an outdoor banquet in the streets of the winning contrada, sonnets are written, vast bets and other huge sums of money are called in. Defeat is invariably acrimonious, recriminations occasionally spilling over into violence, while rumors and memories of dark doings fester for years among the beaten contrade and their members. ■

San Gimignano

TUSCANY'S MOST FAMOUS VILLAGE IS OFTEN CALLED A "medieval Manhattan" after a skyline that bristles with a crop of ancient stone towers. Although popular—perhaps too popular in summer—it is a place that retains its charm, especially after the day-trippers have gone home. It is worth a visit not only for its towers, however, but also for a fascinating art gallery, some beautiful views of the Tuscan landscape, and a pair of superb fresco-filled churches.

San Gimignano existed in Etruscan and Roman times, and then developed during the Middle Ages thanks to its position on the Via Francigena, a trade and pilgrimage route between Rome and the north. The famous towers began to appear around 1150. Their purpose was twofold: to act as a status symbol—your tower had to be higher than your neighbor's—and to provide a defensive retreat in times of trouble.

Plague and the constant strife between aristocratic factions eventually weakened the village, which in 1348 placed itself under the protection of Florence. This immediately undermined the power of local nobles, one reason why so many towers survived (since they posed no threat, there was no need to tear them down).

Exploring the village is easy—you can walk from one end to the other in a few minutes. Start your tour at the southern gateway, the Porta San Giovanni, and then walk north on Via San Giovanni. Stop by **San Francesco** midway up the street, a deconsecrated church now given over, like many places around town, to the sale of the local Vernaccia white wine. Its rear terrace offers memorable views over the Tuscan hills.

At the top of the street, a medieval arch ushers you into the first of two linked central squares, **Piazza della Cisterna** and **Piazza del Duomo.** The first is ringed with towers, medieval buildings, and several tempting cafés. The second is home to the village's two principal sights: the Collegiata and Museo Civico, as well as a

San Gimignano is busy with visitors in summer, but becomes quieter out of season.

San Gimignano
Ⓜ 243 C4
Visitor information
✉ Piazza del Duomo 1
☎ 0577 940 008

frescoed Baptistery, and the **Museo d'Arte Sacra** (*Tel 0577 940 008, closed Mon.*), a modest museum of sacred art and archaeological finds.

The **Collegiata** was once San Gimignano's cathedral, but forsook its title when the village lost its status as a bishopric. Founded in the tenth century, it was consecrated in 1148 and enlarged by the architect and sculptor Giuliano da Maiano between 1466 and 1468.

Beyond the blandest of facades (1239) lies an extraordinary interior almost completely covered in frescoes. Three principal cycles adorn the walls, beginning on the rear (entrance wall) with a **"Last Judgment"** (1410) by leading Sienese painter Taddeo di Bartolo (1363–1422); "Inferno" is portrayed on the left, "Paradiso" on the right.

Between these two scenes, which are painted on protruding walls, is a fresco by Benozzo Gozzoli of "St. Sebastian" (1465), a saint invoked against infectious diseases and often painted during or after plague epidemics (one such epidemic had struck San Gimignano a year before the painting was commissioned). The two wooden statues flanking the fresco, the "Archangel Gabriel" and the "Madonna Annunciate" (1421), are the work of the Sienese master, Jacopo della Quercia.

The church's second cycle (1356–1367), on the left (north) wall, was executed by Bartolo di Fredi and depicts scenes from the Old Testament with biblical scenes from the Creation in the lunettes above. The most celebrated scene, if only because it includes a

The famous towers of San Gimignano: Most Italian towns would once have had a similar skyline.

Collegiata

✉ Piazza del Duomo
☎ 0577 940 316
💲 Church: free. Cappella di Santa Fina: $

graphically depicted penis, is the "Drunkenness of Noah." (Tradition has it that Noah was the first to cultivate the vine, and the first to abuse its fruits.) Also note the lovely scene portraying the "Creation of Eve" (fourth lunette from the left), in which Eve is shown emerg-

Above: Memmo di Filipuccio's fresco in the Museo Civico is probably a warning against the wiles of women.

Opposite: Visitors admire the Salvucci family towers flanking Piazza del Duomo.

Museo Civico

 Palazzo del Popolo, Piazza del Duomo

☎ 0577 940 340

🕐 Closed Mon.

$ Museum: $$. Torre Grossa: $$

ing from Adam's rib. The cycle of New Testament scenes on the opposite wall is earlier (from around 1333) and is attributed to one of two Sienese artists, Lippo Memmi or Barna da Siena.

Elsewhere in the church, be sure to admire the Cappella di San Gimignano (left of the high altar), which contains an altar by Benedetto da Maiano (brother of Giuliano), and to pay the small admission fee for the **Cappella di Santa Fina** off the south aisle. It is dedicated to one of San Gimignano's patron saints, the subject of lunette frescoes (1475) by the important Florentine painter Domenico Ghirlandaio (1449–1494). Benedetto was responsible for the chapel's altar, marble shrine, and bas-reliefs (1475).

MUSEO CIVICO

San Gimignano's civic museum is divided in two. One ticket admits you to the museum proper, another to the **Torre Grossa,** the only one of San Gimignano's towers currently open to the public. You enter both via a pretty courtyard dotted with archaeological fragments and three frecoes (1513) by Sodoma. The museum opens with the **Sala del Consiglio,** dominated by Lippo Memmi's majestic Maestà (1317). Upstairs is the picture gallery proper, crammed with masterpieces by a host of Sienese and Florentine painters, most notably Benozzo Gozzoli and Filippino Lippi. The most beguiling pictures, the work of a minor local painter, Memmo di Filipuccio, hang in a separate room (turn left at the top of the stairs): The early 14th-century panels portray three wedding scenes, including two remarkable vignettes in which the couple share a bath and then a bed.

Take a circuitous route north from Piazza della Cisterna to San Gimignano's third major set piece, the church of Sant'Agostino (*Piazza Sant'Agostino*), and enjoy some of the pretty backstreets on the way. Also spare a few moments to explore the remains of the **Rocca,** or castle (1353), and its peaceful public gardens to the west of Piazza del Duomo. On entering the church, the west wall on your left contains the **Cappella di San Bartolo,** the tomb holds another of San Gimignano's saints. The reliefs (1495) of three episodes from his life are by Benedetto da Maiano. Frescoes also adorn the chapel, and parts of the side walls, although these and other paintings here are overshadowed by Benozzo Gozzoli's stunning **fresco cycle** around the high altar. Painted between 1463 and 1467, it depicts scenes from the "Life of St. Augustine." ∎

Southern Tuscany

FEW AREAS OF TUSCANY DISAPPOINT, BUT FOR SHEER variety of landscape, historical interest, and outstanding villages, none quite compare with the area south of Siena. This is quintessential Tuscany, a region filled with vineyards, cypress-ringed villas, and olive-cloaked hills. Two of the region's finest abbeys are here, along with several of its loveliest little towns, all of which are linked by a tangle of quiet roads that wend through beautiful countryside.

Asciano
⚑ 243 D3
Visitor information
✉ Corso Matteotti 18
☎ 0577 719 510

Abbazia di Monte Oliveto Maggiore
⚑ 243 D3
✉ Near Chiusure
☎ 0577 707 611

Buonconvento
⚑ 243 D3
Visitor information
✉ Via Soccini 18
☎ 0577 807 101

The best way to tackle the region is by car from Siena, heading east in the first instance on the SS438 road. This takes you through the **Crete,** a distinctive landscape of almost bare, sun-drilled clay hills centered on the village of **Asciano**. Pause here to admire the Collegiata di Sant'Agata, a late 13th-century Romanesque-Gothic church, and the surprisingly rich collection of medieval Sienese paintings in the Museo d'Arte Sacra *(Piazza F. Bandiera, book visits through visitor center, tel 0577 719 510).*

From Asciano, take the minor, but very scenic, road south to **Abbazia di Monte Oliveto Maggiore,** a large and beautifully located 14th-century Benedictine abbey. Sant'Antimo (see facing

page) may be more pleasing architecturally, but it does not have Monte Oliveto's majestic artistic offering—a consummately executed fresco cycle (1497–1508) by Sodoma and Luca Signorelli on the "Life of St. Benedict" in the main cloister.

From Monte Oliveto, the SS451 takes you west to **Buonconvento,** a village whose ugly outskirts conceal a pretty medieval kernel. The main draw here is the little-known **Museo d'Arte Sacra** *(Via Soccini 18, tel 0577 807 181, closed Wed., & Mon.–Fri. Nov.–mid-March),* which, like the similar museum in Asciano, has an art collection out of all proportion to the size of the village.

A road south of Buonconvento climbs to **Montalcino,** a village

that from afar appears close to medieval perfection, its pristine hill-top almost untouched by the modern sprawl that detracts from many Italian hill towns. Close up, the town is almost equally alluring, enclosed by walls, crowned by a picture-perfect castle, and privy to magnificent views over the hills of the Crete and the wooded slopes of the Val d'Orcia (see below). The town probably dates from Palaeolithic or Etruscan times, although its chief moment of glory came in 1555, when as the last bastion of the Sienese Republic it held out for four years against the besieging Florentines.

Many people are lured here by one of Italy's greatest red wines, Brunello di Montalcino, which you can buy, along with its cheaper cousin, Rosso di Montalcino, in many local shops. There is also plenty to see, beginning with the **Rocca,** or castle *(Piazzale della Fortezza, tel 0577 849 211, closed Mon. in winter),* which has a little wine shop and offers bracing views from its battlements. Just up the street is the **Museo Civico e Diocesano d'Arte Sacra** *(Via Ricasoli, tel 0577 846 014, closed*

Mon.), full of superbly displayed medieval paintings and sculptures. Walk down to the main square, the tiny **Piazza del Popolo,** and take time out in the Fiaschetteria, a fine 19th-century café.

Isolated in verdant countryside 6 miles (10 km) south of Montalcino, is the **Abbazia di Sant'Antonio,** the most glorious of central Italy's many medieval abbeys. It was founded in the eighth century, possibly by Charlemagne, and built in its present form in 1118. In its day, the abbey lay astride several ancient trade and pilgrimage routes. The most important of these was the Via Francigegna, which also led directly to the growth of towns such as Siena and San Gimignano. Today, the abbey church is beautiful in its simplicity, its interior, based on French Romanesque models, a vision of honey-colored stone and fine medieval carving.

From Sant'Antimo, drive east on the lovely country road into the **Val d'Orcia,** the valley of the Orcia River, where a trio of little villages makes a worthwhile detour before continuing to Pienza

Tuscany at its best in a view toward Monte Amiata from the Val d'Orcia

Montalcino
⚑ 243 D3
Visitor information
✉ Costa del Municipio 8, off Piazza del Popolo
☎ 0577 849 331

Abbazia di Sant'Antimo
⚑ 243 D2
✉ 6 miles (10 km) S of Montalcino
☎ No phone. Contact Montalcino visitor information for further details.

Montalcino's hilltop setting provides far-reaching views over the sun-drenched Tuscan countryside.

and Montepulciano (see facing page). First up, 12 miles (20 km) from Sant'Antimo, is **Castiglione d'Orcia,** huddled around an imposing fortress. Close by lies the hamlet of **Bagno Vignoni,** famed for its main square, which is, in fact, not a square at all, but a large open *piscina*, or pool, that bubbles with water from sulfurous hot springs below. You can bathe in waters from the same source in the nearby Posta Marcucci hotel for a small fee.

Some 3.5 miles (6 km) to the north lies **San Quirico d'Orcia,** a village known for the Collegiata, an outstanding Romanesque church just off Piazza Chigi. Built in the 12th century, the building is renowned for its earlier main portal (1080), considered the region's finest work of its kind. The interior is equally admirable—take time to see Sano di Pietro's 15th-century Sienese painting of the "Madonna and Saints" in the north transept. Also visit the Horti Leonini by the Porta Nuova, a simple Renaissance garden, and the little 11th-century church of Santa Maria Assunta in Via Dante.

A few miles east of San Quirico is **Pienza,** a sleepy hamlet known as Corsignano until 1459, the year Pope Pius II decided to transform the place of his birth into a model Renaissance city. Pius died as the project was barely underway, but not before architects had created a cathedral, papal residence, and a palace-ringed central piazza. This hint of city survives, forming the heart of one of Italy's most charming villages. Although there are few sights to see, images of the flower-decked streets and magnificent views—extending over some of the region's loveliest countryside—will stay with you long after other Italian memories have faded.

The **cathedral** has one of Tuscany's earliest Renaissance facades (1462), while inside are five specially commissioned 15th-century Sienese altarpieces. To its left are two palaces, one of which, the Palazzo Borgia, or Palazzo dei Vescovi, plays host to the **Museo Diocesano** (*Piazza Pio II, tel 0578 749 071, closed Mon.–Fri. in winter*), and its outstanding collection of medieval art and artifacts. To the cathedral's right is the **Palazzo**

Castiglione d'Orcia
🅰 243 D2
Visitor information
✉ Via Marconi 13
☎ 0577 887 363

San Quirico d'Orcia
🅰 243 D3
Visitor information
✉ Via Dante Alighieri 33
☎ 0577 897 211
🕐 Closed Nov.–March

Piccolomini *(Closed Mon.)*, where you can join guided tours around Pius's former state apartments.

Walk west on the main street, Corso Rossellino, and you come to the church of San Francesco, a survivor from pre-Pius Pienza. Beyond it lies Piazza Dante, from which a tempting small lane runs along the walls for more sensational views. Another road drops downhill to the signposted **Pieve di Corsignano,** the village's lovely tenth-century parish church.

Montepulciano is the sort of classic hill town you want to roll up and take home. Ranged over a narrow volcanic outcrop, it consists of little more than a single main street—known as the Corso—a steep thoroughfare that climbs past a group of mostly 16th-century churches and palaces. Start a tour of the town at the bottom of the street at the Porta al Prato. Things

to look out for as you climb include the **Palazzo Bucelli** at No. 70, whose base is studded with Roman and Etruscan remains; the church of **Sant'Agostino,** designed by Michelozzo in 1472; and the small **Museo Civico** *(Via Ricci 10, tel 0578 758 787, closed Mon., & p.m. in winter)*, a collection of medieval paintings and sculptures.

At the top of the climb, you come to the main **Piazza del Duomo,** one of several places around town with stores selling the famed local Vino Nobile wine. Dominating the square is the Duomo, known for Taddeo di Bartolo's astounding high altarpiece (1401) and the sculpture-filled Baptistery. Be sure to follow Via di San Biagio to **San Biagio** (ten minutes' downhill walk), a harmonious Renaissance church designed by Antonio da Sangallo at the beginning of the 16th century. ■

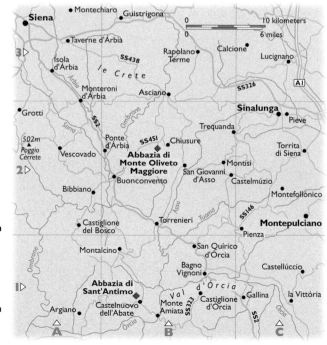

Lucca

"EVERYTHING IN LUCCA IS GOOD," WROTE HILAIRE BELLOC in 1902 in *The Path to Rome*. A few years earlier, Henry James described the city as "overflowing with everything that makes for ease, for plenty, for beauty, for interest and good example" (*Italy Revisited*, 1877). Little has changed since. Peaceful, urbane, and embraced by tree-topped walls, the city today is still an attractive mix of atmospheric piazzas, tiny churches, museums, galleries, and cobbled lanes. Among Tuscan towns and cities, only Florence and Siena are more compelling.

Lucca

 242 B5

Visitor information

✉ Vecchia Porta di San Donato, Piazzale Verdi

☎ 0583 419 689

Lucca owes the gridiron plan of its center to the Romans. Under the Goths and Lombards, it served as the Tuscan capital, rising to medieval prominence as a result of a trade in silk—lingerie is still a major Lucchese money-earner. During the 14th century, the city captured both Pisa and Pistoia, and came close to conquering Florence. Thereafter, the city declined, but retained its independence until the arrival of Napoleon. The Bourbons assumed control until Italian unification.

Today, everything you want to see lies within the old walls. The best plan of attack is to start either at the Duomo and work east, or in the central square, Piazza San Michele, and work north.

Few churches are quite as breathtaking at first glance as **San Michele in Foro** (*Piazza San Michele*), built on the site of the old Roman *foro*, or forum. Its stupendous **facade** combines the marble-striped veneer that distinguishes most Pisan-Romanesque buildings with an astounding confection of miniature loggias, blind arcades, and inventively twisted columns. The plain interior is less arresting, largely because most of the church's funds were lavished on the exterior. It does have one major work of art, however, Filippino Lippi's "Santi

Jerome, Sebastian, Roch, and Helena" (end of the south nave).

Lucca's most famous son, the composer Giacomo Puccini (1858–1924), was born a stone's throw from the church. His birthplace, the **Casa di Puccini** *(Carte San Lorenzo 9, Via di Poggio, tel 0583 584 028, closed Mon.)*, contains a museum devoted to the composer.

Another wonderful **facade** (1060–1241) fronts Lucca's cathedral, **Duomo de San Martino,** in Piazza San Martino, its most important feature is a series of 13th-century carvings around the atrium and the entrance doors. The left-hand door reliefs are by the celebrated Pisan sculptor Nicola Pisano (1200–1278), while the panels between the doors on the "Life of St. Martin" are the work of the facade's principal architect, Guidetto da Como (active early 13th century). Midway down the nave inside, you come to the **Tempietto** (1482–84), a gaudy octagonal chapel built by local sculptor Matteo Civitali (1435–1511) to house the much venerated **Volto Santo** (Holy Face), a cedarwood crucifix said to be a true likeness of Christ carved by Nicodemus, an eyewitness to the Crucifixion. In truth, it is probably a 13th-century copy of an original 8th-century work.

Of greater artistic merit is the "Tomb of Ilaria del Carretto" (1410), dedicated to the wife of Paolo Guinigi, one of Lucca's leading medieval rulers, and housed in the sacristy. The masterpiece of Sienese sculptor Jacopo della Quercia, it is one of Italy's loveliest sculptures. Especially touching is the little dog, a symbol of Ilaria's faithfulness.

The ticket for the sacristy also admits you to the **Museo della Cattedrale** outside in Piazza Antelminelli, which has an excellent collection of paintings, sculptures, and religious ephemera. It also allows you in to the nearby church of **Santissime Giovanni e Reparata,** where excavations have revealed Roman buildings and the medieval remains of Lucca's first cathedral and Baptistery *(Sacristy, museum, & church tel 0583 490 530, closed Mon. & p.m. daily in winter).*

Just south of the cathedral is a good place to climb up to Lucca's magnificent walls (1544–1645). Here you can follow the broad 2.5-mile (4 km) tree-lined walk around the city. Walk east and you soon look down on the **Giardino Botanico,** a peaceful botanic garden entered from Via del Fosso *(Tel 0583 442 160, closed Tues.–Sat.).*

Right: Part of the facade of San Michele in Foro. The pillars and tiny arcades are typical of the so-called Pisan style of Romanesque architecture.

Museo della Cattedrale

 Via Arcivescovado

☎ 0583 490 530

🕐 Closed Mon.

💲 $

Stopping for a chat: Lucca is one of the most pleasant and relaxing of all Tuscan towns.

Green-thumb visitors might also want to explore the gardens of the nearby **Villa Bottini** *(Via Elisa, tel 0583 442 140, closed Sun. p.m.).* A few steps west stands the 13th-century Santa Maria Forisportam (it means outside the walls), a charming but unfinished Pisan-Romanesque church that once marked the city's Roman and medieval limits.

Walk north from here and you come to Lucca's strangest sight, the **Casa Guinigi** *(Via Guinigi 29, tel 0583 48 524),* a medieval town house built by the Guinigi, Lucca's preeminent noble family. It is best known for its tower—which provides lovely city views—and the pair of holm oaks sprouting from the roof! Another former Guinigi dwelling houses the **Museo Nazionale di Villa Guinigi** *(Via della Quarquonia, tel 0583 496 033, closed Mon., & p.m. in winter),* built in 1418 and today given over to an extensive and varied collection of archaeological remains, medieval paintings, sculptures, textiles, and other applied arts.

From Piazza San Michele, pick up Via Fillungo, Lucca's main street,

which takes you to **Piazza dell'Anfiteatro,** a wonderfully distinctive square whose medieval houses were built into the oval of the old Roman amphitheater. A couple of blocks east lies another gem of a church, the small **San Pietro Somaldi.** A similar distance to the northwest stands the larger **San Frediano** (1112–1147), distinguished by its 13th-century facade mosaic and interior treasures that include a sublimely carved 12th-century font, glazed terracottas by the della Robbia family, carvings and pavement tombs by Jacopo della Quercia (fourth chapel on the left), and Amico Aspertini's 16th-century frescoes of the "Arrival of the Volto Santo in Lucca" (second chapel of the north wall).

Southwest of the church, explore the formal 18th-century gardens of the **Palazzo Pfanner** *(Via degli Asili 33, tel 0583 49 1243, closed Dec.–Feb.)* and, farther west, the **Museo Nazionale di Palazzo Mansi** *(Via G. Tassi 43, tel 0583 55 570, closed Sun. p.m. & Mon.),* whose superb rococo decoration provides the backdrop for a fine collection of paintings. ■

Pisa

MOST PEOPLE KNOW PISA'S FAMOUS LEANING TOWER. Rather fewer know that it is one component in a lovely ensemble of medieval buildings; fewer still that the rest of the city—sadly—is a largely modern place (the result of bombing during World War II). Allow an hour to see the tower and its surroundings, and the same again to explore Pisa's remaining medieval highlights.

The **Leaning Tower,** was originally one of the more modest components of the **Campo dei Miracoli,** or Field of Miracles, a grassy piazza that also contains the cathedral, Baptistery, and Camposanto. The tower was begun in 1173 as the cathedral's campanile, and started to lean almost immediately, the result of the weak sandy subsoil underpinning its foundations.

The **Duomo** was begun about a century earlier and with its array of pillars, columns, and colored marbles would provide the model for similar Pisan-Romanesque churches across central Italy. It is known primarily for its bronze south doors (1180), Cimabue's apse mosaic of "Christ in Majesty" (1302), and Giovanni Pisano's astounding pulpit (1302–1311) at the top of the north aisle. An equally staggering pulpit by Giovanni's father, Nicola Pisano, stands in the circular **Baptistery** (begun in 1152). Treasures from both the cathedral and Baptistery can be seen in the nearby **Museo dell'Opera del Duomo.** The Campo's last component, the Camposanto, is a medieval cemetery.

Highlights of the rest of the town are **Piazza dei Cavallieri,** a square ringed by medieval buildings; **Santa Maria della Spina,** an exquisite little church on the riverbank at Lungarno Gambacorti; and the **Museo Nazionale di San Matteo** (*Piazza San Matteo, tel 050 541 865, closed Sun. p.m. & Mon.*), a wide-ranging collection of mostly Tuscan paintings and sculptures. ∎

The Campo dei Miracoli, or Field of Miracles, is home to Pisa's cathedral, Baptistery, and famous Leaning Tower.

Pisa
◭ 242 B4
Visitor information
✉ Via C. Cammeo 2
☎ 050 560 464

TICKETS
The Duomo, Baptistery, Museo dell'Opera, and Camposanto all open daily between 8 a.m. and 7:30 p.m. (shorter hours in winter). A choice of combined tickets are available for two, three, or four of the sights (*Tel 050 561 820*). ∎

A drive through the Chianti countryside

There are many possible routes through the vineyards, olive groves, small towns, and wooded hills of Chianti, Tuscany's most visited region. This loop drive allows you to see the best of the area on a day trip from Siena.

Leave Siena on the SS2 road (the Via Cassia) to the west, keeping your eyes peeled for signs to Castellina in Chianti and the SS222 road to the north, a specially designated scenic route known as the Chiantigiana. Ultimately, you could follow this beautiful road all the way to Florence by way of Greve in Chianti, an excellent way of linking Siena with the Tuscan capital. The route offers a good look at the Chianti region, and is prettier—although far more meandering—than the *superstrada*, or two-lane highway, between the two cities.

For a circular but equally representative tour of Chianti from Siena you should remain with the SS222 as far as Castellina. All manner of diversions are possible from the basic route outlined here, but note that while roads in Chianti are well made, they are also often full of twists and turns. Distances on the ground and journey times are usually much greater than they appear on the map. The region's towns are often relatively unmemorable, making the roads themselves—and the countryside they travel—Chianti's main attractions.

With the countryside come vineyards, hundreds of them. Their grapes produce Chianti's famous wine, a vintage that these days is far superior to the watery, acidic reds found once in cheap Italian restaurants almost the world over. Most of the vineyards are well-signposted and open to the public for buying and tasting.

For an introduction to the region's viticulture, you could do worse than pause in **Castellina in Chianti ❶,** 13 miles (21 km) from the center of Siena, where local wines and olive oils are sold at the Bottega del Vino Gallo Nero at Via della Rocca 10 (the Gallo Nero, or Black Cockerel, is one of the most respected federations of Chianti producers). Also, be sure to walk along the town's intriguing Via delle Volte, a medieval vaulted street just inside the walls.

From Castellina head east on the SS429 to **Radda in Chianti ❷,** an especially scenic stretch of road that runs for 6 miles (10 km). Radda's modern outskirts are unappetizing, although the inner core still retains it medieval aspect. Beyond Radda continue east into the heart of the heavily wooded **Monti del Chianti,** the Chianti hills, and after 2 miles (3 km) take a left turn to **Badia a Coltibuono ❸,** a beautifully located 11th-century Vallambrosan abbey, some 6 miles (10 km) from Radda, now given over to a restaurant and wine cellars. Just south of the abbey, the road joins with the SS408, where you should turn right toward **Gaiole in Chianti,** another important wine town with a quaint old center ringed by more modern development.

Three miles (5 km) south of Gaiole ignore the turns to Radda and Castagnoli off the SS408, and continue on, the same distance again, to the next main junction. Turn left on the SS484 and follow signs for the **Castello di Brolio ❹** *(Near San Regolo, tel 0577 7301, closed in winter).* This vast crenallated castle, approached by a lovely cypress avenue, has been in the Ricasoli family since the 12th century. The battlements offer sweeping views of the Arbia valley and the Chianti hills, while the on-site *cantina* sells the noted wines produced by the castle estate.

Several minor roads, most of them light-color gravel-surfaced *strade bianche* (white roads), lead back to the SS408, either via San Felice or Cacchiano and Monti, the quickest route. Once back on the SS408, turn right and it is another 10 miles (16 km) to Siena.

Alternatively, return from Castello di Brolio to the SS484 and continue 5 miles (8 km) past Villa a Sesta to an intersection beneath **San Gusme,** one of the region's most picturesque villages. From here the return to Siena is slightly longer and more circuitous. ∎

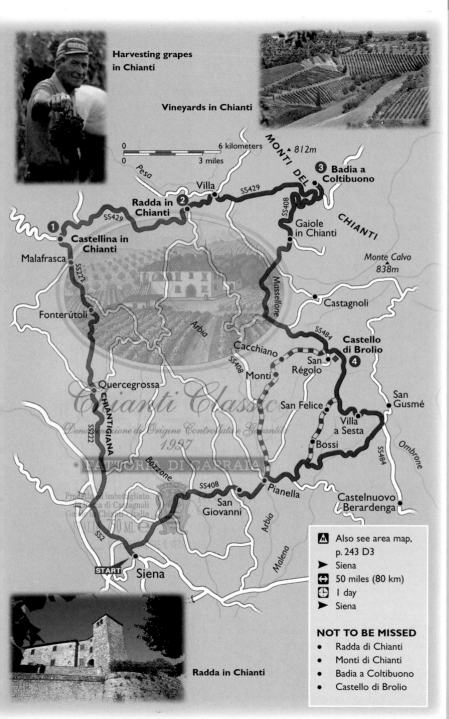

Harvesting grapes in Chianti

Vineyards in Chianti

MONTI DEL ▲ 812m

3 Badia a Coltibuono

0 — 6 kilometers
0 — 3 miles

Pesa

Villa

SS429

SS408

Gaiole in Chianti

2 Radda in Chianti

CHIANTI

1 Castellina in Chianti

SS429

Malafrasca

Monte Calvo ▲ 838m

SS222

Fonterútoli

Massellone

Castagnoli

Arbia

Cacchiano

SS484

Castello di Brolio

SS408

Monti

San Régolo

4

Quercegrossa

CHIANTIGIANA

SS222

San Felice

San Gusmé

Bozzone

Villa a Sesta

Bossi

SS484

Ombrone

Pianella

SS408

San Giovanni

Arbia

Castelnuovo Berardenga

Molena

SS2

START

Siena

Also see area map, p. 243 D3

► Siena

↔ 50 miles (80 km)

⊕ 1 day

► Siena

NOT TO BE MISSED

- Radda di Chianti
- Monti di Chianti
- Badia a Coltibuono
- Castello di Brolio

Radda in Chianti

Arezzo

Arezzo

⚐ 243 E4

Visitor information

✉ Piazza della
Repubblica

☎ 0575 377 678

AREZZO WAS AN IMPORTANT ETRUSCAN CITY THAT
maintained its elevated status during Roman and early medieval
times, when its position astride important trade routes over the
Apennines brought it considerable prosperity. Today, its well-being
derives from a flourishing gold and jewelry industry, and from the
visitors lured by Piero della Francesca's "Legend of the True Cross,"
one of Italy's most celebrated fresco cycles.

**An important
antique fair is
held every month
in Arezzo's
Piazza Grande.**

PIERO TRAIL
Devotees of Piero
della Francesca
(1416–1492) visit
the old school in
Monterchi *(Via della
Regia, closed Mon.)*
to see his "Madonna
del Parto," or preg-
nant Madonna.
Sansepulcro's muse-
um *(Via Niccolò
Aggiunti 65)* has two
further paintings:
the "Resurrection"
and "Madonna della
Misericordia." ∎

Arezzo is not the prettiest of Tuscan
towns—World War II bombing
saw to that—but its modern veneer
conceals an almost perfect medieval
core. Most visitors make straight
for the church of **San Francesco**
in Piazza San Francesco, where
Piero's famous frescoes (1457)
adorn the walls of the apse.

Most of Arezzo's other highlights lie on or close to **Piazza
Grande,** the town's oddly sloping
main square. At the top of the slope
stands the **Palazzo delle Logge**
(1573), fronted by an attractive
Renaissance loggia designed by the
Arezzo-born artist and art historian
Giorgio Vasari (1512–1574). In
the square's top left-hand corner
stands the **Fraternità dei Laici,**
a Gothic palace known for its doorway and lunette sculptures (1434),
the latter the work of Bernardo

Rossellino. Lower down the square
is the rear apse of **Santa Maria,** a
magical 12th-century Romanesque
church whose entrance lies around
the corner on Corso Italia. Pop
inside to admire Pietro Lorenzetti's
high altarpiece painting of the
"Madonna and Saints" (1320).

North of the square stretches the
Passeggio del Prato, a pleasant
public park flanked by the cathedral
and the remnants of the Fortezza
Medicea, the latter a 16th-century
castle built by Florence's Medici
family (Florence captured Arezzo
in 1384). The **cathedral** warrants
a visit for its stained glass (1523),
a fresco of "Mary Magdalene" by
Piero della Francesco (north aisle
beyond the organ), and the bizarre
tomb (1327) of Guido Tarlati, a
14th-century bishop of Arezzo
(located next to Piero's fresco). ∎

Cortona

CORTONA LORDS OVER THE SURROUNDING COUNTRYSIDE, views from its hilltop ramparts extending for miles across the hazy hills and plains of Tuscany and Umbria. As old as Troy, at least according to myth, the town was already a flourishing center when the Etruscans arrived in the eighth century B.C. Today, Cortona has a prevailing medieval look and the town's two museums, several churches, steep old streets, and pleasant feel make it a fine place to visit.

Cortona
🅰 243 E3
Visitor information
✉ Via Nazionale 42
☎ 0575 630 352

As in most medieval Italian towns, you can have as much fun simply wandering Cortona's streets as in seeing the museums and galleries. Brave the steep grades to reach the town's upper levels and the ruined **Fortezza Medicea** (Medici fortress), in particular, where the views are especially good.

Just off Piazza della Repubblica, the central square, the chief attraction is the **Museo Diocesano** *(Piazza del Duomo, tel 0575 62 830, closed Mon.)*, a collection of Renaissance art dominated by two riveting paintings by Fra Angelico: the "Annunciation" and "Madonna and Child with Saints" (1428–1430). Close by stands the **Museo dell'Accademia Etrusca** *(Piazza Signorelli 9, tel 0575 637 235, closed Mon. Oct.–Nov.)*, whose displays are devoted largely to Cortona's Etruscan heritage.

Several churches around town are well worth a visit: **San Nicolò** off Via San Nicolò, for example, has an intriguing double-sided altarpiece by Luca Signorelli (1441–1523), a noted Renaissance painter born in Cortona. Another work by the same painter is found in **San Domenico** *(off Piazza Garibaldi)*, which also boasts a poetic "Coronation of the Virgin" (1402) by Lorenzo di Niccolò Gerini. The most celebrated local church is the austere **Santa Maria del Calcinaio,** often considered— with the similar San Biagio in Montepulciano— as Tuscany's finest Renaissance church. It is located 2 miles (3 km) east of Cortona on the twisting road that climbs to the town from the valley below. ∎

Above left: Views from Cortona's commanding hill-top position stretch for miles across the plains of Tuscany and nearby Umbria.

Above right: "The Annunciation" by Fra Angelico, the Florentine painter and monk who spent ten years in Cortona's Dominican monastery

More places to visit in Tuscany

BARGA

If you are in or around Lucca, consider driving north to this delightful village in a little-visited region known as the Garfagnana. The village sits in the lee of the Orecchiella mountains, nestled on green slopes overlooking the Serchio valley and jagged peaks of the distant Apuane Alps. Its highlight is a captivating tenth-century **Cathedral,** a vision of honey-colored stone fronted by a beautiful panoramic terrace. The facade is adorned with shallow reliefs and other carvings, while the interior boasts a huge tenth-century statue of St. Christopher and a glorious carved pulpit by the 13th-century sculptor Bigarelli da Como.

▲ 242 B5 **Visitor information** ✉ Piazza Angelio 4 ☎ 0583 723 499

THE MAREMMA

The Maremma region encompasses the dismal town of Grosseto, and the medieval charms of **Massa Marittima,** the one town in the region worth a special visit, especially for the magnificent cathedral. The area's coastline is dotted with small resorts and beaches—the best are the undeveloped sands at the Marina di Alberese, the village of Castiglione della Pescaia, and the glitzy resorts of Porto Ercole and Porto Santo Stefano on Monte Argentario. The best coastal scenery is protected by the **Parco Naturale della Maremma,** visited on foot from Talamone, another pretty little resort village, or by shuttle bus (the park is closed to cars) from Alberese south of Grosseto.

Several inland villages are also worth a detour: Isolated Capalbio is a hill-top maze of old streets; **Pitigliano** (*Visitor information, Viale Monterosa, Grosseto, tel 0564 454 510*) is a village of Etruscan vintage superbly located on a narrow rocky ridge; while **Sovana** (*Visitor information, Viale Monterosa, Grosseto, tel 0564 454 510*) is a single-street gem with a sublime parish church, Santa Maria, an ancient cathedral, and a collection of Etruscan tombs. To Sovana's north rises 5,702-foot (1,738 m) **Monte Amiata,** a forest-covered peak surrounded by a coronet of little-known villages.

▲ 243 C2–D1 **Park visitor information** ✉ Parco Naturale Headquarters, Via del Fante, Alberese ☎ 0564 407 098

PISTOIA

Pistoia lies in unprepossessing country between Florence and Lucca, its position and the lure of its rivals accounting for its second-division status among most visitors. However, this is a town with plenty to recommend it. Start exploring in the central **Piazza del Duomo,** ringed by medieval palaces, small museums, and a Baptistery, and visit the 12th-century Duomo, which contains the famous Dossale di San Jacopo (Altarpiece of St. James). One of Italy's most impressive pieces of silverware, the work was begun in 1287 and only completed some 200 years later. It contains 628 sculpted figures and weighs close to a ton. Among the many superb churches, pay special attention to **Sant'Andrea,** which contains a magnificent carved pulpit (1297) by Giovanni Pisano. Also search for the **Ospedale del Ceppo** at the end of Via Pacani, a medieval hospital adorned with a colorful terra-cotta frieze (1526–29).

▲ 243 C5 **Visitor information** ✉ Piazza del Duomo 4 ☎ 0573 21 622

VOLTERRA

Volterra sits on the type of craggy, easily defended hill favored by its Etruscan founders. The rather somber, brooding atmosphere that permeates the town is one that invariably, if unfairly, attaches itself to a civilization most commonly remembered for its cult of the dead. The **Museo Etrusco Guarnacci** is one of Italy's most important outside Rome and Florence (*Museo Etrusco Guarnacci, Via Don Minzoni 15, tel 0588 86 347 or 0588 86 347*). The admission for the museum also allows access to the nearby **Pinacoteca,** a gallery that contains Rosso Fiorentino's mannerist masterpiece, "Descent from the Cross" (1521).

As is often the case in Tuscan towns, the museums are complemented by an old center whose medieval streets are a pleasure to explore for their own sake. From your starting point in the central **Piazza dei Priori,** make a tour of the Rocca (castle), the Balze (part of the town's crumbling rock bastions), and the Parco Archeologico (a park with Roman and other ruins).

▲ 243 C3 **Visitor information** ✉ Via G. Turazza 2 ☎ 0588 87 257 or 0588 86 150 ■

U mbria is the peaceful
land of St. Francis, sun-
hazed hills, dulcet countryside,
and snow-tinged mountains; an
unassuming region whose wonderful food, wine, and unspoiled
medieval towns now rival those
of neighboring Tuscany.

Umbria

Ubaldo, an Umbrian saint

Umbria

FOR YEARS, UMBRIA WAS KNOWN AS TUSCANY'S UNASSUMING SISTER, BUT not any more. These days the region has emerged from the shadow of its more famous neighbor and stands alone as an appealing destination in its own right. Intimate and pretty, the so-called green heart of Italy is tailor-made for a self-contained holiday, thanks not only to its coronet of closely linked hill towns—each a cornucopia of museums, galleries, and secret medieval corners—but also to its wonderfully varied scenery, excellent wines, and honest, unelaborate cuisine.

Umbria shares much with its neighbor Tuscany, including cypresses, traditional rural farmhouses, and vineyards—the last seen here tinged with fall color.

Umbria's earliest known inhabitants were the Umbrii, a farming tribe who were absorbed by the Etruscans after about the seventh-century B.C. Then came the Romans, whose important road through the region, the Via Flaminia, spawned numerous towns. Of these, the most important was Spoleto, a city adopted by the Lombards, the region's next rulers, as the capital of their central Italian duchy.

Powerful city states emerged around the 12th century. Only Perugia, still Umbria's capital today, achieved national prominence. Its fall to the papacy in the 16th century precipitated a long period of stagnation, a period whose effects have only really been reversed with Umbria's emergence as a tourist destination over the last 20 years.

As the birthplace of Francis (1181/2–1226) and Benedict (480–550), Europe's foremost saints and founders of the Western world's

most significant monastic orders, Umbria has an unrivaled claim to fame. So many other saints were also born here that Umbria is sometimes called *Umbra santa*, or *Umbra mistica*—holy or mystical Umbria.

There are two essential stops in Umbria: Orvieto, with its majestic Gothic cathedral, and Assisi, home to the astounding Basilica di San Francesco. The latter is the burial place of Assisi-born St. Francis, Italy's patron saint, and a building that helped alter the course of Italian, and thus European, art. Giotto, Cimabue, and all the other leading Italian artists of their day painted here, beginning a move away from the stilted conventions of Byzantine art to a more naturalistic style of painting that would culminate in the Renaissance.

But to leave Umbria having seen only these sights would be a mistake. One of the region's

Area of map detail

strengths is the proximity of its many towns and villages so you can easily visit other attractions even on a short trip. Perugia is the biggest place, and worth a day's visit. Stay in Spoleto, one of central Italy's most charming towns, or in one of the smaller hill-top centers such as Todi, Spello, or Montefalco. Assisi is also a good base, despite its popularity, as it quietens down considerably after the day-trippers have gone.

More remote towns, such as Gubbio, a medieval gem, are intriguing, as is Norcia in Umbria's wilder and more mountainous eastern margins. The town is a gourmet's paradise and an excellent base for exploring the Parco Nazionale dei Monti Sibillini, one of Italy's newest national parks. Scenery in the park embraces the Sibillini mountain, situated in the Marche, one of the Apennines' major massifs, and the extraordinary Piano Grande, a beautiful flower-filled plain enclosed by a vast bowl of mountains. Hiking in the park is excellent, thanks to the scenery and the availability of good maps, a rarity in central and southern Italy.

Landscapes in western Umbria are more pastoral, their beauty subtle and insinuating and many are similar to Tuscany at its best. ■

Perugia

Perugia
▲ 271 B3
Visitor information
✉ Piazza IV
Novembre 3
☎ 075 572 3327 or
075 573 6458

PENETRATE THE JUMBLE OF HIGHWAYS AND DISPIRITING
suburbs encircling Umbria's capital, and you discover a wonderfully
atmospheric old center still resonating with the echoes of its
Etruscan, Roman, and medieval past. As well as the sights clustered
around Piazza IV Novembre, the main square, there is plenty to see
farther afield, so put on your walking shoes and be prepared to cover
plenty of ground during the course of a day's sightseeing.

**Perugia's Piazza IV
Novembre con-
tains the cathedral
and the Fontana
Maggiore, one
of Italy's loveliest
fountains.**

Start your visit by strolling Corso
Vannucci, the pedestrians-only
street that cuts through Perugia's
medieval heart. In Piazza IV
Novembre, at its northern end,
is the Fontana Maggiore (1277), a
fountain created by the father-and-

son team of Nicola and Giovanni
Pisano, Pisan-based sculptors
best known for their pulpits in Siena
and Pisa (see pp. 244–49
and p. 263). To its rear rises the
Duomo (begun in 1345), whose
interior contains the tombs of two
popes who died in the city (Urban
IV was almost certainly poisoned
and Martin IV expired after eating
a surfeit of eels). Paintings here
include the late 15th-century
"Madonna delle Grazie" (third pillar
of the south nave), a work reputed
to have miraculous powers, hence
its many votive offerings. Also see
the **Cappella del Sant'Anello**
(first chapel in the north aisle),
which contains a piece of agate said
to be the Virgin's wedding ring.

PALAZZO DEI PRIORI
The corner of Piazza IV Novembre
and Corso Vannucci is filled by
one of Italy's most formidable
civic palaces, the Palazzo dei Priori
(1293–1443), home to four separate
sights. The first, the **Sala dei
Notari** (Closed Mon. except
July–Sept.), a meeting place for the
city's medieval lawyers, contains an
impressive vaulted ceiling and the
coats of arms of Perugia's medieval
podestà, or magistrates. Its main
hall is entered via the fan-shaped
steps off the piazza.

Farther down the Corso at No.
15 lies the entrance to the **Sala del
Collegio della Mercanzia** (Tel
075 573 0366, closed p.m. Sun. &
Mon.), former meeting place of the

city's merchants' guild. The tiny 15th-century room is almost completely covered in magnificently detailed wood paneling. A few steps away at No. 25 lies the entrance to the **Collegio del Cambio** *(Tel 075 573 0366, closed p.m. Sun. & Mon.)*, which once hosted the money changers' guild. The city's favorite son, painter Pietro Vannucci (1446–1523), better known as Perugino, provided the decoration—the frescoes (1496) here are considered to be his masterpiece.

Save the palace's pride and joy for last, the **Galleria Nazionale dell'Umbria** *(Tel 075 574 1247, closed p.m. Sun. & first Mon. of every month)*, a large picture gallery on the fourth floor (enter via the palace's main door). Its paintings combine the best of Umbrian art over the centuries with superlative Tuscan works, such as the two paintings of the "Madonna and Child with Saints" by Fra Angelico and Piero della Francesca (1437 and 1460).

Head west from the Corso on Via dei Priori, the most picturesque of Perugia's many medieval streets. You pass a collection of towers and tiny churches before emerging in front of the **Oratorio di San Bernardino,** celebrated for Agostino di Duccio's sculpted and multi-colored facade (1457). Swing north toward Piazza Fontebraccio, where you can see the Arco di Augusto (third to first century B.C.), an Etruscan-Roman gateway, before following Corso Garibaldi north to the churches of **Sant'Agostino** and **Sant'Angelo.**

West of the piazza, the key sights are an Etruscan well in Piazza Danti and the church of **San Severo** *(Piazza Raffaello, tel 075 573 0366)*, which contains a painting by Raphael. Both are easily seen before heading south on Corso Cavour which brings you to **San Domenico,** Perugia's largest church, known for the early 14th-century Gothic tomb of Benedict XI (right of the altar). Just off the same street are the **Museo Archeologico** *(Piazza Giordano Bruno 10, tel 075 572 7141, closed Sun. p.m.)*, whose displays explore Perugia's Roman and Etruscan heritage, and the beautiful church of **San Pietro,** which must not be missed. ■

The Sala dei Notari (1293) is one of the oldest parts of Perugia's Palazzo dei Priori. The coats-of-arms belonged to the town's medieval magistrates.

Assisi

ASSISI IS CELEBRATED AS THE BIRTHPLACE OF ST. FRANCIS, patron saint of Italy, founder of the Franciscan order, and one of the most influential religious figures of the medieval world. His twin-churched basilica, adorned with frescoes by the greatest painters of their day, is one of Europe's most important artistic and sacred shrines. At the same time, Assisi is an attractive hill town in its own right, full of churches, galleries, flower-decked streets, and lovely, pinky-stoned medieval buildings.

St. Francis in the simple garb of a Franciscan monk. The saint was never a priest and held no formal office.

Assisi's principal sight, the Basilica di San Francesco (begun in 1229), lies at the town's western edge, meaning you are initially likely to find yourself in the more central **Piazza del Comune,** probably the site of the old Roman forum. Its northern flank is dominated by the first-century **Tempio di Minerva,** an almost perfectly preserved six-columned Roman temple pediment. Opposite stands the Palazzo dei Priori, a palace that contains the town's **Pinacoteca,** or picture gallery, a modest but interesting collection of medieval and Renaissance Umbrian paintings *(Piazza del Comune 1, tel 075 812 579).* Tucked away off the western edge of the square, is the **Museo e**

Foro Romano, which offers the chance to explore excavations of the Roman remains below the piazza *(Via Portica 2, tel 075 813 053).*

The **Basicilica di San Francesco** hit world headlines in 1997, when earthquakes brought down part of its Upper Church, killing four people and destroying several of its many frescoes. Artistic damage to the building was exaggerated, however, and the greatest of its frescoes survived. Thus in the **Upper Church,** a soaring Gothic space, you can still see Giotto's peerless fresco cycle on the "Life of St. Francis" (1290–95), together with works by Giotto's teacher, Cimabue. In the subdued, crypt-like **Lower Church,** the walls are

smothered in more frescoes by Giotto, the anonymous "Master of San Francesco," and the leading Sienese artists Simone Martini and Pietro Lorenzetti. The Lower Church also contains the tomb of St. Francis, entered via a stone staircase midway down the nave.

This tomb was discovered in 1818 after two months of digging, Francis having been buried in secret to prevent the theft of his body (holy relics during the Middle Ages had immense value). Francis died in 1226 and was canonized just two years later. Donations from across Europe funded construction of the basilica, an early example of Italian Gothic whose single-naved Upper Church influenced Franciscan and other churches for years to come.

Walking back from the basilica, you should detour south to take in **San Pietro,** a pleasing 13th-century Romanesque church, and then return to Piazza del Comune either on Via Ancaiani, an atmospheric old street, or the busier Via San Francesco. On the latter, look for the 15th-century **Oratorio dei Pellegrini** at No. 11, covered in medieval Umbrian frescoes. Once back in Piazza del Comune, a short walk east brings you to the **Basilica di Santa Chiara,** burial place of St. Clare (Chiara), Francis's early companion and founder of the Clarissan order of nuns. To the north is the **Duomo** (begun in 1140 over an earlier 1029 base), its dull interior redeemed by an outstanding Romanesque facade. Farther north rises the **Rocca Maggiore,** the town's partly ruined castle, whose grassy ramparts offer far-reaching views over Assisi and the surrounding countryside.

Be sure to visit the **Eremo delle Carceri,** a Franciscan monastery secreted in lovely countryside some 2 miles (3 km) from the town center. The interior is fascinating—you get to see the primitive cell once used by St. Francis—and the surrounding woods offer a pretty network of easy trails. Less appealing, but equally important to pilgrims, is **Santa Maria degli Angeli,** a church built over the spot where St. Francis died: It is located in the village of the same name on the plain below Assisi. ◾

Assisi

🅰 271 B3

Visitor information

✉ Piazza del Comune 12

☎ 075 812 450

Pilgrims gather at San Damiano, the church where St. Francis first received his calling from God.

A drive ino the heart of Umbria

The lesser-known hill towns between Spoleto and Assisi are the highlights of this bucolic drive off Umbria's beaten track.

Leave Assisi by going east to the **Eremo delle Carceri ❶** (see p. 275) turning left just beyond the monastery to follow the road as it climbs through the woods to the open slopes of **Monte Subasio ❷,** the whale-backed mountain that rears up above the town. Much of the road is gravel surfaced but sound, although if the weather is poor you may want to take the main SS75 road from Santa Maria degli Angeli direct to Spello. This is very much a second choice, however, for the Subasio road, which reaches 4,232 feet (1,290 m), offers quite unforgettable views and the opportunity to get out of the car for a stroll across the mountain's grassy meadows.

The Subasio road descends to the walled town of **Spello ❸** (Hispellum for the Romans) where you should park outside the cramped medieval center and then explore on foot. Most sights are ranged along the town's main street, beginning at the bottom of the hill with the Porta Consolare, a Roman gateway. Farther up the street stands the church of **Santa Maria Maggiore,** which contains a celebrated **fresco cycle** of scenes from the "Life of the Virgin" (1501) by Pinturicchio, one of Umbria's leading Renaissance painters. More works of art await to the left of the church in the excellent **Pinacoteca Civica** (*Piazza Giacomo Matteotti 10, tel 0742 301 497, closed Mon.*), while another painting by Pinturicchio stands in the south transept of the nearby church of Sant'Andrea. Climb to the top of the town for some excellent views and visit the **Villa Fidelia** (*Via Centrale Umbra, tel 0742 651 726, closed Mon.–Fri. Sept.–June*) for its collection of old furniture, sculpture, and costumes.

Take the main SS75 road from Spello toward Foligno, leaving it at the first major junction and following signs to **Bevagna ❹** on the SS316. A former staging post on the Roman Via Flaminia, Bevagna today is a classic rural backwater centered on **Piazza Filippo Silvestri,** a stunning medieval square. Two lovely 12th-century Romanesque churches face one another across the piazza,

San Silvestro and San Michele. Also see the **Mosaico Romano,** a well-preserved Roman mosaic at Via Porta Guelfa 4—for entry ring for the custodian next door at Via Porta Guelfa 2 (*Tel 0743 360 306*). Close by are the ruins of a classical temple and Roman amphitheater (*Via dell'Anfiteatro*).

A scenic road leads south from Bevagna to **Montefalco ❺** (the name means falcon's mount), testimony to the vast views of the Vale of Spoleto available from the town's hilltop aerie. This is one of the nicest towns for miles around, and a good place to stay if you require a base in the region. It is also famous for its red wines, notably Sagrantino and Sagrantino Passito, the latter an unusual red dessert wine. Chief sight is the magnificent modern gallery housed in the former church of **San Francesco** (*Via Ringhiera Umbra, tel 0742 379 598*), a collection of medieval paintings based around a superb 15th-century fresco cycle by Benozzo Gozzoli. More frescoes can be seen in the churches of Sant'Agostino (*Via Umberto I*), **Sant'Illuminata** (*Via Verdi*), and **San Fortunato,** the last prettily located just off the road that leads south out of the town.

Turn left at the intersection just beyond San Fortunato and follow signs to the village of **Trevi ❻,** which soon appears high above you on a spectacular pyramidal hill. Paintings by Perugino, together with works by more minor local painters, can be seen in the **Museo della Città** (*San Francesco, Largo Don Bosco, tel 0742 781150, closed Mon. year-round & Tues.–Thurs. Oct.–March*) and the churches of San Martino and Madonna delle Lacrime. After exploring the town, return to the valley and turn south on the SS3 toward Spoleto. If time allows, stop off at the **Tempio del Clitunno,** an eighth-century church, and the **Fonti del Clitunno ❼,** limpid pools and springs that have been renowned since classical times. Both are signposted off the road south of Trevi. From the Fonti, continue south 7 miles (11 km) on the SS3 to Spoleto (see p. 278–79). ∎

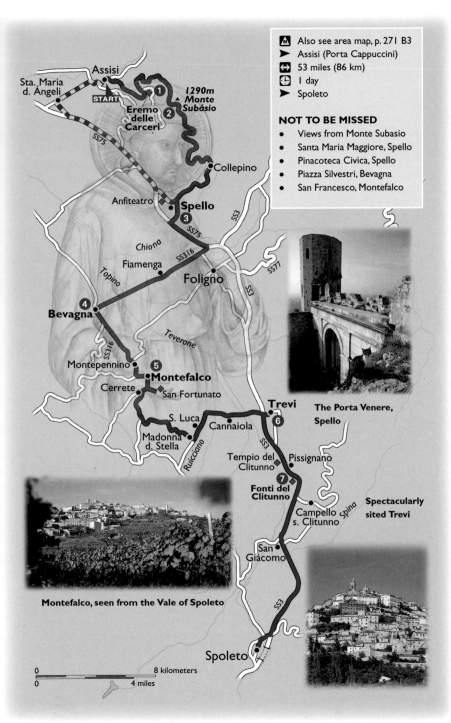

Also see area map, p. 271 B3
Assisi (Porta Cappuccini)
53 miles (86 km)
1 day
Spoleto

NOT TO BE MISSED

- Views from Monte Subasio
- Santa Maria Maggiore, Spello
- Pinacoteca Civica, Spello
- Piazza Silvestri, Bevagna
- San Francesco, Montefalco

Assisi

Sta. Maria d. Ángeli

START

Eremo delle Carceri

1290m ▲ Monte Subásio

SS75

Collepino

Anfiteatro   Spello

Chiona

Fiamenga

SS316

Foligno

SS3

SS77

Topino

Bevagna

Teverone

Montepennino

Cerrete   Montefalco

San Fortunato

S. Luca   Cannaiola

Madonna d. Stella

Ruicciano

Trevi

Tempio del Clitunno   Pissignano

Fonti del Clitunno

Campello s. Clitunno

Spina

San Giácomo

SS3

Spoleto

The Porta Venere, Spello

Spectacularly sited Trevi

Montefalco, seen from the Vale of Spoleto

0   8 kilometers
0   4 miles

Spoleto

Spoleto
🗺 271 B2
Visitor information
✉ Piazza della Libertà 7
☎ 0743 220 311

SPOLETO IS ONE OF CENTRAL ITALY'S MOST CHARMING towns. Founded by the Umbrians, it subsequently became a major Roman colony and later the capital of a far-reaching Lombard duchy. Today, it is best known for its annual Festival of the Two Worlds, one of Europe's leading arts and music festivals, and for the beauty of its cathedral, surrounding countryside, and many Romanesque churches.

The bell tower of Spoleto's beautiful cathedral was built with stone from the town's old Roman amphitheater.

Start a tour of medieval Spoleto in the **Piazza della Libertà,** where you can pick up a detailed map of the town from the well-stocked visitor center. Across the square lies the first-century **Teatro Romano,** a Roman theater that is visited in conjunction with Spoleto's modest

Museo Archeologico (*Via Sant' Agata, tel 0743 223 277, closed Sun. p.m.*). Walk up from the square through Piazza della Fontana to the church of **Sant'Ansano,** whose crypt contains fragments of a Roman temple and well-preserved Byzantine frescoes. Beyond the church lies the **Arco di Druso** (A.D. 23), a Roman arch that opens into **Piazza del Mercato,** site of the former Roman forum.

Pause here to explore the mouthwatering food shops dotting the square. The café with lots of outdoor tables on the west side of the piazza is one of the best places in town to break for refreshments. Then take the alley to the right of the fountain clock to the **Palazzo Comunale,** home of the local **Pinacoteca,** or picture gallery (*Corso Mazzin, Vicolo III No. 2, tel 0743 45 940, closed Mon.*), worth seeing as much for its beautifully decorated salons as the paintings themselves. The ticket to the gallery also allows you to visit the nearby **Casa Romana,** part of a first-century Roman house.

Carry on up the cobbled alley beyond the Palazzo Comunale, and you emerge in Piazza Campitello. From here a quiet lane encircles the Rocca, Spoleto's picture-perfect medieval fortress, offering superb views of the Umbrian countryside and Spoleto's most famous sight, the gargantuan **Ponte delle Torri.** This masterpiece of medieval engineering (it stands 262 feet/80 m high), was built in the 14th century, possibly over an earlier Roman aqueduct, and was designed to carry water from the slopes of Monteluco, the forest-covered hill above Spoleto. You might want to stroll some of the easy trails in the woods across the bridge—climb the steps and bear left and a lovely level path eventually brings you to a peaceful olive grove, or follow the tree-shaded lane here to **San Pietro,** a church known for the 12th-century Romanesque carvings on its facade.

If not, save San Pietro for later and return to Piazza Campitello, where Via Saffi leads down past the fan-shaped piazza fronting Spoleto's idyllic **cathedral** (1198). The cathedral's apse contains one of Umbria's major fresco cycles, "Scenes from the Life of the Virgin" (1467) by the important Florentine painter Fra Lippo Lippi (1406–1469). Other treasures in the church include paintings by Pinturicchio, one of two surviving letters written by St. Francis, and a beautiful 12th-century patterned marble floor.

Return to Via Saffi where a door on the right, a few steps farther down, opens into a court-yard containing the church of **Sant'Eufemia,** a beautifully plain Romanesque church remarkable for its *matroneum,* an upper gallery once used to segregate women from the rest of the congregation. The admission fee for the church also allows you access to the **Museo Diocesano** (*Via Saffi 13, tel 0743 223 245*), the town's principal museum, left of the church. The displays here include numerous interesting medieval paintings from churches in and around Spoleto, as well as Tuscan and Sienese works, the best of which is Filippino Lippi's "Madonna and Child with Saints" (1485). Also fascinating is the museum's collection of votive

tiles, each of which contains a little cartoonlike painting.

Bombing in World War II, and Spoleto's expansion over the last four decades, means that the lower town is largely modern. Three Romanesque churches, however, make a visit here worthwhile. The easiest to see is **San Gregorio** in Piazza Garibaldi, while a short walk east brings you to **San Ponziano,** whose dull interior is redeemed by a tremendous facade and interesting crypt. Nearby, in the town's main cemetery, stands **San Salvatore,** one of Italy's oldest churches, whose fifth-century interior is modeled on an ancient Roman basilica. ■

The church of San Pietro is glimpsed through the arches of the Ponte delle Torri, a huge medieval aqueduct.

Gubbio

Gubbio

⟲ 271 B3

Visitor information

✉ Piazza Oderisi 6

☎ 075 922 0693 or
075 922 0790

BEAUTIFUL FOREST-COVERED MOUNTAINS FRAME GUBBIO'S medieval skyline of towers, battlemented ramparts, and orange-tiled rooftops. Wilder than the bucolic hilltowns to the west, this lovely but isolated town has long been remote from the Umbrian mainstream, having marked the limit of Etruscan expansion in the region. Today, it is known for its ceramics and extravagant May pageant.

Every May, Gubbio holds the Corsa dei Ceri, or Race of the Candles, a pageant in medieval costume.

Most approaches to Gubbio leave you in Piazza Quaranta Martiri, below the old town proper, where it is worth dropping into the church of **San Francesco** to see a series of frescoes (1410) by the Gubbian painter Ottaviano Nelli (left of the high apse). Opposite the church,

note the 14th-century **Loggia del Tiratoio,** once used for drying wool: The washed cloth dried evenly in the loggia's shade. To its right, Via della Repubblica climbs to the medieval quarter, culminating in a series of steps that lead to the central **Piazza Grande.**

This broad piazza provides the stage for the **Palazzo dei Consoli,** the work of local architect Gattapone, the man responsible for Spoleto's imposing Ponte delle Torri (see p. 278). The palace plays host to the **Museo Civico,** the town's main museum and picture gallery (*Piazza Grande, tel 075 927 4298*), best known for the Eugubine Tablets, a unique series of first- and second-century B.C. bronzes inscribed with Latin and Etruscan characters.

North of the square are the **Duomo,** interesting for its grace-fully arched ceiling, and the **Palazzo Ducale** (*Via Federico da Montefeltro, tel 075 927 5872, closed 1st Mon. of the month*), built by Urbino's Federigo da Montefeltro, who briefly ruled Gubbio in the 15th century. West of the square, follow Via dei Consoli, watching for its many **Porte della Morte,** or Doors of Death, so-called because they were reputedly bricked up once a coffin had been taken from a house. At the town's southern end, take the funicular up Monte Ingino: At the top, you can take in wonderful views over the town and the **Basilica di Sant'Ubaldo,** burial place of Gubbio's patron saint. ■

Norcia & the Valnerina

NORCIA IS A REMOTE IMMEDIATELY LIKEABLE MOUNTAIN town that is renowned both as the birthplace of St. Benedict, founder of Western monasticism, and as the producer of some of Italy's best hams, salamis, and sausages. The Valnerina is the name given to the nearby valley of the river's main tributaries, a mountainous region dotted with tiny fortified villages and Umbria's finest abbey.

Norcia

🗺 271 C2

Visitor information

✉ Piazza San Benedetto

☎ 0743 816 701

Norcia's stolid, sturdy air derives mainly from its low buttressed houses and redoubtable walls, both built to resist the earthquakes that periodically shake the region—the last major tremor was in 1979. Of prehistoric origin, the town controlled one of the lowest and therefore most important passes across the Apennines, the mountainous spine that divides the Italian peninsula. Later, it became a Roman outpost, a minor city state, and a papal dominion. Today, it is a quietly prosperous place, and one that attracts ever-increasing numbers of visitors, thanks mainly to the **Parco Nazionale dei Monti Sibillini,** a recently designated national park that protects the magnificent Sibillini mountains immediately east of the town.

The town provides an excellent base for exploring the park, the Valnerina, and the timeless pastoral countryside of the Val Castoriana to the north. As well as being a gastronomic center par excellence, with numerous mouthwatering food stores, it is also an interesting historical town in its own right. The central **Piazza San Benedetto,** in particular, is a delight, as are its principal buildings: the quaint 15th-century Palazzo Comunale; the 14th-century church of San Benedetto, reputedly built over the 5th-century birthplace of St. Benedict; and the Castellina (1554), an imposing papal fortress that contains a small civic museum and art gallery, **Museo Civico**

Diocesano *(Piazza San Benedetto, tel 0743 828 044, closed in winter).*

PIANO GRANDE

The Piano Grande—literally the Big Plain—is one of central Italy's most unusual and magical landscapes. A vast upland plain, it lies

Such is the renown of Norcia as a gastronomic center that "Norcineria" is used across Italy to denote a pork butcher.

The village of Castelluccio crowns a hill above the Piano Grande, one of Europe's wildest and highest upland plains.

high in the Sibillini mountains around 40 minutes' drive from Norcia, its almost eerie expanses ringed by smooth-sloped peaks and overlooked by the wind-battered village of Castelluccio. In spring and summer, the plain becomes a sea of wildflowers, among them rarities such as peonies, orchids, fritillaries, and wild tulips. Glacial in origin, the area was once a huge lake whose lack of a natural outlet meant that it dried slowly over the millennia to produce the almost level plain you see today.

At 4,764 feet (1,452 m), **Castelluccio** is one of Italy's highest continually inhabited settlements, the preserve mainly of shepherds and hang gliders—the steep, smooth slopes of the surrounding mountains make this one of Europe's finest hang gliding areas. All manner of superb hikes, long and short, are possible locally, including a straightforward ascent of Monte Vettore, the highest point at 8,123 feet (2,476m) in the Sibillini range in the Marche. You can pick up good maps from stores in Norcia or from Hotel Sibilla in Castelluccio.

You need a car to explore the Valnerina, the best parts of which can be seen by driving north from Norcia along the Val Castoriana to Preci, with a detour at Piedivalle to see the important Benedictine abbey of Sant'Eutizio. From Preci, you follow the SS209 road southwest along the river. Several diversions are possible, all of which will take you into glorious countryside still scarcely touched by tourism. One excellent circuit would be to turn off the main road at Borgo Cerreto toward Monteleone di Spoleto, dropping back to the Valnerina shortly after Poggiodomo via Gavelli and Caso.

The valley boasts many fortified villages, built because this was a vital trade route from the mountains—**Scheggino** and **Vallo di Nera** are the best. The valley's most famous sight, however, is the picturesque **San Pietro in Valle** (*signposted from Colleponte, tel 0744 71 401*), an eighth-century abbey founded by the Lombard dukes of Spoleto. It contains an important 12th-century fresco cycle, several Roman remains, and a rare Lombard altar dating from 739. ■

Todi

ONCE A SLEEPY AGRICULTURAL BACKWATER, TODI HAS long since been discovered by expatriate incomers, although the influx of outsiders has done little to dent the charm of a hill town that has just about everything: a magnificent location, a history that goes back to Etruscan times, art and culture to spare, picture-perfect streets, and views that seem to stretch across half of Umbria.

Start your day at a café in **Piazza del Popolo**, often described as Italy's most perfect medieval piazza. Pride of place goes to the **Duomo** at its northern end, begun in the 12th century over a temple to Apollo (the square was the site of the former Roman forum). Fragments from this earlier building can be seen inside in the crypt, while in the church's main body the principal attraction is a beautifully inlaid wooden choir (1521–1530). Three major 13th-century palaces guard the piazza's other flanks, one of which, the **Palazzo Comunale,** houses the small Museo Comunale (*Tel 075 894 4148, closed Mon.*), a modern space with archaeological exhibits and a glorious painting depicting the "Coronation of the Virgin" (1511) by Lo Spagna.

Some of Todi's prettiest streets lie north and west of the Duomo. As you explore, note the three separate sets of walls—the town's Etruscan, Roman, and medieval limits. Head south from the piazza and you quickly come to the grandiose Romanesque-Gothic church of **San Fortunato.** The interior holds one undoubted masterpiece: a fresco (1432) in the fourth chapel off the south aisle by the Tuscan painter Masolino da Panicale.

To the church's right you enter Todi's public gardens, passing the stump of the medieval castle. Walk through the gardens and down the snaking footpath at their far end and you emerge in front of **Santa Maria della Consolazione** (1508–1607), among Italy's finest Renaissance churches. ■

The churches of San Fortunato (right) and Santa Maria della Consolazione (left) dominate the hilltop town of Todi.

Todi
◪ 271 B2
Visitor information
✉ Piazza Umberto I 6
☎ 075 894 2686 or 075 894 3395

Orvieto

ORVIETO ENJOYS THE MOST SPECTACULAR LOCATION IN Umbria, spread across a soaring cliff-edged plateau of fractured volcanic rock. Its site attracted the Etruscans, who made this one of their most important cities, but its real fame dates from 1263, the year of a religious miracle that saw the founding of the town's famous cathedral, Orvieto's glorious and undoubted main attraction.

Luca Signorelli's "Last Judgment" in Orvieto cathedral greatly influenced the work of Michelangelo.

Try to approach Orvieto on the scenic **funicular** from the railroad station in Orvieto Scalo, the modern town on the plain. This drops you in **Piazzale Cahen,** where you should visit the ruined medieval fortress, the public gardens—built over the

No visit to Umbria is complete without a visit to Orvieto's **Duomo,** described by Pope Leo XIII as the "Golden Lily of Italian cathedrals." It was inspired by the Miracle of Bolsena (1263), in which blood is said to have dripped from a consecrated host during Mass in the nearby village of Bolsena. The Romanesque-Gothic building distinguished by the most elaborately decorated **facade** of any monument in Italy. All manner of detail dazzles the eye, the most accomplished being the four Sienese bas-reliefs flanking the doors at ground level, one of the masterpieces of 14th-century Italian sculpture.

Inside, the cathedral's apparent sobriety is belied by two heavily frescoed side chapels. On the left (north) side is the **Cappella del Corporale,** which sports a rich casket (1358) encasing the *corporale* (altar cloth) spotted with blood during the miracle of Bolsena. Its walls are blanketed in frescoes (1357–1364) by local painter Ugolino di Prete Ilario, recalling episodes from the miracle (right wall) and assorted miracles of the Sacrament (left wall). The **Cappella di San Brizio,** or Cappella Nuova (*Piazza del Duomo 26, tel 0763 342 477*), opposite holds even more important paintings—a fresco cycle (1499–1504) of the "Last Judgment" by the Tuscan artist Luca Signorelli, one of Italy's great pictorial set pieces.

Opposite the cathedral are the **Musei Faina e Civico** (*Palazzo

Orvieto

🅰 271 A2

Visitor information

✉ Piazza del Duomo 24

☎ 0763 341 772 or 0763 341 911

site of a former Etruscan temple— and the extraordinary **Pozzo di San Patrizio** (*Viale Sangallo, tel 0763 343 768*). The latter is a vast well, commissioned by Pope Clement VIII in 1527 to provide the town with water in the event of a siege. Two 248-step staircases allow you to drop into the structure's dank, dark bowels. Ten minutes' pleasant walk on Corso Cavour from Piazzale Cahen brings you to the heart of the old town.

A total of 33 architects, 152 sculptors, 68 painters, and 90 mosaicists worked on the facade of Orvieto cathedral.

UNDER-GROUND ORVIETO

Several companies offer fascinating tours of the labyrinth of tunnels, galleries, and caves that riddle the volcanic rock below Orvieto. Many tunnels date back to Etruscan times, modern versions of which were used in the making of Orvieto's once notable sweet white wine, on sale at many outlets around town. The visitor center can provide details of tours. ■

Faina, Piazza del Duomo 29, tel 0763 341 511, closed Mon.), whose superbly presented displays encompass a wide variety of Etruscan and other archaeological artifacts. Etruscan fans should also make time to visit the **Necropoli Etrusca-Crocefisso del Tufo** (Tel 0763 343 611), an intriguing series of stone burial chambers a mile (1.6 km) outside town on the SS71 road to Orvieto Scalo.

More archaeological finds are displayed in the less arresting

Museo Archeologico behind the cathedral (Palazzo Papale, Piazza del Duomo, tel 0763 341 511, closed Sun. p.m.).

Elsewhere in the town, you should visit the tiny church of **San Lorenzo** on Via Ippolito Scalza, the larger **Sant'Andrea** in the main Piazza della Repubblica, and **San Giovenale,** hidden away on the town's western margins. The last, in particular, should not be missed, thanks to its medieval frescoes. ■

More places to visit in Umbria

AMELIA

Amelia lies amid pastoral countryside in southern Umbria behind some of Italy's most redoubtable walls. Parts of these ramparts date from the fifth century B.C., but the Roman historian Pliny claimed the town was founded six centuries earlier, which if true would make it one of the oldest settlements in the country. Four gates penetrate the defenses, the main entrance being Porta Romana, from whence medieval streets wend upward to Piazza Marconi, site of the much-altered Romanesque Duomo and a distinctive 12-sided 11th-century tower. Other sights are few and far between, but Amelia's pleasures—like those of similar small hill towns—are those of views, peace and quiet, and the charm of sleepy medieval streets.
🗺 271 B1 **Visitor information** ✉ Via Orvieto 1 ☎ 0744 981 453

CITTÀ DI CASTELLO

Visitors often miss out on Città di Castello, partly because of its location—slightly isolated in the north of the region, where it sprawls across a plain rather than perches on a hilltop like most of its peers. Nevertheless, it is a pleasing and provincial old town, the gridiron plan of its medieval streets a monument to its original Roman builders. The main sight is the **Pinacoteca Comunale** *(Palazzo Vitelli, Via della Cannoniera 22, tel 075 852 0656, closed Mon.)*, notable for Umbria's only painting wholly by Raphael. Also noteworthy are the **Duomo** and its small museum, the latter famed for its collection of Paleo-Christian silverware *(Piazza Gabriotti, tel 075 855 4705)*.
🗺 271 A4 **Visitor information** ✉ Piazza Matteotti ☎ 075 855 4922

DERUTA

Deruta is a modest hill town of pleasant but unremarkable aspect between Todi and Perugia, and would be almost completely ignored were it not for its one claim to fame—its ceramics. Local clay was worked here by the Romans, but it was the discovery of startling new yellow and blue glazes in the 15th century that put the town firmly on the map. The craft continues to this day, as becomes clear as you approach the town, the roadsides being lined with workshops and stalls selling pottery in a multitude of shapes, sizes and designs. The old town contains an interesting museum devoted to the town's specialty, the **Museo Regionale della Ceramica** *(Largo San Francesco, tel 075 971 1000, closed Tues. Oct.–March)*.
🗺 271 B2–B3 **Visitor information** ✉ Piazza dei Consoli ☎ 0759 711 737

LAGO TRASIMENO

Italy's fourth largest lake is a pretty stretch of water nestled amid the low, shadowed hills west of Perugia. Historically, it is known for the battle in 217 B.C. in which the Romans suffered one of their worst ever defeats at the hands of the Carthaginian general, Hannibal. You can visit the site of the battlefield near Tuoro sul Trasimeno, one of several small towns dotted around the lakeshore. Of these, **Castiglione del Lago** is the most pleasant, with a nice old center, a handful of modest beaches, plenty of waterfront fish restaurants, and regular scenic boat trips to the lake's islands. Various watersports, notably windsurfing, are also available here and at other major centers such as Passignano sul Trasimeno.
🗺 271 A3 **Visitor information** ✉ Piazza Mazzini, Castiglione del Lago ☎ 075 96 2484 or 075 965 2738

NARNI

Most Umbrian towns and villages have some appeal, this being a region where it is easier to list the places to avoid than those you should visit. Places to miss would include Terni, a grim industrial city; Cascia, an earthquake-battered pilgrimage center; and Foligno, a relatively modern plain-bound town. Seen from afar, hilltop Narni would also appear to be a town to avoid, largely because proximity to Terni has slightly spoiled its surroundings. Up within the old walls, however, lies yet another wonderful Umbrian hill town. Granted, there are no great set pieces, but there is an evocative fortress, an age-old cathedral, and enough medieval nooks and crannies to warrant an hour or two's aimless exploration.
🗺 271 B1 **Visitor information** ✉ Palazzo del Podestà, Piazza del Popolo 18 ☎ No phone ∎

Southern Italy boasts active volcanoes, the sublime landscapes of Capri and Amalfi, mountains that are still the haunt of bears and wolves, the country's most famous ancient site—Pompeii—and historic cities such as Naples and Lecce.

The South

A flower carpet in Ravello

The South

SOUTHERN ITALY IS ANOTHER COUNTRY, a land separated from the rest of Italy by history, geography, and economics, a world apart that is poorer, wilder, more backward, and more rooted in tradition than its northern counterpart. On the face of things, visitors here are in for a hard time. Towns and cities are culturally less interesting—with some notable exceptions—and the quality and quantity of hotels and restaurants inferior. Roads meander, trains are leisurely, and bureaucracy grinds slow. Distances between points of interest are considerable.

Yet the South is also hugely rewarding, especially if you relish the unknown. This is partly because its landscapes are empty and untrammeled, and partly because you will often have its lonely villages and time-locked towns to yourself. It is also because the South, the so-called Mezzogiorno, or land of the midday sun, comes closest to resembling that fabled phenomenon, "the real Italy," or at least the real Italy that many outsiders, ignorant of the country's modern élan, would like to imagine.

Clichéd Latin vignettes still prevail in the region's rural and urban backwaters—the black-clad peasant woman, the washing hung across streets—as do the classic passions of food, family, soccer, love, and religion. Poverty, crime, and other social ills may be amplified here, particularly in the cities, but so, too, by and large, are the Old World ideals of honor and hospitality.

The region's particular character has been variously molded. Geographically, it is forever isolated, far from markets and the prospect of industrial salvation. Climatically, it bakes under an almost African sun, a blight to agricultural initiative. Geologically, its soils are poor, its mountains devoid of raw materials. Socially, its countryside—although magnificent to the outsider—has been desiccated by emigration. Historically, it has been endlessly conquered—by Phoenicians, Carthaginians, Greeks, Romans, Arabs, Normans, Swabians, Angevins, and Bourbons. And for centuries it remained in thrall to feudal tradition and the deadening hand of Spanish rule, twin afflictions that led to social, economic, and agricultural stagnation that lingers to this day.

This is not to say that the South is universally blighted—far from it. Visitors plumping for its highlights will experience some of Italy's most hallowed names—think of Capri and Pompeii—and visit towns and landscapes every bit as memorable as those of the north.

At its most basic, the area consists of five regions—the Abruzzo, Campania, Calabria, Basilicata, and Puglia—although precisely where the South starts is a matter of debate. The Milanese will tell you Florence, the Florentines say Rome, while the Romans point to the first gas station south of Rome.

Wherever the border, by the time you reach Naples, the region's long-standing capital, there is no doubt that a threshold of some sort has been crossed. Chaotic, noisy, and ebullient, this is one of the most Italian of cities, a microcosm of all that is good and bad in the South. Many people brave its mayhem and admire its many sights as they head for two great archaeological sites to the south, Pompeii and Herculaneum, Roman settlements eerily preserved by an eruption of Mount Vesuvius, the still-active volcano that broods over Naples and its surroundings. A little to the south stretches the fabled Amalfi Coast, Italy's most beautiful stretch of coastline, and the idyllic island retreats of Capri and Ischia.

The Abruzzo is more remote and introspective, low on towns and monuments, high on exceptional mountain scenery, some of the best

of which is protected by the Parco Nazionale d'Abruzzo. To the south stretches Puglia (or Apulia), the heel of the Italian "boot," a long, narrow region whose endless plains and rolling hills are redeemed by the coast and countryside of the Gargano, the boot's spur. Distant Lecce, a city-size shrine to the baroque, is the best of the big urban targets, while the pick of the smaller centers are a string of towns graced with Romanesque churches. The most unusual sights are the *trulli*, strange conical dwellings unique to the region. Few first-time visitors linger in Basilicata, the boot's instep, or in Calabria, its toe, although their empty, mountainous interiors are unspoiled, their coastlines, in places, a perfect place to rest en route to Sicily. ■

Naples

NAPLES (NAPOLI) HAS RARELY WANTED FOR PRAISE. SET ON a peerless bay and backed by Vesuvius's distinctive volcanic profile, the city has been celebrated by poets and painters since classical times as one of the most beautiful and blessed places on earth. That was before crime, poverty, pollution, and traffic chaos took their toll, factors, which until the late 1990s, lent the city an edge that tended to intimidate all but the most resolute visitors. Progress has now been made on several fronts, however, and today this most vibrant and Italian of cities is becoming a mite more amenable.

Naples

- 288 B4

Visitor information
- ✉ Stazione Centrale (railroad station)
- ☎ 081 268 779

- ✉ Piazza Gesù Nuovo
- ☎ 081 551 2701

- ✉ Piazza dei Martiri 58
- ☎ 081 405 311

Museo Archeological Nazionale
- ✉ Piazza Museo Nazionale
- ☎ 081 440 166

This edge and character, of course, are also the city's most distinctive features. Naples is so Italian as to be almost clichéd—a city of pizza, opera, bustling markets, soccer, religion, Sophia Loren (born nearby), family, organized crime, petty crime, and the sort of washing-hung streets used as visual shorthand for Italy in countless movies. Few places bring you quite so close to the teeming realities of life in the Italian south, and few people on earth are quite as exuberant, sharp, fatalistic, and fiercely individual as the Neapolitans—"fiddlers and poets, whores and scoundrels" was how British naval hero Lord Nelson described them in 1798.

The vibrancy of Naples' streets and citizens is matched by a huge artistic and archaeological patrimony, the result of its long history (the

city is at least 3,000 years old) and a succession of rulers and settlers that included the Greeks, Romans, Normans, Germans, French, Aragonese, Spanish, and Bourbons.

Henry James wrote in a letter of 1869 how he "conceived at Naples a tenfold deeper loathing than ever of the hideous heritage of the past—and felt for a moment as if I should like to devote my life to laying railroads and erecting concrete blocks of stores on the most classic and romantic sites." You can see what he meant—Naples has almost too much to see.

A good plan of attack is to take a cab to the Museo Archeologico Nazionale, one of Europe's preeminent archaeological museums and the city's single must-see sight. Then walk south through the most atmospheric part of the old city, the **Spaccanapoli** (meaning split Naples), the area around Via Tribunali and Via Benedetto Croce. Then continue south to arrive at the sights close to the port and waterfront. If time allows, you could also visit two outlying attractions: the Certosa di San Martino and the Palazzo Reale di Capodimonte.

The **Museo Archeologico Nazionale** and its collection of Greek and Roman antiquities, many of them recovered from Pompeii and Herculanum, is stunning. The ground floor is devoted primarily to sculpture, with most of the high-

lights in the first 15 of the floor's 40 or more rooms. Of particular note are statues of Athena, Harmodius and Aristogeiton, Aphrodite, and the much praised Doyphorus, or javelin thrower. More striking still are the "Farnese Hercules," the museum's finest statue, and the "Farnese Bull," the largest surviving sculpture from the ancient world. Much of the mezzanine is devoted to fabulous **mosaics** from Pompeii, the right side to exhibits connected with Naples' early history.

Further treasures grace the first floor, among them the west wing's collection of vases and the Sale della Villa dei Papiri, given over to papyrus, statues, and other exhibits removed from the Villa dei Papiri at Herculaneum. Equally absorbing are the **Sala degli Affreschi,** with wall paintings removed from Pompeii, Herculaneum, and elsewhere, and the **Sala del Tempio di Iside,** a room in which part of Pompeii's Temple of Isis has been re-created and filled with artifacts from the original temple.

Wend east through the streets below the museum to the **Duomo** *(Via del Duomo),* best known for the relics of San Gennaro, a fourth-century martyr and Naples' patron and protector. The saint's chapel contains a phial of blood that is paraded three times yearly— failure of the blood to liquefy during the ceremony bodes ill for the city. Also worth seeing are the saint's impressive Renaissance tomb (1494–1506) and the remnants of the old basilica of Santa Restituta off the right aisle.

The church of **Santa Maria Donnaregina** just to the north *(Vico Donnaregina)* has Tino da Camaino's "Tomb of Mary of Hungary" (1326) and early 14th-century frescoes by Roman painter Pietro Cavallini. A short walk north, **San Giovanni a**

**San Lorenzo
Maggiore**

✉ Piazza San Gaetano

🕐 Roman excavations
beneath church
closed Tues. &
Sun. p.m.

**Monte delle
Misericordia**

✉ Via del Tribunali

Carbonara *(Via Carbonara 5)* is known for Andrea da Firenze's 1414 "Tomb of King Ladislas of Naples."

West of the Duomo stands Gothic **San Lorenzo Maggiore,** one of the city's finer churches, distinguished by Tino da Camaino's "Tomb of Catherine of Austria" (1323) to the right of the high altar. On the same street the **Monte della Misericordia** church houses Caravaggio's majestic "Seven Acts of Mercy" (1607). To the south rises **San Gregorio Armeno** *(Via San Gregorio Armeno 1),* one of the

most opulent of Naple's myriad baroque churches.

Farther west lies **San Domenico Maggiore** *(Piazza San Domenico),* worth visiting for its marvelous funerary sculpture. Across the square, **Sant'Angelo a Nilo** contains Michelozzo's "Tomb of Cardinal Bracciano" (1428). Just off the piazza stands the **Cappella San Severo** *(Via De Sanctis, closed Tues. & Sun. p.m.),* also celebrated for its sculpture, in particular Giuseppe Sammartino's virtuoso "Dead Christ" (1753).

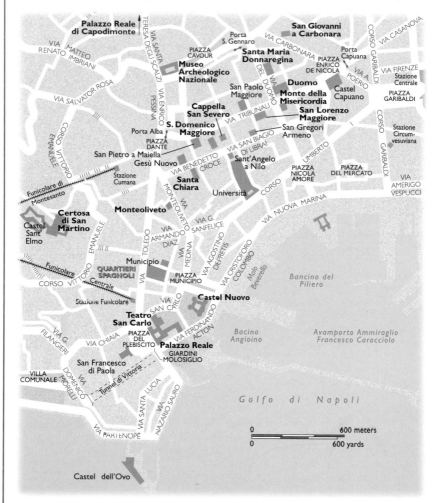

above the altar. The district's rich collection of churches continues on the street to the north, where **San Pietro a Maiella** (*Via San Pietro a Maiella*) and an impressive 17th-century painting cycle by Mattia Preti. The area's last major church, **Santa Chiara** on Via Benedetto Croce has three 14th-century royal tombs by Tino da Camanio and other Florentine sculptors.

Explore south by taking Calata Trinità Maggiore from near Santa Chiara, being sure to see the church of **Monteoliveto** (*Piazza Monteoliveto*), begun in 1411, with more exemplary Florentine tombs and sculptures. Then visit the teeming **Quartiere Spagnoli** west of Via Toledo, full of archetypal Neopolitan street scenes, or continue to the waterfront and **Piazza del Plebiscito**. The latter is dominated by San Francesco di Paola, a neoclassic church modeled on Rome's Pantheon, and by the **Palazzo Reale,** a 17th-century Spanish palace visited for its lavishly decorated royal apartments (*Piazza del Plebiscito, tel 081 580 8111, closed Wed. & Sun. p.m.*). On the palace's northern flank stands the **Teatro San Carlo** (1737), one of Italy's leading opera houses. From here Via San Carlo leads to the **Castel Nuovo** (*Piazza Municipio, tel 081 795 2003, closed Sat. p.m.& all Sun.*), built for Charles of Anjou in 1282. Its stolid ramparts, offset by the delicacy of a lovely entrance arch (1454–1467), conceal several grand salons and a modest civic museum.

This palace and museum complex is Naples' key attraction after the archaeological museum, but you will need to take a cab here as it lies well to the north of the city center (*Parco di Capodimonte, tel 081 744 1307, closed Mon.*). Begun by the Bourbons as a hunting lodge in 1738, its interior is divided between a picture gallery, a series

of former royal apartments, and a top floor display of contemporary art. Of these, the picture gallery is by far the most compelling, its collection on a par with those of more famous galleries in Rome, Florence, and Venice. Virtually all the great names of Italian art are represented, with particularly outstanding works by Titian, Raphael, Michelangelo, Botticelli, Masolino, and Giovanni Bellini. The palace also stands at the heart of a magnificent park.

The gargantuan Carthusian monastery (Certosa) of San Martino and the neighboring 14th-century **Castel Sant'Elmo** look down over Naples from a hilly spur west of the city center. Both buildings are worth a visit in their own right, but as an added bonus the Certosa plays host to the 90-room **Museo Nazionale di San Martino** (*Largo di San Martino 5, tel 081 578 1769, closed Mon. & p.m. daily*), a wide-ranging collection best known for its hundreds of figurines and Neapolitan *presepi*, or Christmas cribs. The Certosa's most memorable sight is the conventual church, one of the city's most pleasing baroque creations. ∎

A fresco from Pompeii, now in Naples' Museo Archeologico Nazionale

SUBTERRANEAN NAPLES
One of southern Italy's most bizarre, but highly memorable, excursions involves exploring the ancient tunnels, cellars, and sewers that riddle underground Naples, or Napoli Sotterraneo (*Piazza San Gaetano 68, tel 081 449 821, guided tours Sat. & Sun. a.m.*). Some tunnels date back to Greek times, but have been extended throughout history for storage, drainage, and similar purposes. ∎

Vesuvius is
dormant, not
extinct. Another
major eruption
is overdue.

Vesuvio
288 B4

Vesuvio

ITALY HAS HIGHER AND MORE ACTIVE VOLCANOES—
notably Sicily's Mount Etna—but none as notorious as Vesuvio
(Vesuvius), whose catastrophic eruption in A.D. 79 famously buried
and preserved the Roman towns of Pompeii and Herculaneum. Today,
the volcano is dormant, for the time being at least (another eruption is
overdue) and can be admired by visitors either as a backdrop to the
Bay of Naples or from the closer proximity of its crater's edge.

ASCENDING VESUVIUS

The easiest way to
the 4,189-foot
(1,277 m) summit
of Vesuvius is from
Ercolano. From
here, you can drive
or take a cab to
Colle Margherita,
where you join an
official guide (small
fee required) for
the final walk to
the summit (wear
sturdy shoes).
Views of the gar
gantuan crater
and the Bay of
Naples below are
unforgettable. ■

People living on the Bay of Naples
in the first century B.C. knew all
was not well with Vesuvius. An
earthquake in 63 B.C., 16 years
before the fateful eruption, had
ravaged the region and given fair
warning of the forces gathering
subterranean strength.

More immediate warning was
issued in the days before the catastrophe, when the volcano began
to smoke and rumble, a warning at
first ignored by the populace—the
volcano, after all, had not erupted
in recorded memory. Vesuvius, or
Vesubius as it was called then, however, means the unextinguished.
On August 24, A.D. 79, it more than
lived up to its name.

On that morning, the cone's
ancient basalt plug collapsed.
Gas, pumice, and other debris
were released with explosive force,
a vast cloud blotting out the sky.
Two days passed before light
returned to the region. Pompeii
was buried by dust and cinders
within hours.

The 2,000 inhabitants who
had not fled were asphyxiated by
superheated gases. By evening, the
volcano's inner walls had also collapsed, unleashing further destruction, including the torrent of
boiling volcanic mud that engulfed
Herculaneum. The most recent
eruption was in 1944–another is
just a matter of time. ■

Ercolano

IN A.D. 79, ERCOLANO (HERCULANEUM) WAS ENGULFED BY the same eruption that devastated nearby Pompeii. But whereas Pompeii was a thriving commercial town, Herculaneum was an exclusive residential district, built to exploit the site's cooling breezes and far-reaching views. Like Pompeii, it remained entombed until the 18th century, and, like its neighbor, remains only half-excavated today. Where it differs from Pompeii is in its more modest and manageable size. You should allow about two hours for the site.

Beyond the entrance, an avenue passes through the ruins of the **Palestra,** or gymnasium. Nearby are the **Casa dell'Atrio,** which still boasts its mosaic pavements, and just beyond it on the left the **Casa a Gratticio** (House of the Wooden Trellis) and **Casa del Tramezzo Carbonizzato** (House of the Burned Partition). Beyond the latter, at the town's major intersection, stands a former dyer's shop (at No. 10), known for its superbly preserved wooden clothes-press.

Across the street stretch the ruins of the **Terme,** or baths. The plan of the **Casa Sannitica**

opposite is typical of simpler dwellings built by the Sannites, a local Italic tribe absorbed by the Romans. Next door is an old weaver's shop, and a couple of doors down the wonderful **Casa del Mosaico di Nettuno e Anfitrite,** noted both for its shop and the blue-green mosaic adorning its rear living quarters. Other outstanding structures include the **Casa del Bel Cortile** (House of the Beautiful Courtyard), the **Pistrinum,** a bakery complete with oven and flour mills, and the **Casa dei Cervi** (House of the Deer), the most sumptuous of Herculaneum's houses. ■

The ruined town of Herculaneum had a population of some 8,000, about one-third of that of nearby Pompeii.

Ercolano

🔺 288 B4

✉ Corso Resina, Ercolano

☎ 081 47 1858

💲 $$

WHY VISIT?
The range of different buildings, and their generally superior state of preservation, makes this the better of the two sites to visit if time constraints force you to choose between Pompeii or Herculaneum. ■

Pompei

BUT FOR ONE OF HISTORY'S MOST FAMOUS CATACLYSMS, Pompeii (Pompei in Italian) would have been one more minor Roman colony lost to the ravages of time. Instead, it was preserved for posterity by the eruption of Vesuvius in A.D. 79, when its buildings and many of its inhabitants were buried beneath a mountain of volcanic debris. There they remained until the 17th century, when the study of old texts suggested Pompeii's existence.

Nowhere in Italy so vividly evokes the reality of the Roman world as Pompeii. "Nothing is wanting but the inhabitants," wrote the diarist Henry Matthews in 1820, adding that "a morning's walk through the solemn streets of Pompeii will give you a livelier idea of their modes of life than all the books in the world."

The main entrance for visitors is the old **Porta Marina,** on the site's seaward (western) flank. Exploring the huge site—Pompeii had a population of some 25,000—requires some forethought. Only about half of the site has been excavated, yet even this requires a day's sight-seeing. Set off early, and be prepared for the crowds, for this is one of southern Italy's most popular excursions. Note, too, that it is worth seeing the town in conjunction with

Naples' Museo Archeologico Nazionale, which houses many of the moveable objects removed from the site over the years. Make for the highlights first, and don't become bogged down with the lesser streets, where one small house soon looks much like another.

Just beyond the entrance, you come to the town's old **forum,** ringed by many of the site's most imposing civic structures: the Tempio di Apollo, Tempio di Giove, and the Basilica, Pompeii's largest building. To the north lie the site's most famous houses: the **Casa del Fauno** and **Casa dei Vettii.** The latter is particularly interesting. Once the property of rich merchant brothers, its painted friezes are some of the finest of their kind. Among the scenes is a mural of a famously rampant Priapus, one of many phallic representations around the site (most probably representing superstitious attempts to ward off the evil eye).

Another well-preserved house, the **Casa degli Amorini Dorati,** lies just to the east, while to the west you should hunt out the **Casa del Poeta Tragica,** known for its famous mosaic and graffiti—"*Cave canem*" ("Beware of the dog"). Some distance out to the west, through the Porta Ercolono a tomb- and cypress-lined lane (Via delle Tombe) leads to a pair of villas, the Villa di Diomede and the **Villa dei Misteri.** Returning to the forum and then heading east on Via dell'Abbondanza, formerly a busy commercial street, brings you to the rest of the site. Off to the right after a short distance (on Via dei Teatri) are the **Teatro Grande,** a 5,000-seat open-air theater, and the smaller 800-seat Teatro Piccolo, or **Odeon,** the name given to a smaller covered theater. Two blocks north, on the corner with Vico del Lupinare,

stretch the ruins of the **Terme Stabiane,** the town's main bath complex. At the end of Vico del Lupinare, once a thriving red-light district, is another visitors' favorite —a small brothel complete with bed stalls and frescoes illustrating the various services available.

Moving on down Via dell'Abbondanza, a right turn takes you to the **Casa del Melandro,** another outstanding patrician house adorned with mosaics and wall paintings. Two more fine houses, both with beautiful gardens, lie on the right toward the end of the street: the Casa di Loreius Tiburtinus and Villa di Giulia Felice. Closing the eastern end of the site is the **Anfiteatro,** one of the oldest (A.D. 80) and best-preserved Roman amphitheaters in existence. ■

This Roman fresco in the Villa dei Misteri shows a young girl being initiated into the rites of the Dionysian cult.

Costiera Amalfitana

THE COSTIERA AMALFITANA, OR AMALFI COAST, IS ITALY'S most beautiful stretch of coastline, a mild-weathered enclave of towering cliffs, idyllic villages tumbling colorfully to the sea, precipitous corniche roads, luxuriant gardens, and magnificent vistas over turquoise waters and green-swathed mountains. It lies along the flanks of the Sorrento Peninsula, a cliff-edged promontory that juts from the mainland close to the southern reaches of the Bay of Naples.

The coast's most convenient access point is **Salerno,** a busy port best known as one of the main Allied beachheads during the 1943 invasion of Italy. From Autostrada A3, you pick up the SS163 at **Vietri sul Mare,** a village celebrated for its ceramics, and one that offers sweeping views of the coastline to come. From here, the road weaves past innumerable viewpoints—the one at **Capo d'Orso** is the best—and skirts the villages of Maiori (small sandy beach) and Minori (ruins of a first-century A.D. Roman villa) before a junction close to **Atrani** (two tempting churches) whisks you inland to Ravello.

Ravello is one of the most romantic and beautiful small towns imaginable. Perched on steep, terraced slopes—"closer to the sky than the sea," in the words of

French novelist André Gide—it is a place blessed with luxuriant gardens, quiet lanes, sleepy, sun-drenched corners, and a lofty position at 1,148 feet (350 m) that provides unforgettable views over the azure coast below. At its heart lie an 11th-century cathedral and the **Villa Rufolo** (*Piazza Vescovado, tel 089 857 657*), the latter one of two villas for which the town is famous. Built in the 13th century, the villa received guests that included popes and emperors, as well as Richard Wagner, who composed part of his opera *Parsifal* here in 1880. Views from its idyllic gardens are magnificent, as are those from the nearby **Villa Cimbrone** (*Tel 089 858 072, closed Nov.–March*).

Dropping back to the coast from Ravello, the corniche road brings you to **Amalfi,** in its day one of Italy's four powerful maritime republics (with Venice, Pisa, and Genoa). All sea trade in the Mediterranean was once governed by the 11th-century Tavole Amalfitane, the world's oldest maritime code. Today, the town's beauty, stunning seafront setting, and mild climate make it a hugely popular resort, so steel yourself for high prices and high-season crowds.

Pride of place goes to the **Duomo di Sant'Andrea,** fronted by a gorgeous and intricately patterned 12th-century facade. Founded in the ninth century, the church's subsequent alterations

Left: The Duomo di Sant'Andrea looks down over the main square in Amalfi.

Costiera Amalfitana
⊠ 288 B4

Ravello
Visitor information
⊠ Piazza del Duomo 10
☎ 089 857 096

Amalfi
Visitor information
⊠ Corso delle Repubbliche Marinare 19–21
☎ 089 871 107 or 089 872 619

have spared the beauty of its principal glory, the main portal's 11th-century Byzantine bronze doors. Next to the church lies the **Choistro del Paradiso** (1268), or Cloisters of Paradise, whose somber Romanesque tone is enlivened by the Arab elements in its sinuous columns.

You can escape much of the town's hustle by hiking into the hills above the town. Consult the visitor center *(Corso Roma, tel 089 871 107)* for more details, or take the popular walk along the **Valle dei Mulini,** a steep-sided ravine dotted with ruined watermills— *mulini*—once used to make paper, an industry for which Amalfi was, and still is, famous. The small **Museo della Carta** *(Palazzo Pagliara, closed Mon. & Fri.)* has displays connected with the industry.

West from Amalfi, the increasingly spectacular corniche road passes **Grotta dello Smeraldo,** a marine cave of luminous emerald waters that you can visit by boat, elevator, or rock-cut steps. Just beyond it, the road passes the **Vallone di Furore,** one of the coast's most impressive gorges (worth exploring on foot), before arriving at the villages of Praiano and **Positano,** two more smart and majestically situated villages. From here the road runs around the tip of the peninsula to **Sorrento,** a popular package tour resort, although none the worse for that. Other roads to Sorrento and the peninsula's northern coast— notably the SS366 from Vettica Minore near Amalfi—provide first-hand views of the interior's beautiful Lattari mountains. ■

The Villa Rufolo in Ravello affords a magnificent view over part of the fabled Amalfi coastline.

Positano
Visitor information
✉ Via del Saracino 4
☎ 089 875 067

Boats at anchor in one of Capri's many small bays. The beautiful coastline is one of the island's main attractions.

Isola di Capri & Isola d'Ischia

BEAUTY IN ITALY OFTEN EXISTS SIDE BY SIDE WITH ugliness. Nowhere is the juxtaposition more marked than off the Neapolitan coast, where Naples' often hellish urban environs give way to the idyllic island havens of Capri and Ischia. A luxury playground of the first rank, Capri has long been a sybaritic retreat for emperors, artists, writers, and the international jet set. Ischia is a less chic island, and more favored by package tour companies, although its views, luxuriant vegetation, quaint villages, and lovely coast are almost equally appealing.

Isola di Capri
🅰 288 B4
Visitor information
✉ Piazza Umberto I
☎ 081 837 0686

Anacapri
Visitor information
✉ Via Orlandi 59
☎ 081 837 1524

The charms of **Capri** have been enjoyed since earliest times. The Emperor Augustus called the island Capri Apragopolis, the City of Sweet Idleness, a fitting epithet for a retreat that has become a byword for decadent self-indulgence. Today hordes of day-trippers flood to the island—which measures a mere 2 miles (3 km) by 4 miles (6 km)—to enjoy its balmy climate, its rugged coastline, its whitewashed villages, and the almost subtropical lushness of its gardens and hilly interior.

Regular boats and hydrofoils from Naples and Sorrento dock at **Marina Grande,** the island's colorful main port and the point of

departure for boat trips around the island. Such trips are an essential part of the Capri experience, offering a firsthand glimpse of the coast's jumble of cliffs, bays, caves, and rocky sea stacks. Beware the separate trips to the famous **Blue Grotto** (Grotta Azzurra) which can be extortionate and overrated.

From Marina Grande a funicular climbs to **Capri,** the island's

Axel Munthe (1857–1949), Swedish physician and author of the best-selling *Story of San Michele* (1929). Be sure to visit the 19th-century **Villa San Michele** (*Off Piazza delle Vittoria, tel 081 837 1401*), on which the book is based, and, in particular, the garden terrace, which offers magnificent views across the island. For more spectacular panoramas, take the chairlift

Above right: The bright lights of Via Cammerelle in Capri. The island's two main villages are full of chic shops and restaurants.

pretty main village, centered on the fashionable Piazza Umberto I. Surrounding streets are lined with cafés, souvenir stores, and chic boutiques, but quieter corners are easily found—try following Via Madre Serafina south to the Belvedere Cannone, for example, or Via Camerelle east to the Belvedere Tragara. Both offer magnificent views. Farther east lies the **Villa Jovis,** or Jupiter's Villa, the remains of the Emperor Tiberius' Capri hideaway. To the south of the village, the exhilarating Via Krupp drops to **Marina Piccola,** one of the island's better—but busier—places to swim and sunbathe.

To the west of Capri lies the island's second village, **Anacapri,** approached by a dramatic corniche road. Quieter than Capri, it is best known as the onetime home of

from Piazza della Vittoria to the summit of nearby **Monte Solaro** (1 hour on foot, 12 minutes by elevator). At 1,932 feet (589 m), this is Capri's highest point.

Ischia is a touch less pretty than Capri, but no less visited. Many visitors are attracted by the island's **hot springs,** a legacy of Ischia's volcanic origins—Monte Epomeo, the island's highest point at 2,585 feet (788 m), is an extinct volcano. The best of the springs bubble under the spa resorts on the northern coast—notably at Forio, Lacco Ameno, and Casamicciola. Villages on the west and south of the island are quieter. Boats dock at the town of Ischia, which divides between the modern Ischia Porto and more picturesque Ischia Ponte. Between the two lie pretty pine woods and a good beach. ■

Isola d'Ischia
▲ 288 B4
Visitor information
✉ Corso Colonna 116
☎ 081 991 146

The fifth-century
B.C. Tempio di
Nettuno at
Paestum is one of
the world's best-
preserved Doric
temples.

Paestum

"INEXPRESSIBLY GRAND," WROTE THE POET SHELLEY OF
Paestum, southern Italy's most evocative and romantic archaeological ensemble. Center stage at the site goes to three almost perfectly
preserved Doric temples, widely considered the greatest in the Greek
world—finer even than those of Greece itself. Much of Paestum's
charm, however, also derives from its flower-filled meadows and the
rural beauty of its tranquil setting.

Paestum

🗺 289 C4

Visitor information

✉ Zona Archeologico,
Via Aquilia

☎ 0828 811 016

Museo Nazionale

✉ Zona Archeologico

☎ 0828 810 023

Paestum began life as Poseidonia,
the city of Neptune or Poseidon,
a colony founded by the Greeks
in the sixth-century B.C. Absorbed
by the Romans in 273 B.C., when it
took its present name, it was almost
completely abandoned following
the ravages of malaria and a devastating Saracen raid in A.D. 877. It
then lay hidden amid the undergrowth for hundreds of years until
its discovery during road building
in the 18th century, when excavations brought its magnificent
temples and other ruins to light
once again.

The grandest and best-preserved
of the temples is the **Tempio di
Nettuno,** or Temple of Neptune
(fifth century B.C.). The temple's
entablature and pediments have
survived nearly intact, but the roof

(Temple of Ceres), actually dedicated to the goddess Athena and probably built some time between its two neighbors.

Paestum's other Greek and later Roman remains are less striking, but it is still well worth exploring the site simply to soak up the atmosphere. For a good overall picture of the area, you could walk the line of the colony's former walls, a distance of just over 2 miles (3 km).

Also be sure to visit the **Museo Nazionale,** a museum of finds from the site located to the east of the temples (tickets for the temples are also valid for the museum). Its most treasured exhibits are wall paintings of the Tomb of the Diver (480 B.C.). These pictures may be the only surviving examples of Greek mural painting from this period. The pictures—five in all—originally formed part of a coffin: Four of them show scenes of a funeral banquet and the songs, games, musicians, and former companions that accompany the deceased into the next world. The fifth panel, which probably formed the coffin's lid, is the most famous of the paintings, and shows a naked diver—hence the tomb's name—diving into a blue sea. The scene may be an unusual allegory of the passage from life to death. ■

is missing. Almost alongside it stands the **Tempio di Hera,** the earliest of the temples, also known as the Basilica after being wrongly identified by 18th-century archaeologists. In a more isolated position, at the site's northern extreme, stands the **Tempio di Cerere**

A wall painting from the Tomb of the Diver in Paestum's Museo Nazionale. The fresco is over 2,000 years old.

The Parco Nazionale d'Abruzzo offers hikers numerous opportunities for spotting wildlife.

Parco Nazionale d'Abruzzo

THE PARCO NAZIONALE D'ABRUZZO IS ITALY'S PREMIER national park, a protected mountain sanctuary that is home to some of Europe's last brown bears, many of its last remaining wolves, and more than 150 varieties of rare indigenous flora. It is also great hiking and driving country, with plenty of marked trails, good maps, and a variety of scenic touring routes. Just beyond its borders lies the appealing town of Sulmona, a good base for exploring this and other nearby mountain enclaves.

Italian parks are often halfhearted affairs, enjoying little genuine protection on the ground. The Abruzzo is a notable exception, its founders having created a well-run park that adroitly balances the needs of visitors, the environment, and the local community. Originally a royal hunting reserve, like many Italian parks, it first achieved protected status in 1917, although the majority of the real work to establish the reserve has been accomplished in the last 30 years.

The park's 155 square miles (401 sq km) of wilderness centers

on the Sangro valley, a broad cleft that almost bisects the park and contains its key villages—Barrea, Villetta Barrea, Alfedena, Opi, and Pescasseroli. For maps and hints for hiking, stop by the largest village, **Pescasseroli,** which has the park's main museum and visitor center *(Viale Santa Lucia 6, tel 0863 910 715 or 0863 91 955).* If you only have time for one walk, try trail 1, a five-hour round-trip from Civitella Alfedena to the Valle delle Rose, which offers a good chance of seeing some of the park's 500 or more Apennine chamois. Shorter walks nearer Pescasseroli include trail C3 to the Valico di Monte Tranquillo (two to three hours) and trail B2 to Monte Valle Carrara. Other favored haunts are the Canala valley (north of Pescasseroli), the Camosciara (southwest of Villetta Barrea), and the Val di Fondillo (east of Opi).

Spring (late May to June) is the best time to enjoy the park's stunning flora—there are more than 1,200 species of flowers and trees, and 267 types of fungus. Two-thirds of the area is forested, so fall is almost equally spectacular, thanks to the ever changing colors of the park's mixed woodlands. Bird-watchers have the chance to spot over 300 species of birds, including at least ten pairs of golden eagles. The park's 40 or more species of mammals are likely to be more elusive—chamois aside—especially the main attractions, the bears and the wolves.

Bears were common here until the 16th century, but were almost extinct by 1915, when bounties on every animal killed were still being paid. Today, between 80 and 100 are thought to exist, both their number and range slowly increasing. Although descended from alpine bears (a species also in decline), the Abruzzo bear has developed enough indigenous features to qualify as a subspecies, *ursus actos marsicanus.* Wolves in the wild total about 30, their number threatened by Italy's huge numbers of feral dogs, with whom they compete for food and with whom they interbreed. A few Apennine wolves are kept in reserves near Pescasseroli and Civitella Alfedena for study purposes and to preserve the subspecies' thoroughbred characteristics.

Once you have seen the park, it makes sense to take in some of the

timeless villages and superb mountain scenery nearby. **Scanno** to the east of the park is a picturesque target—many of the townswomen here still wear traditional dress—as is **Sulmona,** a lovely old mountain town in the shadow of the Maiella, one of the most monumental of all the Apennine massifs. Hiking and touring here are superb—use Sulmona as your base. The same is true of the **Gran Sasso** massif to the north, where the Corno Grande, at 9,560 feet (2,914 m), is the highest peak on the Italian peninsula. Autostrada A25/24 links Sulmona to L'Aquila, the best base for the Gran Sasso. From L'Aquila, be sure to drive up to the Campo Imperatore, a lonely upland plain, and to follow the SS80 road through the scenic Valle di Vomano to the north. ∎

Right: The position of the Apennine wolf—a distinct subspecies—is becoming increasingly precarious.

Pescasseroli
▲ 288 B5
Visitor information
✉ Via Piave
☎ 0863 910 461

Sulmona
▲ 288 B5
Visitor information
✉ Corso Ovidio 208
☎ 0864 53 276

Il Gargano

THE GARGANO IS THE SPUR OF THE ITALIAN "BOOT," AN
upland peninsula jutting into the Adriatic from the Puglian plains.
One of the South's prettiest and most varied scenic ensembles, its
interior is covered in the Foresta Umbra, a protected enclave of wild
and ancient woodlands, while the coastline is a medley of cliffs, coves,
beaches, fishing villages, and increasingly popular small resorts. Off
the coast to the north lie the Isole Tremiti, an archipelago of attractive
islands still little-visited by outsiders.

Manfredonia

🅐 289 C5

Visitor information

✉ Piazza del
Popolo 11

☎ 0884 581 998

Vieste

🅐 289 D5

Visitor information

✉ Corso Lorenzo
Fazzini 8

☎ 0884 707 495

The Gargano largely remains a
closed book to foreigners. Not so
to the Italians, who have discovered
its charms, and its beaches in
parti-cular. As a result, many of the
coastal resorts are busy in summer.
Note, too, that several beaches are
owned by hotels or campgrounds,
so access, unless you are a paying
guest, is not always straightforward.

If you come here in low season,
however, or drive and hike in the
Foresta Umbra, you will barely
meet a soul.

The best approach is from the
south via **Monte Sant'Angelo,**
or St. Michael's Mount, a mountain
town (highest point 2,634 feet/
803 m) famous for three apparitions of the Archangel St. Michael

between 490 and 493. A fourth apparition in the eighth century led to the founding of a monastery, a foundation whose importance was sealed by the Crusades, when soldiers came to pray here before embarking for the Holy Land from Puglia's many ports. Today, the cave in which the apparitions took place is one of Italy's most important points of pilgrimage, although the original grotto has been swallowed up by the **Santuario di San Michele,** a church of 13th-century origins prized for its ornate Byzantine bronze doors (1076).

From Monte Sant'Angelo, you have a choice of two itineraries. One runs north through the **Foresta Umbra** on the SS528 road. This route offers a firsthand view of the beeches, yews, limes, pines, oaks, chestnut, and other trees that comprise this wonderful tranche of relict woodland, one of Italy's newest national parks. Almost at the heart of the forest, near the intersection for Vico, lies the Corpo Forestale, a visitor center where you can pick up details of the region's many trails and other outdoor activities.

The second route, follows the forest road and its continuation (the SS89) north until you come to **Peschici,** one of the smallest and nicest of the villages. To its west lies another resort village, **Rodi Garganico,** as well as several good beaches and the lagoons of Lago di Varano and Lago di Lesina (both noted bird-watching areas).

Head east and you pick up the promontory's coast road, quickly reaching Vieste, the area's most developed village. From here, the road climbs through wooded and rocky landscapes, offering superb coastal vistas, where the beautiful contrast of green woodland and

azure seas and skies provides a constant backdrop.

Continue east and you will complete a return circuit to Monte Sant'Angelo, a distance of about 95 miles (153 km). You will have seen the best the region has to offer. No trip would be complete, however,

without an excursion to the **Isole Tremiti,** which can be reached by regular ferries and hydrofoil *(April–Oct.)* from Manfredonia, Vieste, and Peschici. The trip from Manfredonia gives you sensational views of the promontory's coastline, an added bonus. If you want a quicker approach, the closest port, at 8 miles (12 km), is Rodi Garganico (see above).

The archipelago's principal islands are **San Nicola** and **San Domino,** both renowned for their natural beauty and translucent waters. Opportunities for swimming, diving, and other water sports are all first rate, but the less active can enjoy scenic boat trips, island strolls, and historical sights such as San Nicola's ninth-century Benedictine Abbey of Santa Maria al Mare. ■

Right: Although tourism in the region is increasing, traditional activities such as fishing are still important.

Romanesque Puglia drive

This drive begins in Bari, a busy modern port with an interesting historic quarter, and takes in several towns celebrated for their Romanesque churches, Puglia's chief glory, as well as Emperor Frederick II's great fortress at Castel del Monte.

Begin in the city of **Bari ❶,** whose modern port and ugly suburbs crowd in on the **Città Vecchia** (Old City), an atmospheric labyrinth of streets and alleys that contains most of the city's principal monuments. Chief among these are the late 12th-century **Cattedrale di San Sabino** and the 1087 **Basilica di San Nicola,** both supreme examples of the Romanesque architecture for which Puglia is famed. Such architecture flourished in the region for several reasons. First, the strong government of Norman, Swabian, and Angevin rulers over several centuries provided the money and stability required to create buildings that often took

hundreds of years to complete. Second, the region was a melting pot of ruling and other cultures, with the result that its buildings combined the architectural styles of Roman, Norman, Byzantine, Lombard, Arab, and imported northern Italian craftsmen. Third, Puglia was at a religious intersection, located astride several important pilgrimage routes and close to ports used by pilgrims and crusaders bound for the Holy Land.

After exploring Bari's old center, drive west on the SS16 coast road as far as **Trani ❷,** a

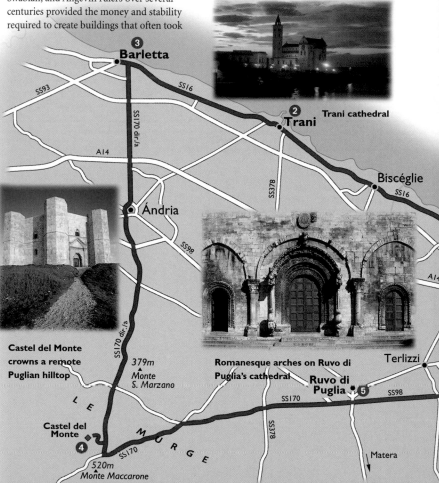

Trani cathedral

Castel del Monte
crowns a remote
Puglian hilltop

Romanesque arches on Ruvo di
Puglia's cathedral

bustling port of whitewashed buildings that boasts an outstanding Romanesque cathedral, a building known both for its unforgettable location—hard against the sea's edge—and its remarkable 12th-century bronze portals. The cathedral is dedicated to St. Nicholas the Pilgrim, an obscure local saint who reputedly arrived in Trani astride a dolphin.

Explore the village and then follow the SS16 to **Barletta ❸,** a relatively drab town enlivened, again, by its Romanesque cathedral, **Chiesa del Santo Sepolcro** *(Corso Garibaldi junction with Corso Vittorio Emanuele),* and by the **"Colosso"** *(Corso Vittorio Emanuele),* the largest Roman bronze in existence. From Barletta drive south on SS170 dir./a through the town of **Andria** and follow signs for Castel del Monte.

Castel del Monte ❹ *(Località Andria, tel 080 521 4361, closed Mon.)* is one of the South's most memorable and mysterious sights. A huge fortress visible for miles around, it sits 1,790 feet (540 m) above Puglia's plains and low limestone hills—a region known as Le Murge—its purpose and distinctive design a puzzle to generations of historians and scholars.

Built between 1229 and 1240, it was the brainchild of Frederick II, Holy Roman Emperor and one of the great personalities of the medieval age. Everything about the building betrays an obsession with mathematical harmony, and, in particular, with the number eight: The building is octagonal in plan, has an octagonal courtyard, and eight octagonal

towers, each of which contains two stories of eight rooms each. Some claim that eight is a symbol of the crown or the union of God and humankind, others that the castle's proportions reflect some astrological configuration of the heavens. Alternative theories suggest it was simply a hunting lodge or a retreat for pilgrims searching for the Holy Grail. That it had some special significance is clear—it was the only octagonal fortress among some 200 quadrilateral castles commissioned by Frederick on his return from the Crusades.

After visiting the castle, turn left onto the SS170 at the junction below the fortress and follow signs to **Ruvo di Puglia ❺,** whose cathedral again encapsulates the best of the Apulian Romanesque style. In Greek and early Roman times, the town was renowned for its distinctive red-black ceramics, the so-called Apulian ware, examples of which can be seen in the local **Museo Archeologico Nazionale Iatta** *(Piazza Giovanni Bovio 35, tel 080 811 042).* From Ruvo, a good road (SS98) runs east to **Bitonto ❻,** a town encircled by olive groves, and one whose Romanesque cathedral bears similarities to the cathedrals of nearby Trani and Bari. Roads from here via Modugno lead back to Bari. ∎

Ⓜ See also area map, p. 289 D4
► Bari
⟷ 78 miles (125 km)
�🕑 1 or 2 days
► Bari

NOT TO BE MISSED
- Trani cathedral
- Castel del Monte

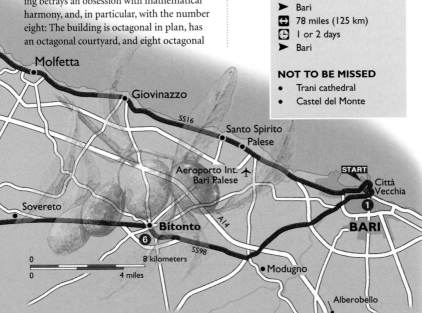

Trulli

Puglia's *trulli* are curious dwellings of mysterious origin. Round, single-story houses, their age is unknown, as are the reasons for their curious conical appearance and oddly tapered roofs. Unknown elsewhere in Europe, they are found scattered across much of the pretty pastoral countryside south of Bari, but especially in the towns and region around Alberobello and Martina Franca. Both places have become popular with visitors eager to experience the trulli at first hand.

Almost everything about the trulli is mysterious. The only simple thing about them is the way they are made and their considerable practicality—they are cool in summer, warm in winter, and cheap and easy to build. But this begs the question of their absence across the Mediterranean, where conditions and locally available building materials are often identical. At their simplest, they consist of uncemented stone walls and roofs. Most are whitewashed and many are topped with strange stone markers, usually a cross or bizarre symbol, tokens of unknown magical or superstitious significance. Roofs are also often painted with arcane hieroglyphics.

The earliest theories for their existence have their roots in peasant artfulness. During the 15th century, Ferdinand I of Aragon prohibited his Puglian subjects from building permanent houses, the idea being that he could move a servile labor force where it was most needed. In response, the Puglians—or so it is claimed—built loose-stoned houses that could be easily dismantled if their occupants needed to move, or if word came of an impending visit from one of the emperor's inspectors. Another theory has it that the houses were a sophisticated form of tax evasion—the Aragonese had imposed a levy on all houses except those that were unfinished, an exemption for which the Puglians could quickly qualify by removing (and later replacing) their loose-stoned roofs.

These theories are quaint, but in truth the origins of the trulli are probably even more exotic. The oldest trulli probably dates back to the 13th century, although the majority are no more than 200 or 300 years old. Some current thinking connects the trulli with similar structures in Mycenae, in Greece, which would link them with a civilization almost 5,000 years old. Such links are not far-fetched, for Puglia's ports are the closest of any in Italy to the Greek mainland. Furthermore, much of the region fell within the realm of Magna Graecia, the area of southern Italy and Sicily colonized by the Greeks between the eighth and third centuries B.C.

Unfortunately, this theory does not explain why trulli are so limited in geographical extent. One that does suggests trulli are based on the "sugarloaf" houses of Syria and other parts of the Middle East, and that one or two were built as tombs or homes in Puglia by monks who settled there from the east. Local people then copied these and adapted them to everyday use. Another idea, along similar lines, suggests that soldiers who disembarked at Puglian ports on their way home from the Crusades introduced the building style to parts of the region.

If you want to see trulli, head for Alberobello where there are some 1,500 examples. Alberobello means "the beautiful tree," from its earlier Latin name, *Silva Arboris Belli*, after the oak woods that once covered the region. Be warned, however, that it is often a busy place, and that while some of the trulli have been converted into evocative hotels and restaurants, others have been turned into stores selling trashy souvenirs.

You can see other trulli in more pastoral surroundings on the road to the nearby town of Martina Franca, and on the road along the Valle d'Itria from Martina Franca to Locorotondo. Martina Franca, despite its off-putting suburbs, is worth a stop in its own right for the baroque architecture of Via Cavour, the Palazzo Ducale (1668), and the church of San Martino (1747–1775). The town walls, and Viale de Gaspari in particular, offer good views over the trulli-dotted countryside. ∎

The traditional trulli in Puglia may have come from Greece or Syria, but scholars are still uncertain of their precise origins.

Lecce

LECCE IS ALMOST UNIVERSALLY KNOWN AS THE "Florence of the baroque," a sobriquet coined as a testimony to an architectural flowering unequalled in southern Italy. Greeks, Romans, Normans, Saracens, and Swabians all left their mark here, but the most lasting legacy was that of Hapsburg Spain, whose ruling denizens, fired by the fervor of the Counter Reformation and financed by wealthy local merchants, effected a sweeping architectural transformation of the city during the 17th century.

Lecce's baroque veneer was applied not only to its major buildings, but also to these buildings' many decorative details: Balconies, porches, pedestals, courtyards, and windows are all smothered in garlands of fruit, chubby statues, gargoyles, and intricately worked curlicues of stone. Almost every surface of a certain age is adorned with the light, golden, and close-grained local limestone—*pietra dorata*—whose easily worked but durable properties proved perfectly suited to the demands of carving

The city's baroque heart is **Piazza del Duomo,** dominated by the cathedral, which was rebuilt by the chief architect of the city's transformation, Giuseppe Zimbalo, between 1659 and 1670. Alongside it stands the **Palazzo Vescovile** (the Bishops' Palace, 1632), and the

glorious **Seminario** (Seminary), built between 1694 and 1709 by Zimbalo's star pupil, Giuseppe Cino. Walk west from the square on Via Vittorio Emanuele and Via Giuseppe Libertini and you come to the **Chiesa del Rosario,** or San Giovanni Battista (1691–1728), Zimbalo's last, and to many eyes, finest work.

Then retrace your steps and head for **Piazza Sant'Oronzo,** Lecce's busy main square, named after the town's first bishop, St. Orontius, a prelate martyred by the Romans in the first century. On the piazza's southern flank lies the partially excavated remains of a Roman amphitheater, along with Lecce's former town hall, the **Sedile,** or Palazzo Seggio (1592). Nearby stands the **Colonna di Sant'Oronzo,** one of two pillars that once marked the end of the old Via Appia, an important Roman road, in the nearby town of Brindisi. Another baroque church, **Santa Maria delle Grazie,** dominates the square's southeast corner. Beyond it rises the unmistakable bulk of the city's **Castello,** a 16th-century fortress built by Emperor Charles V *(Closed to the public).*

From the square, walk north on Via Umberto I to visit **Santa Croce,** the apotheosis of Lecce's vivacious baroque style. Begun in 1549, the church was the work of several architects, including the ubiquitous Zimbalo, who was

Left: **Lecce's local limestone is perfectly adapted to the demands of intricate and detailed carving.**

Lecce

🅰 289 E4

Visitor information

✉ Via Vittorio Emanuele II 24

☎ 0832 248 092

🕐 Closed Sat.–Sun.

responsible for the facade's pediment and rose window. Alongside stands the **Palazzo del Governo** (1659–1695), former residence of the city's governor, also by Zimbalo. (*No admission to visitors.*) Around five minutes' walk to the north on Via Manfredi stands the church of **Sant'Angelo** (1633), a baroque confection by another member of the Zimbalo clan, Francesco Giuseppe Zimbalo.

Return to Piazza Sant'Oronzo and explore the knot of streets to its south, making a special beeline for the church of **Santa Chiara** and its adjacent first-century A.D. **Teatro Romano,** the remains of Puglia's only Roman theater. Continue south toward the limit of old Lecce and you come to the city's principal museum, the **Museo Provinciale Sigismondo**

Castromediano (*Viale Gaalipoli 28, tel 0832 307 415, closed Sun. p.m. & Sat.*). The museum houses a wide-ranging collection, but is best known for its ceramics, its Greek, Roman, and Puglian vases, coins, bronzes, and terra-cottas, reliefs removed from Piazza Sant'Oronzo's amphitheater, and an art gallery containing reliquaries, Byzantine icons, assorted paintings and gold, silver, and ivory artifacts.

The city's final major sight, **Santi Nicola e Cataldo** (1180), lies northeast of the old center on Via del Cimitero, but is well worth the detour. One of the region's finest Norman monuments, the Byzantine, Arab, and early Gothic elements of the original Romanesque church are complemented by a later baroque facade, the work of Giuseppe Cino. ∎

The elaborate facade of the baroque church of Santa Croce in Lecce took over 130 years to build.

More places to visit in the South

CASERTA

Caserta's industrial hinterland is dispiriting but the town itself is redeemed by the **Palazzo Reale** (*Viale Douhet, tel 0823 321 400, closed Mon., & Tues.–Sun. p.m.*), Italy's largest royal palace. It has little to recommend it save for its incredible size—there are some 1,790 windows, 94 staircases, and over 1,000 painted and stuccoed rooms. It was begun in 1752 for the profligate Bourbon King Charles III and finished 20 years later. The **gardens** (*Closed Mon.*) are equally vast: A shuttle bus drops you off at the main points of interest.

Ⓜ 288 B4 **Visitor information** ✉ Palazzo Reale ☎ 0823 322 233

MARATEA

Maratea is an unspoiled seaside resort just south of the Cilento, a knuckle of wild countryside with protected park status. It is a pleasant place to relax, as well as a good base for exploring the park and is also well-placed for exploring the Parco Nazionale del Pollino.

Ⓜ 289 C3 **Visitor information** ✉ Piazza del Gesù 40 ☎ 0973 876 908

MATERA

Matera is widely known for its unique ancient dwellings—the *sassi*—cave settlements excavated from the ravines, or *gravine*, in and around the lower part of the town. You can view the labyrinth of caves, inhabited since prehistoric times, from a specially built Strada Panoramica (panoramic road), but to make the most of this fascinating town, explore the honeycomb of habitations on foot. Make a special point of seeing the 120 or more *chiese rupestri*, or **cave churches**, carved by monks between the eighth and thirteenth centuries, and the **Museo Nazionale Ridola** (*Via Ridola 24, tel 0835 311 239*), a collection of locally discovered archaeological artifacts.

Ⓜ 289 D4 **Visitor information** ✉ Via de Viti de' Marco 9 ☎ 0835 331 983

PARCO NAZIONALE DEL POLLINO

Monte Pollino (7,375 feet/2,248 m) and the national park which protects it form the high mountainous instep of the Italian "boot." Utterly wild and majestic, it is a region that encapsulates the traditional ways of life of the rural south, and until very recently was all but unknown to outsiders. Do not be put off by the fact there is not much to see here—save the scenery—and few places to stay (the village of Terranova di Pollino is the best base). Seasoned walkers will find excellent hiking—the summit of Monte Pollino is the obvious target—and car drivers will also be able to enjoy the uncompromising landscapes.

Just to the east of the region you could also visit **Sibari,** site of the Greek colony of Sybaris, home to the high-living Sybarites, hence the English word "sybaritic." Only one percent of the huge site, which is 20 times larger than Pompeii, has been excavated. The site and small museum can be visited daily.

Ⓜ 289 D3 **Visitor information** ✉ Via Mordini 20, Rotonda ☎ 0973 661 692

LA SILA

The Sila are Calabria's main mountain ranges, a jumble of massifs famous over the centuries for their forests. Timber from these provided, among other things, the wood for many of Rome's church ceilings. Today, parts of the region enjoy national park status (Parco Nazionale della Calabria), although much of the scenery, while wild in the extreme, is more monotonous than that of the Abruzzo and Pollino parks to the north. Some of the most arresting countryside lies along the scenic SS110 road, and around **Camigliatello** and **San Giovanni in Fiore,** the main villages.

Ⓜ 289 D2 **Visitor information** ✉ Via Roma, Camigliatello ☎ 0984 578 091

TROPEA

The drive to Sicily from Rome or Naples is a long haul. One place to break the journey is Tropea on the Calabrian coast, a resort that unlike many on this littoral has largely withstood the modern developments which have tainted other parts of the so-called Calabrian Riviera. Beaches, hotels, restaurants, and surrounding countryside are generally first rate.

Ⓜ 289 D2 **Visitor information** ✉ Piazza Ercole ☎ 0963 61 475 ■

Sicily and Sardinia are worlds apart, two fascinating and rewarding islands whose rich art, culture, language, and history are at once entwined and yet often fiercely separate from those of mainland Italy

Sicily & Sardinia

Mount Etna, Sicily

Sicily

SICILY IS A WORLD APART, AN ISLAND SEPARATED from the rest of Italy not only by the sea, but also by centuries of history and cultural experience. Yet, it is also a vital part of the country—the German writer Johann Goethe observed that "to have seen Italy without seeing Sicily is not to have seen Italy at all, for Sicily is the clue to everything" (*Italian Journey*, 1789). He might have said much the same about Sardinia (see pp. 335–40), a less tempting island for the casual visitor, but as separate in its own way from mainstream Italy as Sicily.

Sicily was once at the hub of the known world. The largest island (Sardinia is the second largest) in the Mediterranean Sea, Sicily lay between the civilizations of Africa and Europe, providing a tempting prize for traders and invaders alike. Originally, the island home to the Siculo and Sicano, ancient tribes from which it takes its present-day name. Between the eighth and third centuries B.C., Sicily's rulers were the Greeks; in the ninth and tenth centuries A.D., it was under Arab control; and in the 11th century it was dominated by the Normans. Between times, The island attracted the Romans, Carthaginians, Vandals, Spanish, Byzantines, French, and Bourbons—and even the British.

Sicily's invaders bequeathed the island its extraordinarily rich heritage, the succession of cultures having molded every aspect of island life from art and architecture to language and cuisine. From the Greeks came the theaters at Syracuse and Taormina, and the great temples at Agrigento, Selinunte, and Segesta. From the Romans came the magnificent mosaics at Piazza Armerina, and from the Arabs a variety of Moorish-influenced architecture and much of Sicily's wonderfully eclectic cuisine—eating is one of the island's great pleasures.

In later centuries, the Normans introduced the majesty of Romanesque architecture, a legacy seen to best effect in the sublime cathedrals of Cefalù and Monreale. From the Spanish, came the decorative exuberance of the baroque, a style incorporated into many Sicilian churches and palaces.

All these artistic, cultural, and culinary strands come together in Palermo, Sicily's capital, a teeming, decaying, fascinating,

and occasionally troubled city which exemplifies writer D. H. Lawrence's observation that Sicily is "where Europe finally ends…beyond is Africa and Asia." (*Sea and Sardinia*, 1921). Palermo provides a telling introduction to Sicily's magnificent past and its occasionally sordid present, the latter manifest in the city's poverty-racked tenements, derelict factories, and unfinished roads and houses.

Similar taints exist on the Sicilian coastline, once one of Europe's loveliest, but now only seen to best effect at places like Cefalù,

San Vincenzo
I. Strómboli
I. Panarea · I. Basiluzzo
Isole Eólie
(Lipari)
I. Filicudi
I. Salina
Canneto
I. Alicudi
Lípari
I. Lípari · Porto Levante
I. Vulcano
Villafranca · Torre Faro
Tirrena
C. di Milazzo
Capo Gallo · C. Calavà · Milazzo · A20 · Messina
Mte. Pellegrino · Capo d'Orlando · Brolo · Barcellona
PALERMO · Sant'Ágata di Militello · Naso · Patti · Pozzo di Gotto
Bagheria · Golfo di · Caronia · Fùrnari · 1287m · A18
Monreale · Términi Imerese · Cefalù · Santo Stéfano · Monti · Pzo. di Vernà
Misilmeri · A19 · Castelbuono · di Camastra · Novara · Roccalumera
Villafrati · Collesano · 1979m · Mistretta · 1847m · di Sicilia
1613m · Pzo. Carbonara · Mte. Soro · Randazzo · Taormina
Rca. Busambra · Caltavuturo · Madonie · Cesarò · SS120 · Fiumefreddo di Sicilia
Corleone · Petralia · Gangi · Bronte · Linguaglossa
Prizzi · Álía · Nicosia · Troina · 3323m · Giarre
Chiusa · Lercara · Pozzillo · Etna · Rifugio
Scláfani · Friddi · Leonforte · Adrano · Sapienza
Santa Caterina · Agira · Nicolosi · Acireale
Mussomeli · Villarmosa · A19 · Paternò · A18
Ribera · Casteltermi · Caltanissetta · Enna · Misterbianco · Aci Castello
Raffadali · San Cataldo · Valguarnera · Catània
Aragona · Pietraperzia · Caropepe · Golfo di Catánia
Montallegro · Canicatti · Barrafranca · Piazza Armerina · Piana di
Agrigento · Favara · Sommatino · Villa Romana · Catánia
Valle dei · Naro · Riesi · Mazzarino · del Casale · Lentini
Templi · Ravanusa · Caltagirone · Francofonte · Augusta
Palma di · Grammichele · Golfo di Augusta
Montechiaro · Niscemi · Vizzini
Licata · 986m · Floridia · Siracusa
Gela · Giarratana · Palazzolo · (Syracuse)
Acréide · A18 · Capo Murro
Vittória · Cómiso · di Porco
Marina di Ragusa · Ragusa · Noto · Avola
Módica · Golfo
Scicli · Íspica · Rosolini · di Noto
Pozzallo · Pachino
Capo Pássero

Taormina, and off-shore islands such as the Aeolian (Eolie) archipelago, best known for the volcanic eruptions of Stromboli.

Inland, the landscapes are less ravaged: They range from the limitless ridged plateaus and shimmering wheatfields of the interior to the Madonie and Nebrodi mountains that rear dramatically from the northern coast and whose wooded ridges run along much of its length.

Finally, there is Mount Etna, Europe's greatest active volcano, a smoldering, snow-capped peak of brooding majesty. ■

Rome

Area of map detail

Palermo

BIG, BATTERED, AND BUSTLING, PALERMO IS NOT A CITY
for all tastes, its traffic, poverty, and decaying sense of baroque
grandeur not for the fainthearted. At the same time, it is one of Italy's
most vibrant and atmospheric cities, founded by the Phoenicians in
the eighth century B.C. and still bearing the stamp of its later Arab,
Norman, and Spanish rulers. Monuments to past glories rise amid
the modern tenements and cramped backstreets, fighting for space in
a city whose Arab bazaars, flourishing port, seedy dives, and teeming
thoroughfares offer a dramatic contrast between past and present.

Palermo

🅰 317 C3

Visitor information

✉ Piazza Castelnuovo
34–35

☎ 091 583 847 or
091 605 8351

Central Palermo's sights are dis-
persed, so arm yourself with a map
and be prepared either for lots of
walking or trips aboard the cabs
or crowded buses that ply the
city's three principal streets: Corso
Vittorio Emanuele, Via Maqueda,
and Via Roma. The most efficient
approach to the key sights is to start
at the western end of the first of
these, Corso Vittorio Emanuele,
working eastward to take in the
clusters of attractions near its seaward conclusion and its intersection with Via Maqueda.

The **Palazzo dei Normanni,**
or Palazzo Reale, occupies the site
of the city's ninth-century Saracen
fortress, a building enlarged by the
Normans and transformed into a
palace complex that became one
of Europe's leading royal courts.

Guided tours conduct you
around the 12th-century **Sala di
Re Ruggero,** or Hall of Roger II
*(Closed Sun., Tues.–Thurs., & p.m.
daily),* a chamber adorned with
mosaics of hunting scenes. Roger, a
Norman king, was also responsible
for the magnificent **Cappella
Palatina** (1132–1140), one of
Palermo's highlights *(Tel 091 705
4317, closed p.m. Sat. & Sun.),* a
glittering private chapel that encapsulates the composite architectural
style that flourished in Sicily under
the Normans. Ancient Roman
columns support its predominantly

Romanesque interior, which is
overarched by a Moorish wooden
ceiling and adorned with Byzantine
mosaics: These mosaics—
along with the similar mosaics in
Ravenna and Istanbul—are considered to be Europe's finest. Also be
sure—if they are open—to stroll
around the palace's palm-fringed
gardens, the **Villa Bonanno.**

Palermo had more than 200
mosques during its period of
Arab rule (831–1072). Many
were subsequently replaced by
Christian buildings, including
San Giovanni degli Eremiti
*(Tel 091 651 5019, closed Sun.
p.m.),* a deconsecrated church,
built between 1132 and 1148, on
Via de Benedettini to the south of
the Palazzo dei Normanni. Its five
bulging ocher domes bear witness
to the architectural legacy of its
Islamic predecessor—the church's
instigator, Roger II, is said to have
employed Arab architects and
personally insisted on the curious
domed motif. As lovely as the
church are its cloister and unkempt
garden, the latter a scented enclave
of palms, lemon trees, and subtropical plants.

Moving east along Corso
Vittorio Emanuele, you come
to Palermo's great honey-stoned
cathedral (begun in 1184), another
monument to the city's Norman
past. Its interior was much altered

**Opposite: Life
is lived outdoors
in Palermo's
cramped but
often colorful city-
center tenements.**

The interior of the Cappella Palatina in the Palazzo dei Normanni, built as a private chapel for the Norman king Roger II

in the 18th century, but the exterior has retained its wonderfully exotic blend of early architectural styles. Note, in particular, the main portal, a 15th-century work executed in a flamboyant Catalan-Gothic manner. Inside, the only surviving points of real interest are the royal tombs of Henry IV, Roger II, and the great Hohenstaufen emperor, Frederick II, and his wife, Constance of Aragon (located in two chapels in the south aisle).

The heart of Palermo is marked by Corso Vittorio's intersection with Via Maqueda, known as the Quattro Canti, or Four Corners. Immediately to the south lies **Piazza Pretoria,** a ring of fine medieval and Renaissance buildings centered on a 16th-century fountain known locally as the "Fountain of Shame" after its lascivious nude figures. Just to the south in Piazza Bellini stands the church of **La Martorana** *(Tel 091 616 1692, closed Sun. p.m.),* also known as Santa Maria dell'Ammiraglio as it was founded in 1143 by Roger II's admiral *(ammiraglio),* Georgios Antiochenos, a Greek Orthodox Christian. Subsequent baroque

alterations spared the church's sensational Greek-crafted 12th-century dome mosaics.

Alongside La Martorana lies the 12th-century Norman church of **San Cataldo,** whose external architecture bears marked Moorish leanings. The interior, like most of Palermo's smaller churches, is a riot of baroque overelaboration. Another example of baroque exuberance is **San Giuseppe dei Teatini** (1612) on the Quattro Canti, whose plain-faced exterior conceals an interior of matchless decorative splendor.

Before continuing east on the Corso, head north on Via Roma, pausing to explore Palermo's vibrant market area in the streets around Piazza San Domenico. This highly colorful district is known as the **Vucciria,** from a dialect phrase meaning a place of noise and confusion. The coinage describes perfectly the teeming, Arablike casbah, a source of junk as well as every variety of food from swordfish to *guasteddi*—rolls filled with calf's spleen, cheese, and a spicy sauce.

While in the vicinity, stop by **San Domenico** *(Piazza San*

Catacombe dei Cappuccini

Long after other memories of your Italian visit have faded, chances are you will recall the sights of the Convento dei Cappuccini *(Via G. Mosca–Via Pindemonte, tel 091 212 117)*. This is Palermo's most unusual and most macabre sight, and one not to be missed. They are some way west of the city center—any cab driver knows how to get there—but the journey is well worth the effort, although only if you can stomach the sight of corpses in various states of decay. Preserving the dead using lime, arsenic, and the drying effects of the sun was a Capuchin tradition, and one seen to eerie effect in the convent's gloomy, subterranean corridors. Row upon row of bodies are hung or splayed in a variety of gruesome poses. Each cluster of corpses is divided according to rank and profession: priests, monks, commoners, aristocrats—even children, the most disturbing of the catacomb's incumbents. All are wearing the clothes they died in, the effect morbid and comical by turns—bones and yellowing flesh poke through moldering gloves; tufts of hair sprout from crumbling top hats. ■

Domenico, closed Sat. p.m. & all Sun. & Mon.), the nearby **Oratorio del Rosario** *(Via Bambinai 2)*, and the **Oratorio di Santa Zita** *(Via Valverde 3)*. All three churches offer object lessons in the finer points of Sicilian baroque decoration.

Farther north, just off Via Roma, Sicily's leading archaeological museum, the extensive **Museo Archeologico Regionale** *(Via Bara all'Olivella 24, tel 091 611 6805, closed p.m. daily except Wed. & Fri.)* is a repository for art and artifacts removed from the island's myriad ancient sites. Highlights include a number of Greek bronzes and the metopes, or friezes, from the Greek temples at Selinunte.

Return to the Quattro Canti and head east to a cluster of sights grouped between the Corso and Via Alloro to the south. Chief among these is the **Galleria Regionale di Sicilia** *(Via Alloro 4, tel 091 616 4317 or 091 662 0220, closed p.m. daily except Tues. & Thurs.)*, an important collection of paintings and sculptures whose highlights are Antonello da Messina's painting of the "Annunciation" (1473) and an exquisite 1471 bust of Eleonora of Aragon by Francesco Laurana.

Immediately north in Piazza Marina stands the Palazzo Chiaramonte (1307), a Gothic palace best known for its garden's mighty magnolia fig *(ficus)* trees. If gardens appeal, walk south to visit the **Villa Giulia**, laid out in 1778, and the 16th-century **Orto Botanico** (Botanical Garden) next door *(Via Lincoln 2b, tel 091 740 4028, closed all Sat. & Sun. p.m.)*. Otherwise, walk to Piazza Marina's southern corner to see the **Palazzo Mirto** *(Tel 091 616 4751, closed p.m. daily)*, filled with gloriously decorated period rooms.

Nearby lies the **Oratorio di San Lorenzo** *(Via Immacolatella 5)*, another baroque gem with an altarpiece by Caravaggio. For something rather more unusual, head to the eastern end of the Corso and the **Museo delle Marionette** *(Via Butera 1, tel 091 328 060, closed Sat. p.m. & all Sun.)*. The museum has a fine collection of puppets from across Sicily—where they were long a source of traditional satire and entertainment—and other parts of the world. ■

One of some 8,000 corpses in the Capuchin Catacombs in Palermo. The first incarceration here was in the 15th century, the last in 1881.

The apse mosaic of "Christ Pantocrater" (Christ Blessing) is a common image in mosaics across Sicily.

Monreale

MONREALE IS ONE OF EUROPE'S SUPREME CATHEDRALS, A monument to the greatest traditions of Arab, Norman, and Byzantine art and architecture. Sadly, it has the misfortune to be stranded in a town almost subsumed by the seething suburbs of present-day Palermo. Brave the surroundings, however, for the church, and its mosaics in particular, constitutes Sicily's single greatest treasure.

Monreale
- 317 C3
- ✉ Piazza Vittorio Emanuele, Monreale
- ☎ Church: 091 640 2424. Cloister: 091 640 4403
- 🕐 Church: open daily. Cloister: closed Sun. p.m., also p.m. daily in winter
- 💲 Church: free. Cloister: $

The cathedral was founded in 1172 by the Norman king, William II, and drew on French, Islamic, and Byzantine models for its design and decoration. A finely carved portal frames its main **bronze doors** (1186), which are adorned with 42 biblical scenes—notice the repeated lion and griffon emblems, symbols of the Norman royal family. Compare the Romanesque scenes here with the more Byzantine-influenced bronze door (1179) on the cathedral's left (north) side.

Inside, the building resembles a giant casket of jewels, shimmering with gold leaf, paintings, and richly colored marbles, its nave and wooden ceiling supported by col-umns salvaged from earlier classical buildings. A glorious mosaic pavement mirrors the greater **mosaics** in the main body of the church—64,000 square feet (5,950 sq m) of decoration in all—a cycle completed around 1182 by Greek, Byzantine, and Sicilian craftsmen. The royal tombs of kings William I and II lie in a chapel to the right of the apse.

On its own, Monreale's interior would be accounted a masterpiece, but the monastery's equally celebrated Norman **cloister** is an added bonus. Some 228 twin columns, most sinuously carved or inlaid with colored marbles, support the quadrangle's Arab-style arches. To the rear, a pleasing terrace and **garden** are one of several points around town offering views of the Conca d'Oro, the name given to the so-called Golden Basin cradling the city of Palermo below. ∎

Cefalù

CEFALÙ HAS LARGELY ESCAPED THE MODERN BUILDING that has done so much to spoil Sicily's once pristine coastline. Charming and compact, this immediately likeable town, built below an immense fortresslike crag, has several pleasant beaches, one of Sicily's most perfect main squares, and a majestic Norman cathedral graced with one of the most sublime images of Christ in Western art.

Cefalù's main **Piazza del Duomo** is as satisfying a spot for a quiet drink or reflective half hour as you could wish for. Gently curved palm trees grow in each corner, overlooked by the amber-stoned facade of the town's wondrous **cathedral** (1131–1240). Legend has it the building was raised to fulfill a vow by Roger II, Sicily's 12th-century Norman king, who survived a shipwreck nearby and pledged a church to the Madonna in gratitude for his escape. Originally, the shrine was intended as Sicily's most important religious building and was designed as a pantheon for Roger's Norman successors. In the event, neither ambition was realized.

The church's interior is as restrained as its exterior—much of it has remained unchanged for over 800 years. Note the redoubtable wooden ceiling and Arab-influenced capitals, the latter perfect examples of the composite Sicilian-Norman Romanesque style. The celebrated **apse mosaic,** which depicts "Christ Pantocrater"— Christ in the act of blessing—dates from 1148, making it the earliest Sicilian example of an image much repeated across the island. A short distance from the cathedral lies the **Museo Mandralisca** (*Via Mandralisca 13, tel 0921 21 547, closed Mon. in winter*), a collection of coins, pottery, vases, Greek and Roman artifacts, and an exceptional painting, the "Portrait of an Unknown Man" (1472), a work by Sicily's most eminent Renaissance artist, Antonello da Messina (1430–1479). ∎

Isole Eolie

SICILY HAS A WHOLE CLUSTER OF RAVISHING OFFSHORE islands—Ustica, Pantelleria, and the Egadi and Pelagie archipelagos. None are as popular or spectacular, however, as the Isole Eolie (Aeolian Islands), legendary home of Aeolus, god of the winds. The coronet of seven islets are the remnants of volcanoes both active and extinct, and visitors come for the chance to witness raw volcanic activity and for the ethereal light, balmy climate, stark beauty, and aquamarine seas.

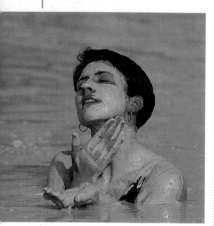

Ferries run to the islands from Naples, Palermo, and Messina, but the most direct access is from Milazzo, a port 16 miles (26 km) away on Sicily's northern coast. Boats also ply between the islands themselves. Walking and snorkeling are major attractions, as are the islands' volcanic black-sand beaches. Excellent wine, dessert wine in particular, is also made locally. However, you won't have the islands to yourself: The big three—Stromboli, Vulcano, and Lipari—are extremely popular, so you need to reserve hotel accommodations in advance. Other islands, notably Salina, are quieter.

Stromboli is the island most people make for, mainly because its volcanic action is the most reliable—spectacular eruptions take place from its summit cone around four times an hour. This makes it the busiest of the Aeolians if you wish to stay overnight, but you can easily visit for the day from Lipari, Salina, or elsewhere. Boats dock near San Vincenzo, a hamlet that with its neighbors (Piscità and San Bartolo) forms a settlement known as **Stromboli Paese.** Most hotels and other facilities are here, as is the island's main black-sand beach (north of Piscità).

The sulfur-streaked crater that provides all the entertainment can be reached by foot (guides available), but it's a long climb to the 3,031-foot (924 m) summit. Allow about seven hours round-trip and take plenty of water. Alternatively, you can admire the eruptions and smoking lava flows at a distance from a boat. The spectacle is all the more dramatic at night, so many people camp near the summit or take evening boat trips from San Vincenzo.

Vulcano is the closest island to Milazzo and the Sicilian mainland. However, it has one major drawback—the last major eruption here was in 1980. The island takes its name from the myth that this was where Vulcan, god of fire, kept his forge, a notion that led to the island lending its name to all things volcanic. If the god's in-house activities are currently diminished, however, they are not entirely curtailed, for all sorts of minor volcanic ructions

Left: Bathing in the natural mud baths of Vulcano. The hot, sulfurous mud can help skin complaints.

Isole Eolie

🄰 317 E4

Visitor information

✉ Corso Vittorio Emanuele 202, Lipari

☎ 090 988 0095

continue unabated—smoke holes smolder, mud baths bubble, and geysers spout.

Boats dock at **Porto Levante,** nestled beneath the so-called **Great Crater** (Vulcano in effect is four separate volcanoes), whose summit offers sensational views of the crater vicinity and the rest of the island. (Allow three hours for the round-trip on foot.) Walks elsewhere reveal landscapes of somber but striking beauty—try the hike to **Vulcanello,** another of the craters. The landscapes can also be enjoyed from one of the highly recommended summer boat trips around the island. Trips leave from **Porto Ponente** (15 minutes' walk from Porto Levante), a place also known for its (busy) black-sand beach and therapeutic sulfurous mud baths. The waters at **Porto Levante** beach are warmed by jets of volcanic steam.

Lipari is the largest and most scenically varied of the Aeolians, making up what it lacks in volcanic activity with some beautiful coastal and other landscapes. Boats dock at **Lipari Town,** cradled between two bays, Marina Lunga, which has a beach, and Marina Corta, from where you can pick up boats for some excellent trips around the coast. The town has a pleasant old walled quarter and a small archaeological museum in the **Castello** *(Tel 090 988 0174, closed p.m.).* In Lipari, you can rent cars, bikes, and scooters to explore the hinterland, whose highlights are the village of **Canneto,** the **Spiaggia Bianco** (the island's best beach), the headland at **Puntazze,** and the matchless viewpoint at **Quattrochi.** ■

Fountains of lava cascade from the top of Stromboli's volcano.

The third-century
B.C. **Teatro Greco,**
or Greek Theater,
in Taormina

Taormina

TAORMINA ENJOYS A FABLED SITE, ITS BEAUTIFUL LOCATION offering views across the blue expanse of the Ionian Sea to one side and the majestic profile of Mount Etna to the other. As well as enjoying some of Sicily's loveliest landscapes, the town boasts sandy beaches, chic designer stores, grand hotels, ancient monuments, and top-notch restaurants. All of these combine to make Taormina the island's most exclusive and visited resort.

Taormina
🅰 317 E3
Visitor information
✉ Palazzo Corvaja,
Piazza Santa
Caterina
☎ 0942 23 243

"I have seen many different types of traveller arrive in Taormina—idle travellers, lying travellers, proud, vain and splenetic travellers—but no sooner do they mount to the Greek theatre in the face of Etna than all their eccentricities disappear, and they become nothing but lotus-eating travellers."
—Walter Starkie,
The Waveless Plain,
1938 ∎

The town is also blessed with a mild climate, which means its matchless views are fringed with borders of palms, bougainvillaea, citrus trees, and swathes of luxuriant subtropical vegetation. Flowers fill the windows and balconies of its medieval houses, most of which twist around steeply rising streets and sun-dappled piazzas. Visitors intent on seeing, or being seen, make for the cafés and bars on the panoramic main square, **Piazza IX Aprile,** or the almost equally seductive establishments on Corso Umberto I, Taormina's main street.

More than most towns, this is a place to be enjoyed off-season, for its charms attract hordes of summer visitors, their numbers swollen by those attending the town's many arts and music festivals. Many of the festivals take place in the town's premier sight, the sublimely situated **Teatro Greco** *(Tel 0942 23 220, closed at dusk).* The German writer, Johann Goethe, considered the theater's setting the "greatest work of art and nature" *(Italian Journey, 1789).*

Other sights are few and far between, but this is not a place you visit primarily for art and architecture. Try exploring the **Giardino Pubblico** (Public Gardens) on Via Croce, or walk or drive the 2 miles (3 km) to the **Castello** on the 1,279-foot (390 m) Monte Tauro. Built on the site of the former Greek acropolis, the medieval fort offers tremendous views of the surrounding countryside. ∎

Etna

ETNA IS EUROPE'S HIGHEST VOLCANO. ANCIENT MARINERS believed its snow-tinged and smoldering summit—visible from far and wide—was the world's highest point. To the Arabs, it was simply the "Mountain of Mountains," while to the Greeks it was known as *aipho* (meaning "I burn"). A visit close to its summit, or a car or train ride around its fertile lower slopes, are essential.

Etna is a youngster geologically. Formed about 60,000 years ago, it sprang from undersea eruptions on what is now the Plain of Catania. Unlike many volcanoes, it tends to rupture rather than explode, creating huge lateral fissures instead of a single crater—some 350 fissures have appeared to date. About 90 major and 135 minor eruptions have been documented, of which the most catastrophic occurred in 1669, when the pyrotechnics lasted for 122 days. Debris was thrown over 65 miles (104 km) and a mile-wide tongue of lava engulfed Catania over 25 miles (40 km) away.

To experience Etna fully, you should visit the summit, which rises to 10,900 feet (3,323 m), *and* explore its lower slopes. For the latter, take the private Circumetnea railroad from Catania, which circles the volcano, or make a road trip along a similar route— the approach from the village of Linguaglossa is superb. As well as views of the mountain, you pass through groves of orange, lemon, figs, vines, olives, and the swathes of forest and other vegetation nurtured by the volcano's fertile soils.

As for the summit, volcanic activity alters the means of access and the areas you can safely approach. Guided tours are possible from Catania, Taormina, Nicolosi, and elsewhere using minibuses and off-road vehicles. Or you can drive yourself to the Rifugio Sapienza, a mountain refuge, take a cable car to the upper slopes, and then walk (allow a full day). Be sure to wear strong boots and clothing. ■

Photographers take pictures as lava flows in a stream during one of Etna's frequent eruptions.

Etna
◭ 317 E3
Visitor information
✉ Piazza Vittorio Emanuele, Nicolosi
☎ 095 914 488
✉ Via Cimarosa 10, Catania
☎ 095 730 6233

Siracusa

SIRACUSA (SYRACUSE) WAS FOUNDED BY THE GREEKS IN 733 B.C. Between the third and fifth centuries B.C., it became Europe's most powerful city. For years, its only rivals were the Greeks, closely followed by the Etruscans and Carthaginians, all of whom it defeated before succumbing to Rome in 214 B.C. Today, its old town, Ortigia, and the extensive archaeological zone (the Parco Archeologico), are essential stops on any Sicilian itinerary. Only the modern town, raised from the ruins of World War II bombing, is a disappointment.

The harbor at Ortigia has been the heart of the ancient city of Siracusa for over 2,500 years.

Start your Syracusean odyssey either in Ortigia, squeezed onto a tiny island linked by a causeway to the mainland and modern town, or in the Parco Archeologico, a pleasant open area ranged across the site

of the ancient Greek city, Neapolis, above the sea and modern suburbs.

The entrance to the **Parco Archeologico** is marked by a small visitor center (*Largo Paradiso, tel 0931 66 206, closed Mon. & p.m. daily*) and a sprawl of souvenir stands. Beyond these on the left lies the site's first major ruin, the **Ara di Ierone II,** created as a vast sacrificial altar in the third century B.C.—anything up to 450 bulls were slaughtered here in a single day. Today, its remains serve as an occasional stage. More survives of the fifth-century B.C. **Teatro Greco,** an amphitheater carved from the hillside's living rock—its 15,000-seat capacity made it one of the largest theaters in the Greek world.

Close to the theater lies the **Latomia del Paradiso,** site of a former quarry in which 7,000 Athenian prisoners were reputedly incarcerated in 413 B.C. and left to perish. Nearby is a grotto known as the **Orecchio di Dionisio** (Ear of Dionysius), christened by the artist Caravaggio in 1608. (Legend has it that the cave's acoustic properties allowed one of Syracuse's erstwhile rulers to overhear prisoners or conspirators talking, hence the strange name.) Another nearby cave, the **Grotta dei Cordari,** was used by Greek rope makers, its humidity preventing hemp breaking as it was being made into ropes.

Syracuse was the birthplace in 287 B.C. of Archimedes, the eminent geometrician and scientist best known for the discovery—made in his tub—that any body in water loses weight equivalent to the weight of the water it displaces. He helped defend Syracuse from the beseiging Romans in 214 B.C. by trying to direct the sun's rays and set fire to the enemy fleet using a system of lenses and mirrors. When the Romans entered the city he was so deep in calculations that he failed to hear them and was killed by a Roman foot soldier.

Before heading for Ortigia (buses and cabs run from outside the ruins), it makes sense to visit the town's **Museo Archeologico Regionale** (*Viale Teocrito 66, tel 0931 464 022, closed Mon. a.m., p.m daily, & 2nd & 4th Sun. of month*). A museum of finds from the archaeological zone and elsewhere, it lies on the grounds of the Villa Landolina, about ten minutes' walk east of the Parco Archeologico. Just west of the villa is the entrance to the **Catacombe di San Giovanni,** the best-preserved catacombs in Italy after those of Rome, although only a fraction of the vast fourth-century network is open to the public (*Viale San Giovanni*).

Ortigia formed the heart of ancient Syracuse for some 2,700 years, its easily defended island location and freshwater springs making it a natural fortress. It was here that the besieging Romans were held at bay for 13 years in the third century B.C. The ancient chronicler Thucydides described the former encounter as the "greatest battle in Hellenic history." Today, much of the island has a pretty baroque and medieval appearance, much of it the result of rebuilding that followed a calamitous earthquake in 1693. The Ponte Nuovo from the mainland leads into Piazza Pancali, home of the fragmentary **Tempio di**

Apollo (565 B.C.), Sicily's oldest Doric temple.

The town's most famous sight is the **Duomo,** whose baroque facade conceals the Tempio di Atena, a fifth-century B.C. temple skillfully incorporated into the fabric of the later Christian building. Also worth seeing are the **Fonte Aretusa,** Ortigia's precious original spring; the **Passeggio Adorno,** a scenic promenade; and the **Museo Regionale** (*Palazzo Bellomo, Via Capodieci 66, tel 0931 69 617, closed p.m. daily*), a museum of paintings (including works by Caravaggio and Antonello da Messina), sculpture, and other artifacts. ∎

Siracusa

▲ 317 E1

Visitor information

✉ Via San Sebastiano 45 (archaeological zone)

☎ 0931 481 200

✉ Via Maestranza 33, Ortigia

☎ 0931 484 255

The morning's catch on sale in Siracusa. The waters around Sicily are rich in fish and seafood.

Piazza Armerina

PIAZZA ARMERINA IS A VILLAGE LOST IN SICILY'S CENTRAL heartlands; a place of little note save for the Villa Romana del Casale, an isolated Roman villa 3 miles (5 km) to the southwest. Here are preserved some of Europe's most extensive and unspoiled Roman mosaics, a priceless treasure buried by a landslip in the 12th century and thus protected from the elements until full-scale excavations between 1929 and 1960 brought their glories to light.

Piazza Armerina
🖽 317 D2
Visitor information
✉ Via Cavour 15, Piazza Armerina
☎ 0935 680 201

Villa Romana del Casale
✉ Paratorre
☎ 0935 680 036
💲 $

No one is sure to whom the Villa Casale belonged, but to judge from its opulence and huge extent—it contains more than 50 rooms—its owner must have been a figure of considerable renown. The most persuasive theories suggest it was a hunting lodge and country retreat built for the Emperor Maximianus Herculius, who reigned as co-emperor with the better-known Emperor Diocletian between A.D. 286 and 305. Its role as a hunting lodge would seem to be borne out by the hunting scenes of many of its floor mosaics, and by its rustic position.

While the villa's superstructure may have gone—skillfully fashioned modern walls and roofs suggest how it might once have appeared—the original mosaics survive in an almost pristine state. Their style resembles similar mosaics discovered in Roman villas across North Africa, suggesting their creators may have been Carthaginian, a notion borne out by the villa's centerpiece, an African hunting scene some 200 feet (59 m) long. Woven into this scene's rippling narrative are vivid depictions of exotic animals such as tigers, ostriches, and elephants, many of them being captured and caged for transportation to Rome for use in circuses and gladiatorial games.

Virtually every room features similarly fascinating mosaics, although the scene that attracts most visitors is the one depicting ten female athletes in bikinis. ■

Agrigento

MODERN AGRIGENTO PROVIDES AN UGLY BACKDROP TO
Sicily's principal archaeological sight—the Valle dei Templi, or Valley
of the Temples, site of the ancient Greek city of Acragas. Once this
"loveliest of mortal cities," as the classical writer, Pindar, described it,
was among the most important of Sicily's Greek colonies. Today, much
of its former grandeur is still apparent in the valley's extensive ruins
and its nine temples, the finest classical Greek remains outside Greece.

A tour group
takes a rest from
the heat in the
Valley of the
Temples. Here
are some of the
finest examples
of classical Greek
architecture.

The city was founded in 582 B.C. by
settlers from nearby Gela, a town
that had originally been established
by pioneers from the Greek island
of Rhodes. Although earthquakes
over the years laid much of the city
low, the worst damage was inflicted
by early Christian settlers, who
deliberately vandalized the temples,
sparing only the **Tempio di
Concordia** (430 B.C.), and only
then because it was converted into a
church in the sixth century.

This magnificent Doric temple
is the finest in Sicily and the finest
in the Greek world after the
Thesion temple in Athens. Other
only marginally less impressive
temples lie close by along the so-
called Via Sacra. Among them are
the 470 B.C. **Tempio di Giunone**
(Juno) and the fifth-century B.C.
Tempio di Ercole (Herakles).
The site's western margins, reached
by crossing the street known as the
Via dei Templi, include the ruins of
the half-finished **Tempio di
Giove** (Jupiter). Had this been
completed—work was interrupted
by a Carthaginian raid in 406 B.C.—
it would have been the largest temple in the Greek or Roman world.

To the north, at the end of the
Via dei Templi, lies the **Quartiere
Ellenistico-Romano,** the ruins
of part of a later Greco-Roman
town. Also here is the **Museo
Archeologico Regionale** (*Viale
Panoramica, tel 0922 401 565, closed
p.m. Sun.–Tues.*), an extensive collection devoted to art and artifacts
discovered in the valley. ∎

Agrigento

🗺 317 C2

Visitor information

✉ Viale delle
  Vittoria 255

☎ 0922 40 1352

Note: Allow a morning to
  explore the site &
  arrive early to
  avoid the crowds.

The Mafia

Everyone has heard of the Mafia. The word first appeared in Italian around 1860. By 1866, it was quoted by Sicily's British consul, who reported to his superiors that "*maffie*-elected *juntas* share the earnings of the workmen, keep up intercourse with outcasts and take malefactors under their wing and protection." Both the word and the organizations of which the consul spoke have ancient origins: The linguistic roots probably lie in an Arab word, *mu'afàh*, which means many things—protection, skill, beauty, ability, and safety.

The organizational roots are more elusive. Many scholars believe the seeds were sown as early as the 12th century, when secret societies were created to resist the imposition of rule by the Holy Roman Empire. Others point to the Bourbons, who used ex-brigands to police the remote Sicilian interior, a system that quickly led to the brigands taking bribes in exchange for turning a blind eye to the activities of their former criminal colleagues. Many also cite the rise of the so-called *gabellotti*, middlemen who acted as rent collectors or mediators between peasants or landowners and quickly grew rich by intimidating the former and acting as agents for the latter. United by similar aims, the *gabellotti* quickly became a separate class, bound by distinct codes of honor, behavior, and semiformal organization.

All theories are linked by a common thread: The centuries-old gulf between Sicilians and agents of authority, a gulf fostered by Sicily's long succession of exploitative foreign rulers. Nowhere was the breach more keenly felt than by landless peasants forced to work on the island's *latifondi*, vast feudal estates owned by absentee landlords in Naples or Palermo. The system went back to Roman times and survived until well after World War II. Where conventional justice and authority were either lacking or despised, it was only a matter of time before the gap was filled by all manner of local arbitrators—the so-called *amici* (friends) or *uomini d'onore* (men of honor).

The traveler Patrick Brydone, writing in *A Tour through Sicily and Malta*, summarized the situation in 1773: "These banditti," he wrote, "are the most respectable of the island, and have the highest and most romantic notions of what they call their point of honour…with respect to one another, and to every person to whom they have once professed it, they have ever maintained the most unshaken fidelity. The magistrates have often been obliged to protect them, and even pay them court, as they are known to be extremely determined and desperate; and so extremely vindictive, that they will certainly put any person to death who has ever given them just cause of provocation." He might easily have been describing events two centuries later. What many people do not know is that Italy once came within a whisker of overturning this state of affairs. Under Mussolini, the legendary police chief Cesare Mori used brutal and entirely illegal measures to combat the Mafia, and, but for World War II, might have crushed it entirely. Ironically, it was the intervention of the Americans that foiled the venture. In preparing for the invasion of Sicily in 1943, the Allies had only one source of intelligence and logistical support—the Mafia—with whom it forged links by exploiting the contacts of Italo-American gangsters such as Lucky Luciano (Luciano's sentence was reassessed in the light of his assistance).

Once the Allies had taken the island, they further reinforced Mafia power by drafting its often highly placed members onto the new Allied Military Government—of 66 Sicilian towns, 62 were entrusted to men with criminal connections. Mafia power was further consolidated in Italy's postwar boom, when huge fortunes were made in construction. Money was then laundered into legitimate businesses or funneled into narcotics, a trade that altered forever the nature of Mafia business. Despite occasional judicial successes, the Mafia's dismemberment remains highly unlikely, largely because its tentacles are now so tightly entwined in Italy's legitimate economy: Not for nothing do the Italians refer to the Mafia as *la piovra*—the octopus. ■

The funeral procession of the bodyguard of anti-Mafia judge Paolo Borsellino

Sardinia

Sardinia has none of Sicily's set pieces, scenic or cultural. Its principal attraction is a peerless coastline, with the Costa Smeralda and other less well-known resorts providing a magnet for those in search of golden sands and emerald seas—opportunities here for diving, sailing, and other water sports are unparalleled. Invaders left their mark on the island as they did in Sicily, but with less spectacular effect, mostly because the island's starkly beautiful interior was far more inhospitable than its Sicilian equivalent. Venture inland today, preferably to the Gennargentu mountains, and you will discover some traditions and ways of life that have remained unchanged for centuries.

Women in Sardinia wearing traditional dress. The island is one of the few places in Italy where such scenes are common, but even here the old ways are disappearing fast.

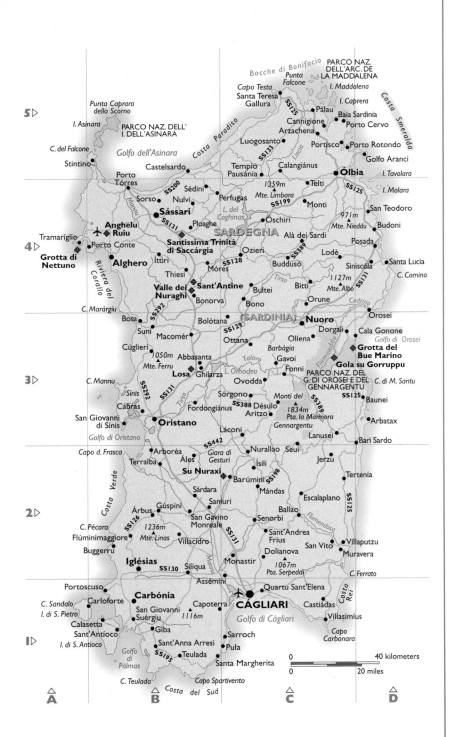

Bocche di Bonifacio

PARCO NAZ. DELL'ARC. DE LA MADDALENA

Punta Falcone

Capo Testa
Santa Teresa Gallura

I. Maddalena

I. Caprera

Pàlau
Baia Sardinia
Porto Cervo

Cannigione
Arzachena
Luogosanto

Portisco
Porto Rotondo

Golfo Aranci

Punta Caprara dello Scorno

I. Asinara

PARCO NAZ. DELL' I. DELL'ASINARA

Costa Paradiso

Costa Smeralda

C. del Falcone

Golfo dell'Asinara

Stintino

Castelsardo

Tempio Pausánia

Calangiánus

Olbia

I. Tavolara

Porto Tórres

Sédini

1359m
Mte. Limbara

Telti

I. Molara

Sorso
Nulvi

Perfugas

Monti

San Teodoro

Sássari

L. del Coghinas

SS199

971m
Mte. Nieddu

Budoni

Ploaghe

Óschiri

Ánghelu Ruiu

Tramaríglio

Porto Conte

SARDEGNA

Alà dei Sardi

Posada

Santa Lucia

Grotta di Nettuno

Alghero

Ittiri

Santissima Trinità di Saccárgia

Ozieri

Lodè

Siniscóla

C. Comino

Thiesi

Móres

Buddusò

1127m
Mte. Albo

C. Marárgiu

Valle dei Nuraghi

Sant'Antine

Bultei

Bitti

Orune

Cedrino

Bonorva

Bono

Orosei

Riviera del Corallo

Bosa

Bolótana

(SARDINIA)

Nuoro

Golfo di Orosei

Suni

Macomér

Oliéna

Dorgali

Cala Gonone

Cúglieri

Ottana

Barbágia

Grotta del Bue Marino

1050m
Mte. Ferru

Abbasanta

Gavoi

Gola su Gorruppu

C. Mannu

Losa

Ghilarza

Ovodda

Fonni

PARCO NAZ. DEL G. DI OROSEI E DEL GENNARGENTU

C. di M. Santu

Sìnis

Cábras

Sórgono

Monti del

Baunei

San Giovanni di Sìnis

Fordongiánus

Désulo
Aritzo

1834m
Pta. la Marmora

Arbatax

Oristano

Láconi

Gennargentu

Lanusei

Golfo di Oristano

Nurallao

Seui

Bari Sardo

Capo d. Frasca

Arboréa

Giara di Gesturi

Ísili

Jerzu

Terralba

Áles

Su Nuraxi

Barúmini

Tertenía

Costa Verde

Sárdara

Mándas

Escalaplano

Árbus

Gúspini

Sanluri

Ballào

C. Pécora

San Gavino Monreale

Senorbi

Flumendosa

Flúminimaggiore

1236m
Mte. Linas

Villacidro

Sant'Andrea Frius

San Vito

Villaputzu

Buggerru

Dolianova

Muravera

Iglésias

SS130

Silíqua

Monastir

1067m
Pta. Serpeddi

C. Ferrato

Portoscuso

Assémini

Quartu Sant'Elena

Costa Rei

C. Sandalo

Carloforte

Carbónia

Capoterra

CÁGLIARI

Castiádas

I. di S. Pietro

San Giovanni Suérgiu

1116m

Golfo di Cágliari

Villasimíus

Calasetta
Sant'Antíoco

Giba

Sarroch

Capo Carbonara

I. di S. Antíoco

Sant'Anna Arresi

Pula

Golfo di Pàlmas

SS195

Teulada

Santa Margherita

C. Teulada

Costa del Sud

Capo Spartivento

0   40 kilometers

0   20 miles

A   **B**   **C**   **D**

Costa Smeralda

ASK ALMOST ANY ITALIAN WHERE THEY WOULD MOST LIKE
to spend an Italian beach vacation and chances are they will say
Sardinia, and more specifically the Costa Smeralda, or Emerald
Coast. The rags-to-riches story of this stretch of the island's northeast
coastline began when the Aga Khan built a single luxury resort
village—Porto Cervo—in the 1960s. Similar resorts followed, turning
the area into one of Europe's most exclusive summer retreats.

Costa Smeralda

🅰 335 D5

Those with time to spare will find a
host of beautiful beaches, turquoise
seas, and unspoiled resorts around
the Sardinian coast. Those with less
time, should make straight for the
Costa Smeralda and any of its
resorts—**Porto Rotondo,
Portisco, Baia Sardinia,** and
the granddaddy of them all, **Porto
Cervo.** All are similarly chic and
exclusive and based mostly around
upscale hotel resorts or self-contained resort villages. Choose well
and you will have a relaxing time—
but don't expect much by way of
local Sardinian color or character.

Relatively undeveloped adjacent
resorts include Santa Teresa
Gallura, Palau, Cannigione, and
the beaches at Punta Falcone, Capo
Testa, and La Marmorata.

Some of the island's northern
highlights are within a morning's
drive. For example, from the SS199
east of Olbia, or from Castelsardo
on the northern coast, you can visit
a succession of Pisan-Romanesque
churches. Take roads south and
west toward Ozieri and Sassari,
and you pass half a dozen of these
churches, including **Santissima
Trinità di Saccargia,** Sardinia's
loveliest religious building. This
itinerary also gives you the chance
to drive along the **Valle dei
Nuraghi** (on the SS131), scattered
with the mysterious *nuraghi*—
ancient prehistoric dwellings—for
which the island is celebrated (see
box, p. 338), and leaves you well
placed for Alghero, one of northern
Sardinia's most attractive towns. ■

Alghero

Sardinian towns are forgettable affairs on the whole, their medieval kernels blighted by modern building and uninspiring suburbs. Not so Alghero, a prettily situated port gathered around a walled and atmospheric old quarter. The town is popular with visitors, but its role as a busy fishing port means that it retains a role of its own.

Alghero owes much of its culture and appearance to the Spanish, and to the Catalans in particular, who ruled the town for some four centuries after landing here in 1354. The Catalan presence was so pervasive that the region acquired the nickname "Barcelonetta" or Little Barcelona. Catalan influence survives to this day, both in language—*plaça* and *iglesia* are used for piazza and church, for example—and in the decidedly Spanish look of the town's religious and domestic architecture.

Key sights in the old town's web of twisting cobbled lanes are the **Cattedrale** in Piazza del Duomo *(Off Via Roma)* and the church of **San Francesco** in Via Carlo Alberto. The former is a Catalan-Gothic building enlivened by an Aragonese portal, the latter a 14th-century Catalan-Gothic affair overlaid with Renaissance detailing and annexed to an exquisite cloister.

The town's best beaches lie to the north, as does the **Grotta di Nettuno** cave system *(Tel 079 979 054, guided tours daily except p.m. Oct.–March)*, best reached by boat, although road access offers far-reaching views of the region's cliff-edged coastline. Arriving by car, however, means climbing down the 654-step **Escala del Cabriol** (Catalan for the "Goat's Steps"). Allow ten minutes. ■

Alghero
335 B4
Visitor information
✉ Piazza Portaterra 9
☎ 079 979 054

Cala Gonone

Cala Gonone
335 C3–D3

Cala Gonone is a small but increasingly popular resort on Sardinian's east coast. It lies at the heart of the island's most spectacular coastal scenery, much of which is accessible by boat from the resort, or visible from above on the gloriously scenic road (SS125) that runs between the neighboring towns of Arbatax and Dorgali.

Ideally, aim to stay in Cala Gonone itself, a former fishing village gradually surrendering its former identity—but not its charm—to the march of modern hotels, restaurants, and other visitor facilities. If accommodations are full, then **Dorgali,** just 6 miles (10 km) inland, makes a good alternative base.

Approaching Cala Gonone from Arbatax and the south offers views of the **Gola su Gorruppu,** one of the island's most breathtaking canyons. Views around Cala Gonone itself are best enjoyed from a boat, the most popular trips being to coves south of the village at **Cala di Luna** and **Cala Sisine.** Cliffs in the vicinity tumble from the 3,000-foot (900 m) mountains that rear up along much of this stretch of coast. Boats will also drop you for the day at secluded coves along the coast, or provide access to the **Grotta del Bue Marino,** a spellbinding cave studded with stalactites and stalagmites *(Tel 0784 96 243, guided tours daily July–Oct.).* ■

Monti del Gennargentu

SARDINIA'S INTERIOR IS ONE OF WESTERN EUROPE'S MOST
traditional rural enclaves, an upland fastness where sheep are often
the only living beings, and where ancient customs, dress, and ceremonies are still preserved in remote, time-forgotten villages. No area
is more starkly beautiful than the mountains of the Gennargentu.

Situated midway down the east
of the island, the Gennargentu rise
to a height of 6,017 feet (1,834 m)
in a succession of mostly barren,
rounded summits. The name means
"Silver Gate," a reference to the snow
that covers them in winter. Their
heart is protected by the **Parco
Nazionale del Gennargentu**
(*Visitor information, Piazza Italia,
Nuoro, tel 0784 30 083*), a national
park that in truth is barely needed,
for this wilderness is so remote
that even the Romans did not
fully penetrate its depths. The only
practical way of seeing the region is
by car, following roads such as the
SS125 from Arbatax to Dorgali
(see p. 337), or the scenic drives
from Aritzo, the main resort center,
to **Arcu Guddetorgiu, Seui,** or
Fonni, the highest of the island's
villages at 3,281 feet (1,000 m). ■

One of the many
ancient *nuraghi*
found across
Sardinia. Some
of the mysterious
structures may
be over 3,000
years old.

Monti del
Gennargentu
🅰 335 C3

Nuraghi

Myth suggests the Sards
are descended from Sardus,
legendary son of Hercules. In truth,
they could have come from almost
anywhere in the Mediterranean.
All that is known for certain is
that an indigenous population
existed before the arrival of the
Phoenicians and Carthaginians in
the first millennium B.C. Evidence
of its presence lies scattered across
the island, from the rock tombs—
Domus de Janas (elves' dwellings) —
of about 2000 B.C. to 1800 B.C.,
to the 7,000 or more mysterious
nuraghi established by the tribes
who inhabited Sardinia from
around 1500 B.C. to 500 B.C.
    Nuraghi were probably houses
or fortified citadels. No two are
the same, but most are conical,
with circular vaulted interiors
linked by passages to terraces
and upper stories. They occur
across Sardinia, but the three most
famous are found at Su Nuraxi,
outside Barumini; Losa, near
Abbasanta; and Sant'Antine,
between Macomer and Sassari.
Anghelu Ruiu, 6 miles (10 km)
north of Alghero, has the best con-
centration of ancient tombs. ■

Cagliari

SARDINIA'S CAPITAL LOOKS A POOR PROSPECT ON PAPER: IT has a large port, substantial population, lots of industry, and a surfeit of modern building. In the flesh, it is a surprisingly appealing place, blessed with a pleasant old center, a couple of major monuments, and easy access to nearby beaches and flamingo-filled lagoons.

Head first for Sardinia's major museum, the **Museo Nazionale Archeologico** (*Piazza Arsenale, tel 070 655 911, closed Mon.*), perched on the northern flanks of the historic quarter, an area enclosed by 13th-century Pisan-built fortifications. The highlights of the museum's wide-ranging collection are a series of bronze statuettes, the artistic highpoint of the island's prehistoric Nuraghic culture. In the same museum complex is a **Pinacoteca,** or art gallery (*Tel 070 670 157, closed Mon. a.m.*), devoted to Sardinian paintings from different eras.

Elsewhere in the old quarter, make for the **Bastione San Remy,** one of several terraces offering views over the city, and the cathedral of **Santa Maria,** whose main portal is guarded by 12th-century carvings originally destined for Pisa cathedral on the mainland. Be certain to descend into the lavishly decorated crypt, hewn from solid rock. Farther afield, try to see the remains of the Roman amphitheater (*Viale Fra Ignazio*) and the churches of **Sant'Agostino** (*near Largo Carlo Felice*), **San Saturno** (*Piazza San Cosimo*), and **Nostra Signora di Bonara** (*Viale Armando Diaz*). San Saturno dates from the fifth century, and is one of the most important early Christian churches on the island. ■

Cagliari's regular Sunday market is held above the city's Bastione San Remy.

Cagliari
🗺 335 C1
Visitor information
✉ Via Mameli 97
☎ 070 664 195

More places to visit in Sicily & Sardinia

BARBAGIA

The Barbagia is one of the wildest regions in Sardinia, which is to say one of the wildest regions in Western Europe. It lies near the island's center, between Nuoro and the almost equally remote Monti del Gennargentu to the south. It is full of tiny villages such as Mamoida, Arizo, and Fonni that in the words of the Sardinian poet Sebastiano Satta (1867–1914) are "as remote from one another as are the stars." Older people still wear traditional costume, one of the few places in Sardinia where this is the case. Sheep farming provides virtually the only income, though in the past banditry and kidnapping were also prevalent. Hiking is possible on the remote hills, but a car is necessary to get the best from the area.
⚠ 335 C3 Visitor information ☎ Piazza Italia, Nuoro ☎ 0784 30 083

ERICE

Some of Sicily's medium-size towns, notably Enna and Erice, are worth a visit if you are in the vicinity. Others, such as Catania and Messina—both mainly modern and earthquake-damaged horrors—you should avoid. Erice appeals by virtue of its panoramic setting, hunched 2,461 feet (750 m) above the port of Trapani, and the charm and medievalism of its alleys, streets, and squares (unusual in Sicily). The main sights are the 16th-century cathedral and **Castello di Venere,** a 12th-century Norman castle that occupies the site of the Eryx, a fortress and ancient shrine dating back to Greek and Phoenician times.
⚠ 316 B3 Visitor information ✉ Viale Conte Pepoli 11 ☎ 0923 869 388

GIARA DI GESTURI

A *giara* is a basalt outcrop, a topographical feature found across Sardinia. The best is the Giara di Gesturi, a high plateau about 2,000 feet high (600 m) and 8 miles (13 km) across. Its summit is cloaked in lush vegetation and forests of cork oak, the last a refuge for the once-common and intensely reclusive Sardinian pony. The plateau is good for walking, and is also known for its birds and spring flora—the best access point is the village of Gesturi. While in the region you should also visit **Las Plassas,** a distinctive conical hill visible for miles around and topped by a ruined 12th-century castle. More importantly, you should visit 15th-century B.C. **Su Nuraxi,** the most important of the island's *nuraghi,* or prehistoric dwellings. It lies about half a mile (1 km) west of Barumini, a village some 30 miles (50 km) north of Cagliari.
⚠ 335 B2–C2 Visitor information ✉ Via Mameli 97, Cagliari ☎ 070 664 195

SEGESTA

Sicily has many splendid Greek temples, but none occupy such dramatic surroundings as the tawny-stoned Segesta. The Doric temple (426–416 B.C.), almost encircled by a shallow ravine, stands in majestic isolation at the heart of glorious countryside. Myth claims the original colony, still largely unexcavated, was founded by Trojan companions of Aeneas. In truth, the site probably dates back to the pre-Hellenic cultures of the 12th century B.C. Work on the temple was probably abandoned after a Carthaginian raid in 409 B.C. A short road from the site leads about a mile (2 km) toward the summit of **Monte Barbaro,** whose hilly slopes offer glorious views and a dainty Greek theater (third century B.C.) still used for performances on summer evenings.
⚠ 316 B3 Visitor information ✉ Located 25 miles (40 km) east of Trapani, signed just south of Calatafimi exit of A29 Autostrada ⏱ Closed 1 hour before dusk–9 a.m.

SELINUNTE

Selinunte was among Sicily's most powerful Greek colonies, but fell into ruin following Carthaginian raids in 409 B.C. and 250 B.C. What survives places it second to Agrigento in archaeological terms, although only portions of its eight massive temples remain standing (much of the site is still being excavated). The best of its treasures have been removed to Palermo's Museo Archeologico Regionale (see p. 321) but a small on-site museum displays some of the lesser artifacts. Like Segesta, the site has a pretty location, making the ruins pleasant to visit for their own sake.
⚠ 316 B2 Selinunte site & museum ☎ 0924 46 277 ⏱ Closed dusk–9 a.m. ■

Travelwise

Street sign, Capri

TRAVELWISE INFORMATION

PLANNING YOUR TRIP

WHEN TO GO

Deciding when to visit Italy depends on the activities you plan during your vacation. Spring and fall (April–June and late September–October) are best for sight-seeing; summer (July–August) is extremely busy, but best for the beach; and winter (January–March) is the time for skiing. Most big cities—Venice is the exception—are quieter in winter, with fewer lines and lower prices. Easter, however, is always busy.

See pp. 387–89 for more details if you wish to plan your trip around one of the many artistic, religious, cultural, and other festivals and events that take place across Italy throughout the year.

Further help in planning your trip is available from Italian State Tourist Offices outside Italy (see p. 348 for details). Some cities and organizations also have useful websites:
www.visiteurope.com/italy
www.itwg.com
www.initaly.com
www.wel.it
www.traveleurope.it
www.tour-web.com
www.doge.it
www.romeguide.it
www.beniculturali.it/home.htm

CLIMATE

As a general rule, Italy has mild winters and hot summers, but its position and varied topography produce a wide range of climatic conditions. Climate is generally warmer and drier the farther south you go. Winters in the Alps, Apennines, and high ground of the south can be severe, with snow and temperatures below freezing. Winter across the rest of northern and central Italy is

shorter, but otherwise broadly comparable to the colder climate of northern Europe. Spring tends to be short and fall more drawn out, but summers are hot across the country—and very hot in the south.

Winter daytime temperatures in Italy range from around 15° to 59°F (-10° to +14°C), and summer temperatures from 65° to 90°F (18° to 33°C), although temperatures may often exceed these extremes. Italy uses degrees Celsius (°C) as its unit of temperature. To convert degrees Celsius to degrees Fahrenheit, multiply °C by 9, divide by 5, and add 32.

WHAT TO TAKE

You should be able to buy everything you need in Italy. Pharmacies offer a wide range of drugs, medical supplies, and toiletries, along with expert advice, but you should bring any prescription drugs you might need. Many brand-name drugs are different in Italy. A pharmacy (farmacia) is indicated by a green cross outside the store. It is also useful to bring a second pair of glasses or contact lenses if you wear them. Sunscreen and anti-mosquito products are advisable in summer.

Clothing will depend on your destination, when you travel, and the activities you plan: You will only really need to dress up for the grandest city restaurants and casinos. Don't be too casual, however, as Italians generally dress more smartly than most U.S., Canadian, and northern European visitors. Make some effort for any meal out, and always dress appropriately in churches—ideally no bare shoulders or shorts for women. Note, too, that dress codes are more conservative in the south and most rural areas. Bring a sweater, even in summer, for evenings can be chilly. Come

prepared for some rain and cool temperatures outside high summer. Hiking, skiing, camping, and other sports equipment can easily be bought or rented, but you may prefer to bring equipment such as hiking boots.

Electricity in Italy is 220V, 50 Hz, and plugs have two (sometimes three) round pins. If you bring electrical equipment, you will need a plug adapter plus a transformer for U.S. appliances.

Lastly, don't forget the essentials: passport, driver's license, tickets, traveler's checks, and insurance documents.

INSURANCE

Make sure you have adequate travel and medical coverage for treatment and expenses, including repatriation and baggage and money loss. Keep all receipts for expenses. Report losses or thefts to the police and obtain a signed statement (una denuncia) from police stations to help with insurance claims.

FURTHER READING

Italy has spawned a huge amount of poetry, fiction, and nonfiction from native and foreign writers over the course of more than 2,000 years. The following is a highly selective list of books you might want to pack or read before your vacation. The Italians, Luigi Barzini (Simon & Schuster, 1996) was first published in 1964, but no writer, before or since, has produced a more penetrating or better-written analysis of Italy and the Italians. This is an essential read.

The best relatively modern Italian or Italian-set novels include The Leopard, Giuseppe di Lampedusa; A Room with a View, E. M. Forster; Christ Stopped at Eboli, Carlo Levi; The Name of the Rose, Umberto Eco; The Aspern Papers, Henry James; and the works of Primo Levi and Italo Calvino. Evocative travelogues and nonfictional accounts include *Italian Journey*, Johann Goethe; *Italian Hours*, Henry James; *Innocents Abroad*, Mark Twain; *Naples '44*, Norman Lewis; *Venice*, James Morris; *The Stones of Florence/Venice Observed*, Mary McCarthy; *Love and War in the Apennines*, Eric Newby; and *Romans*, Michael Sheridan.

HOW TO GET TO ITALY

PASSPORTS

U.S., Canadian, and U.K. citizens require a passport to enter Italy for stays of up to 90 days. No visa is required.

AIRLINES

All the major airlines have flights to Italy, and many arrange package tours and budget-price flights. Alitalia, the main Italian carrier, has booking offices in most major cities around the world. Direct scheduled flights from North America land in Milan or Rome. Rome is the more convenient hub, and has a wider and more easily accessible network of internal flights. Flying time to Italy is about 8–9 hours from New York, 10–11 hours from Chicago, and 12–13 hours from Los Angeles.

Useful numbers
In Italy:
Alitalia, tel 06 65 643 (infor-
  mation) or 06 65 641
  (bookings)
Alitalia, tel 02 24 991
American Airlines, tel 02 6791
  4400 or 06 4274 1240
Continental, tel 06 487 711
Delta, tel 800 864 114
TWA, tel 06 47 241
United, tel 02 482 9800

In the U.S. and Canada:
Alitalia (U.S.), tel 800/223-5730
Alitalia (Canada), tel 514/842-
  8241
American Airlines, tel 800/433-
  7300

Continental, tel 800/231-0856
Delta, tel 800/241-4141
TWA, tel 800/892-4141
United, tel 800/538-2929

AIRPORTS

You will arrive in Italy from the United States and Canada at either Milan's Malpensa airport or Rome's Leonardo da Vinci (better known by its colloquial name of Fiumicino).

Fiumicino-Leonardo da Vinci, tel 06 65 951 or 06 6595 3640, is about 19 miles (30 km) west of Rome's city center. The best way into the city is on the express rail service, which leaves the airport hourly between about 7:30 a.m. and 10 p.m., taking 30 minutes to reach Stazione Termini, Rome's principal railroad station. Onward rail connections to all parts of the country leave from Termini: Florence and Naples, for example, are two hours away by train to the north and south. Tickets for the rail service can be bought from automated machines in the airport arrivals *(arrivi)* terminal, or from a small ticket office *(biglietteria)* on the right as you face the rail station platforms. The same office also sells tickets for the state network: Buying tickets here saves waiting in long lines at Termini.

Cabs outside arrivals are plenti-ful, but be sure to take a licensed cab (yellow or white), and *never* accept offers from taxi (or hotel) touts, however friendly they seem, inside the terminal buildings. Follow the clear signs for "Roma" and "Centro" if you are driving to the center, but be warned that traffic may be intimidating if you are unused to driving in Italy. Parking is also extremely difficult. If you are renting a car to travel onward, it is a good idea to see Rome without a vehicle and then rent a car in the city, or return to the airport to rent a vehicle there. Milan's major intercontinental airport, Milan-Malpensa, tel 02

7485 2200, is an impractical 31 miles (50 km) northwest of the city center.

At present, there is no dedicated rail link and incoming passengers must take either an expensive cab ride (well over L100,000) or board a special bus for the hour's journey to the Stazione Centrale, Milan's main railroad station. Buses are timed to meet incoming and departing interna-tional and intercontinental flights. The Stazione Centrale offers superb onward rail connnections to Bologna (1 hour), Turin (1 hour, 30 minutes), Verona (1 hour, 30 minutes), Florence (2 hours), and Venice (3 hours).

If you begin your holiday in the United Kingdom, you can fly direct to a wide variety of Italian destinations. Scheduled flights with British Airways, tel 0845-722 2111, Alitalia, tel 08705-448259, and a host of smaller cut-rate carriers leave from Heathrow, Gatwick, Stansted, Luton, and Manchester for airports in Rome, Milan, Venice, Genoa, Bologna (for Florence), Florence, Pisa (for Florence), and Naples. Charter flights and smaller operators also often fly to lesser airports such as Verona and Catania (for Sicily). Note that charter flights often use second-string airports near the major cities, namely Ciampino in Rome and Treviso for Venice (both have bus-metro connections to their respective city centers).

GETTING AROUND

TRAVELING IN ITALY

BY AIRPLANE
Some 40 Italian cities are connected by internal flights: Rome and Milan are the main hubs. Flights within Italy are operated mainly by ATI, Alitalia's domestic service, plus smaller companies such as Meridiana and Air One.

Alitalia, tel 06 65 641 or
06 65 643
Meridiana, tel 0789 69300
Air One, tel 1478 48880

BY FERRY
Car and passenger ferries and/or
hydrofoils operate between
Reggio di Calabria and Messina
on Sicily; Naples to Capri and
Ischia; Naples to Palermo (Sicily);
from Genoa, Livorno, and
Civitavecchia to several ports on
Sardinia; between Piombino and
ports on the island of Elba; from
Tuscan ports to islands in the
Tuscan archipelago such as
Capraia; and from Sicilian ports
to a large number of islands off
the Sicilian coast. For more
details, contact visitor centers in
the relevant ports.

BY BUS
Trains are usually quicker and
cheaper than inter-town buses
(pullman orcorriere), but in more
remote areas such buses (usually
blue) may be the only viable
means of public transportation.
Services are operated by many
different companies, but usually
depart from a town's major
square, outside the railroad
station, or from a bus depot.
Tickets must generally be bought
before boarding the bus, usually
from the depot or the nearest
bar or station kiosk. Inquire at
local visitor centers for details.

BY TRAIN
Train is an excellent way of
traveling around Italy. Fares on
the state-run railroad network
(Ferrovie dello Stato or FS) are
inexpensive, and standards of
service and comfort are
improving, especially on the
country's new superfast trains.

Tickets (biglietti) can be bought
at stations and some travel
agents and are issued in first
(prima) or second (seconda)
class. On fast intercity (IC)
trains an extra supplement
(supplemento) must be paid at
the time you pay for your ticket
or (for a higher fee) on the train.
On the superfast Pendolino or

Eurostar services, you must pay
a supplement and make seat
reservations in advance: Seats
are often bookable until a few
minutes before a train departs.

Reservations can be made for
most other services, including
long-distance overnight sleeper
(cucetta) services, available in
first class (single or double
berths) or second class (six-
berth compartments). Note that
larger stations may have
separate ticket windows for
such services, so check you are
in the right line: Look for the
word prenotazioni (reservations).

The FS issues two main rail
passes for nonresident visitors
to Italy (excluding Sardinia): the
BTLC (Biglietto Turistico Libera
Circolazione), a travel-at-will card
(first or second class) available
for 8-, 15-, 21-, and 30-day
periods; and a FlexiCard,
allowing four prespecified days'
travel within a 9-day period (or
8 days within 21, or 12 days
within a month). Supplements
are payable on Pendolino and
Eurostar services. Buy passes at
main stations in Italy or through
CIT Tours in the U.S.

Before traveling, you must
validate all tickets in the special
machines (small gold or yellow
boxes) on platforms and station
ticket halls: A heavy fine is
payable if you travel with a non-
validated ticket. If you intend to
travel extensively on trains, then
buy the pozzorario, a cheap
biannual schedule available in
bookstores and station kiosks.

BY CAR
Italian city centers may be
congested, but the rest of the
country has an excellent
network of clearly signposted
and numbered roads, from the
ordinary highway—known as a
nazionale (N) or strada statale (S
or SS) to the fast four- or six-
lane expressways known as
autostrade, where tolls are
payable. Sometimes you pay a
fixed rate, but usually you take a

card from automated machines
on joining the road and then pay
at a manned booth (alt stazione)
when exiting. Prepaid viacards,
available from autostrada service
stations (24-hour gas and food
stops), make toll payment quicker, especially at busy times.
Gravel-surfaced roads known as
strade bianche (white roads) are
common in rural areas, but are
intended for cars and are often
marked on maps. They are slow
but passable.

Maps are widely available from
bookstores and other outlets:
The best are the Touring Club
of Italy (TCI) 1:200,000 ratio
sheet maps.

Renting a car
It is easy to rent a car in Italy—
international companies have
offices in some railroad stations,
most airports, and all major
cities. Costs are high by U.S.
standards and it may be worth
arranging car rental through
your travel agent before leaving
home. Cheaper deals in Italy can
often be obtained through
smaller local companies—look
under "Autonoleggio" in the
Yellow Pages (Pagine Gialle).
Drivers must be over 21 and
hold a full license to rent a car.

Motoring information
Breakdowns Put on hazard
lights if you break down, and
place a warning triangle behind
the car. Call the Automobile Club
d'Italia (ACI) emergency number
(Tel 116), giving your location, car
make, and registration. The car
will be towed to the nearest ACI-
approved garage. Car rental firms
often have their own arrangements for breakdowns and
accidents. Inquire when renting.

Busy periods Italian roads are
especially busy on Friday and
Sunday evenings and immediately
before and after major public
holidays such as August 15. The
first and last weekends of
August, when many Italians begin
and end their vacations, are also
busy. City traffic builds up in the

early morning, evening, and pre-lunch periods.

Distances All distances on signposts in Italy are shown in kilometers (1 km = 0.62 mile).

Gas In Italy, gas *(benzina)* is expensive and priced by the liter (0.26 U.S. gallons). Gas stations on *autostrade* are open 24 hours and generally accept credit cards. Other gas stations usually close between 1 p.m. and 4 p.m., after 7 p.m., and all day Sunday, and many only accept cash. Be sure all pump meters are set to zero before the attendant starts filling your tank. Some stations have automatic dispensers that take L10,000 or L50,000 notes to use in closed periods.

Parking Parking is often difficult in major towns and Italian cities. Most street slots and parking lots *(parcheggi)* are filled with local cars. Many historic centers, notably Florence and Siena, have "blue zones" *(zona blu)* or similar areas that are completely closed to traffic. Others may have restrictions at busy times of the day. Metered parking *(parcometro)* is gradually being introduced in some cities. Try to park your car in supervised lots and never leave valuables or luggage in parked vehicles. Illegally parked cars, especially those in a "removal zone" *(zona rimozione),* may be towed away or receive a ticket.

Licenses U.S. and Canadian drivers in Italy require a full home driver's license *(patente)* or international driver's license. They are also legally bound to carry a translation of the license to help police, but this obligation is rarely enforced. For details of current regulations and how to obtain translations and an international driver's license contact any branch of the American Automobile Association or Canadian Automobile Association.

Rules of the road Most regulations in Italy are similar to those in the U.S., notably the fact that you drive on the right. Passing is on the left only. Seat belts are compulsory in front and back seats, and licenses, insurance, and other documentation must be carried at all times. Drink-driving penalties are severe, with heavy fines and the possibility of six months' imprisonment. A red warning triangle for use during breakdowns or accidents must be carried by law.

Speed limits The limit in built-up areas is 50 kph (31 mph) and 110 kph (68 mph) outside them, unless marked at 90 kph (56 mph). Autostrade limits are 130 kph (80 mph) and 110 kph (68 mph) for vehicles with engine capacity under 1100 cc.

TRANSPORTATION IN TOWNS & CITIES

Most historic town and city centers are small enough to explore on foot. In some towns, notably Lucca and Ferrara, you can rent bicycles. Elsewhere, motor scooters are available, but inexperienced riders should treat these with caution in busy cities such as Rome.

BY CAB
Cabs are difficult to hail on the streets. Most congregate at taxi stands on main piazzas or outside railroad stations. Supplements can legally be charged for luggage placed in the trunk, rides early or late in the day, on Sundays and public holidays, or trips to airports or outside the city limits. You may wish to settle a non-metered price for longer journeys before setting off. Cabs can usually be reserved by phone: The operator will give you the number and call sign of the cab that has been dispatched. A supplement is payable for reserved cabs. Round up fares to the nearest L5,000, or tip about 10 percent.

BY BUS
In cities and towns, trams and buses *(autobus)* are usually orange, and the procedure for using them is virtually identical across Italy. You buy your ticket beforehand, usually from designated bars—look for bus company logos or bar-tobacconists signs with a white "T" on a blue background. Some cities such as Rome also have ticket machines in the streets. You then validate your ticket by stamping it in a small machine on the bus. Generally you board a bus by the rear doors and leave by its central doors. A bus stop is *una fermata.* Often, as in Rome or Florence, a ticket allows a limited number of journeys within a set period (usually 1 hour, 15 minutes). Otherwise it is valid for a single journey. Day passes giving unlimited travel are available in Rome, Florence, and elsewhere. Inspectors board buses at random and passengers without valid tickets are subject to fines.

BY SUBWAY
Rome and Milan have subways *(la metropolitana* or *metro* for short). Stations and trains are drab, but both systems are generally safe. Although limited in extent, the networks are useful for crossing these cities in a hurry. Buy tickets from the same sources as bus tickets (see above) or from station machines and ticket offices. In Rome, a bus ticket allows one metro trip within its time limit. In Milan, tickets are valid for an unlimited number of journeys within 75 minutes of purchase. Integrated day passes in both cities give unlimited journeys on bus, tram, and metro services.

PRACTICAL ADVICE

COMMUNICATIONS

POST OFFICES
You can buy stamps *(francobolli)* from a post office *(ufficio postale)*

or most tobacconists (tabacchi), the latter indicated by a blue sign with a white "T." Offices are generally open from about 8, 8:30, or 9 a.m. to 2 p.m. Monday to Friday, 8 or 8:30 a.m. to noon Saturday. Main post offices in larger towns and cities usually open from 8, 8:30, or 9 a.m. to 7 or 8 p.m. Monday to Saturday The Italian mail system can be slow. Allow 15 days for letters between Italy and North America, longer for postcards. Priority post is now available. Post is guaranteed to arrive at its destination within three days for the United States and next day in Europe. It costs an average of L500 more than standard postage. Use fax for hotel reservations.

Mail boxes Small red mail boxes (blue in the Vatican) are found outside post offices or on walls in towns and cities. They are marked "Poste," and usually have two slots: one marked "Per La Città" (city mail), the other "Per Tutte Le Altre Destinazioni" (other destinations).

Receiving mail You can arrange to have mail waiting for you poste restante (or fermo posta in Italian) in Italy. Mail must carry your name and be addressed to the "Ufficio Postale Centrale, Fermo Posta" plus the name of the town or city. It must be collected from the town's main post office, and you need to present a passport or photo ID and pay a small fee. American Express also has a general delivery service.

TELEPHONES

Italy's telephone network is operated mainly by Telecom Italia (TI). Public phone booths are found on the streets, bars, restaurants, and TI offices in larger towns. Look for red or yellow signs showing a telephone receiver, or receiver and dial. Most take coins and cards (schede telefoniche), on sale at tabacchi and newspaper stands in L500, L10,000, and L15,000

denominations. Cards have a small perforated corner that must be removed before use. To make a call, simply pick up the phone, insert money or card, and then dial the number. Most booths have instructions in English. All calls can be made direct, without operator (call 10) or long-distance connections. Telephone numbers may have anything between four and eleven digits. Call 12 for information, 176 for assistance in English, 170 for the intercontinental operator (15 for Europe), and 172-1011 for collect calls. Calling rates are lowest on Sundays and between 10 p.m. and 8 a.m. weekdays. Hotels always add a significant surcharge to calls made from rooms.

To call an Italian number within Italy, dial the full number, including the town or city code (for example, 06 in Rome, 055 in Florence, and 041 in Venice). The code must also be used when calling within a city. Thus in Florence, you still add the 055 code when calling another number in the city. To call Italy from abroad, dial the international code (011 from the U.S. and Canada, 00 from the U.K.), then the code for Italy (39), followed by the area code (including the intitial 0) and number.

CONVERSIONS

1 kilo = 2.2 pounds
1 liter = 0.2642 U.S. gallons
1 kilometer = 0.62 miles
1 meter = 1.093 yards

Women's clothing

U.S.	8	10	12	14	16	18
Italian	40	42	44	46	38	40

Men's clothing

U.S.	36	38	40	42	44	46
Italian	46	48	50	52	54	56

Women's shoes

U.S.	6–6½	7–7½	8–8½	9–9½
Italian	38	39	40–41	42

Men's shoes

U.S.	8	8½	9½	10½	11½	12
Italian	41	42	43	44	45	46

ETIQUETTE & LOCAL CUSTOMS

Italians may have a reputation for being passionate and excitable, but they are also generally polite and considerate in social and public situations. On meeting people, or entering or leaving stores, bars, hotels, and restaurants, use a simple buon giorno (good day) or buona sera (good afternoon/evening). Do not use the informal ciao (hi or goodbye) with strangers. "Please" is per favore, "thank you" grazie, and prego means "you're welcome." Before a meal you might say buon appetito (enjoy your meal), to which the reply is grazie, altrettanto (thank you, and the same to you). Before a drink, the toast is salute (good health) or cin cin. Say permesso when you wish to pass people, and mi scusi if you wish to apologize, excuse yourself, or stop someone to ask for help. A woman is addressed as signora, a young woman signorina, and a man as signore. More vocabulary can be found at the end of Travelwise, see p. 389.

Kissing on both cheeks is a common form of greeting among men and women who know each other well. Dress appropriately in churches, respect those at worship, and do not sight-see in churches when services are in progress. Italians dress conservatively for most occasions, and unusual dress will be noticed. For advice on tipping, see p. 348.

Italians are generally more assertive in lines, when they form them at all, and in stores, banks, and other offices you should not expect "fairness" or for people to "wait their turn." You can be equally assertive in such situtations—such pushiness is not generally considered rude in Italy.

Smoking in public places is common and usually not subject to the restrictions common in the U.S.

HOLIDAYS

Stores, banks, offices, and schools close on the following national holidays:
January 1 (New Year's Day)
January 6 (Epiphany)
Easter Sunday
Easter Monday
April 25 (Liberation Day)
May 1 (Labor Day or May Day)
August 15 (Ferragosto or Assumption)
November 1 (All Saints' Day)
December 8 (Immaculate Conception)
December 25 (Christmas)
December 26 (Santo Stefano)

Some cities have special holidays when businesses close: Rome (June 29, St. Peter's Day); Florence and Genoa (June 24, St. John's Day); and Venice (November 21, Festa della Salute).

MEDIA

USEFUL PUBLICATIONS

Most Italian newspapers are sold from a street newsstand (edicola), many of which, in larger cities and tourist centers, also stock American, British, and other foreign language newspapers and periodicals. The International Herald Tribune, USA Today, and most U.K. papers are available on the day of issue from about 2 p.m. Airports and railroad stations often have the largest selection of foreign publications.

Italy has a buoyant newspaper market. Among national papers, Corriere della Sera is one of the most authoritive, while the more populist La Repubblica is also widely read. The best-selling papers of all, however, are sports publications such as the pink Corriere dello Sport. Many papers have strong city or regional links, notably La Stampa in Turin, Il Messagero in Rome, and La Nazione in Florence. Regional and city papers are often read in preference to national newspapers. Newspapers are a good

source of information on local events, museum opening times, and so forth.

English Yellow Pages for Italy lists English-speaking services, shops, and professionals in the towns of Rome, Milan, Bologna, Genoa, Naples, Catania, Florence, and Palermo. Copies are free to foreign residents and people traveling to Italy. Ask at embassies, consulates, and tourist information centers. Tourists may buy copies from international bookstores in all towns listed in the book or consult a copy at most large hotels.

TELEVISION

Italian television has three main state channels, RAI 1, 2, and 3, three prominent privately owned channels (Rete Quattro, Canale 5, and Italia Uno), and a plethora of cable, local, and other private channels. In most parts of the country you can expect to have 15 or more channels. Foreign movies and shows are almost always dubbed into Italian, never with English subtitles, but up-to-date hotels provide access to CNN, Sky, BBC World, and other foreign stations via cable and satellite. The main RAI 1 news bulletin is at 8 p. m.

RADIO

Italian radio is generally of a poor standard, although the number of stations, particularly FM music stations, is enormous. The only English-language broadcasts are those of the BBC World Service and similar organizations.

MONEY MATTERS

On January 1, 1999, the euro became the official currency of Italy, and the Italian lira (L) became a denomination of the euro. Lira notes and coins continue to be legal tender during a transitional period. Euro banknotes and coins are to be introduced by January 2002. Lira coins are issued in denominations of L50, L100,

L200, L500, and L1,000. There is also a telephone token (gettone) worth L200 that can be used as cash. Notes are issued in L1,000, L2,000, L5,000, L10,000, L50,000, L100,000, and L500,000 denominations.

Most major banks, airports, and railroad stations have automatic teller machines (Bancomat in Italian) for money (ATM) cards and international credit cards (carta di credito) with instructions in various languages. Before leaving home, ask your credit card company for a four-digit PIN number to enable you to withdraw money. Currency and traveler's checks—best bought in Italian lire before you leave— can be exchanged in most banks and Bureaux de Change (cambio), but lines are often long and the procedures slow. In rural areas, small towns, and much of the south, ATMs and cambio facilities are rarer— sometimes nonexistent.

Credit cards are accepted in hotels and restaurants in most major towns and cities. Look for Visa, Mastercard, or American Express stickers (Diners Card is less well-known), or the Italian Carta Sì (literally, "yes to cards") sign. Many businesses still prefer cash, however, and smaller stores, hotels, and similar establishments, especially in rural areas, may not take cards. Always check before ordering a meal or reserving a room.

American Express
Rome Piazza di Spagna, tel 06 67 641
Florence Via Dante Alighieri 22r, tel 800 864 046
Venice Salizzada San Moisè, San Marco 1471, tel 041 520 0844

OPENING TIMES

Opening hours present a problem in Italy. There are few hard and fast rules, and opening times of museums and churches, in particular, can change with little or no notice. Stores, banks, and other institutions in big cities are also increasingly moving to northern European hours (with no lunch and afternoon closing). Look for the words *orario contin- uato* displayed. Treat the following times as a general guide only:

Banks 8:30 a.m.–1:30 p.m. Monday to Friday. Major banks may also open for an hour in the afternoon and Saturday morning. Hours are becoming longer and more flexible.

Churches 8 or 9 a.m.–noon and 3 or 4–6 or 8 p.m. daily excluding services; many churches close Sunday afternoon.

Gas stations 24 hours on *autostrade;* store hours elsewhere (see below).

Museums State-run national museums usually close Sunday afternoon and all day Monday. Most close for lunch (1–3 or 4 p.m.), although major museums are increasingly open 9 a.m. to 7 p.m. Winter hours are shorter.

Post offices 8 or 9 a.m.–2 p.m. Monday to Saturday, but larger offices 8 or 9 a.m.–6 or 8 p.m. Monday to Saturday.

Restaurants Many restaurants close on Sunday evening and all day Monday or one other day a week (*la chiusura settimanale*). Many close in January and periods in July or August.

Stores Generally 8:30 or 9 a.m.– 1 p.m. and 3:30 or 4–8 p.m. Monday to Saturday. Many stores close Monday morning and another half-day a week. Depart- ment stores and major city stores may stay open seven days a week from 9 a.m. to 8 p.m. or later (10 p.m.), but Sunday and late hours are still unusual.

TIME DIFFERENCES

Italy runs to CET (Central European Time), one hour ahead of Greenwich Mean Time and six hours ahead of Eastern Standard Time. Noon in Italy is 6 a.m. in New York. Clocks change for daylight saving in May (1 hour forward) and late September/October (1 hour back). Italy uses the 24- hour clock.

TIPPING

In restaurants where a service charge (*servizio*) is not levied leave 10–15 percent; even where it is, you may wish to leave 5–10 percent for the waiter. In bars, tip L100 or L200 for drinks consumed standing at bars, and L500–1,000 for waiter service. In hotel bars be slightly more generous.

Service is included in hotel rates, but tip chambermaids and doormen about L1,000 (L2,000 for calling a cab), the bellhop L3,000–5,000 for carrying your bags and the concierge or porter (*portiere*) around L5,000–15,000 if he has been helpful. Double these figures in the most expensive hotels.

Tip rest room and checkroom attendants up to L500. Porters at airports and railroad stations generally work to fixed tariffs, but tip L1,000–3,000 extra at your discretion. Cab drivers expect around 10 percent. Barbers merit around L3,000–4,000, a hair- dresser's assistant L3,000–8,000 depending on the level of estab- lishment. Tip church or other custodians L2,000–4,000.

RESTROOMS

Few public buildings have restrooms. Generally you need to use facilities in bars, railroad stations, and gas stations where standards are generally low. Ask for *il bagno* (eel ban-yo), take a few tissues, and don't confuse *Signori* (Men) with *Signore* (Women). Tip attendants L200–500.

USA
New York 630 5th Ave., Suite 1565, New York, NY 10111, tel 212/245-4822, fax 212/586-9249

Chicago 500 N. Michigan Ave., Suite 2240, Chicago, IL 60611, tel 312/644-0990, fax 312/644-3109

Los Angeles 12400 Wilshire Blvd., Suite 550, Los Angeles, CA 90025, tel 310/820-0098, fax 310/820-6357

CANADA
Montreal 1 Place Ville-Marie, Suite 1914, Montreal PQ H3B 2C3, tel 514/866-7667, fax 514/392-1492

UNITED KINGDOM
London 1 Princes St., London W1R 8AY, tel 020-7408 1254, fax 020-7493 6695

TRAVELERS WITH DISABILITIES

Museums, galleries, and public buildings across Italy are making great progress in providing wheelchair access, but there remains much to be done. Few buses or trains have dedicated facilities, and virtually no cabs. Many historic cities present special problems, notably Venice, which has a large number of stepped bridges. Only hotels in higher star categories provide dedicated rooms, but hotels and restuarants will almost always do their best to provide appropriate help if you call in advance. Consult your nearest Italian embassy or consulate for details of the special procedures required to bring a seeing eye dog into Italy.

Useful contact bodies in North America include Wheels Up! (tel 888/389-4335), which offers discounted air fares and other travel arrangements; Access First (tel 800/557-2047 or 617/397-8610), which special- izes in vacations to Italy; and information agencies dealing with travel for visitors with disabilities such as AccessAbility Travel (tel 800/610-5640 or 800/228-5379), SATH (Tel 212/447-7284 or 447-0027), and Twin Peaks Press (206/694-2462).

EMERGENCIES

EMBASSIES IN ITALY

U.S. Embassy Via Vittorio Veneto, Rome, tel 06 46 741
U.S. Consulate Lungarno Vespucci 38, Rome, tel 055 239 8276
U.S. Consulate Via Principe Amadeo 2, Milan, tel 02 290 351
Canadian Embassy Via Zara 30, Rome, tel 06 445 981
Canadian Consulate Via Pisani 9, Rome, tel 02 67 581
U.K. Embassy Via XX Settembre 80/A, Rome, tel 06 482 5441

EMERGENCY PHONE NUMBERS

Police, tel 112
Emergency services, tel 113
Fire services, tel 115
Car breakdown, tel 116
Ambulance, tel 118

For legal assistance in an emergency, contact your embassy or consulate (see above) for a list of English-speaking lawyers.

For general help, contact *English Yellow Pages* (tel 06 474 0861).

WHAT TO DO IN A TRAFFIC ACCIDENT

Put on hazard lights and place a warning triangle 165 feet (50 m) behind the car. Call the police (tel 112 or 113) from a public phone (see p. 346): *Autostrade* have emergency telephones at regular intervals. At the scene, do not admit liablity or make potentially incriminating statements to police or onlookers. Ask any witnesses to remain, make a

police statement, and exchange insurance and other relevant details with the other driver(s). Call the car rental agency, if necessary, to inform them of the incident.

LOST PROPERTY

If you lose property, go first to the local visitor center and ask for assistance. Bus, tram, train, and metro systems in cities usually have special offices to deal with lost property, but they can be hard to find and are usually only open a few hours a day. Ask for directions at visitor centers, and also try bus depots and rail stations. Hotels should also be able to provide assistance.

To report a more serious loss or theft, go to the local police station or Questura. In Rome the main Questura is off Via Nazionale at Via San Vitale 15 (tel 06 4686). Many have special English-speaking staff to deal with visitors' problems. You will be asked to help fill in and sign a form *(una denuncia)* reporting any crime. Keep your copy for relevant insurance claims.

Report the loss or theft of a passport to the police and then notify your embassy (see above).

HEALTH

Check that your health insurance covers visits to Italy and that your travel insurance also includes sufficient medical coverage. For minor complaints, first visit a drugstore or pharmacy *(una farmacia)*, indicated by a green cross outside the store. Staff is well trained and will be able to offer advice as well as guidance in finding a doctor *(un medico)* if necessary. Also consult your hotel, the Yellow Pages, or visitor centers for help in finding or choosing a doctor or dentist *(un dentista)*. Be sure to take enough prescription drugs *(medicina)* to cover a journey—

brand names may be different in Italy, leading to confusion at pharmacies. If you need to renew a prescription, pharmacies will direct you to a doctor.

For more serious complaints go immediately to a hospital *(un ospedale)*. Emergency treatment is provided at the *Pronto Soccorso*. Italian hospitals often look run down, but the standards of treatment are generally good.

Before leaving home, consider contacting the International Association for Medical Assistance to Travelers (IAMAT), a nonprofit-making organization that anyone can join free of charge. Members receive a directory of English-speaking IAMAT doctors on call 24 hours a day and are entitled to services at set rates. Tel 716/754-4883 in the U.S. and 416/652-0137 in Canada.

The most common minor complaints in Italy are likely to be caused by too much sun and biting insects such as mosquitoes. Poison ivy is not a major problem, but Italy does have poisonous snakes *(vipere)*, although bites are generally only fatal if you have an allergic reaction.

Tap water is safe across the country. However, do not drink water if marked *acqua non potabile*, and never drink from streams in the mountains or elsewhere. Milk is pasteurized and safe.

Hospitals
Rome Rome American Hospital, Via E. Longini 69, tel 06 22 551
Florence Santa Maria Nuova, Piazza Santa Maria Nuova 1, tel 055 27 581
Venice Ospedale Civile, Campo S.S. Giovanni e Paolo, tel 041 520 5622
Genoa Instituto Giannina Gaslini, Via V. Maggio 39, tel 010 563 6324

HOTELS & RESTAURANTS

HOTELS

Italy has a variety of accommodations to suit all tastes and pockets. Choose from fine hotels in old palaces and castles, intimate family-run establishments, or the increasingly popular *agriturismo,* or farm holidays. The following is a recommended selection of the most comfortable and interesting places to stay in Italy.

Grading system

Hotels are officially graded from one star, the simplest accommodations, to five star (luxury). Grading criteria are complex, but in a three-star establishment and above, all rooms should have private bath/shower rooms, a telephone, and a television. Most two-star hotels also have private bathrooms.

Note that even in the smartest hotels, bathrooms may only have a shower (una doccia) and no tub (una vasca). Always ask to see a selection of rooms—you may be shown the worst first. Rooms are often small by U.S. standards, even in upscale hotels. All-day room service and air-conditioning are also comparatively rare.

Recommended hotels have a restaurant unless stated. A restaurant symbol is given where the restaurant is outstanding in its own right. (Note that the term *pensione,* referring to private rooms or the simplest hotels, is still seen, but is not used as an official designation.)

Location

Hotels that provide the best, centrally located accommodations within a town or city have been chosen for this selection. Noise can be a problem in urban areas, but a quiet, out-of-town option is often provided. Where possible, hotels are also selected for their character, charm, and historical associations. In country areas, the emphasis is on period villas and restored historic properties with pools and grounds and gardens. Choice and quality is generally poorer in remote rural areas, and in much of southern Italy.

Reservations

It is advisable to reserve all hotels in advance, especially in the major cities, and particularly in high season (June–Aug.). Note that in Rome, Florence, and Venice, high season often means Christmas, New Year, and Easter to October.

Make your reservation by telephone and confirm by fax. It is also a good idea to reconfirm reservations a couple of days before arrival. Hoteliers are obliged to register every guest, so when checking in you will be asked for your passport. It will be returned within a few hours, or on the day of departure.

Checkout times range from around 10 a.m. to noon, but you should be able to leave luggage at reception for collection later in the day.

Prices

All prices are officially set, and room rates must be displayed by law at reception and in each room. Prices for different rooms can vary within a hotel, but all taxes and services should be included in the rate.

Hotels often levy additional charges for air-conditioning and garage facilities, while laundry, drinks from minibars, and phone calls made from rooms invariably carry large surcharges.

Price categories given in the entries are for double (una matrimoniale) or twin (una camera doppia) rooms and are for guidance only. Seasonal variations often apply, especially in coastal resorts, where high-season (summer) rates are usually higher.

At busy times, there may also be a two- or three-day minimum stay policy, and you may be obliged to take full- or half-board packages. Half-board (mezza pensione) includes breakfast and lunch; full-board (pensione completa) includes all meals. Such packages are always priced on a per person basis.

Prices usually include breakfast (colazione), but where breakfast is optional (see rate cards in rooms), it always costs less to eat at the nearest bar. Breakfasts in upscale hotels are improving—U.S.-style buffets are now more common—but for the most part colazione means a coffee, a roll, and jelly.

Credit cards

Many large hotels accept the major credit cards. Smaller ones may only accept some, as shown in their entries. Abbreviations used are AE (American Express), DC (Diners Club), MC (Mastercard), and V (Visa). Look for individual card symbols outside establishments, or the Italian Carta Sì sign. As a general rule, AE and DC are less widely accepted than V and MC.

Hotel groups

U.S. contact numbers:
Best Western, tel 800/528-1234
Hilton, tel 800/445-8667
ITT-Sheraton, tel 800/221-2340
Jolly, tel 800/221-2626
Leading Hotels of the World, tel 800/223-6800
Relais & Châteaux, tel 212/856-0115
Italian contact numbers:
Atahotels, tel 02 895 261
Family Hotels, tel 055 462 0080
Jolly, tel 800 17 703 (toll free)
Starhotels, tel 055/36 921 or 1678 60 200

RESTAURANTS

Italy has one of the world's great cuisines, and the pleasures of Italian food and wine are as much a part of a visit to the country as the museums and galleries. Restaurants of different type and quality are found in every town or village, from the humble pizzeria to the great centuries-old classics.

Italian cooking has many common denominators—such as a simple approach and fresh ingredients—but it is also highly regional. Our selection includes restaurants that reflect the best regional cooking, but don't be afraid to experiment, especially in small towns and rural areas. If in doubt, look where local people choose to eat.

Types of restaurant

Categories of restaurants in Italy are increasingly blurred. Once an *osteria* was a simple inn, a trattoria was a basic neighborhood eating place, and a *ristorante* was an upscale establishment with culinary pretensions. Now some of the best places to eat can be *osterie*, increasingly being revamped by young owners as informal restaurants with innovative cooking.

Old-fashioned trattorias with bright lights and checkered tablecloths are also largely consigned to the past while ristorante is a term now applied to just about any eating place. A pizzeria remains the one constant—a simple, usually modern place that often serves basic pasta, main courses, and desserts as well as pizzas.

Wherever you eat, remember that neither a restaurant's appearance nor price necessarily reflect the quality of the dining experience. A pizza in a boisterous Neapolitan pizzeria may be every bit as good—and memorable—as a five-course feast in a sleek Milanese restaurant full of business people.

Where the number of seats in a restaurant is given as a range, the larger figure accounts for outdoor dining.

Dining hours

Breakfast (*colazione*) usually consists of a cappuccino and bread roll or sweet pastry (*una brioche*) taken standing in a bar between about 7 and 9 a.m. Lunch (*pranzo*) starts around 12:30 p.m. and finishes at about 2 p.m.—the infamous long lunch and siesta are increasingly a thing

of the past. Dinner (*cena*) begins about 8 p.m., with last orders at around 10 p.m., although hours may be later in southern Italy and earlier in rural areas or smaller towns.

Pizzerias often only open in the evenings, especialy those with wood-burning ovens (*forno a legno*) that take time to fire. Most restaurants in every category close once a week (*la chiusura settimanale*), and many take long vacation breaks (*ferie*) in July or August.

Meals

Italian meals traditionally begin with appetizers or hors d'oeuvres (antipasto—literally "before the meal"), a first course (*il primo*) of soup, pasta, or rice, and a main course (*il secondo*) of meat or fish. Vegetables (*contorni*) or salads (*insalata*) are often served separately with or after il secondo. Desserts (*dolci*) may include or be followed by fruit (*frutta*) and cheese (*formaggio*). Italians often round off a meal with an espresso (never cappuccino) and brandy, grappa (a clear, brandylike spirit), or an *amaro* (a bitter digestif).

You don't need to order every course—a primo and salad is acceptable in all but the grandest restaurants. Many Italians choose to go to an ice-cream parlor (*gelateria*) as part of an after-dinner stroll instead of dessert.

Meals are usually accompanied by bread and mineral water, for which you pay extra.

Set menus

The menu in Italian is *il menù* or *la lista*. Fixed-price menus are available in many restaurants in tourist areas. The *menù turistico* usually includes two courses, a simple dessert, and half a bottle of wine and water per person. Quantity and quality of food are invariably poor. Of better value in more upscale restaurants is the *menù gastronomico*, where you pay a fixed price to sample a selection of the restaurant's special dishes.

Bars, cafés, & snacks

Bars and cafés are perfect for breakfast and often provide snacks such as filled rolls (*panini*) or sandwiches (*tramezzini*) throughout the day. A few may offer a light meal at lunch. Stands or small stores selling slices of pizza (*pizza al taglio*) with different toppings are common.

It always costs less to stand at the bar. Specify what you want and pay at the separate cash desk (*la cassa*), then take your chit (*lo scontrino*) to the bar and repeat your order. A small coin slapped on the bar often helps secure prompt service.

Where a bar has a waiter and tables, especially outside tables, you pay more to sit and place your order with the waiter. Only in small rural bars can you pay at the bar and then sit down.

Wine bars (*enoteche*) are becoming more common. All serve wine by the glass or bottle, often in informal surroundings, and most provide bread, cheeses, other snacks, and good quality light meals. A *birreria*, or beer cellar, is similar, but usually appeals to a younger crowd.

You must retain your receipt when you leave the bar. If you are stopped outside of the bar by plain clothes finance police and you do not have a receipt, you will be liable to pay for what you ordered again plus a fine.

Paying

The check (*il conto*) must be presented by law as a formal receipt. A price scrawled on a piece of paper is illegal, and you are within your rights to demand an itemized *ricevuta*. Bills once included a cover charge (*pane e coperto*), a practice the authorities are trying to outlaw. Many restaurants attempt to get around the law by charging for bread brought to your table whether you want it or not.

Smaller, simpler restaurants, and those in rural areas, are less likely to accept credit cards, and it can be worth checking if your card is acceptable even in places displaying card signs outside.

Tipping & dress
Tip between 10 and 15 percent where service has been good and where a service charge (servizio) is not included. As a rule, Italians dress well but informally to eat out, especially in better restaurants. A relaxed casual style is a good rule of thumb. Jacket and tie for men are rarely necessary, but often the better dressed you are, the better service you receive.

Smoking
Smoking is common in Italy, and there are very few non-smoking areas in restaurants. Italians will be unlikely to move or desist from smoking if you protest.

The hotels and restaurants listed here have been grouped first according to their region, then listed alphabetically by price category. For disabled access, it is recommended that you check with the establishment to verify the extent of their facilities.
L = lunch   D = dinner

ROME

🏨 HASSLER
🍴 $$$$$ ✪✪✪✪✪
PIAZZA TRINITÀ DEI MONTI 6
TEL 06 699 340
FAX 06 678 9991
Rooms in this hotel above the Spanish Steps are in the grand style and have views of Rome or the gardens of the Villa Medici. The rooftop restaurant is renowned, but more for the views than the food.
ⓘ 85 + 15 suites 🚇 Metro: Spagna 🅿 ⬧ ⬧ ⬧ All major cards

🏨 HOLIDAY INN CROWNE MINERVA PLAZA
$$$$$ ✪✪✪✪✪
PIAZZA DELLA MINERVA 69
TEL 06 6994 1888
FAX 06 679 4165

It is hard to imagine a better centrally placed hotel than the Minerva, which occupies a beautifully restored 17th-century palazzo almost directly behind the Pantheon. Its position, comfort, service, facilities, rooms, and the stylish reception are beyond reproach. Non-smoking rooms available.
ⓘ 131 + 3 suites 🚌 Bus: 119 to Piazza della Rotonda or 70, 81, 87 to Corso del Rinascimento 🅿 ⬧ ⬧ 🈂 All major cards

🏨 D'INGHILTERRA
🍴 $$$$–$$$$$ ✪✪✪✪
VIA BOCCA DI LEONE 14
TEL 06 69 981
FAX 06 6992 2243
First choice if you are looking for a hotel that retains the old-fashioned charm and traditions of the 19th century. Past guests have included the composer Franz Liszt and Ernest Hemingway. Its central position is convenient to the Spanish Steps and the major shopping streets.
ⓘ 95 + 10 suites 🚇 Metro: Spagna 🅿 ⬧ ⬧ ⬧ All major cards

🏨 SCALINATA DI SPAGNA
$$$$ ✪✪✪
PIAZZA TRINITÀ DEI MONTI 17
TEL 06 679 3006
FAX 06 6994 0598
Especially popular with U.S. visitors, this romantic, quiet, and welcoming hotel is able to charge over the going rate thanks to its rambling charm and wonderful position at the top of the Spanish Steps. Rooms are Old World in style and furnished with antiques. There is a lovely roof terrace, but no restaurant
ⓘ 16 🚇 Metro: Spagna ⬧ All major cards

🏨 COLUMBUS
🍴 $$$$ ✪✪✪✪
VIA DELLA CONCILIAZIONE 33
TEL 06 686 5435
FAX 06 686 4874

Ideally placed for St. Peter's, this hotel is housed in a 15th-century monastery, and still preserves a calm and slightly old-fashioned atmosphere. It is a favorite among visiting religious dignitaries. The hotel's Veranda restaurant is excellent.
ⓘ 92 🚌 Bus: 64 🅿 ⬧ ⬧ All major cards

🏨 CARRIAGE
$$$–$$$$ ✪✪✪
VIA DELLE CARROZZE 36
TEL 06 699 8124
FAX 06 678 8279
Rooms here are relatively small but prettily furnished with reproduction antiques and furniture, and the position close to Via dei Condotti and the Spanish Steps is good.
ⓘ 27 🚇 Metro: Spagna ⬧ ⬧ All major cards

🏨 GRAND HOTEL DEI CESARI
$$$ ✪✪✪
VIA DI PIETRA 89/A
TEL 06 679 2386
FAX 06 9879 0835
A hotel has existed on this site since 1787. Today's version is a reliable family-run concern tucked away in a central back street between

the Corso and Pantheon.

ⓘ 72 🚌 Bus: 56, 60, 62, and others to Via del Corso 🛗 ⚙ All major cards

🏨 LOCARNO
$$$ ✪✪✪
VIA DELLA PENNA 22
TEL 06 361 0841
FAX 06 321 5249
On a relatively quiet side street a stone's throw from Piazza del Popolo. Attractive art nouveau decor distinguishes many of the rooms and public spaces.

ⓘ 28 🚌 Bus: 119 to Via di Ripetta ℗ 🛗 ⚙ ⚙ All major cards

🏨 PORTOGHESI
$$$ ✪✪✪
VIA DEI PORTOGHESI 1
TEL 06 686 4231
FAX 06 687 6976
A peaceful hotel housed in a 17th-century palazzo just north of Piazza Navona close to the Palazzo Altemps gallery. Rooms are simple but pleasant, and there is the bonus of a summer terrace for breakfast.

ⓘ 27 🚌 Bus: 70, 81, 87 🛗 ⚙ ⚙ All major cards

🏨 TEATRO DI POMPEO
$$–$$$ ✪✪✪
LARGO DEL PALLARO 8
TEL 06 6830 0170
FAX 06 6880 5531
A central and intimate hotel near Campo de' Fiori, with enchanting wood-beamed rooms and vestiges of the site's Roman past—parts of Pompey's ancient theater, supposedly the scene of Julius Caesar's death, are incorporated into the building.

ⓘ 13 🚌 Bus: 64 and others along Corso Vittorio Emanuele II 🛗 ⚙ ⚙ All major cards

🏨 NAVONA
$$ ✪
VIA DEI SEDIARI 8, OFF CORSO DEL RINASCIMENTO
TEL 06 686 4203
FAX 06 6880 3802
A star among Rome's

inexpensive hotels, thanks to its tremendous position—just off the southeastern corner of Piazza Navona—and the welcome of its English-speaking Italo-Australian family owners. The quality of the rooms, many of which have been upgraded, is good for this class of hotel.

ⓘ 30 🚌 Bus: 70, 81, 87, 115 to Corso del Rinascimento ⚙ In some rooms ⚙ No credit cards

🏨 CAMPO DE' FIORI
$–$$ ✪✪
VIA DEL BISCIONE 6
TEL 06 6880 6865
FAX 06 687 6003
Rooms vary in size and quality (some are tiny and sparsely furnished), but the position is excellent—close to Campo de' Fiori and Piazza Navona, two of Rome's loveliest squares. Traces of fresco and open brickwork in the public spaces create a homey and romantic atmosphere. No elevator or restaurant.

ⓘ 27 🚌 Bus: 64 and all other buses along Corso Vittorio Emanuele II ⚙ All major cards

🍴 LE SANS SOUCI
$$$$$
VIA SICILIA 20
TEL 06 482 1814
Rome has a number of grand and glamorous places for a celebratory treat, and this is perhaps the best. The elaborate setting is theatrical and almost de trop, the service is impeccable, and the food is a one-star Michelin combination of sophisticated French and Italian cuisine. Be sure to dress the part.

🍴 80–100 🚌 Bus: 57 ℗ ⏰ Closed Mon. L & 2 weeks Aug. ⚙ ⚙ All major cards

🍴 IL CONVIVIO
$$$$–$$$$$
VIA DEI SOLDATI 28
TEL 06 686 9432
The sublime and often inventive Roman-based cuisine at

this tiny restaurant north of Piazza Navona has earned a Michelin star. The wine list is one of the best in the capital. Reservations essential.

🍴 30 🚌 Bus: 70, 81, 87 to Corso del Rinascimento ⏰ Closed all Sun. & Mon. L ⚙ ⚙ All major cards

🍴 LA ROSETTA
$$$$–$$$$$
VIA DELLA ROSETTA 8
TEL 06 686 1002
A small restaurant of long-standing repute in a small street immediately north of the Pantheon. Patrons usually include politicians from the nearby parliament building. Fish and seafood only.

🍴 50 🚌 Bus: 119 to Piazza della Rotonda ⏰ Closed Sat. L, all Sun., & 20 days Aug. ⚙ ⚙ All major cards

🍴 ALBERTO CIARLA
$$$$
PIAZZA SAN COSIMATO 40
TEL 06 581 8668
This enduring fixture of the Trastevere restaurant scene is the best place to eat fish and seafood in Rome.

🍴 70 🚋 Tram: 8. Bus: 44, 56, 60, 75 to Viale di Trastevere ⏰ Closed L, all Sun., & 2 weeks each Jan. & Aug. ⚙ ⚙ All major cards

🍴 CHECCHINO DAL 1887
$$$–$$$$
VIA MONTE TESTACCIO 30
TEL 06 574 6318
Checchino has a Michelin star, but the cooking at this historic restaurant in the old cattle yards area south of the historic center is of a very particular kind. Dishes revolve largely around offal and such quintessential Roman ingredients as *cervello* (brain), *trippa* (tripe), and *pajata* (intestine).

🍴 70–100 🚌 Bus: 13, 23, 27, 57. Metro: Piramide ℗ ⏰ Closed Sun. D, all Mon., Aug., & June–Sept. ⚙ ⚙ All major cards

---

HOTELS & RESTAURANTS

🍴 PARIS
$$$–$$$$
PIAZZA SAN CALLISTO 7/A
TEL 06 581 5378
An understated and elegant restaurant just off Piazza Santa Maria in Trastevere. Good fish and pasta dishes, and outdoor dining in summer.
🔌 70–100 🚌 Bus: 44, 56, 60, 75 to Piazza S. Sonnino. Tram: 8 🕐 Closed Sun. D, Mon., & Aug. 🔲 🔲 All major cards

🍴 PIPERNO
$$$–$$$$
VIA MONTE DEI CENCI 9
TEL 06 6880 6629
Rome has a strong tradition of Jewish culture and cooking, and this old-fashioned and rustic restaurant in the former Ghetto is the best place to sample specialties such as *carciofi alla giudìa* (deep-fried artichoke) and *fiori di zucca ripieni* (deep-fried zucchini flowers filled with mozzeralla).
🔌 100 🚌 Bus: 23 🕐 Closed Sun. D, all Mon., & Aug. 🔲 🔲 All major cards

🍴 VECCHIA ROMA
$$$–$$$$
PIAZZA CAMPITELLI 18
TEL 06 686 4604
One of the city's prettiest restaurants, situated on a charming piazza at the heart of the old Ghetto—be sure to reserve a table outside. The food is not as good as the setting, but certainly not bad. Salads are excellent, pastas are innovative—*stringhelli con basilico e pecorino* combines basil, cheese, and chewy noodles—while the main courses tend toward fish and seafood.
🔌 100–120 🚌 Bus: 64 & other buses to Piazza Venezia 🕐 Closed Sun. 🔲 🔲 AE, DC

🍴 SORA LELLA
$$$
VIA DI PONTE QUATTRO CAPI 16, ISOLA TIBERINA
TEL 06 686 1601
The two cozy dining rooms and their wood-paneled walls and rows of bottles still bear witness to the simple trattoria origins of this restaurant on the Tiber Island. Both the prices and sophistication of the fine Roman cooking have increased since the death of the legendary owner, the matronly Sora Lella.
🔌 45 🚌 Bus: 15, 23, 57, & others to Piazza Bocca della Verità 🕐 Closed Sun. & Aug. 🔲 🔲 All major cards

🍴 ORSO 80
$$–$$$
VIA DELL'ORSO 33
TEL 06 686 4904
Invariably filled with vacationers, but none the worse for that, this big restaurant close to Piazza Navona is a reliable standby for basic meat and fish dishes at a moderate price in a convenient location.
🔌 170 🚌 Bus: 70, 81, 87 to Corso del Rinascimento 🕐 Closed Mon. & some of Aug. 🔲 🔲 All major cards

🍴 AL 34
$$
VIA MARIO DE' FIORI 34
TEL 06 679 5091
A cozy and romantic spot on a quiet side street off Via dei Condotti. The menu is long and varied, but the Roman-based cooking occasionally suffers as a result of the restaurant's sheer popularity.
🔌 60 🚇 Metro: Spagna 🕐 Closed Mon. & Aug. 🔲 🔲 All major cards

🍴 NERONE
$$
VIA DELLE TERME DI TITO 96
TEL 06 481 7952
This friendly, old-fashioned trattoria is noted for its buffet of cold antipasti (appetizers) and robust Abruzzese and Roman cooking. In summer, there is a handful of tables outdoors.
🔌 30–50 🚇 Metro: Colosseo 🕐 Closed Sun. & Aug. 🔲 All major cards

🍴 GRAPPOLA D'ORO
$–$$
VIA PALESTRA 4
TEL 06 494 1441
Food in this timeless old trattoria close to Campo de' Fiori is classic Roman, with excellent *saltimbocca alla Romana* (veal with ham and sage). Fewer locals and more tourists than in days gone by, but the easygoing atmosphere remains unchanged.
🔌 140 🚌 Bus: 64 & all other buses along Corso Vittorio Emanuele II 🕐 Closed Sun. & Aug. 🔲 All major cards

🍴 ANTICO CAFFÈ DELLA PACE
$
VIA DELLA PACE 3, OFF PIAZZA NAVONA
TEL 06 686 1216
By night, this pretty ivy-covered café is one of Rome's trendiest places, but by day it is quieter, its enchanting old mirror-and-wood interior providing a perfect place for a coffee or a predinner drink.
🚌 Bus: 70, 81, 87 to Corso del Rinascimento 🕐 Closed Mon.

🍴 CAFFÈ GRECO
$
VIA DEI CONDOTTI 86
TEL 06 678 2554
Rome's oldest and most atmospheric coffeehouse was founded in 1767 and has hosted the likes of Goethe, Casanova, and Lord Byron.
🚇 Metro: Spagna. Bus: 119 to Piazza di Spagna 🕐 Closed Sun.

🍴 CAVOUR 313
$
VIA CAVOUR 313
TEL 06 678 5496
Perfect for a snack or glass of wine after visiting the Forum.
🚌 Bus: 11, 27, 81, 85, 87 🕐 Closed Sun. in summer

🍴 ENOTECA CORSI
$
VIA DEL GESÙ 88

KEY 🏨 Hotel 🍴 Restaurant 🛏 No. of bedrooms 🔌 No. of seats 🚌/🚇 Transportation 🅿 Parking 🕐 Closed

TEL 06 679 0821
Little has changed at this simple wine bar-trattoria in over 30 years. The food is simple Roman cooking at its best—you can eat a full meal or simply have a glass of wine and a snack.
🚍 Bus: 64 🕐 Closed Sun., Aug., & D

🍴 GELATERIA DELLA PALMA
$
VIA DELLA MADDALENA 20
TEL 06 654 0752
A big, bright, and modern emporium just north of the Pantheon selling over 100 flavors of ice cream, cakes, chocolates, and other calorie-filled treats.
🚍 Bus: 119 to Piazza della Rotonda 🕐 Closed Wed.

🍴 GIOLITTI
$
VIA UFFICI DEL VICARIO 40
TEL 06 699 1243
Once the most celebrated of Rome's café-ice cream parlors—and noted for its sulky service—although now challenged by the nearby Gelateria della Palma (see above).
🚍 Bus: 119 to Piazza della Rotonda 🕐 Closed Mon.

🍴 IL PICCOLO
$
VIA DEL GOVERNO VECCHIO 74–75
TEL 06 6880 1746
This intimate small *enoteca* or wine bar just a few steps west of Piazza Navona is perfect for a quiet glass of wine by candlelight.
🚍 Bus: 46, 62, 64 to Corso Vittorio Emanuele II

🍴 IVO
$
VIA DI SAN FRANCESCO A RIPA 158
TEL 06 581 7082
Everybody should sample the Ivo experience at least once. This is one of the biggest and most popular of

Trastevere's many pizzerias. You may have to wait in line, but turnover is quick and the atmosphere lively.
🔧 200 🚍 Bus: 44, 56, 60, 75 to Viale di Trastevere. Tram: 8 🕐 Closed Tues. & 3 weeks Aug. 💺 🚍 All major cards

🍴 LA TAZZA D'ORO
$
VIA DEGLI ORFANI 84, OFF PIAZZA DELLA ROTONDA
TEL 06 678 9792
Stand at the bar (there are no seats) at the "Cup of Gold" and indulge in what is by common consent the best coffee in Rome.
🚍 Bus: 119 to Piazza della Rotonda 🕐 Closed Sun.

🍴 LEONCINO
$
VIA DEL LEONCINO 28
TEL 06 687 6306
Once all small restaurants in Rome would have looked like this central pizzeria just off Via del Corso. Tiny and cramped, its marble tables and unadorned interior have hardly changed in 30 years. Popular, so be prepared to wait in line.
🔧 30 🕐 Closed Wed. 🚍 Bus: 81, 119 to Via del Corso 🚍 No credit cards

🍴 ROSATI
$
PIAZZA DEL POPOLO 4/5A
TEL 06 322 5859
Rosati's historical rival across the square, Canova, has the sunnier café terrace, but Rosati has the better interior (a 1922 art nouveau delight) and the more tempting cakes, pastries, and cocktails.
🚍 Bus: 119 to Piazza del Popolo 🕐 Closed Tues. Nov.–March

🍴 TRASTÈ
$
VIA DELLA LUNGARETTA 76
TEL 06 589 4430
A modern tea and coffee shop in Trastevere whose

easygoing atmosphere makes it a pleasant place to linger. Snacks and light meals are also available.
🚍 Bus: 44, 56, 60, 75 to Piazza S. Sonnino. Tram: 8 🕐 Closed L daily & Aug.

🍴 TRE SCALINI
$
PIAZZA NAVONA 30
TEL 06 6880 1996
Tre Scalini would be just one more bar among many on Piazza Navona were it not for its magnificent *tartufo*, probably the world's finest chocolate chip ice cream.
🚍 Bus: 70, 81, 87 to Corso del Rinascimento 🕐 Closed Wed.

NORTHWEST ITALY

CINQUE TERRE

🏨 PORTO ROCCO
$$$ ◆◆◆◆
VIA CORONE 1, MONTEROSSO
TEL 0187 817 502
FAX 0187 817 692
Set on steep slopes affording fine views of the sea and village, this hotel has a romantic, flower-filled terrace, pleasant bar and restaurant. Rooms are filled with pictures, rugs, antiques, and old furniture.
🛏 44 🕐 Closed Nov.–Feb. 💺 🚍 All major cards

🏨 CA' D'ANDREAN
$$ ◆◆◆
VIA LO SCALO 101, MANAROLA
TEL 0187 920 040
FAX 0187 920 452
A former mill, wine cellar, and private home that opened as a hotel in 1988. Rooms are plain, simple, and clean.
🛏 10 🕐 Closed Nov. 🚍 All major cards

🏨 STELLA MARIS
$$ ◆◆
VIA MARCONI 4, LEVANTO
TEL 0187 808 258
FAX 0187 807 351
Levanto is not one of the

Cinque Terre, but lies nearby and makes a good base for exploring the villages. The well-run Stella Maris occupies part of an 19th-century palazzo. Half of the rooms are modern, the remainder having original frescoes and old furniture.
🛏 15 🕐 Closed Nov.
🖎 All major cards

🍴 GAMBERO ROSSO
$$$
PIAZZA G. MARCONI 7, VERNAZZA
TEL 0187 812 265
This is the pick of several good fish and seafood restaurants on this pretty square, although Vulnetia and Gianni Franzi at Nos. 29 and 5 respectively offer almost equally good food. All three have outdoor tables in fine weather.
🪑 20–50 🕐 Closed Mon. except July–Aug. 🔄 🖎 All major cards

🍴 MORESCO
$$$
VIA JACOPO DA LEVANTO 24, LEVANTO
TEL 0187 807 253
Innovative Ligurian cooking with dishes such as *zuppa rustica di funghi e fiori di zucca* (a rustic soup with mushrooms and zucchini flowers) and superb fish and seafood. The food in this small but superb restaurant is complemented by impeccable service. The lovely dining room decorated with frescoes and trompe l'oeil.
🪑 60 🅿 🕐 Closed Nov., Feb., & Tues. except July–Aug.
🖎 All major cards

🍴 GIGANTE
$$
VIA IV NOVEMBRE 9, MONTEROSSO
TEL 0187 817 401
Good fish and seafood dishes, combined with a warm welcome and courteous service, have made this large trattoria popular with locals and visitors alike.
🪑 150–190 🕐 Closed Mon.
🖎 All major cards

🍴 MANANAN
$$
VIA FIESCHI 117, CORNIGLIA
TEL 0187 821 166
An appealing, old-fashioned trattoria housed in the former wine vaults of the 14th-century Palazzo Fieschi. Fish and seafood dominate the menu, but other pasta dishes are also available.
🪑 25 🕐 Closed Tues. except in summer & L June–Sept. 🖎 No credit cards

🍴 ARISTIDE
$–$$
VIA LO SCALO 138, MANAROLA
TEL 0187 920 000
Simple Ligurian fish and seafood. Play it safe with *zuppa di pesce* (fish soup) and other traditional staples such as *pesce del giorno alla griglia* (grilled fish of the day).
🪑 60 🕐 Closed Mon.
🖎 No credit cards

GENOA

🏨 BRISTOL PALACE
$$$–$$$$ ○○○○
VIA XX SETTEMBRE 35
TEL 010 592 541
FAX 010 561 756
The best known of Genoa's grand old hotels, although the grandeur and elegance are a little faded in places.
🛏 133 🅿 🔄 🔄 🖎 All major cards

🏨 CITY
$$$ ○○○○
VIA SAN SEBASTIANO 6
TEL 010 5545
FAX 010 586 301
A comfortable, central hotel affiliated with the reliable Best Western chain.
🛏 63 🅿 🔄 🔄 🖎 All major cards

🏨 METROPOLI
$$$ ○○○
PIAZZA FONTANA MOROSE
TEL 010 246 8888
FAX 010 246 8686
Another upscale hotel affiliated with the Best Western

chain, in a romantic square at the heart of Genoa's historic center. First floor rooms are especially pleasant.
🛏 45 🅿 🔄 🔄 🖎 All major cards

🍴 GRAN GOTTO
$$$$
VIALE BRIGATE BISAGNO 69r
TEL 010 583 644
Winner of a Michelin star, this venerable restaurant has been in the same family since 1937 and serves classic Ligurian food with a creative twist. An emphasis on fish, but meat dishes and pasta are also available. Widely considered Genoa's best.
🪑 60 🕐 Closed Sat. L, all Sun., & 2 weeks Aug. 🔄 🖎 All major cards

🍴 LA BITTA NELLA PERGOLA
$$$$
VIA CASAREGIS 52
TEL 010 588 543
A refined Michelin star winner, although unlike the Gran Gotto, fish and seafood reign supreme. Menu combines the maritime cuisines of two great Italian culinary traditions: Ligurian and Neapolitan.
🪑 40–60 🕐 Closed Sun. D, Mon., & 3 weeks Aug. 🔄 🖎 All major cards

🍴 SAINT CYR
$$$
PIAZZA MARSALA 8R
TEL 010 815 039
Modern, elegant, and central restaurant. The varied and often extravagant menu changes daily, and embraces regional meat and fish dishes. *La zuppa di cipolle* (onion soup), *trenette al pesto* (pasta with a basil, cheese, and pine nut sauce) and rice *(riso)* with asparagus tips *(punti di asparagi)* are all memorable.
🪑 40 🕐 Closed Sat. L, all Sun., & 10 days Aug. 🔄 🖎 All major cards

ANTICA OSTERIA DELLA FOCE
$
VIA RUSPOLI 72r
TEL 010 553 3155
A rustic, family-run *osteria* of the old school, with a handful of tables around a large wood-burning oven. A warm welcome and robustly flavored Genovese specialties.
🍴 35 🕐 Closed Sat. L, all Sun., Aug., & 1 week at Christmas & Easter 🅰 All major cards

PARCO NAZIONALE DEL GRAN PARADISO

BELLEVUE
$$$$ ✪✪✪✪
VIA GRAN PARADISO 22, COGNE
TEL 0165 74 825
FAX 0165 749 192
The best of this resort's many hotels. Communal areas are decorated with rustic antiques, and rooms, although varying in age and style, are all attractively decorated. The smart hotel-restaurant, Le Petit Restaurant, is the town's finest.
🛏 37 🅿 🕐 Closed Mon., & Oct.–Dec. 🛗 🅰 🏊 🅰 All major cards

PETIT DAHU
$$ ✪✪
FRAZIONE VALNONTEY 27, VALNONTEY
TEL 0165 74 146
FAX 0165 74 146
A tiny hotel with small, simple rooms fashioned from two traditional wooden houses built in 1729. Situated in the pretty village of Valnontey, 1 mile (1.5 km) from Cogne—perfectly positioned for hiking.
🛏 8 🅿 🕐 Closed May & Oct.–Nov. 🅰 AE, V

LOU RESSIGNON
$$
VIA MINES DE COGNE 23, COGNE
TEL 0165 74 034
Warm welcome, homey atmosphere, rustic appearance—wooden ceiling

and old fireplace—and authentic Valle d'Aosta cooking, with many dishes that have all but vanished from most local menus such as *soupetta alla cogneintze* (a soup of rice, local fontina cheese, herbs, and croutons).
🍴 60 🕐 Closed Mon. D, Tues. except summer & Christmas, & 2-week periods Sept., Oct., & Nov. 🅰 All major cards

PORTOFINO

SPLENDIDO
One of Italy's finest, most notable, and most expensive hotels. Originally a medieval monastery, it opened as a hotel in 1901. Stunning location set on four acres (1.5 hectares) of semitropical gardens. All rooms are individually styled, but all are exceptional. Sauna, tennis courts, and countless other facilities.
$$$$$ ✪✪✪✪
VIALE BARATTA 16
TEL 0185 269 551
TEL 0185 269 614
🛏 69 🅿 🕐 Closed Jan.–mid-March 🛗 🅰 🏊 🅰 All major cards

EDEN
$$$ ✪✪
VICO DRITTO 18
TEL 0185 269 091
FAX 0185 269 047
A traditional Ligurian house dating from 1929 near the village square. Set in a small palm-dotted garden, which is available for alfresco eating in summer at the Da Ferruccio restaurant. Hotels in this lower price range are rare here.
🛏 8 🅿 🛗 🅰 All major cards

PICCOLO HOTEL
$$$ ✪✪✪✪
VIA DUCA DEGLI ABRUZZI 31

TEL 0185 269 015
FAX 0185 269 621
A comfortable and intimate hotel set among parkland and gardens. Most rooms have balconies with sea views.
🛏 23 🅿 🕐 Closed Nov.–Dec. 🛗 🅰 🅰 All major cards

DA PUNY
$$$
PIAZZA MARTIRI DELL' OLIVETTA 5
TEL 0185 269 037
A Portofino institution, this long-established restaurant is set on the chic square overlooking the harbor, with two comfortable salons and tables set under trees on a terrace. The menu features predominantly fish and seafood.
🍴 40–70 🕐 Closed Thurs. & mid-Dec.–mid-Feb. 🅰 All major cards

LA GRITTA
$$
CALATA MARCONI 20
TEL 0185 269 126
One of Portofino's oldest bars. Rex Harrison once shared cocktails here with the Duke of Windsor, just two among many illustrious past habitués.
🕐 Closed Thurs.

TURIN

JOLLY HOTEL PRINCIPI DI PIEMONTE
$$$$$ ✪✪✪✪
VIA GOBETTI 15
TEL 011 562 9693
FAX 011 562 0270
A ten-story, centrally located hotel, built in 1939, and renovated in elegant, traditional style and much favored by VIPs.
🛏 99 + 8 suites 🅿 🛗 🅰 🅰 All major cards

TURIN PALACE
$$$$ ✪✪✪✪
VIA P. SACCHI 8
TEL 011 562 5511
FAX 011 561 2187
A classy hotel, close to the railroad station, dating from

HOTELS & RESTAURANTS

1872. The spacious, quiet rooms are either modern in appearance or decorated in a more traditional manner with Louis XV-style furnishings.
(i) 121 All major cards

VICTORIA
$$$ ◐◐◐
VIA NINO COSTA 4
TEL 011 561 1909
FAX 011 561 1806
An elegant hotel distinguished by its courteous service and fine attention to detail. Modern and older wings, with uniformly good rooms in various styles.
(i) 85 All major cards

AMADEUS E TEATRO
$$ ◐◐◐
VIA PRINCIPE AMEDEO 41 BIS
TEL 011 917 4951
FAX 011 817 4953
First choice among the mid-range hotels. Close to the Mole Antonelliana and convenient for the city-center sights.
(i) 26 P All major cards

BALBO
$$$$
VIA ANDREA DORIA 11
TEL 011 839 5775
Outstanding Piedmontese cooking has earned this elegant restaurant—often described as the region's best—a Michelin star and the plaudits of most leading Italian food writers. Housed in a 19th-century palazzo in the historic center.
60–80 Closed Mon. & some of Jul.–Aug. All major cards

DEL CAMBIO
$$$$
PIAZZA CARIGNANO 2
TEL 011 543 760
A historic restaurant founded in 1757 that boasts a beautiful interior, complete with chandeliers, ornate lamps, and huge mirrors. Cooking is good and Piedmontese in inspiration. The wine list is superb.
60–150 Closed Sun.,

Aug., & 1 week Jan. All major cards

SPADA REALE
$$
VIA PRINCIPE AMADEO 53
TEL 011 817 1363
Almost as old as the Tre Galline (see below), this family-run restaurant is a favorite with Turin's artistic and media crowd, and it has a lively, informal atmosphere. Carefully selected ingedients add a Tuscan twist to Piedmontese tradition.
120 Closed Sun. & some of Aug. All major cards

TRE GALLINE
$$
VIA BELLEZIA 37
TEL 011 436 6553
There has been an inn of this name here for three centuries, perhaps longer. The present patrons continue a strong tradition of classic Piedmontese cooking in a tranquil city-center setting just northwest of Piazza Reale.
70 P Closed Mon. L, Sun., & 3 weeks Aug. All major cards

VALLE D'AOSTA

ROYAL E GOLF
$$$$
VIA ROMA 87, COURMAYEUR
TEL 0165 846 787
FAX 0165 842 093
One of Courmayeur's best hotels. Its Michelin-starred restaurant is even more renowned, and boasts elaborate cooking with regional and French influences. Reservations essential.
20–30 P Closed L & Mon. except Aug. & Christmas All major cards

HOLIDAY INN AOSTA
$$$ ◐◐◐◐
CORSO BATTAGLIONE AOSTA 30, AOSTA
TEL 0165 236 356
FAX 0165 236 837

On the western edge of town with the predictable comfort and modern fittings associated with a chain hotel. Mountain views from some rooms.
(i) 50 P All major cards

PALACE BRON
$$$ ◐◐◐◐
VIA PLAN GORRET 14, COURMAYEUR
TEL 0165 846 742
FAX 0165 844 015
This hotel is attractively situated in pine woods about a mile (1.5 km) from the town center (a free bus shuttle is available). Comfortable, modern rooms and appealing public areas with magnificent views of Mont Blanc.
(i) 27 P Closed May–June & Oct.–Nov. All major cards

VECCHIO RISTORO
$$$
VIA TOURNEUVE 4, AOSTA
TEL 0165 33 238
A wonderfully labyrinthine restaurant housed in a former water mill by the old town walls. Cooking adds a twist to local regional dishes such as *ravioli di asparagi con salsa al parmigiano* (asparagus-filled

pasta served with a parmesan cheese sauce).
🍴 34 🕐 Closed Sun., Mon. L, & 3 weeks June 💳 All major cards

LOMBARDY & THE LAKES

BERGAMO

🏨 EXCELSIOR SAN MARCO
$$$ ●●●●
PIAZZA DELLA REPUBBLICA 6
TEL 035 366 111
FAX 035 223 201
Modern Bergamo boasts any number of modern, characterless hotels, but this is the most comfortable. Plus points are the roof terrace and easy walking distance from the historic hilltop part of the city.
🛏 155 🅿 🛗 💳 All major cards

🏨 SAN VIGILIO
$$–$$$ ●●●
VIA SAN VIGILIO 15
TEL 035 253 179
FAX 035 402 081
The best of only a handful of hotels in or close to Bergamo's historic Città Alta, or Upper City. It lies midway between the old Cittadella fortress and the medieval castle. The hotel restaurant, I Musicanti, has a terrace with broad city views.
🛏 7 🅿 🛗 💳 All major cards

🍴 COLLEONI DELL'ANGELO
$$$$
PIAZZA VECCHIA 7
TEL 035 232 596
Both the position—in the upper city's finest square—and the regional Lombardesque food in this restaurant are outstanding.
🍴 100 🕐 Closed Mon. & 2 weeks Aug. 💳 All major cards

🍴 DA VITTORIO
$$$–$$$$
VIALE PAPA GIOVANNI XXIII 21
TEL 035 213 266

Tremendous cooking, with fish, seafood, mushrooms, and truffles, has earned this venerable restaurant two Michelin stars. In spring, try perfect grilled tuna, in the fall, a fillet of monkfish with potatoes and porcini (mushrooms).
🍴 120 🅿 🕐 Closed Wed. & Aug. 💳 All major cards

LAGO DI COMO

SOMETHING SPECIAL

🏨 GRAND HOTEL 🍴 VILLA D'ESTE
The lakeside Villa d'Este was built in 1568 and became a hotel in 1873. Today, it is not only one of Italy's grandest and most luxurious hotels, but also has one of the country's finest gardens. Public areas are magnificent —full of frescoes, statues, vast chandeliers, and precious antiques—while rooms are decorated in a similarly grand 19th-century style.
$$$$$ ●●●●●
VIA REGINA 40, CERNOBBIO
TEL 031 3481
FAX 031 348 844
🛏 150 + 9 suites 🅿 🛗 💳 🏊 🏊 💪 All major cards

SOMETHING SPECIAL

🏨 GRAND HOTEL 🍴 VILLA SERBELLONI
The first choice for a treat in Lake Como's prettiest village. Rooms are all superlative, but vary in size and splendor—the best look out over the lake.
$$$$–$$$$$ ●●●●●
VIA ROMA 1, BELLAGIO
TEL 031 950 216
FAX 031 951 529
🛏 72 rooms + 11 suites 🅿 🕐 Closed Nov.– March 🛗 💳 🏊 💪 All major cards

🏨 TERMINUS 🍴
$$$–$$$$ ●●●●
LUNGO LARIO TRIESTE 14, COMO
TEL 031 329 111
FAX 031 302 550
A 19th-century, family-run villa hotel in the center of town near the lakefront. It has a pleasant terrace for sunny days with lakeside views for dining, and good rooms with floral fabrics and elegant furniture.
🛏 36 + 2 suites 🅿 🍴 Restaurant closed Tues. 🛗 💳 All major cards

🏨 DU LAC
$$–$$$ ●●●
PIAZZA MAZZINI 32, BELLAGIO
TEL 031 950 320
FAX 031 951 624
Charming Anglo-Italian-run hotel at the center of the village, close to the ferry landing stage. Roof terrace and plenty of rooms offering views of the lake.
🛏 48 🅿 🛗 💳 All major cards

🍴 TERRAZZO PERLASCO
$$$–$$$$
PIAZZA DE GASPERI 8
TEL 031 303 936
A refined, modern restaurant just east of the town center whose major attraction is a terrace with panoramic views of the lake.
🍴 90 🕐 Closed Mon. & 2–3 weeks Aug. 💳 All major cards

🍴 BARCHETTA
$$$
SALITA MELIA 13, BELLAGIO
TEL 031 951 389
Dine on the charming terrace in summer or indoors in front of the fire, amid a clutter of objets d'art and antiques. Fish and meat dishes, including excellent *maialino arrosto del Monte Primo* (local roast suckling pig).
🍴 30–80 🕐 Closed Tues. mid-Sept.–mid-June, 3 weeks Oct.–Nov., & Mon.–Fri. Dec.–March 💳 AE, MC, V

🛗 Elevator 💳 Air-conditioning 🏊 Indoor/🏊 Outdoor swimming pool 💪 Health club 💳 Credit cards **KEY**

LAGO MAGGIORE

🏨 GRAND HOTEL DES ÎLES BOROMÉES
$$$$$ ⭕⭕⭕⭕⭕
CORSO UMBERTO I 67, STRESA
TEL 0323 938 938
FAX 0323 32 405
A classic villa hotel set on the lakeside amid gardens and parkland. Opened as a hotel in 1863, it has been a byword for luxury and elegance ever since. Note that the 27 rooms in the hotel's *residenza* (annex) are less costly and decorated in a more contemporary style.
🛏 129 + 11 suites 🅿 ➡ 🔲 🏊 📺 🅾 All major cards

🏨 VERBANO
🍽 $$$ ⭕⭕⭕
VIA UGO ARA 12, ISOLA DEI PESCATORI
TEL 0323 30 408
FAX 0323 33 129
This is one of the few places to stay on the Borromean Islands. The restaurant is good and offers outdoor terrace dining in summer.
🛏 12 🅿 🕐 Hotel closed Jan.–Feb.; restaurant closed Wed. Oct.–mid-April 🅾 All major cards

🍽 LA PIEMONTESE
$$$
VIA MAZZINI 25, STRESA
TEL 0323 30 235
A pleasant family-run restaurant in the town center where you can dine outside under a vine-covered pergola in summer. Robust local dishes, with an emphasis on fish.
🪑 60 🅿 🕐 Closed Mon. 🅾 All major cards

LAGO D' ORTA

🏨 VILLA CRESPI
🍽 $$$$–$$$$$ ⭕⭕⭕⭕
VIA FAVA 8–10 (1 MILE/2 KM E OF ORTA SAN GIULIO)
TEL 0322 911 902
FAX 0322 911 919
An outstanding place to eat and sleep. The restaurant has a Michelin star and the handful of rooms in the park-enclosed 19th-century villa boast ornate Moorish decoration, canopied beds, marble bathrooms, and valuable furniture and antiques.
🛏 6 rooms + 8 suites 🅿
🕐 Hotel closed Jan.; restaurant closed Mon. in low season ➡ 🔲 🏊 🅾 All major cards

🏨 SAN ROCCO
$$$ ⭕⭕⭕⭕
VIA GIPPINI 11, ORTA SAN GIULIO
TEL 0322 911 977
FAX 0322 911 964
A converted 17th-century monastery with a panoramic view of the lake. Rooms are comfortable and modern, if a little dated; half have lake views.
🛏 74 🅿 ➡ 🏊 📺 🅾 All major cards

MANTOVA

🏨 SAN LORENZO
$$$ ⭕⭕⭕⭕
PIAZZA CONCORDIA 14
TEL 0376 220 500
FAX 0376 327 194
In the heart of the historic center, and, for the most part, decorated with period furniture and antiques. The terrace offers good views of the city. Breakfast is served, but there is no restaurant.
🛏 64 🅿 ➡ 🔲 🅾 All major cards

🏨 BROLETTO
$$ ⭕⭕⭕
VIA ACCADEMIA 1
TEL 0376 223 678
FAX 0376 221 297
Central Mantova (Mantua) has few good hotels. This adequate but unexceptional establishment lies just a stone's throw from the Palazzo Ducale. Some rooms suffer traffic noise. No restaurant.
🛏 16 ➡ 🔲 🅾 All major cards

🍽 AQUILA NIGRA
$$$$
VICOLO BONACOLSI 4
TEL 0376 327 180
Mantua's best restaurant has a Michelin star, a central location, frescoed walls, medieval vaulted ceilings, and a refined range of Mantuan specialties such as *tortelli di zucca* (pasta parcels with sweet squash filling) and *filetto di manzo* (beef fillet).
🪑 75 🅿 🕐 Closed Mon., Sun. D April–May & Sept.–Oct., all Sun. rest of year, & 2 weeks in Aug. 🔲 🅾 All major cards

MILAN

🏨 FOUR SEASONS
🍽 $$$$$ ⭕⭕⭕⭕⭕
VIA GESÙ 8
TEL 02 77 088
FAX 02 7708 5000
Milan's finest luxury-class hotel is a converted 14th-century monastery on one of the city's premier shopping streets, northeast of the Duomo. Its La Veranda restaurant is highly rated, but expensive.
🛏 82 + 16 suites 🅿
🚇 Metro: Montenapoleone ➡ 🔲 📺 🅾 All major cards

🏨 RADISSON SAS BONAPARTE
$$$$–$$$$$ ⭕⭕⭕⭕
VIA CUSANI 13
TEL 02 85 601
FAX 02 869 3601
A good central location in front of the Castello Sforzesco to the northwest of the Duomo. Attentive service and spacious rooms furnished with sobriety and style.
🛏 55 + 10 suites 🚇 Metro: Cairoli 🅿 ➡ 🔲 🅾 All major cards

🏨 SPADARI AL DUOMO
$$$–$$$$$ ⭕⭕⭕⭕
VIA SPADARI 11
TEL 02 7200 2371
FAX 02 861 184
A tremendous position on a side street just off the central Piazza del Duomo. Decor is elegant and sophisticated, and the hotel is particularly known for its precious collection of contemporary art.

ⓘ 38 🚇 Metro: Duomo
🅿 🔼 Closed some of Aug.
⬌ ❄ 💳 All major cards

🏨 CASA SVIZZERIA
$$$ ❂❂❂
VIA SAN RAFFAELE 3
TEL 02 869 2246
FAX 02 7200 4690
Hotels this good, this central,
and at this price are rare in
Milan, so reservations are
essential. No restaurant.
ⓘ 45 🚇 Metro: Duomo
🔼 Closed for some of late
July & Aug. ⬌ ❄ 💳 All
major cards

🍴 SADLER
$$$$$
VIA ETTORE TROILO 14,
AT VIA CONCHETTA
TEL 02 5810 4451
Superlative meat and fish
cooking has earned Sadler a
Michelin star, as well as plaudits
from Italian food writers.
However, you'll need to take a
cab here, as the restaurant lies
south of the city center.
🍴 55 🔼 Closed L, Sun., Jan.
1–15, & Aug. ❄ 💳 All
major cards

🍴 AIMO E NADIA
The best restaurant in
Milan—some say the best
in Lombardy. Known for its
fanatical use of the best ingre-
dients available and inventive
interpretations of Milanese
and other northern Italian
dishes. Menus change regu-
larly and can range from
simple dishes such as *crostini*
(toasts) with the finest olive
oil and sweetest tomatoes to
melanzane farcite d'aragosta
(eggplant stuffed with lob-
ster). Less expensive for lunch.
$$$–$$$$$
VIA MONTECUCCOLI 6
TEL 02 416 886
🍴 40 🚇 Metro:
Primaticco 🔼 Closed
Sat. L, Sun., & Aug. ❄
💳 All major cards

🍴 PECK
$$–$$$$$
VIA VICTOR HUGO 4
TEL 02 876 774
This superb contemporary
one-star Michelin restaurant
near the Palazzo dell'
Ambrosiana offers excellent
fixed-price *degustazione* menus
as ways of sampling local
dishes, most notably a variety
of *classici risotti* (risottos) and
scaloppina alla Milanese
(breaded veal cutlet).
🍴 50 🚇 Metro: Duomo
🔼 Closed Sat. L, Sun., &
3 weeks July or Aug. ❄
💳 All major cards

🍴 OLIVIA
$$$
VIA GABRIELE
D'ANNUNZIO 7–9
TEL 02 8940 6052
A reliable mid-priced restaurant in the Navigli canal district with a modern and
welcoming interior on several
levels. Cooking can be adventurous, as in dishes such as
ravioli di faraona—pasta
parcels filled with guinea fowl.
🍴 55 🚇 Metro: Sant'
Agostino 🔼 Closed Sat. L,
Sun., & Aug. ❄ 💳 All
major cards

🍴 TRATTORIA MILANESE
$$$
VIA SANTA MARTA 11
TEL 02 8645 1991
A busy, central, traditional,
two-room trattoria that's
been in the same family for
over 60 years. Popular with a
range of Milanese, from
business people to young
lovers. Located just west of
the Biblioteca Ambrosiana.
🍴 80 🔼 Closed Tues. &
Aug. 💳 All major cards

🍴 CHARLESON
$–$$
PIAZZA DEL LIBERTY 8
TEL 02 798 631
Big, busy, and often noisy, just
as pizzerias should be, and
convenient to the center, just
west of the Duomo. Antipasti
(appetizers) and non-pizza

dishes, such as simple pastas,
are also available.
🍴 180 🚇 Metro: Duomo
🅿 🔼 Closed Mon. & Aug.
❄ 💳 All major cards

🏨 CIPRIANI
🍴 $$$$$ ❂❂❂❂
FONDAMENTA SAN
GIOVANNI, ISOLA DELLA
GIUDECCA 10
TEL 041 520 7744
FAX 041 520 3930
The Cipriani is different
because it lies on the island of
the Giudecca rather than the
Grand Canal. This makes it
quieter and calmer—guests
also have use of a pool, garden, and tennis courts—but
you may feel cut off from the
life of the city.
ⓘ 59 + 12 suites 🚤 Zitelle
52 or private hotel launch
from San Marco ⬌ ❄
🏊 💳 All major cards

🏨 DANIELI
🍴 $$$$$ ❂❂❂❂❂
RIVA DEGLI SCHIAVONI-CALLE
DELLE RASSE, CASTELLO 4196
TEL 041 522 6480
FAX 041 520 0208
To indulge fully in the hotel's
opulent Old World splendor,
be sure to reserve a room in
the original hotel, housed in
a 13th-century palazzo on
St. Mark's waterfront, not the
1948 annex.
ⓘ 221 + 9 suites 🚤 San
Zaccaria 1, 4, 52, 82 ⬌ ❄
💳 All major cards

🏨 GRITTI PALACE
🍴 $$$$$ ❂❂❂❂❂
CAMPO SANTA MARIA DEL
GIGLIO, SAN MARCO 2467
TEL 041 794 611
FAX 041 520 0942
A more peaceful location than
the Danieli (see above) and
housed in an equally historic
building—the 15th-century
palace home of a former
doge. Similar levels of comfort
and elegance.
ⓘ 87 + 6 suites 🚤 Santa

Maria del Giglio I 🚌 🛥
🚶 All major cards

🏨 LUNA HOTEL
🍴 BAGLIONI
$$$$–$$$$$ ✪✪✪✪
CALLE LARGA
DELL'ASCENSIONE, SAN
MARCO 1243
TEL 041 528 9840
FAX 041 528 7160
Venice's oldest hotel, and
once the Venetian head-
quarters of the Knights
Templars. Public spaces have
beautiful old touches, such as
the frescoes of the Marco
Polo lounge, while rooms—
some of which look out over
the Grand Canal—are elegant
and well designed. The hotel's
Canova restaurant is one of
the city's best.
ⓘ 111 + 7 suites 🚌 San
Marco 1, 3, 4, 82 🚌 🛥
🚶 All major cards

🏨 ACCADEMIA VILLA
MARAVEGE
$$$ ✪✪✪
FONDAMENTA BOLLANI,
DORSODURO 1058–1060
TEL 041 521 0188
FAX 041 523 9152
A well-known and popular
hotel, thanks to its location,
garden, setting—a 17th-
century palazzo that once
housed the Russian Embassy—
and the grand style and
antique decoration of its
rooms and public spaces.
Some rooms are very small
and there is no restaurant.
Reservations essential.
ⓘ 27 🚌 Accademia 1, 3,
4, 82 🛥 🚶 All major cards

🏨 ALA
$$$ ✪✪✪
CAMPO SANTA MARIA DEL
GIGLIO, SAN MARCO 2494
TEL 041 520 8333
FAX 041 520 6390
The Ala is a short walk from
St. Mark's and shares the
same square as the presti-
gious Gritti Palace hotel (see
p. 361). Rooms are generally
either small and decorated in
a contemporary manner or

large and furnished in an older
style. No restaurant.
ⓘ 85 🚌 Santa Maria del
Giglio I 🚌 🛥 🚶 All
major cards

🏨 AMERICAN
$$$ ✪✪✪
FONDAMENTA BRAGADIN-
SAN VIO, DORSODURO 628
TEL 041 520 4733
FAX 041 520 4048
A perfect mid-priced hotel in
a quiet and pretty canalside
location within a few minutes'
walk of the Accademia and
Guggenheim galleries. Rooms
range in quality, size, and price.
No restaurant.
ⓘ 28 🚌 Accademia 1, 82
🚌 🚶 All major cards

🏨 FLORA
$$$ ✪✪✪
CALLE DEI BERGAMESCHI,
SAN MARCO 2283/A
TEL 041 520 5844
FAX 041 522 8217
A small inner garden—a rarity
in Venice—lends this hotel
much of its charm. Period-
style rooms are a bit small, but
the location, just off Calle
Larga XXII Marzo to the west
of St. Mark's, is perfect.
ⓘ 44 🚌 Santa Maria del
Giglio I 🚌 🛥 🚶 All
major cards

🏨 GIORGIONE
$$$ ✪✪✪✪
CAMPO SS. APOSTOLI,
CANNAREGIO 4587
TEL 041 522 5810
FAX 041 523 9092
The hotel has a small court-
yard garden and tranquil posi-
tion, plus a range of facilities
and well-presented rooms that
raise it above the standard of
most other four-star hotels.
ⓘ 68 🚌 Ca' d'Oro I 🚌
🛥 🚶 All major cards

🍴 GRAN CAFFE
RISTORANTE QUADRI
$$$$$
PIAZZA SAN MARCO 120–124
TEL 041 528 9299
The classical Venetian cooking
here is good, but does not

rival Harry's. The fantastically
opulent setting and views over
St. Mark's Square are likely to
linger longer in the memory.
Reservations essential.
🪑 74 🚌 San Marco 1, 3, 4,
82 🕑 Closed Tues. L, Mon.,
& L July–Aug. 🛥 🚶 All
major cards

🍴 HARRY'S BAR
$$$$$
CALLE VALLARESSO, SAN
MARCO 1323
TEL 041 528 5777
This is Venice's most famous
restaurant (and bar), and, in
1999, one of only two eating
places in the city holding a
Michelin star. Dress up and
expect a large U.S. presence
among the international
clientele in the busy dining
room upstairs. The lively bar
downstairs serves the city's
best martinis and the popular
cocktail—the Bellini (fresh
white peach juice and
champagne)—was invented
here. Reservations essential.
🪑 80–100 🚌 San Marco 1,
3, 4, 82 🛥 🚶 All major
cards

🍴 ANTICO MARTINI
$$$$–$$$$$
CAMPO SAN FANTIN, SAN
MARCO 1983
TEL 041 522 4121
The refined Venetian cuisine is
almost overshadowed by the
decor, a grand ensemble of
chandeliers, paneled walls, and
precious paintings. The
restaurant, in the shadow of
Teatro La Fenice opera house,
is almost three centuries old,
and has been run by the same
family since 1920. The 350-
label wine list is outstanding.
🪑 40–85 🚌 Santa Maria del
Giglio I 🕑 Closed Wed. L &
Tues. 🛥 🚶 All major cards

🍴 AL COVO
$$$–$$$$
CAMPIELLO DELLA PESCARIA,
CASTELLO 3968
TEL 041 522 3812
Texas-born Diane and her
Italian husband have created a

wonderful little two-room (smoking and non-smoking) restaurant that produces exquisite and often innovative takes on Venetian classics such as *fritto misto* (mixed fish and seafood grill). Fixed-price lunch menus are less expensive than evening à la carte.
🍴 50 🚇 Arsenale 1, 52 or San Zaccaria 1, 52, 82 🕐 Closed Wed., Thur., & 2 weeks each Jan. & Aug. 🔇 🃏 All major cards

🍴 ANTICO MONTIN
🏨 $$$–$$$$
FONDAMENTA DI BORGO, DORSODURO 1147
TEL 041 522 7151
FAX 041 520 0203
Artists, writers, and the rich and famous have patronized the Montin for decades. For a long while it lived off its reputation, but standards in the kitchen have risen to former levels. The rear garden is one of the loveliest places in Venice to eat alfresco, but the main dining rooms are equally cozy and appealing. Steeped in history, they have an old-fashioned atmosphere and painting-covered walls.
🍴 125 🚇 Zattare or Ca' Rezzonico 1, 52, 82 🕐 Closed Tues. D, Wed., & some of Aug. 🃏 All major cards

🍴 CORTE SCONTA
$$$–$$$$
CALLE DEL PRESTIN, CASTELLO 3886
TEL 041 522 7024
It is increasingly difficult to secure a table in this simple, trattoria-style restaurant, a favorite of locals and foreigners in the know. The atmosphere is lively, at times almost chaotic, and there is no real menu. The wait staff brings a selection of appetizers and a limited choice of main and pasta dishes. Quality is good, but perhaps not reflective of the price and reputation.
🍴 50–70 🚇 Arsenale 1 🕐 Closed Sun., Mon.,

4 weeks Jan.–Feb., & 4 weeks from 3rd Sun. July 🔇 🃏 All major cards

🍴 FIASCHETTERIA TOSCANA
$$$–$$$$
SALIZZADA SAN GIOVANNI CRISOSTOMO, CANNAREGIO 5719
TEL 041 528 5281
This pleasantly stylish restaurant close to the Rialto has been a safe bet for good Venetian fish dishes—despite its Tuscan name—since 1956. Tables are close together, and the atmosphere can be busy. The wine list is intriguingly eclectic, and in summer you can dine outdoors.
🍴 80–110 🚇 Rialto 1, 3, 82 🕐 Closed Tues. & 3–4 weeks July & Aug. 🔇 🃏 All major cards

🍴 FLORIAN
$$$
PIAZZA SAN MARCO, SAN MARCO 56–59
TEL 041 528 5338
Venice's oldest (founded in 1720), most opulent, and most expensive café. Well worth at least one visit to enjoy its beautiful 18th-century interior.
🚇 San Marco 1, 3, 4, 82 🕐 Closed Wed.

🍴 TRATTORIA ALLA MADONNA
$$$
CALLE DELLA MADONNA, SAN POLO 594
TEL 041 522 3824
A trattoria of the old school: big, busy, and low on frills. The mainly fish-oriented cooking is unexceptional, but as a dining experience it is far more genuine and earthy than the pricier tourist-filled haunts on the nearby Rialto waterfront.
🍴 220 🚇 Rialto 1, 3, 82 🕐 Closed Wed. & some of Jan. & Aug. 🔇 🃏 All major cards

🍴 VINI DA GIGIO
$$$
FONDAMENTA SAN FELICE, CANNAREGIO 3628/A
TEL 041 528 5140
A perfect little canalside restaurant for a quiet lunch or romantic dinner. Simple but elegantly cooked and presented Venetian cooking, friendly service, and two plain dining rooms with bar, beamed ceilings, and pretty wooden cabinets around the walls. Try the *carpaccio di spada* (thin slices of swordfish).
🍴 40 🚇 Ca' d'Oro 1 🕐 Closed Mon. & some of Jan. & Aug. 🔇 🃏 All major cards

🍴 DONA ONESTA
$$
PONTE DE LA DONA ONESTA, DORSODURO 3922
TEL 041 710 586
The "Honest Woman" is true to her name, and this simple trattoria charges fair prices for good, basic Venetian fish and meat dishes in a plain, one-room restaurant near San Rocco and the Frari.
🍴 70 🚇 San Tomà 1, 82 🕐 Closed Sun. 🔇 🃏 All major cards

🍴 HARRY'S DOLCI
$$
FONDAMENTA SAN BIAGIO 773, ISOLA DELLA GIUDECCA
TEL 041 522 4844
Cross the water to the Giudecca island to take tea, coffee, and cakes (meals, too) in a fashionable but pleasantly relaxed offshoot of Harry's Bar (see p. 362).
🚇 Sant'Eufemia 52, 82 🕐 Closed Tues. Nov.–March

🍴 ACIUGETA
$–$$
CAMPO SS. FILIPPO E GIACOMO, CASTELLO 4357
TEL 041 522 4292
An old-fashioned pizzeria-trattoria just west of St. Mark's, and one of the most reasonably priced places in this busy quarter for a simple meal.

70 inside + 70 outside
San Zaccaria 1, 4, 52, 82
Closed Wed. in winter
MC, V

ANTICA DOLO
$
RUGA VECCHIA SAN GIOVANNI, SAN POLO 778
TEL 041 522 6546
Not quite as old as nearby Do Mori (see below), but an almost equally authentic and atmospheric source of wines and snacks (*cicheti* in Venetian dialect).
Rialto 1, 3, 82 Closed Sun.

DO MORI
$
CALLE DO MORI, OFF RUGA VECCHIA SAN GIOVANNI, SAN POLO 429
TEL 041 522 5401
Venetians and market traders have been crowding this dark, cramped *bacaro*, or wine bar, since 1462. No chairs or tables, but tasty snacks and more than 350 different wines. An essential Venetian experience.
Rialto 1, 3, 81 Closed Sun. & Wed. D

IL CAFFÈ
$
CAMPO SANTO MARGHERITA, DORSODURO 2963
TEL 041 528 7998
A tiny red-fronted café with a spread of busy outdoor tables on a lovely and lively square a few minutes' walk from the Frari church.
Ca' Rezzonico 1
Closed Sun.

PAOLIN
$
CAMPO SANTO STEFANO, SAN MARCO 3464
TEL 041 522 0710
The best bar on one of the city's prettiest piazzas, with excellent ice cream and plenty of sunny tables where you can watch the world go by.
Accademia 1, 3, 4, 82
Closed Fri.

VINO VINO
$
CALA DEL CAFFETTIER, PONTE DELLE VESTE, SAN MARCO 2207D
TEL 041 523 7027
Two rooms with old wooden cabinets and marble-topped tables, a few paces from Teatro La Fenice opera house. More than 250 wines by the glass or bottle, plus snacks and light meals. Open until 11 p.m. or midnight.
Santa Maria del Giglio 1
Closed Tues.

NORTHEAST ITALY

DOLOMITI

PARKHOTEL LAURIN
$$$$ ✪✪✪✪
VIA LAURIN 4, BOLZANO (BOZEN)
TEL 0471 310 000
FAX 0471 311 148
This hotel is an art nouveau gem on the eastern edge of the old town. Over the years it has played host to royalty and other visiting VIPs. The belle epoque restaurant is good, but more expensive than the superior Amadè (see below).
96 P
All major cards

LUNA-MONDSCHIEN
$$$ ✪✪✪✪
VIA PIAVE 15, BOLZANO (BOZEN)
TEL 0471 975 642
FAX 0471 975 577
This central but peaceful garden-fringed hotel dates from 1798; the superior wood-paneled rooms have balconies overlooking the garden.
85 P All major cards

GOLF
$$–$$$$ ✪✪✪✪
VIA CIMA TOSA 3, CAMPO CARLO MAGNO (2 MILES/3 KM FROM MADONNA DI CAMPIGLIO)
TEL 0465 441 003
FAX 0465 440 294

PRICES

HOTELS
An indication of the cost of a double room without breakfast is given by $ signs.

$$$$$	Over $280
$$$$	$200–$280
$$$	$120–$200
$$	$80–$120
$	Under $80

RESTAURANTS
An indication of the cost of a three-course dinner without drinks is given by $ signs.

$$$$$	Over $80
$$$$	$50–$80
$$$	$35–$50
$$	$20–$35
$	Under $20

There are numerous hotels in the winter and summer resorts of the Dolomites. This hotel, as the name suggests, stands out by virtue of its nine-hole golf course.
115 P All major cards

SCHLOSS KORB
$$$ ✪✪✪✪
MISSIANO, STRADA CASTEL D'APPIANO 5, BOLZANO (BOZEN)
TEL 0471 636 000
FAX 0471 636 033
If you wish to be out of Bolzano, then drive 3 miles (5 km) west of town to this evocative 13th-century castle up in the hills. Both the building, with its old tower, and much of the decoration retains a suitably antique period feel.
56 P Closed Nov.–Easter
No credit cards

CHALET HERMITAGE
$$ ✪✪
VIA CASTELLETTO INFERIORE 69, MADONNA DI CAMPIGLIO
TEL 0465 441 558
FAX 0465 441 618
Set among gardens and woodland, with wonderful mountain views, about 1 mile

(1.5 km) from the center of Madonna. The hotel restaurant is one of the best in town. This is now a bio-ecological hotel, awaiting four star approval.
(i) 24 **(clock)** Closed Oct.–mid-Dec. & Easter–late June All major cards

AMADÈ
$$–$$$$
VIA CAVOUR-VICOLO CA' DE' BEZZI 8, BOLZANO (BOZEN)
TEL 0471 971 278
A restaurant whose often innovative cuisine combines the flavors of the Veneto and the Tyrol. Fish and meat dishes are both available. There is an excellent and inexpensive fixed-price lunch menu.
30–40 Closed Sun. D, Mon. L, & 3 weeks July–Aug. All major cards

EL FILÒ
$–$$
PIAZZA SCUOLE 5, MOLVENO
TEL 0461 586 151
A medieval house at the center of town where you can go for a snack and a glass of wine or a full meal. Choose from game specialties such as *cervo* (venison), *cinghiale* (wild boar), and Trentino dishes like *gnocchi alle ortiche* (small potato dumplings with a nettle sauce).
55 Closed Nov.–April All major cards

LAGO DI GARDA

PALACE HOTEL VILLA CORTINE
$$$$$
VIA GROTTE 6, SIRMIONE
TEL 030 990 5890
FAX 030 916 390
Sublime, almost overly luxurious 1905 villa hotel set on parkland away from the town center overlooking the lake.
(i) 49 + 2 suites Closed Nov.–Easter All major cards

HOTEL DU LAC DU PARC
$$$–$$$$$
VIALE ROVERETO 44, RIVA

DEL GARDA
TEL 0464 551 500
FAX 0464 555 200
Riva has numerous mid-range hotels, but for style and recreational activities (sauna, tennis courts), this smart, Spanish-style villa hotel has no equal.
(i) 170 + 4 suites All major cards

LAURIN
$$$$
VIALE LANDI 9, SALÒ
TEL 0365 22 022
FAX 0365 22 382
One of Italy's finest art nouveau villas, this romantic hotel is set on the lake and surrounded by parks and gardens.
(i) 36 + 2 suites All major cards

GARDA & SUISSE
$$$–$$$$
VIA ZANARDELLI 126, GARDONE RIVIERA
TEL 0365 290 485
FAX 0365 20 777
In its day, the 180-room Grand hotel nearby was more famous, but today this much more intimate villa on the lake is Gardone's most elegant hotel.
(i) 17 Restaurant closed Mon., Tues. L All major cards

VILLA DEL SOGNO
$$$–$$$$
VIA ZANARDELLI 701, GARDONE RIVIERA (BRESCIA)
TEL 0365 290 181
FAX 0365 290 230
This grand 1920s mock-Renaissance "Villa of the Dream" overlooks the lake and surrounding countryside. Both the hotel, which is the area's best, and its grounds, are oases of seclusion and tranquility.
(i) 32 + 4 suites Closed mid-Oct.–March All major cards

LA RUCOLA
$$$$
VIA STRENTELLE 3, SIRMIONE
TEL 030 916 326

Exemplary modern Italian cooking with seasonal specialties that embrace meat, fish, and seafood dishes.
45 Closed Thur. & Jan. All major cards

VILLA FIORDALISO
$$$$
CORSO ZANARDELLI 132, GARDONE RIVIERA
TEL 0365 20 158
FAX 0365 290 011
A temple to refined regional Lombard and Veneto cooking that has earned a Michelin star. This 19th-century villa—once home to Mussolini's mistress—is surrounded by parkland. There are six three-star standard rooms, some with lake views.
60 Closed Jan. & Feb. Restaurant closed Mon., Tues. L All major cards

VECCHIA RIVA
$$$
VIA BASTIONE 3, RIVA DEL GARDA
TEL 0464 555 061
An intimate and refined restaurant whose cooking is largely, but not exclusively, based on fish from the lake.
60 Closed Tues. & L All major cards

OSTERIA DELL'OROLOGIO
$–$$$
VIA BUTTURINI 26, SALÒ
TEL 0365 290 158
A real find among the generally expensive restaurants in Lake Garda's resorts. The setting is simple and informal, and there are good cheeses, wines, snacks, and a handful of hot dishes.
70 Closed Wed. & June All major cards

PADOVA

MAJESTIC TOSCANELLI
$$$
VIA DELL'ARCO 2
TEL 049 663 244
FAX 049 876 0025

HOTELS & RESTAURANTS

Housed in a 16th-century palazzo on a tranquil square just south of the central Piazza delle Erbe. The rooms are decorated in a 19th-century style.
ⓘ 32 🚫 ⊗ 🚫 All major cards

🏨 AL FAGIANO
$-$$ ○○
VIA LOCATELLI 45
TEL 049 875 3396
FAX 049 875 0073
A plain and inexpensive hotel with a courteous welcome and perfect central position close to the Basilica di Sant'Antonio.
ⓘ 29 🚫 ⊗ 🚫 All major cards

🍴 ANTICO BROLO
$$$-$$$$
CORSO MILANO 22
TEL 049 664 555
An elegant restaurant with first-rate service and good, if rarely exceptional, food. Signature dishes include *ravioli ai fiori di zucca* (filled pasta with zucchini flowers) and *testina di vitello all'aceto cotto e cipolla* (veal head with vinegar and onion).
🪑 90 🕐 Closed Sun. L, Mon., & 3 weeks Aug. ⊗ 🚫 All major cards

🍴 L'ANFORA
$-$$
VIA DEI SONCIN 13
TEL 049 656 629
Meat and fish dishes are available at this gracious little restaurant near Piazza delle Erbe at the heart of the old city. Try the grilled fish of the day, *zuppa di vongole e cozze* (a soup of clams and mussels), or *tagliatelle ai porcini* (pasta with wild mushrooms).
🪑 30 🕐 Closed Sun. ⊗ 🚫 No credit cards

VERONA

🏨 GABBIA D'ORO
$$$$$ ○○○○
CORSO PORTA BORSARI 4/A
TEL 045 800 3060

FAX 045 590 293
This superb, discreet hotel lies close to Piazza delle Erbe at the center of the city. All its rooms are different and beautifully appointed with beamed ceilings, frescoes, canopy beds, and many other period touches. No restaurant.
ⓘ 27 🚫 ⊗ 🚫 All major cards

🏨 VICTORIA
$$$$ ○○○○
VIA ADUA 6
TEL 045 590 566
FAX 045 590 155
This well-run, centrally located hotel has calm and understated rooms, some of which retain traces of mosaic and fresco from medieval and Roman buildings on the site. No restaurant.
ⓘ 67 + 4 suites 🅿 🚫 ⊗ 🚫 All major cards

🏨 COLOMBA D'ORO
$$$-$$$$ ○○○○
VIA C, CATTANEO 10
TEL 045 595 300
FAX 045 594 974
A bright and enticing family-run hotel housed in a thoughtfully restored 14th-century palazzo close to Piazza Brà.
ⓘ 49 🚫 ⊗ 🚫 All major cards

🏨 TORCOLO
$$ ○○
VICOLO LISTONE 3
TEL 045 800 7512
FAX 045 800 4058
A welcoming, good-value hotel that looks onto a peaceful square close to the main Piazza Brà. No restaurant.
ⓘ 19 🚫 ⊗ 🚫 AE, MC, V

🍴 IL DESCO
$$$$$
VIA DIETRO SAN SEBASTIANO 7
TEL 045 595 358
Justly ranked among northern Italy's best restaurants by many critics, including Michelin, which has awarded it two stars. Try appetizers such as small

medallions of quail or exquisite flans of tomato and mussels, and main courses like duck breast with honey and a purée of zucchini and eggplant.
🪑 50 🕐 Closed Sun., 1st week Jan., Easter, 2 weeks June, & some of Aug. ⊗ 🚫 All major cards

🍴 ANTICO CAFFÈ DANTE
$$-$$$
PIAZZA DANTE
TEL 045 800 3593
A historic café in one of the city's most romantic and beautiful medieval squares. Well cooked light meals are served.
🕐 Closed Mon. except in summer, 10 days each Jan. & June ⊗ 🚫 All major cards

🍴 LA GREPPIA
$$-$$$
VICOLO SAMARITANA 3
TEL 045 800 4577
A bright, spacious restaurant with vaulted ceilings at the heart of the city's historic center. Local and regional cooking.
🪑 80-150 🕐 Closed Mon. & some of Aug. ⊗ 🚫 All major cards

🍴 TRATTORIA AL CALMIERE
$$-$$$
PIAZZA SAN ZENO 10
TEL 045 803 0765
One of only a handful of historic trattorias to have survived in Verona, this restaurant on a pretty piazza in front of San Zeno offers reliable roast meats, robust pastas, and good basic Veronese specialties.
🪑 120 + 60 outdoors 🕐 Closed Thurs. & Sun. D in summer, Wed. D & Thurs. in winter, & 3 weeks July ⊗ 🚫 All major cards

🍴 LA STUETA
$$
VIA REDENTORE 4/B
TEL 045 803 2462
A little two-room restaurant

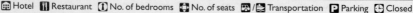

of huge popularity, and no wonder, for the local cooking is superb and the prices are low. Try the polenta dishes, the gnocchi, and delicious *zuppa di patate* (potato soup).

🔲 45 🕐 Closed Mon., Tues. L, & Aug. 🅰 All major cards

VICENZA

🏨 DUE MORI
$$ ✪✪

CONTRÀ DO RODE 26
TEL 0444 321 886
FAX 0444 326 127

Vicenza has several bland modern hotels on its outskirts, but remarkably few places to stay in the city's historic heart. This simple hotel lies close to Piazza dei Signori, the central piazza.

🛏 46 🅰 AE, MC, V

🍴 ANTICA CASA DELLA MALVASIA
$$

CONTRÀ DELLE MORETTE 5
TEL 0444 543 704

A rather unusual restaurant at the heart of the city whose bustle and atmosphere lend it the feel of a large medieval diner. Food can be innovative and is strictly regional, and includes *puledro* (horse meat), a major local specialty. Good salads are among the wide choice of alternatives. Excellent drinks, including 177 different teas, 75 herbal infusions, 70 malt whiskies, and 150 grappas.

🔲 140–180 🕐 Closed Mon. 🅲 🅰 All major cards

EMILIA-ROMAGNA & THE MARCHE

ASCOLI PICENO

🏨 GIOLI
$$ ✪✪✪✪

VIALE DE' GASPERI 14
TEL 0736 255 550
FAX 0736 255 550

A modern, functional hotel just a minute's walk east of the cathedral.

🛏 56 🔄 🅰 All major cards

🍴 RISTORANTE DEL CORSO
$$–$$$

CORSO MAZZINI 277–79
TEL 0736 256 760

A restaurant in the historic center devoted solely to fish and seafood. The *minestrina di pesce* (fish soup), when available, is delicious.

🔲 40 🕐 Closed Sun. D, Mon., & Sept. 🅲 🅰 V

🍴 TORNASACCO
$$–$$$

PIAZZA DEL POPOLO 36
TEL 0736 254 151

On Ascoli's beautiful main square, this is the perfect spot to sample local specialties such as *olive ascolane* (big, juicy olives stuffed with minced meat and deep fried).

🔲 56 🕐 Closed Fri. & 2 weeks July 🅲 🅰 All major cards

BOLOGNA

🏨 GRAN HOTEL BAGLIONI
$$$$–$$$$$ ✪✪✪✪✪

VIA DELL'INDIPENDENZA 8
TEL 051 225 445
FAX 051 234 840

English royalty has stayed at the Grand during visits to Bologna. It is the city's finest hotel, and both its rooms and public areas are extremely opulent and elegant.

🛏 121 + 4 suites 🅿 🔄 🅲 🅰 All major cards

🏨 CORONA D'ORO 1890
$$$–$$$$ ✪✪✪✪

VIA OBERDAN 12
TEL 051 236 456
FAX 051 262 679

Art nouveau decoration in the public areas and medieval touches such as painted wooden ceilings in the rooms make this a memorable place to stay. No restaurant.

🛏 35 🅿 🔄 🅲 🅰 All major cards

🏨 OROLOGIO
$$–$$$ ✪✪✪

VIA IV NOVEMBRE 10

TEL 051 231 253
FAX 051 260 552

Perfect for sight-seeing, the hotel lies just off Piazza Grande in a quiet pedestrians-only zone of the historic city center.

🛏 31 🅿 🔄 🅲 🅰 All major cards

🏨 ROMA
$$–$$$ ✪✪✪

VIA MASSIMO D'AZEGLIO 9
TEL 051 226 322
FAX 051 239 909

A calm atmosphere, professional service, and central position are the hallmarks of the Roma.

🛏 85 🔄 🅲 🅰 All major cards

🍴 BATTIBECCO
$$$–$$$$$

VIA BATTIBECCO 4
TEL 051 223 298

A stylish, centrally located restaurant with a bias toward fish and seafood, but plenty of pastas, risottos (including porcini mushrooms and saffron), and meat dishes such as *maialino* (roast suckling pig).

🔲 60 🅿 🕐 Closed Sun. 🅲 🅰 All major cards

🍴 ROSTERIA LUCIANO
$$$

VIA N. SAURO 19
TEL 051 231 249

Lunch at this intimate central restaurant is fast and furious. Dinner is more relaxed, with a chance to savor delicious dishes such as *tagliolini al tartufo* (thin pasta strands with truffle) and the Luciano's signature dish, *braciolina all' antica Bologna* (cuts of pork with a ham filling).

🔲 45–60 🕐 Closed Wed. & 4 weeks July–Aug. 🅲 🅰 All major cards

🍴 DA CESARI
$$–$$$

VIA DEI CARBONESI 8
TEL 051 237 710

One of the city's classic old trattorias—in the same family for over 30 years—with traditional Bolognese dishes,

HOTELS & RESTAURANTS

home-produced wine, and occasionally adventurous offerings such as *capretto* (goat) and *ravioli di coniglio* (pasta and rabbit).
🍴 65 🕐 Closed Sat. in summer, Sun., & 3 weeks Aug. 🉐 🚫 All major cards

🍴 LA FARFALLA
$–$$
VIA BERTIERA 12
TEL 051 225 656
Sample classic Bolognese dishes such as *tortellini in brodo* (filled pasta parcels in broth) and *zucchine ripiene* (stuffed zucchini) at this simple two-room trattoria in the university district.
🍴 30 🕐 Closed Sat. D, Sun., & Aug. 🚫 No credit cards

FERRARA

🏨 ANNUNZIATA
$$$ ✪✪✪✪
PIAZZA DELLA REPUBBLICA 5
TEL 0532 201 111
FAX 0532 203 233
It is impossible to be more central than this reliable family-run hotel directly in front of the Castello Estense. No restaurant.
🛏 23 🅿 🚌 🉐 🚫 All major cards

🏨 CARLTON
$$–$$$ ✪✪✪
VIA GARIBALDI 93
TEL 0532 211 130
FAX 0532 205 766
A pleasant and comfortable family-run hotel a few minutes' walk west of the central Piazza della Repubblica.
🛏 63 🅿 🚌 🉐 🚫 All major cards

🍴 L'OCA GIULIVA
$$–$$$
VIA BOCCACANALE DI SANTO STEFANO 38
TEL 0532 207 628
A tiny establishment run by young owners where the menus change weekly and make innovative use of fish and meat. Dishes may include simply grilled fish or a

more decadent pâté of pheasant with *uva passita* (rich, sugary grapes).
🍴 15–30 🕐 Closed Tues. L, Mon., & 2 weeks in summer 🉐 🚫 All major cards

🍴 QUEL FANTASTICO GIOVEDÌ
$$–$$$
VIA CASTELNUOVO 9
TEL 0532 760 570
"That Fantastic Thursday" is named after a John Steinbeck story. Its food can be as unusual as its sobriquet, with dishes such as salmon and bream sushi with an herb mayonnaise and tagliatelle with saffron and squid.
🍴 38 🕐 Closed Wed. & 4 weeks July–Aug. 🉐 🚫 All major cards

PARMA

🏨 BUTTON
$$ ✪✪✪
VIA DELLA SALINA 7
TEL 0521 208 039
FAX 0521 238 783
Parma has smarter hotels in more outlying positions, but this is the best choice for sight-seeing at the heart of the historic quarter. No restaurant.
🛏 40 🅿 🚌 🚫 All major cards

🍴 ANGIOL D'ORO
$$$$
VICOLO SCUTELLARI 1
TEL 0521 282 632
The food here is good, without meriting the high prices, but what you pay for is the location—in summer you dine at tables laid out on the corner of the beautiful Piazza del Duomo.
🍴 70 🕐 Closed Sun. 🉐 🚫 All major cards

🍴 PARIZZI
$$$–$$$$
STRADA DELLA REPUBBLICA 71
TEL 0521 285 952
Parma-based cuisine in this comfortable and relaxed Michelin one-star restaurant that has been a byword for

fine food and courteous service in the city for years. Try the *manzo stracotta* (beef steak in a rich sauce) as a main course.
🍴 60 🅿 🕐 Closed Sun. D in summer & Mon. 🉐 🚫 All major cards

🍴 LA BARRICATA
$–$$
BORGO MARODOLO 8/A
TEL 0521 281 307
A small trattoria, west of the river near the Annunziata church, whose cooking combines the local and southern Spanish cuisine of the Italo-Spanish family owners.
🍴 35 🕐 Closed Tues. & Aug. 🉐 🚫 No credit cards

RAVENNA

🏨 BISANZIO
$$$ ✪✪✪✪
VIA SALARA 30
TEL 0544 217 111
FAX 0544 32 539
A stylish Best Western hotel at the center of town with opulent public spaces, a pretty internal garden, and attractive, restful rooms. No restaurant.
🛏 38 🚌 🉐 🚫 All major cards

🍴 LA GARDELA
$$
VIA PONTE MARINO 3
TEL 0544 217 147
An unpretentious dining room with straightforward local cooking in a convenient spot between the Basilica di San Vitale and Piazza del Popolo.
🍴 80–95 🕐 Closed Thurs. & some of Feb. & Aug. 🉐 🚫 All major cards

URBINO

🏨 BONCONTE
$$–$$$ ✪✪✪✪
VIA DELLE MURA 28
TEL 0722 2463
FAX 0722 4782
Some rooms can be small, especially on upper floors, but the Bonconte's comforts and location—by the town

walls—make it a perfect sight-seeing base.

ⓘ 23 🅿 ⬌ ⓢ ⓐAll major cards

🍽 VECCHIA URBINO
$$–$$$
VIA DEI VASARI 3–5
TEL 0722 4447
This pretty, central restaurant comes into its own in the fall and winter when the menu is enlivened with seasonal truffle and mushroom dishes.
🍴 50–120 ⏲ Closed Tues. in winter ⓐAll major cards

🍽 FRANCO
$–$$
VIA DEL POGGIO 1-PIAZZA RINASCIMENTO
TEL 0722 2492
The eponymous Franco hails from Rome, so Roman fare like carbonara (pasta with egg and ham) is on offer along with tasty local dishes such as *coniglio* (rabbit) with an herb stuffing. In a lovely setting by the Palazzo Ducale.
🍴 110 ⏲ Closed Sun. ⓐAll major cards

FLORENCE

🏨 HELVETIA & BRISTOL
$$$$$ ✪✪✪✪✪
VIA DEI PESCIONI 2
TEL 055 287 814
FAX 055 288 353
First choice in Florence if money is no object. Luxurious and exclusive, this superb hotel has been in business since the 18th century. Facilities and bathrooms are state of the art, but rooms (some of which are relatively small) are in a more sober, traditional style with antiques and old paintings.
ⓘ 34 + 15 suites 🅿 ⬌ ⓢ ⓐAll major cards

🏨 EXCELSIOR
$$$$$ ✪✪✪✪✪
PIAZZA OGNISSANTI 3
TEL 055 264 201
FAX 055 210 278
Florence's second grandest

hotel is undermined only by its location on one of the city's less attractive piazzas. Otherwise, the antique-filled rooms are visions of Old World elegance, while the public areas—all marble, columns, and ornate ceilings—are on a sumptuous scale.
ⓘ 146 + 7 suites 🅿 ⬌ ⓢ ⓐAll major cards

🏨 BRUNELLESCHI
$$$$–$$$$$ ✪✪✪✪
PIAZZA SANTA ELISABETTA 3
TEL 055 27 370
FAX 055 219 653
Designed by leading Italian architect Italo Gamberini, this central hotel has been stylishly converted from a Byzantine chapel and fifth-century tower. Ancient brick and stone have been preserved in the public areas and complemented by the use of wood. Rooms are bright, airy, and comfortable.
ⓘ 88 + 8 suites 🅿 ⬌ ⓢ ⓐAll major cards

🏨 TORRE DI BELLOSGUARDO
$$$–$$$$$ ✪✪✪✪
VIA ROTI MICHELOZZI 2
TEL 055 229 8145
FAX 055 229 008
This glorious Renaissance villa lies amid hilltop gardens with lovely views, just a five-minute drive south of the Oltrarno. The frescoes and vast stone fireplaces of the vaulted public areas create a wonderful atmosphere, while the spacious rooms are individually decorated in an old-fashioned style. Breakfast and light meals served, but no restaurant.
ⓘ 10 + 6 suites 🅿 ⬌ ⓢ 3 rooms only 🏊 ⓐAll major cards

🏨 J & J
$$$$ ✪✪✪✪
VIA DI MEZZO 20
TEL 055 26 312
FAX 055 240 282
This converted 15th-century convent appears bland from the outside, but conceals a beautifully romantic little hotel

within. Patches of old fresco and vaulted ceilings distinguish the public areas, while the rooms combine fine fabrics, modern fixtures, and an array of antiques. The hotel is in the quiet Sant'Ambrogio district, but remains an easy walk from all the sights. No restaurant.
ⓘ 18 + 5 suites 🅿 ⓢ ⓐAll major cards

🏨 MONNA LISA
$$$$ ✪✪✪✪
BORGO PINTI 27
TEL 055 247 9751
FAX 055 247 9755
A somber facade conceals a marvelous 14th-century palazzo complete with sweeping staircase, frescoed ceilings, and terra-cotta floors. Rooms vary in size, but preserve an aristocratic, Old World feel, with oil paintings and expensive antiques. Some rooms overlook a peaceful rear garden, others an inner courtyard.
ⓘ 30 🅿 ⬌ ⓢ ⓐAll major cards

🏨 LOGGIATA DEI SERVITI
$$$ ✪✪✪
PIAZZA SS. ANNUNZIATA 3
TEL 055 289 592
FAX 055 289 595
This hotel occupies a former convent building in a distinguished square designed by leading Renaissance architect Filippo Brunelleschi. Rooms vary in style, but all have tasteful, understated lines, and decor that recalls the simplicity of the original structure. Some have vaulted ceilings and canopied beds, and all are enlivened by rich fabrics and pieces of period furniture.
ⓘ 25 + 4 suites 🅿 ⬌ ⓢ ⓐAll major cards

🏨 MORANDI ALLA CROCETTA
$$$ ✪✪✪
VIA LAURA 50
TEL 055 234 4747
FAX 055 248 0954
This quiet and intimate hotel—part of a former monastery—near Piazza S.S.

Annunziata is a gem, thanks both to the charm and friendly welcome of the owner, and the considerable style with which the rooms and public spaces have been decorated. Colorful rugs cover polished wooden floors, and old prints and antiques decorate the walls. No restaurant. Reserve well in advance.

🛏 10 ⬛ 🅰 All major cards

🏨 CASCI
$$ ✪✪
VIA CAVOUR 13
TEL 055 211 686
FAX 055 239 6461
This excellent two-star hotel is the best in its class, and enjoys a perfect position just two minutes' walk north of the cathedral. The modestly sized rooms are immaculate and modern, and the courtesy and welcome of the multilingual family owners is faultless. Buffet breakfast but no restaurant.

🛏 25 ⬛ ⬛ 🅰 All major cards

🏨 HOTEL BELLETTINI
$$ ✪✪
VIA DEI CONTI 7
TEL 055 213 561
FAX 055 283 551
More than a hint of the 19th-century pervades this central and friendly hotel, with the type of terra-cotta floors and wood-beamed ceilings you would expect of a period Florentine town house. Rooms can be a little spartan but are spotless (the two on the top floor have views) and the staff is unfailingly helpful.

🛏 28 🅿 ⬛ ⬛ 🅰 All major cards

🍴 CIBREO
$$$–$$$$
VIA DE' MACCI 118
TEL 055 234 1100
The first choice of most Florentine gastronomes, and the best place in the city to enjoy creative interpretations of traditional Tuscan dishes

such as *trippa in insalata* (a cold tripe salad—better than it sounds) and the celebrated *fegato brasato* (braised liver). The dining room is plain—simple wooden tables and painted walls—and the service and atmosphere relaxed. Prices are set for each course—be sure to leave room for the mouthwatering desserts. A reservation several days in advance is essential.

🍽 70 🅿 🕐 Closed Sun. & Mon. ⬛ 🅰 All major cards

🍴 OLIVIERO
$$$
VIA DELLE TERME 51R
TEL 055 287 643
Oliviero enjoys a reputation—shared with Cibreo (see this page)—for excellent regional cooking with a twist, but unlike its rival usually also offers a selection of fish and seafood dishes. Typical dishes include *tagliatelle all'ortica* (pasta with a green nettle sauce) or pigeon with a purée of peas and potato. The ambience is warm and welcoming.

🍽 80 🕐 Closed Sun. & Aug. ⬛ 🅰 All major cards

🍴 ANGIOLINO
$$–$$$
VIA SANTO SPIRITO 36R
TEL 055 239 8976
A pretty trattoria of the old school. Colorful festoons of dried flowers, chilis, pumpkins, and tomatoes hang from the ceiling; wicker-covered Chianti bottles and red-checked table cloths add another traditional touch. Cooking has a good Florentine flavor, with appetizers such as *crostini* (small toasts with liver or olive paste) and hearty soups such as *ribollita* (vegetables with black cabbage) and *pappa al pomodoro* (tomato and basil).

🍽 110 ⬛ 🅰 All major cards

🍴 BALDOVINO
$$–$$$
VIA SAN GIUSEPPE 22R
TEL 055 241 773
This bustling, innovative, and pleasantly chic restaurant, just behind Santa Croce, offers pizzas baked in traditional Neapolitan style in wood-fired ovens or a choice of Tuscan pasta and meat dishes. It is run by a young Scottish couple—making its success among visitors and Italians all the more remarkable—who

have also opened an equally appealing wine bar and food store just across the street.
🍴 130 🕐 Closed Mon.
🗞 All major cards

CAFFÈ ITALIANO
$$–$$$
VIA ISOLE DELLE STINCHE 11–13R
TEL 055 289 368
This restaurant is split into three areas: a formal restaurant, a wine bar for snacks and lighter meals, and a simple trattoria for lunches and less formal dining. All serve good-value Tuscan food and have a fine medieval setting, with vast beams, brick vaults, and terra-cotta floors.
🍴 50–120 🕐 Closed Mon.
🗞 MC, V

OSTERIA DE' BENCI
$$
VIA DE' BENCI 13r
TEL 055 234 4923
A busy dining room painted in tasteful pastel colors that lend it a fresh modern air. Staff is young, energetic, and informal, and the food offers light, well-cooked takes on Tuscan staples such as *zuppa di verdura* (vegetable soup) and *agnello scottaditto* (grilled lamb).
🍴 50–80 🕐 Closed Sun. & some of Aug. 🗞 All major cards

PAOLI
$$
VIA DEI TAVOLINI 12R
TEL 055 216 215
A tempting place to eat at the very heart of the city (just off Via dei Calzaiuoli), although the temptation lies not so much in the food, a predictable mixture of Tuscan grilled meats, pastas, and soups, as in the beautiful frescoed dining room.
🍴 80 🕐 Closed Tues. & Aug. 🔆 🗞 All major cards

BELLE DONNE
$–$$
VIA DELLE BELLE DONNE 16R/A
TEL 055 238 2609

This tiny venue is a good spot for lunch. Cascades of fruit and fresh flowers provide a startling backdrop to a handful of shared paper-covered tables. Daily specials—Tuscan to a fault—are posted on a blackboard. The service is informal, the atmosphere lively.
🍴 30 🅿 🕐 Closed Sat., Sun., & Aug. 🔆 🗞 No credit cards

CAFFÈ RIVOIRE
$$
PIAZZA DELLA SIGNORIA 5R
TEL 055 211 302
Founded in 1827 as a bar specializing in hot chocolate. Today, it is the city's premier central café, its position on Piazza della Signoria ensuring it is constantly thronged. Prices are high, however, and mass tourism has somewhat tarnished its allure.
🕐 Closed Mon. 🗞 All major cards

ROSE'S
$–$$
VIA DEL PARIONE 26R
TEL 055 287 090
Imagine a sleek New York designer bar given a Florentine makeover and you have Rose's, perfect for lunch, coffee, afternoon tea, light supper, or late-night drinks. Modern without being impersonal, it provides a welcome contrast to the mainly wood and terra-cotta interiors of many restaurants in the city.
🍴 50 🗞 All major cards

CAFFÉ CIBREO
$
VIA DEL ANDREA DEL VERROCCHIO 5R
TEL 055 234 5853
This entrancing café lies some way off the beaten track, to the north of Santa Croce, but is well worth the detour. The interior is beautifully old-fashioned, and cakes, snacks, and light meals come from the Cibreo restaurant, just across the street (see p. 370).
🕐 Closed Sun. & Mon.

CAFFÈ GILLI
$
PIAZZA DELLA REPUBBLICA 39R
TEL 055 239 6310
This vast characterless square is distinguished only by its four historic cafés, of which Gilli is the best. Founded in 1733, it moved to its present corner site in 1910, the date of its magnificent belle epoque interior. Its large terrace is a fine place for an aperitif as you watch the Florentines on early evening parade.
🕐 Closed Tues. 🗞 All major cards

CAFFÈ ITALIANO
$
VIA DELLA CONDOTTA 56R
TEL 055 291 082
A remarkably well-kept secret, given its position just a few steps from the busy Via dei Calzaiuoli. Upstairs is a cozy den with a handful of tables for coffee, cakes, and light lunches, while downstairs there is a stylish stand-up bar with lots of dark wood and a relaxed, faintly arty atmosphere.
🕐 Closed Sun. & Aug.

CANTINETTA DEI VERRAZZANO
$
VIA DEI TAVOLINI 18R
TEL 055 268 590
A tempting retreat for take-out snacks, cakes, or slices of pizza, or a more leisurely lunch and glass of wine at the tables to the rear. Choose from the mouthwatering array of food under the huge glass-fronted display. Owned by a notable Chianti vineyard, so the wines are as good as the food.
🕐 Closed Sun. & Aug. 🗞 All major cards

LE VOLPI E L'UVA
$
PIAZZA DEI ROSSI 1R
TEL 055 239 8132
A discreet wine bar tucked away just off Piazza di Santa Felìcita a little way south of the Ponte Vecchio. It offers a

HOTELS & RESTAURANTS

well-chosen and interesting selection of regularly changing wines and a first-rate selection of cheese and snacks as an accompaniment. ⊕ Closed Sun. & 1 week Aug. ⊗ AE, MC, V

TUSCANY

AREZZO

⊞ CASTELLO DI ⊕ GARGONZA
$$–$$$ ✪✪✪
CASTELLO DI GARGONZA, MONTE SANTO SAVINO
TEL 0575 847 021
FAX 0575 847 054
A converted medieval hamlet complete with castle and church, in the countryside 4 miles (6 km) west of Monte San Savino, a village 10 miles (16 km) southwest of Arezzo. Rooms must be taken for a minimum of three nights; apartments and cottages in the village are available for weekly rental. ⓘ 32 ⓟ ⊕ Closed Nov. & some of Jan. ⛴ ⊗ All major cards

⊕ BUCA DI SAN FRANCESCO
$$–$$$
VIA SAN FRANCESCO 1
TEL 0575 23 271
The central Buca has been serving simple Tuscan staples such as thick *ribollita* (vegetable soup) and *agnello* (roast lamb) since 1929. The dining room, with its ancient floor and medieval paintings, is well placed for the church of San Francesco and Piero della Francesca's noted fresco cycle. ⊞ 60 ⊕ Closed Mon. D, Tues., & July ⊗ All major cards

CHIANTI

⊞ CASTELLO DI ⊕ SPALTENNA
$$$–$$$$ ✪✪✪✪
PIEVE DI SPALTENNA, GAIOLE IN CHIANTI

TEL 0577 749 483
FAX 0577 749 269
A splendid former castle-monastery on the outskirts of Gaiole. The hotel buildings and rooms retain many medieval features. The first-rate restaurant occupies the old refectory. ⓘ 26 ⓟ ⊕ Closed Jan.–mid-March, restaurant closed Mon. L ⛴ ⊠ ⊗ All major cards

⊞ RELAIS FATTORIA VIGNALE
$$$–$$$$ ✪✪✪✪
VIA PIANIGIANI 8, RADDA IN CHIANTI
TEL 0577 738 300
FAX 0577 738 592
A roadside setting makes this hotel less enticing than some Chianti hotels, but the gardens and the rooms in the old farmhouse building, with their simple country furniture and wooden beams, more than compensate. ⓘ 34 ⓟ ⊕ Closed Jan.–March, restaurant closes Wed. ⛴ ⊠ ⊗ All major cards

⊞ TENUTA DI RICAVO ⊕
$$$–$$$$ ✪✪✪
LOCALITÀ RICAVO 4, CASTELLINA IN CHIANTI
TEL 0577 740 221
FAX 0577 741 014
Nestled in pastoral countryside about 2 miles (3 km) from Castellina, this converted medieval hamlet is perfect both as a base and as a place to relax in a peaceful setting. The Pecora Nera restaurant serves refined Tuscan cuisine. ⓘ 23 ⓟ ⊕ Closed Oct.–April, restaurant closed Tues. & Wed. ⊠ ⊗ All major cards

⊕ BADIA A COLTIBUONO
$$$
BADIA A COLTIBUONO, (3 MILES/5 KM NE FROM GAIOLE)
TEL 0577 749 424
Housed in the refectory of a restored monastery founded in 770, this well-known and

exclusive restaurant forms part of a family-owned Chianti vineyard and estate. ⊞ 65–110 ⓟ ⊕ Closed Jan.–Feb., & Mon. except in summer ⛴ ⊗ All major cards

CORTONA

⊞ IL FALCONIERE ⊕
$$$–$$$$ ✪✪✪✪
LOCALITÀ SAN MARTINO A BOCENA 370
TEL 0575 612 679
FAX 0575 612 927
A beautifully restored 17th-century villa located about 2 miles (3 km) outside the town walls, off the SS71 road for Arezzo. All rooms are exquisitely furnished in period style and some retain original frescoes. The restaurant (with summer terrace) offers fine meat and fish dishes and boasts an excellent wine list. ⓘ 12 ⓟ ⊕ Hotel closed some of Nov., restaurant closed Mon. Nov.–March ⛴ ⊠ ⊗ All major cards

⊞ SAN MICHELE
$$–$$$ ✪✪✪✪
VIA GUELFA 15
TEL 0575 604 348
FAX 0575 630 147
Comfortable converted Renaissance palace at the town's historic heart. The building retains many of its original features, and the room in the old tower is a gem. ⓘ 35 ⓟ ⊕ Closed mid-Jan.–Feb. ⊟ ⛴ ⊗ All major cards

⊕ LA LOGGETTA
$$
PIAZZA PESCHERIA 3
TEL 0575 630 575
A tasteful restaurant with a simple brick-vaulted medieval interior, white walls, and honest Tuscan cooking. The central position just off the main square is another plus, as is the chance to eat outdoors on the terrace in fine weather. ⊞ 70 ⊕ Closed Nov. & Mon. Sept.–June ⊗ All major cards

TONINO
$–$$
PIAZZA GARIBALDI 1
TEL 0575 630 500
Big, busy, modern, and noisy—but that's how many Italians like their restaurants. Locals flock here for the famous *antipastissimo* (15 different appetizers) and the views across the Val di Chiana.
🍴 400 🕐 Closed Tues. in winter 🅂 🅂 All major cards

LUCCA

LOCANDA L'ELISA
$$$$$ ●●●●●
VIA NUOVA, MASSA PISANA
TEL 0583 379 737
FAX 0583 379 019
A superlative luxury hotel in a neoclasssic villa 2 miles (3 km) south of Lucca on the road to Pisa. It has just two rooms and eight sumptuous suites, plus lush gardens, discreet service, and a dazzling collection of antiques and furniture.
🛏 2 + 8 suites 🅿 🅂 🖾 🅂 All major cards

LA LUNA
$$ ●●●
VIA FILLUNGO-CORTE COMPAGNI 12
TEL 0583 493 634
FAX 0583 490 021
A family-run hotel in a sleepy courtyard just off old Lucca's main street. No restaurant.
🛏 30 🅿 🕐 Closed some of Jan. 🅂 All major cards

PICCOLO HOTEL PUCCINI
$$ ●●●
VIA DI POGGIO 9
TEL 0583 55 421
FAX 0583 53 487
Bright, tasteful rooms in a Renaissance palace at the heart of the old city. It is essential to request private parking in advance of your stay. No restaurant.
🛏 14 🅿 🅂 All major cards

LA MORA
$$$
VIA SESTO DI PONTE A MORIANO 1748, PONTE A MORIANO
TEL 0583 406 402
A Michelin star underlines the quality of La Mora's cooking, the region's best, although to enjoy its sublime Lucchese dishes you need to travel 5 miles (8 km) northwest of Lucca to the hamlet of Ponte a Moriano.
🍴 40–60 🅿 🕐 Closed Wed. & some of Jan. & June 🅂 All major cards

BUCA DI SANT'ANTONIO
$$
VIA DELLA CERVIA 3
TEL 0583 312 199
Established in 1787, this is the best of Lucca's city-center restaurants. Cooking is based on old Lucchese traditions, but does not shy from innovation. Try the celebrated *semifreddo Buccellatto*, the house dessert, a mix of chilled cream and wild berries.
🍴 90 🕐 Closed Sun. D, Mon., & some of July 🅂 🅂 All major cards

MONTALCINO

DEI CAPITANI
$$ ●●●
VIA LAPINI 6
TEL 0577 847 227
FAX 0577 847 227
A comfortable, modern hotel in an old town house with a panoromic terrace, bar area, and swimming pool. No restaurant.
🛏 29 🅿 🅂 🖾 🅂 All major cards

TAVERNA DEI BARBI
$$–$$$
FATTORIA DEI BARBI, LA CROCE, LOCALITÀ PODERNOVI
TEL 0577 849 357
Annexed to a well-known Brunello vineyard 3 miles (5 km) southeast of Montalcino, this wonderful restaurant

serves superb local dishes washed down with home-produced wine. The tasteful, rustic dining room is dominated by a huge stone fireplace.
🍴 80 🅿 🕐 Closed Jan., 2 weeks July, Tues. D, & Wed. except in Aug. 🅂 All major cards

GAPPOLO BLU
$$
VIA SCALE DI MOGLIO 1
TEL 0577 847 150
In a stepped alley off the main Via Mazzini, the cool stone walls of the medieval interior house two small dining rooms. The high-quality pasta dishes are all good.
🍴 35 🕐 Closed Fri. 🅂 All major cards

MONTEPULCIANO

DUOMO
$$ ●●●
VIA SAN DONATO 14
TEL 0578 757 473
FAX 0578 757 473
Just a few steps from the town's cathedral and main piazza, this is a friendly, family-run hotel with bright, straightforward rooms.
🛏 13 🅂 🅂 All major cards

LA CHIUSA
$$$$
VIA DELLA MADONNINA 88, MONTEFOLLONICO
TEL 0577 669 668
FAX 0577 669 593
For the best food close to Montepulciano, you need to drive 5 miles (8 km) northwest to the village of Montefollonico. Here, this former mill has become a Michelin one-star hotel-restaurant, with just 12 rooms. Meals are expensive and outstanding. A light creative touch enhances the mostly Tuscan cuisine.
🍴 45 🅿 🕐 Closed Tues. & mid-Jan.–mid-March 🅂 All major cards

LA GROTTA
$$
LOCALITÀ SAN BIAGIO 16
TEL 0578 757 607
For a town of its size, Montepulciano has few good restaurants. La Grotta is a good place for lunch, thanks largely to its location opposite the noted church of San Biagio. Without a car or cab, however, it is a steep climb back up to town.
🍴45 🅿 🕐 Closed Wed. & Jan.–Feb. 🅰 All major cards

PIENZA

IL CHIOSTRO DI PIENZA
$$$ 000
CORSO ROSSELLINO 26
TEL 0578 748 400
FAX 0578 748 440
Part of the exclusive Relais hotel group, this centrally located hotel takes its name from the *chiostro* (courtyard) of the 15th-century convent from which it was converted. The simple but elegant rooms evoke the flavor of the old building.
🛏37 🅿 🔄 🏊 🅰 All major cards

FALCO
$–$$
PIAZZA DANTE ALIGHIERI 7
TEL 0578 748 551
A trattoria with a medieval interior, on a square just outside the village, frequented by locals as well as visitors. Try the famed local pecorino cheese melted and wrapped in prosciutto.
🍴80 🅿 🕐 Closed Fri. 🅰 All major cards

PISA

ROYAL VICTORIA
$$–$$$ 000
LUNGARNO PACINOTTI 12
TEL 050 940 111
FAX 050 940 180
An exception to Pisa's generally lackluster and predominantly modern hotels. On the banks of the Arno, and ten minutes' walk from the Leaning Tower, it has been in the same family for five generations (since 1839). Service is courteous and attentive, and the fine rooms recall times past.
🛏48 🅿 🔄 🅰 All major cards

AL RISTORO DEI VECCHI MACELLI
$$$–$$$$
VIA VOLTURNO 49
TEL 050 20 424
Pisa's most noted restaurant lies on the city's western fringe. Dishes that brought it fame include *spaghetti verde con i frutti di mare* (green pasta with mixed seafood).
🍴45 🕐 Closed Sun. L, Wed., & 2 weeks Aug. 🅰 All major cards

OSTERIA DEI CAVALIERI
$$
VIA SAN FREDIANO 16
TEL 050 580 858
A plain but welcoming trattoria at the heart of the old city. The well-priced classic Tuscan dishes include *cinghiale* (wild boar) and a sprinkling of more adventurous meat and fish dishes.
🍴60 🕐 Closed Sat. L, Sun., & Aug. 🅰 All major cards

SAN GIMIGNANO

LA COLLEGIATA
$$$$$ 0000
LOCALITÀ STRADA 27
TEL 0577 943 201
FAX 0577 940 566
A dazzlingly stylish hotel with a good restaurant housed in a converted 16th-century convent 1 mile (1.5 km) from the town wall. Fine views of San Gimignano and its towers.
🛏20 🅿 🔄 🅰 All major cards

LA CISTERNA
$$ 000
PIAZZA DELLA CISTERNA 24
TEL 0577 940 328
FAX 0577 942 080
The village's oldest established hotel occupies a central position on the main piazza. Rooms with a view command higher prices.
🛏49 🅿 🕐 Closed Jan.–Feb. 🔄 🅰 All major cards

LEON BIANCO
$$ 000
PIAZZA DELLA CISTERNA 13
TEL 0577 941 294
FAX 0577 942 123
This hotel shares La Cisterna's perfect position, but is smaller and more intimate.
🛏25 🕐 Closed mid-Jan.–Feb. 🅿 🔄 🅰 All major cards

DORANDÒ
$$$–$$$$
VICOLO DELL'ORO 2
TEL 0577 941 862
A small, welcoming, and intimate restaurant in a medieval setting but with a modern ambience. Unusually, it re-creates ancient recipes from Etruscan, Medici, and early medieval periods.
🍴50 🕐 Closed mid-Jan.–mid-March & Mon. except in summer 🅰 All major cards

SIENA

SOMETHING SPECIAL

CERTOSA DI MAGGIANO
Much favored by honeymoon and anniversary couples, this magnificent converted 14th-century abbey, on beautiful grounds 2 miles (3 km) east of Siena, is one of central Italy's finest and most romantic hotels.
$$$$$ 0000
STRADA DI CERTOSA 82
TEL 0577 288 180
FAX 0577 288 189
🛏7 rooms + 11 suites
🅿 🅰 All major cards

ANTICA TORRE
$$-$$$ ✪✪✪
VIA FIERAVECCHIA 7
TEL 0577 222 255
FAX 0577 222 255
Siena's most appealing small hotel has just eight rooms squeezed into an old medieval tower (torre) a few minutes' walk southeast of the historic center. No restaurant.
🛏 8   All major cards

DUOMO
$$-$$$ ✪✪✪
VIA STALLOREGGI 38
TEL 0577 289 088
FAX 0577 43 043
Rooms here are unexceptional, but the hotel's position, close to the sights, is perfect. No restaurant.
🛏 23   All major cards

PALAZZO RAVIZZA
$$-$$$ ✪✪✪
VIA PIAN DEI MANTELLINI 34
TEL 0577 280 462
FAX 0577 221 597
Siena's most charming mid-range hotel occupies an 18th-century palace on the fringes of the old center. It retains many old features, original antiques, and furniture.
🛏 36   All major cards

AL MARSILI
$$-$$$
VIA DEL CASTORO 3
TEL 0577 47 154
The most attractive old restaurant in a city not renowned for its eating establishments. It has a large, formal dining room with medieval touches of decor and serves reliable regional cooking.
🍽 80-140   Closed Mon.   All major cards

CAMPANE
$$-$$$
VIA DELLE CAMPANE 6
TEL 0577 284 035
Voted the city's favorite restaurant in a readers' poll in the local La Nazione newspaper. Unusually for Siena, it offers fish and seafood dishes.
🍽 40-60   Closed Mon. in winter   All major cards

LE LOGGE
$$-$$$
VIA EL PORRIONE 33
TEL 0577 48 013
No Sienese restaurant is prettier than this former medieval pharmacy just off the Campo, complete with period furniture and fittings. Innovative but occasionally hit-and-miss Sienese cuisine.
🍽 40-80   Closed Sun. & some of June & Nov.   AE, DC

VOLTERRA

SAN LINO
$$ ✪✪✪✪
VIA SAN LINO 26
TEL 0588 85 250
FAX 0588 80 620
A converted convent within the town walls, and Volterra's best central option. Not as polished as some Italian hotels in the four-star category.
🛏 43   All major cards

SACCO FIORENTINO
$-$$
PIAZZA XX SETTEMBRE 18
TEL 0588 88 537
A centrally located restaurant offering innovative creations such as coniglio in salsa di aglio e Vin Santo (rabbit in a garlic and sweet wine sauce) along with more traditional dishes such as salsicce e fagioli (Tuscan sausages and beans).
🍽 50   Closed Fri., 10 days June & mid-Nov.–March   All major cards

UMBRIA

ASSISI

FONTEBELLA
$$$ ✪✪✪
VIA FONTEBELLA 25
TEL 075 812 883
FAX 075 812 941
An intimate hotel with attractive, antique-furnished rooms (all different) and good views from upper floors. Its Frantoio restaurant is also excellent.
🛏 43   P   All major cards

MEDIO EVO
$$$
VIA ARCO DEI PRIORI 4B
TEL 075 813 068
A beautiful medieval vaulted dining hall is the setting for refined and exquisite food that mixes Italian and pan-European culinary styles.
🍽 80-120   Closed Sun. D, Wed. & some of Jan. & July   All major cards

GUBBIO

BOSONE PALACE
$$-$$$ ✪✪✪
VIA XX SETTEMBRE 22
TEL 075 922 0688
FAX 075 922 0552
A converted medieval palace in a central location combining modern facilities with period touches such as decorative antiques and frescoed ceilings.
🛏 30   All major cards

TAVERNA DEL LUPO
$$-$$$
VIA DELLA REPUBBLICA 47
TEL 075 927 4368
Pretty medieval dining rooms and well-presented Umbrian specialties, including truffle, game, and mushroom dishes.
🍽 150   Closed Mon.   All major cards

MONTEFALCO

VILLA PAMBUFFETTI
$$$ ✪✪✪✪
VIA DELLA VITTORIA 20
TEL 0742 378 823
FAX 0742 379 245
Tastefully converted villa in gardens on the edge of the village. Excellent restaurant.
🛏 15   P   All major cards

COCCORONE
$$–$$$
LARGO TEMPESTIVI, OFF VIA TEMPESTIVI
TEL 0742 379 535
Attractive medieval dining room whose open fire is used to cook meats and other Umbrian specialties. The *crespelle* (stuffed pancakes) and tiramisu are notable.
🛏 40   ⏱ Closed Wed.
🖲 All major cards

NORCIA

SALICONE
$$$ ✪✪✪
VIALE UMBRIA, STRADA COMMMUNALE, MONTEDORO
TEL 0743 828 076
FAX 0743 828 081
A comfortable modern hotel just outside Norcia's town walls, affiliated with Best Western. Rooms are spacious and tastefully decorated, and all have hydro-massage tubs.
🛏 71   🅿 ⬌ 🖲 📺
🖲 All major cards

GRANARO DEL MONTE
$$–$$$
VIA ALFIERI 7–12
TEL 0743 816 513
Large, bustling restaurant in a fine medieval setting (an old papal granary), complete with tapestries, roaring fires, and suits of armor. Umbrian country cooking, with many regional and truffle-based specialties.
🛏 50–150   ⏱ Closed Tues.
⬌   🖲 All major cards

ORVIETO

LA BADIA
$$$ ✪✪✪✪
LOCALITÀ LA BADIA 8
TEL 0763 301 959
FAX 0763 305 396
In a beautiful pastoral setting, 2 miles (3 km) from Orvieto, this glorious hotel was converted from a 12th-century Romanesque *badia* (abbey).
🛏 26   🅿   ⏱ Closed Jan.–Feb.   🖲 ⬌ 🖲 All major cards

MAITANI
$$$ ✪✪✪✪
VIA MAITANI 5
TEL 0763 342 011
FAX 0763 342 012
Located just off Piazza del Duomo, this hotel and its rooms combine the old and the new, but can be a touch spartan in places.
🛏 40   🅿   ⏱ Closed some of Jan.   ⬌   🖲   🖲 All major cards

GIGLI D'ORO
$$–$$$
PIAZZA DEL DUOMO 8
TEL 0763 341 903
The evocative dining rooms occupy a 16th-century town house in the shadow of the cathedral. The refined regional cuisine matches the elegance of the surroundings.
🛏 50   ⏱ Closed Wed.   🖲
🖲 All major cards

ETRUSCA
$$
VIA MAITANI 10
TEL 0763 344 016
A trattoria of old-fashioned charm set in a 16th-century building, with courteous service, pleasantly relaxed atmosphere, and traditional Umbrian dishes at fair prices.
🛏 90   ⏱ Closed Mon. & some of Jan. & Feb.   🖲
🖲 All major cards

PERUGIA

LOCANDA DELLA POSTA
$$$ ✪✪✪✪
CORSO VANNUCCI 97
TEL 075 572 8925
FAX 075 572 2413
There has been a hotel on this central street since the 18th century. Good, modern rooms, but no restaurant.
🛏 40   🅿 ⬌ 🖲 🖲 All major cards

ALADINO
$$$
VIA DELLE PROME 11
TEL 075 572 0938
A welcoming restaurant with

PRICES

HOTELS
An indication of the cost of a double room without breakfast is given by $ signs.
$$$$$ Over $280
$$$$ $200–$280
$$$ $120–$200
$$ $80–$120
$ Under $80

RESTAURANTS
An indication of the cost of a three-course dinner without drinks is given by $ signs.
$$$$$ Over $80
$$$$ $50–$80
$$$ $35–$50
$$ $20–$35
$ Under $20

---

an interesting wine list. The menu combines Umbrian and Sardinian dishes.
🛏 55–65   ⏱ Closed Mon., L & 2 weeks Aug.   🖲   🖲 All major cards

SPELLO

PALAZZO BOCCI
$$$ ✪✪✪✪
VIA CAVOUR 17
TEL 075 301 021
FAX 075 301 464
Converted 17th-century palazzo on the main street, with superb frescoed public areas and large modern rooms. The co-owned Il Molino restaurant *(Tel 075 651 305, closed Tues.)* opposite is the best in town.
🛏 23   ⬌   🖲   🖲 All major cards

CACCIATORE
$$
VIA GIULIA 42
TEL 075 651 141
Food here is not exceptional, but the outdoor terrace on summer evenings is one of the most poetic places to dine in Umbria. There are 17 rooms available in the two-star hotel.
🛏 100–150   🅿   ⏱ Closed Mon. & 3 weeks July   🖲 All major cards

---

SPOLETO

🏨 GATTAPONE
$$$ ◆◆◆◆
VIA DEL PONTE 6
TEL 0743 223 447
FAX 0743 223 448
A marvelous hotel in a spectacular location overlooking a wooded gorge. Intimate and discreet with individually decorated rooms. No restaurant.
🛏 18 🅿 ⬗ 🄲 🄲 All major cards

🍴 APOLLINARE
$$
VIA SANT'AGATA 14
TEL 0743 223 256
Cozy medieval dining rooms with striking gold and blue seating. Innovative and carefully prepared food—the truffle-filled *caramella soffiata* appetizer is sensational.
🍽 55–95 🅿 🕐 Closed Tues. 🄲 All major cards

TODI

🏨 FONTE CESIA
$$$ ◆◆◆◆
VIA LORENZO LEONI 3
TEL 075 894 3737
FAX 075 894 4677
Consummately restored 17th-century palace at the heart of the town, with rooms decorated in different period styles.
🛏 35 🅿 ⬗ 🄲 🄲 All major cards

🍴 CAVOUR
$
CORSO CAVOUR 21–23
TEL 075 894 3730
A simple trattoria-pizzeria patronized by locals and visitors alike.
🍽 180 🕐 Closed Wed. except summer 🄲 All major cards

THE SOUTH

CAPRI

🏨 GRAND HOTEL
🍴 QUISISANA
$$$$–$$$$$ ◆◆◆◆◆
VIA CAMERELLE 2
TEL 081 837 0788
FAX 081 837 6080
The grandest of many grand hotels on Capri, and much patronized by U.S. visitors. The hotel's restaurant Quisi is the island's best, but, like the hotel, is very expensive.
🛏 150 + 13 suites 🅿 🕐 Closed Nov.–Easter ⬗ 🄲 🄲 🄲 🄲 🄲 All major cards

🏨 VILLA SARAH
$$–$$$ ◆◆◆
VIA TIBERIO 3/A
TEL 081 837 7817
FAX 081 837 7215
A welcoming family-run hotel with garden, about ten minutes' walk from the center of Capri town. No restaurant. Reserve well in advance.
🛏 20 🕐 Closed Nov.–Easter 🄲 All major cards

🍴 LA CAPANNINA
$$$–$$$$
VIA LE BOTTEGHE 12–14
TEL 081 837 0732
A glamorous but unstuffy restaurant just off the main piazzetta, with the American-born, fifth-generation owner, Signora de Angelis, often at the front of the house. Predominantly modern fish-based creations, with some meat dishes.
🍽 100–120 🕐 Closed mid-March–mid-Nov. 🄲 🄲 All major cards

COSTIERA AMALFITANA

🏨 HOTEL PALUMBO
$$$$$ ◆◆◆◆◆
VIA SAN GIOVANNI DEL TORO 16, RAVELLO
TEL 089 857 244
FAX 089 858 133
Most of Ravello's top hotels, including the nearby Palazzo Sasso, are something special, but the Palumbo is something else again. Past guests at the magnificent 12th-century palace hotel include Richard Wagner, Ingrid Bergman, Tennessee Williams, and a young John and Jacqueline Kennedy. Try for rooms in the old hotel, not the newer (but less expensive) annex.
🛏 13 + 2 suites 🅿 ⬗ 🄲 🄲 All major cards

🏨 SAN PIETRO
$$$$$ ◆◆◆◆◆
VIA LAURITO 2, POSITANO
TEL 089 875 455
FAX 089 811 449
Positano has a surfeit of glorious five-star hotels, with little to choose between them. San Pietro, about 1 mile (1.5 km) from the village, is probably the best, thanks to its pool, views, beach (reached by elevator), tennis courts, and tastefully understated rooms.
🛏 52 + 6 suites 🕐 Closed Nov.–March 🅿 ⬗ 🄲 🄲 🄲 All major cards

🏨 SANTA CATERINA
🍴 $$$$$ ◆◆◆◆◆
VIA NAZIONALE 9, LOCALITÀ PASTENA, AMALFI
TEL 089 871 012
FAX 089 871 351
This sumptuous hillside mansion on the coast road just outside Amalfi is probably the best hotel in the region and provides a luxurious base for exploring.
🛏 55 + 12 suites 🅿 ⬗ 🄲 🄲 🄲 All major cards

🏨 HOTEL POSEIDON
🍴 $$$$ ◆◆◆◆
VIA PASITEA 148, POSITANO
TEL 089 811 111
FAX 089 875 833
A romantic hotel with a superb panoramic location overlooking the sea and village. Elegant rooms and a pretty terrace garden with bar and restaurant.
🛏 50 🅿 ⬗ 🄲 🄲 🄲 All major cards

🏨 VILLA CIMBRONE
$$$–$$$$
VIA SANTA CHIARA 26, RAVELLO
TEL 089 857 459
FAX 089 857 777

Greta Garbo vacationed at this lovely villa set among gardens before it was converted into a hotel. Although a beautiful place to stay, it is a steep walk from the rest of the village. No restaurant.
[1] 19 **[⊕]** Closed Nov.–March **[⟁]** All major cards

🏨 MIRAMALFI
$$$ ✪✪✪✪
VIA QUASIMODO 3, AMALFI
TEL 089 871 588
FAX 089 871 287
A modern hotel just outside Amalfi, where most of the simply but pleasantly decorated rooms have balconies with sea views.
[1] 48 **[P]** **[⇄]** **[⟁]** **[⟐]**
[⟁] All major cards

🏨 CARUSO BELVEDERE
🍴 $$–$$$ ✪✪✪✪
VIALE SAN GIOVANNI DEL TORO 2, RAVELLO
TEL 089 857 111
FAX 089 857 372
Run by the Caruso family since 1893, this old-fashioned and characterful hotel, at the heart of the Ravello, stands in a splendid garden with glorious views.
[1] 24 **[P]** **[⇄]** **[⟁]** All major cards

🍴 LA CARAVELLA
$$$–$$$$
VIA MATTEO CAMERA 12, AMALFI
TEL 089 871 029
This restaurant has been in the same family for three generations. Much thought goes into re-creating traditional, and sometimes unusual, fish and seafood dishes such as *fettucine nere con sugo nero* (black pasta noodles with a squid's ink black sauce).
[⟐] 40–50 **[P]** **[⊕]** Closed Nov. & Tues. except Aug. **[⟁]**
[⟁] All major cards

🍴 DA GEMMA
$$$
VIA FRA GERARDO SASSO 10, AMALFI
TEL 089 871 345

Be sure to reserve a table on the enchanting terrace of this long-established family-run restaurant that has been described as the best trattoria on the Amalfi coast. Fish, seafood, and pastas are excellent. Try the *ziti alla genovese*, an unusual pasta with a sauce of meat and onions.
[⟐] 45 **[⊕]** Closed Wed. except in summer **[⟁]** All major cards

🍴 CUMPÀ COSIMO
$$
VIA ROMA 44–46, RAVELLO
TEL 089 857 156
A simple pizzeria-restaurant in the middle of the village that has been run by the Bottone family for more than 70 years.
[⟐] 100 **[⊕]** Closed Mon. in winter **[⟁]** All major cards

🍴 'O CAPURALE
$$
VIA REGINA GIOVANNA 12, POSITANO
TEL 089 875 374
Positano is hard on the wallet, so this popular and moderately priced local trattoria comes as a pleasant surprise. Cooking is simple, with specialties such as *bucatini all capuralessa* (thick spaghetti with tomatoes, mozzarella, and eggplant).
[⟐] 70 **[⊕]** Closed Tues. except in summer **[⟁]** All major cards

IL GARGANO

🏨 PIZZOMUNNO
🍴 VIESTE PALACE
$$$$$ ✪✪✪✪✪
SPIAGGIA DI PIZZUMUNNO, VIESTE
TEL 0884 708 741
FAX 0884 707 325
More a luxurious hotel-village than a hotel, this is the Gargano's premier establishment. It boasts many sports facilities and a private beach, but is not for those in search of an intimate atmosphere.
[1] 183 **[⊕]** Closed Nov.–March **[P]** **[⇄]** **[⟁]** **[⟐]**
[⟐] **[⟁]** All major cards

🏨 SEGGIO
$$ ✪✪✪
VIA VIESTE 7, VIESTE
TEL 0884 708 123
FAX 0884 708 727
A small hotel with a private beach housed in a 17th-century palazzo in a pedestrianized quarter of Vieste.
[1] 28 **[P]** **[⊕]** Closed Nov.–March **[⇄]** **[⟁]** **[⟐]** **[⟁]** All major cards

ISCHIA

🏨 REGINA ISABELLA
$$$$–$$$$$ ✪✪✪✪✪
PIAZZA SANTA RESTITUTA, LACCO AMENO
TEL 081 994 322
FAX 081 90 190
Ischia's top luxury hotel is situated in the northwest of the island and has every comfort.
[1] 117 + 7 suites **[P]**
[⊕] Closed mid-Jan.–early April **[⇄]** **[⟁]** **[⟐]** **[⟁]** **[⟐]**
[⟁] All major cards

🍴 IL MELOGRANO
$$$
VIA GIOVANNI MAZZELLA 110, LOCALITÀ FORIO D'ISCHIA
TEL 081 998 450
Just south of the village of Forio on the island's west coast, this small, modern restaurant with garden offers creative dishes such as *fiori di zucchono ripeno di ricotta e basilico* (baby zucchini flowers stuffed with basil and ricotta cheese), meat dishes such as *coniglio* (rabbit), and perfectly cooked fish and seafood.
[⟐] 45 **[P]** **[⊕]** Closed Nov.–March **[⟁]** All major cards

LECCE

🏨 PATRIA PALACE
$$$ ✪✪✪✪
PIAZZETTA GABRIELE RICCARDI 13
TEL 0832 245 111
FAX 0832 245 002
A beautifully restored 18th-century palazzo at the heart of the historic city center.
[1] 67 **[P]** **[⇄]** **[⟁]** **[⟁]** All major cards

🍽 BARBABLU
$$–$$$
VIA UMBERTO I 7
TEL 0832 241 183
The "Blue Beard" is a central restaurant that presents carefully researched traditional local recipes executed with a modern twist, using only the finest ingredients.
🛏 40–60 🅿 🕐 Closed Sun. D, Mon., & some of June & Nov. 🅢 🅢 AE, MC, V

NAPLES

🏨 GRANDE ALBERGO
🍽 VESUVIO
$$$$ ✪✪✪✪
VIA PARTENOPE 45
TEL 081 764 0044
FAX 081 764 4483
Built in 1882, this fine hotel has welcomed the likes of Humphrey Bogart and Errol Flynn over the years. The rooftop Caruso restaurant, with its superb views, is named after the opera star, another famous guest.
🛈 149 + 16 suites 🅿 🔁 🅢 🅢 All major cards

🏨 GRAND HOTEL
🍽 PARKER'S
$$$–$$$$ ✪✪✪✪
CORSO VITTORIO EMANUELE 135
TEL 081 761 2474
FAX 081 663 527
Its position west of the center, between the teeming Spanish Quarter and Vomero hill, affords wonderful views of the Bay of Naples. Built in 1870, the hotel's atmosphere and style are traditional. The Bellevue restaurant rates highly on its own account.
🛈 70 + 9 suites 🅿 🔁 🅢 🔽 🅢 All major cards

🏨 REX
$$ ✪✪✪
VIA PALEPOLI 12
TEL 081 764 9389
FAX 081 764 9227
Located close to the waterfront, just south of San Carlo. Rooms are mostly small and plain, but reasonable prices

mean they are in high demand. No restaurant.
🛈 36 🅿 🅢 🅢 All major cards

🍽 LA SACRESTIA
$$$$
VIA ORAZIO 186
TEL 081 664 1051
Not only the best food in Naples—try the *pesce spada* (swordfish)—but also one of the best settings—in a villa at the top of a labyrinth of streets (take a cab) with a terrace that offers incomparable views over the Bay of Naples.
🛏 100 🕐 Closed Mon. in winter, Sun. in summer, & 2 weeks Aug. 🅢 🅢 All major cards

🍽 LA BERSAGLIERA
$$$–$$$$
VIA SANTA LUCIA 10–11, BORGO MARINARI
TEL 081 764 6016
Most visitors of note who have visited Naples since 1923 have eaten at this waterfront restaurant. Prices are perhaps higher than the food merits, and it can be busy with vacationers, but the busy atmosphere and sense of history make this a fun place to visit at least once.
🛏 200 🅿 🕐 Closed Tues. & some of Jan. & Aug. 🅢 🅢 All major cards

🍽 LA CANTINA DI TRIUNFO
$$
RIVIERA DI CHIAIA 64
TEL 081 668 101
A venerable wine shop/trattoria with marble bars and old wooden tables. You can drink a glass of wine with cheese, salami, and other snacks, or choose a meal from the daily menu.
🛏 40 🕐 Closed L, Sun., & Aug. 🅢 AE, V

🍽 BRANDI
$–$$
SALITA SANT' ANNA DI PALAZZO 1–2, OFF VIA CHIAIA
TEL 081 416 928

The most famous pizzeria in Naples and birthplace of the *Margherita* (tomato, basil, and mozzarella cheese). It is often full of vacationers, but the atmosphere, pizzas, and pasta dishes are good.
🛏 100 🅢 🅢 All major cards

🍽 GRAN CAFFÈ GAMBRINUS
$
VIA CHIAIA 1-PIAZZA TRENTO E TRIESTE
TEL 081 417 582
Dating from 1860, this is the city's most famous and most opulent café. Wonderful coffees and widely celebrated cakes and pastries.
🛏 170 🅢 All major cards

PAESTUM

🏨 ESPLANADE
🍽 $$ ✪✪✪
VIA STERPINIA
TEL 0828 851 043
FAX 0828 851 600
Most people see Paestum as a day trip, but this Best Western hotel on the edge of pine woods close to the sea with its own pool and private beach makes a comfortable overnight stop.
🛈 28 🅿 🔁 🅢 🏊 🅢 All major cards

PARCO NAZIONALE DEL ABRUZZO

🏨 VILLINO MON REPOS
$$–$$$ ✪✪✪✪
VIA SANTA LUCIA 2, PESCASSEROLI
TEL 0863 912 858
FAX 0863 912 818
A century-old villa in a peaceful park setting.
🛈 17 🅿 🅢 All major cards

🍽 PAGNANI
$$ ✪✪✪
VIALE CABINOVIA, PESCASSEROLI
TEL 0863 912 866
FAX 0863 912870
A modern mountain hotel

just outside the village with bright, spacious rooms, many with flower-filled balconies.

🛈 37 🅿 ⬌ ⬳ 📺 ⬳V

🏨 ARMANDO'S
$$ ✪✪✪
VIA MONTENERO 15, SULMONA
TEL 0864 210 787
FAX 0864 210 783
A simple, clean hotel a few minutes from the town center in peaceful surroundings.
🛈 21 🅿 ⬌ ⬳All major cards

POMPEI

🏨 FORUM
$$ ✪✪✪
VIA ROMA 99
TEL 081 850 1170
FAX 081 850 6132
Most people visit Pompeii on a day trip, but if you do stay, this is the best of the hotels near the excavations.
🛈 19 ⬌ ⬳ ⬳All major cards

🍴 IL PRINCIPE
$$$$
PIAZZA BARTOLO LONGO 8
TEL 081 850 5566
Prices at this Michelin one-star venue are high for dishes that combine modern regional cooking with dishes revived from ancient times, such as *garum,* a Roman sauce served with fish.
🪑 40–150 🕐 Closed Sun. D & Mon. except April–June & Sept.–Oct. ⬳ ⬳All major cards

PUGLIA

🏨 PALACE
🍴 $$$ ✪✪✪✪
VIA LOMBARDI 13, BARI
TEL 080 521 6551
FAX 080 521 1499
Bari's best and most prestigious Old World hotel lies within walking distance of the old quarter. The Murat hotel restaurant is also first-class.
🛈 178 + 19 suites 🅿 ⬌ ⬳ ⬳All major cards

🍴 LA PIGNATA
$$–$$$
CORSO VITTORIO EMANUELE 173, BARI
TEL 080 523 2481
An elegant restaurant that offers a mixture of Italian and regional Pugliese cusine.
🪑 85 🅿 🕐 Closed Sun. D, Mon., & Aug. ⬳ ⬳All major cards

TRULLI COUNTRY

🏨 DEI TRULLI
Rooms in this unusual luxury hotel are arranged around an attractive collection of *trulli,* the distinctive ancient dwellings for which Alberobello and its surroundings are celebrated.
$$$$–$$$$$ ✪✪✪✪✪
VIA CADORE 29, ALBEROBELLO
TEL 080 932 3555
FAX 080 932 3560
🛈 28 🅿 ⬳ ⬳
⬳All major cards

🍴 IL POETA CONTADINA
$$$–$$$$
VIA INDIPENDENZA 21, ALBERBELLO
TEL 080 721 917
An elegant, understated central restaurant with one of Italy's best wine cellars and delightful local cooking, including an appetizer (in season) of warm salad with *cappesante* (scallops) and wild porcini.
🪑 70 🅿 🕐 Closed Sun. D, Mon., 2 weeks Jan., & 10 days June–Aug. ⬳ ⬳All major cards

🍴 TRULLI D'ORO
$$–$$$
VIA CAVALLOTTI 27, ALBERBELLO
TEL 080 721 820
The local rustic cooking may lack the refinement of Il Poeta Contadina (see above), but the setting, in five *trulli* with

wooden beams and white-washed walls, makes for a memorable meal.
🪑 100–150 🕐 Closed Mon. except in summer & Jan. ⬳ ⬳All major cards

SICILY & SARDINIA

SICILY

AGRIGENTO

🏨 VILLA ATHENA
$$$ ✪✪✪✪
VIA DEI TEMPLI 33
TEL 0922 596 288
FAX 0922 402 180
Early reservations are needed for this peaceful 18th-century villa at the heart of the archaeological zone. A pool and pretty rooms complement the superb location.
🛈 40 🅿 ⬳ ⬳ ⬳All major cards

🏨 COLLEVERDE PARK HOTEL
$$–$$$
VIA DEI TEMPLI
TEL 0922 29 555
FAX 0922 29 012
A modern hotel surrounded by gardens and set just north of the temples and archaeological zone.
🛈 48 🅿 ⬌ ⬳ ⬳All major cards

🍴 LE CAPRICE
$$–$$$
VIA PANORAMICA DEI TEMPLI 51
TEL 0922 26 469
A busy, rustic-style restaurant close to the temples with a pleasant panoramic terrace. Fish and grilled meats are the menu's main staples.
🪑 100 🅿 🕐 Closed Fri. & 2 weeks July ⬳ ⬳All major cards

CEFALÙ

🏨 KALURA
$$$ ✪✪✪
VIA V. CAVALLARO 13, LOCALITÀ CALDURA

TEL 0921 421 354
FAX 0921 422 501
About 1 mile (1.5 km) east of the town, so you may need a car or cab, but worth the inconvenience for its lovely setting above the sea, private beach, simple rooms (some with sea views), and sports facilities.
🛏 65 🅿 🛗 🅢 🏊
🅢 All major cards

🍴 LA BRACE
$$
VIA XXV NOVEMBRE 10
TEL 0921423 570
A Dutch-Indonesian couple has run this atmospheric restaurant for over 20 years, offering traditional regional food to rival that of Italian-born chefs. Try the *spaghetti all'aglio e peperoncino* (pasta with garlic and chili), and the cannoli for dessert. Both are classic Sicilian dishes.
🍽 45 🅢 🕐 Closed Mon. & mid-Dec.–mid-Jan. 🅢 All major cards

ISOLE EOLIE

🏨 GATTOPARDO PARK HOTEL
$$$–$$$$ ✪✪✪
VIALE DIANA, LIPARI
TEL 090 981 1035
FAX 090 988 0207
Choose from comfortable rustic-style rooms in a pretty 19th-century villa or peaceful bungalows in the surrounding gardens. Breakfast and lunch must be reserved with accommodations.
🛏 47 🅿 🅢 🅢 All major cards

🏨 LA SCIARA RESIDENCE
$$–$$$
VIA SOLDATO CINOTTA, STROMBOLI
TEL 090 896 004
FAX 090 986 284
A central residence close to the sea surrounded by several small villas in a park setting.
🛏 62 🛗 🅢 🏊 🅢 All major cards

🍴 FILIPPINO
$$$–$$$$
PIAZZA MUNICIPIO 8–16, LIPARI
TEL 090 981 1002
A pretty Michelin one-star restaurant founded in 1910 with lovely views from its terrace and first-rate fish and seafood.
🍽 200 🅿 🕐 Closed Mon. except June–Sept. 🅢
🅢 All major cards

🍴 E PULERA
$$$
VIA DIANA, LIPARI
TEL 090 981 1158
Less renowned than the Filippino (see above), but the predominantly fish-based cooking is almost as good and less expensive. A pretty garden setting among lemon, grapefruit, and mandarin trees.
🍽 100 🕐 Closed daily L & Oct.–May 🅢 All major cards

PALERMO

🏨 GRANDE HOTEL ET DES PALMES
$$$ ✪✪✪✪
VIA ROMA 398
TEL 091 583 933
FAX 091 331 545
The Grand has a whiff of Palermo in the 1950s and is slightly living on past glories, but remains the first choice among the big central hotels if you are searching for character and a sense of history.
🛏 187 🅿 🛗 🅢 🅢 All major cards

🍴 CAPRICCI DI SICILIA
$$–$$$
VIA ISTITUTO PIGNATELLI 6, PIAZZA STURZO
TEL 091 327 777
Not much to look at, inside or out, but the welcome is warm. The simple, highly accomplished cooking embraces Palermitan specialties like *sarde ripiene* (stuffed sardine), *pasta con sarde* (pasta with sardines), *spada alla brace* (grilled swordfish), and sublime *cassata* (traditional Sicilian ice cream). Outdoor seating in summer.

🍽 80–120 🅿 🕐 Closed Mon. & 15 days Aug. 🅢
🅢 All major cards

🍴 SANTANDREA
$$
PIAZZA SANT'ANDREA 4
TEL 091 334 999
The best among several unpretentious trattorias close to the busy Vucciria market in the city center. Food never strays far from its Palermitan roots, with lots of grilled fish and seafood dishes.
🍽 55–65 🕐 Closed Tues. & some of Jan. 🅢 All major cards

SIRACUSA

🏨 GRAND
$$$–$$$$ ✪✪✪✪
VIALE MAZZINI 12
TEL 0931 464 600
FAX 0931 464 611
A comfortable hotel of Old World style founded in 1898 on the western edge of Ortigia, the town's ancient heart. Its roof terrace restaurant has fine sea and harbor views.
🛏 39 🅿 🛗 🅢 🅢 All major cards

🏨 DOMUS MARIAE
🍴 $$ ✪✪✪
VIA VITTORIO VENETO 76
TEL 0931 24 854
FAX 0931 24 858
The second of old Ortigia's attractive hotels, the Domus is warmly and professionally run by Orsoline nuns.
🛏 16 🅿 🅢 🅢 AE, V

🍴 ARCHIMEDE
$$–$$$
VIA GEMMELLARO 8
TEL 0931 69 701
Contented diners have come to this restaurant in Ortigia since 1930 to enjoy mainly fish and seafood dishes. The three dining rooms are divided by 14th-century arches.
🍽 150 🕐 Closed Sun. D 🅢 🅢 All major cards

🍴 MINOSSE
$$–$$$
VIA MIRABELLA 6
TEL 0931 66 366
A big, reliable trattoria at the heart of Ortigia's tangle of streets with winning fish and seafood. *Pesce del giorno* (grilled fish of the day) is always a good choice.
🔲 140 🕐 Closed Mon. 🔳
🔷 AE, MC, V

TAORMINA

🏨 VILLA DUCALE
$$$–$$$$ ✪✪
VIA LEONARDO DA VINCI 60
TEL 0942 28 153
FAX 0942 28 710
There are lovely views from the terrace of this romantic little hotel, part of a late 19th-century villa. No restaurant.
🛏 12 🅿 🔳 🔷 All major cards

SOMETHING SPECIAL

🏨 SAN DOMENICO PALACE
A central and consummately converted 15th-century convent with gorgeous garden, splendid rooms decorated with antiques, and views of Etna and the sea.
$$$$$ ✪✪✪✪✪
PIAZZA SAN DOMENICO 5
TEL 0942 23 701
FAX 0942 625 506
🛏 102 + 9 suites 🅿
🔄 🔳 🔺 🔷 All major cards

🏨 VILLA BELVEDERE
$$–$$$ ✪✪✪
VIA BAGNOLI CROCE 79
TEL 0942 23 791
FAX 0942 625 830
Panoramic views distinguish this comfortable hotel, situated amid palm and olive trees a little east of the town center by the public gardens. No restaurant.
🛏 47 🅿 🕐 Closed Dec. & mid-Jan.–mid-March 🔄
🔳 🔺 🔷 All major cards

🍴 MAFFEI'S
$$$–$$$$
VIA SAN DOMENICO DI GUZMAN 1
TEL 0942 24 055
Easily Taormina's best cooking, with superlative fish and seafood dishes. Elegant, small, and popular with locals, so reservations essential.
🔲 40 🕐 Closed Tues. except in summer 🔷 All major cards

🍴 VECCHIA TAORMINA
$
VICO EBREI 3
TEL 0942 23 761
You don't need a fortune to eat well in Taormina, as this good central pizzeria proves.
🔲 80 🕐 Closed L & all Wed. 🔳 🔷 No credit cards

SARDINIA

ALGHERO

🏨 VILLA LAS TRONAS
$$$ ✪✪✪✪
LUNGOMARE VALENCIA 1
TEL 079 981 818
FAX 079 981 044
A lovely art nouveau villa on a promontory overlooking the sea. The town is close at hand, but the hotel's gardens and beach provide a wonderful sense of peace and privacy.
🛏 29 🅿 🔄 🔳 🔺 🔻
🔷 All major cards

🍴 AL TUGURI
$$–$$$
VIA MAIORCA 113
TEL 079 976 772
A tiny place whose cuisine combines Sardinian and Catalan traditions, with an emphasis on fish and seafood. Try the homemade pasta with *cozze*, *piselli*, and *gamberi* (mussels, peas, and lobster).
🔲 30 🕐 Closed Sun. except in summer 🔳 🔷 All major cards

CALA GONONE

🏨 COSTA DORADA
$$–$$$
LUNGOMARE PALMASERA
TEL 0784 93 333
FAX 0784 93 445
A straightforward and comfortable hotel in a pleasant coastal setting.
🛏 30 🕐 Closed Nov.–Easter 🔳 🔷 All major cards

CAGLIARI

🏨 REGINA MARGHERITA
$$$ ✪✪✪✪
VIALE REGINA MARGHERITA 44
TEL 070 670 342
FAX 070 668 325
The best of the hotels close to Cagliari's old quarter. No restaurant.
🛏 99 🅿 🔄 🔳 🔷 All major cards

🍴 DAL CORSARO
$$$
VIALE REGINA MARGHERITA 28
TEL 070 664 318
Impeccable and often creative Sardinian cooking from a family-run, elegant two-room restaurant. A local institution, it has been known for many years as one of the best places to eat on the island. Reservations essential.
🔲 80 🅿 🕐 Closed Sun. & Aug. 🔳 🔷 All major cards

COSTA SMERALDA

🏨 CALA DI VOLPE
$$$$$ ✪✪✪✪✪
CALA DI VOLPE, PORTO CERVO
TEL 0789 976 111
FAX 0789 976 617
The Emerald Coast's leading hotel is an elegant re-creation of a traditional Sardinian village. Its many facilities include tennis courts and access to a nine-hole golf course.
🛏 112 + 11 suites 🅿 🔄
🔳 🔷 All major cards

SHOPPING

Shopping is one of the great pleasures of visiting Italy. From the smallest mountain town to the grandest city street, Italian stores offer superb arrays of food and wine, wonderful clothes, inspired design, beautiful fabrics, precious jewelry, exquisite shoes, leather-ware and accessories, precious art, antiques, objets d'art, and a host of craft and artisan articles such as ceramics, metalware, and marbled paper. Unfortunately, most of these come at a high price, for Italy is not a country of bargains, although you don't necessarily have to part with your money—you can have almost as much fun window-shopping or simply browsing the country's many street markets and antique fairs.

STORES

Most Italian stores are small, family-run affairs, even in big cities. Many neighborhoods still have their own baker (panifico), fruit seller (fruttivendolo), pastry store (pasticceria), butcher (macellaio), and food shop (alimentari). Department stores and supermarkets are gradually gaining ground, especially in larger towns and cities, but the shopping mall in Italy is still an almost alien concept.

MARKETS

All towns and cities have at least one street market (un mercato). In cities, these usually run daily except Sunday, starting at dawn and closing early afternoon. Opening times are the same in towns, but generally such provincial markets are held just once weekly. Many larger towns also hold antique fairs, usually once monthly or over a weekend, or coinciding with special events devoted to local food or artisanal produce. These are the only places you may be able to bargain—haggling over prices in food markets or other stores is not appropriate.

SPECIALTIES

Many Italian products are unique to one area and to one season of the year. Fruit and vegetables only appear in stores when they are in season, so don't expect to find grapes in spring or cherries in fall. All regions, and many towns, have their own food and wine specialties. Some are found across Italy—such as Parma ham and Parmesan cheese—but often, as in the truffles of Umbria and Piedmont, or the the spicy panforte cake of Siena, the products are confined to a small area. The same applies to handicrafts, with glassware and lace both specialties of Venice, for example, or the marbled paper and fine leatherware typical of Florence.

WHAT TO BUY

Italy is a cornucopia of exquisite gifts and treats. Food delicacies are obvious purchases, but check import restrictions on meat and produce into North America. Lingerie, silks, lace, linens, soaps, shoes, bags, wallets, marbled paper products, and jewelry are all easily trans-portable items. Also leave space for wine, clothes, and design objects, particularly kitchenware, an area in which Italian designers excel. Most reputable stores should be able to arrange shipping for larger items such as ceramics, furniture, and antiques.

OPENING HOURS

Most small stores open Tuesday to Saturday from around 8 a.m. to 1 p.m and 3:30 to 8 p.m. Most close on Monday morning or one other half day a week. Hours often alter slightly in summer, with a later afternoon opening to avoid the heat of the afternoon. In cities, especially in clothes, book, and department stores, there is a move toward full-time opening (orario continuato) from 9 a.m. to 8 p.m, Monday to Saturday (and occasionally Sunday).

PAYMENT

Supermarkets and department stores usually accept credit cards and traveler's checks, as do larger clothes and shoe stores, but cash is required for virtually all transactions in small food and other stores.

EXPORTS

Most Italian luxury items and many clothing purchases include a value-added goods and services tax of 19 percent (known as IVA in Italy). Non-European Union residents can claim an IVA refund for pur-chases over L300,000 (before tax) made in one store. Shop with your passport and ask for invoices to be made out clearly, showing individual articles and tax components of prices. Many department stores have special counters for this purpose.

Keep all receipts and invoices and have them stamped at the customs office at your airport of departure, or the last exit from EU territory if you are traveling beyond Italy. Then mail the invoice to the store, within 90 days of arriving home, for your rebate.

Many stores are members of the Tax-Free Shopping System, and issue a timesaving "tax-free check" for the amount of the rebate which can be cashed directly at special tax-free counters at airports or rebated to your bank or credit card account.

ROME

Rome's key shopping streets cluster around Via dei Condotti, home to most of the big names in designer clothes and shoes. Less expensive stores line Via del Corso, Via Nazionale, and Via del Tritone. Antique and art stores are found on Via del Babuino, Via Margutta, Via Giulia, Via Monserrato, and Via dei Coronari. The best food stores are on Via Santa Croce and Via Cola di Rienzo.

SHOPPING

CERAMICS

Ginori Via del Tritone 177, tel 06 679 3836. Fine porcelain and other ceramics from a company founded in 1735.

DEPARTMENT STORE

La Rinascente Via del Corso 189, tel 06 679 7691. The largest and most stylish of Rome's big stores.

DESIGN

Culti Via della Vetrina 16/a, tel 683 2180. Linens, plates, glasses, and other articles for the home.
Spazio Sette Via dei Barbieri 7, tel 06 6880 4261. Several floors filled with objects for the home and office.

FOOD & WINE

Ai Monasteri Piazza Cinque Lune 2, tel 06 6880 2783. Jams, preserves, honey, liqueurs, chocolates, soaps, and perfumes, all made in monasteries and convents across Italy.
Buccone Via di Ripetta 19–20, tel 06 361 2154. One of Rome's best-stocked wine stores.
Castroni Via Cola di Rienzo 196, tel 06 687 4383. The ultimate Roman food store.
Trimani Via Goito 20, tel 06 446 9661. A wine store that opened in 1821 and will ship bottles home.

JEWELRY

Bulgari Via dei Condotti 10, tel 06 679 3876. Italy's foremost jewelers, but prices start high and climb to stratospheric.

LINEN & FABRICS

Bassetti Corso Vittorio Emanuele II 73, tel 06 689 2326. A large selection of Italian silks and fabrics.
Frette Via del Corso 381, tel 06 678 6862; Via Nazionale 84, tel 06 488 2641. A national chain selling superb sheets, towels, and other household linens.

MARKETS

Campo de' Fiori Colorful and central food, fruit, and flower market held in Campo dei Fiori (Mon.–Sat.). Also see p. 63.

Porta Portese Massive flea market held in streets off Viale Trastevere near Porta Portese. Very crowded. Beware of pickpockets (Sun. a.m.).

MEN'S CLOTHES

Davide Cenci Via Campo Marzio 1–7, tel 06 699 0681. A huge store, founded in 1926, selling clothes in classic Italian-English country gentleman styles.

PENS & PAPER

Pineider Via dei Due Macelli 68, tel 06 678 9013; Via della Fontanella Borghese 22, tel 06 687 8369. Everyone from Napoleon to Elizabeth Taylor has shopped for pens and paper at Pineider.

PICTURES & PRINTS

Alberto di Castro Via del Babuino 71, tel 06 361 3752. Hundreds of old prints and engravings.

RELIGIOUS OBJECTS

Gaudenzi Piazza della Minerva 69/a, tel 06 679 0431. A treasure trove of religious objects and souvenirs. Similar stores in the nearby Via dei Cestari sell everything from rosaries to cardinals' hats.

SHOES

Ramirez Via del Corso 176, tel 06 679 5928. One of Rome's largest shoe stores, with hundreds of modern, mid-priced styles for men and women.

TURIN

Turin's streets are filled with good stores, especially Via Roma and Via Garibaldi. Antique shops abound on Piazza San Carlo, Via Maria Vittoria, and the streets around Via Pietro Micca. The city is especially known for its vermouths and chocolates.

FOOD & WINE

Paissa Piazza San Carlo 196, tel 011 562 8364. Selection of food and drinks, including Turin's

locally produced vermouths such as Cinzano and Martini.
Peyrano Corso Moncalieri 47, tel 011 660 2202. Superlative chocolates.

MARKETS

Balôn Piazza della Repubblica. Flea market on Saturday morning plus huge "Gran Balôn" antiques and flea market every second Sunday of the month.

GENOA

Genoa's Via Soziglia is a good place to pick up Ligurian handicrafts such as lace, ceramics, marble, gold, and silverware. Jewelers line Via dei Orefici, and luxury shops cluster on Via XX Settembre and Via Luccoli.

DEPARTMENT STORES

COIN Via XX Settembre 16a, tel 010 570 5821.
La Rinascente Via Vernazza 1, tel 010 586 995.

FOOD & WINE

Pietro Romanengo Via Soziglia 74r, tel 010 247 4574. Fantastic chocolates and candies.
Sattanino Via Ponte 19r, tel 010 580 972. Sells Liguaria's classic pizzalike focaccia bread with a huge range of fillings.
Vinoteca Sola Piazza Colombo 13r, tel 010 561 329. Hundreds of wines from Italy and around the world.

MILAN

Milan is probably Italy's premier shopping city, especially for clothes and shoes. Armani, Prada, Versace, Ferré, Krizia, Moschino, and Dolce & Gabbana all originated here. Most of these, and other designer names, abound on the so-called Golden Quadrangle, a quartet of streets on and around Via Montenapoleone. Antique, accessory, and other luxury stores are also found here. Less expensive high quality clothing can be found on Corso

Buenos Aires and Corso Vittorio Emanuele, and the more attractive Brera district has an oasis of interesting and unique stores: Via Solferino, Via Madonnina, and Via Fiori Chiari are the key streets.

CLOTHES
Giorgio Armani Via Sant' Andrea 9, tel 02 7600 3234. The most famous name in Milan's fashion firmament.
Prada Via della Spiga 1, tel 02 7600 2019. Fashionable bags, accessories, and clothes.

DEPARTMENT STORE
La Rinascente Piazza del Duomo, tel 02 88 521. Has Italy's largest fashion floors within a single store, plus household and other goods.

JEWELRY
Mario Buccellati Via Montenapoleone 4, tel 02 7600 2153. Only Rome's Bulgari rivals Buccellati for the title of Italy's finest jeweler.
Meru Via Solferino 3, tel 02 8646 0700. Cutting-edge contemporary designs.

LACE
Jesurum Via Verri 4, tel 02 7601 5045. Huge range of machine- and handmade lace.

MARKETS
Mercantone dell' Antiquariato Via Brera-Via Fiori Chiari. Massive antiques market (3rd Sat. of each month).
Mercato Papiniano Viale Papiniano. New and secondhand goods (Sat.).

PAPER & STATIONERY
Papier Via San Maurilio 4, tel 02 865 221. A large selection of beautiful, and often unusual, papers.

PERFUME
Profumo Via Brera 6, tel 02 7202 3334. An encyclopedic selection of Italian scents and colognes for men and women.

PORCELAIN & GLASS
Ginori Corso Buenos Aires 1, tel 02 2951 6611. An Italian institution since 1735. Specializes in porcelain, but also sells glass and silverware.

PRINTS & ENGRAVINGS
Raimondi di Pettinaroli Corso Venezia 6, tel 02 7600 2412. Hundreds of old prints and engravings.

VENICE

Venice's most famous products are glass, lace, fabrics, and marbled paper. Beware, however, for much cheap glass and lace is foreign and machine-made. Many glass shops are on the Fondamenta dei Vetrai on the island of Murano (take boat 52 from San Marco), but there are also numerous stores around San Marco. Lace can be found on the island of Burano (boat 12 from the Fondamente Nuove), and paper and fabric stores are dotted across the city.

The key shopping streets are around Calle dei Fabbri, the Frezzeria, and Le Mercerie between San Marco and the Rialto Bridge and on and around Calle Largo XXII Marzo west of Piazza San Marco. Antiques stores cluster around the churches of San Maurizio and Santa Maria Zobenigo, west of Piazza San Marco. Antiques fairs are held periodically in Campo San Maurizio: Details of forthcoming fairs are available from the visitor center.

BEADS
Anticlea Campo San Provolo, Castelo 4719/a, tel 041 528 6946. A tiny gem of a store, crammed with thousands of new and antique Venetian beads in all colors and sizes.

DEPARTMENT STORE
COIN Salizzada San Giovanni Crisostomo, San Marco, tel 041 239 8000. The city's easiest place to shop under one roof.

FOOD
Aliani Campo della Corderia, Ruga Vecchia San Giovanni, San Polo 214, tel 041 520 6525. Venice's best food emporium has myriad cheeses, hams, fresh pasta, and lots of ready-made delicacies.

GLASS
Pauly Ponte Consorzi-Piazza San Marco 73–77, tel 041 520 9899. A huge store-showroom with everything from glass dolphins to chandeliers costing a king's ransom.
Venini Piazzetta Leoncini, San Marco 314, tel 041 520 4045. Innovative and precious designs.

GONDOLIERS' GOODS
Ceccato Sottoportico di Rialto, San Polo 1617, tel 041 522 2700. If you must buy a gondolier's straw hat as a souvenir, then at least buy the real thing from this store, which sells hats, tunics, and pants to real gondoliers.

JEWELRY
Missiaglia Piazza San Marco 125, tel 041 522 4464. Classic and contemporary gold and silver at top prices from Venice's best jeweler.
Nardi Piazza San Marco 69–71, tel 041 522 5733. The only place that produces work to come close to nearby Missiaglia.

LACE
Jesurum Piazza San Marco 60–61, tel 041 522 9864. A wide range of impressive and expensive lacework products.
Mercerie del Capitello San Marco 4857, tel 041 520 6177. Venice's finest lace retailer since 1868. Products and quality are guaranteed.

LEATHER
Marforio Campo San Salvador, San Marco 5033, tel 041 522 5734. Italy's largest and oldest leather store (founded 1875), with a wide range of bags and accessories by all the big designer names.

MARKETS

Rialto Do not miss the general goods and food markets (the Erberia) in the streets north of the Rialto Bridge—a medley of sights and sounds (Mon.–Sat. 8 a.m.–1 p.m.).
Pescheria The fish market operates alongside the Erberia north of the Rialto Bridge and is equally captivating (Tues.–Sat. 8 a.m.–1 p.m.).

MASKS

Mondonovo Rio Terrà Canal, Dorsoduro 3063, tel 041 528 7344. Mask stores are everywhere in Venice. This is perhaps the best.

PAPER

Legatoria Piazzesi Campiello della Feltrina, San Marco 2511, tel 041 522 1202. Workshop still employing traditional methods to produce papers, books, and stationery.
Polliero Campo dei Frari, San Polo 2995, tel 041 528 5130. Tiny shop by the Frari church selling beautiful leather- and paper-bound books and diaries and other marbled paper products.

FLORENCE

Florence is a great shopping city for luxury goods. Leather, clothes, jewelry, and antiques are top buys, thanks to a long tradition of outstanding artisanal work. Less expensive gift possibilities include marbled paper and goods from the city's thriving markets. Most clothes and other luxury goods stores are found on and around Via de' Tornabuoni. Antique stores group together south of the Arno River on and around Via Maggio. Jewelers congregate on the Ponte Vecchio.

DEPARTMENT STORES

COIN Via de' Calzaiuoli 56r, tel 055 280 531. Florentines crowd this central mid-range store, which sells a wide range of quality goods.

La Rinascente Piazza della Repubblica 1, tel 055 239 8544. Of generally higher quality than COIN, but with less stock and a less inviting atmosphere.

DESIGNER CLOTHES

Gucci Via de' Tornabuoni 73r, tel 055 264 011. The famous double "G" label originated in Florence.
Pucci Via dei Pucci 6, tel 055 628 7622; Via della Vigna Nuova 97r, tel 055 294 028. With Gucci and Ferragamo, Emilo Pucci is one of the city's best-known designers, having made his name with signature silks and prints in the 1960s.

FABRICS

Casa dei Tessuti Via de' Pecori 20r, tel 055 215 961. A staggering collection of sumptuous silk, linen, wool, and other fabrics.

JEWELRY

Torrini Piazza del Duomo 10r, tel 055 230 2402. Torrini registered its half cloverleaf trademark in 1369. Traditional and modern designs, with an emphasis on gold.

LEATHER

Cellerini Via del Sole 37, tel 055 282 533. Wallets, shoes, suitcases, belts, but most of all, bags—over 600 types to choose from.
Desmo Piazza de' Rucellai 10r, tel 055 292 395. A long-established name with a huge selection of leather goods under one roof.

LINENS

Loretti Caponi Piazza Antinori 4r, tel 055 213 668. Beautiful embroidery, linens, lingerie, and lace.

MAPS & GUIDES

Geografica Via dei Cimatori 16r, tel 055 239 6637. The only store in Italy where you can buy or order the full range of 1:25,000 Italian military (IGM) maps for hiking. Other Italian hiking and

driving maps and guides are also available.

MARKETS

Cascine Parco del Cascine. A vast weekly flea market held in a large park to the west of the city center (Tues. 8 a.m.–2 p.m., Bus: 1, 9, 17).
Mercato Centrale Piazza del Mercato Centrale. Europe's largest indoor food market is a bustling must-see, even if you don't want to buy anything (Mon.–Sat. 9 a.m.–5 p.m.).
San Lorenzo Piazza San Lorenzo. The square and its surrounding streets are crammed with stalls selling clothes and other general goods (Mon.–Sun. 9 a.m.–7 p.m.).

PAPER & PENS

Pineider Piazza della Signoria 14r and Via de' Tornabuoni, tel 055 284 655. This exclusive store has branches around the world, but was founded in Florence in 1774.

SHOES

Salvatore Ferragamo Via de' Tornabuoni 14r, tel 055 292 123. Ferragamo made his name in the U.S., but his Italian base was Florence. Also sells clothing and accessories.

SOAPS & PERFUMES

Farmaceutica di Santa Maria Novella Via della Scala 16r, tel 055 282 128. A beautiful store selling soaps, perfumes, and cosmetics, many made to ancient recipes created in monasteries and convents.
Farmacia del Cinghiale Piazza del Mercato Nuovo 4r, tel 055 212 128. A store that has sold natural cosmetics and other toiletries since the 18th century.

ENTERTAINMENT

Italy has a plethora of fascinating and colorful festivals, religious ceremonies, historic pageants, fairs, markets, and local events. A few are vast, showy affairs such as the Venice Carnival or Siena's Palio (horse race). Many are cultural extravaganzas of Europe-wide significance, notably Verona's magnificent summer opera festival or Venice's international film festival. The majority, however, are tiny affairs, restricted to a town or village, and often held in honor of a saint, historic event, or local products such as wine, food, or craft items.

You may wish to plan your trip around some of the larger events, but be sure to reserve accommodations and make travel arrangements well in advance, as tickets and hotel rooms go quickly. It is more likely, however, that you will simply stumble across a smaller festival *(festa)* as you travel, especially at Easter or during the summer, when virtually every village in the country finds an excuse to put on a show.

Most smaller events follow a similar pattern, especially those with a religious inspiration. Generally there are processions, often in traditional costume, followed by special church services, fireworks, village marching bands, and lots of eating and drinking. Keep your eyes peeled for flyers advertising a *festa* or *sagra* (a wine or food fair), or consult local visitor information centers, which always have lists of forthcoming events, large or small.

The selection of events below details by town the main arts and musical festivals, plus a selection of the largest and most colorful historical and other events throughout the year.

ARTS & MUSIC

Città di Castello A major international festival of chamber music takes place here each summer. *(Aug.–Sept., tel 075 855 4922)*

Fiesole The Estate Fiesolana (Fiesole Summer) is an important festival of music and other performing arts held in a hill town above Florence. *(Mid-June–Aug., tel 055 219 851)*

Florence The city's Maggio Musicale is widely considered Italy's most prestigious festival of classical music. *(Late April–early July, tel 055 211 158 or 055 213 535)*

Lucca The Estate Musicale Lucchese is one of Tuscany's leading summer musical festivals. *(July–Aug., tel 0583 419 689)*

Macerata This town in the Marche hosts a small but highly regarded opera festival. *(Mid-July–mid-Aug., tel 0733 261 334)*

Milan Opera season and other classical music is staged at La Scala, Italy's premier opera house. *(Opera: Dec.–July; classical: Sept.–Nov., tel 02 86 791)*

Naples The San Carlo is Italy's second-ranked opera house after Milan's La Scala. *(Opera season: Dec.–May; classical music and ballet: June–Nov., tel 081 797 2111)*

Perugia Umbria Jazz attracts the world's leading jazz musicians to venues in Perugia and smaller centers around the region. *(July, tel 075 5732 2432)*

Pesaro The opera festival in this Marche town is devoted to the composer Giacchino Rossini. *(Aug., tel 0721 30 161)*

Ravenna A wide-ranging festival with opera, jazz, and contemporary music. *(Mid-June–mid-July, tel 0544 213 895)*

Siena Siena's Settimane Musicali Senesi (Musical Weeks Festival) is a series of classical recitals. *(July–Aug., tel 0577 46 152 or 0577 42 209)*

Siracusa A biennial festival of Greek drama with performances in the Sicilian town's original outdoor Greek theater. *(May–June in even-numbered years, tel 0931 67 415)*

Spoleto The prestigious and wide-ranging Festival dei Due Mondi, or Festival of the Two Worlds, is especially popular with U.S. visitors, thanks to its links with a sister festival of arts and music in Charleston, South Carolina. *(Late June–July, tel 0743 44 325 or 0743 28 120, fax 0743 40 396)*

Stresa Stresa Settimane Musicale (Stresa Musical Weeks) is a short season of classical concerts. *(Late Aug.–Sept., tel 0323 31 308 or 0323 30 171)*

Taormina This Sicilian town hosts a prestigious international film festival, plus plays and concerts in its stunning outdoor Greek theater. *(July–mid-Sept., tel 0942 23 243)*

Torre del Lago An outdoor opera festival on the Tuscan coast near Viareggio devoted to composer Giacomo Puccini. *(Mid-July–mid-Aug., tel 0584 359 322)*

Urbino This Marche town hosts the Festival Internazionale di Musica Antica, one of Europe's leading festivals of early and baroque music. *(10 days late July, tel 0722 2613)*

Venice (art) The Biennale, founded in 1895, is one of Europe's most important contemporary art shows. It is held in pavilions (galleries) in the Giardini Pubblici, or public gardens. *(June–Sept. in odd-numbered years, tel 041 522 6356)*

Venice (film) The Venice International Film Festival, founded in 1932, ranks second only to Cannes among European movie festivals. *(10 days late Aug.–early Sept., tel 041 526 0188)*

Venice (opera) Concerts are held at temporary venues after the fire that damaged La Fenice opera house in 1996. *(Nov.–June, tel 041 786 562)*

Verona Italy's major opera festival is staged in the city's vast Roman amphitheater, the Arena. *(July–Aug., tel 045 801 5151)*

ENTERTAINMENT

CALENDAR OF EVENTS

January

Epiphany Celebrations across Italy to celebrate the feast of the Epiphany, especially in Rome where a 3-week Christmas fair concludes in Piazza Navona. *(Jan. 5–6)*

Festa di Sant'Orso Aosta, Valle d'Aosta. An ancient local festival celebrating Aosta's patron saint. *(Late Jan.)*

Festival della Canzone Italiana San Remo, Liguria. This 3-day "Festival of Italian Song" is hugely popular in Italy, where it is televised nationwide, but little known outside the country. *(3 days late Jan.)*

February

Carnevale Italy's most celebrated carnival festivities take place in Venice (street parties, costumes, and masked balls) and Viareggio on the Tuscan coast where a huge procession of floats takes place. *(10 days to Ash Wednesday)*

Sagra del Mandorla in Fiore Agrigento, Sicily. International festival of folk music, dancing, and folklore held to coincide with the "Festival of the Almond Blossom." *(1st week Feb.)*

Sagra del Tartufo Norcia, Umbria. One of the biggest of several rural food and truffle *(tartufo)* fairs held across truffle-producing areas of Italy, notably Tuscany, Umbria, and the Marche. *(Late Feb.)*

March–April

Easter Celebrations take place in every town, village, and city across Italy to mark Pasqua (Easter). Torchlit and other processions, plus religious services take place on Good Friday and Easter Sunday. The pope traditionally leads Rome's Good Friday procession past the Colosseum, and conducts a service broadcast worldwide from St. Peter's on Easter Sunday. Ceremonies in Sicily and rural areas are often especially memorable.

Festa di San Marco Venice. The city's patron saint, St. Mark, is commemorated with a gondola race and other festivities. *(April 25)*

Scoppio del Carro Florence. The "Explosion of the Cart" concludes Florence's Easter Sunday ceremonies. A cart of flowers and fireworks is ignited at noon by a mechanical dove that "flies" along a wire from the altar of the cathedral to the piazza outside.

May

Cavacata Sassari, Sardinia. Sardinia's grandest festival involves thousands of people in traditional island dress parading on foot and horseback, followed by horse races and traditional songs and dances. *(40 days after Easter—usually last Sun. May)*

Corsa dei Ceri Gubbio, Umbria. Processions and medieval pageantry precede a race of teams carrying huge wooden candles, or *ceri,* to the hill above the town. *(Early or mid-May)*

Festa di San Domenico Abat Cocullo, Abruzzo. One of Italy's strangest festivals, in which live snakes are handled by local people and draped over a statue of the village's patron saint. *(1st week May)*

Festa di San Gennaro Naples. Celebrations to honor the city's patron saint, including the miraculous liquefaction (or otherwise) of a phial of the saint's blood. *(Three times yearly: 1st Sun. May, Sept. 19, & Dec. 16)*

Festa di Sant'Efisio Cagliari, Sardinia. Mass processions on foot or horseback, with participants in medieval dress, to commemorate the city's patron saint. *(May 1)*

Sagra di San Nicola Bari. Festivities centered on a boat carrying the image of Bari's patron saint for a ceremony at sea. *(1st weekend May)*

Vogalunga Venice. The "long row" is a popular 20-mile (32 km) race for a wide variety of old and new rowing boats to the island of Burano, returning along the Grand Canal in the early afternoon. *(One Sun. in May)*

June

Calcio Storico Florence. Three mass soccer games played in medieval dress in Piazza Santa Croce or Piazza della Signoria to commemorate a game first played in 1530. *(Last week June)*

Festa di San Pietro St. Peter's, Rome. Important religious festival to celebrate the feast day of St. Peter. *(June 29)*

Festa di San Ranieri Pisa, Tuscany. Candlelit processions followed by a rowing regatta in medieval dress to celebrate Pisa's patron saint. *(June 16)*

Festa di Sant'Andrea Amalfi, Campania. Festivities to celebrate Amalfi's patron saint. *(June 27)*

Gioco del Ponte Pisa, Tuscany. The "Game of the Bridge" is a tug-of-war in medieval costume held on Pisa's Ponte di Mezzo. *(Last Sun. June)*

July

Festa del Redentore Venice. Pontoon bridges are laid across the Giudecca canal to link Venice with the church of the Redentore (Redeemer), a celebration of Venice's deliverance from the plague in 1576. People traditionally picnic in boats and fireworks close the event. *(3rd Sat. & Sun. July)*

Festa di Noiantri Rome. Eight days of festivals, pageants, outdoor feasts, and folk music in Rome's colorful Trastevere quarter. *(Mid-July)*

Il Palio Siena. Italy's best-known festival begins with processions and displays of flag throwing by participants in medieval costume before a bareback horse race around the Campo, the city's main square. The race is held twice yearly and is usually broadcast on national television. *(July 2 & Aug. 16)*

August

Bravio delle Botte Montepulciano, Tuscany. A barrel-rolling contest up the town's steep main street, plus

processions and displays of medieval drumming and flag throwing. (*Last Sun. Aug.*)
Luminara di Santa Croce Lucca, Tuscany. Torchlit procession bearing the Volto Santo, the city's most sacred relic, around the streets. (*Aug. 14*)
Torneo della Quintana Ascoli Piceno, Marche. Jousting involving knights in armor plus medieval pageant. (*1st weekend Aug.*)

September
Giostra del Saracino Arezzo, Tuscany. Jousting knights and processions and events in medieval costume. (*1st Sun. Sept.*)
Regata Storica Venice. A magnificent medieval pageant involving a procession of boats on the Grand Canal, followed by a boat race. (*1st Sun. Sept.*)

October
Sagra del Tartufo Alba, Piedmont. A fair held in the country's white truffle (*tartufo*) capital to celebrate the expensive fungus. (*2 weeks mid-Oct.*)

November
Festa della Salute Venice. The "Festival of Health" sees a pontoon bridge built across the Grand Canal to the church of the Salute to commemorate the passing of a plague epidemic in 1630. (*Nov. 21*)

December
Festa di Sant'Ambrogio Milan. Large market and other celebrations to commemorate the city's patron saint. (*Early Dec.*)
Presepi Ornate and often precious old Christmas cribs (*presepi*) are features of churches across Italy in the lead up to Christmas, but especially in Naples, where the tableau figures are a popular craft tradition.
Christmas Eve Special religious services across Italy. (*Dec. 24*)
Christmas Day Rome. Papal blessing in St. Peter's Square. (*Dec. 25*)

LANGUAGE GUIDE

USEFUL WORDS & PHRASES
Yes/No *Sì/No*
OK/that's fine/sure *Va bene*
I don't understand *Non capisco*
Do you speak English? *Parla inglese?*
I don't know *Non lo so*
I would like... *Vorrei...*
Do you have...? *Avete...?*
How much is it? *Quant'è?*
What is it? *Che cos'è?*
Who? *Chi?*
What? *Quale?*
Why? *Perchè?*
When? *Quando?*
Where? *Dove?*
What's the time? *Che ore sono?*
Good morning *Buon giorno*
Good afternoon/good evening *Buona sera*
Good night *Buona notte*
Hello/goodbye (informal) *Ciao*
Goodbye *Arrivederci*
Please *Per favore*
Thank you *Grazie*
You're welcome *Prego*
What's your name? *Come si chiama?*
My name is... *Mi chiamo...*
I'm American (man/woman) *Sono Americano/Americana*
How are you? (polite/informal) *Come sta/stai?*
Fine, thanks *Bene, grazie*
And you? *E lei?*
I'm sorry *Mi dispiace*
Excuse me/I beg your pardon *Mi scusi*
Excuse me (in a crowd) *Permesso*
good/bad *buono/cattivo*
big/small *grande/piccolo*
with/without *con/senza*
more/less *più/meno*
enough *basta*
near/far *vicino/lontano*
left/right *sinistra/destra*
straight ahead *sempre dritto*
hot/cold *caldo/freddo*
early/late *presto/ritardo*
here/there *qui/là*
today/tomorrow *oggi/domani*
yesterday *ieri*
morning *la mattina*
afternoon *il pomeriggio*
evening *la sera*
entrance/exit *entrata/uscita*
open/closed *aperto/chiuso*

bathroom/toilet *il bagno/il gabinetto*
Let's go *Andiamo*

EMERGENCIES
Help! *Aiuto!*
Can you help me? *Mi puo aiutare?*
I'm not well *Sto male*
Call a doctor *Chiamate un medico*
Where is the police station? *Dov'è la polizia/la questura?*
first aid *pronto soccorso*
hospital *l'ospedale*

SIGHT-SEEING
art gallery *la pinacoteca*
castle *il castello/la fortezza*
church *la chiesa*
garden *il giardino*
museum *il museo*
postcard *la cartolina*
stamp *il francobollo*
visitor center *l'ufficio di turismo*

IN THE HOTEL
hotel *un albergo*
room *una camera*
single room *una camera singola*
double rooms *una camera doppia*
room with private bathroom *una camera con bagno*
I have a reservation *Ho una prenotazione*

SHOPPING
shop/store *il negozio*
market *il mercato*
Do you have some...? *Avete un po' di...?*
this one/that one *questo/quello*
a little/a lot *poco/tanto*
enough/too much *abbastanza/troppo*
Do you accept credit cards? *Accetate carte di credito?*
expensive/cheap *caro/a buon prezzo*

STORES/SHOPS
bakery *il forno/il panificio*
bookstore *la libreria*
butcher *la macelleria/il macellaio*
cake store *la pasticceria*
delicatessan *la salumeria/ la norcineria*
drugstore/pharmacy *la farmacia*
food store *l'alimentari*
ice cream parlor *la gelateria*
post office *l'ufficio postale*
supermarket *il supermercato*
tobacconist *il tabaccaio*

MENU READER

GENERAL

breakfast *la colazione*
lunch *il pranzo*
dinner *la cena*
waiter *il cameriere*
I'd like to reserve a table *Vorrei riservare una tavola*
Have you a table for two? *Avete una tavola per due?*
I'd like to order *Vorrei ordinare*
I'm a vegetarian *Sono vegetariano/a*
The check, please *Il conto, per favore*
cover charge *il coperto*
Is service included? *Il servizio è incluso?*

THE MENU

l'antipasto appetizer
il primo first course
la zuppa soup
il secondo main course
il contorno vegetable, side dish
insalata salad
la frutta fruit
il formaggio cheese
i dolci sweets/desserts
la lista dei vini wine list

TERMS

affumicato smoked
ai ferri grilled
alla griglia grilled
alla Milanese in breadcrumbs
allo spiedo on the spit
arrosto roasted
bollito boiled
costoletta chop
fritto fried
in umido stewed
ripieno stuffed/filled
stracotto braised, stewed
sugo sauce

PASTA & SAUCES

agnolotti large filled pasta parcels
al pomodoro tomato sauce
amatriciana tomato and bacon sauce
arrabbiata spicy chilli tomato sauce
bolognese veal or beef sauce
cannelloni filled pasta tubes
carbonara cream, ham, and egg sauce
farfalle butterfly-shaped pasta
fettucine flat, thick pasta ribbons

gnocchi potato and dough cubes
lasagne layers of meat, cheese, and pasta
parmigiano Parmesan cheese sauce
pasta e fagioli pasta and beans
penne tubular pasta quills
peperoncino oil, garlic, and chilli
pesto pine nuts, basil, and cheese
puttanesca tomato, anchovy, oil, and oregano sauce
ragù any meat sauce
ravioli filled pasta parcels
rigatoni large pasta tubes
spaghetti long, thin pasta strands
tagliatelle long, flat pasta ribbons
tagliolini very thin pasta ribbons
tortellini filled pasta twists
vongole wine, clams, and parsley

MEATS

agnello lamb
anatra duck
bistecca beef steak
cinghiale wild boar
coniglio rabbit
fritto misto mixed grill
maiale pork
manzo beef
ossobuco cut of veal
pancetta pork belly/bacon
pollo chicken
prosciutto cotto cooked ham
prosciutto crudo cooked (Parma) ham
salsiccia sausage
saltimbocca veal with ham and sage
trippa tripe
vitello veal

FISH & SEAFOOD

acciughe anchovies
aragosta lobster
baccalà dried salt cod
calamari squid
cappesante scallops
cozze mussels
dentice sea bream
gamberi prawns
granchio crab
merluzzo cod
ostriche oysters
pesce spada swordfish
polpo octopus
rospo monkfish
salmone salmon
sarde sardines
seppie cuttlefish
sgombro mackeral
sogliola sole

tonno tuna
triglie red mullet
trota trout
vongole clams

VEGETABLES

aglio garlic
asparagi asparagus
basilico basil
capperi capers
carciofi artichokes
carotte carrots
cavolo cabbage
cipolle onions
fagioli beans
funghi mushrooms
funghi porcini ceps, boletus mushrooms
insalata mista mixed salad
insalata verde green salad
melanzane eggplant
patate potatoes
patate fritte French fries
peperoni peppers
piselli peas
pomodoro tomato
radicchio red salad leaf
rucolo/rughetta rocket, arucola
spinaci spinach
tartufo truffle
zucchini zucchini

FRUIT

albicocca apricot
ananas pineapple
arance oranges
banane bananas
ciliegie cherries
ficchi figs
fragole strawberries
limone lemon
mele apples
melone melon
pere pears
pesca peach
pompelmo grapefruit
prugna plum

DRINKING

acqua water
una birra beer
una bottiglia bottle
una mezza bottiglia half-bottle
caffè coffee
caffè Hag/caffè decaffeinato decaffeinated coffee
latte milk
tè tea
vino wine
vino della casa house wine
zucchero sugar

INDEX

Bold page numbers
indicate illustrations

CREDITS

ILLUSTRATIONS CREDITS

Cover, (tl) Vittoriano Rastelli/Corbis UK Ltd. (tr) SuperStock. (bl) PowerStock/Zefa. (br) Robert Harding Picture Library Ltd. Spine, SuperStock. 1, Tony Stone Images. 2/3, Tony Stone Images. 4, Robert Harding Picture Library. 9, Francis G. Mayer/Corbis UK Ltd. 11, Vittoriano Rastelli/Corbis UK Ltd. 12/13, 14, Jonathan Blair/Corbis UK Ltd. 15, William Allard/National Geographic Society. 16/17, Michael Freeman/Corbis UK Ltd. 19, Jim Holmes/AA Photo Library. 20, Museo Archeologico Nazionale, Naples, Italy/Bridgeman Art Library. 21, Museo Archeologico Nazionale, Naples, Italy/Bridgeman Art Library. 23, Chateau de Versailles, France/Index/Bridgeman Art Library. 24/25, Museo de Firenze Com' era, Florence, Italy/Bridgeman Art Library. 26 (l), Archivio Iconografico, S.A./Corbis UK Ltd. 26 (r), Bettmann/Corbis UK Ltd. 27, Mussolini/Corbis UK Ltd. 28/29, George Steinmetz/Katz Pictures. 31, Sandro Vannini/Corbis UK Ltd. 32/33, Francis G. Mayer/Corbis UK Ltd. 34, Archivio Iconografico, S.A./Corbis UK Ltd. 35, Philadelphia Museum of Art/Corbis UK Ltd. 36, Araldo de Luca/Corbis UK Ltd. 36/37, Hubert Stadler/Corbis UK Ltd. 38 (l), Archivio Iconografico, S.A./Corbis UK Ltd. 38 (r), Hulton-Deutsch Collection/Corbis UK Ltd. 39, Robbie Jack/Corbis UK Ltd. 41, Everett/Corbis UK Ltd. 43, James Stanfield/National Geographic Society. 44/45, Marka. 48/49, Riccardo Musacchio/Farabolafoto. 49, Vanni Archive/Corbis UK Ltd. 50/51, Vince Streano/Corbis UK Ltd. 52/53, Angelo Hornak Library. 55, Jean-Marc Charles/Franca Speranza Srl. 56, Archivio Iconografico, S.A/Corbis UK Ltd. 57, Sandro Vannini/Franca Speranza Srl. 58, Gianni Dagli Orti/Corbis UK Ltd. 59, Ruggero Vanni/Corbis UK Ltd. 60, Michael S. Yamashita/Corbis UK Ltd. 61, Vanni Archive/Corbis UK Ltd. 62, Clive Sawyer/AA Photo Library. 63, Ted Spiegel/Corbis UK Ltd. 64/65, Donadoni/Marka. 65, Joseph Martin/Piazza della Minerva, Rome, Italy/Bridgeman Art Library. 68/69, Jim Holmes/Axiom. 70 (t), Santa Maria del Popolo, Rome, Italy/Bridgeman Art Library. 70 (b), Nicolas Sapieha; Kea Publishing Services/Corbis UK Ltd. 71, Massimo Listri/Corbis UK Ltd. 73 (t), Museo di Goethe, Rome, Italy/Bridgeman Art Library. 73 (b), Gianni Dagli Orti/Corbis UK Ltd. 75, Adam Woolfitt/Corbis UK Ltd. 76, Grzegorz Galazka/Corbis UK Ltd. 79, Vatican Museums and Galleries, Vatican City, Italy/Bridgeman Art Library. 80, James Stanfield/National Geographic Society. 81, Vatican Museums and Galleries, Vatican City, Italy/Bridgeman Art Library. 83, Mike King/Corbis UK Ltd. 86/87,

Enzo & Paolo Ragazzini/Corbis UK Ltd. 88, C. Penna/Marka. 89, M. d'Ottavio/Farabolafoto. 91 (t), Owen Franken/Corbis UK Ltd. 91 (c), Vittoriano Rastelli/Corbis UK Ltd. 91 (b), Owen Franken/Corbis UK Ltd. 92, Maurizio Lanini/Corbis UK Ltd. 92/93, Tim Thompson/Corbis UK Ltd. 94, D. Donadoni/Marka. 95, Clive Sawyer/AA Photo Library. 96, Curzio Baraggi/Farabolafoto. 98, D. Donadoni/Marka. 99, Curzio Baraggi/Farabolafoto. 100, Simon Harris/Robert Harding Picture Library. 101, Virgili/Marka. 103, David Lees/Corbis UK Ltd. 107, Roberto Benzi/Marka. 108, T. di Girolamo/Marka. 110, Shaun Egan/Tony Stone Images. 111, Farabolafoto. 112, Archivio Iconografico, S.A./Corbis UK Ltd. 113, T. Conti/Marka. 114, Electa Archive. 115, John Heseltine/Corbis UK Ltd. 116/117, Vince Streano/Corbis UK Ltd. 119 (t), Schuster/Robert Harding Picture Library. 119 (c), D. Donadoni/Marka. 119 (b), Peter Bennett/AA Photo Library. 120, Peter Wilson/Corbis UK Ltd. 121, Dennis Marsico/Corbis UK Ltd. 122, D. Donadoni/Marka. 123, John Heseltine/Corbis UK Ltd. 124, Franca Speranza Srl. 125, T. Di Girolamo/Marka. 127, Massimo Mantovani/Tony Stone Images. 129, Gerard del Vecchio/Tony Stone Images. 132, Clive Sawyer/AA Photo Library. 132/133, S. Tauqueur/Franca Speranza Srl. 134, Massimo Listri/Corbis UK Ltd. 135, Adam Woolfitt/Corbis UK Ltd. 136, Ken Mclaren/Life File. 137, Clive Sawyer/AA Photo Library. 139, Clive Sawyer/AA Photo Library. 141, John Heseltine/Corbis UK Ltd. 142, David Lees/Corbis UK Ltd. 143, San Marco, Venice, Italy/Bridgeman Art Library. 144, Dennis Marsico/Corbis UK Ltd. 145, Dario Mitidieri/AA Photo Library. 146, Bettmann/Corbis UK Ltd. 147, Galleria dell'Accademia, Venice, Italy/Bridgeman Art Library. 148, Archivio Iconografico, S.A./Corbis UK Ltd. 148/149, David Lees/Corbis UK Ltd. 150, David Lees/Corbis UK Ltd. 151, Wolfgang Kaehler/Corbis UK Ltd. 152, Robert Harding Picture Library. 153, Santa Maria Gloriosa dei Frari, Venice, Italy/Bridgeman Art Library. 154/155, Dario Mitidieri/AA Photo Library. 158, Scuola di San Giorgio degli Schiavoni, Venice, Italy/Bridgeman Art Library. 159, Archivio Iconografico, S.A./Corbis UK Ltd. 160, San Giovanni e Paolo, Venice, Italy/Bridgeman Art Library. 161, San Giovanni e Paolo Square, Venice, Italy/Bridgeman Art Library. 162/163, Thad Samuels Abell II/National Geographic Society. 163, Todd Gipstein/Corbis UK Ltd. 164/165, Yann Arthus-Bertrand/Corbis UK Ltd. 167, Galen Rowell/Corbis UK Ltd. 170/171, Simon Harris/Robert Harding Picture Library. 172/173, Marka. 174, Vanni Archive/Corbis UK Ltd. 175, Carmen Redondo/Corbis UK Ltd. 176, Sandro Vannini/Corbis UK Ltd. 177, Roberto Soncin Gerometta/Franca Speranza Srl. 179 (t), K. Carlson/Nature Photographers. 179 (c), Clive Sawyer/AA Photo Library. 179 (b), Roberto Sonsin

Gerometta/Franca Speranza Srl. 180/181, Hart/Robert Harding Picture Library. 182, Elio Ciol/Corbis UK Ltd. 183, Christel Gerstenberg/Corbis UK Ltd. 186/187, Kim Hart/samfoto/Robert Harding Picture Library. 188, John Sims. 189, Tony Gervis/Robert Harding Picture Library. 190, John Sims. 191, Scala. 192/ (t), Owen Franken/Corbis UK Ltd. 192/ (b), R. Meucci/Marka. 193, Vanni Archive/Corbis UK Ltd. 194/195, Dennis Marsico/Corbis UK Ltd. 195, Robert Harding Picture Library. 196, Gian Berto Vanni/Corbis UK Ltd. 197, Sandro Vannini/Franca Speranza Srl. 198, F.Giaccone/Marka. 199, Michele d'Ottavio/Farabolafoto. 200, Galleria Nazionale delle Marche, Urbino, Italy/Bridgeman Art Library. 201, Clive Sawyer/AA Photo Library. 203, Clive Sawyer/AA Photo Library. 206/207, M.Christofori/Marka. 208, Dennis Marsico/Corbis UK Ltd. 209, M.Christofori/Marka. 210/211, Robert Harding Picture Library. 211, Opera del Duomo, Florence, Italy/Bridgeman Art Library. 212, David Lees/Corbis UK Ltd. 213, David Lees/Corbis UK Ltd. 214, A. Martinuzzi/Farabolafoto. 215, Dennis Marsico/Corbis UK Ltd. 216, Dennis Marsico/Corbis UK Ltd. 217, Galleria degli Uffizi, Florence, Italy/Bridgeman Art Library. 218/219, Galleria degli Uffizi, Florence, Italy/Bridgeman Art Library. 219, Galleria degli Uffizi, Florence, Italy/Bridgeman Art Library. 220, Arte & Immagini Srl/Corbis UK Ltd. 221, Bargello, Florence, Italy/Bridgeman Art Library. 222, Opera di Santa Croce, Florence, Italy/Bridgeman Art Library. 223, Chris Haigh/Tony Stone Images. 224, San Lorenzo, Florence, Italy/Bridgeman Art Library. 225, Cappella Medici, Florence, Italy/Bridgeman Art Library. 226, Palazzo Medici-Riccardi, Florence, Italy/Bridgeman Art Library. 227, Dennis Marsico/Corbis UK Ltd. 228, Dennis Marsico/Corbis UK Ltd. 229, Museo di San Marco dell'Angelico, Florence, Italy/Bridgeman Art Library. 232/233, Roy Rainford/Robert Harding Picture Library. 233, Santa Maria Novella, Florence, Italy/Bridgeman Art Library. 234, Sandro Vannini/Corbis UK Ltd. 235, Brancacci Chapel, Santa Maria del Carmine, Florence, Italy/Bridgeman Art Library. 236/237, Vittoriano Rastelli/Corbis UK Ltd. 237, Vittoriano Rastelli/Corbis UK Ltd. 238, Palazzo Pitti, Florence, Italy/Bridgeman Art Library. 239, Massimo Listri/Corbis UK Ltd. 240, Todd Gipstein/Corbis UK Ltd. 241, John Sims. 244/245, Jean-Pierre Lescourret/Corbis UK Ltd. 247, Agostino Quaranta/Farabolafoto. 248, Archivio Iconografico, S.A./Corbis UK Ltd. 249, Sandro Vannini/Franca Speranza Srl. 250/251, Owen Franken/Corbis UK Ltd. 251, Owen Franken/Corbis UK Ltd. 252, Dennis Marsico/Corbis UK Ltd. 252/253, Sandro Vannini/Corbis UK Ltd. 254, Archivio Iconografica, S.A./Corbis UK Ltd. 255, Marka. 256/257, James Nelson/Tony Stone Images. 258/259, Clive Sawyer/AA

Photo Library. 260/261, B. Morandi/ Franca Speranza Srl. 261, Macduff Everton/Corbis UK Ltd. 262, Dennis Marsico/Corbis UK Ltd. 263, Gavin Hellier/Robert Harding Picture Library. 265 (tl), John Sims. 265 (tr), Ken Paterson/AA Photo Library. 265 (b) Ken Paterson/AA Photo Library. 266, Dennis Marsico/Corbis UK Ltd. 267 (l), Clive Sawyer/AA Photo Library. 267 (r), Museo Diocesano, Cortona, Italy/Bridgeman Art Library. 269, Pacciani/Franca Speranza Srl. 270, Vince Streano/Corbis UK Ltd. 272, Robert Harding Picture Library. 273, John Heseltine/Corbis UK Ltd. 274, Musacchio/Farabolafoto. 274/275, Roger Antrobus/Corbis UK Ltd. 275, Ken Paterson/AA Photo Library. 277 (t), Clive Sawyer/AA Photo Library/. 277 (c), Ken Paterson/AA Photo Library. 277 (b), Ken Paterson/AA Photo Library. 278, Bastin & Everard/Franca Speranza Srl. 279, Joe Cornish/Tony Stone Images. 280, L. Sechi/Marka. 281, Tony Gervis/Robert Harding Picture Library. 282, D.Donadoni/Marka. 283, Sandro Vannini/Corbis UK Ltd. 284, Orvieto Cathedral, Italy/Bridgeman Art Library. 285, Giuseppe Carfagna/Franca Speranza Srl. 287, Jonathan Blair/Corbis UK Ltd. 290, John Sims. 291, John Sims. 293, Museo Archeologico Nazionale, Naples, Italy/Bridgeman Art Library. 294, Jonathan Blair/Corbis UK Ltd. 295, Garry Hunter/Tony Stone Images. 296, R. Rainford/Robert Harding Picture Library. 297, R Frerck/Robert Harding Picture Library. 298, AA Photo Library/Tony Souter. 298/299, R.Rainford/Robert Harding Picture Library. 300/301, G.Sosio/Marka. 301, Massimo Amendola/ Franca Speranza Srl. 302/303, R.Frerck/ Robert Harding Picture Library. 303, Museo Archeologico Nazionale, Paestum, Italy/Bridgeman Art Library. 304/305, D.Donadoni/Marka. 305, Marcello Calandrini/Corbis UK Ltd. 306/307, Nevio Doz/Marka. 307, V.Arcomano/ Marka. 308 (bl), Clive Sawyer/AA Photo Library. 308 (br), Tony Souter/AA Photo Library. 308 (t), F.Stella/Marka. 311, Bouchet/Marka. 312, John Sims. 312/313, Vince Streano/Corbis UK Ltd. 315, Kevin Schafer/Corbis UK Ltd. 319, F.Giaccone/ Marka. 320, Ruggero Vanni/Corbis UK Ltd. 321, Yami Arthus-Bertrand/Corbis UK Ltd. 322, F.Giaccone/Franca Speranza Srl. 323, E.Rooney/Robert Harding Picture Library. 324, R.Francis/Robert Harding Picture Library. 324/325, Roger Ressmeyer/Corbis UK Ltd. 326, Clive Sawyer/AA Photo Library. 327, Vittoriano Rastelli/Corbis UK Ltd. 328, V.Arcomano/ Marka. 329, James Marshall/Corbis UK Ltd. 330, Farabolafoto. 331, S.Vannini/ Franca Speranza Srl. 333, A.Ramella/ Marka. 334, John Sims. 336/337, A & L Sinibaldi/Tony Stone Images. 338, John Heseltine/Corbis UK Ltd. 339, Clive Sawyer/AA Photo Library. 341, Richard T. Nowitz/Corbis UK Ltd.

Published by the National Geographic Society

John M. Fahey, Jr., *President and Chief Executive Officer*

Gilbert M. Grosvenor, *Chairman of the Board*

Nina D. Hoffman, *Senior Vice President*

William R. Gray, *Vice President and Director, Book Division*

David Griffin, *Design Director*

Elizabeth L. Newhouse, *Director of Travel Publishing*

Barbara A. Noe, *Associate Editor*

Caroline Hickey, *Senior Researcher*

Carl Mehler, *Director of Maps*

Joseph F. Ochlak, *Map Coordinator*

Gary Colbert, *Production Director*

Richard S. Wain, *Production Project Manager*

DeShelle Downey, *Staff Assistant*

Edited and designed by AA Publishing (a trading name of Automobile Association Developments Limited, whose registered office is Norfolk House, Priestley Road, Basingstoke, Hampshire, England RG24 9NY. Registered number: 1878835).

Betty Sheldrick, *Project Manager*

David Austin, *Senior Art Editor*

Rachel Alder, *Senior Editor*

Bob Johnson, *Designer*

Inna Nogeste, *Senior Cartographic Editor*

Nicky Barker-Dix, Amber Banks, *Cartographers*

Richard Firth, *Production Director*

Steve Gilchrist, *Prepress Production Controller*

Picture Research by Zooid Pictures Ltd.

Drive maps drawn by Chris Orr Associates, Southampton, England

Cutaway illustrations drawn by Maltings Partnership, Derby, England

Library of Congress Cataloging-in-Publication Data

Jepson, Tim.
   The National Geographic Traveler : Italy / Tim Jepson.
      p. cm.
   Includes index.
   ISBN 0-7922-7562-4
   1. Italy—Guidebooks. I. Title.
DG416 .J48 2000

                                                      00-021916
                                                              CIP

Printed and bound by R.R. Donnelley & Sons, Willard, Ohio. Color separations by Leo Reprographic Ltd., Hong Kong. Cover separations by L.C. Repro, Aldermaston, U.K. Cover printed by Miken Inc., Cheektowage, New York.

Visit the Society's Web site at http://www.nationalgeographic.com

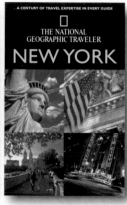 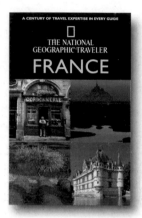 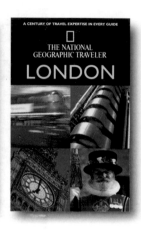

THE NATIONAL GEOGRAPHIC TRAVELER

A Century of Travel Expertise in Every Guide

- **Australia** ISBN: 0-7922-7431-8
- **California** ISBN: 0-7922-7564-0
- **Canada** ISBN: 0-7922-7427-X
- **The Caribbean** ISBN: 0-7922-7434-2
- **Florida** ISBN: 0-7922-7432-6
- **France** ISBN: 0-7922-7426-1
- **Great Britain** ISBN: 0-7922-7425-3
- **Italy** ISBN: 0-7922-7562-4
- **London** ISBN: 0-7922-7428-8
- **Miami and the Keys** ISBN: 0-7922-7433-4
- **New York** ISBN: 0-7922-7430-X
- **Paris** ISBN: 0-7922-7429-6
- **Rome** ISBN: 0-7922-7566-7
- **San Francisco** ISBN: 0-7922-7565-9
- **Sydney** ISBN: 0-7922-7435-0

AVAILABLE WHEREVER BOOKS ARE SOLD